DICTIONARY OF
THE NAPOLEONIC WARS

*Napoleon at the entry-port of H.M.S. Bellerophon
on his way into exile on St. Helena, 1815.*

Dictionary of the
NAPOLEONIC
WARS

❖

David G. Chandler

WORDSWORTH EDITIONS

Maps and diagrams drawn by Sheila Waters and Hazel Watson
from sketches prepared by the author.

First published in 1993 by
Academic Reference Division
Simon & Schuster
15 Columbus Circle, New York, New York 10023

This edition published 1999
by Wordsworth Editions Limited
Cumberland House, Crib Street, Ware,
Hertfordshire SG12 9ET

ISBN 1 84022 203 4

Printed and bound in Great Britain
by Mackays of Chatham plc, Chatham, Kent.

THIS BOOK IS RESPECTFULLY DEDICATED
TO THE MEMORY OF

Peter V. Ritner

WHO MANY YEARS AGO
ENCOURAGED THE AUTHOR TO STUDY THE

'...sweet sound of a distant drum,'

AND TO TRACE AND DESCRIBE THE
INCOMPARABLE MILITARY CAREER OF NAPOLEON BONAPARTE
AGAINST THE SETTING OF HIS LIFE AND TIMES,
HIS OFFICERS, MEN AND BRAVE OPPONENTS.

Contents

Explanatory Keys to Maps

viii

List of Maps

ix

Author's Note

xii

Acknowledgments

xiii

Introduction

xv

Chronological Table

xxiii

Dictionary

1

Appendix:
Napoleon's Military Movements, 1796–1815

497

Bibliography

558

Explanatory Key
TO MILITARY SYMBOLS USED ON MAPS & DIAGRAMS

General Note: Throughout the volume, with the exception of a few tactical diagrams, French forces are depicted in dark shades and their adversaries in lighter. A sequence of moves in a complex engagement is indicated by progressive variation of texture within the dark and light symbols. Where applicable, maps include their own keys to explain these sequences.

1 Symbols showing the presence but not the physical location of military units

ARMY — NAPOLEON 180,000 / RÜCHEL 15,000

CORPS

DIVISION

BRIGADE (& Demi-Brigade) — ½

REGIMENT

BATTALION

N.B. Names and arabic numerals adjacent to symbols, where included, reveal the identity of unit commanders and the approximate strengths of their formations.

2 Symbols showing the approximate physical location of units on the ground

CORPS — VI NEY 32,000 / VI MILLER 15,000

DIVISION

BRIGADE

REGIMENT

BATTALION

GENERAL UNIT AREA — e.g. areas of bivouacs, assembly, concentration etc.

UNITS IN ACTION ETC.

N.B. The Roman numeral within the Corps symbol reveals the identity of the formation. An adjacent name & arabic numeral reveals the commander & strength of the unit.

The protrusion atop any symbol indicates the direction in which the unit is facing.

3 Formation Boundaries

ARMY — xxxx — — xxxx —

CORPS — xxx — — xxx —

DIVISIONAL — xx — — xx —

LINES OF BATTLE at given moment — 1700 hrs. / 1200 hrs.

4 Movement Symbols

ATTACKS

ADVANCES ---▸ ---▸

RETREATS •••••▸ •••••▸

TACTICAL WITH-DRAWALS ▪▪▪▪▪▸ ▪▪▪▪▪▸

N.B. Different phases in an attack sequence are shown by differentiations within these basic symbols (see relevant keys). When more than one map is allocated to a subject, each map recommences with the basic symbol.

5 Miscellaneous Symbols

INFANTRY — INFANTRY SQUARES

CAVALRY — CAVALRY PICQUETS

ARTILLERY — HEADQUARTERS G.Q.C / A.H.Q.

CONVOYS & TRAINS

BRIDGES)( )(— PONTOON BRIDGES)( )(

CAMPS ▲ ▲ — PERMANENT DETACHED FORTS ★ ★ or ☆

PERMANENT LINEAR FORTIFICATIONS

ENTRENCHMENTS SIEGE WORKS ETC.

FIELD FORTIFICATIONS

NAVAL VESSELS — SMALL BOAT FLOTILLAS

SITES OF ENGAGEMENTS

List of Maps

BATTLE, CAMPAIGN, AND TACTICAL DIAGRAMS

Battles of Abensberg and Eckmühl, 20–22 April 1809   1
Night (or Second) Battle of Aboukir, 21 March 1801   3
Battle of Albuera, 16 May 1811   6
Battle of Arcis-sur-Aube, 20–21 March 1814   13
Battle of Arcola, 15–17 November 1796   14
Artillery of *La Grande Armée*   22–23
Battle of Aspern-Essling, 21–22 May 1809   24
Battle of Aspern-Essling: Day One   25
Battle of Aspern-Essling: Day Two   26
Battle of Assaye, 23 September 1803   28
Battle of Austerlitz, 2 December 1805: General Situation—Morning   32–33
Battle of Austerlitz: Final Attack   34
Battle of Austerlitz: Allied Attack (*left*);   35
    Battle of Austerlitz: Napoleon's Counterattack (*right*)   35
Siege of Badajoz, 6 April 1812   38
Battle of Barrosa, 5 March 1811   43
Battle of Borodino, 7 September 1812   65
Battle of Bussaco, 27 September 1810   73
Battle of Castiglione, 5 August 1796: Phase One   81
Battle of Castiglione: Phase Two   82
Battle of Champaubert, 10 February 1814   88
Siege of Ciudad Rodrigo, 19 January 1812   92
Battle of Copenhagen, 2 April 1801   104
Battle of Corunna, 16 January 1808   107
Battle of Dresden, 26–27 August 1813   125
North Italy, 1800   132–133
Danube Theater, 1805   137
Battle of Elchingen, 14 October 1805: Morning   139
Battle of Eylau, 7–8 February 1807: Day One   144
Battle of Eylau: Day Two   145
Battle of the First of June, 1794   150
Battle of Friedland, 14 June 1807   161
Battles of Fuentes de Oñoro, 3 and 5 May 1811   164
Battle of Golymin, 26 December 1806: Positions at about 5:00 P.M.   173
Grand Tactics: The Strategic Battle   179
Grand Tactics: *Le Bataillon Carré*   180

[ix]

List of Maps

Grand Tactics 181
Grand Tactics 182
Grand Tactics: Cavalry Screen Concealing Davout's March to Austerlitz, 1805 183
Battle of Hanau, 30 October 1813 192
Battle of Heilsberg, 10 June 1807 196
Battle of Hohenlinden, 3 December 1800 200
Saxony, 1806 206
Battle of Jemappes, 6 November 1792 214
Poland, 1807 228–229
Battles of Laon and Craonne, 9–10 March, 1814 237
Battle of La Rothière, 1 February 1814 238
Battle of Leipzig, 16–18 October 1813 247
Battle of Ligny, 16 June 1815: Positions at 2:15 P.M. 250
Battle of Lützen, 2 May 1813 257
Battle of Marengo, 14 June 1800: The Afternoon Battle 267
Battles of Maya and Roncesvalles, 25 July 1813 277
Battle of Montmirail, 11 February 1814 287
Russian Campaign of 1812 292–293
Battle of New Orleans, 8 January 1815 313
Battle of the Nile, 1 August 1798: Positions at 8:00 P.M. 316
Crossing of the Douro at Oporto, 12 May 1809 320
Battle of Orthez, 27 February 1814 322
Spain, 1808–09 330
The Peninsula 337
Battle of Pultusk, 26 December 1806 350
Battle of Quatre Bras, 16 June 1815: Positions at 3:00 P.M. 353
The Danube, 1809 356–357
France, 1814 362
Battle of Rivoli, 14 January 1797 380
Germany, 1813 388–389
Battle of Cape St. Vincent, 14 February 1797 395
Battle of Salamanca, 22 July 1812 397
Siege of San Sebastian, 25 July–31 August 1813 400
Battles of Sorauren, 28 and 30 July 1813 415
Strategy: Maneuver of the Central Position—The Attack at Piedmont,
    April 1796 422
Strategy: The Maneuver Preceding Lodi 423
Strategy: The Maneuver of Envelopment (Schematic) 424
Strategy: Envelopment—The French Advance to the Danube at Ulm, 1805 425
Strategy: Maneuver of the Central Position (Schematic) 426
Strategy: The French Offensive, 1806 427
Battle of Talavera, 28 June 1809: Final Attack 434
Lines of Torres Vedras, 1810 443
Siege of Toulon, 7 September–19 December 1793 446
Attack at Trafalgar, 21 October 1805: Positions at 12:05 P.M. 449
Battle of Vauchamps, 14 February 1814 459
Battle of Vimiero, 21 August 1808 466

List of Maps

Battle of Vitoria, 21 June 1813   469

Battle of Wagram, 5–6 July 1809: Day One   472–473

Battle of Wagram: Day Two   474–475

Battle of Wavre, 18 June 1815: Positions at 4:00 P.M.   485

AUTHOR'S NOTE

FOR the convenience of readers who may find difficulty in recognizing the English equivalent of certain military ranks when these are given in French, here is an explanatory table:

Maréchal*	Field Marshal
Général d'armée	General
Général de corps d'armée	Lieutenant General
Général de division	Major General
Général de brigade	Brigadier General
Colonel	Colonel
Lieutenant Colonel	Lieutenant Colonel
Commandant, Chef de bataillon	Major
Capitaine	Captain
Lieutenant	Lieutenant
Sous-Lieutenant, Ensigne, Cornette	Second Lieutenant, Ensign (infantry), Cornet (cavalry)
Aspirant	Candidate Officer or Cadet
Adjudant-chef, Adjudant-Sous-Officier	Regimental Sergeant-Major, Warrant Officer, 1st Class
Adjudant	Company Sergeant-Major, Warrant Officer, 2nd Class
Sergent-chef	Staff Sergeant, First Sergeant
Sergent, Maréchal-des-logis	Sergeant, Corporal of Horse
Caporal, Brigadier (cavalry and artillery)	Corporal
Soldat première classe	Senior soldier
Soldat	Private

STAFF RANKS

Major général, Général-en-chef	Chief of Staff
Adjudant général (Adjudant commandant after 1800)	Staff Officer (First Class), a colonel or lieutenant colonel often serving as a corps or divisional chief of staff
Adjudant Major	Staff Officer (usually grade of Major)
Officier d'état-major	Staff Officer
Chef de brigade	Brigade-Major

* The title of "Marshal" was technically a dignity rather than a specific rank. The highest permanent rank in the French armies at this period was General of Division. Higher ranks and service appointments were held in only an acting capacity. See Nouveau Dictionaire Militaire, Paris, 1892.

ACKNOWLEDGMENTS

THE PUBLISHERS AND AUTHOR record their indebtedness to the following individuals and institutions for permission to reproduce certain of the illustrations to be found in this book: The National Maritime Museum, Greenwich; The British Museum, London; Cliché des Musées Nationaux, Versailles; Musée d'Armée, Paris; The Victoria and Albert Museum, London; John R. Freeman & Co., London; H. Roger Viollet, Paris; Etablissement Cinématographique des Armées, Paris; and (for photographic services) Marshalls of Camberley.

Maps on pages 13, 22-23, 25, 26, 32-33, 34, 81, 82, 88, 125, 132-33, 137, 144, 145, 179, 180, 181, 182, 183, 206, 228-29, 237, 238, 257, 267, 287, 292-93, 330, 337, 356-57, 362-63, 381, 388-89, 422-27, 446, 459, 472-75 are reprinted with permission of Macmillan Publishing Co., Inc. from *The Campaigns of Napoleon* by David G. Chandler, © 1966 by David G. Chandler, © 1966 by Macmillan Publishing Co., Inc.

Introduction

"THE ART OF WAR . . . has many words unknown, or at least not familiar to any but those whose profession and duty obliges to be masters of them. . . . These difficulties are generally pass'd by unregarded, as if not material for the understanding of what is read; and yet, in reality, they are as necessary and proper to be known as any other part of the relation, which without them becomes but a confus'd notion of something done or acted, without any distinct judicious knowledge of the methods, parts and circumstances of the action. . . ." This passage, penned some 67 years before Napoleon's birth by the anonymous author of the *Military Dictionary*, with the addition of ". . . some broad indications of the characters and achievements of sundry of the principal personages," could serve equally well as a description of the rationale and purpose behind the publication of this volume.

It is now a dozen years since *The Campaigns of Napoleon* was published. The world in general and the reading public in particular have been kind to this book, and it has gone through a number of printings in the United States, Great Britain, and Italy and—whether deservedly or not—continues to be in demand. Over this period of time it has become increasingly evident that there is a genuine need for a dictionary of the type represented by this present book. Even with almost 1,200 pages, 78 maps, and 84 halftone illustrations at my disposal, supported by 10 appendices on related aspects, it just was not possible to do proper justice to so daunting and yet deserving a subject within such a compass—at least not in terms of the type of treatment that was felt to be necessary. Although the textual coverage was restricted to a consideration of only those campaigns that Napoleon commanded in person, with the sole exception of a reasonable treatment of Sir Arthur Wellesley's and Sir John Moore's expeditions to the Peninsula in 1808–09, it proved impracticable to cover even these subjects in sufficient detail. A great deal of important ancillary material had, *faute de mieux*, to be left out, including by far the greater part of the Peninsular War and the equally significant naval struggle, and almost in its entirety the Anglo-American War of 1812. Given the impact of these subjects upon the succession of great European campaigns—the naval war from the very beginning and the other two from 1808 and 1812 respectively—this was a serious deficiency in the earlier volume, as was the virtual exclusion of all reference to the French Revolution *per se* and to the campaigns it spawned between 1792 and 1796, except insofar as Napoleon Bonaparte was personally

[xv]

involved. Furthermore, with a cast of noteworthy leaders running into several hundreds, it was inevitable that many deserving soldiers would receive little beyond the bare mention of their names and thus remain insubstantial shadows in the reader's mind. This, too, was frustrating for author and reader alike.

These particular deficiencies in *The Campaigns* have been brought home to the author practically every week since publication by the arrival of one or more letters from genuinely interested and impressively motivated readers, seeking guidance on and clarification of myriad points, and above all asking for further information on individuals and events not properly treated in the book's pages. The great majority who took the trouble to write had clearly found the work of interest and of value, and it is always a particular pleasure for an author to make even this transient form of contact with his readership. The scope and depth of the questions asked have been vast, ranging from scholarly appeals for documentary and bibliographical guidance to points raised by individuals seeking information on military ancestors; from war-gamers striving to reconstruct parts of one of the campaigns or battles to schoolboys seeking "instant inspiration" for completion of some pedagogic requirement; from fellow-authors wrestling with some aspect of Napoleon's military career to a considerable number of ladies (whom H. G. Wells would have certainly regarded as "girls of the better sort and a few rare and gifted women" at the turn of the century) caught up by the colorful appeal and drama of one of the most important personalities and periods of modern history. "What a romance my life has been," Napoleon once half ruefully remarked during the last, frustrating years on St. Helena. The truth of this is in large measure borne out by the continuing appeal of the subject more than a century and a half since Napoleon quitted the terrestrial scene. Some, admittedly, are critical of and infuriated by the less pleasant sides of both his personality and achievements—and there were indubitably blemishes on both counts; but the overwhelming majority are caught up by the awesome range of Napoleon's attributes and talents and react according to temperament and inclination by either regarding him with near-idolatry or with a simpler admiration based upon straightforward recognition of his considerable attainments.

As these lines are written, there lies on the table the latest of these letters, this one from an 11-year-old schoolboy living in Wiltshire. "Please could you tell me as much as possible about Napoleon's campaigns," this seeker after knowledge hopefully begins. "I ask this because I am doing a project on Napoleon's campaigns and the French Revolution." No inconsiderable request for an author to receive on a Monday morning—but with a deft display of persuasive powers considerably in advance of his years the correspondent continues: "Also Professor ——— of Sidney Sussex College, Cambridge, kindly told me that you were the leading authority on the subject." Apart from making a mental note to be sure and refer some appallingly abstruse subject to the attention of my Cantabrian patron at some future date, what can one do but set out to cooperate to the best of one's ability and limited time? The choice is even more preordained by the discovery in the same envelope of a compliments' slip from the young man's headmaster inscribed, "This is a genuine request and is made with my support and encouragement." Who knows? Perhaps we have a future Oman or Fortescue in the making, and it would be rash as well as discourteous to disregard the appeal. So one does what one can.

Authors write in the field of military history for a number of reasons, and often for a combination of them. Some are mainly concerned with maintaining the historical record of military events, policies, and organizations. A number write essentially for the benefit of a very small clientele of equally superior minds who represent the very quintessence of historical scholarship in the often ultra-specialized fields. Others set out to assist the student of greater or lesser expertise in the subject, or to inform that indeterminate but hopefully vast species of potential readers so beloved of the writers of book-jacket blurbs—"the intelligent layman." In this case it is necessary to blend scholarly research with an easy-to-read literary style and to contain the scholarly apparatus of footnotes and references within reasonable proportions. More write to cater to the growing numbers of *kriegsspiel* players, collectors of militaria, and other military buffs, not to forget the memberships of the burgeoning historical re-enactment societies such as the Sealed Knot, the Napoleonic Association, the Peninsular and Waterloo Association, or the American Brigade of the Revolution, who individually and collectively often embody very considerable areas of knowledge and are certainly never to be discounted as representing an intellectually lightweight readership. Still others write in the hope of interesting the young in a fascinating subject with all its many facets and aspects, so that some of them in their turn may one day become the serious readers, researchers, and writers of tomorrow. Many of these types of historiography are not mutually exclusive, and it is hoped that this *Dictionary of the Napoleonic Wars* will prove of use and interest to several categories of readers and help answer at least some of the myriad questions that surround the life and times of Napoleon Bonaparte. That is the prime purpose of this book.

It is hoped therefore, that the pages that follow will both supplement and complement what was written in the *Campaigns of Napoleon* and in the large number of excellent titles by other authors working in this seemingly inexhaustible field. It is also intended that this book should stand or fall on its own merits. Thus some of the information—for example, the descriptions of the 60 battles, both great and small, in which Napoleon played an important part—will be found in the earlier book, although many points of detail have been added and new information incorporated to make the most of the fruits of 12 further years of reading, writing, and research by the author and others. For a full overview of Napoleon's generalship as such, however, the reader's attention is respectfully directed toward the *Campaigns of Napoleon*, for inevitably the format of a book such as this has to be fragmentary, although certain steps have been taken, as will be described in later paragraphs, to enable the first-time reader to relate the particular episodes and personalities one to another with the sole use of the present volume.

Inevitably and quite properly the massive shadow of Napoleon hovers over every one of the pages that follow, but the real heart of this book is dedicated to the thousand or so entries devoted to the officers and men (although predominantly to the former, because the serried ranks of the *Grande Armée,* of Moore's and Wellington's Peninsular, Kutusov's Russian, or the Archduke Charles' Austrian armies, and of Nelson's, Villeneuve's, and Gravina's fleets, remain mainly silent and anonymous for the latter-day historian and writer, with a number of notable and noteworthy exceptions), who lived through, fought in, and endured these stirring but terrible campaigns and battles over every type of European, Levantine, and North American terrain.

"No man is an island," declared the 17th-century poet and philosopher John Donne, and that is certainly true of historians and chroniclers. Each generation is to a marked degree dependent on the work and inspiration of both predecessors and contemporaries. This work owes an immense debt to the two-volume *chef d'oeuvre* of Georges Six, *Dictionnaire biographique des généraux et amiraux Français de la Révolution et de l'Empire 1792–1814* (1934), as well as to the earlier work of C. Gavard, *Galerie des maréchaux de France* (1839), and the two collections of prints and information published in 1818 by C. Panckoucke, entitled *Portraits des Généreaux Francais . . . 1792 à 1815.* Schuerman's *Itinéraire général de Napoléon* (1911) proved invaluable for the preparation of the simplified and condensed treatment of Napoleon's movements which will be found in the Appendix. Other titles that I have found most illuminating and useful in the preparation of the book include Brigadier Peter Young's studies of *Napoleon's Marshals* (1976) and Dr. C. J. Duffy's works on *Austerlitz* (1977) and *Borodino* (1972). No less helpful have been the books of Antony Brett-James, *Wellington at War* (1961), *The Life of General Graham, Lord Lynedoch* (1959), *The Hundred Days* (1964), *1812* (1966), *Europe against Napoleon* (1972) and *Life in Wellington's Army* (1973). For the Peninsular War in all its phases and complexities, the volumes of the incomparable Sir Charles Oman provided many of the answers, as did the earlier classic works of Sir Charles Napier and the recent writings of Jac Weller, *Wellington in the Peninsula* (1962). For the naval struggle, the great twin volumes of Admiral Mahan formed the basis, supplemented by the many excellent volumes published by the *Naval Records Society* and numerous biographies devoted to individual admirals and monographs tackling aspects of the war at sea in the days of the "wooden-walls." Any such list of secondary sources would fill many pages, but mention must also be made of the five volumes by F. L. Petre on individual Napoleonic campaigns, Colonel Phipps' great work (in five volumes), *The Armies of the First French Republic and of the Consulate* (1935–39), General Foy's *Histoire de la guerre de la Péninsule* (4 vols., 1827), and a number of Commandant Lachouque's flamboyantly Gallic works, including *Waterloo* and (with Anne S. K. Brown) *The Anatomy of Glory*. The works of Richard and Michael Glover also proved of the greatest value. Equally important—albeit all too rarely acknowledged—were the volumes of the *Dictionary of National Biography, La petite Larousse illustrée,* and the encyclopaedias *Britannica* and *Americana,* as well as other works of ready reference. From these sources, together with the not inconsiderable notes and archives that have accumulated over some 20 years from reading and research in the British Museum, the Public Records Office, and other documentary repositories, the present volume has been slowly created.

No claim is made that the coverage is anywhere near complete, even of the more important figures and events. Perhaps the hardest task of all was the initial selection of the 1,200 subjects for inclusion. Frenchmen appear more frequently than Russians or Germans; soldiers receive ten times the space allotted to politicians and statesmen; numerous actions at sea and on land have been left out; women appear hardly at all—all these are criticisms that may be leveled at this book with ample justification. However, any compiler has, in the last analysis, to trust to his own judgment of what can be included and what must, for reasons of space, regretfully be laid aside. It is felt that a fair representative selection has been made, and bearing in mind that the work needs to stand on its own rather than to serve purely as a supplementary volume of background information in support of the *Campaigns of Napoleon,* it is hoped that the reader will find at least something of use in its pages. In such a work errors, alas, will have escaped the closest scrutiny of the author and publisher's readers, but the forebearance of the reader is requested, and every attempt will be made to correct such slips in future printings.

As the entries are arranged in alphabetical order, certain steps have been taken to help orientate the reader. First, every name of a place, person, or aspect that is the subject of an entry in the body of the work is marked with an asterisk wherever it appears. The only exception is the case of Napoleon himself: neither Buonaparte, Bonaparte, nor Napoleon is so marked, as it is obvious that this name will appear several thousand times. In two cases a special circumstance pertains: it has been decided to treat "*coalitions*" and "*coups d'état*" in consolidated entries; thus descriptions of, for example, the "Third Coalition" or "the *coup d'état de Brumaire*" will be found under the relevant collective heading and not under "Third" or "Brumaire" (although in some cases a single-line cross-reference is provided to direct the reader to the relevant entry).

When the dates of an individual are uncertain, the convention of "fl." (i.e., *floreat* or flourished) is included after the name with a date at which the person's career reached its high (or low) watermark.

In the second place, to aid the reader to relate a particular entry to its wider setting or period, a fairly extensive chronology has been provided (see

p. xxiii). Reference to this for a particular event will give some indications of what other linked subjects are to be found elsewhere, and as a further help each item included in the chronology is supported by an italicized coding in parentheses to indicate whether the subject is political, diplomatic, personal (to the subject's career), or military; in the last instance, the geographical location of the event is also indicated. Thus under "1793 16 September Buonaparte given command of the artillery before Toulon" there is the coding "*(pers./ mil./France)*," indicating that this was an important moment in his personal career, an event of some military significance, and that Toulon is to be found in France. Later, under 19 December for the same year, "the fall of Toulon" is labeled "*(pol./mil./France)*," the recapture of the great arsenal and naval base being an event of great political importance to the struggling Republican government in Paris as well as a notable military happening.

Thirdly, to provide the reader with a ready means of acquiring an overview of a particularly important subject, nine key article-entries (ranging from 2,000 to 7,000 words apiece) have been included at the appropriate alphabetical point. These are as follows:

Coalitions
Coups d'état
Napoleon Bonaparte, Emperor
Naval Wars
Peninsular War
Revolution, the French
Revolutionary Wars
War of 1812
Wellesley, Field Marshal Sir Arthur, First Duke of Wellington

Cross-references are indicated in eight of these article-entries by use of asterisks. In the case of that devoted to Napoleon himself, however, the convention has *not* been employed, as almost every fifth word would have needed to be marked. In these articles special attention has been paid to treating the subject in general rather than completely specific terms. Many events are mentioned without repeating the specific dates, as these will be found in the individual entries and in the chronology. This general rule also holds good for mentions of other asterisked events within all individual entries.

Fourthly, to assist the reader who is interested to know exactly where Napoleon was on a particular date during the campaigns he personally conducted, a section entitled "Napoleon's Military Movements, 1796–1815" will be found in the Appendix. Whenever possible, besides the points of departure and arrival on each date, some idea of the route followed is included in simplified form, while in the final column reference is made to any special event or circumstance that took place on that date—those placed in parentheses being occasions at which the Emperor was not personally present. It did not prove feasible to indicate the physical distances covered, and not every place name will be found on the general maps incorporated in the volume, but the great majority of major staging posts and stopping points will be discoverable, and reference to the scale-lines provided on the maps will make it possible to estimate the distances involved.

Fifthly, to illustrate key engagements, particularly those fought at sea or during the Revolutionary and Peninsular wars, a total of 42 specially commissioned battle maps and diagrams have been included. Additionally, by kind permission of Macmillan Publishing Co., Inc., of New York, further maps from the *Campaigns of Napoleon* have been republished in photogravure and on a reduced scale to support the descriptions of major battles and to cover major campaign areas. Over 125 illustrations are also incorporated in the text, the greater number being portraits.

It remains, finally, to thank a number of people whose advice, assistance, and enthusiasm have greatly aided the production of this dictionary. First there are those colleagues and friends in the Department of War Studies and International Affairs at the Royal Military Academy Sandhurst who have afforded the author the benefit of their knowledge and expertise, including Antony Brett-James, John Keegan, and Christopher Duffy of the "Old Guard" (not to forget Brigadier Peter Young, sometime Reader in Military History at Sandhurst, who qualifies for the honorable title of "Oldest of the Old"); Michael Orr and Richard Holmes of what may be termed "the Middle Guard"; and Paddy Griffith, John Pimlott, Nigel de Lee, and Hew Strachan of the "Young Guard." The Sandhurst Central Library staff, headed by John Hunt and his predecessor, Lieutenant Colonel Alan Shepperd, and the devoted personnel of the Ministry of Defence Library (Central and Army) in Whitehall have also made notable contributions which are gratefully acknowledged. Much advice and information has also been forthcoming from certain colleagues of many nations who are fellow-members of the International Commission for Comparative Military History, particularly the *président d'honneur, Général* Fernand Gambiez, the current president, Colonel Bengt Ähslund of Sweden, and three of the author's fellow vice-presidents, Professor André Corvisier of the Sorbonne, Professor Jack Jessup of the U.S.A., and Lieutenant General Pavel Zhilin, chief of the Military History Institute of the Soviet Union. American men of letters who have aided the author include Colonel John Elting, U.S.A. (ret.), Colonels Tom Greiss and John Britt III of the United States Military Academy, West Point, and Professors Ted Ropp, Gunther Rothenburg, Claude Sturgill, and John Shy, while Canadian scholars and friends include Professor Jim Stokesbury, Commander Alec Douglas, and Mr. Ben Weider, the noted collector of Napoleonic art and relics. Much is also owed to members of the British Commission for Military History and those devoted and hardy groups who have accompanied the author abroad on many a tour to France and the Peninsula under the aegis of Captain Gordon Battlefield Tours and the Mili-

Introduction

tary History Society. The cartographers, Sheila Waters and Hazel Watson, converted the author's rough sketches and near-illegible scrawls into fine maps and diagrams; Dr. Christopher Duffy also contributed his photographic skills, while Messrs. S. P. Cullen and R. Sweet of Marshalls Ltd. (Photographers) of Camberley provided prompt and swift printing services. Mrs. Janet Gillette and Mrs. Janette Ingram bravely and accurately saw to the typing of the various drafts of the manuscript. The author also acknowledges his debt to Mr. Fred Honig, formerly of the Macmillan Company of New York (who originally commissioned this work), and to Mrs. Elizabeth Scharlatt and Miss Deborah Hastings, members of the editorial department of that publisher, for their many services in preparing the volume for publication. Lastly, he owes (as always) an inestimable debt to his wife Gillian and three sons, Paul, John, and Mark, for cheerfully tolerating (usually anyway) the steadily creeping tide of books and papers which at times threatened to engulf the whole house, and for sustaining him through the long months of preparation and particularly those times when the spirit temporarily flickered and the inspiration faltered. This book is as much the achievement of all those mentioned above as it is of the author, although its defects, errors, and oversights are wholly his responsibility and are in no way to be laid at their door.

DAVID G. CHANDLER
The Royal Military Academy Sandhurst

[xxii]

Chronological Table

THE EVENTS LISTED BELOW denote highlights of the life and times of Napoleon Bonaparte. Inevitably, a highly selective approach has been adopted, and there is no claim that anything approaching a comprehensive coverage has been achieved. To assist the reader, the following conventions have been adopted. Any event that has merited an entry in the Dictionary is marked with an asterisk, e.g., 1815 Battle of Waterloo* (*mil., Belgium*). Placed in parentheses after the item is information on the category of event and (when relevant) the geographical location.

dip.	diplomatic
mil.	military
pol.	political
pers.	personal

N.B.: Napoleon's name is spelled in the Italo/Corsican form until he adopted the French style.

1769	29 April	Arthur Wellesley* born (*pers.*)
	15 August	Napoleone Buonaparte born (*pers.*)
1779	1 January	Napoleone and Giuseppe Buonaparte enter College of Autun (*pers.*)
	15 May	Napoleone enters School of Brienne (*pers.*)
1784	30 October	Napoleone enters *l'Ecole Militaire* in Paris as a gentleman-cadet (*pers.*)
1785	24 February	Death of Carlo Buonaparte* (*pers.*)
	1 September	Napoleone commissioned into the French Royal Artillery* (*mil.*)
1786	1 September	Napoleone begins first leave in Corsica (until June 1788 with extensions) (*pers.*)
	June	Napoleone joins Auxonne Training School (*mil.*)
1789	5 May	Meeting of States-General at Versailles (*pol.*)
	17 June	Third Estate declares itself the National Assembly (*pol.*); start of French Revolution*
	14 July	Storming of the Bastille (*pol.*)
	15 September	Buonaparte starts further period of leave in Corsica (*pers.*)

1790	14 July	Paoli* returns to Corsica (*pol.*)
1791	10 February	Buonaparte returns to regimental duty at Auxonne (*mil.*)
	1 April	Buonaparte promoted to *premier lieutenant* (*mil.*)
	20 June	Louis XVI* flees to Varennes (*pol.*)
	1 September	Buonaparte begins third period of leave in Corsica (*pers.*)
1792	6 February	Buonaparte promoted to *capitaine en second* (with ante-date) (*mil.*)
	3 March	Siege of Seringapatam* (*mil./India*); falls on 19th
	1 April	Buonaparte elected lieutenant colonel of 2nd Bn., Ajaccio Volunteers (*mil./pol.*)
	20 April	French Assembly declares war on King of Bohemia (*dip.*)
	26 June	The First Coalition* comes into existence (*dip.*)
	5 September	The September Massacres in Paris; start of the "Terror"* (*pol.*)
	20 September	The battle of Valmy* (*mil./France*)
	21 September	National Convention established in Paris (*pol.*)
	22 September	Abolition of French monarchy; start of Revolutionary Calendar (*pol.*)
	6 November	The battle of Jemappes* (*mil./Netherlands*)
1793	21 January	Execution of Louis XVI* (*pol.*)
	1 February	France declares war on Great Britain and Holland (*dip.*)
	22 February	Attack on La Maddalena* fails (*mil./Sardinia*); French evacuate on 25th
	3 March	Buonaparte breaks with Paoli* (*pol.*)
	9 March	The Convention declares war on Spain (*dip.*)
	18 March	The battle of Neerwinden* (*mil./Netherlands*)
	5 April	General Dumouriez* defects to the Allies (*pol.*)
	6 April	Establishment of Committee of Public Safety (*pol.*)
	2 June	Girondin party overthrown by Jacobins* (*pol.*)
	13 June	Buonaparte arrives in France with his family from Corsica (*pers.*)
	27 August	Toulon* admits the Allies (*pol./mil./France*)
	7 September	French forces begin to besiege Toulon* (*mil./France*)
	16 September	Buonaparte given command of the artillery before Toulon* (*pers./mil./France*)
	15–16 October	The battle of Wattignies* (*mil./Holland*)
	18 October	Buonaparte promoted to *chef de bataillon* at Toulon* (*pers.*)
	19 December	Fall of Toulon* (*pol./mil./France*)
	22 December	Buonaparte promoted to *général de brigade* (*pers.*)
1794	6 February	Buonaparte given command of the Artillery in the Army of Italy (*pers.*)
	13–14 March	The battle of Hotham and Martin (*mil./naval*)
	5 April	Execution of Danton in Paris (*pol.*)
	24 April	Action of Villers-en-Cauches* (*mil./Netherlands*)

	1 June	The battle of the First of June* (*mil./naval*)
	26 June	The battle of Fleurus* (*mil./Netherlands*)
	27 July	*Coup d'état** of *9 Thermidor;* fall and death of Robespierre;* end of the "Terror"* (*pol.*)
	9–20 August	Buonaparte imprisoned at Antibes (*pers./pol.*)
	15 September	Action of Boxtel* (*mil./Netherlands*)
795	1 April	*Coup d'état* of *12 Germinal, An III* (*pol.*)
	16 May	Peace of Basle (*dip.*)
	20 May	*Coup d'état* of *1 Prairial* (*pol.*)
	21 June	Allies and émigrés land at Quiberon (*mil./pol.*)
	19 August	Peace with Spain (*dip.*)
	21 August	Buonaparte appointed to *Bureau Topographique** in Paris (*pers.*)
	4–5 October	*Coup d'état* of *13 Vendémiaire, An IV* (*pol.*); "whiff of grapeshot" (*pers.*)
	16 October	Buonaparte promoted to *général de division* (*pers.*)
	26 October	Buonaparte appointed to command Army of the Interior (*pers.*)
	27 October	Formal creation of Directory* (*pol.*); Constitution of the Year Three (*pol.*)
	22–24 November	The battle of Loano (*mil./Italy*)
1796	2 March	Bonaparte appointed to command Army of Italy (*pers.*)
	9 March	Bonaparte marries Josephine Beauharnais* (*pers.*)
	26 March	Bonaparte assumes command at Nice (*mil.*)
	10 April	Combat of Voltri* (*mil./N. Italy*)
	12 April	The battle of Montenotte* (*mil./N. Italy*)
	13 April	The battle of Millesimo* (*mil./N. Italy*)
	14 and 15 April	First and second battles of Dego* (*mil./N. Italy*)
	21 April	The battle of Mondovi* (*mil./N. Italy*)
	28 April	Armistice of Cherasco* (*dip.*)
	7 May	Passage of the river Po (*mil./N. Italy*)
	8 May	Combat of Fombio (*mil./N. Italy*)
	10 May	The battle of Lodi* (*mil./Italy*)
	15 May	Occupation of Milan (*mil./pol./N. Italy*)
	30 May	The battle of Borghetto* (*mil./N. Italy*)
	4 June	First siege of Mantua* (*mil./N. Italy*); to 31 July (abandoned)
	23 June	Armistice of Bologna with Papal States (*dip.*)
	2 August	First battle of Lonato* (*mil./N. Italy*)
	5 August	Second battle of Lonato* and battle of Castiglione* (*mil./N. Italy*)
	19 August	Treaty of Idelfonso with Spain (*dip.*)
	4 September	The battle of Roveredo* (*mil./N. Italy*)
	8 September	The battle of Bassano* (*mil./N. Italy*)
	8 October	Spain declares war on Great Britain (*dip.*)
	15–17 November	The battle of Arcola (*mil./N. Italy*)

	16 November	Accession of Tsar Paul (*dip.*)
	16 December	General Hoche* sails for Ireland (*mil.*)
	21–27 December	Attempted landing at Bantry Bay fails (*mil./naval*)
1797	14 January	The battle of Rivoli (*mil./N. Italy*)
	2 February	Surrender of Mantua (*mil./N. Italy*)
	14 February	The battle of Cape St. Vincent* (*mil./naval*)
	19 February	Treaty of Tolentino* (*dip.*)
	22–24 February	Attempted landing at Fishguard (*mil./naval*)
	16 April	Beginning of Spithead Mutiny* (*naval*); ends 15 May
	18 April	Preliminary Peace of Leoben* (*dip.*)
	12 May	Beginning of the Nore Mutiny* (*naval*); ends 13 June
	16 May	Bonaparte occupies Venice (*mil./pol.*)
	28 June	French occupation of the Ionian Isles (*mil./naval*)
	4 September	*Coup d'état* * of *18 Fructidor, An V* (*pol.*)
	11 October	The battle of Camperdown* (*mil./naval*)
	16 October	Bonaparte appointed to command Army of England (*pers.*)
	17 October	Treaty and Peace of Campo Formio* (*dip.*)
1798	20 February	Pope Pius VI* deported to France (*pol.*)
	5 March	Directory* abandons plans for invasion of England (*mil.*)
	12 April	Bonaparte appointed to command Army of the Orient (*pers.*)
	26 April	Annexation of Geneva and creation of Helvetic Republic (*dip.*)
	19 May	Bonaparte sails from Toulon for Egypt (*mil.*)
	May	*Coup d'état* * of *22 Floréal, An 5* (*pol.*)
	10 June	Occupation of Malta* (*mil./pol.*)
	1 July	Army of the Orient disembarks at Embabeh (*mil./Egypt*)
	2 July	Storm of Alexandria* (*mil./Egypt*)
	13 July	The battle of Shubra Khit* (*mil./Egypt*)
	21 July	The battle of the Pyramids* (*mil./Egypt*)
	1 August	The battle of the Nile* (*naval*)
	2 September	The Sultan declares war on France (*dip.*)
	5 September	France introduces conscription* (*pol.*)
	21 October	Revolt of Cairo suppressed (*pol./mil.*)
	29 December	Formation of Second Coalition* against France (*dip.*)
1799	8 February	Siege of El Arish* (*mil./Sinai*); falls on 19th
	1 March	War breaks out between Second Coalition and France (*dip.*)
	3 March	First attack on Jaffa* (*mil./Syria*); stormed on 7th; massacre
	11 March	Bonaparte visits the Pestiferies at Jaffa* (*pers.*)
	19 March	Start of the siege of Acre* (*mil./Syria*); abandoned 20 May
	25 March	Battle of Stockach* (*mil./Germany*)
	16 April	Battle of Mount Tabor* (*mil./Syria*)
	20 May	French retreat from Syria begins (*mil./Syria*)
	4–7 June	First battle of Zurich (*mil./Switzerland*)
	14 June	Bonaparte reaches Cairo (*mil./pol.*)
	18 June	*Coup d'état* * of *30 Prairial, An VII* (*pol.*)

	25 July	Battle of Aboukir* (*mil./Egypt*)
	15 August	Battle of Novi* (*mil./N. Italy*)
	23 August	Bonaparte sails for France (*pol./pers.*)
	27 August	Allied landing under Duke of York* in Holland (*mil.*)
	26–30 September	Second Battle of Zurich* (*mil./Switzerland*)
	9 October	Bonaparte lands in France. (*pol./pers.*)
	9–10 November	*Coup d'état* of *Brumaire;* abolition of Directory* (*pol.*)
	10 November	Provisional Consulate* set up (*pol.*)
	19 November	The Duke of York* evacuates Holland (*mil.*)
	14 December	Constitution of the Year VIII (*pol.*); Bonaparte made First Consul (*pers.*)
	26 December	*Conseil d'état* formed (*pol.*)
1800	20 January	Caroline Bonaparte* married to Murat* (*pers.*)
	28 January	Convention of El Arish (*dip./Sinai*)
	14 March	Election of Pope Pius VII (*dip.*)
	20 March	The battle of Heliopolis (*mil./Egypt*); Kléber* defeats Turks
	5 April	Austrian offensive opens in northwest Italy (*mil.*)
	20 April	Siege of Genoa* opens (*mil./Italy*)
	3 May	The second battle of Stockach* (*mil./Germany*)
	15 May	Crossing of the Alps by the Army of the Reserve begins (*mil./Switzerland—Italy*)
	21 May	Siege of Fort Bard* begins (*mil./Italy*)
	4 June	Fall of Genoa* (*mil./Italy*)
	5 June	Fall of Fort Bard* (*mil./Italy*)
	9 June	The battle of Montebello* (*mil./Italy*)
	14 June	The battle of Marengo* and death of Desaix* (*mil./Italy*)
	15 June	Convention of Alessandria (*dip.*)
	19 June	The battle of Höchstädt (*mil./Bavaria*)
	28 July	Austro-French preliminaries of peace (*dip.*)
	5 September	Fall of Malta* (*mil.*)
	7 October	Second treaty of Idelfonso cedes Louisiana to France (*dip.*)
	5 November	Austro-French hostilities resume (*dip./mil./Austria*)
	3 December	The battle of Hohenlinden (*mil./Bavaria*)
	18 December	Formation of Second Armed Neutrality (*dip./Baltic*)
	24 December	Bomb attempt on First Consul's life in Paris (*pers./pol.*)
1801	15 January	Franco-Austrian Armistice of Treviso (*dip.*)
	9 February	Peace of Luneville* (*dip.*)
	22 March	Second (or night) battle of Aboukir (*mil./Egypt*)
	23 March	Assassination of Tsar Paul I;* accession of Alexander I* (*pol./dip.*)
	2 April	The battle of Copenhagen* (*naval*)
	6 and 13 July	The battles of Algeçiras* (*naval*)
	15 July	The Concordat* with Rome is signed (*pol./dip.*)
	14 September	The French evacuate Egypt (*dip./mil.*)
	1 October	The Preliminaries of Amiens are signed (*dip.*)

	14 December	Leclerc* sails from Brest for Santo Domingo* (*mil./West Indies*)
1802	5 February	Leclerc* reaches Santo Domingo* (*mil./West Indies*)
	25 March	Peace of Amiens* (*dip.*)
	8–14 May	Plebiscite on the Life Consulship; proclaimed 2 August (*pers./pol.*)
	19 May	Institution of *légion d'honneur** (*pol.*)
	2 August	French annex Elba (*dip./mil.*)
	2 September	French annex Piedmont (*dip./mil./N. Italy*)
	15 October	French invade Switzerland (*mil.*)
1803	19 February	French Act of Mediation in Switzerland (*dip.*)
	11 March	Fleet told to prepare for invasion of England (*dip./naval*)
	3 May	French sell Louisiana to the U.S.A. (*dip.*)
	16 May	Britain declares war on France (*dip./mil.*)
	1 June	Mortier* occupies Hanover (*mil./Germany*)
	15 June	Camp of Bologne* manned (*mil./France*)
	23 August	Camps formed at St. Omer and Bruges; invasion flotillas assemble (*mil./naval*)
	9 October	Franco-Spanish alliance signed (*dip.*)
	29 November	The battle of Argaum* (*mil./India*)
1804	13 February	Cadoudal* plot uncovered (*pol.*)
	19 & 28 February	Arrests of Moreau* and Pichegru* (*pol.*)
	21 March	Duc d'Enghien* kidnapped and executed (*pol./dip.*)
	24 March	Promulgation of Civil Code* (*pol.*)
	18 May	Napoleon proclaimed Emperor (*pers./pol.*)
	19 May	Creation of the Marshalate* (*mil./pol.*)
	2 December	Coronation of Napoleon at Notre Dame (*pol.*)
	14 December	Spain declares war on Britain (*dip.*)
1805	11 April	Anglo-Russian alliance signed (*dip.*)
	26 May	Napoleon crowns himself King of Italy (*pol./dip.*)
	4 June	France annexes Genoa (*pol./dip.*)
	7 June	Eugène Beauharnais* appointed Viceroy of Italy (*pol.*)
	22 July	Action of Ferrol between Calder* and Villeneuve* (*naval*)
	9 August	Adhesion of Austria completes Third Coalition* (*dip.*)
	3 September	Last major formations leave Camp of Boulogne* (*mil.*)
	10 September	General Mack's* Austrians invade Bavaria (*dip./mil.*)
	25 September	The *Grande Armée* crosses the Rhine (*mil.*)
	7 October	First French units cross the Danube (*mil./Bavaria*)
	8 October	Combat of Wertingen* (*mil./Bavaria*)
	11 October	Combat of Haslach* (*mil./Bavaria*)
	14 October	Action of Elchingen* (*mil./Bavaria*)
	17 October	Convention of Ulm* (*dip.*)
	20 October	Capitulation of Ulm* (*dip./mil./Bavaria*)
	21 October	The battle of Trafalgar* (*naval*); death of Nelson*
	28–31 October	The second battle of Caldiero* (*mil./N. Italy*)

	3 November	Treaty of Potsdam* (*dip.*)
	8 November	The battle of Maria Zell* (*mil./Danube*)
	11 November	Action of Durrenstein* (*mil./Danube*)
	14 November	Napoleon enters Vienna (*dip./mil.*)
	16 November	Battle of Hollabrünn* (*mil./Danube*)
	2 December	The battle of Austerlitz* (*mil./Moravia*)
	26 December	Peace of Pressburg* (*dip.*)
1806	23 January	Death of William Pitt* (*pol./dip.*)
	15 February	France forces Prussia to grant concessions (*dip.*)
	1 April	Joseph Bonaparte* created King of Naples (*dip.*)
	April	Murat* made Grand Duke of Berg and Cleves (*dip.*)
	16 May	British blockade of French ports begins (*dip./naval*)
	20 June	Louis Bonaparte* created King of Holland (*dip.*)
	4 July	General Stuart* wins battle of Maida (*mil./Italy*)
	12 July	Creation of the Confederation of the Rhine* (*dip.*)
	18 July	Massena* captures Gaeta (*mil./Naples*)
	20 July	Franco-Russian peace treaty (*dip.*)
	6 August	Dissolution of Holy Roman Empire (*dip.*)
	9 August	Prussian army mobilizes (*mil.*)
	24 August	Tsar Alexander* refuses to ratify peace with France (*dip.*)
	1 October	Prussia issues ultimatum to France (*dip.*)
	6 October	Formation of Fourth Coalition* (*dip.*)
	7 October	French troops invade Saxony (*mil.*)
	9 October	Action of Schleiz* (*mil./Saxony*)
	10 October	The battle of Saalfeld* (*mil./Saxony*)
	14 October	The battle of Jena-Auerstädt* (*mil./Saxony*)
	20 October	Start of siege of Magdeburg* (*mil./Prussia*)
	27 October	Napoleon enters Berlin (*mil./Prussia*)
	28 October	Hohenlohe* surrenders to Lasalle* at Prenzlau (*mil./Prussia*)
	7 November	Blücher* surrenders to Bernadotte* at Lubeck (*mil./Prussia*)
	11 November	Surrender of Magdeburg* to Ney* (*mil./Prussia*)
	21 November	Promulgation of Berlin Decrees (*dip.*) Inauguration of Continental System* (*dip.*)
	10 December	Saxony signs Treaty of Posen with France; its Elector proclaimed King (*dip.*)
	18 December	Napoleon enters Warsaw (*mil./Poland*)
	26 December	The battles of Golymin* and Pultusk* (*mil./Poland*)
1807	1 January	Napoleon meets Marie Walewska* at Warsaw (*pers.*)
	7 January	British Orders in Council* against contraband (*dip./naval*)
	30 January	Start of siege of Stralsund* (*mil./Poland*)
	7 and 8 February	The battle of Eylau* (*mil./Poland*)
	19 February	British squadron forces the Dardanelles (*dip./naval*)
	18 March	Start of siege of Danzig* (*mil./Prussia*)
	26 April	Franco-Russian Convention of Bartenstein (*dip.*)

29 April	Surrender of Stralsund* (*mil./Poland*)
27 May	Fall of Danzig* (*mil./Prussia*)
10 June	The battle of Heilsberg* (*mil./Poland*)
14 June	The battle of Friedland (*mil./Poland*)
25 June	The meeting on the river Niemen (*dip.*)
5 July	British fiasco before Montevideo* (*mil./South America*)
7–9 July	The Peace and Treaties of Tilsit* (*dip.*)
16 August	British forces bombard and land at Copenhagen* (*naval/ mil./Denmark*)
7 September	British forces take over Danish fleet (*mil./naval*)
13 October	Decree of Fontainebleau (*dip.*)
27 October	Secret treaty of Fontainebleau with Spain (*dip.*)
7 November	The Tsar recalls his ambassador from London (*dip.*)
23 November	First Milan Decree (*dip.*)
27 November	Regent John* of Portugal sails for Brazil (*pol./dip.*)
30 November	General Junot* occupies Lisbon (*mil./Portugal*)
17 December	Second Milan Decree (*dip.*)

1808	20 February	Murat* appointed Napoleon's "Lieutenant" in Spain (*dip.*)
	29 February	French seize Barcelona* (*mil./Spain*)
	16 April	Start of Conference of Bayonne (*dip.*)
	2 May	Revolt of Madrid suppressed (*pol./mil.*)
	6 June	Joseph Bonaparte* proclaimed King of Spain (*dip.*)
	8 June	General Dupont takes Cordova*
	15 June	Attempted storm of Saragossa* (*mil./Spain*)
	16 June	Start of first siege of Saragossa (*mil.*)
	14 July	The battle of Medina del Rio Seco* (*mil.*)
	20 July	End of Conference of Bayonne (*dip.*)
	21 July	Capitulation of Bailen* (*mil./Spain*)
	25 July	Massacre of Evora* (*mil./Spain*)
	1–8 August	Wellesley* lands at Mondego Bay (*mil./Portugal*)
	14 August	Raising of siege of Saragossa (*mil./Spain*)
	16 August	Action of Obidos* (*mil./Portugal*)
	17 August	Action of Roliça* (*mil./Portugal*)
	21 August	The battle of Vimiero* (*mil./Portugal*)
	30 August	The Convention of Cintra* (*dip./mil./Portugal*)
	27 September	Start of Congress of Erfurt* (*dip.*)
	14 October	End of Congress; Russo-French convention (*dip.*)
	27 October	General Moore* leaves Lisbon for Spain (*mil.*)
	31 October	Combat of Pan Corbo* (*mil./Spain*)
	5 November	Combat of Valmaceda* (*mil./Spain*) Napoleon takes command of Army of Spain (*pers.*)
	14 November	Action of Reynosa* (*mil./Spain*)
	23 November	The battle of Tudela* (*mil./Spain*)
	30 November	The battle of Somosierra* (*mil./Spain*)
	4 December	Napoleon occupies Madrid (*pol./mil.*)
	20 December	Start of second siege of Saragossa* (*mil.*)
	21 December	Action of Sahagun* (*mil./Spain*)

	22 December	Napoleon crosses the Guadarrama Pass (*mil.*)
	24 December	Moore* begins to retreat (*mil./Spain*)
	26 December	Action of Benavente; Moore* captures Lefebvre-Desnouëttes (*mil./Spain*)
1809	3 January	Action of Villafranca* ,(*mil./Spain*)
	9 January	Combat of Lugo; Moore's success (*mil./Spain*)
	16 January	The battle of Corunna;* Moore* killed (*mil./Spain*)
	24 January	Napoleon leaves Valladolid for Paris (*pol.*)
	24 February	British capture Martinique (*mil./naval/West Indies*)
	29 March	Soult captures Oporto (*mil./Portugal*)
		The battle of Medellin (*mil./Spain*)
	9 April	Creation of Fifth Coalition* (*dip.*); Austria attacks Bavaria (*mil.*)
	20 April	The battle of Abensberg* (*mil./Bavaria*)
	21 April	Storming of Landshut* (*mil./Bavaria*)
	22 April	The battle of Eckmühl* (*mil./Bavaria*)
	23 April	The storming of Ratisbon* (*mil./Bavaria*)
	26 April	Wellesley lands at Lisbon (*mil./Portugal*)
	3 May	The combat of Ebelsberg* (*mil./Austria*)
	12 May	The battle of Oporto (*mil./Portugal*)
	13 May	Napoleon enters Vienna (*mil./pol.*)
	21 and 22 May	The battle of Aspern-Essling* (*mil./pol.*)
	4 June	Start of siege of Gerona (*mil./Spain*)
	14 June	The battle of the Raab* (*mil./Germany*)
	5 and 6 July	The battle of Wagram* (*mil./Austria*)
	10 July	Action of Znaim* (*mil./Austria*)
	12 July	Armistice of Znaim* (*dip.*)
	28 July	The battle of Talavera* (*mil./Spain*)
	29 July	British landing at Walcheren* (*mil./Holland*)
	4 August	Combat of Arzobispo* (*mil./Spain*)
	16 August	The battle of Flushing* (*mil./Holland*)
	19 October	Treaty of Vienna and Peace of Schonbrunn* (*dip.*)
	19 November	The battle of Ocaña* (*mil./Spain*)
	11 December	Surrender of Gerona (*mil./Spain*)
	15 December	Napoleon divorces Josephine* (*pers.*)
1810	5 February	Start of siege of Cadiz* (*mil./Spain*)
	11 February	Start of blockade of Ciudad Rodrigo* (*mil./Spain*)
	2 April	Napoleon marries Marie-Louise* (*pers.*)
	17 April	Massena* appointed to command in Portugal (*mil.*)
	16 June	Start of siege of Ciudad Rodrigo* (*mil./Spain*)
	9 July	Napoleon annexes Holland (*pol.*)
		Fall of Ciudad Rodrigo (*mil./Spain*)
	16 August	Start of siege of Almeida* (*mil./Portugal*)
	21 August	Bernadotte* elected Crown Prince of Sweden (*dip.*)
	28 August	Fall of Almeida (*mil./Portugal*)
	27 September	The battle of Bussaco* (*mil./Portugal*)

	10 October	Massena halted by the lines of Torres Vedras* (*mil./Portugal*)
	18 October	The Fontainebleau Decrees* (*pol.*)
	15 October	The action of Fuengirola (*mil./Spain*)
1811	26 January	Start of first siege of Badajoz* (*mil./Spain*)
	5 March	The battle of Barrosa* (*mil./Spain*)
		Massena retreats from lines of Torres Vedras* (*mil./Portugal*)
	11 March	Fall of Badajoz* (*mil./Spain*)
	3 April	Action of Sabugal* (*mil./Portugal*)
	3–5 May	The battle of Fuentes de Oñoro (*mil./Portugal*)
	7 May	Start of second siege of Badajoz* (*mil./Spain*)
	12 May	Raising of siege of Badajoz* (*mil./Spain*)
	16 May	The battle of Albuera* (*mil./Spain*)
	24 May	Start of siege of Tarragonna* (*mil./Spain*)
		Resumption of siege of Badajoz* (*mil./Spain*)
	25 May	The action of Usagre* (*mil./Spain*)
	19 June	Abandonment of siege of Badajoz* (*mil./Spain*)
	28 June	Fall of Tarragonna* (*mil./Spain*)
	25 September	The battle of El Bodon* (*mil./Portugal*)
	28 October	The battle of Arroyo dos Molinos* (*mil./Spain*)
	19 December	Start of siege of Tarifa* (*mil./Spain*)
	23 December	Napoleon starts military preparations against Russia (*mil./dip.*)
	31 December	Tsar Alexander* issues *ukase* against French trade (*pol./dip.*)
1812	5 January	Fall of Tarifa* (*mil./Spain*)
	8 January	Start of second siege of Ciudad Rodrigo* (*mil./Spain*)
	10 January	France occupies Swedish Pomerania (*pol./dip.*)
	19 January	Fall of Ciudad Rodrigo* (*mil./Spain*)
	26 February	Alliance between France and Prussia (*dip.*)
	10 March	Alliance between France and Austria (*dip.*)
	16 March	Start of third siege of Badajoz* (*mil./Spain*)
	24 March	Secret Russo-Swedish agreement (*dip.*)
	6 April	Storm of Badajoz* (*mil./Spain*)
	17–28 May	Conference of Dresden (*dip.*)
	28 May	Peace of Bucharest* (*dip.*)
	18 June	War declared between the U.S. and Great Britain (*dip.*)
	20 June	Sixth Coalition* formed (*dip.*)
	24 June	French cross the river Niemen (*mil./Poland*)
	28 June	Battle of Vilna* (*mil./Poland*)
	21 July	Action of Alba de Tormes* bridge (*mil./Spain*)
	22 July	The battle of Salamanca* (*mil./Spain*)
	23 July	Action of Garcia Hernandez (*mil./Spain*)
	25 and 26 July	Combats of Ostronovo* (*mil./Russia*)
	28 July	The battle of Vitebsk* (*mil./Russia*)

8 August	Action of Inkovo* (*mil./Russia*)
13 August	Wellington enters Madrid (*pol.*)
17–19 August	The battles of Smolensk* and Valutino (*mil./Russia*)
17 and 18 August	The first battle of Polotsk* (*mil./Russia*)
24 August	Abandonment of siege of Cadiz* (*mil./Spain*)
7 September	The battle of Borodino* (*mil./Russia*)
14 September	Napoleon enters Moscow* (*dip./pol.*)
15 September	Outbreak of the great fire of Moscow (*pol.*)
19 September	Start of first siege of Burgos* (*mil./Spain*)
13 October	The battle of the Queenstown Heights (*mil./Canada*)
18 October	The battle of Vinkovo* (or Taruntino) (*mil./Russia*)
19 October	The French begin to leave Moscow (*mil./pol.*)
22 October	Abandonment of siege of Burgos* (*mil./Spain*)
23 October	Action of Venta del Pozo (*mil./Spain*)
	Conspiracy of General Malet* in Paris (*pol.*)
24 & 25 October	The battle of Maloyaroslavetz (*mil./Russia*)
2 November	French reoccupy Madrid (*mil./Spain*)
3 November	The battle of Fiodoroivskoy (*mil./Russia*)
14 November	The second battle of Polotsk* (*mil./Russia*)
17 November	The battle of Krasnöe* (*mil./Russia*)
27–29 November	The battle of the river Beresina* (*mil./Russia*)
5 December	Napoleon quits the *Grande Armée* at Smorgoni* (*pol.*)
9–15 December	Actions of Alba de Tormes (*mil./Spain*)
14 December	French rear guard reaches the river Niemen (*mil./Russia*)
18 December	Napoleon reaches Paris (*pol.*)
29 December	Action of Plechenitski (*mil./Poland*)
30 December	Convention of Tauroggen* (*dip.*)

1813	25 January	Napoleon and Pius VII sign second Concordat (*pol.*)
	26 February	Secret convention of Kalisch (*dip.*)
	10 March	Start of first siege of Torgau* (*mil./Germany*)
	16 March	Prussia declares war on France (*dip.*)
	1 May	Action of Poserna* (*mil./Germany*); Bessières killed
	2 May	Battle of Lutzen (*mil./Germany*)
	11 May	Fall of Torgau (*mil./Germany*)
	18 May	Bernadotte* lands Swedish troops (*dip./mil.*)
	20 and 21 May	The battle of Bautzen* (*mil./Germany*)
	26 May	Action of Hanau (*mil./Germany*)
	28 and 29 May	Battle of Sackett's Harbor (*mil./U.S.*)
	30 May	Start of siege of Hamburg (*mil.*)
	31 May–2 June	Crossing of the river Esla (*mil./Spain*)
	2 June	Armistice of 1813* (or Pleischwitz) (*dip.*)
	8 June	Crossing of the river Ebro* (*mil./Spain*)
	12 June	French evacuate Madrid (*mil./Spain*)
		Suchet* repulses Murray's* landing at Alicante (*mil./Spain*)
	21 June	The battle of Vitoria* (*mil./Spain*)
	22 June	Start of the siege of Pamplona (*mil./Spain*)

27 June	Start of the siege of San Sebastian* (*mil./Spain*)
	Secret convention of Reichenbach* (*dip.*)
25 July	Battles of Maya and Roncesvalles* (*mil./Spain*)
	Failure of attempted storm of San Sebastian (*mil./Spain*)
27–30 July	Battle of Sorauren* (*mil./Spain*)
2 August	Massena* abandons offensive (*mil./Spain*)
12 August	Austria declares war on France (*dip.*)
17 August	Renewal of hostilities in Germany (*mil.*)
23 August	Battle of Gross-Beeren* (*mil./Germany*)
25 August	Suchet evacuates Tarragonna* (*mil./Spain*)
26 August	Actions of Katzbach and Pirna (*mil./Germany*)
26 & 27 August	The battle of Dresden* (*mil./Germany*)
30 August	The battle of Kulm* (*mil./Germany*)
31 August	Action of San Marcial* and fall of San Sebastian* (*mil./Spain*)
1 September	The battle of Vera* (*mil./Spain*)
6 September	The battle of Dennewitz* (*mil./Germany*)
10 September	The battle of Lake Erie (*naval*)
12 September	The battle of Ordal* (*mil./Spain*)
13 September	The battle of Villafranca* (*mil./Spain*)
3 October	Blücher* defeats Bertrand* at Wartenberg (*mil./Germany*)
4 October	Start of second siege of Torgau* (*mil./Germany*)
7 October	Crossing of the river Bidassoa* (*mil./Spain*)
	The second battle of Vera (*mil./Spain*)
12 October	Action of Colditz* (*mil./Germany*)
14 October	Action of Liebertwolkwitz* (*mil./Germany*)
16 October	The battles of Lindenau* and of Mockern* (*mil./Germany*)
16–19 October	The battle of Leipzig* (*mil./Germany*)
18 October	Bavaria and Saxony join the Allies (*dip.*)
30 October	The action of Hanau* (*mil./Germany*)
	Fall of Torgau* (*mil./Germany*)
9 November	Action of St. Jean-de-Luz* (*mil./France*)
10 November	The battle of the Nivelle* (*mil./France*)
9–12 November	The battle of the river Nive* (*mil./France*)
11 December	The treaty of Valençay* (*dip.*)
13 December	The battle of St. Pierre* (*mil.*)
1814 11 January	Murat signs peace with the Allies (*dip.*)
29 January	The battle of Brienne* (*mil./France*)
1 February	The battle of La Rothière* (*mil./France*)
5 February	Conference of Châtillon-sur-Seine (*dip.*)
10 February	The battle of Champaubert* (*mil./France*)
	Châtillon Conference suspended (*dip.*)
11 February	The battle of Montmirail* (*mil./France*)
14 February	The battle of Vauchamps* (*mil./France*)
17 February	Conference of Châtillon resumes (*dip.*)
22 February	Treaty of Troyes* (*dip.*)

	23 February	Crossing of the river Adour (*mil./France*)
	25 February	Conference at Bar-sur-Aube* (*dip.*)
	27 February	The battle of Orthez* (*mil./France*)
	1 March	Combat of Aure (*mil./France*)
	7 March	The action of Craonne* (*mil./France*)
	9 March	Treaty of Chaumont* (*dip.*)
	9–10 March	The battle of Laon* (*mil./France*)
	13 March	The battle of Rheims* (*mil./France*)
	17 March	The battle of Fismes* (*mil./France*)
	19 March	End of Châtillon Conference
	20 March	The battle of Tarbes* (*mil./France*)
	20–21 March	The battle of Arcis-sur-Aube* (*mil./France*)
	24 March	Conference of Sommagices* (*dip.*)
	25 March	Marmont* and Mortier* defeated at La-Fère-Champenoise (*mil./France*)
	30 March	Action of Montmartre (*mil./France*)
	31 March	The Allies enter Paris (*dip./pol./mil.*)
	6 April	First abdication of Napoleon at Fontainebleau (*dip.*)
	10 April	The battle of Toulouse* (*mil./France*)
	11 April	Treaty of Fontainebleau* (*dip.*)
	14 April	The sortie from Bayonne (*mil./France*)
	16 April	The second treaty of Fontainebleau (*dip.*)
	3 May	Louis XVIII* enters Paris (*pol.*)
	4 May	Napoleon lands on Elba* (*pers.*)
	27 May	End of siege of Hamburg* (*mil./Germany*)
	29 May	Death of Josephine* (*pers.*)
	30 May	First treaty of Paris* (*dip.*)
	25 July	The battle of Lundy's Lane (*mil./Canada*)
	24 August	The battle of Bladensburg (*mil./U.S.*)
	1 November	Congress of Vienna opens (*dip.*)
	24 December	Treaty of Ghent signed (*dip.*)
1815	8 January	The battle of New Orleans (*mil./U.S.*)
	26 February	Napoleon escapes from Elba* (*pol./pers.*)
	1 March	Napoleon lands near Fréjus (*mil./France*)
	7 March	The affair of the Defile of Laffrey (*mil./France*)
	13 March	Allies at Vienna outlaw Napoleon (*dip.*)
	20 March	Napoleon reaches Paris (*pol.*)
	25 March	Seventh Coalition* formed (*dip.*)
	31 March	Murat* declares war on Austria (*dip.*)
	4 April	Wellington* reaches Brussels (*mil.*)
	3 May	Murat* defeated at Tolentino (*mil./Naples*)
	9 June	First Congress of Vienna ends (*dip.*)
	12 June	Napoleon leaves Paris for the northeast frontier (*mil.*)
	15 June	Crossing of the Sambre and action of Frasnes* (*mil./Belgium*)
	16 June	The battles of Quatre Bras* and Ligny* (*mil./Belgium*)

[xxxv]

	18 June	The battle of Waterloo* and the battle of Wavre* (*mil./Belgium*)
	22 June	Napoleon's second abdication (*pol.*)
	7 July	Allies re-enter Paris (*pol.*)
	15 July	Napoleon boards H.M.S. *Bellerophon* (*pers.*)
	7 August	Napoleon sails on H.M.S. *Northumberland* for St. Helena* (*pers.*)
	13 October	Murat* court-martialed and shot (*pol.*)
	17 October	Napoleon lands on St. Helena* (*pers.*)
	20 November	Second Treaty of Paris* (*dip.*)
	7 December	Execution of Marshal Ney* (*pol.*)
1821	5 May	Death of Napoleon on St. Helena (*pers.*)
1836	29 July	Arc de Triomphe inaugurated by Louis-Philippe (*pol.*)
1840	15 December	Napoleon's body placed in *Les Invalides*, Paris (*pol.*)

Dictionary of the Napoleonic Wars

Abensberg, battle of, 20 April 1809. The Austrian attack on the French forces in Bavaria on 9 April achieved surprise, and it was only after Napoleon's arrival at the front (17th) that the confusion was halted. Placing Lannes* in command of a provisional corps of 25,000 men in the center, with Davout's* III Corps on his left and Lefebvre's* VII Corps on the right, Napoleon launched a major attack against the Archduke Charles' overextended center, passing south of Abensberg. This split the Austrian army in two, Charles retreating on Eckmühl* with his right wing while his left retreated south under General Hiller* to Landshut.* The French

(113,000 strong) thus regained the initiative in the Campaign of 1809 and defeated some 161,000 Austrians, killing and wounding 2,700 and taking some 4,000 prisoners of war.

Abercromby, General Sir Ralph (1734–1801). A British soldier of great distinction who did much to restore the British Army's morale following the setbacks of the American Revolution, he began his military career in the cavalry (1756). By 1773 he had risen to lieutenant colonel, but following a number of political setbacks in Parliament he retired from the service to live in Edinburgh. At the out-

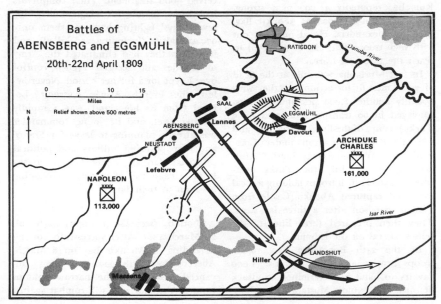

Battles of
ABENSBERG and EGGMÜHL
20th-22nd April 1809

set of the Revolutionary wars he was recalled and appointed a major general. After taking part in the Flanders Campaign of 1794 he led a force to the West Indies, capturing St. Lucia, Demerara, and Trinidad from the French. After periods of command in Ireland and Scotland, he took part in the abortive Helder Campaign* and was defeated at the battle of Bergen. Sent to command in the Mediterranean in June 1800, he failed to take Cadiz but was then ordered to clear the French from Egypt. He landed successfully on 8 March 1801 but was mortally wounded during the night battle of Aboukir* on the 22nd, just as victory was won, and he died a week later. He inspired a group of officers destined to earn future distinction, including Moore,* Hope,* Graham,* and Hill.*

Aboukir, (first) battle of, 25 July 1799. Following his repulse from Acre* and return to Cairo, General Bonaparte learned on 15 July that a Turkish army commanded by Mustapha Pasha, Seraskier of Rumelia, reputedly 15,000 men strong, had landed on the coast at Aboukir Bay, hard by Alexandria. He at once set out with such troops as could be collected to reach the threatened area.

In fact Mustapha was only at the head of 7,000 men fit for action, together with possibly another 8,000 sick and servants, conveyed in 60 transports escorted by 5 Turkish ships-of-the-line, 3 frigates, and a small British squadron under Commodore Sir William Sidney Smith.* After landing on 14 July the Turks overwhelmed 300 French troops holding a local fort, and captured Aboukir Castle from a small garrison after a three-day siege. They then prepared three lines of defenses to seal off the isthmus.

By the 24th Bonaparte had 10,000 troops nearby, and with Murat's* 1,000 cavalry to hand he determined to attack at once and exploit Mustapha's total in-

action, even though Kléber's* division had not yet reached the scene. Early on 25 July the French launched their first frontal onslaught on the Turkish positions. At midday the moment of decision came when Murat led a brilliant charge to reach the fort, and there captured Mustapha Pasha personally after receiving a wound in the jaw. Meanwhile Lannes* was making himself master of the Turkish redoubt at the head of two battalions. Very soon the Army of Rhodes disintegrated into a horde of fugitives: perhaps 2,000 were cut down at the water's edge, and as many as twice that number drowned trying to reach the ships.

A large party of Turks sought sanctuary in Aboukir Castle, which was promptly besieged by General Menou.* Desperately short of food and water, 1,000 Turks died over the following week, and only on 2 August did the remaining 1,500 survivors sue for terms. With memories of Bonaparte's massacre at Jaffa* in mind, few expected quarter, but in fact they received good treatment. Their conquerors had some reason for magnanimity, for seven days' fighting had cost them only 970 casualties (including 220 killed), and in return they had eliminated the Army of Rhodes and secured French control over Egypt for a further period. Nevertheless, the French Armée d'Orient, isolated from its homeland, was a rapidly waning asset, and its young commander was already planning to leave for France and more alluring military and political prospects. On 23 August he put to sea from Alexandria, effectively abandoning his men to their fate.

Aboukir, (second—or night) battle of, 22 March 1801. After successfully forcing a landing at Aboukir Bay on 8 March, Abercromby's* 18,000-strong army advanced west along the narrow isthmus toward Alexandria. A stiff combat against

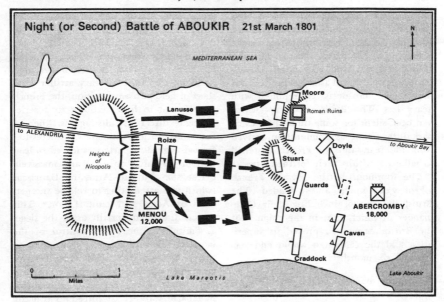

General Friant's* garrison on the 13th induced the British to retire into a strong defensive camp some five miles from the city, while the French continued to hold a fortified ridge, with numerous cannon in position, about two miles to their front.

The arrival of General Menou* with 10,000 reinforcements from Cairo and Upper Egypt induced the French to risk a night attack on the British position. Late on the 20th, 12,000 French troops silently filed out of Alexandria's defenses, and forming themselves into three columns set out for the British camp. Indications that an attack was in the wind had reached the British from an Arab spy the previous afternoon, so surprise was not complete. Nevertheless, the timing and direction of the onslaught were not foreseen, and soon a highly confused action was raging from the hour before dawn on the 22nd.

The brunt of the attack was borne by Major General Sir John Moore* and the 8,000 men of the Reserve Division. Their position extended through the ruins of a Roman palace and included a half-built redoubt. The first French attack came in against the extreme left of this position, but this was only a feint, and soon the main onslaught was unleashed against the redoubt sector—the key to the British position, as Moore was well aware. A period of chaotic fighting ensued. The 28th Foot on the right wing, heavily engaged to their front, found their flank turned and their rear threatened by a force of French cavalry and grenadiers, but Colonel Chambers coolly ordered "Rear rank Twenty-Eighth; right about face," and engaged the new threat. Moore then led up the 42nd Highlanders against the flank of the French column in its turn, and a fierce bayonet charge shattered the enemy and retrieved the overall situation.

Unfortunately the Highlanders pursued their foes too vigorously, and French cavalry at once exploited the situation.

[3]

As the light increased, the British line's cohesion again seemed threatened, and both Sir Ralph Abercromby (now come forward to command the battle) and Moore were wounded. Fortunately Doyle's troops arrived to aid their comrades, and the French were decisively repulsed with heavy loss. The British artillery—which had been silent for some time—now came back into action as ammunition arrived from the rear, and the French hastened to fall back within their fortified lines.

The four-hour battle cost the French all of 3,000 killed and wounded. The British lost 1,376, including their Commander in Chief, shot in the thigh. But the British Army had proved its superiority, and the campaign would end successfully six months later.

Aboukir, naval battle of, 2 August 1798. *See* **Nile**

Acre, siege of, 18 March–20 May 1799. The "key of Palestine" stands on a small peninsula abutting the Mediterranean, and in 1799 it proved the scene of a serious setback to General Bonaparte's ambitions in Syria. Following his successful advance from Egypt, he did not anticipate a long delay before Acre's antiquated de-

fenses fell, but the determination of the governor, Djezzar-Pasha,* backed by Sidney Smith* and his R.N. flotilla, which had already robbed the French of much of their siege train, proved Bonaparte's undoing. Deprived of heavy artillery and short of field gun ammunition, the French were forced to have recourse to a series of eight direct assaults against the defenses, all of them ultimately unsuccessful. In mid-siege Bonaparte was forced to lead part of his forces to meet and massively defeat the Turkish Army of Damascus (which was attempting to relieve the garrison of Acre) at Mount Tabor.* This success did not materially assist the siege, as Smith's unquestioned control of the local seas enabled supplies and succor to reach the garrison, while British naval landing parties fought alongside Djezzar's men. With plague decimating his ranks, Bonaparte was at last forced to concede failure after a final attempt at a storming on 10 May, and ten days later the French burned their remaining stores and set out toward Egypt, accompanied by 2,300 sick and wounded. Over 2,000 lay dead in Syria, half of them victims of bubonic plague.

Adam, General Sir Frederick (1781–

St. John of Acre

1853). Commissioned in 1795, Adam later served in Egypt and Sicily and was present at Maida* in 1806. After a spell as ADC to the Prince Regent, he fought in eastern Spain and was twice wounded. Promoted to major general in 1814, he commanded a brigade at Waterloo* and helped in the repulse of the Middle Guard.

Addington, Henry, 1st Viscount Sidmouth (1757–1844). A friend of William Pitt* from childhood, Addington entered Parliament in 1783 and served as Speaker for 11 years from 1789. He helped raise revenue for the French wars, but eventually disagreed with Pitt over Ireland and Catholic Emancipation. In 1801 King George III invited him to form a government, and he at once entered negotiations with France which led to the Peace of Amiens* a year later. Believing in Napoleon's sincerity, he implemented force reductions. This and other policies earned him Pitt's open criticism, and a combination of opponents from both main parties compelled his resignation, 30 April 1804. By then war had been renewed for 11 months. After a temporary reconciliation with Pitt, he was created a viscount in January 1805 and for a few months was President of the Council before a further dispute caused his resignation from the ministry. Only in 1812 did he re-enter public affairs under Percival,* whose successor as premier, Lord Liverpool,* appointed him Secretary of the Home Department. He continued in this post until 1821, earning a reputation for severity, suppressing discontent in the country with a ruthlessness worthy of Fouché.* A major target of the abortive Cato Street Conspiracy, he also became involved in the unsavory divorce proceedings brought against Queen Caroline. He remained in the Cabinet until 1824, and later opposed the Great Reform Bill. Well-intentioned and hard-working by nature, he was also noted for his personal dullness.

Adour River, the crossing of, 23 February 1814. General Hope* ferried a force over this considerable obstacle west of Bayonne and then held his bridgehead against the strong French garrison with the aid of Congreve's* rockets. Next day a bridge was completed which enabled Bayonne to be blockaded while Wellington* moved against Soult* at Orthez.*

Alava, General Miguel de (1771–1843). This Spanish commander replaced General Romana* as Wellington's favored liaison officer. In 1805 he served aboard the Spanish fleet at Trafalgar.* Present at Salamanca,* he was wounded in the rump at Orthez* in 1814, to Wellington's mirth, just before Wellington himself was hit by a spent round. He was a member of the Duke's staff, as Spanish Commissioner, during the Waterloo campaign, and as such attended the Duchess of Richmond's ball and was present at both Quatre Bras* and Waterloo.*

Alba de Tormes, bridge of. Wellington ordered General d'España* to place a strong force at this point on 21 July 1812. That officer, however, decided to withdraw the Spaniards on his own authority without informing his superior, and as a result the French, retreating in disorder from Salamanca,* were able to escape from the pursuing Allies.

Albuera, battle of, 16 May 1811. As Marshal Soult* advanced to relieve besieged Badajoz,* Marshal Beresford* moved with 35,000 Allies to intercept his approach. Taking up a position to block the River Albuera crossings at the village of that name, Beresford awaited the French attack. Soult (with 24,260 men and some 48 guns) sent a strong force of infantry against the town and bridge, but launched his cavalry and more infantry over fords far to the south. The 4,000 cavalry and 19 battalions of this outflanking attack scattered the weaker Span-

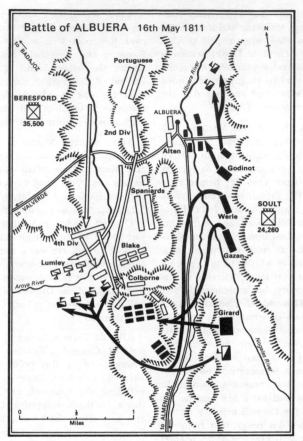

Battle of ALBUERA   16th May 1811

iards in this sector and were soon threatening to roll up Beresford's line in one of the best French attacks of the whole Peninsular War.

Beresford ordered General Blake* to form a defensive flank, but he did not do so in sufficient strength. Soon a mere four Spanish battalions holding a small rise were under attack by two French divisions, but they gallantly held off the leading columns and gave General Stewart time to bring up his 2nd Division on their right. The counterattack did not go precisely as Beresford intended, and Colborne's* brigade had 60% casualties when it was charged in flank by the Polish Lancers in a torrential rain. A howitzer was taken by the French, and the Allied line was only just stabilized with heavy loss as the rain stopped. After a pause the French came on again in a huge column, with close artillery support, and Houghton's Brigade sustained 80% casualties. In growing alarm, Beresford ordered d'España to support the survivors, but he refused. Confused orders then held up two Portuguese brigades and the position became increasingly desperate.

The situation was saved by General Lowry Cole* and Sir Henry Hardinge,* who on their own initiative brought up the 4,000 men of the 4th Division in an oblique attack. Infantry firepower repulsed the French cavalry and then an infantry brigade, and soon the 4th linked up with the few survivors of the 2nd Division. A celebrated charge by the Fusilier Brigade—"Nothing could stop that astonishing infantry"—routed the French; Alten* cleared Albuera of the enemy, and after four hours' fighting the battle was over as rain returned. The French lost some 8,000 casualties, the Allies about 6,000 in this severe action. The siege of Badajoz was resumed, but controversy about this battle continued for many years.

Alcantara, bridge of. Built on the order of the Emperor Trajan by Caius Julius Lacer in A.D. 105, the bridge has six arches of uncemented granite, the two main spans are 210 feet above the river, and the total length is 670 feet. Its military importance as one of the few bridges over the central reaches of the Tagus, close to the frontier with Portugal in the general direction of Castelo Branco, made it a significant point. In 1809, the second arch from the right bank was demolished by General Mayne to preclude its use by the French, and in July 1811 Napoleon ordered Marshal Marmont* to construct a suspension bridge and a defended bridgehead. This task, however, proved beyond the resources of *l'Armée de Portugal.*

The same idea occurred to Wellington in the spring of 1812, after his successful capture of Ciudad Rodrigo* and Badajoz.* The storming of these two fortresses had given him control of the two main routes into Spain through the "corridors," but a third road halfway between the two would confer obvious advantages. Accordingly, on 24 May 1812 Colonel Sturgeon and

Major Todd of the Royal Staff Corps were sent to report on the feasibility of the task of bridging the gap. With commendable efficiency they constructed a simple form of suspension bridge built of ropes. Heavy beams were secured to the massive Roman stone pillars at either end, and 18 cables, tightened by winches, were stretched between them. On top of the ropes were placed eight notched crossbeams, supporting a floor made of rope yarn with planks above. A screen of tarpaulins served as a parapet on each side. So strong did this bridge prove that even cavalry and heavy guns were able to pass with complete safety, and when danger threatened, the bridge's roadway could be rolled up and subsequently relaid.

Aldea Tejada, village of. Wellington* moved General Pakenham's 3rd Division to this place during the morning of 21 July 1812 from the River Tormes. This formation subsequently advanced to scatter the leading French division of Marmont's* army, thus opening the Allied attack at Salamanca.*

Alessandria, Convention of, 15 June 1800. Following his defeat at Marengo,* the Austrian General Melas* sued for an armistice, and quickly agreed to surrender all remaining posts in the Milanese, Piedmont, and Lombardy and to withdraw his forces east of the River Ticino. Active operations were not to be resumed until an offer of peace terms had been considered by the Austrian government.

Alexander I, Tsar of Russia (1777–1825). Succeeding his father, the mad Tsar Paul I,* on 24 March 1801, Alexander's initial fascination with Napoleon faded after the Enghien* incident, and Russia joined the Third Coalition.* Hostilities continued through the campaigns of Austerlitz,* Eylau,* and Friedland,* but the famous meeting with Napoleon at Tilsit* in mid-1807 caused a major switch in the Tsar's policy. Once again deeply impressed by Napoleon, he joined the Continental System* and declared war on Great Britain. It was not long, however, before friction developed between France and Russia, important bones of contention being economic conditions, creation of the Grand Duchy of Warsaw by Napoleon, the treatment of Alexander's relative the Duke of Oldenburg, and Napoleon's refusal to countenance a Russian attack on Constantinople. Relations deteriorated rapidly from 1809, and in 1812 Napoleon invaded Russia with well-known results. The Tsar refused to treat with the Emperor even after the loss of Moscow, but waged a relentless campaign that ultimately led to the virtual destruction of the French army. In the next years the Tsar sent his armies into central and western Europe and furthered the collapse of the First Empire.

Following the fall of Napoleon, Alexander protected France from the most vindictive attentions of the Prussians and played a leading role at the Congress of Vienna.* He insisted on the need to maintain European equilibrium, and was the inspirer of the Holy Alliance. In later years he became something of a mystic and took little direct part in the ruling of Russia.

Alexandria, storming of, 2 July 1798. Immediately after landing at Marabout in Egypt, Bonaparte launched 5,000 men of *l'Armée d'Orient* against the western fortifications of Alexandria after an eight-mile night march. Almost crazy with thirst, troops under Menou* stormed the Triangular Fort, and Generals Kléber* and Bon* captured two gates into the city. By midday, Alexandria had fallen. This success cost the French some 300 casualties.

Alexandria, night battle of. *See* **Aboukir,** second battle of

Tsar Alexander I

Algeçiras, naval battles of, 6 and 13 July 1801. A small French squadron under Admiral Durand Linois sailed from Toulon for Cadiz, as part of a naval scheme to challenge the Royal Navy's command of the western Mediterranean. His three ships-of-the-line and single frigate joined up with four Spanish warships at Cadiz and sailed for Ferrol, but were intercepted by Admiral Sir David Saumarez* and took refuge in Algeçiras Bay opposite Gibraltar. Saumarez launched an attack against the anchored vessels, but was driven off on 6 July by shore batteries and gunboats, losing H.M.S. *Hannibal* in the process. This vessel ran aground directly beneath the Spanish batteries and could not be recovered.

The French and Spaniards sent a scratch squadron of six ships to rescue Linois' squadron and bring it back to Cadiz for repair, but contrary winds delayed Admiral Moreno's sailing. Saumarez by terrific efforts completed his own repairs and was able to pursue Moreno when he set out for Algeçiras. He caught up with the enemy between Cadiz and Algeçiras, and in a fierce night action sank two Spanish three-deckers while a 74-gun ship struck its colors. This was achieved with minimal British losses, and the effect of the success was to ruin all chance of the larger Franco-Spanish plan being achievable. The Spaniards accused the French of sacrificing Spanish ships for a relatively minor objective—the rescue of Linois—and withdrew their cooperation from the First Consul's naval plans.

Almaraz, capture of the bridge of, 18 May 1812. In early May 1812 a captured French dispatch revealed that Marshal Marmont* was planning to make a sudden attack over the Tagus using the bridge at Almaraz. Wellington accordingly ordered General Hill* to execute a surprise attack on the bridge and its defenses, the only sizable French force within supporting distance being Foy's* 5,000 men at Talavera, two days' march away.

Hill left Almendalejo with two brigades of the British 2nd Division on 7 May, passed through Merida and Truxillo by the 15th, and then led his force of 7,000 men and its six howitzers over three ranges of hills to reach the Pass of Miravete on the 17th. French outworks, including the castle of Miravete, were to be attacked frontally by Ashworth's Portuguese brigade and the cannon while Wilson's brigade attacked from the left, but the approach was slowed by rough going, and Hill changed his plan. After using the 17th for a reconnaissance, he decided to mask Miravete, leave his guns behind, and attempt a bold direct assault on Fort Napoleon (which mounted nine guns) and Fort Ragusa (six guns), which stood on heights on opposite banks of the Tagus. The French had 1,000 troops in the area, 300 of them in Miravete castle.

After moving up through the Pass of Cueva, Howard's brigade (comprising the first battalions of the 50th, 71st, and 92nd

Regiments of Foot) reached within 300 yards of Fort Napoleon by dawn on the 18th and stormed the position at 6:00 A.M. with 900 men. The attack was successful, and the French garrison of Fort Ragusa fled. Thus 900 men captured two strong forts and the bridge they were designed to defend. The British (and the 6th Portuguese Regiment) lost a total of 189 casualties and inflicted 400. The bridge itself had been demolished during the Talavera campaign of 1809, but the pontoon bridge that the French had established was now also dismantled, and as a result the forces of Marmont were cut off from those of Soult* operating away to the south. Later on the bridge was repaired and used by the Allies as a major route over the Tagus.

Almeida, siege and blockade of, 1810 and 1811. This Portuguese fortress, guarding the Northern Corridor,* fell to Marshal Ney* on 28 August 1812 after a 12-day siege. Brigadier General Cox's defense was compromised by the explosion of his magazine on the 27th. Following Massena's* retreat from Portugal early in 1811, the Allies invested Almeida on 4 April. French attempts to relieve General Brennier's* garrison of 1,300 led to the battle of Fuentes de Oñoro.* Thereafter Brennier broke out with his garrison on 10 May, to Wellington's rage. Almeida remained in Allied possession for the rest of the war.

Alten, General Sir Charles, Count von (1764–1840). Of Hanoverian extraction, Alten served in the army of that state from 1783 to 1803, before transferring to the British service in the latter year. He fought in Hanover (1805), at Copenhagen* two years later, and then campaigned in Sweden and the Peninsular War with the King's German Legion.* He served with the Walcheren* expedition (1809) and then returned to the army in

Spain. Present at Waterloo,* he was promoted to major general in 1816 and ultimately became a field marshal in the reconstituted Hanoverian army.

Alva, River. A tributary of the River Mondego, the heights above which were fortified by the Allies in 1810 and were briefly occupied by the divisions of General Hill* and General Leith* immediately before the battle of Bussaco.* Their troops were moved over the Mondego to hold the southern end of the Bussaco ridge on 26 September.

Alvintzi, General Josef, Baron (1735–1810). A native of Transylvania, Alvintzi first fought in the Seven Years' War against the Turks and then against the French. Commanding an Austrian force, he defeated Dumouriez at Neerwinden* (1794), but was defeated by Bonaparte at Arcola* (1796) and Rivoli* the next year. He subsequently became a field marshal and served as Governor of Hungary from 1798. He died at Buda.

Amalgame, l', of 21 January 1793. The practice of amalgamating two battalions of the Volunteers of 1792 with one battalion of line infantry (as at Valmy*) was ordered to be adopted by the French army as a whole by decree of the Committee of Public Safety. Implementation was not achieved until early 1794, but from that date some 213 *demi-brigades* of infantry were formed, these formations replacing the old *régiments*.

Amiens, Preliminaries of, 1 October 1801, and Peace of, 25 March 1802. A series of circumstances induced the British government to seek a general pacification with France during 1801. Late 1800 had seen the re-creation of the Armed Neutrality of the North,* which halted the British trade in Baltic grain, and February 1801 had seen the further isolation of Great Britain when Austria, after Marengo* and Hohenlinden,* signed the Peace of Luneville* with France. Two poor harvests, the continuing possibility of a French invasion, and finally the fall of Pitt's* ministry of 4th March, increased the desirability of seeking a settlement.

Prime Minister Addington,* feeling his negotiating position to be strengthened by the naval attack on Copenhagen (March 1801)* and the satisfactory progress of the British campaign in Egypt, opened serious negotiations in September, and on 1 October 1801 Lord Hawkesbury signed preliminaries of peace the day before news reached London of the surrender of the last French troops in Egypt. The terms were very one-sided. France agreed to restore the Kingdom of the Two Sicilies and the Papal States, but was to retain Nice, Savoy, Piedmont, and the territories seized on the left bank of the Rhine, as well as Holland. Britain, on the other hand, agreed to return the Cape, Egypt, Malta, Tobago, Martinique, Demerara, Berbice, and Curaçao, and was to retain only Trinidad and Ceylon. Vague French undertakings concerning the restoration or compensation of the Kings of Piedmont and Holland, and general agreements reaffirming the terms of earlier treaties, were accepted at face value. Small wonder that Paris was jubilant at the terms M. Otto had negotiated—but the pacification was equally hailed in London, for a time.

Addington appointed Lord Cornwallis as Ambassador-Extraordinary to conclude the definitive treaty, in which it was optimistically hoped that some of the vague agreements would be honored. After a visit by the delegation to Paris in November 1801, the negotiations were resumed at Amiens in the Hôtel de Ville, the French team being led by Joseph Bonaparte,* who was soon popular with the British representatives. It soon became clear that the French were going to concede little or nothing over such issues as remuneration for the maintenance of prisoners of war or the restoration of the Prince of Orange. Some progress was made over the matter of Malta's future; its future independence was to be guaranteed by six powers.

The First Consul never regarded the peace as more than a breathing space, and he was soon increasing his grip on the Cisalpine Republic, sending General Leclerc* to conquer Santo Domingo, and creating the Batavian Republic.* However, peace was signed on 25 March 1802. It was destined to survive barely a year.

Ancien Régime, l'. A phrase used to describe the highly centralized Bourbon monarchical government that was overthrown by the Revolution, it also reflected the former social system based upon the three estates of the realm—the nobility, the clergy, and the Third Estate (or professional middle classes). Until the processes of national bankruptcy were far advanced, the ministers of Louis XVI governed France through powerful provincial governors and *intendants*, trying to finance the administration by ever

Andréossy

greater recourse to loans at ruinous interest rates together with farming out the regular taxes to speculators. The whole system was compromised by the prevalent concept of privilege, and was the antithesis of the revolutionary principles of "liberty, equality, and fraternity." The viability of the system was largely undermined from within by the *philosophes* during the generation before 1789, and the passion for equality that swept France sounded the death knell of *l'ancien régime*. Political liberty, however, did not survive the revolution for long, and the excesses of the early governments ultimately led to the restoration of despotism for a considerable period in the interests of firm government and public order.

Anciens, Conseil des. This higher chamber of the French legislative system was created by the Constitution of Year III. It comprised 250 members with a minimum age of 40 years, and one third were renewed each year. The Council could not initiate legislation, only deliberate upon the proposals of the *Conseil des Cinq-Cents* (or Five Hundred)* and accept or reject them, in which case they could not be reintroduced for one year. The first meeting was on 28 October 1795, when it selected the first five Directors. As a rule it met in the former Hall of the Convention in the Tuileries Palace.

Andréossy, Général Antoine-François, comte (1761–1828). Of noble origin, he entered the artillery in 1781 and saw service in Holland (1787). From June 1796 he commanded the bridging train of the Army of Italy, serving with distinction at Arcola* and before Mantua.* Promoted to *général de brigade* in November 1797, the following July he commanded the French flotilla on the Nile, and then served as Berthier's* assistant in Syria. He returned to France with Napoleon, assisted him at Brumaire,* and became *général de* *division* in 1800. After holding various artillery appointments, he was ambassador to Great Britain briefly in 1803. Later diplomatic appointments included that of ambassador to Constantinople (1812–14). He was reconciled with the Bourbons and held high military administrative posts; in 1827 he was elected a *député*.

Angoulême, Louis de Bourbon, duc de (1775–1844). A nephew of Louis XVIII, he landed in southern France in early 1814 to inspire and lead a popular movement

Duc d'Angoulême

in support of the House of Bourbon. He entered Bordeaux in triumph on 12 March, the date usually associated with the foundation of the Bourbon Restoration.

Anna, Grand Duchess of Russia (1793–1827). The younger sister of Tsar Alexander I,* her hand was briefly sought by Napoleon in 1809. Romanov family hostility doomed the negotiations to failure, and the Emperor switched his attention to Marie Louise of Austria,* who in due course became his second wife after the divorce from Josephine (1810).*

Arapiles, los. Small village southeast of Salamanca* in Spain, adjacent to two heights, the Greater and the Lesser Arapiles, which played an important part in the battle of 20 July 1812. Clausel's* counterattack in the late afternoon almost reached the village but was repulsed by Wellington's* rapid redeployment of Clinton's* 6th Division.

Arc de Triomphe, l'. On 18 February 1806 Napoleon selected a site on the western limits of Paris for an imposing memorial to his martial successes. The *Arc* was inaugurated on 29 July 1836 by Louis-Philippe. Designed by the architects Chalgrin and Joust, the pediment stands just under 50 meters high, and beneath it burns a perpetual flame. On its sides are inscribed 126 military battles and engagements, together with the names of 662 marshals, generals, and admirals who served with distinction between 1792 and 1815.

Arcis-sur-Aube, battle of, 20–21 March 1814. This town in Champagne, situated on the river Aube 38 kilometers north of Troyes, was the scene of Napoleon's last battle against the Allies of the 6th Coalition* during the Campaign of France. Faced by converging enemy armies, Napoleon decided to launch a blow at Schwarzenberg's* forces before rushing the small French army north to attack Blücher's* communications on the upper Marne. By 11:00 A.M. on the 21st Ney* and Sebastiani* had driven General Wrede* out of Arcis, and at 1:00 P.M. Napoleon arrived along the northern bank of the Aube and crossed the bridge. A fierce cavalry action occupied the late afternoon and part of the night, the French gaining the advantage. Overnight Schwarzenberg brought up some 80,000 men to face the 28,000 available French. However, Schwarzenberg suspected a trap and did not press his advantage of num-

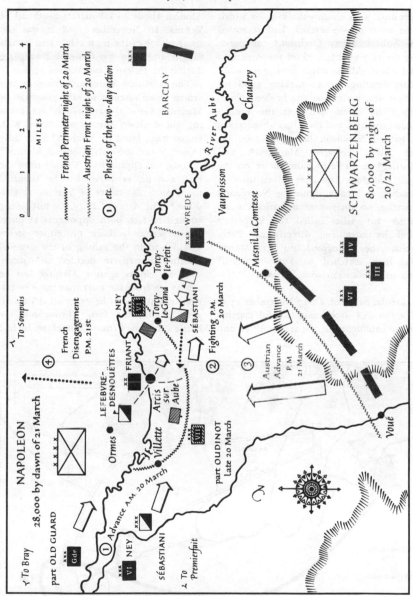

Battle of Arcis-sur-Aube, 20–21 March 1814

bers until 3:00 P.M. on the 21st, by which time most of the French had recrossed the Aube to safety. Oudinot,* commanding the rear guard, held off the Austrians and their Allies until 6:00 P.M. amid bitter fighting, before making good his retreat and destroying the bridge behind him. The battle had cost the French 3,000 casualties, and the Allies about 4,000. It gained Napoleon little, however, for the Allies defeated Marmont* and Mortier* at La-Fère-Champenoise on the 25th, and three days later linked up with Blücher at Meaux. Ignoring Napoleon's situation on their communications at St. Dizier, the Allies called the Emperor's bluff by advancing directly on Paris, which they occupied on 31 March. Napoleon marched to Fontainebleau,* and his abdication soon followed.

Arcola, battle of, 15–17 November 1796. The town of Arcola stands amid marshes at the confluence of the rivers Adige and Alpone, about 40 kilometers southeast of Verona. In November 1796 it was the scene of one of the most celebrated battles fought and won by General Bonaparte during the Italian Campaign of 1796.

The Austrians were advancing in two armies in an attempt to raise the siege of Mantua.* General Davidovitch* was pressing ahead down the upper Adige with 18,000 men, faced by Vaubois* with only 10,000. Simultaneously, General Alvintzi* (28,000) was approaching Verona from the east, and on 11 November he repulsed the French defenders of Verona at Caldiero.* The Army of Italy was not strong enough to face both opponents at once, but a serious setback on either sector would lead to the raising of the siege of Mantua. Bonaparte decided to concentrate his efforts against Alvintzi, but he was aware from the start that these operations might have to be canceled if Vaubois gave ground too fast. Throughout the battle's three-day course, therefore, he had

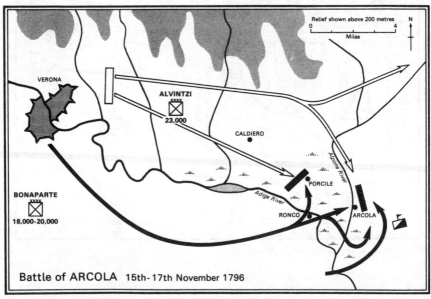

Battle of ARCOLA 15th–17th November 1796

to keep careful note of the latest tidings from the distant northern sector—and also of news from Mantua, for only 9,000 men could be spared to contain General Wurmser's* garrison of 23,000, and a serious Austrian attempt to break out through the French siege lines was a possibility. General Bonaparte was thus effectively caught between three fires.

Leaving 3,000 troops to hold Verona, on the night of 14 November Bonaparte set out with his 18,000 men along the south bank of the river Adige to force a surprise crossing at Ronco, some 7 kilometers southwest of Arcola. Andréossy* established a pontoon bridge there by dawn on the 15th, and the French poured over into the marshes beyond as if their intention was to threaten Alvintzi's lines of communication running east from Verona. Sending part of Massena's* division to secure his bridgehead's left flank at Porcile, Bonaparte led Augereau's* 6,000 men toward the bridge over the Alpone opposite Arcola. Alvintzi lost no time in reinforcing his initial 2,000 troops in Arcola with a further 7,000, and sent General Provera* with 4,000 more to attack Porcile. All day the battle for Arcola bridge raged, but the French never secured it. Aware that time was fast passing, Bonaparte sent General Guieu* to seek a crossing place near Albaredo to the south, but his force of 3,000 men only completed its mission and came up on the flank of Arcola in the late evening. All this time the Austrian wagon trains and guns were escaping through Villanova toward Vicenza. Outside Arcola, Bonaparte was almost drowned when he was pushed into a dyke by an overzealous officer as the Commander in Chief led forward yet another attack, tricolor in hand. The French were just gaining the upper hand near the town when disturbing news reached headquarters: Vaubois had been forced back in the

northern sector to Bussolengo. There was nothing for it but to call off the action, so nearly won, and retire the French troops to Ronco. Overnight, the Austrians regarrisoned Arcola and reoccupied Porcile.

As no graver news arrived from the north, the next morning Bonaparte returned to the attack. Everything had to be fought for again without the benefit of surprise. A day-long fight restored Porcile to the French, but Arcola remained untaken. General Vial* failed to establish another crossing near the mouth of the Alpone. Casualties were mounting on both sides, but Alvintzi now had all of 11,000 in action around Arcola. At dusk, Bonaparte again felt constrained to retire his weary men over the Adige, leaving only a small party on the northern bank to secure the bridgehead. Overnight, however, 3,000 reinforcements reached the French from Mantua. Alvintzi's army was now in full retreat from Verona.

As the 17th dawned with no more alarming news from Vaubois, Bonaparte ordered a third attempt to defeat Alvintzi. Massena was given the task of keeping the Austrians busy among the marshes on the north bank of the Adige, while part of Augereau's division was preparing to cross at Albaredo. The mission of this formation was to capture Arcola from the rear and then to advance on Villanova to trap whatever part of the Austrian army was still west of the Alpone.

Massena carried out his role most skillfully. Sending only 3,000 of his men to tie down Provera's force near Porcile, after a difficult crossing of the Adige (the pontoon bridge almost collapsed but was repaired) Massena placed the remainder of his men in an ambush amid the dykes and marshes, leaving only one unit in view. This the Austrians duly attacked, and fell straight into the other troops awaiting them. Massena's men charged after the fleeing Austrians, crossed the Arcola bridge, and took possession of part of the town. Augereau meantime had been making heavy weather of the Albaredo crossing, and part of his division was sent off to the south to find another crossing point near Legnano. Aware that Austrian morale was sinking rapidly, Bonaparte devised a stratagem to secure Augereau's crossing at Albaredo. The Commander in Chief sent off a small force of his Guides* with four trumpeters to find a ford over the Alpone unseen by the Austrians. Once safely over, this detachment suddenly emerged, making as much din as possible, on the rear of the Austrians holding Albaredo and Arcola. As their attention was distracted, Augereau launched an all-out attack and captured Albaredo. Alvintzi, who could see signs of troops appearing from afar in the direction of Legnano, ordered his men to retreat north toward the main road and then toward Vicenza without further delay. By the next morning the Austrians had all gone —and the major attempt to break through to Mantua had been abandoned.

The three-day struggle cost the French 4,500 casualties, and in its course they probably inflicted 7,000 on the Austrians. The attritional nature of this action was marked, but it had achieved Bonaparte's overriding purpose by ensuring that Alvinzti had no chance whatsoever of linking up with Davidovitch coming from the northern sector of the Adige near Lake Garda. With typical energy, Bonaparte at once made every effort to trap Davidovitch near Dolce on 21 November, but the French forced marches narrowly failed to accomplish this, and the Austrian second column made good its escape back to Trento in the Tyrol. The siege of Mantua could be continued: such was the ultimate effect of the battle of Arcola.

Argaum, battle of, 29 November 1803. Following the great victory of Assaye* in the Second Anglo-Mahratta War, Major General Arthur Wellesley* entered the state of Berar in Central India. After linking up with Colonel James Stevenson's column, the joint force of perhaps 10,000 British and sepoy troops advanced against the Sultan of Berar's far larger army (including 38 cannon), which was drawn up before the village of Argaum. The first attack was repulsed when the Indian guns engaged Wellesley's vanguard with telling effect, but he rallied the sepoy battalions, steadied his line, and led them forward again in a second onslaught at 4:30 P.M. The cavalry on Wellesley's right routed Berar's horsemen, while Wellesley in person directed the infantry attack against the center, moving light guns up in support. Berar's elite Arab infantry was decimated, and his center collapsed. For the loss of 46 killed and 315 wounded, Wellesley inflicted possibly 5,000 casualties on Berar and captured all his guns. This victory ended the Second Mahratta War in Central India.

Ariñez, hill of. This was the key feature, overlooking a large bend in the River Zadorra, on the plain of Vitoria in northern Spain. It was captured by Lieutenant General Sir Thomas Picton* and his 3rd Division at 3:00 P.M. on 21 June 1813, during the climax of the battle of Vitoria.*

Armed Neutrality of the North, of 1800. British claims to the right of search* of neutral shipping for contraband cargoes was bitterly resented by the Baltic powers, and following the collapse of the Second Coalition* after Marengo* and Hohenlinden* steps were taken to revive the Armed Neutrality of 1780. Denmark, Sweden, and Russia were the original signatories, and on 18 December 1800 the adherence of Prussia to the Northern Convention completed the league. The implications for Great Britain were grave: not only did it threaten the effectiveness of the naval blockade of France (almost Britain's last weapon, as her continental allies and their armies had been defeated), but it also constituted a grave peril to her national security by cutting her dockyards off from the major source of crucial naval stores—timber (particularly for masts and yards) and also pitch (for caulking) and hemp (for rigging).

Equally disruptive was the halting of grain shipments from the Baltic region. The British harvests of 1799 and 1800 had both been of poor quality and yield, and by late April 1801 the price of wheat had risen to 151 shillings a quarter (or treble the price of 1798). Agrarian and urban misery threatened social and political consequences within the country, and William Pitt's* ministry was forced to pass oppressive political and labor legislation to control the situation.

Early in 1801 the British government sent a powerful fleet under Admiral Sir Hyde Parker* to deliver an ultimatum to Crown Prince Frederick of Denmark, regent for the insane Christian VII, King of Denmark and Norway. Its rejection led to the first battle of Copenhagen,* which Rear Admiral Nelson* pressed to a conclusion in disregard of his superior's orders, on 2 April 1801. Next day the Danes accepted a truce. This strong action, associated with the assassination later the same year of the mad Tsar Paul,* effectively dissolved the Armed Neutrality of the North. During its period of existence, however, the Northern Convention had demonstrated the vulnerability of Great Britain to overt economic pressure, and did more damage than the French squadrons and invasion flotillas assembling in the Channel ports. The economic damage it caused was one of several factors that induced the British mercantile classes to press for a general pacification—which Addington's* ministry eventually signed with France at Amiens.*

Armistice, of 2 June–13 August 1813. After the great battle of Bautzen* in late May, both the French and the Allies desired a breathing space. Although both sides made a show of negotiating for a permanent peace, neither was wholly genuine in pacific intent. Napoleon used the respite to bring up reinforcements, while Russia and Prussia persuaded the Emperor of Austria to enter the war on their side. Sweden also joined the Allies. The collapse of the armistice on 13 August when Blücher* advanced from Breslau surprised nobody, and soon the second phase of Campaign of Germany, 1813, was in full swing. Ahead lay Dresden* and Leipzig.*

Arroyo dos Molinos, battle of, 28 October 1811. Wellington* sent General Hill* with 10,000 Allied troops to surprise the French division of General Girard,* which comprised six weak infantry battalions, two regiments of cavalry, and half a battery of guns, or about 4,000 men in all. Girard was marching from Montanchez, and halted at Arroyo dos Molinos for the night of 27 October. Hill had been marching parallel to Girard from Aldea del Cano and had halted at Alcuescar for the same night, but decided to march without delay against Girard, setting out at 2:30 A.M. through torrential wind and rain. Disguised by the elements, Hill's force reached within half a mile of Arroyo dos Molinos before the alarm was raised.

Sending Wilson's brigade to seal off the town with three Portuguese battalions from the south, Hill led the remainder (Howard's brigade and Stewart) with the cavalry in the center to seize the roads leading to Medellin and Merida. Soon all three roads were blocked. In fact an unsuspecting Girard was already on the move, Renard's brigade having already moved off, and accordingly he was left with only 4,000 men under command. The

British 71st and 92nd Regiments penetrated the village and captured Girard's baggage, taking General Bron prisoner, and pressed on to attack Dombrouski's brigade beyond. In growing confusion, Girard tried to break out along one road after another, but in vain. In a confused cavalry action, the French cavalry were defeated by the 9th Light Dragoons and the 2nd Hussars of the King's German Legion amid a dense morning mist, and once this began to lift Hill ordered a general charge. The French gave ground; 1,000 surrendered at the foot of the 1,000-foot-high cliffs, and the remainder fled towards Truxillo and were pursued for 24 miles by the British cavalry. For the loss of only 7 killed and 64 wounded, Hill killed an estimated 300 French, captured 1,300 more, and took three guns. The Spanish forces under Morillo also lost 30 men fighting with Hill. This proved the last episode in the campaign of 1811, and Napoleon recalled Girard to France in disgrace.

Art of War, the. Military reforms in the army of Louis XVI bore full fruit only after the advent of the French Revolution in 1789. For the first time, in 1792, an entire nation was organized to defend *la patrie en danger*, and the concept of the nation-at-arms came into being under the inspiration of Lazare Carnot.* Mass conscription provided larger armies than previously; natural leaders were encouraged to emerge; and a simplified logistical system, based upon living off the countryside, was introduced to feed the new forces, which were imbued with a strong sense of patriotism and proselytizing zeal. Added to the improved artillery* introduced a generation earlier by Gribeauval,* the improved musket issued in 1777, significant tactical developments in the infantry arm, and a doctrine of total war enunciated by Guibert*—all inheritances from *l'ancien*

*régime**—these developments implied a revolution in the art of war, provided a great leader would emerge to make the most of the new opportunities.

Napoleon was no great innovator as a soldier. He distrusted novel ideas, disbanding the balloon companies inherited from the armies of the Revolution and rejecting Roger Fulton's offer of submarines and naval mines. His genius was essentially practical, and his military concepts evolved from the close study of earlier commanders, particularly Frederick the Great.* He made the fullest use of the ideas of his predecessors and breathed life into them. The result was a devastatingly effective mastery of the military art and science which knew no peer for almost two decades.

Napoleon did make a number of important improvements. He greatly developed the staff organization, defining the functions of the *Grand-Quartier-Général* with the aid of Berthier,* and adding simpler but effective staffs at corps and divisional level. The adoption of the *corps d'armée** as the standard major formation was an important step forward, for the flexibility, independence of action, speed, and operational capacity which each of these balanced, all-arm formations represented enabled their master to wage warfare on a scale and with an effectiveness that astounded France's opponents. By 1812 all major powers, save Great Britain, had adopted similar organizations. Aware of the importance of forming powerful reserves, Napoleon also massed much of his heavy cavalry and artillery* into special formations retained under army command for use at the critical moment in a battle or campaign, and the creation of the Imperial Guard* as a *corps d'élite* was intended to provide an ultimate reserve of the most experienced and loyal veterans.

As a grand strategist, Napoleon always

sought (but did not always achieve) a rapid, decisive knockout blow against his enemies. Such short, sharp wars as the conquest of Prussia in 1806* were his ideal. Long wars of attrition were not to his taste, but in 1796 (North Italy), 1812 (Russia), and above all in the lengthy struggle in the Iberian Peninsula (1807–14) he found his armies involved in them despite his best endeavors. The latter two instances, which effectively doomed France to defeat, arose from the Emperor's attempt to wage all-out economic warfare against the most elusive of his opponents—Great Britain—and this policy as embodied in the Continental System* proved a fatal mistake.

At the level of strategy Napoleon had no contemporary peer. To make the utmost use of the superior mobility and inspiration of his armies, he developed two major strategic systems. When facing a foe superior in numbers, the strategy of the central position* was employed to split the enemy into separate parts, each of which could then be eliminated in turn by adroit maneuvering to gain the French a local superiority of force in successive actions by bringing the reserve into action at the critical time and place. This system he first employed along the Ligurian coast in April 1796, and it was also the strategic basis of the ill-fated Waterloo campaign of 1815. Conversely, when the enemy was inferior to the French, Napoleon would often employ a maneuver of envelopment—pinning the foe's attention with a detachment while the bulk of the army swept against the hostile lines of communication to sever the enemy's links with his bases. Convoy-bound armies were particularly vulnerable to this form of attack, and it was employed with telling effect in one variant or another numerous times, including the Marengo,* Ulm,* and Jena-Auerstadt* campaigns. On occasion, Napoleon would merge features of these

two classic strategies. They were by no means new concepts, but they were highly suited to the *corps d'armée* system, and time and again brought success to French armies until the enemy came to appreciate the main features of them and developed the necessary counterstrategies. Thus Wellington* refused to be psychologically dominated and developed superior means of logistical support, and Prince Schwarzenberg* and Blücher* learned by 1813 to ignore the presence of the French threatening their rear areas, and to press ahead for their own objectives and thus call Napoleon's bluff.

All Napoleonic strategy was aimed to achieve a favorable battle situation, and once again the Emperor often excelled in the art and science of grand tactics. Ideally he sought to achieve a "strategic battle," in which, after drawing all the enemy into action, the abrupt and disconcerting appearance of a force on the enemy's flank and rear was the preliminary to the unleashing of the French reserves for the *coup de grâce* against the predetermined sector. Castiglione* (1796) and Bautzen* (1813) were planned along these lines, and so (originally) were Jena* and Friedland.* Correct timing of the stages was vital, and at this Napoleon excelled. He regarded frontal attritional battles such as Borodino* (1812) as far less likely to produce a good result. At Waterloo, however, the French paid the penalty for relying on stereotyped strategic and grand tactical schemes, and found themselves the victims of an enveloping attack.

French minor tactics,* particularly the combination of infantry in column with others in line (*l'ordre mixte*) and the use of clouds of skirmishers to the fore, also proved effective against traditional 18th-century linear tactics, but once again Napoleon's opponents came to appreciate the systems and learned how to counter them. Only the British army pursued its own way; other armies adopted methods based on those of the French.

One great secret of French success lay in simplified logistical support methods—but these proved inadequate in Russia and Spain. All in all, however, the French concept of the art of war remained the dominant one for at least 30 years.

Artigas, José Gervasio (1764–1850). South American patriot leader who masterminded a patriotic struggle against the Spanish authorities which began in 1810 at Buenos Aires.* After mixed fortunes, he was finally forced to relinquish the large areas of Argentina and Uruguay that he had conquered with Portuguese forces. In 1820 he fled to Paraguay, where he died.

Artillery. "It is with guns that war is made," declared Napoleon, and as a soldier who had started his career in the artillery *Régiment de la Fère* it is hardly surprising that his interest in the artillery continued throughout his campaigns to the very end.

The reforms of Gribeauval* in the 1770s had virtually revolutionized the French artillery of *l'ancien régime.** Cannon were transformed from a considerable liability into an undoubted asset in the field by being standardized, lightened in gross weight, and redesigned. The standard calibers became 12-, 8-, and 4-pounders, with a proportion of 6-inch howitzers. The design of gun carriages was improved, and much equipment became interchangeable. The use of pre-packaged rounds improved rates of fire, and the introduction of better sights and inclination markers improved accuracy. Gribeauval's reforms also extended into the administrative field. Gunners were subjected to progressive training, and the arm was reorganized into seven regiments, each comprising 20 companies and

equipped with a depot and training school. *Le système Gribeauval* underlay the French artillary of the revolutionary and consular periods and, with certain adjustments, dominated the Empire as well.

Gribeauval's sound work was carried on by his pupils, including the Baron du Teil*—a particular influence on Lieutenant Bonaparte during his period at Auxonne. During the Revolutionary Wars, the artillery proved the pride of the army, being less affected than either the cavalry or the infantry by the exodus of aristocratic officers. Guns were organized into *compagnies* (batteries) of eight pieces, six being of one caliber, the remaining two being howitzers. The campaigns between 1792 and 1796 also saw a substantial increase in the number of horse artillery batteries, and the introduction of galloper-guns (*artillerie volante*) capable of keeping up with cavalry.

The Consulate and the Empire saw further advances. The First Consul himself was responsible for the militarization of the artillery services, ending the traditional employment of civilian drivers. He also encouraged the creation of an operational Artillery Reserve, an organization that held up to 25% of the guns of the *Grande Armée*, including a high proportion of the redoubtable 12-pounders, the Emperor's "beautiful daughters"—a concept he had first experimented with in 1796. Many of these reforms were the work of the able Marmont.* By 1803 there were eight regiments of foot artillery, six of horse, two battalions of *pontonniers,* and eight battalions of artillery train troops. Two years later the French possessed 4,506 heavy (including fortress) guns, 7,766 intermediate and light, 8,320 howitzers, and 1,746 mortars. By the *Système de l'An XI* (1803), 4-pounders were largely replaced by 6-pounders to make effective use of the large numbers of Prussian and Austrian guns of that caliber captured between 1794 and 1800. Redesigned 12-pounders were brought into use, being placed in corps reserves and in the Artillery Reserve. A proportion of heavier howitzers also replaced some of the 6-inch variety. Eight- and 6-pounders were allocated to advance guard and divisional batteries. After 1809, however, it was found that the declining quality of the French infantry required the reintroduction of regimental artillery, and the 4-pounder reappeared. The target was to provide five guns for every 1,000 men, but a proportion of over three per thousand was the best attained.

Several European armies—for example, those of Prussia and Austria—tended to pattern their cannon on French models, but most retained at least some national features. Thus the Prussian army at Waterloo,* besides having 12- and 6-pounders, included 5.8-inch and 6.7-inch howitzers. The Russian artillery, in addition to 12- and 6-pounders, also held large numbers of 20-, 10-, and 3-pounder "unicorns" (long-barreled howitzers) that were introduced in Arakcheev's "System of 1805." The British Royal Artillery contained 9- and 6-pounder cannon and 5.5-inch howitzers. The last two pieces were considerably lighter than their French equivalents and were regarded as superior in rate of fire and general accuracy. British cannon were distinguishable by their single (rather than double) trails.

Cannon fired spherical round-shot, bagged grape, and canister shot (anti-personnel ammunition of varying numbers of shot contained in each round), and howitzers employed explosive shells. A British invention, introduced in 1803, was shrapnel* shell, hollow spheres packed with balls and an explosive charge with a range of up to 1,000 yards when employed in the howitzer variety. By comparison, a 12-pounder could fire a ball to some 1,000 meters, an 8-pounder to 900 meters, a 4-pounder to some 850 meters—but under the right conditions ricochet fire might attain longer ranges. Grape had a carry of about two thirds, canister of one half, at these ranges. Ammunition was carried in ready-to-use chests (or *coffrets,* slung between the twin-trails), in artillery limbers, and in caissons.

Most guns were drawn by between four and six horses according to size and classification—horse artillery batteries and Guard units having the higher allocations. Gun crews (to include drivers) varied from 15 for the larger pieces to 8 for the smaller. In "Foot Artillery" units these crews marched beside their pieces; in the horse artillery they rode on horseback or on the gun-limbers; in *l'artillerie volante* they invariably rode horses.

Gun drill was much the same in all armies, being designed to obtain the highest rate of accurate fire possible. A high degree of teamwork was a vital prerequisite of success, and frequent practices were enjoined by all artillery commanders. The use of prepackaged rounds (serge bags holding powder and ball) was common if not universal.

Artillery tactics varied. The French advocated the bold handling of guns, commanders being encouraged to shorten the range by advancing in bounds whenever practicable. *Général de brigade* Senarmont's* handling of his guns at Friedland* in 1807 was one outstanding example: he shortened the range from 600 to 60 paces in three rapid advances. Napoleon became increasingly convinced of the value of massed batteries; those employed at Jena* and Wagram* (1806 and 1809 respectively) to hold sectors of the battlefront, and the large batteries in action at Borodino* and Waterloo are notable examples. By way of contrast, Wellington* tended to advocate small detachments placed in hull-down positions

CALIBRE AND SPECIFICATION	CANNON	DIRECT FIRE RANGES IN METRES
		300　　　　600　　　　900　　　　120
12 POUNDER Calibre　　　　= 121 mm Length of barrel = 7ft 7ins Weight of barrel = 2172 lbs Carriage weight = 2192 lbs		
8 POUNDER Calibre　　　　= 100 mm Length of barrel = 6ft 7ins Weight of barrel = 1286 lbs Carriage weight = 1851 lbs		
4 POUNDER (see Note A) Calibre　　　　= 84 mm Length of barrel = 5ft 3ins Weight of barrel = 637 lbs Carriage weight = 1454 lbs		
6" HOWITZER Calibre　　　　= 166 mm Length of barrel = 2ft 4ins Weight of barrel = 701 lbs Carriage weight = 1895 lbs		

NOTE A: Pre-1803 and post 1809; during the period 1804-1809 the 6 Pounder was widely employed in lieu, its ranges being approx. 50 metres longer than the 4 Pounder (ball) and approx. 30 metres longer in the case of canister. Length of barrel was approx. 5 ft. 10 ins, weighing 850 lbs

KEY

●●●●●●●➤ Ball: effective range

⟋➤ Ball: maximum range

▬▬▬ Canister range

⟍➤ Shell ranges } variable ch and fuse se

	GUN CREWS ■ Specialist ⊠ Non-specialist	AMMUNITION Trail Chest Caisson			AVERAGE RATE of FIRE	LOCATION (see Note B)
0 ▬▬ 1800	8 ⊠▲▲⊠⊠▲▲⊠ 👤👤👤👤👤👤👤👤 👑👑👑👑👑👑👑 ⊠⊠⊠⊠⊠⊠⊠ 15 👤👤👤👤👤👤👤 7	Ball	Ball	Canister	One round per minute	Artillery Reserve and Corps Reserves (One battery of eight guns per Corps)
		9	48	20		
	8 ⊠▲⊠▲⊠▲⊠▲ 👤👤👤👤👤👤👤👤 👑👑👑👑👑 13 ⊠⊠⊠⊠⊠ 5	Ball	Ball	Canister	Two rounds per minute	Divisional Reserves
		15	62	20		
	5 ⊠▲⊠▲⊠ 👤👤👤👤👤 👑👑👑 8 ⊠⊠⊠ 3	Ball	Ball	Canister	Two to three rounds per minute	Advance Guards and Divisional Reserves and Artillery Reserve (horse batteries)
		18	100	50		
Shell burst danger zone 40 metres diameter	8 ⊠▲⊠▲⊠▲⊠▲ 👤👤👤👤👤👤👤👤 👑👑👑👑👑 13 ⊠⊠⊠⊠⊠ 5	Shell	Shell	Canister	One shell per minute	Divisional Reserves and Artillery Reserve
		4	49	11		

n the case of the 12, 8, and 4 Pounders, the employment
f ricochet fire could increase the maximum range
y between 50% and 75%; each 'bound' of the cannon-
all theoretically decreased in distance by 50% each
ime it hit the ground. i.e. 600 ⊳ 300 ⊳ 150 ⊳ 75 ⊳ 37 yards.

NOTE B: Most guns were organised into
'companies' of eight cannon; in the case of many
Divisional and Artillery Reserve formations
(and some Corps reserves) a proportion of six
cannon to two howitzers was observed.

Artillery of La Grande Armée

along the crest of his position, and under close cavalry attack his gunners were trained to leave their pieces to shelter in neighboring infantry squares. On occasion, particularly in the French army, light pieces were attached to infantry squares (as at the battle of the Pyramids,* 1798), generally being placed to cover the vulnerable corners.

Notable artillerists besides Napoleon included Marmont,* Drouot,* and Senarmont in the French army. If the French tended to set the standards, they were eventually emulated by their foes, who included the Russian Major General Kutaisov and the British gunners Colonels Wood, Dickson, and Frazer.*

Arzobispo, crossing at, 4 August 1809. Sir Arthur Wellesley* led his British army over the Tagus and out of Spain into Portugal toward Almeida through Arzobispo, following the successful battle of Talavera.* The threat of being enveloped

by Soult* from the north and his distrust of his Spanish allies had persuaded Wellesley to order this retreat.

Aspern-Essling, battle of, 21–22 May 1809. After regaining the initiative on the Danube front by the battles of Abensberg* and Eckmühl,* Napoleon occupied Vienna on 13 May and at once sought crossing places over the Danube which would permit the French army to reach the north bank, the bridges in the city having been destroyed by the Austrian rear guard. His object was to hunt down and fight Archduke Charles and the main Austrian army, thought to be near Brünn, but in fact far closer to the Danube as events would soon show.

Eventually a bridging site was selected four miles below the city, and on the 18th troops occupied Lobau Island near the north bank and serious bridging work began. On the 20th Massena's* IV Corps moved over the single bridge to occupy

Battle of ASPERN-ESSLING   21st-22nd May 1809

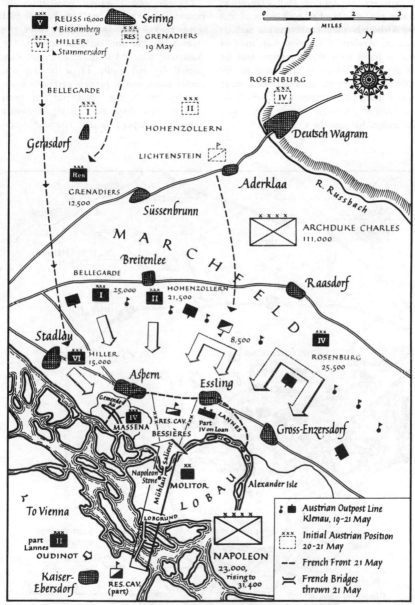

Battle of Aspern-Essling: Day One

the villages of Aspern and Essling as cavalry pushed ahead to seek signs of the foe. Although they reported no serious contacts, Archduke Charles was in fact close at hand with 95,000 troops, and he was kept fully informed of French moves by an observatory on the Bissamberg near Vienna. Late that afternoon a heavy hulk sent down on the swollen current breached the bridge, halting the crossing.

On the 21st a second breakdown occurred in the morning. The French had some 24,000 men and 60 guns over the river when, in the early afternoon, the Austrians attacked in great strength, supported by 200 guns. Their timing was rather awry, so the French garrisons managed to retain the great part of both villages after desperate fighting, Massena defending Aspern while Lannes* com-

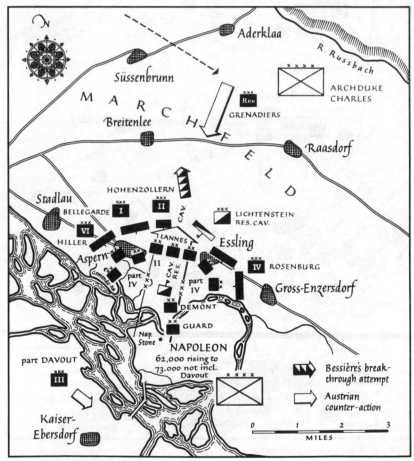

Battle of Aspern-Essling: Day Two

manded in Essling; Bessières* used his 7,000 cavalry to dominate the area between the villages and to draw enemy fire. By nightfall the French had been reinforced (the bridge being open again) to 31,500 men and 90 guns, but the odds were still strongly against them, and the flooding Danube and a succession of waterborne missiles continually threatened the tenuous link to the south bank.

By 3:00 A.M. on the 22nd, Napoleon had doubled his force over the river, the II Corps, more cavalry, and the Imperial Guard having made the crossing overnight. A dawn attack regained all of Aspern for the French, and the garrison of Essling repulsed an Austrian assault at 5:00 A.M. Although Davout's* III Corps had not yet reached the field, Napoleon decided to launch a large attack against the center of the Austrian line. Three divisions of II Corps, supported by the cavalry, advanced under Lannes at 7:00 A.M. and at first made excellent progress. However, Archduke Charles in person rallied his wavering line, and a new breach smashed in the bridge meant that Davout would not be in time to enter the battle. With ammunition running low, Napoleon ordered Lannes to fall back to the village line, but Austrian attacks captured most of Essling, apart from the granary, and threatened the French right flank.

Napoleon's situation was fast becoming critical. His troops repelled a major attack at 1:30 P.M., but the position was almost untenable. At 2:00 P.M. Napoleon ordered a retreat into Lobau Island, and this was facilitated by the recapture of Essling by the Young Guard in a celebrated attack. The withdrawal proceeded in good order, but the mortal wounding of Lannes was a sad loss. The evacuation continued overnight, and at 3:30 A.M. on the 23rd the bridge to the north bank was dismantled.

The French had 21,000 casualties and inflicted possibly 23,340. Their repulse was due to poor reconnaissance, an underestimation of the character of the Danube in flood, and a miscalculation of their opponent's zeal. Six weeks later, however, a carefully prepared second crossing would result in the great victory of Wagram.*

Assaye, battle of, 23 September 1803. For the Second Mahratta War, the governor general of India, the Earl of Mornington, deployed two field armies. One, in north India, was commanded by General Lake; the second, in south-central India, was entrusted to Lord Mornington's younger brother, Arthur Wellesley.* Major General Wellesley advanced with a force of some 13,500 British and sepoy troops and 22 guns to challenge the vast army of the Princes of Scindia and Berar, which included over 20,000 famous Mahratta cavalry, perhaps as many effective infantry, and 98 guns, besides numbers of ill-trained levies. After six weeks of marching, Wellesley caught up with his opponents near the small town of Assaye; they were occupying a seven-mile position behind the river Kaitna.

Appreciating that a frontal attack against so strong an opponent was out of the question, Wellesley decided to mount an oblique attack against the enemy's left flank in the vicinity of Assaye itself. Using the British and Allied cavalry to pin the attention of the main enemy army by placing them in a position overlooking the south bank of the Kaitna, he advanced his British infantry from the River Purna to cross a ford opposite Waroor a mile and a half to the southeast of Assaye. Once this maneuver was completed, the British cavalry would move to join the infantry over the river, and Wellesley's battle line would swing left to face the extreme left of the enemy position, its own flanks resting securely on the banks of the Kaitna and its tributary the Juah.

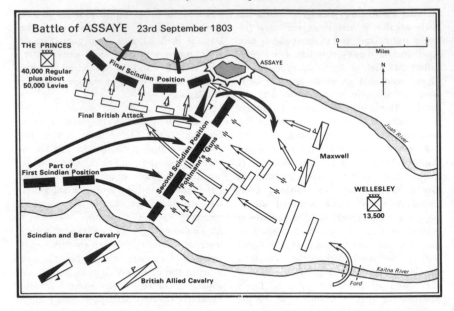

Colonel Maxwell's cavalry successfully countered an attack by the Mahratta horsemen as the infantry crossed the ford, but the enemy realized what was happening sooner than Wellesley had hoped, and thanks to a German mercenary, Pohlmann, the Indian army's guns were rapidly redeployed to face the threat to their flank, while Scindia's regular battalions were repositioned to face the small British army. Despite mounting casualties, Wellesley pressed home his attack, silenced the enemy guns, and forced the Scindian infantry beyond to give ground. However, assaults on Assaye itself came to grief against the defenses and guns manned by Berar's troops. Then the Mahratta cavalry charged down, but Maxwell met and routed them in a spirited engagement on Wellesley's right flank, and then proceeded to exploit his success by falling on the columns of Mahratta infantry beyond. These also were induced to flee, and the situation on Wellesley's right was thus made safe.

Much fighting had still to be faced, however, for the enemy center and reserves took up a new position with their backs to the Juah. Wellesley immediately ordered Maxwell to watch his flank while he swung his handful of battalions in a tight arc toward Assaye. Now the Mahratta infantry broke and fled for the Juah, hotly pursued by Maxwell, who was killed. Wellesley turned his attention to the matter of recapturing some cannon which the enemy had managed to reman and turn against his rear. The battle drew to a close at about 6:00 P.M. as the princes abandoned the field and fell back. Wellesley's army was utterly exhausted, having sustained some 1,600 casualties and inflicted perhaps 6,000. This was to prove one of the hardest-fought battles Wellesley ever undertook. Later in the year he would fight the battle of Argaum,* but the Second Mahratta War would drag on until 1805.

Atrocities. All armies, subjected to extreme stress, committed military excesses at one time or another during the Napoleonic Wars. The French often looted indiscriminately, and when subjected to guerilla or partisan activities, as in Spain, Portugal, and Russia, responded with brutal ferocity. Spanish and Russian patriots, and German resistance movements, meted out terrible treatment to stragglers and isolated small units. Colonel Trant's* Portuguese irregulars, for example, massacred French wounded at Coimbra* in 1810. The etchings by Goya,* "The Horrors of War," bring the point graphically home. Wellington's army, especially when exposed to the temptations of drink, could also get out of hand—as its behavior after the stormings of Ciudad Rodrigo,* Badajoz* (both 1812), and San Sebastian* (1813) illustrates.

Auerstädt, battle of. *See* **Jena-Auerstädt**

Augereau, *Maréchal* Pierre François Charles, duc de Castiglione (1757–1816). Born in Paris of humble parents, Augereau remained coarse and brutal for the rest of his life, nicknamed "child of the people" and "proud brigand." He was a fine tactical commander, although Napoleon remarked that he was incapable of understanding the orders issued by the *Grand-Quartier-Général*, needing to be shown exactly what was required of him on a map.

His first military service was in 1774, in the *Régiment de Clare Irlandais*, and over the next dozen years he changed regiments several times, serving at one time in the Prussian army and at another (1786) with a French training mission to Naples. Expelled at the time of the French Revolution, in 1790 he joined the Parisian National Guard and later a volunteer regiment. In 1793 he was arrested at Tours for political reasons but was soon freed, and thereafter his career flourished. Promoted to Captain of Hussars (26 June

Augereau

1793), the same year saw him as a lieutenant colonel and ADC to General Rossignol during the revolt in La Vendée.* On 27 September he was made *adjutant général* and *chef de brigade* (or full colonel). On 23 December he was promoted to *général de division*. In 1794 he served in the Pyrenean and Catalonian campaigns, winning an action at St. Laurent de la Monga on 13 August, and later being involved in the sieges of Figueras and Rosas. The following year he was transferred to the Army of Italy and fought with distinction at Loano (24–5 November). On Schèrer's* relinquishment of command, he passed under that of General Bonaparte and soon distinguished himself in the Campaign of 1796 at Millesimo* and Montenotte,* storming Cosseira Castle, and at Lodi.* His services at Castiglione* on 5 August—particularly his staunch morale when everything seemed lost—earned him Napoleon's lasting esteem, and (later) his ducal title. Later in the same campaign he fought at Primolano, Bassano,* Arcola,* and La Favorita outside

Mantua,* and after the surrender of that fortress was sent back to Paris with the 60 captured Austrian colors. He later served as Military Governor of Verona and neighboring Venetian territory, but in July 1797 he was recalled from Italy to command the 17th Military Division at Paris.

At this juncture he became politically ambitious and played a leading part in the coup of 18th Fructidor* which purged the Directory and the Councils of royalist elements: In 1799 he was elected to a seat in the *Conseil de Cinq-Cents*,* but opposed the coup d'état of Brumaire* after Napoleon's return from Egypt. He subsequently was reconciled with the First Consul.

Some trace of this disagreement lingered, however. Although 1800 saw Augereau campaigning successfully in Germany (where he captured Würzburg and Burg-Eberbach), followed by a command in Holland, from October 1801 to August 1803 he received no appointments, but lived on his estate at La Houssaye-en-Brie in semi-retirement. He then received command of camps at Bayonne and Brest, and was clearly restored to favor by 19 May 1804, when he was included in the original creation of the Marshalate.* The following February he was appointed a Grand Eagle of the Legion of Honor, and from 30 August 1805 began his 18-month association with the VII *corps d'armée*. As its commander, he served in Austria in 1805, forcing General Jellacic to surrender at Feldkirch in November. The next year found him at Jena,* commanding Napoleon's left wing. On 24 December he won the action of Kolozomb. The next February, despite serious illness, he gallantly led his corps to virtual destruction at the bitter battle of Eylau,* and was shot in the arm.

Despite his renewed criticism of Napoleon's generalship, on 19 March 1808

he was created Duke of Castiglione. The following February he married his second wife (his first had died in 1806), and despite the difference in their ages this proved a success. Three months later he was ordered to Spain to replace Gouvion St. Cyr,* and assumed command of a new VII Corps. Serving in Catalonia, he took Gerona (10 December), but in April 1810 he was transferred to command the II Corps in Germany. There he remained for some years; he occupied Prussia during the French invasion of Russia, and successively served as commandant of Berlin and governor of Frankfurt in the first quarter of 1813. The major campaign of that year found him at the head of first the IX and then the XVI Corps, and leading the latter he won the battle of Naumburg on 9 October. He subsequently fought at Leipzig.* As the Allied armies invaded France in 1814, he commanded the so-called Army of the East (or of the Rhone). Defeated at St. Georges (18 March), he lost Lyons five days later.

At this point he abandoned Napoleon's cause. The first Bourbon Restoration created him a Chevalier of St. Louis, and he was given command of the 19th Military Division at Lyons and later transferred to Caen. He did not rally to Napoleon in 1815 and was struck from the roll of the Marshalate on 10 April that year. After Waterloo* he lived in obscurity on his estate after serving on the Council of War which refused to convict Marshal Ney*; this caused the Bourbons to deprive him of all emoluments. He died on 12 June 1816.

As a soldier he was a good tactician, capable of making decisions, and very gallant. As a man he was uncouth, endowed with an excessive sense of humor and a lust for money. But his troops took to him, and he was not the least distinguished Marshal of the Empire.

Aulic Council, the. This august body of senior Austrian commanders nominally controlled their country's strategy in time of war. Until the aftermath of Austerlitz,* the Aulic Council's ultraconservative and deadening hand was very influential, and hampered the field commanders with gratuitous advice and demands for ever more reports and paperwork. Its powers were reduced during the reforming work of the Archduke Charles,* whose authority transcended it.

Austerlitz, battle of, 2 December 1805. The climax to the great Campaign of 1805,* which finally established the military reputation of the one-year-old First French Empire and its dynamic leader, was fought out a few miles east of Brünn in Moldavia on a cold winter's day. Napoleon feigned weakness to induce his Austrian and Russian enemies to advance from Olmütz and attack him, but managed to bring up two distant *corps d'armée** (Bernadotte's* 1st and Davout's* 3rd from Iglau and Vienna respectively) to build up his strength to 73,200 men and 199 guns. The Allied army, commanded by General Kutusov* and accompanied by both the Tsar Alexander* and the Emperor Francis I,* deployed 85,400 men and 278 guns, and despite the misgivings of its Commander in Chief, the advice of the hotheads such as Dolgoruki* prevailed, and on 1 December the army pressed forward to occupy the Pratzen Heights (abandoned by the French) and their environs. Napoleon meanwhile anchored his left wing on the Santon mount (entrusted to Lannes*), placed Soult's* IV Corps to hold the villages along the valley of the Bosenitz and Goldbach streams in his extended center, and relied on Davout's recently arrived divisions to reinforce the extreme right around Zokolnitz and Telnitz. This frontage was almost five miles long. The

mass of his cavalry, Oudinot's* grenadiers, the Imperial Guard,* and Bernadotte's I Corps were concealed on and behind the Zurlan Heights toward the French left. His dispositions made, Napoleon made a night walk through part of his army, being greeted with cheers from the men, who organized an impromptu torchlight procession to honor their leader, who just one year earlier had crowned himself Emperor at Notre Dame.

Across the valley, the Allied leaders were discussing their plans for the morrow, confident that victory would be theirs. Kutusov catnapped while General Weyrother read out the orders. Some 45,000 men were to advance under General Buxhowden* in a broad outflanking movement south of the Pratzen Heights, which would sever the French links with Vienna and roll their battle line up the Bosenitz and Goldbach valley, aided by a further 15,000 men from the Pratzen. Meanwhile a secondary movement by General Bagration* and 17,600 men would attack the Santon on the French left. The Russian Imperial Guard (8,500 strong) was to form a central reserve, initially near the village of Austerlitz, east of the Pratzen. They little guessed that Napoleon hoped that they would execute just such a plan.

By 4:00 A.M. on the 2nd both armies were astir. A dense mist inconvenienced the Allied advance, but within three hours Telnitz and Zokolnitz were under attack and eventually were occupied. However, part of Davout's corps intervened, and the situation was stabilized. At 8:30 A.M. Buxhowden summoned Kollowrath from the Pratzen to enter the battle. Napoleon on the Zurlan was scrutinizing these moves as the mist slowly dispersed. Judging the Pratzen to be cleared of almost all Allied troops, at 9:00 A.M. Napoleon ordered Marshal Soult to attack the Heights with two divisions from the vicinity of Puntowitz.

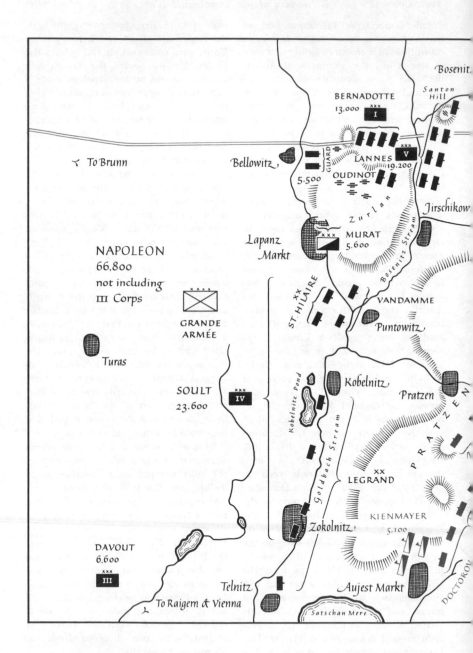

Bosenit.

Santon
Hill

BERNADOTTE
13,000
xxx
I

To Brunn

Bellowitz,

GUARD
5,500

LANNES 19,200
xxx
V

OUDINOT

Jirschikow

Zurlan

Bosenitz Stream

Lapanz
Markt

MURAT
5,600

NAPOLEON
66,800
not including
III Corps

GRANDE
ARMÉE

ST. HILAIRE
xx

VANDAMME

Puntowitz

Turas

Kobelnitz Pond

Kobelnitz

Pratzen

SOULT
23,600
xxx
IV

Goldbach Stream

P R A T Z E N

xx
LEGRAND

KIENMAYER
5,100

DAVOUT
6,600
xxx
III

Zokolnitz

Telnitz

To Raigem & Vienna

Aujest Markt

DOCTOROV

Satschan Mere

[32]

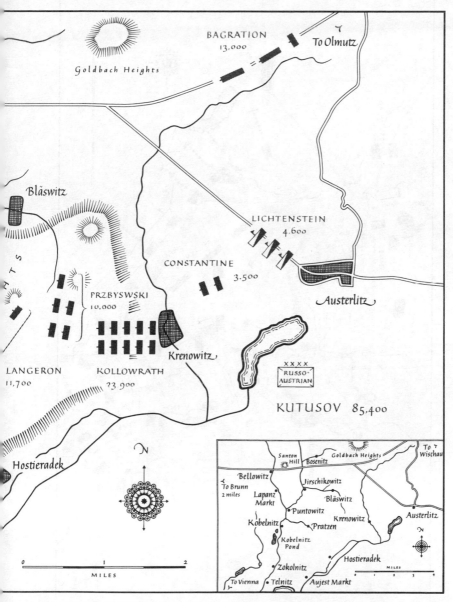

Battle of Austerlitz, 2 December 1805: General Situation—Morning

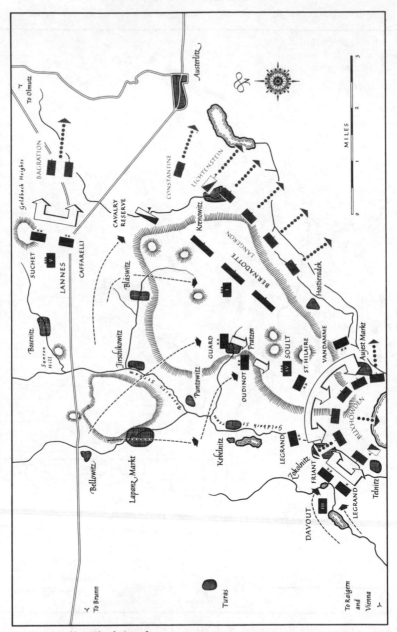

Battle of Austerlitz: Final Attack

The Allies were surprised by this unanticipated development, and too late tried to reinforce the threatened sector. Napoleon ordered Bernadotte's corps forward to Blaswitz on Soult's left. Meanwhile a violent fight was flaring around the Santon hill, but Lannes held his ground, aided by Murat's* massed cavalry, which clashed with Prince Lichtenstein's squadrons in the open plain to the Santon's south. The battle in the Goldbach valley was once again in full swing, and Napoleon sent down Oudinot's grenadiers to reinforce the tiring French right wing, which was having to give some ground.

At 10:30 A.M. Kutusov counterattacked Soult's two divisions on the Pratzen from three sides, and the Marshal barely stopped his line from collapsing by skillful deployment of his corps artillery. The French Imperial Guard advanced toward the fighting but did not engage at this juncture. However, at 1:00 P.M. the Russian Guards stormed up from Austerlitz and some of Soult's weary troops broke and abandoned the summit. Fortunately for the French, the Guard cavalry under Bessières* and Rapp* charged and flung back the foe, while Bernadotte rushed up a division to Soult's aid on his own initiative. Thus the crisis in the center passed, and Napoleon began to plan his battle-winning maneuver.

Summoning the Imperial Guard on to the Pratzen, he ordered it and Soult's survivors to move south along the feature to envelop Buxhowden's unwieldy column. By 3:30 P.M. the move was completed, and French guns and infantry were firing from the Pratzen onto the massed enemy below. Trapped among some frozen meres, Buxhowden tried to extricate his men. Some tried to escape over the ice, but it broke under the French bombardment, and retreat became an all-out rout. By now Kutusov and the Allied monarchs were leaving the field and Bagration also broke off the

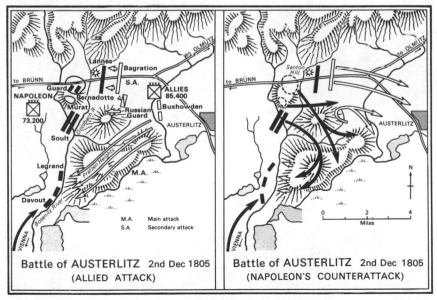

Battle of AUSTERLITZ 2nd Dec 1805
(ALLIED ATTACK)

M.A.   Main attack
S.A.   Secondary attack

Battle of AUSTERLITZ 2nd Dec 1805
(NAPOLEON'S COUNTERATTACK)

action on the northern side of the battle-field and headed back up the highroad toward Olmütz. Sometime after 4:00 P.M. the last gun fell silent, and the "Battle of the Three Emperors" was over.

Casualties had been high. An eighth of the *Grande Armée* was stricken, including 1,300 killed, 6,490 wounded, and 500 missing. Fully one third of the Austro-Russian army had been accounted for: some 16,000 killed and wounded and possibly 11,000 prisoners. The French had also taken 180 cannon and 45 colors. The battle sounded the death knell of the Third Coalition.* The day after the battle the Emperor Francis of Austria applied for an armistice, and before the end of the month the Peace of Pressburg* was signed. The Russians retired to their own territory, and soon Great Britain was left alone to sustain the fight against France. News of Austerlitz reputedly hastened the death early in 1806 of William Pitt.* This battle

raised Napoleon's martial reputation to a new height, and he had every reason to declare at the opening of his victory bulletin, "*Soldats! Je suis content de vous.*"

Aux Champs. Played on the drums and fifes, this piece of military music served as both a "General Salute" for high-ranking officers and as a signal for the troops to move off toward the field of battle. It was introduced in 1802.

Axamitowski, Général Vincent (1760–1828). A distinguished Polish artillery officer who entered the French service in 1800. Given command of the artillery of the Grand Duchy of Warsaw in 1807, he later served on Murat's* personal staff and commanded a cavalry brigade (1813). He finished his service as the senior gunner of the new kingdom of Poland in 1825.

Bacler d'Albe, Général Baron Louis-Albert G. (1761–1824). A painter by profession, he volunteered for the army in 1793. He was wounded at Toulon* in 1793 and soon gravitated to the staff as a geographical expert, serving in the Italian Campaigns of 1794 and 1796. In late 1799 he was appointed chief geographical engineer at the *Dépôt de la Guerre,* and on 23 September 1804 he became chief of the Emperor's topographical office in the *Bureau.** In this capacity he served through the campaigns of 1805–07, being promoted to colonel, and then through the campaigns of 1808–13. He was made a Baron of the Empire in 1809 and received promotion to *général de brigade* in 1813. He became director of the *Dépôt* next year, and later served the Bourbons in various capacities before retiring in 1820. Napoleon found him an indispensable staff assistant during the great campaigns, and when in the field invariably held early-morning or late-night map conferences with him.

Badajoz, sieges of 1811 and 1812. This fortified town guarded the Spanish side of the southern corridor* linking Portugal and Spain and was besieged four times during the Peninsular War.* The first siege was from 26 January to 9 March 1811, when Soult* bluffed the Spanish garrison into surrender after the death of General Menacho, the governor, although the French were at the time gravely worried about the outcome of the battle of Barrosa* near Cadiz. Wellington* ordered Marshal Beresford* to undertake its re-capture the same May, but he was forced to abandon the siege after only five days on 12 May as Soult moved up to relieve General Phillipon's* garrison. The relief army never arrived, but the French were able to sally from the town to destroy the Allied siegeworks as Beresford moved off to fight and win the battle of Albuera* (16 May).

The town was reblockaded on 19 May, and the full Allied siege was resumed from the 24th. Wellington massed 14,000 men, but critical shortages of trained engineers and of suitable siege guns made progress very slow. Soon 60,000 French troops were converging on Badajoz, and Wellington, with only 44,000 men available, decided to abandon the siege and retire on 19 June. Next day a relief force reached Phillipon's hungry garrison.

As he prepared to assume the offensive in 1812, Wellington needed to secure control of the corridors as a preliminary step. The capture of Ciudad Rodrigo* on 19 January secured the northern invasion route, and the Allies then turned against Badajoz once more. Wellington brought 32,000 men to the area, placing four divisions to cover the operation and using four more in the siege lines. Phillipon had some 5,000 defenders, including over 600 sick. This time the Allies had a proper complement of engineers and heavy guns. The town was invested on 16 March, and nine days later a volunteer force captured Fort Picurina, an outlying post guarding the eastern defenses. This success enabled the Allied gunners to concentrate their

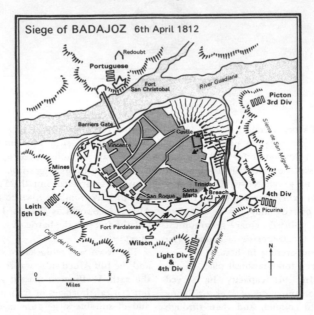

Siege of BADAJOZ 6th April 1812

fire on the weakest sector—the south-eastern wall.

By 6 April three breaches had been battered, and Wellington (aware that French forces were on the move) ordered a full-scale assault for the same night. The 4th and Light Divisions were to storm the breaches, Picton's* 3rd Division was to attempt to storm the castle by escalade, and the 5th Division with Portuguese aid was to mount a diversion. Phillipon had prepared the defense of the breaches with care, and Wellington's "forlorn hope" was driven back with heavy loss by 10:30 P.M. Thereafter no less than 40 assaults were vainly attempted and casualties soared. Fortunately for the Allies, Picton's force managed to capture the castle by 11:30 P.M., and half an hour later General Leith's* division also entered the town from the northwest side. The 3rd and 5th Divisions were then able to drive through the town to attack the rear of the breaches by 1:00

A.M., whereupon Phillipon ordered his garrison to retreat into Fort San Christobal on the further bank of the river Guadiana, where he surrendered on terms the next day, having lost a total of 1,350 killed and wounded.

To capture Badajoz had cost the Allies 3,350 during the assault and a further 1,410 during the preparatory phases. Six generals had been wounded, and four colonels killed. The troops vented their fury on the heads of the hapless Spanish population, and for three days the town was put to the sack. Wellington could not regain control until the 11th, and this episode did not redound to the credit of the British army. However, the Allies had now gained control of both corridors and could prepare their invasion of Spain, which would in due course lead them to the great success at Salamanca.*

Bagavut, General Karl Federovitch (1761–1812). This Russian soldier was of

Estonian extraction, and made his reputation fighting the Turks in the Crimean region (1783–84). He later served with distinction in Poland and Moldavia (1780–89) and took part in the Campaign of 1805 against Napoleon. Three years later he defeated the Swedes at Aabo. He was killed at the action of Tarutino during the Campaign of 1812.

Bagration, General Peter (1765–1812). This notable Russian commander came from a noble Georgian family, entering the army in 1782. Service in the Caucasus and Poland earned him the favor of Suvorov, whom he accompanied on his Italian and Swiss campaigns (1799), during which he captured Brescia. In 1805 he commanded against Murat* at Hollabrunn,* accepting odds of five to one to enable the main Allied army of Kutusov* to make good its retreat. He was present

Bagration

at the battles of Austerlitz,* Eylau,* Heilsberg,* and Friedland,* where he particularly distinguished himself. Successful campaigns against the Swedes and Turks followed in 1808 and 1809, and in 1812 Bagration was appointed to command the Second Army of the West. He was defeated at Moghilev in July, but evaded French attempts to trap his army and eventually joined Barclay de Tolly* at Smolensk.* Kutusov gave him command of the Russian left wing at Borodino,* and he was wounded in the battle. Just over two weeks later he succumbed to an infection and was greatly mourned by the Russian army and people.

Bailen, capitulation of, 21 July 1808. General Dupont* was entrusted with the pacification of Andalusia in southern Spain by Napoleon, but after sacking Cordoba the French commander found himself faced by a massive popular rising and the 30,000-strong army of General Reding. Instead of retreating over the Sierra Morena immediately, Dupont unwisely lingered in the plain of Andujar, and when at last he did decide to retire, his column, burdened by wounded and loot, found the road toward distant Madrid threatened by the Spaniards. Dupont sent his subordinate General Vedel with 10,000 men to reopen the road, whereupon Reding and Castaños* swooped on his remaining 13,000 troops to trap them near Bailen amid inhospitable and waterless hills. On the 19th Dupont made five attempts to break out, but in vain. Vedel's return from the North did not improve the situation, and after two days of negotiation both French forces agreed to capitulate. This event caused a sensation throughout Europe, and its repercussions, together with Junot's* defeat at Vimiero,* persuaded Napoleon of the need for his personal intervention in the Peninsula.

Baird, General Sir David (1757–1829). Commissioned in 1772, Baird served with distinction in India, surviving almost four years of captivity, and capturing Pondicherry in 1793. Service at the Cape of Good Hope led to his promotion to major general (1798), and after returning to India he led the storm of Seringapatam,* 1799. In 1801 he led a force from India to Egypt in support of Abercromby's* invasion. Returned to India, he fell out with Wellesley* and left for England. He was captured at sea but soon exchanged, and at last he reached England after a total absence of 24 years. In 1806 he became Governor of the Cape, but was dismissed after the Montevideo* fiasco. In 1807 he commanded a division at Copenhagen,* and next year sailed for Portugal to reinforce Moore.* He shared in the Corunna* campaign, losing an arm in the battle. This proved his last active command, but in 1820 he was made Commander in Chief of Ireland. His last post was as governor of Fort George, which he held until his death. A popular commander, the phrase "not Baird but Bayard" was often applied to him.

Ballesteros, General Francisco (fl. 1810). A Spanish general of mediocre martial skill but vast political and military ambition. Jealousy at Wellington's appointment as Generalissimo led him to make a bid for power on 23 October 1812. The attempt failed, and the Cortes promptly ordered him to be incarcerated in North Africa.

Bantry Bay, attempted landing at, December 1796. On the Directory's* order, 20,000 French troops under General Hoche* embarked on Admiral Morard de Galles'* fleet at Brest, and on 15 December sailed to attempt an invasion of Ireland. The Royal Navy's blockading ships were eluded, and a landfall was made by the majority of the ships on the 21st. The wind, hitherto favorable to the French, now turned adverse, and the inexperienced crews of many of the 35 vessels present proved incapable of entering Bantry Bay, where it was hoped to land the expedition. The weather moderated on the 24th, but hopes of effecting a landing were dashed next day when a full gale blew up. Several ships dragged their anchors, and soon all were desperately putting out to sea, where many were scattered. On the 27th, a council of war decided to call off the invasion attempt, and on 14 January 1797 the bulk of the expedition safely returned to the harbor of Brest. Four vessels had been sunk or scuttled, and six more were taken by the Royal Navy. However, the inability of the Channel fleet to intercept the expedition on its outward voyage caused a considerable furor, and Admiral Hood* was much criticized.

Barbé-Marbois, Ministre François (1745–1837). A sometime diplomatic official of the *Ancien Régime,* he later became a member of the *Conseil des Anciens,* and served as Minister of Finance from 1802–05. Three years later he was appointed the first president of the *Cour des Comptes,* and he remained an influential figure throughout the Empire. Reconciled to Louis XVIII,* he served as Minister of Justice from 1815–16.

Barcelona, seizure of, 29 February 1808. A French force commanded by General Duhesme* masqueraded as a party of wounded, and under this disguise entered the castle of Barcelona, which they promptly occupied. It thereafter became the base for a French corps, was intermittently blockaded for the next six years by Spanish irregulars, and proved difficult to maintain.

Barclay de Tolly, Field Marshal Prince Mikhail (1761–1818). A Livonian of Scottish ancestry, he joined the Russian army in 1776 as an ordinary soldier. He came to the notice of Prince Repnin while fighting against the Turks in 1790 and became his adjutant. He later served against the Swedes and the Poles, but only emerged to real significance during the Winter Campaign of 1806–07. He distinguished himself at Pultusk* and again at Eylau,* where he was seriously wounded. His conduct at the latter battle earned him the favor and confidence of the Tsar Alexander,* as well as promotion to lieutenant general. The next year he accompanied Bagration* to seize Sweden's Aaland Islands by means of a bold march across the frozen Gulf of Bothnia. From 1810 he was Minister of War, and to that position was added the *de facto* command of the First Army of the West in 1812. The responsibilities of the double appointment proved too much for him, for he found it hard to delegate authority. Nevertheless, since 1810 he had managed to introduce many important reforms into the army, effectively modernizing it.

His conduct of the defense of the Russian homeland in mid-1812 attracted much criticism. From his original position around Vilna, his strategy was one of evasion and retreat—drawing the French deeper into Russia. He thus successfully escaped from several French envelopment attempts, and eventually linked up with Bagration's army at Smolensk,* where a major battle was fought (16–17 August). The battle was lost, partly because of the mutual dislike he and Bagration felt for one another, but again the Russian army escaped to the east. On the Tsar's order, the senior command was now given to Kutusov,* and at the famous battle of Borodino* Barclay de Tolly commanded only the right wing, but he fought with skill. After the battle he resigned, but next year returned to the service to lead a Russian army into Silesia to link up with Russia's new Prussian allies. He accompanied the Tsar on both the campaigns of 1813 and 1814, and fought at Bautzen,* Dresden,* Kulm,* and Leipzig.* In 1814 he became Commander in Chief of the Russian forces occupying France. In 1815 he was put at the head of the Russian army that set out for France after Napoleon's return from Elba,* but Waterloo* had been fought before he reached the frontiers. By this time he was a prince and a field marshal. He died at Insterburg on 26 May 1818. A great administrator and reformer rather than a brilliant field commander, Barclay de Tolly deserved well of his master the Tsar.

Bard, Fort, siege of, 21 May to 5 June 1800. Held by Colonel Bernkopf and a garrison of 400 grenadiers of the Austrian Kinsky Regiment, with some 26 cannon, Fort Bard held up the Army of the Reserve for several critical days during the latter stages of the crossing of the Alps by way of the St. Bernard Pass. Bonaparte was able to pass infantry and cavalry around the obstruction, but his artillery and trains were tied to the only road. Overnight on the 24th and 25th the French managed to slip six guns past the Fort, and this enabled the advance into the North Italian plain to continue, but the mass of their cannon was bottled up until Bernkopf was induced to surrender early in June.

Barham, Charles Middleton, Admiral Lord (1726–1813). A friend of the younger Pitt,* Barham was for many years Controller of the Navy. After Addington* left office in 1804, he was brought back from retirement in his late 70s to serve as First Lord of the Admiralty in place of Lord Melville. Barham retired again soon after Trafalgar.*

Baring, Major George (fl. 1815). A British officer serving in the King's German Legion, he commanded the 376 men who constituted the garrison of the farm of La Haie Sainte* during the battle of Waterloo.* After a gallant defense, Baring, out of ammunition, was forced to relinquish his post, and escaped with 42 other survivors.

Barnard, General Sir Andrew Francis (1773–1855). Commissioned into the 90th Foot in 1794, he later served in both the First Guards and the 95th, amassing military experience in the West Indies, the Helder, Sicily, Canada, and above all, in the Peninsula. He received two wounds at Barrosa,* and served at Ciudad Rodrigo,* Badajoz,* Salamanca,* Vitoria,* and San Sebastian* before sharing in the Pyrenean campaign of 1813–14 and the battle of Toulouse,* where he rose to command the Light Division. He fought at Quatre Bras* and Waterloo* (again being wounded), and commanded the British division sharing the occupation of Paris. He later held various posts in the Royal Household, and steadily rose in rank to full general (1851). Colonel of the Rifle Brigade from 1822, one of his last appointments was Lieutenant Governor of Chelsea Hospital (1849).

Barras, Directeur Paul (1755–1820). Until 1788 he served as an army officer in the French West Indies. Returning to France in difficult financial circumstances, he seized the opportunities posed by the Revolution and was elected Deputy for Var, the region where he had been born. He was one of the political commissars at the siege of Toulon,* and remembered Bonaparte when he became a Director after helping plot the fall of Robespierre.* At the crisis of *Vendémiaire** in 1795, he appointed Bonaparte to defend the Tuileries Palace against the impending insurrection—a duty that once and for all launched Napoleon's meteoric career.

Barras's cast-off mistress, Josephine de Beauharnais,* soon became the young general's wife. Barras's political career came to an abrupt end at the *coup d'état* *de Brumaire* in November 1799. Thereafter he retired to enjoy his amassed wealth. An immoral man with an insatiable appetite for material advantages and honors, Paul Barras did much to set the low tone of the Directory* regime.

Barrosa, battle of, 5 March 1811. As 15,000 Spanish and British troops, commanded by General Graham,* marched from Tarifa toward Cadiz* intent on disrupting the French blockade of that city, contact was made with 7,000 French troops on the Cerro del Puerco above the tower of Barrosa. The 28th Foot, abandoned by its Spanish allies, fell back from the Cerro, but on Graham's order charged back up the hill supported by the two British brigades that ultimately defeated General Laval's French troops. The 87th took an eagle, and scattered two French battalions. The loss of 1,200 British casualties secured the march to Cadiz, but General La Peña's Spaniards had merely observed the action.

Bar-sur-Aube, Conference of, 25 February 1814. The scene of the defeat of Gérard's* corps on 24 January, next month the town became the location of an Allied council of war. Attended by the Tsar Alexander,* the Austrian Emperor,* the King of Prussia, and Lord Castlereagh,* it saw great criticism of General Schwarzenberg* when he proposed that the main Allied army should retreat to the Langres Plateau, following the rough handling recently meted out by Napoleon to the Army of Bohemia at Montereau.* In the end his proposal was grudgingly adopted until Napoleon turned north, and orders were sent to the distant Blücher* and the Army of Silesia to operate independently for the time being. A week later the Allies met again at Chaumont.*

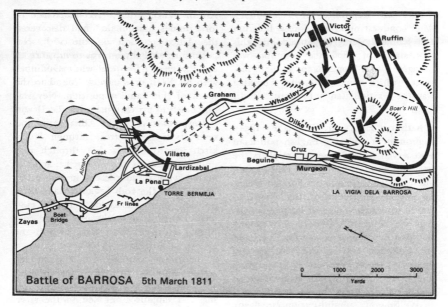

Battle of BARROSA 5th March 1811

0   1000   2000   3000
Yards

Bassano, battle of, 8 September 1796. Following his repulse at Castiglione,* General Count Wurmser* retired up the Adige Valley to Trent and set about devising another plan for the relief of the Austrian garrison besieged in Mantua.* Calculating that Bonaparte would march on Trent in support of Moreau's* belated offensive into south Germany, Wurmser left General Davidovitch* with 15,000 Austrians to contest the French advance and set out early in September with some 20,000 men to march down the Brenta Valley to the southeast. He hoped to break into the Po Valley from the east, using Trieste as his forward base, and thus both threaten Bonaparte's lines of communication and relieve Mantua.

Not until after the battle of Roveredo* against Davidovitch and the occupation of Trent (5 September) did Bonaparte learn of Wurmser's bold move. He at once set off in pursuit with 22,000 men,

leaving Vaubois* to contain Davidovitch. By dint of forced marches down the Valsaguna and Upper Brenta Valley, which started on the 6th, Bonaparte was soon on Wurmser's tail, and in some alarm the Austrians turned at bay at Bassano, leaving a rear guard of Croatians at Primolano in an attempt to delay the French arrival. Bonaparte brushed this force aside on 7 September, and next day attacked the main Austrian position. Sending Augereau* to outflank Bassano from the east, and Massena* to envelop the town from the west, Bonaparte soon had the Austrians in full flight. Some 3,000 escaped east to Trieste; Wurmser himself, with 12,000 troops, fled west and in due course forced a way into Mantua, which was promptly besieged again (15 September). As a result of the battle on the 8th, the French, with minimal loss, took almost 4,000 prisoners, 35 cannon, 5 colors and 2 pontoon trains.

Batavian Republic, the (1795–1806). After conquest by French forces, Belgium and Holland were reorganized into this new state. In 1806 the republic was changed into a kingdom for Louis Bonaparte,* which lasted until 1810. The area was then assimilated into France until 1814.

Bathurst, Henry, 3rd Earl (1762–1834). A prominent and able English politician who served in Pitt's* second ministry, he was Master of the Mint in 1804. Later, after a brief period at the Foreign Office, he became President of the Board of Trade under the Duke of Portland. During the ministry of Lord Liverpool,* Bathurst became Secretary for War and the Colonies, and in this post he did much to support Wellington's* protracted war in the Peninsula. In later years he became Lord President of the Council in Wellington's administration (1828–30), but took no active part in politics after the Great Reform Bill.

Battle of the Nations. *see* **Leipzig**

Bautzen, battle of, 20–21 May 1813. Following their defeat by Napoleon at Lützen,* the Russian and Prussian army of Prince Wittgenstein,* 96,000 men and some 450 guns strong, fell back eastward between the rivers Elbe and Oder to the vicinity of Bautzen, a Saxon town on the upper reaches of the river Spree, about 60 kilometers east of Dresden. The Tsar and the King of Prussia ordered a stand to be made, as Napoleon—hampered by shortage of cavalry from an all-out pursuit—closed up to the Spree, after occupying Dresden and making it his center of operations. At this juncture the Emperor had 115,000 men and 150 guns under immediate command, but a further 85,000 men and as many guns under Marshal Ney* were approaching from the north, and Napoleon planned a classical example of a battle of envelopment (*see*

Art of War). After a reconnaissance in force under Macdonald* had discovered the Allied position on the 16th, Napoleon ordered three corps to advance to pin the enemy frontally while Oudinot* with his XII Corps moved around to the south of the Bautzen position. Ney was instructed to march south with the II and V Corps to envelop the Allied army and sever its line of retreat through Hochkirch toward Görlitz, but through misunderstanding of his orders he actually moved with all four corps in his sector, and late on the 20th began to take up a position near Maukendorf facing eastward rather than southward. These confusions on Ney's part were to rob the French of a decisive victory.

Meanwhile, Napoleon had spent the 19th examining the Allied positions beyond the Spree. Wittgenstein* was occupying a seven-mile front behind the river, holding a series of spurs and ridges and fortified villages organized into two lines of positions, with the town of Bautzen slightly to the fore of the left center. The Allies had seven corps in position, but Napoleon overcalculated their strength, estimating it to be 150,000. Placing Marmont's* VI and Macdonald's XI Corps to hold the center, Napoleon ordered Bertrand's* IV Corps and the mass of the cavalry to hold the left (the entire wing being under the coordinating control of Soult*), while Oudinot's XII Corps prepared to cross the Spree on the army's left. The Imperial Guard was held in reserve near Kleinförstchen.

On the 19th an Allied investigation to the north of their position was driven back by Kellermann's* cavalry and part of Lauriston's approaching corps without revealing the true nature of the French envelopment plan. Napoleon's plan was to pin the enemy frontally with the corps of his center and right until Ney could arrive in strength to turn the Allied right wing and thus distract all of Wittgenstein's reserves to face the northern threat. At the critical moment, Bertrand's corps would attack the exposed "hinge" of the Allied battle line and sever it, while Ney's troops pressed ahead for Hochkirch. Given the strength of the enemy's position and erroneously estimated numbers, Napoleon decided to devote the first day to a battle of attrition, and to hold over the critical moves and the *coup de grâce* for the second day. The Tsar's conviction that Napoleon would strike to the south so as to keep the Allies away from neutral Austrian territory caused Wittgenstein to mass troops on his left wing—thus unintentionally playing Napoleon's game by leaving his right wing more lightly held.

At noon on the 20th the French guns opened fire, and three hours later the first major attacks began as trestle bridges were rapidly built over the Spree. By 6:00 P.M., after much heavy fighting, the French were masters of the main ridge, comprising much of the Allied first position, and were also holding Bautzen itself. To the south, Oudinot was also making good progress, attracting more and more enemy reserves. Ney's approach toward Klix was by now known to the Allies, but his strength and probable role remained secret. At the close of the first day, therefore, Napoleon had reason to be satisfied with the course of events to date.

Early on the 21st Napoleon, aware that Ney would not be fully in action before 11:00 A.M., adjusted his plans so that his III Corps would attack the Allied right and link up with Soult while Lauriston's V Corps was to press ahead for Hochkirch and the vital road beyond. Soult was to supervise the critical attack by Bertrand once the situation was ripe for it, as the enemy tried to make a new front to face Ney's advance. All other formations would continue their pinning

roles in the center and to the south, pending the collapse of the second Allied line.

The battle resumed with the greatest ferocity on all sectors, and soon Oudinot was vainly appealing for aid. By noon, however, a little farther north, Marmont was crossing the Blossaer Wasser—a tributary of the Spree near Basankwitz—and part of the Young Guard moved forward to the VI Corps' left flank. Macdonald also made some progress. At 1:30 P.M., judging from the din to the north that Ney was fully engaged, Napoleon ordered Soult to unleash the IV Corps from the earthworks it had been holding just east of the Spree, and the Young Guard began to mount a supporting attack against Kreschwitz to Bertrand's right. The IV Corps made good progress at first, and by 2:00 P.M. was master of the plateau to its front after defeating Blücher's* Prussian Corps. Sixty guns of the Guard Reserve poured fire into Kreschwitz from the flank. But by 3:00 P.M. Bertrand's attack was losing momentum short of its ultimate objective, Klein-Burschwitz, and he lost many men.

One reason for this was the failure of Ney to carry out his instructions correctly. Arriving near Preititz too late to trap Blücher as he retired from the plateau, Ney then allowed his men to become deeply involved in costly attacks against the village, and only at 2:00 P.M. was he reinforced by Reynier's* VII Corps and able to attack the plateau of Klein-Burschwitz. Thus the enveloping attack also lost momentum, and at 3:30 P.M. Ney was still using both corps in wasteful frontal attacks on Preititz and the plateau. On Ney's left meanwhile, Lauriston's V Corps pushed the Allies back to Baruth, but this was all of three miles short of Hochkirch to the south.

By 4:00 P.M., the Allies were everywhere giving some ground, and Napoleon ordered up the Imperial Guard. Blücher's men shrank back before the veterans, and Wittgenstein ordered a general retreat. The Allies were able to perform this in good order, as their line of retreat was still intact, and they successfully evacuated most of their guns. Each side had lost some 20,000 casualties over the two days—and Napoleon had won a notable success as his enemies reeled back toward Silesia. It had not, however, been truly decisive, and the French could not pursue with full effectiveness owing to their shortage of cavalry and the general inexperience and exhaustion of their troops after this protracted ordeal. On 4 June both sides agreed to an armistice* pending the possibility of negotiations.

Bayonne, Conference of, 16 April–20 July 1808. Napoleon summoned the members of his family and the Spanish royal house to a series of important meetings. Charles IV* and Prince Ferdinand* of Spain were induced to surrender the Spanish throne into Napoleon's care (by 6 May). The Emperor found his own relations more troublesome. Neither Louis* nor Lucien* would accept the Spanish throne, and in the end Joseph* was persuaded to exchange the throne of Naples and assume the crowns of Spain and the Indies.

Bayonne, sortie from, 14 April 1814. Although small in itself, this episode is of some importance as constituting the very last military engagement of the Peninsular War. It was fought four days after the battle of Toulouse,* and was thus well after Napoleon's abdication on 6 April, but only rumors of the ending of the war had reached southwestern France. General Hope* was in charge of the investment of the citadel of Bayonne but was proving very slow in pressing the siege, which had already been in progress for over six weeks. The French governor, General Thou-venot,* although he had received indications that the Emperor had abdicated, determined on a sortie, and at 3:00 A.M. on the moonless night of the 14th he attacked at the head of 5,000 men. The French advance on Etienne took the British troops holding the sector (a brigade of 5th Division, a company of Guards, and Hinuber's brigade of the King's German Legion*) by surprise, despite a warning of what was afoot given by a deserter to General Hay.* The French captured the church and village of Etienne at the charge, all except one house gallantly held by Captain Forster of the 38th (later the 1st Staffordshire Regiment). The British fled in disorder before the French up the Peyrehorade road; General Lord Hay was killed and Colonel Townshend of the Guards taken prisoner. The French broke through the Allied siege lines and forced their way to the rear of the Allied right wing, causing dire confusion. Fortunately, Hinuber brought up his Germans to rally part of the 5th Division and counterattacked at Etienne, aided by a battalion of Bradford's Portuguese. He recaptured the church and village as the massed guns of the arsenal thundered overhead, causing serious fires. General Hope was wounded twice in a defile—once by a British bullet—but at dawn a determined attack by General Howard at the head of the reserve Brigade of Foot Guards drove the French back within their lines. In this affair the French lost 905 casualties and the British 838; Hope was fortunate to have survived what at one time looked like a major disaster. Definite news soon arrived from Paris, and on 27 April the Governor surrendered Bayonne.

Beauharnais, Viceroi Eugène de (1781–1824). The son of General Alexandre de Beauharnais (guillotined in 1794) and Josephine Tascher and the stepson of

Eugène Beauharnais

Napoleon, he served as his aide-de-camp during the campaigns of 1796 and 1798–99. Promoted to general in 1804, the next year saw him made a prince of the Empire, Viceroy of Italy, and Colonel General of the Chasseurs of the Guard. An able soldier, he served with particular distinction at Wagram,* Borodino,* and during the retreat from Moscow, assuming the senior command from Murat* toward its close. In 1813 he played an important part in winning Lützen,* and thereafter organized an effective defense of Italy against the Austrians. He remained loyal to Napoleon until the first abdication, but did not rejoin him in 1815, having promised his father-in-law, the King of Bavaria, not to become involved any further in French affairs. He became Prince of Eichstadt and Duke of Leuchtenberg and lived the rest of his life in Munich, devoting his time to helping old soldiers and servants of his stepfather. His undoubted qualities as both man and soldier earned him Napoleon's respect during the great years of the Empire.

Beauharnais, Hortense de (1783–1837). The daughter of General Beauharnais and Josephine,* sister of Eugène,* and stepdaughter of Napoleon, she was married on his direction to his brother Louis Bonaparte,* later King of Holland. The marriage was not a success, and the couple eventually separated.

Beauharnais, Josephine de (1763–1814). Born Marie Rose Josephine Tascher de la Pagerie, this beautiful Creole spent her earliest years in the French West Indian colonies. In 1779 she married the Vicomte Alexandre de Beauharnais, by whom she had two children, Eugène* and Hortense.* After being widowed in 1794, she was at various times mistress to Directors Tallien, Gohier, and Barras,* becoming closely associated with *les incroyables*, the most chic and frivolous Parisian social set. She first met General Bonaparte in 1795 when she applied for the return of her late husband's sword, and the 25-year-old Napoleon fell deeply in love with her.

Josephine Beauharnais

They were married by civil ceremony on 9 March 1796. Josephine, six years older than her husband, felt affection rather than passion for Napoleon, and riskily continued flirtations with other men, including Captain Hippolyte Charles.* She was hated by the Bonaparte family, who continually tried to bring about her downfall, and Napoleon almost divorced her for infidelity in October 1799. She retained her hold over him, however, and was crowned Empress in December 1804. Ultimately, on 15 December 1809, the marriage ended in divorce, largely because of her inability to produce an heir for Napoleon. Thereafter she lived in luxurious retirement at Malmaison until her death on 29 May 1814. Her name was spoken by Napoleon minutes before his death on the island of St. Helena.

Beaulieu, General Johann Peter, baron (1725–1819). Born in Brabant, he earned notice during the Seven Years' War, serving in the Austrian army. In 1792 he defeated General Biron at Valenciennes, and in 1794 vanquished General Jourdan* at Arlon. In 1796 he was appointed Austrian Commander in Chief in North Italy but proved no match for Bonaparte, who ultimately expelled him from the Po Valley into the Tyrol.

Bedoyère, Général C. de la (1786–1815). Imperial aide-de-camp, he carried a critical message from Napoleon to Marshal Ney* on 16 June 1815, and before delivering it ordered General d'Erlon* to march with his corps toward Ligny. After the second Bourbon Restoration, he was shot for having rallied to Napoleon's cause.

Beethoven, Ludwig van (1770–1827). Born in Cologne, after an impecunious youth he eventually became established in Vienna (from 1792), where he first earned notice as a pianist. From 1800 he began to produce his great compositions; draw-

ing some inspiration from the events of the French Revolution, he originally dedicated his Third Symphony to Bonaparte. He tore up the dedication after Napoleon became Emperor, and renamed it "The Heroic Symphony." His growing deafness embittered his later years, and he died a lonely man.

Belem Rangers, the. Ironic nickname given to the convalescent British soldiers at Belem hospital in the Peninsula who became notorious for indiscipline and looting.

Bellerophon, H.M.S. British ship-of-the-line, commanded by Captain Maitland R.N., in which Napoleon embarked from the vicinity of Rochfort on 15 July 1815 in the hope of gaining sanctuary in Great Britain from the Prince Regent.

Belliard, Général, comte Auguste-Daniel (1769–1832). His early military career was in the National Guard, but in 1792 he began a series of staff appointments, serving at Valmy* and Jemappes.* After Arcola* he became *général de bri*

Belliard

gade, and commanded a division under Kléber* in Egypt. He surrendered Cairo to the British on terms (1801). He later served Murat* as chief of staff from 1805 to 1808, fighting in all the great campaigns, and later served King Joseph* in the same capacity. He fought in Russia under Murat again, and held further senior posts in 1813 and 1814. After joining the Bourbon cause in 1814, he rallied to Napoleon in 1815 and was sent to negotiate with Murat in Italy, but in vain. He was later reconciled again with the Bourbons.

"Bellitote." *See* **Fourés,** Madame Pauline

Benavente, battle of, 29 December 1808. As Sir John Moore retreated toward Corunna from Sahagun, Napoleon sent General Lefebvre-Desnouëttes* at the head of 600 *Chasseurs-à-Cheval* to harass the British rear guard as it fell back over the River Cea. The French successfully forded the river to the east of the bridge, which the British engineers had demolished in the early hours, but Lieutenant Colonel Otway and the cavalry picquets won a breathing space for Lord Paget to deploy the 10th Hussars and some King's German Legion cavalry. Several charges and countercharges took place, but the French were lured into an ambush in the environs of Benavente itself, and to the delight of the local populace, who were watching from the walls of the town, were briskly repulsed. The British cavalry, joined by the 7th and 18th Hussars, pursued the French back to the river, and killed a number and captured many more as the *Chasseurs* of the Guard tried to cross. Among the prisoners was Lefebvre-Desnouëttes himself, who had been wounded. The British lost a dozen or so casualties; the French about 150, of whom 100 were taken prisoner. This minor affair added further luster to the repuation of the British

cavalry, and took place under the eyes of Napoleon himself, who watched from an eminence on the southern bank of the river. The rebuff earned Moore sufficient time to evacuate his rear guard toward Astorga.

Bennigsen, General Levin A.T., Count (1735–1826). A German soldier who entered Russian service in 1773, he caught the notice of the Tsarina Catherine and earned distinction in campaigns in Poland. In 1806 he fought at Pultusk, and was in command at Eylau* in February 1807. At Borodino* he commanded the center of Kutusov's* army. He defeated Murat* at the action of Tarutino later in 1812 (18 October). Disagreements with Kutusov led to his temporary retirement, but after the latter's death he returned to command the Russian Army of Reserve. His conduct at Leipzig* in 1813 earned him the title of Count—an honor bestowed upon him by Tsar Alexander* on the field of battle.

Beresford, General William Carr, Viscount (1764–1854). Of Irish origin, he entered the 6th Foot in 1785. Next year he lost an eye in a shooting accident in Nova Scotia. After several changes of regiment on promotion, he served with the 69th Foot as a marine in the Mediterranean (1793–94), fighting at Toulon* and later storming the Martello tower in Corsica. In 1794 he became Lt. Colonel of the 88th Foot (the Connaught Rangers) and was sent to India. From 1801–03 he served in India under Baird* as a brigadier general, and later helped in the recapture of the Cape of Good Hope (January 1806). He captured Buenos Aires* that year, but later, seriously outnumbered, he had to surrender. After escaping he returned to England and was appointed Governor of Madeira, where he learned Portuguese and was promoted to major general. He was next sent to join Wellesley* at Lisbon (1808), and subsequently served under Moore* throughout the Corunna campaign of 1808–09. He was sent back to Lisbon to train a Portuguese army and was promoted Marshal in that force on 2 March 1809. A skillful trainer of men, he raised the famous *Caçadores* regiments and earned Wellington's commendation. He received a knighthood after Bussaco,* and then set about training Portuguese brigades from 1810–11. Sent to besiege Badajoz,* he emerged the victor from the hard-fought battle of Albuera,* but as his true gifts were as an administrator and trainer he was restored to these roles. He was present at Salamanca,* Vitoria,* and the later campaigns in the Pyrenees and in the south of France, and in 1814 was sent to join the Duc d'Angoulême* at Bordeaux. He was created Lord Beresford of Albuera, took his seat in the Lords, and was appointed Governor of Jersey. He later served the King of Portugal, putting down rebellions in Rio de Janeiro, but, tiring of the fluctuations of Portuguese affairs, he twice refused the senior command in the civil wars and returned to follow his political career in England. A staunch supporter of Wellington as premier, he was promoted to full general in 1825 and served as Master General of the Ordnance, 1828–30. Following his retirement, he was involved in a celebrated dispute with Napier* the historian over his description of Albuera in his famous *History of the War in the Peninsula*.

Beresina, battle of the river, 27–28 November 1812. As the *Grande Armée* continued its retreat from Moscow and Smolensk under ever-worsening conditions, its chances of ultimate survival became increasingly remote. By 22 November only some 49,000 troops remained under arms with about 250 cannon, but a mass of over 40,000 stragglers dogged the heels of the column. The return of Marshal Ney* with the survivors of the rear guard after a heroic march on the 21st had temporarily raised morale, but next day grim tidings arrived from the west announcing that Admiral Tshitsagov* and 34,000 Russians had reached the river Beresina and were effectively severing the French line of retreat toward Poland and safety. Another Russian army, 30,000 strong, was closing in from the northeast under General Wittgenstein,* and all of 80,000 more under Kutusov* were moving up from the east. It seemed that the French were already caught in a trap. Even worse, Oudinot's* patrols reported that the Beresina—normally frozen solid by late November and thus passable —had been turned into a roaring torrent by an unseasonable thaw (and Napoleon had only a few days before ordered the pontoon train to be burned at Orsha). The staff ordered the destruction of more coaches and wagons, and Napoleon's state papers were burned; a number of the prized tricolor standards shared the same fate to avert any possibility of their falling into enemy hands.

A combination of factors helped to save the *Grande Armée*. An act of intelligent disobedience on the part of General Baron Eblé* at Orsha had saved two field forges, two wagons of charcoal, and six more of sapper tools from the conflagration, and, provided a source of timber could be found near a possible bridging site, it might still prove feasible to extemporize a crossing. Next, the arrival of a cavalry officer named Corbineau* with the news that he had discovered an unmarked ford over the Beresina near the village of Studienka to the north of Borisov (where the Russians had already destroyed the bridge) suggested the existence of a suitable bridging site. Thirdly, the wily Kutusov, confident that his colleagues and the swollen river—together with "General Winter"— would be more than sufficient to deal with the French army, had allowed his pursuit to lag until a gap of 30 miles divided him from the French rear guard. This meant that the numerical odds the French were likely to face in a contested river crossing were less daunting than might otherwise have been the case.

These circumstances operating in his favor caused Napoleon to regain all of his old fire and dash as he turned to tackle the not inconsiderable problems of forcing a crossing over a broad river in full spate in the presence of a posted opponent. First, to distract Tshitsagov's attention from the intended crossing place, Oudinot was ordered to make a feint along the riverbank well to the south near Uchlodi. This the Marshal undertook on the 25th, and the Admiral obligingly moved south, falling for the bait. As soon as it was clear that Studienka was uncovered, Eblé* and his *pontonniers* and engineers got down to work. The houses of the village were demolished to provide timbers, and despite the bitter conditions and having to work up to their armpits in freezing water, by the afternoon of the 26th two rickety 300-foot bridges had been built. Corbineau's cavalry had splashed over the ford the previous night to cover the bridge building, but now, at 1:00 P.M., Oudinot's II Corps of 11,000 men hastened over the first bridge to create a secure bridgehead, followed by a division of heavy cavalry and two guns. Two hours later the second bridge was open to traffic, and more artillery passed over. So far the French plan was working well. More troops crossed.

However, Tshitsagov was soon aware of his error, and early on the 27th a spoiling battle began as he advanced northward. Oudinot proved capable of hurling the Russians back, and soon after noon Imperial Headquarters and the Imperial Guard had safely passed the Beresina. Meanwhile, on the eastern bank, Marshal Victor* and the IX Corps repulsed Wittgenstein's first attacks. Unfortunately, at 4:00 P.M. the larger bridge broke down, and a panic set in. Eblé eventually restored order, repaired the breach, and then forced a way through a massive block of corpses and abandoned vehicles so the fighting remnants of Eugène's* IV and Davout's* I Corps could cross the river. By evening these formations had passed over safely, and the bridges were open for the noncombatants to cross, but despite all pleas they refused to move at night, and thus threw away their best chance of survival. A further setback during the night of the 27th–28th occurred when a French division of Victor's corps lost its way and was forced to surrender. This would complicate the rear guard's task on the morrow.

All morning on the 28th a bitter battle raged as Wittgenstein tried to reach the bridges. Victor's diminished line held firm, although Russian guns were able to fire on the crossings, which occasioned another panic. The artillery bridge again broke under bombardment, but the Russians were forced back by the fire of massed French guns sited along the west bank, and the greater part of Victor's rear guard had passed the remaining bridge by 1:00 A.M. on the 29th. Meanwhile, the battle on the west bank had also continued throughout the 28th, as Oudinot and Ney grappled with massively superior numbers of Russians. At one critical juncture, when II Corps' cohesion almost broke, the situation was saved by a fine charge by Dumerc's cuirassiers—and Tshitsagov again fell back.

Once more the stragglers refused to cross the bridges, preferring to wait for daylight, but at 9:00 A.M. Eblé set fire to the bridges, and a stampede by the pitiful masses still on the eastern bank marked the start of a human tragedy as thousands perished in the press or in the river. Cossacks butchered an estimated 10,000 survivors.

Nevertheless, Napoleon was across the Beresina. For the loss of 25,000 battle casualties and perhaps 30,000 noncombatants, the *Grande Armée* had inflicted 20,000 losses on the Russians and shaken off its pursuers. Only 25 guns had been lost, and the road to the west toward Smorgoni and distant Vilna lay open before the survivors. The retreat went on.

Berg, Grand Duchy of. A principality on the right bank of the Rhine, stretching from the river Lippe to the north through Hesse to the Westerwald, its chief town being Düsseldorf. An ancient fief of the Holy Roman Empire, Napoleon bestowed it on his brother-in-law, Murat,* in 1806. After 1815 it was awarded to Prussia.

Bernadotte, Maréchal Jean-Baptiste Jules, prince de Ponte Corvo, King of Sweden (1763–1844). The only member of the marshalate to found a lasting royal dynasty, Bernadotte was in his early years an out-and-out republican. The son of a lawyer of Pau, he enlisted in the *régiment de Brassac* in 1780, and eight years later had risen to the rank of sergeant major in the *régiment Royal-Marine.* After saving his colonel from a Marseilles mob, he was commissioned into the 36th Regiment in November 1791. Between 1792 and 1796 he served in succession in the Armies of the Rhine, the North, and the Sambre-et-Meuse, steadily rising in rank to *général de division* (22 October 1794). After seeing considerable action along the Rhine and winning an action at Limburg in July 1796, early the next year he was sent to join the Army of Italy and, commanding the 4th Division, helped Bonaparte cross the river Tagliamento. He was later put in charge of the Frioul area. Various commands in Italy followed, but in April

Bernadotte

1798 Bernadotte was sent by the Directory as ambassador to Vienna. When a mob burned the French flag he left the city on 14 April. During the War of the Second Coalition* that followed he commanded divisions in the Army of Mainz, and in August 1798 found time to marry Désirée Clary, Napoleon's sometime sweetheart. In 1799 he successively commanded the Army of Observation of the Lower Rhine and the left wing of the Army of the Danube. Disgusted by the conduct of the war, he threw up his command and traveled to Paris, where he was dismissed. However, from July to September 1799 he found himself Minister of War, before he was once again sacked. Still an ardent republican (he had the slogan "Death to Tyrants" tattooed on his arm), he refused to be involved in the *coup d'état* of Brumaire, but in January 1800 he was nominated a Councillor of State, and from April commanded the Army of the West in place of Brune.* In 1803 he was about to travel to America as ambassador when war with England broke out, and the appointment was canceled.

In 1804 he was made Governor of Hanover, and in May became a Marshal. On 30 August 1805 he took command of the I Corps of the *Grande Armée*, served with distinction in the Ulm Campaign*— though he violated Prussian territory at one stage—and played a significant part at Austerlitz.* The following June he was created Prince of Ponte Corvo.

The Prussian campaign of 1806 almost brought his ruin, for his failure to involve his corps at either Jena* or Auerstädt* in October infuriated Napoleon, and he was nearly court-martialed. Napoleon relented, however, possibly misguidedly, and Bernadotte served well in the pursuit of the Prussian army, taking Halle, and later forcing Blücher* to surrender at Lübeck, where he also took the surrender of a newly arrived division of Swedes. The courtesy he displayed to their officers was to lead to important future events. He also captured Elbing in December.

In 1807 he won the action of Mohrungen,* but was wounded in the head at the river Passarge in March, and again in the throat at Spanden in June. Forced to relinquish his command, he was made Governor of the Hanseatic Towns in July, and occupied Jutland. In March 1809 he was made commander of the Saxon army —which became the IX Corps of the *Grande Armée*—and won an action at Linz. At Wagram,* however, he mishandled his command and abandoned the key village of Aderklaa. He had already rashly criticized Napoleon's handling of the battle, and the Emperor dismissed him from both his command and the army.

He returned to Paris in semi-disgrace, but the Council of Ministers appointed him to command a force sent to counter the British landing at Walcheren* on 12 August. However, after issuing an indiscreet proclamation he was summoned to Vienna by Napoleon and was removed from his appointments on 24 September 1809. From this date his association with Napoleon and his fortunes rapidly waned.

However, on 21 October 1810 he was elected Crown Prince of Sweden by the States General, as King Charles XIII had no heir, and Bernadotte's earlier association with Swedish notables in 1806 thus bore unexpected fruit. He became a Lutheran and was formally adopted by Charles XIII in November, changing his names to Charles-Jean. Napoleon approved this development with some hesitation, and indeed it was not to work out to the Emperor's ultimate advantage. Bernadotte from the first adopted the interests of his new country as his own, and when Napoleon seized Swedish Pomerania in March 1812, he began to draw close to Tsar Alexander,* at first declaring only a state of friendly neutrality. Then in July 1813, Bernadotte led Sweden into the Sixth Coalition* against France, and next month took command in person of the Army of the North. On 23 August he defeated Oudinot* at Gross-Beeren,* and Ney* at Dennewitz* two weeks later. In the days before Leipzig,* Barnadotte was accused of deliberate delays, but he was present at the Battle of the Nations.

Furthering Swedish aims, Bernadotte forced Denmark to cede Norway to Sweden by the Treaty of Kiel on 14 January 1814. During the Campaign of France, he advanced his troops only as far as Liège, and then proceeded to Paris alone—for he had some hopes of being asked to succeed Napoleon after his abdication. This did not, however, materialize, for many Frenchmen regarded him as a traitor. In 1815 Bernadotte refused to join the Seventh Coalition, but took possession of Norway. He became King Charles XIV on 5 February 1818 and proved a moderate ruler despite trouble with Swedish liberals from 1830. He reordered Sweden's administration along more modern lines, and his descendants rule to the present day. Charles XIV died of apoplexy at Stockholm on 8 March 1844.

Berthier, Maréchal Louis-Alexandre, prince de Neuchâtel et de Wagram (1753–1815). The son of a geographical engineer ennobled by Louis XV, Berthier was commissioned into the same branch in 1766. After service with infantry and cavalry units, he was appointed to the staff of Marshal Rochambeau in America in 1781. He was promoted to lieutenant colonel in 1789 and helped organize the Versailles National Guard once the Revolution broke out. His protection of the royal family from extremist factions caused his motives to be questioned, but he held a number of staff posts under Rochambeau and Lafayette* until August 1792, when he was dismissed from the service. Next year, however, after a period of voluntary service, he was made Chief of Staff to Biron's army. Another period of unemployment followed a mission to Paris, but

Berthier

in March 1795 he was promoted to *général de brigade* and sent as Chief of Staff to the Army of the Alps and Italy. Promoted to *général de division* the same June, after service with the Army of the Alps he was transferred to become Bonaparte's Chief of Staff on 2 March 1796. Thus began a close association that was to last with hardly a break until 1814. Bonaparte rapidly realized Berthier's gifts as a hardworking senior staff officer, and his promptness in sending accurate written orders to subordinate commanders was particularly appreciated. Berthier shared in the tribulations and triumphs of the First Italian Campaign, and on Bonaparte's departure for Paris in December 1797, he was appointed commander of the Army of Italy. As such, he occupied Rome in February 1798 and declared it a republic.

After being appointed Chief of Staff to the short-lived Army of England, he became a member of the *Conseil des Cinq-Cents** for a brief period before his election was annulled. Berthier next accompanied Bonaparte to Egypt and Syria, 1798–99, greatly missing his mistress, Madame Giuseppina Visconti. He returned to France with Napoleon and aided him during Brumaire,* and from November 1799 to April 1800 he was Minister of War. He was made Commander in Chief of the Army of Reserve for the Second Italian Campaign (in fact serving as Chief of Staff to Bonaparte, who, as First Consul, was technically debarred from senior command) and received a bullet wound in the arm at Marengo.*

Following an administrative appointment in Piedmont, he again became Minister of War in October 1800, a post he retained until August 1807. In May 1804 he was one of the 18 marshals appointed, and on 30 August 1805 he was made Chief-of-Staff to the *Grande Armée*.

In this capacity he served as Napoleon's indispensable assistant in all the major campaigns between that year and 1814, and over the years received many honors and large grants of money. He was created Prince de Neuchâtel in 1806, and next year gave up the Ministry of War to General Clarke* in order to devote all his attentions to the *Grande Armée*. He married the daughter of the brother-in-law and cousin of the King of Württemberg and held important posts in the Imperial Court, including that of Grand Huntsman.

In 1809 he was for a time general in chief of the French army on the Danube, but he proved his incapacity in this position very rapidly when the Austrians attacked under Archduke Charles.* Napoleon arrived just in time to remedy the situation, and Berthier gratefully resumed his staff appointment. Nevertheless, his master was sufficiently pleased with his subsequent performance to make him Prince of Wagram* on 15 August 1809, and further conferred on him the great *château de Chambord* with benefit of its vast estates and rents. As Chief of Staff of the *Grande Armée en Russie*, he accompanied Napoleon to Moscow, and later, during the retreat, he was not chosen to accompany the Emperor back to Paris from Smorgoni, but stayed to assist first Murat* and later Viceroy Eugène* in the final stages of the disastrous campaign. Reunited with Napoleon, he continued to serve him throughout the campaigns of 1813 and 1814, but became increasingly war weary. He received a lance blow on his head at the battle of Brienne.* On 11 April 1814 he joined the "mutineers" and supported the Provisional Government that took over on Napoleon's first abdication. The Bourbon regime appointed him Captain of the 5th Company of *Gardes du Corps* and made him a peer of France and Commander of Saint Louis. In March 1815 he stayed by Louis XVIII

and escorted him and the court from Paris to Ghent, before traveling to Bavaria. Refusing to rejoin Napoleon, his name was struck off the register of the Marshalate on 10 April. Overcome by remorse— or possibly pushed—he fell to his death from a window at Bamberg on 1 June 1815 after watching Allied formations marching past toward France.

Berthier's gifts as a staff officer were immense, although he proved a feeble commander when left on his own. A short, stout, bustling, and often jolly man, he proved a good intermediary between Napoleon and the other marshals, although he incurred the dislike of not a few of them. Napoleon allowed Berthier more familiarity than anybody else, but worked him mercilessly. He once sneeringly referred to him as being merely a "chief clerk," and on at least one occasion physically assaulted him in a rage. In fact, however, the Emperor found him indispensable and was genuinely fond of him.

Berthollet, Comte Claude-Louis (1748–1822). French theoretical chemist who worked on the uses of chlorine and analyzed ammonia, as well as aiding Lavoisier in his researches into gunpowder. Elected to the Academy of Sciences in 1781, during the Revolution he became an expert on metal smelting and the conversion of iron into steel. After accompanying Bonaparte to Egypt in 1798, he later became a senator and a count.

Bertrand, Général Henri-Gatien, comte (1773–1844). An engineer officer from 1793, he served in Italy (1797) and then in Egypt and Syria. Promoted to *général de brigade* in 1800, four years later he was appointed Inspector General of Engineers and an imperial aide-de-camp. He served with distinction in 1805, 1806, and 1807, and was promoted to *général de division* in May 1807. Made a count

Bertrand

the next year, in 1809 he built the bridges over the Danube below Vienna involved in the battles of Aspern-Essling* and Wagram.* From 1811–12 he served as governor of the Illyrian provinces, but in March 1813 took command of the IV Corps of the *Grande Armée*. He fought in most of the battles of that campaign, but in November 1813 became Grand Marshal of the Palace, succeeding Caulaincourt.* After fighting through the Campaign of 1814, he accompanied Napoleon to Elba,* and thence back to France in March 1815. After Waterloo,* he accompanied Napoleon to St. Helena,* and remained in his service until the Emperor's death. From 1830 Bertrand became commandant of the *Ecole Polytechnique*, and played a role in politics. Retired in 1832, he was chosen eight years later to accompany the Prince de Joinville to St. Helena, and thence escorted Napoleon's remains back to Paris. From first to last he proved one of the Emperor's most loyal and faithful servants.

Bessières, Maréchal Jean-Baptiste, duc d'Istrie (1768–1813). The son of a surgeon,

he almost entered the medical profession, but the Revolution intervened and instead he became a grenadier captain in the National Guard, and later in Louis XVI's Constitutional Guard. In this capacity he fought alongside the Swiss at the Tuileries on 10 August 1792. Fortunate to survive, he next served as a common soldier in the Army of the Pyrenees and was recommissioned in 1793. Three years later Bonaparte chose him to command his Guides, and he served with distinction at Rivoli.* Promoted to major, he accompanied Bonaparte to Egypt and Syria, serving at Acre* and Aboukir.* At Brumaire he commanded the Guard of the *Corps Législatif,* and moved from that to command the horse grenadiers of the Consular Guard. After Marengo* he was promoted to *général de brigade* and second-in-command of the Consular Guard and then to *général de division* in September 1802. Bessières was created a marshal two years later and appointed colonel general commanding the Cavalry of the Imperial Guard. He led a celebrated charge at Austerlitz,* fought at Jena,* and in 1807 distinguished himself at

Bessières

Eylau* and Friedland.* After a spell as Ambassador to Württemberg, he was put in command of a provisional corps, and in Spain defeated General Cuesta* at Medina del Rio Seco,* before entering Madrid with Joseph.* He later commanded the II Corps, but was relegated to command of the cavalry, his proper métier, by Napoleon, who appointed Soult* in his place. With the cavalry he participated at Somosierra* and in the pursuit of Sir John Moore* toward Corunna.*

In the Danube campaign of 1809 he commanded the Reserve Cavalry, serving with special distinction at Aspern-Essling* and later at Wagram,* where he was slightly wounded. On 28 May, he had been made Duke of Istria, and after Bernadotte's* recall from the Army of the North he took over command of that force and recaptured Flushing.* In 1810 he became commander of the Imperial Guard in Paris, and later served in northern Spain, being present at Fuentes de Oñoro* on 5 May 1811.

As war with Russia approached in 1812, he was given charge of the Cavalry of the Guard for that campaign. During the early stages of the retreat, he rescued Napoleon and his staff from an attack by Cossacks at Gorodnia. Next year he took command of the Guard formations serving in the Army of the Main, but was killed at Rippach near Weissenfels* on 1 May by a cannonball. Napoleon thus lost one of his most valorous and loyal assistants as well as a genuine friend.

Béthencourt, Général Antoine de (1759–1801). Of noble birth, he was arrested in 1794 but freed 15 months later. Reinstated, he served briefly in the Army of the West before being transferred to that of the Reserve in late March 1800. On 16 May he took command of the force ordered to hold the Simplon Pass, and later passed the Alps under command of

Moncey* (late May). He besieged and took the town of Arona (20 June). In December he was sent out to Guadeloupe as Commander in Chief, but died there in August 1801.

Bianchi, General Vicenz Friedrich, Baron, later Duke of Casalanza (1768–1855). Of Viennese origin, he was commissioned an officer of engineers in 1787. After notable service against the Turks and the French, he was promoted to brigadier general in 1807. Severely defeated at Dresden* in 1813, the next year he led a force against Lyons, and in 1815 helped expel Murat* from the Kingdom of Naples in favor of Ferdinand de Bourbon—who made him a duke.

Bidassoa, crossing of the river, 7 October 1813. The lower reaches of this river formed the frontier between France and Spain, flowing into the Bay of Biscay near Hendaye and Irun. Local fishermen informed Wellington* that at low tide the estuary was fordable, and this enabled the Allied army to cross to French soil. Next day, the French defenses on the *Grande Rhune* feature were outflanked and abandoned, Soult's* army falling back to the river Nivelle* defense line.

Blake, General Joachim (1759–1827). Of Irish descent, Blake was born at Malaga. In 1808 he was given command of the Army of Galicia as captain general of that province, but was defeated by Bessières* at Medina del Rio Seco* on 14 July 1808. He was later defeated at Pan Corbo* and Espinosa by Lefebvre* and Victor* respectively and again at Murviedro. Despite these setbacks he was no mean commander, and fought with small regular forces and guerrillas until 1812, when he was taken prisoner. In later years he earned a reputation as a political liberal, particularly from 1820. Brave and approachable, and strict for a

Spanish commander, he had a tendency toward bad luck.

Blockade, naval. The Royal Navy's command of the seas during most of these wars was secured by two main methods— by obtaining a decisive battle victory, and by use of the weapon of blockade. Naval blockades were of two main types, close and open. A close blockade was a matter of making it impossible for an enemy squadron to put out to sea, and this was very hard to achieve owing to the effects of weather, wear and tear, and overall cost to the blockaders in terms of men and shipping. An open blockade, on the other hand, was frequently resorted to. In the simplest terms, this was a matter of keeping an enemy's ports under close surveillance—a role often entrusted to frigates—so that when and if his ships put out to sea a British naval force could be rapidly alerted and move to intercept. Thus an open blockade was really a means of forcing a battle, a decisive action. The main force had to be sufficiently far off to tempt the foe to leave his ports, yet close enough to ensure an interception.

An open blockade was extremely costly to maintain. Besides the vigilant frigates, powerful squadrons had to be kept at sea ready to act. Brest was one French base kept under constant surveillance. Its proximity to the British Isles always held the possible threat of an escorted French expeditionary force slipping off to effect a landing in Ireland or elsewhere, or to mount a raid in the West Indies, and a squadron had to be perpetually in the vicinity of the Scilly Isles or Ushant, ready to head off any such enterprise. The wear and tear on both ships and personnel was immense; at least one ship in every five was at any one time back in a home port undergoing repair or refitting, and the boredom of blockade duty was immense. Yet the effort was necessary if national security was to be maintained—

and if every chance of bringing the foe to battle was to be utilized. Bad weather could of course interrupt a blockade, as when Bonaparte's expedition to the east slipped out of Toulon undetected by Nelson* in 1798. As Emperor, Napoleon came to appreciate that he could keep the Royal Navy at full stretch by merely threatening the possibility of slipping a squadron out to sea from Brest or Toulon, and even if he had no intention of doing so the possibility had to be guarded against.

Another form of blockade was the economic variety—the commercial blockade. This involved using light fleet elements to disrupt the enemy's trade and to cut France off from sources of supplies and strategic material. At one end of the scale this involved intercepting major convoys and their escorts and fighting a virtual naval battle; at the other it entailed using brigs and corvettes to interrupt coastal traffic. Sometimes, when a large and crucial convoy was involved, considerations of getting it safely into port might persuade the enemy to send out a strong squadron, and thus a battle situation might develop. Inevitably, the status of neutrals raised problems, and British claims to the "right of search"* for contraband was one factor that led to the War of 1812* with the United States.

Blücher, Field Marshal Gebhard Leberecht von, Prince of Wahlstadt (1742– 1819). Born at Gross-Renzow near Rostock in Mecklenburg, the son of a retired infantry captain, Blücher almost became a farmer, but instead, at age 14, he enlisted in the Swedish Morner Regiment of cavalry in 1757 and served three campaigns against the Prussian army of Frederick the Great. Taken prisoner near Friedland* in 1760, he was allowed to change sides and join the Prussians, being commissioned a cornet in the Belling (or 8th) Hussars, with whom he fought for the remainder of the Seven Years' War. Garrison peacetime life proved boring to his wild spirit, and in 1773 he was virtually cashiered by Frederick because of the many complaints about his wild behavior.

Captain Blücher retired to become a farmer and was married in 1773. His farming prospered, but in 1786 he was recalled to the army at his own urgent request after Frederick's death, with the rank of major backdated for eight years. In 1793 he served with great valor against the French Revolutionary armies, and his reputation for a dashing "hussar complex" became confirmed over the next two years. In March 1794 he was given command of the Black Hussars—the name now sported by the 8th Hussars. Near Landau on 28 May he defeated a French force in brilliant style, and in mid-June was promoted to major general. After the Peace of Basel (1795) more years of peacetime soldiering followed, and as usual brought Blücher trouble through his contentious nature. His dislike of the French grew into hatred, and he was bitterly critical of Prussia's hesitation to re-enter the wars.

When at last war did come in 1806, it proved disastrous for Prussia. Blücher served at Auerstädt* against Davout,* and after the stinging defeat of the Prussian army he commanded the rear guard during successive stages of the retreat all the way back to the Baltic coast. At length he was forced to surrender to Bernadotte* at Rackau near Lübeck on 6 November. Years of great frustration followed, for Napoleon—virtual master of Prussia after Tilsit* until 1813—refused to permit his re-employment in an active capacity, appreciating his ability and his hatred of France. For a time he was Governor General of Pomerania, and he did what he could to aid the reform movement stirring within the Prussian army, keeping in close touch with von Scharn-

horst* and von Gneisenau.* He was seriously ill through much of 1807–08, and his sanity was for a time despaired of. Later he busied himself refortifying Colberg but had to go into hiding in early 1812 as Napoleon prepared to march on Russia.

After the Convention of Tauroggen,* however, Prussia at last moved to throw off French tutelage. Lieutenant General Blücher was appointed to command the first Prussian forces to enter the field on 28 February 1813 and was promoted to general. After von Scharnhorst's death, von Gneisenau became his irreplaceable Chief of Staff and added his brains to the older man's valor: between them they made a strong command team. In the War of Liberation, Blücher fought in most of the major engagements—Lützen* (2 May) and Bautzen* (20 May) before the armistice;* at the Katzbach* (26 August), where he defeated Marshal Macdonald;* and finally at Leipzig* (16–18 October). His determined advance from the north toward Leipzig before the battle there called Napoleon's bluff, and Blücher further kept the dilatory Bernadotte up to the mark. In reward for his services King Frederick-William III* promoted him to general field marshal. Despite his 70 years, the old warrior was full of energy and wrath in the prosecution of his personal vendetta against the French.

The invasion of France opened in midwinter, and despite Napoleon's tactical skill the numerical superiority of the Allies began to tell. While Schwarzenberg* advanced from the plateau of Langres toward the Seine, Blücher led his army toward the Marne and Paris. The Emperor checked Blücher in four battles in five days between 10 and 14 February, namely at Champaubert,* Montmirail,* Château-Thierry,* and Vauchamps,* and then turned south to check the Austrians at

Montereau.* Doubling back to the north again, Napoleon won a small action against the Prussians at Craonne* (7 March), but at Laon* on the 9th the French were repulsed with heavy loss. The advance on Paris was resumed as the Emperor moved south once more, and eventually the Allied armies linked up outside Paris, won the action of Montmartre,* and occupied the French capital. This forced Napoleon's first abdication.*

Blücher's·health again deteriorated, and he prepared to retire to Berlin. However, he recovered sufficiently to pay a visit to England, where the old soldier was lionized. Back on his Silesian estates, he believed his military days were over, and he prepared to resign all his posts. Then on 8 March 1815 came news of Napoleon's return to France, and the old warhorse was once more summoned to head the army in Belgium. His over-bold decision to concentrate well forward in mid-June led to the defeat of Ligny,* and Blücher himself was thought to be a casualty. However, he reappeared on 17 June in a battered but determined condition, and after heavy doses of gin and rhubarb insisted on his army marching from Wavre* to support Wellington* at Waterloo* the next day. The Prussian approach complicated Napoleon's handling of the battle from 1:00 P.M., and from four o'clock the Prussians were in heavy action against Plancenoit, threatening the French flank and rear. This attack absorbed all French reserves at a critical moment and enabled Wellington to defeat the final French onslaught. The two leaders met at La Belle Alliance at 9:00 P.M. and the Prussians headed the pursuit.

After Napoleon's final abdication, Blücher was created Prince of Wahlstadt and loaded with many other honors. He died at Kribolwitz in Silesia on 12 Sep-

tember 1819. Despite certain mental limitations, he was a fine fighting commander loved by his troops, who dubbed him "Papa Blücher" and "Alte vorwärts" ("Old Forward") for his personal valor, strong character, and loyalty to both his men and allies.

Bock, General Eberhardt von (fl. 1812). Commander of the Heavy Brigade of the King's German Legion, von Bock led the most effective part of the pursuit of Marmont's* army after Salamanca,* and inflicted a severe blow to General Foy's* rear guard at Garcia Hernandez,* during which a French infantry square was broken by cavalry.

Bon, Général Louis André (1758–1799). From 1776 he was a private soldier but he left the army in 1784. In 1792 he was elected lieutenant colonel of the Grenadiers of Drôme, and after service in the Army of the Alps was present at Toulon* next year. He was wounded four times in 1794 but was promoted *général de brigade* in June 1795. Wounded at Arcola,* in 1797 he commanded a division for the first time. In 1798 he served with distinction in Egypt at Alexandria,* the Pyramids,* and El Arish,* and later at Mount Tabor* in Syria. He was mortally wounded, however, in the storming attempt of 10 May 1799 at Acre.*

Bonaparte, Carlo (1746–1785) After law studies in Rome and Tuscany, Napoleon's father set up as a lawyer in Ajaccio, Corsica. Descended from a minor noble family originally of Italian extraction, he supported the link of Corsica with France and would not support Paoli's* separatist movement. This attitude earned him certain favors, including subsidized education for his two eldest sons in France. He fathered eight surviving children and died of cancer in 1785.

Carlo Bonaparte

Bonaparte, Caroline, Reine de Naples (1782–1839). Napoleon's youngest sister married Murat* in 1800, became Grand Duchess of Berg in 1806 and Queen of Naples two years later. She proved popular with her adopted people and inspired a brilliant court. After the King's death in 1815 she retired first to Austria and then to Florence, where she died.

Bonaparte, Elisa, Grande Duchesse de Toscana (1777–1820). The eldest of Napoleon's three sisters, she married a Corsican, Felix Bacciochi, in 1797, who duly became Prince of Piombino eight years later. She left her husband soon after, and at Napoleon's request became Grand Duchess of Tuscany, 1809–14. After retiring to Germany, she became reconciled with her first husband and lived out her life with him at Trieste in great luxury. Disliked by Napoleon for her bitter tongue, she in later life befriended the exiled Fouché.*

Bonaparte, Jérôme, Roi de Westphalie (1784–1860). Napoleon's youngest brother first served as a naval officer from 1800, and three years later married the American Elizabeth Patterson, to his elder brother's great displeasure. Promoted to rear admiral in 1806, he was reconciled with Napoleon and commanded a Bavarian division in the Prussian Campaign of that year. Later he was given the Bavarian Corps, besieged Glogau, overran Silesia, and was promoted to *général de division* in 1807. On 7 July 1807 he was proclaimed King of Westphalia, and at Napoleon's insistence married Catherine of Wurttemberg after divorcing his first wife. In 1809 he commanded the X Corps, and three years later was given command of the right wing of the *Grande Armée de Russie*. His inaction earned Napoleon's wrath, and he left the army on 14 July. After losing his kingdom to the Allies in 1813, he returned to France, and escorted Marie Louise* from Paris in 1814. Next year he rallied to his elder brother, landing in France on 22 May, and was given a divisional command under Reille.* At Waterloo* he was responsible for escalating the fight for Hougoumont and was slightly wounded. After long and varied wanderings in many countries, in 1847 he was allowed to return to France. He became Governor of the Invalides, a Marshal of France (1850), President of the Senate, and First Prince of the Blood (both 1852). Next year he morganatically married the Marquise Giustina Bertholini. Jérôme was probably the gayest of the Bonaparte clan, and not devoid of talent.

Bonaparte, Joseph, Roi de Naples, then Roi d'Espagne (1768–1844). Napoleon's respected elder brother, he shared his education at Autun. He settled with the family near Toulon after their expulsion from Corsica in 1793 and there married

Joseph Bonaparte

Julie Clary. Employed as an aide to various Representatives of the People in 1793 and 1794, he followed Napoleon to Italy in 1796 before undertaking a mission to Corsica. Next year he was elected to the Council of Five Hundred.* Joseph served as French ambassador to Parma and Rome, and later proved a successful negotiator of the treaties of Luneville* and Amiens.* Honors and promotions followed his younger brother's success; in 1806 he was given command of the Army of Naples, and then the crown of that country (31 March 1806). He unwillingly agreed to abdicate this throne in favour of Murat* at Napoleon's insistence, and became King of Spain (6 June 1808). His reign was dominated by quarreling marshals and the varying fortunes of the Peninsular War, and his genuine liberal interests found scant chance to flourish. Decisively defeated at Vitoria* in 1813, he retired to France, but next year was made Napoleon's lieutenant general and commander of the Paris National Guard. After 1815 he settled in Philadelphia until 1832, and again from 1837–39, paying visits to England (1832) and Florence, where he spent the last three years of his life.

Bonaparte, Empress Josephine. *See* **Beauharnais,** Josephine.

Bonaparte, Letizia, *"Madame Mère"* (1750–1836). Mother of Napoleon and wife of Carlo Bonaparte,* whom she married at the age of 14, Letizia came from a long-established Corsican family called Ramolino. She bore her husband 13 children, of whom five died in infancy. After being expelled from her home at Ajaccio by Paoli,* she re-established the family base near Toulon in 1793, and later near Marseilles. Widowed at the age of 35, she had a long and hard struggle to bring up her family, but was always renowned for her common sense. During the great years of her family's prosperity she would always warn ". . . just so long

Letizia (Ramolino) Bonaparte, "Madame Mere"

as it lasts," and she prudently put money aside against a change of fortune. This helped mitigate the disasters of 1814 and 1815. She retired to Rome, continuing her simple style of life, and eventually died respected by all who knew her.

Bonaparte, Louis, Roi d'Hollande (1778–1846). Napoleon's third brother was also a gunner in his early career, but made only slow initial progress. He accompanied his brother as an aide-de-camp on the first Italian Campaign, and was present at Caldiero,* Arcola,* and Rivoli* as well as at the siege of Mantua.* He traveled to Malta and Egypt in 1798 but was sent home with captured colors after the capture of Alexandria. In June 1799 he transferred to the cavalry, and after various postings was promoted *général de brigade* in March 1803, and *général de division* in March 1804. Created Constable of the Empire in May of that year, he was given command over all troops in Holland from September 1805. On 24 May 1806 he was crowned King of Holland. In 1809 he commanded the Dutch army during the Walcheren* invasion, but soon quarreled with Napoleon over economic policy, refusing to accept the full implementation of the Continental System.* On 1 July 1810 he abdicated the throne and never again took up a senior appointment, living first in Germany, then France, Switzerland (1814), and ultimately in Italy, where he died at Livorno. He married Hortense de Beauharnais* at his brother's behest, but the match proved unhappy. Louis was dogged by ill health and lived a solitary life.

Bonaparte, Lucien (1775–1840). This brother never chose to share in the advancement of the clan, although he was often pressed to do so. He had played a political role in the earlier years, serving as a Deputy for a Corsican district, then as a member of the Council of Five Hundred.* He supported Napoleon during the *coup d'état* *de Brumaire,* swinging the Council behind him at the crisis. Later he served for a time as Minister of the Interior and as ambassador to Madrid, but in 1804, disdainfully rejecting all offers of royal honors, he retired to live in Rome. Later, after a vain attempt to settle in the United States, he returned to Italy (1815), where he passed the remainder of his life.

Bonaparte, Napoleon. *See* **Napoleon.**

Lucien Bonaparte

Bonaparte, Pauline, Princesse Borghese (1780–1825). Napoleon's second sister married General Leclerc* but was widowed in 1802. The next year she married the Italian Prince Borghese, but the marriage was not a great success and the flirtatious and brilliant Pauline spent most of her time in Paris, earning a reputation for profligacy. Napoleon's favorite sister, she remained loyal to him and visited him on Elba.* She retired to Rome and died in Florence.

Pauline Bonaparte

Bonet, Général Jean Pierre François, comte (1768–1857). The son of a pastry cook, he first joined the army in 1786, but twice deserted. Nevertheless, his talents soon secured his rise during the Revolution, and he fought at Hohenlinden* (1800) and in many other battles. He then served in Belgium, aboard the fleet at Brest, and from 1808 in Spain. In July 1812 he succeeded briefly to the command of the Army of Portugal when Marmont* was wounded at Salamanca,* but was almost immediately seriously wounded himself. In later years he served as a divisional commander under Marmont again in Germany, fighting at Lützen,* Bautzen,* and Dresden,* but was taken captive in November 1813. He was freed within a year, and took part in the Hundred Days,* commanding part of the garrison of Paris. After the second Bourbon Restoration, Bonet eventually became Inspector General of infantry in various divisions, and a peer of France (1831), finally retiring from duty in May 1848. In 1852 he became a senator.

Borghese, Prince Camille (1775–1832). The scion of an ancient noble Tuscan family, Prince Borghese married Pauline Bonaparte* in 1803. After the couple separated, Napoleon gave his brother-in-law an honorific appointment in the French Cisalpine department. After 1815 Pauline was reconciled with her husband, and they lived together first in Rome and later in Florence.

Borghetto, battle of, 30 May 1796. After the battle of Lodi* and the subsequent occupation of Milan, General Bonaparte prepared to press after General Beaulieu,* who was regrouping his shaken Austrian forces behind the river Mincio. The Austrian commander spread his 19,000 available troops along the river between Lake Garda and the great fortress of Mantua, attempting to hold a 20-mile

front. Leaving Berthier* to command the approaches to the Mincio, Bonaparte led a punitive expedition to repress local revolts against the French in both Milan and Pavia (the latter city being pillaged), but by the 29th he was back with the main army, some 28,000 men strong, at Brescia, as it prepared to attack Beaulieu's position and cross to Venetian territory. On the 30th, the French suddenly pounced on Borghetto, and the French grenadiers stormed the bridge with little loss. Beaulieu's overextended forces, trying to carry out a cordon-type defense, were given no chance to concentrate to meet this blow, and the Austrians were fortunate to be able to retreat over the river Adige and head north toward the Tyrol. During the follow-up of this operation, Bonaparte was almost captured at Valeggio by the scouts of Sebettendorf's division (1 June). After Borghetto, only Mantua remained in Austrian hands in North Italy.

Borodino, battle of, 7 September 1812. Borodino is a small village on the banks of the river Kaluga, near its confluence with the Moskowa, some 50 kilometers west of Mojaisk and 115 kilometers from Moscow. It was the scene of the largest battle of the Campaign of 1812.

After making the decision to continue his advance on Moscow after the battle of Smolensk,* Napoleon led the *Grande Armée* to close with the combined Russian First and Second Armies of the West, whose newly appointed Commander in Chief, General Kutusov,* had selected the vicinity of Borodino for a serious stand. The French had some 133,000 troops and 587 guns; the Russians, 120,000 men and 640 cannon. On 5 September the French advance guard captured the Schivardino redoubt about three miles southwest of Borodino, and the next day saw the French pouring up the New Post Road from Smolensk while Napoleon

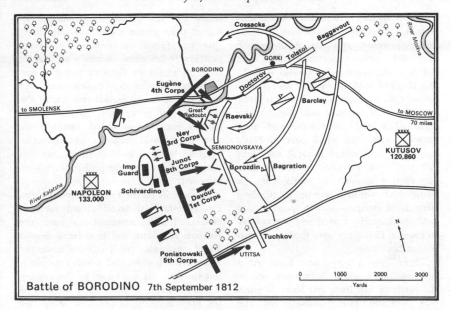

Battle of BORODINO 7th September 1812

conducted a careful reconnaissance of the Russian position. At this stage Kutusov had Borodino in front of the center of his array, half his army facing northward along the south bank of the Kalatsha River; the left wing, facing west, ran from the Raevski redoubt* to the south of Borodino (mounting 18 cannon) through the ruined village of Semionovskaya, past some earthworks called *flèches* to the hamlet of Utitsa and its knoll on the Old Post Road; and the southern part of the line was in thick woodland. From these dispositions, it appeared that Kutusov expected a French attempt to turn his right flank, but this Napoleon ruled out, as the Kalatsha's banks were steep. Similarly, he rejected Davout's* plan for a wide sweep to the south around the Russian left. Instead, he proposed a massive onslaught against Kutusov's left, and ordered his dispositions accordingly. Napoleon was suffering

from a heavy cold and associated complaints, and these factors were to affect his performance on the morrow. Kutusov, meanwhile, worked upon his peasant soldiers' mysticism, building up their morale. He had established his headquarters at Gorki.

At 5:00 A.M. on the 7th Ney* reported the army to be in position. An hour later 100 French guns opened fire against General Bagration's* positions, but the range was found to be too great and the cannon had to be moved forward to 1,300 yards from the foe. At first fate seemed to be favoring the French attacks. Eugène Beauharnais'* Italian divisions captured Borodino village on the French left, Davout made good progress with two divisions against the Semionovskaya sector, and on the right Prince Poniatowski* was in control of Utitsa and part of the neighboring woods. Russian reserves were being committed in large numbers,

[65]

and Kutusov had to draw many formations from his disengaged right wing to reinforce his center and left. A premature attempt by Eugène to send his men over the Kalatsha toward the Raevski redoubt was checked with heavy loss, and Poniatowski's progress in the south also petered out. Davout's advance was met by the corps of Raevski, Borozdin, and Baggavout,* and even when part of Ney's corps and the whole of Junot's* were sent *"au feu,"* the Russians refused to give any further ground. By 10:00 A.M. the battle had already become a grinding struggle of attrition—and Napoleon only held the Imperial Guard and the cavalry in reserve. Casualties were rapidly mounting on both sides.

Three French corps now launched a new onslaught against Semionovskaya, in the teeth of fire from 300 Russian guns. Ney received four wounds, but the Russian General Bagration was also mortally wounded. Exploiting a slight lull, Murat* attacked with cavalry in force, and the *flèches* at last passed into French possession; however, the Russians only fell back as far as the neighboring Psarevo plateau. Appeals to Napoleon for the release of the Imperial Guard to exploit the success met stony refusal. The Emperor felt ill and would play only a negative role.

By midday the Russians had ceded some ground in the center, but were holding elsewhere. Tolstoi's IV Corps was redeployed from the right wing, and Generals Platov* and Uvarov led 12,000 cavalry and Cossacks over the Kalatsha to counterattack Borodino itself. This onslaught caused the postponement of an impending full-scale attack on the Raevski Redoubt as Eugène returned to the north bank of the Kalatsha with his command to stabilize the situation there. By 2:00 P.M. this had been done, and Eugène's three divisions were ready to

storm the key objective. An earlier attempt, prior to the Russian cavalry diversion, had failed, but now a coordinated attack was launched. While the infantry tried to storm in through the gun embrasures, Auguste de Caulaincourt* led the 5th Cuirassiers against the rear of the redoubt, and successfully burst in. The cavalry general was killed, but by 3:00 P.M. the Raevski Redoubt was at last in French hands, and the linchpin of Kutusov's battle line seemed to have been removed.

Meanwhile on the French extreme right, Poniatowski had faced mixed fortunes around Utitsa. Attempts to turn the Russian left flank had foundered despite Junot's assistance, as Tutchkov made the most of the broken and wooded terrain—but the Russian was killed in the process. Victory, therefore, could only be won by the French in the center, and Murat led two cavalry corps over the ravine near Semionovskaya to attempt the rout of Bagration's Second Army. A new desperate encounter resulted, but the Russian line held, and five Russian cuirassier regiments repulsed the attack. Appeals to the Emperor for the use of the Guard were again refused. Eugène had tried to exploit his success at the Raevski Redoubt, but Barclay de Tolly,* commanding the First Army of the West, had checked his advance, and without reserves the French could make no further progress.

When Kutusov authorized General Doctorov and the Russian Guard Corps to launch a counterattack near Semionovskaya, Napoleon grudgingly permitted the release of the reserve artillery, and the 80 guns pulverized the assembling Russian columns so effectively that the attack never materialized. By this time both sides were almost exhausted.

There was still some fight left in Poniatowski's Poles, and at 4:00 P.M. he managed to retake Utitsa and its knoll.

The arrival of fresh Russian troops on the horizon—in fact the Moscow Militia —caused the Prince to pause, and by five o'clock the battle had almost petered out. The French were in possession of almost the whole original Russian line, but Kutusov's army had fallen back only to the next ridge.

Overnight the Russians decided to evacuate their positions rather than face a renewal of the battle. The French had lost an estimated 33,000 casualties; the Russians all of 44,000. It had been a desperate day, and the result was inconclusive. Seven days later, it is true, the French entered Moscow, but the Russian army was still very much a force to be reckoned with, and the Tsar's determination to continue the war remained undiminished.

Boulogne, Camp of, 1803–05. After the outbreak once again of formal hostilities with Great Britain on 16 May 1803, the First Consul ordered the formation of a new Army of England, 160,000 strong, and massed it along the Channel coast. The largest of a series of encampments was that developed at Moulin-Herbert near Boulogne, where the camp eventually took on the appearance of a town. Napoleon held several reviews there, and on 16 August 1804 he presented the first mass awards of the *légion d'honneur.** A month earlier, an invasion exercise carried out in foul weather had led to serious loss of life. From March 1805 the army was ready to invade England, but Admiral Villeneuve's* fleet failed to appear and the embarkation was postponed. On 25 August 1805 the main forces began to leave the coast and head for the Rhine, although Napoleon himself lingered at Boulogne until 3 September. The campaigns of Ulm* and Austerlitz* followed.

Bourcet, Général Pierre-Joseph de (1700–1780). French officer and writer,

commissioned into the artillery and engineers, who served with distinction under Marshal Maillebois in Italy (1733 and 1741). In 1756 he commanded these arms of the service in the Army of Germany, and ended the Seven Years' War as second-in-command in Dauphiné. An expert cartographer, he mapped the Alpine frontier. His book, *Principes de la Guerre des Montagnes*, greatly influenced the young Bonaparte, who absorbed Bourcet's beliefs in the need for alternate strategic plans and in the value of skillful tactical outflanking movements in battle.

Bourrienne, Louis Antoine Fauvelet (1769–1834). A schoolmate of Napoleon's at Brienne, Bourrienne followed him to Italy and in 1797 became his private secretary, a post he held until 1804 when he was sacked for theft and peculation. He was next sent to Hamburg as *chargé d'affaires*, but was again removed from his post for the scale of his exactions and profiteering from evasions of the Continental System.* He later joined the Bourbons, who made him a Minister of State. His three-volume *Mémoires* are of dubious accuracy but still throw much light on the years of his close association with Napoleon.

Bourmont, Général (later Maréchal) Louis August Victor, comte de Ghaisnes (1773–1846). An ensign in 1789, he fought with the Vendean rebels in 1794. He fled abroad after being suspected of complicity in the bomb plot of 1800 against the First Consul's life, but in 1807 rejoined the French army when Junot* reached Lisbon, and was soon made Chief of Staff to Loison.* Thereafter he served in many campaigns and battles, was wounded at Lützen,* and was promoted to *général de division* in 1814. Placed in command of part of Gérard's* corps in 1815, he deserted to the Allies on 15 June. Reconciled with the Bourbon regime, he served as Minister of War in 1829, commanded the expedition to Algiers the next year, and earned his Marshal's baton there. Unemployed under Louis-Philippe, he spent several years in Rome before finally returning to France in 1840.

Bowles, Captain (later General) George (1786–1876). Commissioned into the Coldstream Guards in 1804, he served in North Germany, Denmark, and most particularly the Peninsular and Waterloo* campaigns. In 1815 he was ADC to the Duke of Richmond.* He later served as Military Secretary in Canada and commanded the Coldstream during the suppression of the Lower Canada Revolt of 1838. Retiring from the active list in 1843, Bowles held a number of court appointments and became a major general in 1846. From 1851 he was Lieutenant of the Tower of London.

Boxtel, action of, 15 September 1794. This small affair in Holland was notable for being Lieutenant Colonel Arthur Wesley's (later Wellesley and Wellington*) baptism of fire. He was commended for reserving the fire of the 33rd Foot and defeating a French infantry column by well-directed volley firing at close range.

Braganza, John of, Regent (and later King) of Portugal (1763–1826). When his mother became mad, he ruled in her name from 1792 and took the title of Prince Regent in 1799. Supporting links with England, he became enmeshed in the plots of Godoy* and France, and fell out with Napoleon over the Berlin Decrees instituting the Continental System.* The French invasion of Portugal under Junot* began on 18 October 1807, and instituted the Peninsular War.* He moved to Brazil with his court shortly before the French reached Lisbon. On his mother's death in 1816, he succeeded as King John VI. During his ten-year reign he lived to see the separation of Brazil from Portugal.

Brennier, Général Antoine-François, comte (1767–1832). First a cadet in the Spanish army, Brennier (or Brenier de Montmorand) later served Louis XVI before being absorbed into the Revolutionary forces in June 1793 as a major. A veteran of many campaigns, he achieved fame in the Peninsula as governor of Almeida,* blowing up the fortress and evacuating his garrison through Wellington's* forces on 10 May 1811. Promoted to *général de division* later that year, he was gravely wounded two years later at Lützen.* Brennier eventually accepted the Bourbon regime and served in various capacities and political posts until 1831.

Bridport, Lord. *See* **Hood,** Admiral Alexander

Brienne, battle of, 29 January 1814. As the Allies invaded France, Napoleon pounced on Blücher's* dispersed army at Brienne, the scene of the Emperor's schooldays, bringing some 30,000 troops, mostly raw conscripts, into action against possibly 25,000 Prussians. Pinning the enemy with Grouchy's* cavalry and horse artillery in the late morning, Napoleon sent in Ney's* two divisions and part of Victor's* corps against the town as the rest of the II Corps moved to outflank the Prussian right wing. The fighting was uneven but dragged on until 10:00 P.M., the French eventually gaining possession of the town and the chateau. At one moment Napoleon was almost taken by Cossacks; at another Blücher and Gneisenau* narrowly escaped from the castle. The French lost some 3,000 casualties and inflicted about 4,000. Next day the French pressed on to La Rothière,* soon to be the scene of a second and more serious conflict as the Allies mounted a counteroffensive.

Broglie, Maréchal Victor Francois, duc de (1718–1804). Appointed a Marshal of France in 1762, he proved an able commander during the Seven Years' War although he was weak at cooperation with colleagues. In 1789 Louis XVI commanded him to lead the royal troops gathering near Versailles, and he very briefly served as Minister of War. He retired to Germany and later led the corps of *emigrés** in Champagne. He lived out the remainder of his life in England and Russia. During the 1780s he had experimented with tactical reforms, and in the 1760s had tried out new major formations of all arms in the field.

Brougham, Henry Peter, Baron (1778–1868). British lawyer and statesman, born in Edinburgh, he came to London in 1805. Called to the Bar in 1808, he served various terms in Parliament. His defense of Queen Caroline during George IV's divorce action in 1825 made him a popular idol. He contributed a great deal to education and legal reform. Made Lord Chancellor (1830), Brougham played a large part in the Great Reform Bill. Leaving office in 1834, he continued his legal work with great distinction.

Brueys d'Aigalliers, Vice Amiral François Paul (1753–1798). After first going to sea in 1766, he had an eventful career in the French Royal Navy. He was promoted to captain in 1792, was arrested and cashiered on political grounds the next year, and was reinstated in 1795. After service in the Adriatic, he became rear admiral in 1796 and vice admiral in April 1798. He was given the naval command of the expedition to Egypt, sailing with the convoy from Toulon on 19 May 1798, and escorted Bonaparte to Alexandria* via Malta.* Attacked by Admiral Nelson on 1 August 1798 at Lake Aboukir (see the battle of the Nile*), he was killed in

action shortly before his flagship, *l'Orient,* blew up.

Bruix, Vice Amiral Eustache (1759–1805). His first naval experience came in 1778, and as a junior officer he saw much service in the West Indies. Promoted to captain in 1793, he was cashiered for political reasons later the same year but reinstated in mid-1794. After various staff appointments at Brest, he took part in the abortive raid against Ireland in 1796. Next year he was promoted to rear admiral, and from 1798–99 he served as Minister of Marine and the Colonies, eventually being promoted to vice admiral. Given an active command again, Bruix escaped the blockade* outside Brest in March 1799, and after making a bold cruise down the Mediterranean toward Egypt with the possible intention of reinforcing the French army isolated in the Orient, a combination of Royal Naval pressure and sickness on board compelled him to abandon the enterprise. He reached Carthagena in June, and ultimately re-entered Brest in August,

Bruix

where he was reblockaded. In 1802 he was made a Councillor of State, and from mid-1803 commanded the naval forces at Boulogne.* In July 1804 he was appointed Inspector of the Ocean Coasts, but died in Paris early the following year.

Brumaire. *See* **Coups d'État**

Brune, Maréchal Guillaume Marie Anne (1763–1815). First a clerk and then a printer, he became an ardent republican at the Revolution, and in 1789 was promoted to captain in the National Guard of Paris. In 1793 he was appointed *général de brigade* while serving with the Army of the North, and three years later, after various appointments within France, was sent to the Army of Italy, fighting under Massena* at Arcola* and Rivoli.* On Bonaparte's recommendation, Brune became *général de division* in November 1797. Next year he commanded a small army on the Swiss frontier before being given command of the Army of Italy for seven months.

In January 1799 he was transferred to command the French forces in Holland, and in this capacity engaged the Anglo-Russian army. He was beaten at Alkmaar but won the action at Castricum. In the end the Allies were induced to give up the invasion after the Convention of Alkmaar. Brune was appointed a Councillor of State (December 1799).

Following two brief commands in the west and east of France, he was called to Italy to replace Massena,* and conducted a notable campaign against various Austrian forces between August 1800 and January 1801, completing the conquest begun at Marengo.*

After service on the Council of State in Paris, in 1802 he went as Ambassador to Turkey for two years and received news of his appointment to Marshal (May 1804) in Constantinople. In late 1806, he became Governor General of the Hanseatic

Brune

Towns. The next April he was given command of a *corps d'observation* in the area, and he captured Stralsund in July. However, Brune fell from Napoleon's favor shortly thereafter because of his strong republican feelings, which he openly expressed, and he remained unemployed until 1814, receiving neither titles nor favors from the Emperor. In that year, embittered by treatment that he considered very unfair, he joined the Bourbon cause. But when Napoleon returned from Elba in 1815 Brune rejoined him, and was given a command on the Var and made a peer of France. He flew the *tricolor* over Toulon until late July, when he was arrested. He was murdered by a royalist mob at Avignon on his way to Paris.

Brunswick, General Charles William Ferdinand, Duke of (1735–1806). After serving under his uncle Ferdinand of Brunswick and Frederick the Great,* he first rose to high command in the Prussian Army during the Seven Years' War. After further experience in Bavaria and Holland, during which he became regarded as a fine commander of infantry, he was appointed Allied *généralissime* for the invasion of France in 1792. After issuing the Brunswick Manifesto, he captured Longwy and Verdun, but was decisively repulsed at Valmy.* He retreated into Germany and retained his command in 1793, but proved incapable of cooperation with Wurmser* and the Austrians. He was defeated by Hoche* at Wissemburg, and thereafter retired to his estates. However, in 1806, he was reappointed to high command in the Prussian army when war broke out with France, and was mortally wounded at the battle of Auerstädt.*

Brunswick, General William Frederick, Duke of (1771–1815). Fourth son of Charles William of Brunswick,* he was unable to take possession of his inheritance in 1806 and was formally deprived of his estates by the Peace of Tilsit.* Not surprisingly he became a bitter opponent of Napoleon, and played a large part in the raising of the "Black Brunswickers" in 1809. After living in England and Portugal, he eventually was restored to his Duchy in 1813. In 1815 he was killed at the battle of Quatre Bras* at the head of his Brunswick Corps in 6th Division.

Bubna-Littitz, Field Marshal, Count of (1768–1826). An Austrian commander who first campaigned (against the Turks) in 1788. He saw much service against French armies and was appointed a field marshal at Wagram* in 1809. He undertook several diplomatic missions to Paris in 1813, and served at Lützen,* Bautzen,* Dresden,* and Leipzig.* He was made governor of Lombardy in 1818, and three years later repressed a Piedmontese revolt with great severity.

Bucharest, Peace of, May 1812. This pacification between Russia and the Turks cleared the Tsar's hands of a struggle in the Balkans just prior to the French invasion of Russia. Negotiated between Admiral Tshitsagov* and Khaleb Effendi, the Grand Vizier's plenipotentiary, the agreement hinged upon Russia's willingness to withdraw her forces from Moldavia and Wallachia.

Buenos Aires, invasions of, 1806 and 1807. As part of the strategy of conquering the colonies of France and her Allies, a small British force, 1,500 strong, landed near Buenos Aires on 27 June 1806 under command of Colonel Beresford.* Despite some initial success—the capture of Montevideo* on 3 February 1807—Beresford was not strong enough to hold his acquisitions, and he was counter-attacked by Santiago de Liniers, a French officer in the service of Charles IV* of Spain, and forced to surrender.

Next year a larger British expedition under General John Whitelock* captured Montevideo and marched, 10,000 strong, to attack Buenos Aires. Once again de Liniers proved more than a match for them, and after an abortive assault on 5 July, Whitelock was forced to abandon all operations in the region of the river Plate. These successes helped to inspire the Argentinian independence movement.

Bugeaud de la Piconnerie, Maréchal Thomas Robert, duc d'Isly (1784–1849). After service as a grenadier in the *velites* of the Imperial Guard* (from 1804), he was commissioned in 1806. He rose to notice for gallantry during the sieges of Saragossa* and Pamplona* in the Peninsula, but in 1814 he rallied to the Bourbons. Next year, however, he rejoined Napoleon and defeated an Austrian force in Savoy. He subsequently retired to his estates until 1830, when he was recalled. He held various military and political appointments and earned a name for severity, but in 1836–37 he became a national hero for his skill at completing the conquest of Algeria. He was made governor general from 1840, appointed a marshal three years later, and created a duke in 1844. He expanded French control over the Sahara and defeated the Moroccans. Sacked for political reasons in 1847, next year he was appointed commander of the Army of the Alps by the new Prince-President, later Napoleon III. He died of cholera.

Bülow, General Friedrich Wilhelm von, Count Dennewitz (1755–1816). Of distinguished ancestry, Bülow first took command of a division of the Prussian army in 1813. He won several notable actions

Bülow

during the War of German Liberation, starting with Luckau. On 23 August he defeated Oudinot* at Gross-Beeren,* and on 6 September defeated Ney* at Dennewitz,* receiving the title of Count for this success. He served well at Leipzig,* and next year at Laon,* where his corps enabled Blücher* to hold his ground and repulse Napoleon. On 18 June 1815 it was the arrival of Bülow's corps near Plancenoit at 4:00 P.M. that was a critical event in the battle of Waterloo.* He died next year at Königsberg.

Bureau Topographique, le. Instituted by Lazare Carnot* in 1792 to serve as a

General Staff organization, the Bureau was organized into a series of commissions, each charged with supervising the military activities on one of the major war fronts. In 1795, prior to *Vendémiaire,** *général de brigade* Bonaparte was for a time attached to the section overlooking the Italian struggle.

Burgos, sieges of, 19 September–22 October 1812 and 10–12 June 1813. Napoleon had ordered the modernizing of the fortifications in 1808, for Burgos controlled a vital part of the important highway linking Madrid to France. After Salamanca,* Wellington* first marched on Madrid and then north to besiege Burgos. The garrison of 2,000 French troops commanded by *général de brigade* Dubreton* fought a doughty defense, and although the Allies captured the Great Hornwork on 20 September by a *coup de main*, they thereafter made only very slow progress. Shortage of siege artillery, much rain which flooded the trenches of the siege lines, and the determined defense inspired by Dubreton combined to defeat Wellington. Despite the explosion of several mines and the eventual capture of the lower levels of the fortress, the Allies never attained the citadel where the Napoleon Battery was situated. By early October a state of stalemate had developed, and as French forces under Souham* and Cafarelli* began to mass north of the city, Wellington had to abandon his intention. After the failure of one last assault on 18 October, the order to retreat was issued on the 21st. Burgos had cost the Allies over 2,000 casualties; the French lost only 623.

Next year, however, a renewed Allied attack on the fortress shortly before the great battle of Vitoria* was crowned with success. The garrison held out for only two days before surrendering on 12 June.

Burrard, Lieutenant General Sir Harry (1755–1813). An ensign in the Coldstream Guards in 1772, he later saw extensive service in North America under Generals Howe and Cornwallis. From 1780 he was MP for Lymington. After service in Flanders, 1793–95, he was promoted to colonel, and in 1798 to major general. In 1807 he commanded the 1st Division at Copenhagen* (serving as second in command to Lord Cathcart*), and was made a baronet. Next year he was sent to the Peninsula to supersede Wellesley,* taking over after Vimiero* and forbidding a full pursuit of the routed Junot.* He in turn was superseded by Sir Hew Dalrymple,* but he shared responsibility for the Convention of Cintra* and was recalled to London. After the inquiry he never again held an active command, but commanded the Guards Brigade in London, 1810.

Bussaco (or Busaco), battle of, 27 September 1810. After the capture of Ciudad Rodrigo* and Almeida,* Massena's* Army of Portugal advanced into the country toward Coimbra.* Ahead of them, Wel-

lington* gathered his Allied army upon the Serra do Bussaco, an eight-mile long, steep-sided ridge, intent upon at least delaying the French advance by offering battle, and thus winning time for a further withdrawal to the prepared lines of Torres Vedras.*

Massena was at the head of three corps, totalling 65,974 men and 114 guns, with Ney,* Reynier,* and Junot* as his key subordinates. Wellington's army comprised seven divisions and 60 guns—perhaps 51,340 men in all, including some 5,000 Portuguese. His position on the long ridge was extended, but he put only two divisions on the eastern half of the ridge (under Leith* and Hill*). He massed the rest in concealed positions to dominate the main road which climbed from Moura to pass the Bussaco Convent on the left center of his position (the extreme left being held by Cole's 4th Division) and to hold the crest above San Antonio do Cantaro, where a secondary road breasted the ridge near his center.

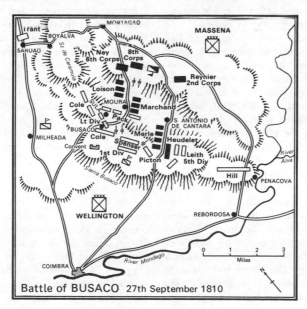

Battle of BUSACO 27th September 1810

To ease communication along the ridge, Wellington had a rough lateral road constructed.

The French plan was for Reynier's II Corps to advance from San Antonio to seize the crest before swinging right to roll up the Allied position and attack the Coimbra road while Ney's VI Corps stormed up from Moura. Junot's VIII Corps was to be held in reserve. Massena underestimated the British strength as that of merely a rear guard, and was both dilatory in his approach and unthorough in reconnoitering the position. Thus the 26th was wasted.

At 5:45 A.M. on the 27th Reynier's leading divisions under Generals Heudelet and Merle appeared out of a dense mist to attack part of Picton's* 3rd Division from the direction of San Antonio. Merle reached the crest but was flung back by a charge by the 88th Foot. In the meantime Hill and Leith moved part of their divisions to Picton's assistance, and by 6:30 A.M. two more French assaults had been repulsed with heavy loss. Thus 22 battalions were defeated, and Massena's outflanking move came to naught.

At 8:15 A.M., unaware of what had transpired to his left, Ney sent Loison* and Marchand* into action up the Coimbra highroad. Ahead of Loison the troops of Craufurd's* Light Division fell back; the French took the hamlet of Sula but were then halted short of the crest by rifle fire and the effect of shrapnel shells from the British artillery. On the left of this attack, Marchand led 11 battalions against Pack's Portuguese and almost reached the convent before being repulsed with 1,200 casualties. Desultory fighting continued until 4:00 P.M., when Massena called off the battle without sending in his reserves. For his part, Wellington wisely forebore to counterattack into the valley. The French had lost 4,486 casualties including five generals; the Allies had only 1,252 killed and wounded

during this model defensive battle. Next day Massena found a way around the Serra to the west, and Wellington at once headed for Torres Vedras, but the battle had raised the morale of the Allied troops, especially the Portuguese, even if it had not served to turn the French back.

Buxhowden, Field Marshal Friedrich Wilhelm, Count of (1750–1811). He first gained attention during Suvorov's* campaigns in Poland (1793–94), and was made governor of the region after its conquest. In 1805 he commanded the Austro-Russian left wing at Austerlitz* which made the main attack against Napoleon's positions—and failed. After Tilsit* he was given the task of organizing the new Russian possession of Finland, 1808–09.

Byng, Field Marshal Sir John, Earl of Strafford (1772–1860). Commissioned into the 33rd Foot, he served in Flanders under Wellesley* (1793–95). Wounded during the Irish Rising of 1798, in 1804 he exchanged into the 3rd Guards. Service in Hanover, Copenhagen,* and Walcheren* followed, and in 1810 he moved to the Peninsula and soon received command of a brigade under Hill.* Byng served at Vitoria* and Roncesvalles,* and at the latter won Wellington vital time to prepare for the battle of Sorauren.* Wounded at Nivelle,* he distinguished himself at Nive.* A major general since June 1813, he went on to fight at Orthez,* Aire, and Toulouse,* receiving the K.C.B. in 1814. The next year he commanded the 2nd Guards Brigade at Waterloo.* After taking part in the occupation of France he received no more active commands, but was promoted to lieutenant general in 1825, commanded in Ireland 1828–31, and in the latter year he became M.P. for Poole. Created a Baron in 1835, he was ultimately made a field marshal in 1855 and became an earl two years later.

Cadiz, siege of, 5 February 1810–24 August 1812. The great seaport and naval arsenal of southwestern Spain stands on a peninsula and constituted a strong and defensible position. In early 1810 Cadiz—the seat of the Spanish Supreme Junta since its flight from Madrid—was virtually undefended, but Soult's* preference for occupying Seville gave the Spanish general, the Duke of Albuquerque, time to march in his 10,000 men from Merida (3 February) to reinforce the 2,400 volunteers of the garrison, while a further 3,000 men arrived by sea. Marshal Victor* approached the defenses on the 5th—just too late.

The Regency Council (replacing the Junta) appealed to Wellington* for aid, and later in February three British and two Portuguese battalions arrived by sea. Supplied by the Royal Navy, and defended on the landward side by the San Petri River, its marshes, and the man-made lines of defenses, Cadiz proved impregnable. Some 60,000 French troops were tied down in its vicinity until mid-1812, exposed to guerrilla attacks and forays of the sort that led to the battle of Barrosa,* won by Lieutenant General Graham,* commander of the British forces in Cadiz. Soult and the Army of the South doggedly clung to their siege lines until August 1812, when the works were demolished as the French prepared to abandon Andalusia in the aftermath of Salamanca.*

Cadogan, Colonel Henry (1780–1813). Commissioned into the 18th Foot in 1797,

two years later he exchanged into the Coldstream Guards, the first of several transfers. After service in Scotland, the Channel Isles, and Curaçao, he joined the 71st Highlanders. Serving as aide-de-camp to Wellesley* in 1809, he fought at Oporto,* negotiated with Cuesta,* the Spanish commander, and was present at Talavera.* In 1810 he took command of the 71st on their arrival in the Peninsula, and distinguished himself at Fuentes de Oñoro* next year. He was given command of a brigade and died at the battle of Vitoria* leading his men to storm the Puebla Heights.

Cadoudal, Georges (1771–1804). The Chouan chief and royalist conspirator

Cadoudal

fought against the Revolutionary forces in La Vendée from 1793 and refused the amnesty offered in 1795. In 1799 he attempted to stir up a new royalist rising, and rejected several overtures from Bonaparte. The Comte d'Artois appointed him lieutenant general, and he traveled to Paris and helped mastermind the attempt to blow up the First Consul with an "infernal machine" on 24 December 1800. He escaped to England, but returned to Normandy on 21 August 1803. He plotted with Pichegru* and Moreau,* but was arrested and executed (25 June 1804) after the failure of the conspiracy that bears his name, which came to a climax with the abortive attempt to seize Bonaparte in an ambush on 16 January 1804. His conspiracy was used by Fouché* as a convenient excuse for eliminating many critics of the regime.

Caffarelli du Falga, Général Louis Marie Joseph Maximilien de (1756–1799). An officer of engineers, first commissioned in 1775, he enjoyed very mixed fortunes under the Revolution, being cashiered several times and imprisoned once, but following the loss of his left leg on the Rhine front he was promoted to *général de brigade* in December 1795. Subsequently he became chief engineer of the Army of England and the Army of the Orient, and accompanied Bonaparte to Egypt in 1798. He fortified Cairo after its capture and, in Syria, served before Jaffa* and Acre.* During the siege of Acre he was mortally wounded and died on 27 April 1799.

Caffarelli du Falga, Général Marie François Auguste, comte (1766–1849). Brother of Louis, he served in the Sardinian army from 1785–92, and then entered the French dragoons. Enjoying a variegated career, he served in the Consular Guard in 1800 and fought at Marengo.* After a mission to the Vati-can, he became *général de division* in 1805 and an imperial aide (to 1806). Further service in Italy eventually led to transfer to Spain, 1809–13. He replaced Dorsenne in command of the Army of the North in 1812, but in January 1813 again became Napoleon's aide. Thereafter he held Paris appointments, and in 1814 accompanied Marie Louise* and the King of Rome* to Vienna. In 1815 he rallied to Napoleon and was retired by the Bourbons on 1 August. He was made a peer of France in 1831 and employed on various commissions.

Calder, Admiral Sir Robert (1745–1818). After entering the Royal Navy in 1759, he was promoted to post captain in 1780. Selected by Jervis* to take dispatches to London after the victory of St. Vincent* (1796), he was knighted, became a baronet in 1798, and was promoted to rear admiral in 1799 and, after long service with the Channel fleet, to vice admiral in 1804. Commanding the blockade off Brest, he intercepted Villeneuve's* fleet returning from the West Indies and fought an indecisive action on 22 July 1805, which induced the French to sail for Ferrol and, later, Cadiz. Reprimanded by the Admiralty, he never again received an active command, but became a full admiral by seniority in 1810.

Caldiero, battles of, 12 November 1796 and 30 October 1805. In a second attempt to relieve Mantua,* General Alvintzi* led 28,000 Austrians toward Verona and the river Adige from the east, associating his move with Davidovitch's* southward march from Trent. Bonaparte's resources were overstretched trying to contain both threats and at the same time continue the siege of Mantua. Alvintzi drove back the French outposts east of the Adige with some loss, and on 11 November Bonaparte sent Massena* and Augereau* with 12,000 men from Verona to attack the

Austrian advance guard of 8,000 men. Their eastward advance, however, was delayed by a severe sleet storm, and the French halted at Caldiero after covering only five miles. Next day the French attack was held by the advanced elements of the Austrian army, and Alvintzi brought up his main body to defeat the French, causing them 2,000 casualties. This, arguably Bonaparte's first defeat in battle, caused the French to retire on Verona. However, their young commander, benefiting from the continued inactivity of Davidovitch on the northern sector, at once launched the maneuver that led to the victory of Arcola.*

Nine years later, as a complementary offensive to the great advance into central Germany, Napoleon ordered Massena at the head of 37,000 troops to drive the Archduke Charles* and his 50,000 men out of North Italy. The Austrian commander, wishing to extricate his forces and retire toward the major theater in the Danube valley, launched a surprise attack against Massena at Caldiero on 30 October. The French held their ground, but the action won Charles enough time to evacuate his baggage trains to the east. Massena followed the retiring foe with energy, and Charles was never able to take part in the Danubian operations that led first to the loss of Vienna to the French and ultimately to the crushing defeat of the Austrians and Russians at Austerlitz.*

Cambacères, Second Consul Jean Jacques Regis, duc de (1753–1824). An able lawyer and statesman, Cambacères belonged to a legal family from Languedoc. Elected a deputy for the department of Hérault in the Convention, he cunningly avoided compromising himself over the issue of voting for the execution of Louis XVI. He survived the Terror, burying himself in his legal work on the new codes of law under preparation. He became a member of the *Conseil des Cinq-Cents,** and served briefly as Minister of Justice in June 1799. At *Brumaire** he backed Bonaparte's cause and was rewarded with appointment as Second Consul. Thereafter he made large contributions to the formulation of what became the Civil Code.* Under the Empire, he was one of the few men to whom Napoleon would always listen seriously, and became Prince-Archchancellor of the Empire and Duke of Parma. He joined the Bourbons in 1814, but rallied to Napoleon the next year. After Waterloo* he lived in exile in Brussels until 1818, when he was permitted to return to France. He took no further part in public affairs.

Cambronne, Général Pierre Jacques Etienne, vicomte (1770–1842). His first military service came in 1792 as a volunteer; rising to sergeant major in 1793, he was commissioned the same year. After valorous service on the Rhine, in Switzerland, and in the campaigns of 1805–07,

Cambronne

he was transferred to the Imperial Guard in 1809. Service in Spain and Russia followed, and his reputation grew through 1813 (when he was promoted to *général de brigade*) and 1814. Napoleon selected him to serve as staff officer to the battalion of the Guard that accompanied him to Elba. He commanded the advance guard on Napoleon's return to France, was made a count, and commanded part of the Guard at Waterloo,* where the famous *"mot de Cambronne"* became legendary. Wounded and taken prisoner, he was pardoned by the Bourbons despite a sentence of death passed in his absence, in 1816. After a period on half-pay, he commanded the 26th Division in 1820, and was created a viscount two years later. He finally retired at his own request in early 1823, and lived out his days at Nantes.

Campbell, Major General Alexander (fl. 1809). A friend of the Prince Regent, he commanded the 4th Division at Talavera* (where he was wounded) with distinction, but later earned Wellington's* criticism for his part in the failure to forestall and prevent Brennier's* escape from Almeida* in 1811.

Campbell, Lieutenant Colonel Sir Colin (1776–1847). After running away to sea in 1792, he served on an East Indiaman. Commissioned into the militia, 1795, it was as an officer of the 78th Foot that he saw much service in India (1802–06), including the battle of Assaye.* After taking part in the Copenhagen campaign of 1807, he was sent to the Peninsula as Wellesley's* senior aide-de-camp. He took part in most of the major campaigns including nine battles and sieges, being promoted to brevet-lieutenant colonel in 1810 and to assistant quartermaster general two years later. Knighted in 1814, he was present at Waterloo.* He became a major general in 1825, and later served as Governor of

Nova Scotia (from 1833) and of Ceylon (from 1839).

Camperdown, naval battle of, 11 October 1797. A Dutch fleet of 16 vessels under Admiral Jan Willem de Winter sailed from the Texel to carry aid and 15,000 troops to the Irish rebels. Despite the problems caused by the mutinies at the Nore and Spithead,* Admiral Adam Duncan prevailed upon his men to put to sea, and intercepted the fleet with 16 Royal Naval units. With the wind in his favor and superior gun power at his disposal, Duncan soon gained the upper hand in a savage engagement ten miles off the Dutch coast. Each side lost over 1,000 killed and wounded, but the Dutch lost nine ships-of-the-line, several frigates, and 5,000 prisoners, while the British lost no vessels. This victory effectively ensured the isolation of the Irish rebels from the prospect of any large-scale aid.

Campo Formio, Treaty and Peace of, 17 October 1797. Following the preliminaries of Leoben,* Austria and France signed a formal peace at Passeriano near Campo Formio. By its terms, Austria ceded Belgium (the Austrian Netherlands) to France and (by secret clause) agreed to the French occupation of the left bank of the Rhine. French possession of Corfu and the Ionian Isles was also accepted, and Lombardy was abandoned. In return Austria received Dalmatia, the Frioul, and Venetian territory east of the Adige, and acknowledged the existence of the Ligurian and Cisalpine Republics.* Compensation was to be afforded the dispossessed Rhennish princes from secularized ecclesiastical lands.

Canning, George (1770–1827). The son of a barrister but brought up by a banker uncle, he was educated at Eton and Oxford. After legal training, he entered Parliament in 1793 and became Pitt's*

Canning

Under Secretary of State for Foreign Affairs from 1796–99. In 1807 he became Foreign Secretary, and planned the attack on Copenhagen.* His notorious quarrel with Castlereagh* after the Walcheren* fiasco led to a duel (1809) in which he was wounded. He refused to serve under Perceval* or (for some years) under Liverpool,* but carried out special diplomatic missions. In 1816 he did in fact become President of the India Board under Liverpool, a post he resigned in 1821. He returned next year as Foreign Secretary, acknowledged the independence of Spain's colonies, and championed Greece against Turkey. In April 1827 he became Prime Minister but died of dysentery in August the same year.

Carnot, Général Lazare, comte (1753–1823). The son of a Burgundian notary, the future "organizer of victory" was educated at Autun and the Engineer School at Mezières, where Monge* was a professor. After being commissioned in 1773, he served in various garrisons, and was for a time imprisoned for unau-

thorized publication of a military document. In August 1791 he was elected Deputy for Pas-de-Calais and became a key politician with military responsibilities. Re-elected to the Convention in 1792, he voted for Louis XVI's execution, and masterminded the *levée en masse* and the *députés-en-mission* system, leading many missions in person. He helped win the battle of Wattignies,* and was from August 1793 an influential member of the Committee of Public Safety. He quarreled with Robespierre* and thus did not share in his eclipse, and in 1795 he was elected a Director and again given charge of military affairs. For some months in 1796 he was President of the Directory,* but was forced to flee abroad after the *coup d'état* of *Fructidor*. He was allowed to return to France after *Brumaire,* and Bonaparte appointed him Inspector General of the Army (1800). From April to December of that year he served the Consulate as Minister of War, but then was relegated to membership of the Tribunate (1802–07). His opposition to the honors system and the proclamation of the Empire caused him to be virtually

Carnot

unemployed until January 1814, when he was appointed to command the defense of Antwerp and promoted to *général de division*. In March 1815 he rallied to Napoleon, who made him a count, a peer of France, and Minister of the Interior. Exiled in July, he lived in many places, including Cracow and Warsaw, before finally settling in Magdeburg in October 1816, where he devoted his remaining years to writing.

Carteaux, Général Jean François (1751–1813). After service as a soldier in the infantry and dragoons, 1776–79, he became a court painter. In 1789 he was an aide to Lafayette,* and held various staff appointments before being promoted to *général de brigade* in July 1793 and to *général de division* just one month later, after suppressing rebels in Provence. That September he was appointed to command against the rebels in the Midi and at Toulon,* but was transferred first to the Army of Italy and then to that of the Alps. He was disgraced, tried, and imprisoned (December 1793–August 1794), and retired from the service in 1795. However, he took part in the *coup d'état* de Vendémiaire, and was thereafter given various active commands, including one in the Army of Batavia (1800). After running the National Lottery (1801–04) he became administrator of the Principality of Piombino (1803–05), and finally retired from public life in 1810.

Castaños, Francisco Xavier, Duke of Bailen (1756–1852). Born in the Spanish province of Biscay, he studied for a military career in Germany and first saw active service against the French in Navarre. In 1808 he forced General Dupont* to surrender at Bailen*—his greatest moment—and five years later played a useful part at Vitoria.* From 1825 he was a member of the Council of State, and later became President of the Council of Castille (1843) and tutor to Queen Isabella II of Spain.

Castellane-Novejean, Général Boniface Louis André, comte de (1758–1837). First commissioned in 1774, he was a representative of the nobility at the States-General in 1789. Dismissed in 1792, and later imprisoned until 1794, he was eventually reinstated and promoted to *général de brigade* in June 1794. He was made a baron and a count in 1810, and was mostly employed on the *Conseil d'état*. He joined the Bourbons in 1814, and became a Peer of France in August 1815. In 1816 he was made a lieutenant general.

Castiglione, battle of, 5 August 1796. From 3 June the great fortress of Mantua* was closely besieged by the Army of Italy, and it was destined to dominate the next eight months of the campaign. Vienna was determined to prevent its fall, and in July two main Austrian forces began to converge on the river Mincio. General Quasdanovitch* (18,000 men) advanced to the west of Lake Garda, while General Würmser* (24,000) marched from Trent on Verona, and a small force (5,000) moved down the Brenta valley under Meszaros. To meet these converging forces Bonaparte had 46,000 men, but many of these were engaged on garrison and occupation duties, while the siege of Mantua's garrison of 12,700 men tied down many more.

Faced by a complex situation, Bonaparte called off the siege of Mantua on 31 July, and Würmser and Meszaros duly resupplied Count d'Irles' garrison. Meanwhile, Massena* and Augereau* had repulsed Quasdanovitch and Liptay (Würmser's advance guard commander) on 3 August around Lonato* and Castiglione, as Bonaparte took up a central position between his two adversaries. As Quasdanovitch fell back north, the

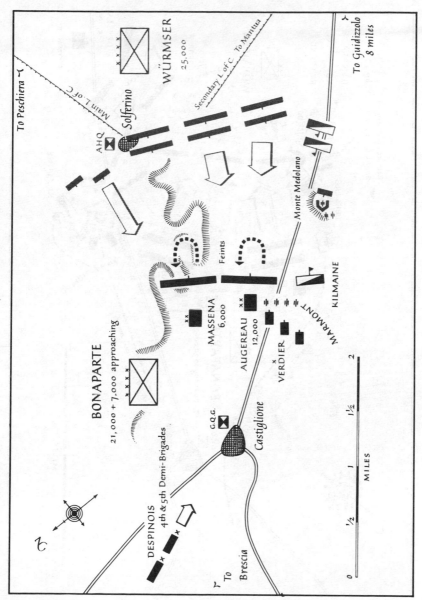

Battle of Castiglione, 5 August 1796: Phase One

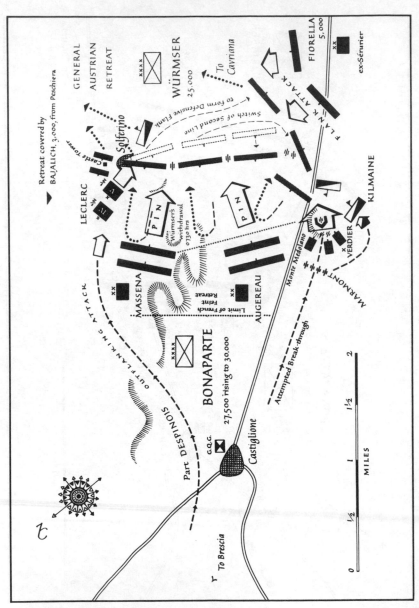

Battle of Castiglione: Phase Two

French prepared to turn their full attention upon Würmser—who had to be prevented from falling back into Mantua at all costs. By the 4th Würmser was occupying a position between Solferino in the north and the knoll of Monte Medolano—in advance of his left wing—with 25,000 troops.

Bonaparte's plan was to build up his 21,000 men already present to some 30,000 men by the crisis of the battle. Troops were arriving at Castiglione from the north, but most important would be the arrival of Sérurier's 5,000 men (commanded by Fiorella, as Sérurier was sick) on Würmser's left flank and rear from the distant town of Marcaria, where they had fallen back after evacuating the Mantuan siege lines. If correctly timed, this force's intervention would distract the Austrians, giving the French the chance to break through the Austrian left center and achieve a convincing victory. A special force of grenadiers, aided by guns and cavalry, would be held in reserve for the vital breakthrough.

Early on the 5th Massena and Augereau launched their frontal attacks and, as prearranged, fell back in front of the Austrians in a deliberate attempt to lure Würmser forward from his strong position. The Austrian front-line units obliged, pivoting on their left flank, but not the second line, nor the strong force holding Monte Medolano. The subsequent timings of the battle phases went awry for the French. Fiorella intervened before all the Austrians had been drawn into the frontal battle, and Würmser was able to redeploy his reserves to meet the new threat. The French special force therefore faced not only the original Austrian first-line troops but also the garrison of Monte Medolano, and the breakthrough attempt failed as a result. Worse still, the French front-line divisions failed to pin the troops opposing them, and the Austrians were able to fall back to their original strong position. The French took Monte Medolano with the bayonet, but Würmser was by now (early afternoon) in full retreat for Peschiera. The Austrians had lost 2,000 killed and wounded and another 1,000 prisoners, as well as 20 guns; the French possibly had 1,500 casualties, but Bonaparte was not wholly satisfied with the outcome. Nevertheless, Castiglione is important as showing the development of Bonaparte's concept of the "strategic battle," and its grand tactical sequence would be repeated with variations (and greater success) on many future occasions.

Castlereagh, Robert Stewart, Viscount (1760–1822). This distinguished British statesman proved an inveterate opponent of Napoleon's France, second only to Pitt.* He first entered Parliament in 1794, and by 1798 he was the Irish Lord Privy Seal. Until 1805, most of his time was taken up by Irish affairs, but in that year Pitt appointed him to the War and Colonial Offices. He planned Wellesley's* expedition to the Peninsula and supported him consistently from 1808, but in 1809 the Walcheren* failure led to his eclipse in the Cabinet, and his duel with Canning* further damaged his reputation. Nevertheless, he served as Foreign Minister from 1812–22 under Lord Liverpool,* and masterminded two major coalitions against France. He was senior British representative at the Congress of Vienna,* 1814–15, selected St. Helena* as Napoleon's place of confinement, and later championed the Congress System as a means to reduce international tensions. His severe attitude toward domestic policies made him an unpopular figure in his last years, and in 1822, a year after being made Marquess of Londonderry, he took his own life.

Cathcart, General Charles Murray, Earl

(1783–1859). First commissioned in 1800, he saw service in Sicily and Italy (1805–06), and was present at Maida.* He took part in the Walcheren* expedition (1809) and served in the Peninsula from 1810–12. Quartermaster General from 1814–22, he was present at Waterloo.* In later life Cathcart became governor of Edinburgh Castle (1837–42), and was Commander in Chief in Canada, 1846–49. He was made a full general in 1854.

Caulaincourt, Général Armand Augustin Louis de, marquis de, duc de Vicenza (1773–1827). After varied service in the Bourbon infantry, the Army of the North, and the Parisian Guard, in 1794 he became a trooper in the 16th *chasseurs-à-cheval* and worked his way up to Captain and aide-de-camp in 1795. Next year he served on a mission to Constantinople, and later, after returning to France, fought at Stockach,* Moesskirch, and Neresheim before being sent to St. Petersburg on another diplomatic mission. In July 1802 he was appointed an aide to the First Consul, and was promoted to

Auguste Caulaincourt

général de brigade the next year. In 1804 he became Master of the Horse and as such served Napoleon until 1813, taking part in several of the great campaigns. Promoted to *général de division* in 1805, he also became ambassador to St. Petersburg from 1807–11, being created a duke in 1808. He was at Napoleon's side through the Russian campaign of 1812, and returned with him to Paris from Smorgoni.* He succeeded Duroc* as Grand Marshal of the Palace for six months in 1813 and led many diplomatic missions to the Allies over the years 1813–14. Caulaincourt was appointed Foreign Minister from November 1813 until the first abdication, a post he resumed from March to July 1815. After Waterloo,* his period of disgrace was short, and in August 1815 he was allowed back into France, on retirement. His *Mémoires* form a vital source for events from 1812–14.

Caulaincourt, Général Auguste Jean Gabriel, comte (1777–1812). The younger brother of Armand, he served in the cavalry from 1792 in many varied ca-

Armand Caulaincourt

pacities. He impressed Massena* in Switzerland, was wounded at Marengo,* and in 1804 he became a member of Louis Bonaparte's* staff. After service at Austerlitz,* Caulaincourt passed into Dutch service, 1806–08, as King Louis' Master of the Horse. Returning to France, he was promoted to *général de brigade* (1808) and saw much active service in Spain, becoming *général de division* in 1809. Ill health led to extended leave in France, and he was made a count in 1810. In charge of the Imperial Headquarters in 1812, he took over Montbrun's* 2nd Cavalry Corps at Borodino,* and was killed leading the charge that captured the Raevski Redoubt.

Cavalry, the. "Cavalry is useful before, during and after the battle," wrote Napoleon, and he stressed the need for audacity in its employment and careful training to achieve true discipline. He was also insistent that careful categorization according to role was of great importance. For battlefield domination he relied upon *cuirassiers* and *carabiniers,* large men upon powerful horses, equipped with back and breastplates as well as helmets, and armed with long straight swords, a pair of pistols, and (eventually) a carbine apiece. There were 14 regiments of *cuirassiers* in the *Grande Armée* and two of *carabiniers* (who first adopted the cuirass in 1809). Using their weight and the full benefit of shock, these formidable troopers were expected to be able to ride down their mounted adversaries and to be able to exploit gaps blown through infantry formations by the artillery.

The second category of cavalry was the dragoon. Originally a mounted infantryman, by the early 19th century the dragoon was becoming regarded as basically a cavalryman, although in Spain the dismounted role was employed often enough, and after 1812 there were sometimes as many as two dismounted squadrons in a regiment, owing to the dearth of horses. Armed with a sword, pistols, dragoon-musket, and bayonet, dragoons were expected to perform many roles—ranging from forming the cavalry screen to providing escorts for convoys—and they were also to the fore on the battlefield. Napoleon had 30 regiments of dragoons, but in 1811 six were converted into lancers, or *chevau-légers.*

The two elite formations of lancers forming part of the Imperial Guard Cavalry were the Poles and the Dutch. The lance was reintroduced to the former in 1809, proving a useful weapon for tackling infantry drawn up in square at close range. A saber and pistols were also carried.

The remainder of the French horsemen formed the Light Cavalry, comprising 13 regiments of hussars, some 30 regiments of *chasseurs-à-cheval,* and certain other formations which included the Mamelukes of the Guard, the *gendarmerie d'élite* and (from 1814) the *éclaireurs-à-cheval.* All sported distinctive uniforms, wielded sabers and pistols, and in many cases carried carbines in addition. Pre-eminently used for reconnaissance and pursuit roles, the light cavalry regarded themselves as the *beaux sabreurs* of the army.

The basic administrative and tactical unit was the squadron, usually divided into two *compagnies,* each of two *pélotons* holding between 36 and 60 cavalrymen. A *cuirassier* regiment held 1,040 troopers in four squadrons; a dragoon regiment comprised 1,200 men in five squadrons (two of which might be dismounted); a regiment of light horse had anywhere between 1,200 to 1,800 cavalrymen in four to eight squadrons.

Cavalry regiments were organized into brigades and divisions, and even complete corps in the later years of the Empire. Each *corps d'armée* had either a brigade or division of mounted troops attached to it, usually of dragoons and light cavalry. The heavy units were generally massed in the Cavalry Reserve, together with more dragoons, and kept under army command. Murat* was the most notable cavalry leader of his time, but he was ably backed by corps and divisional commanders who included Grouchy,* Nansouty,* Colbert, and Lasalle.* It was some time before the French cavalry reached its full potential, as it had suffered the loss of many officers during the·Revolutionary period, but by 1807 it was reaching its prime. The great charges led by Murat at Eylau* and Grouchy at Friedland* played vital parts in the outcome of these battles.

Of the European powers, Austria's cavalry—some 58,000 strong—was widely regarded as the finest in Europe in the 1790s, and under such commanders as Prince Lichtenstein they were generally well handled at Austerlitz,* Aspern-Essling,* and Wagram,* although they were generally beaten by the French. In 1805 there were eight *cuirassier* regiments, six of dragoons, six of 'light horse,' twelve of hussars, and three of lancers. The cavalry of Prussia was bold in action but outdated in organization and role in 1806. Prussian horses were of particular quality, and the arm was greatly modernized by 1813 when it comprised two Guard, seven heavy, and thirteen light regiments —or 12,600 regular horsemen, besides 18,500 *landwehr* troopers. The forces of the Tsar contained cavalry that was rated as highly as that of France, while in the Cossacks they possessed a particularly effective form of irregular light cavalry for skirmishing, patrolling, and raiding roles. In 1812, Russia fielded six regiments of Guard cavalry, eight *cuirassier*, and thirty-six dragoon regiments, a further eleven of hussars and five of Uhlans, besides a total of 30,000 Cossacks, who rated as irregular horse. The Russians had

cavalry corps of two divisions (of two or three brigades apiece), and rode tough and fast mounts. Had their commanders employed them in mass formations to gain maximum shock effect after the French style, their repute would indeed have been formidable. Platov,* *hetman* of the Cossacks, bore an almost legendary reputation for his skillful handling of irregular horsemen.

British cavalry bore a mixed reputation. Their horses were rated far superior to those of the French, and this gave British cavalrymen the edge in many an encounter like Sahagun* or Benavente.* On the other hand they were not noted for their ability to rally after a charge and often ran into difficulties, as at Vimiero,* Talavera,* and Waterloo.* Divided into heavy (Life Guards, Dragoons, and Dragoon Guards) and light (Hussar) categories, they were relatively few in number, but in Le Marchant, Uxbridge,* and Cotton* they produced some excellent leaders. The Hanoverian, King's German Legion, and Brunswicker units were among the best. British cavalry lacked a uniform drill, and rarely fought in formations larger than the brigade.

Cervoni, Général Jean Baptiste (1765–1809). After enlisting as a private in 1783, he later rose to notice at Toulon* and in North Italy (1796), where he fought at Voltri,* Lodi,* Castiglione,* Arcola,* Rivoli,* and at the siege of Mantua.* Promoted to *général de division* in February 1798, he served in Italy and Brussels. As Chief of Staff to Lannes* in 1809 he was killed at Eckmühl* on 22 April that year.

Ceva, battle of, 16–17 April 1796. This fortified position was held by Colli* and an Austro-Piedmontese force (13,000 strong) after their retreat from Montenotte.* Bonaparte twice had to cancel a main attack because of crises at Dego,* and on the 16th Augereau's* premature assault was defeated with loss. On the 17th, however, Augereau and Serurier* massed 24,000 troops for a new attack the next day, but Colli beat a skillful retreat to a stronger position near San Michele, and then again to Mondovi,* where he was at last brought to action.

Ceylon, occupation of, 1796. Long a Dutch colony, Ceylon was conquered by an expedition mounted by the East India Company in 1795–96. It was retained at the Peace of Amiens,* and became a British Crown Colony in 1802.

Chabran, Général Joseph, comte (1763–1843). Elected a captain of volunteers in 1792, he held a number of staff appointments under Massena,* whom he served in Italy (1796), fighting at Lodi,* Lonato,* Roveredo,* and Bassano.* His promotion to *général de brigade* was confirmed in May 1797, and after more active service in Italy, Switzerland, and on the Danube, he was promoted to *général de division* in June 1799. Next year he was given the 5th Division of the Army of Reserve, and after crossing the Alps was entrusted with the siege of Fort Bard.* More staff and garrison duties followed, but in March 1808 Chabran was given a command in Catalonia, and later that year took over a division of V Corps under Gouvion St. Cyr.* He was appointed Governor of Barcelona, but in May 1810, following a scandal, he was relieved of his post. The Bourbons recalled him to service in 1814 and made him a count, and he finally retired in 1827.

Chambarlhac de Laubespin, Général Jacques Antoine, baron de (1754–1826). Following service in the Bourbon infantry (1769–1776), he re-entered military life in 1792 as a lientenant colonel of volunteers. He distinguished himself at Arcola,* was promoted to *général de*

brigade on the battlefield (subsequently confirmed in December 1796), and gravely wounded. He was again wounded at Verona in 1799 and, recalled to France, served with skill in operations against the Chouan revolt in the west of France. He fought under Victor* at Marengo,* and after garrison appointments was promoted to *général de division* in July 1803. Numerous garrison and staff posts followed, and in 1811 he was made a Baron of the Empire. After service in the Campaign of France (1814), he was removed from command by the Bourbons and, after refusing several proffered commands, was finally retired in October 1815.

Champaubert, battle of, 10 February 1814. Learning that Blücher's* Army of Silesia was becoming considerably strung out as it marched westward toward Paris to the south of the river Marne, Napoleon decided to take the opportunity of destroying it in detail. Marching northward from Nogent-sur-Seine on 9 February through heavy rain at the head of 30,000 hungry and tired men, including many raw conscripts, and 120 guns, the Emperor surprised the 5,000 Russians of General Olssufiev near the village of Baye, south of Champaubert. The French forces engaged were the corps of Marmont* and Ney,* and for once in this campaign they enjoyed a massive superiority of force, as much as six to one. By 10:000 A.M. on the 10th Olssufiev's pickets were being driven in, but their commander rashly decided to fight it out in the belief that Blücher might come up to his aid. This proved a vain hope, and by 3:00 P.M. the Russians had been pressed back through Champaubert; Olssufiev tried to retreat toward Etoges but found himself enveloped by French cavalry on both flanks. His force lost some 4,000 casualties, the French only some 200 men. Olssufiev himself was taken prisoner in a wood that evening.

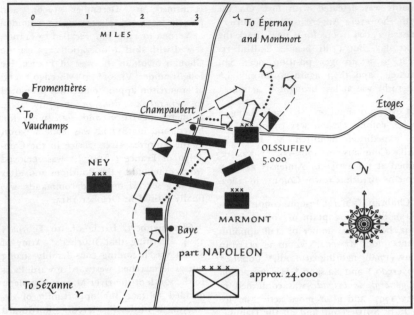

Battle of Champaubert, 10 February 1814

This success proved the prelude for two more French victories over the next few days, at Montmirail* and Vauchamps.*

Charles, Field Marshal, Archduke of Austria, Duke of Teschen (1771–1847). The third son of the Emperor Leopold II, and brother of his successor, Francis I,* the Archduke Charles proved one of the ablest—and youngest—of Napoleon's opponents. Brought up by the Duke of Saxe-Teschen, he first saw action at Jemappes* in 1792. Next year, as Governor General of the Austrian Netherlands, he faced a French invasion and fought with success against Dumouriez* at Neerwinden,* but was beaten at Wattignies* and Fleurus.* His developing martial talents justified his promotion to field marshal in 1796, and at the head of the Army of the Rhine he faced the combined attacks of Jourdan* and Moreau,* driving them back over the river after successes at Rastadt, Amberg, and Würzburg. He was then transferred to the Italian theater after the fall of Mantua,* and fought a tenacious rear-guard campaign through the Frioul and eastern Alps against the victorious Bonaparte. Although ultimately defeated, Charles preserved the greater part of his army intact for the peace. In 1799, he won the battles of Biberach and Stockach* against Jourdan, but proved incapable of cooperating with his Russian allies under Suvorov.* He gave up his military career and became first Governor of Bohemia and later Minister of War, but in 1805 he was given command of the Italian front and checked Massena* at Caldiero.* After Austerlitz,* he masterminded the reconstruction of the Austrian army, and in 1809 led it with considerable distinction against Napoleon. Defeated at Abensberg-Eckmühl,* he had the better of Napoleon at Aspern-Essling* only to be seriously defeated at Wagram* in July 1809.

Thereafter he left field command of the Austrian forces to Prince Schwarzenberg.* Bedeviled by epilepsy, he was nevertheless both an able reformer and field commander.

Charles IV, King of Spain (1748–1819). Charles succeeded to the Spanish throne in 1788. Dominated by his wife, he proved little more than a cipher; his country was governed by the Queen and her lover, Prince Godoy,* who from 1795 forced Spain into alliance with France. In the crisis of 1808, he agreed to abdicate the throne on 18 March, then reconsidered, but ultimately abdicated at Bayonne* on 1 May, in favor of Joseph Bonaparte.* He then lived in exile at Valençay until 1814, when he moved to Marseilles. He died in obscurity in Rome.

Charles XIII, King of Sweden (1748–1818). Succeeding his nephew, Gustavus IV, to the throne in 1809, Charles XIII selected Bernadotte* as his heir in 1810, as he had no children. The long antagonism with Russia was brought to a conclusion, the price being the cession of Finland to the Tsar. Charles XIII also brought his country into the Allied coalition, and the Congress of Vienna* awarded Sweden possession of Norway, at the expense of Denmark, in 1815.

Charles XIV, King of Sweden. *See* **Bernadotte**

Chassé, Général David Henri, baron de (1765–1849). After service in the Dutch army (1775–1792), he transferred to the French forces for three years. Returning to Holland, he became a major general in 1806, and in 1808 was posted to Spain. After fighting at Durango and Talavera,* in November 1810 he became a French *général de brigade* and a baron one year later. Serving under d'Erlon,* he greatly distinguished himself at Maya* (1813), saving the army. Wounded at Arcis-sur-Aube* in 1814, he returned to Dutch service and became a lieutenant general in April 1815. He commanded a division under the Prince of Orange* at Waterloo.* In 1830 he defended Antwerp against the insurgents and held out in the citadel until 1832, when he capitulated. After a period as a prisoner, he was released and promoted to general of infantry.

Chasseloup-Laubat, Général François, comte de (1754–1833). An engineer of great reputation, he was commissioned in 1778. After service with revolutionary armies, he became chief engineer to Bonaparte in Italy (1796 and 1800), being present at most battles and sieges. Promoted to *général de division* in 1799, he spent many years in Italian appointments. In 1807 he supervised the sieges of Danzig* and Stralsund,* and next year was made a count. He served in Russia in 1812 and retired the next year. Chasseloup-Laubat espoused the Bourbon cause in 1814 and took no part in the events of 1815. In 1817 he was made a

Chasseloup-Laubat

marquis, and three years later became president of the *Ecole Polytechnique*.

Chateaubriand, François René de (1768–1848). Of noble origin and a royal officer, Chateaubriand became a celebrated literary figure. He went to America during the Revolution, and after his return in 1791, served briefly in Condé's army but was wounded, and thereafter he lived in Britain until 1799. He returned to France during the Consulate, but greatly disapproved of the execution of d'Enghien,* and resigned his diplomatic post in Rome. After travels in the Middle East, Chateaubriand lived in France out of the public eye, welcomed the return of the Bourbons, and was made a peer. After service as ambassador to Berlin (1820) and London (1822), he undertook his greatest written work, and opposed the regime of Louis-Philippe from 1830. He is regarded as the founder of the French romantic literary movement.

Château-Thierry, action of, 12 February 1814. As Blücher's* army fell back following its series of defeats culminating at Montmirail,* Napoleon and Mortier* set out to pursue the discomfited corps of Generals Sacken* and Yorck.* The latter's rear guard attempted a stand at Château-Thierry on the river Marne, but Ney* soon blasted his way through their position, defeating the cavalry on the left, to capture the hills overlooking the Marne. This complicated the Allied retreat, but the Prussian infantry got away, aided by the fire of a covering battery. Two Russian regiments under General Heidenreich, on the right of the line, were forced to surrender. For a cost of 600 men, the French inflicted 1,250 casualties on the Prussians and 1,500 on Sacken's Russians and captured a total of nine guns and much baggage and transport. The Emperor spent the night at Château-Thierry and next day, the bridge having been restored, Mortier set out to follow Sacken and Yorck with part of the Old Guard and Colbert's cavalry. However, this delay allowed the Allies to break contact and reach Fismes. That same afternoon Napoleon realized that it was time to transfer his attentions to the army commanded by Prince Schwarzenberg,* but first he launched a final blow at Blücher's Army of Silesia at Vauchamps.*

Chatham, Second Earl of. *See* **Pitt,** Sir John

Chaumont, Conference and Treaty of, 9 March 1814. Following their discussions at Bar-sur-Aube* in late February, the Tsar, Austrian Emperor, King of Prussia, and British representatives reconvened the meeting at Chaumont on 1 March. By the terms of the resulting treaty (signed on 9 March but in fact dated the 1st) the powers agreed that Napoleon should be offered the French frontiers of 1791 in return for a general cease-fire. In the event of these terms being rejected, the Allies pledged themselves to wage an implacable war against Napoleon, and to forego any unilateral negotiations with France. The Emperor rejected the offer with scorn, and so ended the last attempt to achieve a negotiated settlement.

Cherasco, Armistice of, 28 April 1796. Ten days of action sufficed to bring Piedmont to the conference table. After the battle of Mondovi,* the King of Savoy realized that defeat faced him. By the terms of the temporary armistice agreed upon with Bonaparte, a cease-fire took place along the river Stura; Piedmont handed over Ceva, Cuneo, and Tortona (or Alessandria if Tortona were still in Austrian hands), and also granted the French free passage right over the river Po at Valenza. The terms were referred to the Directory* in Paris, and approval reached Bonaparte at Milan on 21 May.

Christian VIII, King of Denmark (1786–1848). The nephew of Christian VII, who became insane, this Danish ruler proved incapable of resisting the power of Sweden and the wishes of the Allied powers, and agreed to surrender Norway to Sweden in January 1814 at Bernadotte's* demand. In 1839 he became King of Denmark by election.

Cinq-Cents, Conseil des (the Five Hundred). Called into existence by the Constitution of the Year III, this Council, together with the *Conseil des Anciens,** formed the legislature of the Directory.* Its members had to be age 30 or over and were elected for three years. Its task was to propose and pass legal drafts, and to re-examine any laws rejected by the *Anciens.* The *Cinq-Cents* also had the power to declare war and make peace, as well as to draw up a list of Directors, but for any decision a quorum of at least 200 members had to be present. This Council became the mainstay of republicanism, which in large measure accounts for its opposition to the *coup d'état de Brumaire** in 1799.

Cintra, Convention of, 22 August 1808. Wellesley's* victory over Junot* at Vimiero* in Portugal led to his supersession by the more senior generals Burrard* and Dalrymple.* These commanders agreed to negotiate with the French, whose team was ably led by Kellermann the Younger,* and by the terms of the Convention the French were permitted free evacuation and repatriation for 26,000 troops with their baggage and booty by British shipping. These easy terms caused a furor in England, and all three British commanders were recalled to London to face a court of enquiry.

Cisalpine Republic, the. Formed by Bonaparte on 29 June 1797 from the Lombard possessions on both banks of the river Po in North Italy (merging the two short-lived earlier Cispadane and Transpadane republics), this state was recognized by Austria at Luneville.* Several adjoining territories were added, and in 1805 the area became the Kingdom of Italy.

Ciudad Rodrigo, sieges of, 1810 and 1812. This Spanish fortress guarded one exit of the northern corridor* linking Spain and Portugal, and became the focal point of major operations several times during the Peninsular War. Blockaded by Marshal Ney* from 11 February 1810, and

invested from 16 June, a regular siege against General Herrasti's garrison of 6,500 only began on 25 June, as Massena* prepared for the third French invasion of Portugal. Wellington* decided against trying to relieve the fortress, and after a gallant defense Herrasti surrendered on 9 July after a large breach had been blown. The French pillaged the town.

Two years later, Wellington, preparing his invasion of Spain, appeared before the fortress on 8 January 1812 in bitter weather. Five divisions were in the vicinity, one prosecuting the siege (in turn), the remainder covering the opera-

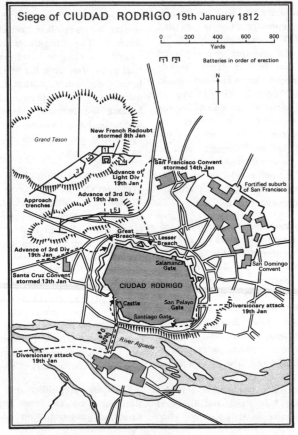

Siege of CIUDAD RODRIGO 19th January 1812

tion. Some 38 siege guns were available, and Lieutenant Colonel Fletcher RE* headed the team of engineers. On 8 January the overlooking hill north of the town—the Greater Teson—was captured from the French, and on the 16th, despite a French sortie, the intervening Lesser Teson was also secured. General Barrié and his French garrison of 1,937 fought a determined defense, but by the 19th the Allied guns had blasted two breaches. That evening the breaches were stormed and the town captured after a fierce fight. The Allies lost 568 in the assault, including General Craufurd.* The town was again plundered by the victorious troops, but Wellington had secured the northern corridor and would soon turn south to besiege Badajoz.*

Civil Reforms, of Napoleon. The constructive side of Napoleon's work, as both First Consul and Emperor, forms the positive aspect and in many instances the most lasting achievement of his period of rule. To the present day many French and European institutions and legal codes remain based upon the great body of Napoleonic reforms.

It is evident that his interest in civil and legal affairs began in his twenties. The interest he took in 1796–97, when military affairs permitted, in setting up the Cisalpine Republic* in North Italy, the rapid reordering of the affairs of Malta* in June 1798, and his subsequent work in Egypt are evidence of this. His greatest constructive work, however, dates from *Brumaire** in late 1799, and continued intermittently until at least as late as 1812.

Appreciating that effective civil reforms must be based on a sound financial basis, one of his earliest acts as Consul was to set up an efficient taxation system. Eight officials were appointed to oversee each *département*, and soon some 660 million francs were being received each year from income tax and public property

sources. Much more revenue was raised by indirect taxation, levied on such commodities as wine, playing cards, coaches, salt, and tobacco. He paid great attention to balancing his budgets, and for a number of years the cost of living remained remarkably stable. Ministerial budgets were critically examined, the public debt limited to 80 million, and the worthless paper money of the revolution progressively called in. To reduce reliance on costly loans negotiated with private bankers, in February 1800 the First Consul created the Bank of France with an initial capital of 30 million francs and a permitted dividend of 6%. From 1807, a Public Audit Office supervised all expenditures. The result of these and other measures was a sevenfold rise in the value of government stock between 1799 and 1807. Thereafter, however, the economic repercussions of ceaseless wars began to take an ever greater toll, and by 1812 the French were complaining of the excessive level of both direct and indirect taxation. The implications of the Continental System* from 1806 had at least a partial effect on this deterioration.

The Civil Code set out to bring logical order to the confused condition of France's courts of law and the over 14,000 decrees that had been passed since 1789. From the days of the *ancien régime,** the north of France had basically adhered to the Germanic concept of customary law, while the south had supported Roman law. Napoleon wished to end anomalies and to liberalize many aspects of law. Aided by the lawyers Tronchet and Portalis and a team of other experts, Napoleon supervised this massive task; between July and December 2,281 articles of the Civil Code were drafted and debated in over 100 sessions of the Council of State, Napoleon finding time to preside at no less than 57 of them in person.

The task was daunting, and not without

disagreements among those who undertook it. All agreed that equality before the law, the complete destruction of relics of feudal privilege, and the inviolability of property were basic principles, as well as freedom of conscience and the civil nature of the marriage contract. Under Napoleon's urging, the importance of the father in the family unit was emphasized, but he failed to gain acceptance for other liberalizing ideas involving the family, laws of inheritance, and the status of convicted political criminals. However, he won over the issues of the wife owing obedience to her husband, and over the admissibility of divorce.

Although the draft was prepared by early 1801, it required three years of negotiation to gain the acceptance of the Tribunate, whose members raised many objections. Ultimately the Civil Code was published on 21 March 1804. Three years later it was renamed the *Code Napoléon,* and as such was applied in many European countries beyond France's boundaries, and still remains of great significance today.

The implementation of the Code within France was entrusted to the departmental prefects, eventually 83 in number, officials chosen with considerable care and entrusted with very considerable local powers. Aided by subprefects and local councils of notables, and controlling the police detachments of the national police force created in 1802, the prefects were responsible for the maintenance of law and order. Until the refractory conscript problem grew out of hand from 1812 onward, there was a slight fall in the crime index.

In 1808 the Criminal Code was promulgated. Napoleon insisted upon appointing judges by constitutional right, and in 1804 had established judicial circuits on the British model. His strong preference for the jury system did not ultimately impress the Council of State, and in 1808 juries were excluded from courts of first instance in favor of courts of arraignment, which decided whether a *prima facie* case had been made out against the accused. However, the Emperor was united with his jurists in resisting the pretensions of the military in legal matters; the soldier in peacetime was fully responsible to civil law. The year 1810 saw the production of a Penal Code.

To produce a contented and prosperous people required an enlighted educational system and a guaranteed right to free labor for reasonable return. Where education was concerned, Napoleon reopened the primary schools, created 39 *lycées* run on broadly military lines for the elite, and a further 350 state secondary schools (for boys only). A single state school for girls who were orphans of holders of the *légion d'honneur** was opened in 1807. Private secondary schools were also encouraged. At the tertiary level, a dozen schools of law were founded as well as teacher-training institutions linked to the University of France, a supervisory and examining body opened in 1808. Plans for a supreme college of professors which would embrace every discipline never materialized, but all in all Napoleon achieved a great deal in laying firm foundations for widespread basic literacy.

But for the strains of continual wars, France would have prospered greatly. The Commercial Code of 1807 regulated many aspects of trade and industrial life, and both agriculture and industry prospered, freed from ancient restrictions and provided with genuine incentives and, when needed, government aid.

Clarke, Maréchal Henri Jacques Guillaume, duc de Feltre (1765–1818). First commissioned in 1781, he was a member of the embassy in London in 1790. After a fluctuating career during the Revolution, he was attached to the *Bureau Topographique** and was promoted to *général de division* in December 1795. Sent to Italy the next November to watch Bonaparte secretly, he became his loyal subordinate. After various diplomatic roles, he backed Bonaparte at *Brumaire,** and in 1805 became Napoleon's secretary of the cabinet. After holding governorships in Austria and Prussia, he replaced Berthier* as Minister of War in August 1807 and held this post until April 1814, being made Duc de Feltre in 1809. Rallying to the Bourbons, he accompanied Louis XVIII to Ghent in 1815. The next July he was appointed *maréchal*, but gave up the War Ministry in September 1817.

Clausel, Maréchal Bertrand, comte (1772–1842). He first served in the National Guard in 1789, and eventually rose to *général de brigade* in 1799 after experience in the Pyrenees* and Spain. He fought in Italy at Novi* (1799), in Santo Domingo under Leclerc* (1801–02), and was promoted to *général de division* in 1802. He was shipwrecked off Florida but eventually returned to France. He later held posts in Holland, Italy, and Dalmatia before being posted to the Army of Portugal (1810–12). He was wounded at Salamanca,* but took over command from Marmont* and Bonet,* launched a telling counterattack, and led the retreat. Appointed to replace Caffarelli* in command of the *Armée du Nord*, he subsequently served with distinction under Soult* in the Pyrenees and south of France, fighting at Nivelle,* Nive,* St. Pierre,* and Orthez,* as well as at Toulouse.* In 1815 he rallied to Napoleon and attempted to quell the Bourbonist rising around Bordeaux. After Waterloo* he lived in exile in the U.S.A. until 1820. He next commenced a political career, but in 1830 was sent to command in Algeria; next year he was appointed a Marshal of France. In 1835 he became Governor General of Algeria, but after a defeat at Constantine and the subsequent retreat (1836) he was recalled and retired. He resumed his political career.

Clausewitz, General Karl Maria von (1780–1831). Joining the Prussian army, he fought the French on the Rhine (1793–94), and after training at the Berlin Academy was transferred to the staff on Scharnhorst's* recommendation. Captured after Auerstadt* (1806), he was released and aided Scharnhorst remodel the Prussian army. He was tutor to the Crown Prince and served with the French in Russia (1812) before defecting to the Russians. He helped negotiate the convention of Tauroggen* with General Yorck.* From 1814 he resumed service in the Prussian army and was Chief of Staff to General Thielmann* at Ligny* and Wavre* in 1815. Promoted to major general in 1818, he directed the Berlin staff college and began his historical and theoretical writing. His most celebrated work, *On War*, influenced many subsequent generations of soldiers down to the present day, particularly his beliefs that "war is the continuation of policy by other means" and that the decisive battle was the supreme moment in war. He died of cholera in 1831.

Clinton, Lieutenant General Sir Henry (1771–1829). First commissioned in 1787, he served in Holland 1788–89, and in 1793 became an aide-de-camp to the Duke of York.* Promoted to lieutenant colonel in 1795, he was a prisoner in France 1796–97. In 1799 he served as a liaison officer to Suvorov's* Russian army in North Italy. From 1802–05 he was adjutant general in India, but on returning to Europe he was again attached to the Russian army for the campaign that ended at Austerlitz,* at which battle he was present. From 1806–07 he was commandant of Syracuse in

Sicily. In 1808 he was elected a member of Parliament and began a political career that continued until 1818, with interruptions for military service. He served Sir John Moore* as adjutant general during the Corunna* campaign, and in 1810 was promoted to major general. From 1811–14 he commanded the 6th Division under Wellington* in the Peninsula, and played a notable part at Salamanca.* In 1814 he was made a lieutenant general (having been knighted the previous year), and in 1815 he fought at Waterloo.*

Coalitions, the First to Seventh (1792–1815). The energy and ideological inspiration released by the French Revolution, and later channeled into rampant nationalism by Napoleon, threatened the established European monarchies, and their reaction was to form a series of alliances in the hope of containing, and of overthrowing, the French military and political menace.

On 26 June 1792, Austria and Prussia formed the *First Coalition*. Distaste for developing French republicanism, anxiety for the Bourbon royal family, and the presence of growing numbers of *émigrés** in the Imperial fief of Trier, were the major motives. The final incentive was the French declaration of war against the King of Hungary and Bohemia (the secondary titles of the Austrian emperor) on 20 April 1792. The campaigns of Valmy* and Jemappes* followed, and after the execution of Louis XVI* in January 1793 Great Britain joined the coalition, followed by Spain in March. Russia, Holland, Naples, and Tuscany were loosely associated, but contributed little. The effectiveness of Carnot's* armies began to tell, and in February 1795 Tuscany made peace with France. The same April Prussia left the alliance by the Treaty of Basel, the new Batavian

Republic* (Holland) joined France (16 May), and Spain also left the war on 19 August by the treaty of San Idelfonso. Sardinia and Piedmont made peace with France in May 1796 after Mondovi* and Cherasco.* Bonaparte's conquest of North Italy and limited French successes on the Rhine led to Austria signing the preliminaries of Leoben* (18 April 1797), and the First Coalition finally collapsed on 17 October 1797 when Austria and France signed the Peace of Campo Formio.* Lack of coordination, sparsity of common interests, and the problem of Poland—together with French energy and martial skill—were the main causes of failure.

French actions in Switzerland, Italy, and on the Rhine, and her ambitions in the Middle East, led Britain, Austria, Russia, Naples, and Turkey to form the *Second Coalition*. Many individual treaties were signed from May 1798 onward, but the Coalition was only completed on 22 June 1799 with the conclusion of the formal Austro-British alliance. Activity centered upon Sardinia, Rome, and (from July) Egypt in 1798; the next year fighting spread to Naples, Syria, the Rhine, North Italy, Switzerland, and Holland—with Russian forces under Suvorov* joining the Austrians and British in the last two theaters. Early French reverses (as at Novi* in North Italy) gave way to successes (as at Zurich,* 26 September, which caused the Russians to retreat) and then Bonaparte returned from Egypt. The *coup d'état** of *Brumaire** led to the Consulate, and in 1800 the French counteroffensives on the Rhine and in North Italy (the Marengo* campaign) led to substantial Austrian setbacks, culminating in Moreau's* victory at Hohenlinden* on 3 December. Russia had made peace with France on 8 October, and that autumn the Armed Neutrality of the North* against Britain took effect. On 9 February 1801

Austria and France signed the treaty of Luneville*; this left only Britain in the war, but the preliminaries and the Peace of Amiens* (finally signed on 25 March 1802) brought a short period of general peace.

The Enghien* affair, Britain's wish to recover Hanover (seized by France in 1803), and a desire to restrict French expansionism led to the *Third Coalition*, formed on 11 April 1805 but effective from 9 August that year. Great Britain, Austria, Russia, and Sweden were members, with some German princes. The loss of the battles of Ulm* and Austerlitz*— and operations in North Italy around Caldiero*—doomed the Coalition to failure in its turn; an Austro-French armistice was signed on 6 December, and 20 days later came the Peace of Pressburg.* William Pitt's* death was hastened by the news of this new collapse, largely due to weak coordination, poor planning, and to the proven genius of Napoleon.

Friction with Prussia over Hanover induced Berlin to seek allies, and a series of Russo-Prussian treaties and an agreement with Great Britain led to the formation of the *Fourth Coalition*, effective from 6 October 1806. The whirlwind campaign of October-November ruined Prussia militarily (see Jena-Auerstadt), but neither Prussia nor Russia made peace. The French occupation of Warsaw led in early 1807 to the bitter Winter Campaign of Eylau,* in which Napoleon received his first serious check in battle, but in the following spring the French victory of Friedland* led to the conference and Treaty of Tilsit.* Prussia was dismembered, Russia became an ally of France, and Napoleon's power and repute appeared at their zenith. Once again Britain was left the sole opponent to Napoleon, but his attempts to set up the Continental System* to cow London proved a failure and a liability.

Growing disillusion with life in a French-dominated Europe and the transfer of French troops to Spain led Austria to seek a new British Alliance, and on 9 April 1809 the *Fifth Coalition* came into being. The Danube Campaign of April–July, with associated Italian operations, followed, but at Abensberg-Eckmühl* Napoleon regained the initiative. The setback of Aspern-Essling* proved only the curtain-raiser to the great French victory of Wagram,* and on 11 July Austria sought an armistice at Znaim. The British expedition to Walcheren* failed (August–September), and on 14 October Austria and France signed the Treaty of Vienna. Britain was again alone, but her armies were permanently in Portugal from April 1809, and the "Spanish Ulcer" would soon be exercising its long-term ill effects on France.

Following Napoleon's invasion of Russia in June 1812, Russia and Great Britain formed the nucleus of what became the *Sixth Coalition*. Spain and Portugal acceded, and after Borodino,* the retreat to the Beresina,* and subsequent French retreat into Poland, Prussia left Napoleon's alliance and joined the Coalition (27 February 1813) by the Convention of Kalisch.* Following the battles of Lützen* and Bautzen* and the armistice of 1813,* Austria also joined the alliance, followed by Sweden and numbers of German states. The French were driven west of the Rhine after Leipzig,* and the Allies invaded French soil early in 1814. On 9 March 1814 the Treaty of Chaumont* bound the Allies together most effectively, with common undertakings and aims, and the triumphant outcome of the Campaign of France led to Napoleon's first abdication and the restoration of the Bourbons.

The Allies were meeting at the Congress of Vienna* when news arrived, in March 1815, that Napoleon had returned to

France from Elba. On 25 March the *Seventh Coalition* was formed—all signatories of the Sixth becoming parties to the new agreement. Refusing to open negotiations with Napoleon, the Allies promised 500,000 men, backed by British money, to bring about his final downfall. The Waterloo* campaign of June 1815 followed, and on 22 June Napoleon again abdicated. Allied armies poured into France in July, and with Napoleon's departure for exile on St. Helena,* the need for military coalitions against France came to an end. An exhausted Europe looked forward to a period of rest, reconstruction, and peace.

Cochrane, Admiral Thomas, Earl of Dundonald (1775–1860). This famous British sailor entered the navy in 1793. Renowned for his skill at capturing prizes, he was knighted in 1809 after a bold raid against the French shipping in Aix Roads, which was compromised by Admiral Gambier's absence from the scene. Since 1807 he had been an MP, proving very outspoken concerning naval abuses, and this made him highly unpopular with his superiors. His foes achieved his ruin in 1814, but his constituents remained loyal and again returned him to Parliament. In 1818 he transferred his services to Chile during its war of liberation against Spain, and achieved major successes at sea for both that country and Peru, including the capture of Lima. After further disputes he joined the Brazilian navy in 1823, and following their successful campaign for independence from Portugal he once more transferred his allegiances in 1827—this time to aid Greece in her fight for independence against Turkey. In 1832 he was reappointed to the Royal Navy and resumed his original career, championing the cause of steam propulsion, and becoming full admiral in 1851.

Cocks, Lieutenant Colonel Charles

Somers (1786–1812). Commissioned into the 16th Light Dragoons in 1803, he saw early service in Ireland before entering Parliament in 1807. He first reached Portugal in March 1809 and fought at Talavera* before falling seriously ill. Recovered, in December he was attached to Spanish forces as an intelligence officer, and in 1810 began a long series of special missions and fact-finding tours that proved of the greatest assistance to Wellington.* He fought at Fuentes de Oñoro* and before Badajoz* in 1811, and watched the storm of the latter the following April, before transferring to the 79th Highlanders as a major. He was present at Salamanca,* entered Madrid, but was killed during the siege of Burgos* after having led a successful raid to seize the great hornwork a week after being promoted to lieutenant colonel. Wellington deplored the death of a skilled officer whom he regarded as one of the most promising men in the British army. His effectiveness as an intelligence officer was highly regarded.

Coignet, Capitaine J.R. (fl. 1805–15). French soldier and member of the Imperial Guard, whose *Cahiers* or notebooks form a colorful source of firsthand information on several Napoleonic campaigns.

Coimbra, massacre of, October 1810. After the battle of Bussaco* in Portugal, the French occupied and looted Coimbra. Massena* marched on to Torres Vedras* on 5 October, leaving 5,000 French wounded. Colonel Trant* and Portuguese irregulars raided the town and killed many of the wounded.

Colborne, Colonel Sir John, Baron Seaton (later Field Marshal) (1778–1863). Commissioned in 1794, he fought in Egypt (1801) and in Sicily (1806). He was Sir John Moore's* secretary during the

Corunna* campaign of 1808–09, and was promoted to lieutenant colonel at Moore's dying wish. He later commanded the 52nd Foot with great distinction in the Peninsular War* and at Waterloo,* being dubbed KCB in 1815. After a period as Lieutenant Governor of Guernsey, he was given the same post in Upper Canada, and crushed a revolt there in 1838. Promoted to general in 1854, he commanded in Ireland (1855–60) and became a field marshal in 1860.

Colditz, action of, 12 October 1813. This Saxon town some 30 miles southeast of Leipzig,* famed for its ancient castle and ceramic industry, was the scene of an able French rear-guard action commanded by Murat* against Schwarzenberg's* Army of Bohemia and elements of Bennigsen's* Russian forces. The French retired toward Leipzig in good order.

Cole, General Sir Galbraith Lowry (1772–1842). Commissioned a cornet in 1787, he served in the West Indies, Ireland, and Egypt. He was MP for Inniskillen from 1798–1800 and for Fermanagh, 1803–23, and fought as a brigadier general in Sicily, 1806–08. Cole was promoted to major general in 1808 and commanded the 4th Division in the Peninsula from 1809 to 1814. He was knighted in 1813 and promoted to lieutenant general in 1813. He subsequently became Governor of Mauritius (1823–28) and of Cape Colony (1828–33), and was promoted to full general in 1830.

Colli, General Michael, Baron von (fl. 1795). As Piedmontese Commander in Chief in 1795–96, Colli found it difficult to cooperate wholeheartedly with his Austrian colleagues and superiors, including de Wins and Beaulieu.* He was rapidly defeated by Bonaparte in April 1796 at Ceva* and Mondovi,* but put up a fair resistance until the armistice of Cherasco* was signed.

Collingwood, Vice Admiral Cuthbert, Baron (1750–1810). He first went to sea in 1750, and after service in American waters and in the West Indies, rose to prominence at the battle of the First of June* in 1794, and at Cape St. Vincent* (1797). He later commanded the blockades of Cadiz and Brest, and in 1805 assumed command of the fleet at Trafalgar* after Nelson's* death. Later commands included the Mediterranean (1807–08) and supervision of the blockade of Toulon* (1808–10). He died at sea and was buried in St. Paul's.

Colonna-Cesari, Colonel Giacomo (fl. 1793). A Corsican by birth, and nephew to the patriot Paoli,* Colonna-Cesari, an elderly officer of the *Gendarmerie*, commanded the abortive attack against the island of La Maddalena* (23–25 February 1793). Bonaparte, a member of the expedition, was very critical of his competence, and accused him of deliberately courting failure.

Commerce, War of (1793–1814). France waged a determined *guerre de course* against British shipping from 1793. Privateers* out of French ports made numerous attacks on British shipping in the Channel, the Mediterranean, and the West Indies. Some privateers were of large design; most were very small, but fast, heavily armed and well manned. Between 1793 and 1814 a total of 10,871 sail of British merchant shipping fell into French hands—or over 500 ships a year on the average, representing 2½% of British shipping (the average entries and departures from British ports being 21,369 *per annum*), and totaling possibly 1,375,000 tons. British losses would have been considerably higher but for the adoption of the convoy system, but Mahan estimates that one fortieth of British trade was lost.

On the other hand, British countermeasures virtually destroyed the French mercantile marine by 1799, long before the economic struggle was fully extended to involve neutral shipping following the Continental System's* implementation and the British Orders in Council.* By 1811 some 4,000 sail of French shipping was operating under the British flag.

Compans, Général Jean Dominique, comte (1769–1845). After first seeing service in 1791, he served at Toulon* and on the Italian front in many staff and command appointments. In 1805 he was Lannes'* Chief of Staff, and was wounded at Austerlitz.* After Jena,* he was promoted to *général de division* (November 1806). He was made a count three years later. In Russia, 1812, he captured the Schivardino Redoubt two days before Borodino,* and was again wounded in the main battle. He served through the campaign of 1813, being twice wounded at Mockern. Compans accepted the Bourbons in 1814 but returned to Napoleon next year. However, he refused a proffered command in the *Armée du Nord* and was retired on 7 June 1815.

Compans

Concordat, of 15 July 1801. After nine months of secret negotiations with the Papacy, the First Consul reached agreement with Pope Pius VII's* representatives after the consideration of 26 successive projects. The final 17 articles brought France back within the Roman fold, but the head of state retained the right to nominate candidates for vacant bishoprics, and bishops were required to take the oath before the First Consul. Ecclesiastical lands and goods seized at the Revolution were to remain in their new owners' hands, but the French government promised some compensation for individual losses.

The Concordat's terms faced much opposition in the Council of State, the Tribunate, and the Senate, but were finally approved on 8 April 1802. Despite later disputes with the Papacy it remained in force until 1905. Its terms served as a model for many similar agreements between the Papacy and numerous German and Italian states, as well as with Switzerland. In its original form, it was part of Bonaparte's plan to rally the Catholics of France behind the Consulate.

Congreve, Sir William, Baronet (1772–1828). The eldest son of an official of the Royal Laboratory at Woolwich, Congreve served with the Royal Artillery in 1791 before being attached to the Royal Laboratory's staff. In 1808 he invented the Congreve rocket, and next year he raised two rocket companies for the British army. Wellington* was not impressed with the weapon, but Congreve accompanied one company abroad which served at Leipzig* (the only British troops present), and later in the south of France (1814). He succeeded to the family baronetcy in 1814, and was Controller of the Royal Laboratory from that year until 1828. He was also an MP from 1812 to 1828. He wrote several works.

Conscription. In the first years of the Revolutionary wars, the French government relied upon the "volunteers of 1791" and the *fédérés* of 1792 to make up the numbers required for the armies. These measures failed to produce a satisfactory result, and in August 1793 the Committee of Public Safety decreed the *levée-en-masse* by the Requisition Law, which made all males between 18 and 25 liable for military service. The actual term "conscription" was not, however, employed until 5 September 1798, when the Jourdan* Law established it as a permanent principle. A fixed number of men were to be called to the colors in annual classes—all available manpower being divided into five groups according to age, profession, and marital status. Those who were to serve were to be chosen by either lot or conscription. From 1799, however, men about to be drafted had the right to find volunteer replacements to achieve their communal quotas, and Napoleon later extended this to include individual replacements. As the wars unfolded the demand for men grew steadily, and conscription became hated throughout the Empire. Some 2 million were called up between 1804 and 1815. Evasions of the system led to the problem of refractory conscripts.*

Conseil des Cinq-Cents. *See* **Cinq-Cents,** Conseil des

Conseil des Anciens. *See* **Anciens,** Conseil des

Conseil d'Etat, le. Created by the law of 26 December 1799, the Council of State's function was to decide upon the legality of proposed statutes and laws and to rule in cases based upon their interpretation. In view of the wide nature of its duties, the Council was divided into six sections. Certain high officers of state were members by right of their positions, the rest were appointed for life. *Auditeurs*—

bright young men with futures in the administration before them—were allowed to attend, and on occasion to participate in discussions.

Constant, Wairy, called "Constant" (1778–1845). Born in Belgium, the son of an innkeeper, he entered the First Consul's service in 1800 and remained his valet until 1814. He retired to Breteuil, where he died. His *Mémoires* were largely the work of another hand, and are accordingly suspect.

Constantine, Grand Duke (1779–1831). Born the second son of Tsar Paul I,* he served his elder brother, Tsar Alexander I* in many capacities. He commanded the Russian Guard Corps at Austerlitz* and fought at several other battles. In 1816 he became Viceroy of Poland, but proved very unpopular. He renounced his rights of succession to the Russian throne in order to marry the Polish Countess Grudzinska. A Polish revolt drove him out of his palace in November 1830, and next year he died of cholera.

Consulate, the (1799–1804). The *coup d'état** of *Brumaire* overthrew the Directory,* and on 10 November 1799, General Bonaparte, Siéyès,* and Roger Ducos* were declared "Provisional Consuls." Siéyès and Roger Ducos were soon induced to retire, and their places were filled by the ex-Jacobin Cambacérès* and the crypto-royalist Lebrun. A plebiscite approved the new arrangements by a large majority, and on 14 December the Constitution of the Year VIII came into force. Already Bonaparte was recognised as *de facto* First Consul. In 1802, between 8 and 14 May, Bonaparte was made Consul for Life, and in early August a plebiscite on the issue revealed three and a half million votes in favor and only eight thousand against. This was some measure of the First Consul's popularity in France as a whole and of his ability to cow opposition; matters were carried one stage farther when a new constitution was approved on 4 August, by which the First Consul could present for the Senate's approval the name of his proposed successor. In effect Bonaparte was now only one step away from the throne—a step that would be taken on 18 May 1804 and confirmed by a further plebiscite in November of that year. His coronation as Emperor of the French was held on 2 December 1804.

Conté, Nicolas Jacques (1775–1805). This celebrated chemist and inventor originally set up in Paris as a painter and scientist. He proposed the use of balloons for military purposes, and after their successful use at Fleurus* he was given command of the company of *aerostatiers*, but this was subsequently disbanded by the First Consul. Conté subsequently developed an artificial fabric.

Continental System, the. The idea of an economic blockade as a means to bring effective pressure to bear on Great Britain dated from the Convention, when the Committee of Public Safety decreed such a measure in 1793. Similar edicts were issued during the Directory and Consulate with varying effect, but the idea was taken up again by Napoleon with new determination in late 1806. In the hope of causing Britain grave commercial and economic trouble, to the profit of French industry and agriculture, the Emperor responded to the British maritime blockade of 16 May 1806 by issuing the Berlin Decrees (21 November 1806). By these instruments, it was proclaimed that all commerce between Britain and the Continent was to cease, and that all British goods discovered in areas occupied by the French army and its allies were to be confiscated.

The System began to bite following the Treaty of Tilsit,* which saw the ad-

herence of Russia to its aims, but Napoleon was still dissatisfied with its comprehensiveness. By the Decree of Fontainebleau (13 October 1807) and the First Milan Decree (23 November the same year), the Berlin Decrees were reinforced. In the hope of extending the restrictions to include neutrals, France declared that all colonial goods would be considered British unless a certificate of place of origin was produced on demand, and that any ships that touched at an English port were to be confiscated together with their entire cargo. These steps were taken in part on account of the British Orders in Council* of January 1807 and various other dates, which applied serious sanctions on seaborne trade with France—and which the Royal Navy proved far more effective in enforcing than Napoleon's customs officials. By the Second Milan Decree (17 December 1807), Napoleon insisted that any neutral vessel submitting to English requirements, including the Right of Search* for contraband articles, would be considered denationalized and British property, and accordingly it would constitute a legal prize. In effect this made the blockade a full act of warfare rather than a mere mercantile device. The neutrals were unable to avoid Royal Naval patrols, so the Continent was effectively closed to them. However, because much of the Continent rallied to Napoleon's call, at least at first, considerable damage was caused to British interests and prosperity. Further regulations were issued in 1810 and 1813, and at least in some measure the French economy was stimulated.

However, the neutral countries soon came to resent the trade restrictions with great bitterness, and illicit smuggling developed on a vast scale. Within a short space of time, even France's allies were resenting the effects of the system which effectively banned coffee, cotton, and cane sugar even from Paris, and evasions sprang up on every hand. Louis Bonaparte,* King of Holland, connived at his merchants' continuing to trade with Great Britain clandestinely, and his refusal to enforce the system was a major reason for his enforced abdication in 1810 and for France's subsequent takeover of the United Provinces. Many another Imperial servant was deeply involved in illegal trading, including Bourienne* at Hamburg and Massena* in North Italy.

His belief that the full Continental System must be applied eventually led Napoleon to invade Portugal, take over Spain, and, in 1812, to invade Russia. It was common knowledge that France herself was prepared to avoid the regulations and indulge in some illicit trade with Great Britain when highly favorable terms could be obtained, and this caused great resentment in St. Petersburg. Russian trade with Great Britain in corn, minerals, and naval stores had formed an important part of the economy, and it was the desire to resume these lucrative trades that led to the rapid cooling of Russo-French relations from 1810. Thus in the end the implications of the Continental System led to serious developments for France, and may be said to have rebounded with a vengeance on Napoleon's head.

Cooke, Lieutenant General Sir George (1768–1837). Commissioned into the Foot Guards in 1784, he was promoted to captain eight years later. He fought in Flanders (1794) and Holland (1799). He became a major general in 1811, and from that year until 1813 served in the Cadiz* garrison. In 1815 he commanded the Guards Division at Waterloo* and was awarded the KCB later that year. He was promoted to lieutenant general in 1821.

Copenhagen, naval battle of, 2 April 1801. The need to counter the formation of the Second Armed Neutrality of the North* induced the British government to order Admiral Sir Hyde Parker,* with Vice Admiral Nelson* as his second-in-command, to take a fleet of 26 ships-of-the-line, 7 frigates, and 23 smaller craft to the Baltic in March 1810.

The fleet anchored outside the Sound on 21 March, while diplomatic efforts continued in Copenhagen in an attempt to persuade Crown Prince Frederick, regent for the insane Christian IV, to detach Denmark from the Northern Convention. Although the failure of these talks was announced on the 23rd, it was not until the 30th that the fleet sailed through the Sound, hugging the Swedish shore to avoid the Danish gunfire from Kronborg castle, and anchored again off Hven.

The Danes had moored 18 naval vessels in a line off the shore of Amager Island, on which stands the greater part of Copenhagen, with the 66-gun Trekoner Battery at its northern end guarding the channel leading to the city. More shipping was present inside Copenhagen's port. The British admirals reconnoitered this position on the 30th, and Nelson was given command of a dozen ships-of-the line and other craft to attack the Danish fleet while Parker and the remainder stood guard off the mouth of the harbor.

On 1 April the fleet sailed east of the Middle Ground shoals (lying east of Amager Island) and reanchored; when the wind was favorable, Nelson moved his squadron to the southernmost point of the shoal and there awaited first light, spending part of the night on a further reconnaissance and in issuing his orders. Two small ships-of-the-line were to engage the Trekoner Battery, while the frigates attacked the northernmost Danish vessels, and light gunbrigs were to tackle the southern end of the line. A flotilla of bomb vessels was to station itself opposite the Danish center on the west side of the

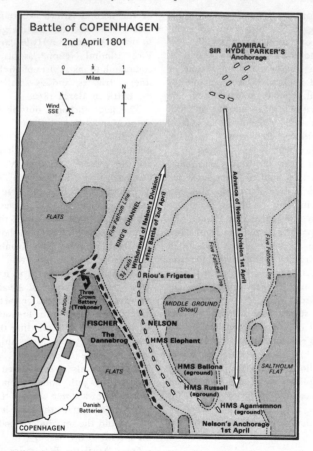

Battle of COPENHAGEN
2nd April 1801

Middle Ground. Nelson, meantime, with his 12 "74s," would sail around the Middle Ground and head north in line ahead to engage the main enemy vessels. Once in their prescribed positions, they were to anchor by the stern and engage their selected opponents.

At 9:00 A.M. on the 2nd the wind allowed Nelson to set sail; the first firing started at 10:30 A.M. and the first British ships reached their posts without delay. Then, however, matters began to go wrong. First, H.M.S. *Agamemnon* and then two more ships-of-the-line went

aground on the shoal, and the gunbrig flotilla also failed to round the obstacle. Nelson, commanding from H.M.S. *Elephant,* reorganized his depleted force and pressed on, but this meant that the frigates would have to attack the powerful Trekoner Battery unsupported. Seeing the developing problems, Admiral Parker tried to sail southward against the wind to aid his subordinate, but made slow progress, and at 1:15 P.M. he signaled Nelson to discontinue the action. Nelson placed his telescope to his blind eye and pretended not to observe the signal, but the hard-pressed frigates prepared to comply. Nelson pressed on with his attack and captured the burning Danish flagship, the *Danneborg*. The Danish commander, Commodore Fischer, twice transferred his flag, and at 2:00 P.M. Nelson sent a message ashore under flag of truce suggesting negotiations. At 3:00 P.M. a cease-fire began. In return for landing the wounded Danes, the British (who had lost 941 casualties) removed 12 prizes. The Danes suffered 790 sailors killed, 900 wounded, and 2,000 taken prisoner. More British ships went aground during the withdrawal, but the armistice held. Further operations followed against Sweden and Russia, but the death of Tsar Paul I* ended the Armed Neutrality soon afterward, and British naval prestige reached a new height.

Copenhagen, bombardment of, 16 August–7 September 1807. Learning that the French planned, by a secret clause of the Treaty of Tilsit,* to seize the Danish fleet, the British government sent Admiral Gambier with 20 sail-of-the-line and 18,000 troops under Lord Cathcart* to forestall this possibility. The soldiers landed on 16 August and began to besiege Copenhagen; 13 days later a Danish relief attempt was beaten off by Sir Arthur Wellesley's* divisional command. The fleet then moved inshore and joined in the bombardment of Copenhagen (2–5 September). On the 7th, the Regent, Crown Prince Frederick, agreed to hand over the Danish fleet of 18 sail. The last British troops were evacuated in October. This bold action—without declaration of war—was dictated by necessity and proved completely effective.

Copenhagen (horse). Named after the 1807 bombardment, the foal belonged to General Lord Grosvenor and was later bought by Wellesley.* A chestnut, 15 hands high, Copenhagen remained Well-

ington's favorite mount through the Peninsular War, and was ridden by him all day at Waterloo.* The horse died in 1836, age 28, and was buried at Stratfield Saye.

Corbineau, Général Jean-Baptiste Juvenal, comte (1776–1848). Commissioned into the 18th Cavalry in 1792, Corbineau fought in the Armies of the North, Sambre-et-Meuse, Danube, Switzerland, and in that of the Rhine between 1792 and 1800. He later served in Hanover and Poland (1807) and was made a baron (1808). He fought in Spain (1808–11), being promoted to *général de brigade* (1811). Attached to Oudinot's* II Corps in Russia (1812), he discovered the vital ford over the Beresina* near Studienka which enabled the French to escape. He became a *général de division* and an imperial aide-de-camp in 1813, saving Napoleon's life from Cossacks at Brienne* in 1814. He finally retired in 1848.

Cornwallis, Admiral Sir William (1744–1819). He entered the Royal Navy in 1755 and saw much service in the West Indies over the next 30 years. He was appointed Commander in Chief in the East Indies in 1789, and was promoted to rear admiral in 1793 and to vice admiral in 1794. Despite a major disagreement with the Admiralty in 1796, he was promoted to full admiral in 1799, and commanded the Channel fleet in 1801 and again between 1803 and 1806. He was appointed GCB in 1815.

Corps d'armée, and its System. The *corps d'armée* was the pre-eminent executive instrument of French conquest and military success during the Napoleonic wars. The subdivision of an army into large, self-contained units was by no means a new concept. The Roman legion of antiquity had inspired Marshal de Saxe* to experiment with an all-arms force of reasonable proportions in the 1740s, and Marshal de Broglie had used a similar concept for maneuvers during the 1770s. During the earlier years of the French Revolution Dubois-Crancé had called for the creation of all-arms divisions, and *corps d'armée* formed the basis of General Moreau's* *Armée d'Allemagne* in 1800. Only with Napoleon's reform of the French army between 1802 and 1804, however, did the army corps become the standard strategic and grand tactical formation.

An individual *corps d'armée* was, in effect, a miniaturized army. Commanded by a marshal or senior general, it comprised varying numbers of infantry divisions (always the basis), one division of cavalry (or occasionally only a brigade), supporting services, and a small staff. Each division had its allocation of field artillery, the cavalry had horse artillery batteries, and under corps command was at least one battery of 12 pounders. The composition was flexible; corps would be built up by the attachment of extra divisions or reduced according to their intended task, and in size might fluctuate between 9,000 men and as many as 21,000 or more. Napoleon's habit of changing the composition of some of these formations in mid-campaign—including the creation of new *corps* if he saw a need—did much to confuse enemy intelligence.

A *corps d'armée* system conferred a number of advantages. First, each corps was a balanced force, and as such was capable of engaging several times its own number of opponents for a time—Napoleon believed up to a day—while awaiting reinforcement. Secondly, because of this tactical fighting power, the various corps could march through the theater of war in dispersion, making the best possible use of the available roads and local resources, rather than in one vast, slow-moving army. Providing each corps was

within one day's hard marching of one or more neighboring formations, the system could operate effectively, aiding both speed of movement and flexibility of employment. Thus the French army under Napoleon could march dispersed until a target came in view, and then rapidly concentrate for battle.

The ultimate development of the *corps d'armée* system was *le bataillon carré* (or the "square battalion") that was used in the devastatingly short Prussian campaign of 1806 prior to Jena-Auerstadt.* Symmetrically arranged, with an advance guard, flank corps, and a reserve in rear, the *Grande Armée* could adjust itself to strategic circumstances rapidly. The previous year had seen the great concentric sweep of 210,000 men marching in dispersion from the Rhine to the Danube in the space of 11 days, leading to the positive demoralization of General Mack,* who subsequently surrendered at Ulm.* As for the fighting power of individual corps, Davout's* achievement at Auerstadt in 1806 with only his III Corps against the main part of the Prussian army, or the showing of Lannes'* V Corps against Bennigsen's* Russians during much of the battle of Friedland* in June 1807, form convincing examples.

All in all, the *corps d'armée* system was one major factor in Napoleon's successes, and similar organizations were adopted by Austria (after 1805), Prussia, and Russia (after 1806) during the rebuilding of their outclassed 18th-century-type armies.

Corridors, the, Northern and Southern. These were the two most convenient invasion routes between Spain and Portugal. The Northern Corridor was guarded by Almeida* on the Portuguese side and by Ciudad Rodrigo* and Fort San Concepcion on the Spanish side. Far to the south, the Southern Corridor also had two fortresses—Portuguese Elvas* and

Spanish Badajoz*—on each side of the arid and rocky frontier region. Both corridors saw much fighting between Wellington* and various French marshals between 1809 and 1812, when Wellington finally gained control.

Corsica, struggle for independence of. The island that saw Napoleon's birth in 1769 had a long history of turbulence. A Genoese possession from 1347, its population was constantly in revolt, and in 1768 the island was sold to Louis XV. The French regime proved equally unpopular, and resistance soon sprang up around the

patriot leader Paoli.* In 1789 the National Assembly formally assimilated Corsica into France, and Paoli recognized French sovereignty, but the passing of the Civil Constitution of the Clergy rekindled his hostility and from 1793–96 the island passed into British hands.

Corunna, battle of, 16 January 1809. The town of Corunna (or Coruña) stands on a peninsula jutting into the Atlantic on the northwest coast of Spain, and in early 1809 it was the scene of an important rear-guard battle fought by Lieutenant General Sir John Moore* against

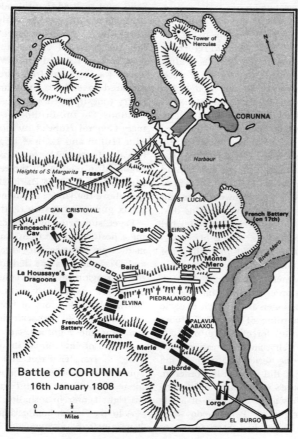

Battle of CORUNNA
16th January 1808

Marshal Soult.* Following his bold advance from Salamanca* to Sahagun* in the hope of surprising Soult's scattered divisions in December 1808, Moore had learned that Napoleon in person was leading an army over the Guadarrama Pass from Madrid to trap the British, and at once ordered a full-scale retreat to Corunna through Benavente,* Astorga,* Villafranca,* and Lugo (detaching part of his army under General Craufurd* at Astorga with orders to march west to Vigo), and under appalling winter conditions his army passed through the Cantabrian Mountains, its cohesion and discipline steadily slipping, but always managing to keep one step ahead of the pursuing French. On 2 January Napoleon handed over command to Soult prior to returning to France, and on 11 January 1809, after suffering many vicissitudes and over 5,000 deaths on the retreat, Moore brought his army to Corunna, there to await the arrival of the fleet, intending to evacuate his bedraggled men by sea.

One hundred transports escorted by twelve ships-of-the-line appeared on the 14th, and embarkation of the cavalry and artillery began at once, but many horses had to be shot. The gunpowder store had already been exploded the previous day. The 15th saw the arrival of Marshal Soult's first formations, and a brisk skirmish was fought around the village of Piedralonga, but the Duke of Dalmatia postponed a general attack until the following day in order to allow time for the rest of his 16,000 men and 40 guns to come up. By the morning of the 16th, Moore had run down his forces ashore to 15,000 infantry, 90 cavalry, and nine cannon. All morning nothing serious happened, and only at 1:30 P.M. did Soult at last order an attack, to Moore's undisguised relief. The French had drawn up their line of battle along the Heights of Penasquedo—high ground that Moore had been forced to

relinquish to the foe on account of his slight numbers. Soult placed two divisions of cavalry on the left, Mermet's and Merle's infantry divisions, with a large battery, in his center, and Delaborde's infantry and Lorge's dragoons down toward and beyond the river Mero on his right. The French aim was to hold Moore's left and center while sending the cavalry to cut his divisions off from Corunna and the waiting shipping by means of a left hook. As for Moore, his intention was simply to fight Soult off and gain sufficient time to embark his army. Moore knew that Marshal Ney's* corps was marching to reinforce Soult, and realized that the odds would be too long once the two marshals had joined forces—hence his relief when he learned that the Duke of Dalmatia was on the move at last. General Fraser's* reserve division was recalled from the port as it prepared to embark, and the British infantry took up their predesignated battle positions. On the British left near the estuary General Hope's* division took post, with Hill's* and Leith's* brigades on the forward slopes of Monte Mero with Catlin Craufurd in reserve. In the center, Moore deployed General Sir David Baird's* division above the village of Elvina, supported by six guns. The British right was refused —Paget, supported by three cannon, holding a position to the right and rear of the main line between the villages of Eiris and Oza, with Fraser's division farther to the rear again on parts of the Heights of Santa Margarita, a bare mile from the landward fortifications of Corunna. Linking his flank and rear with the main position was the highroad, and Moore felt confident of his ability, should the need arise, to transfer Paget and Fraser to a point of crisis. His main position would hinge upon Elvina, slightly in advance of his right center in a shallow valley.

A heavy French bombardment from the Penasquedo battery signaled the advance of 600 *tirailleurs* under General Jardon, followed by Mermet's packed columns, toward Elvina, while on Soult's left Lahoussaye* and Franceschi began to edge northward toward the intervening ridge of San Christobal at the head of their horsemen. Soon a heavy fight was raging around Elvina and the ridge behind it. Baird* was an early casualty, and Moore rode up to control the situation; at 3:00 P.M. he sensed an opportunity to counterattack the French 31st Regiment, which had become split by the village below, and the 42nd charged downhill. The French were taken aback, but rallied, and soon Major Napier,* commanding the 50th Foot, felt constrained to move his men to the relief of the Highlanders. Meanwhile, Moore had sent the third regiment of General Bentinck's brigade, the Fourth, to form a new line at right angles to the ridge to head off an outflanking attempt by the French 47th Regiment. The brigade commander was amiably but inconsequentially ambling to and fro on a mule, and was perfectly content to leave the tactical detail to his subordinates.

The struggle for Elvina was long and bitter, and by 3:30 P.M. both the 42nd and the 50th were spent forces, and Napier wounded and a prisoner. However, the superb fighting of these two formations had blunted Mermet's ardor, and the French advance had petered out. Sir John Moore summoned General Warde's Guards Brigade from divisional reserve, and rode off to visit Paget farther to the right. Paget had moved five of his battalions forward along the valley of the Monelos stream to head off the advancing French cavalry, which was making slow progress over the broken and rocky terrain. As the 95th weaved forward in skirmishing order, Lahoussaye ordered his cavalry to dismount and fight on foot with their carbines, but they proved no match for the British green-clad riflemen, and,

aided by the 28th and 91st, the 95th brought down such a hail of fire that the French retired. At the same time, Paget sent the 20th and 52nd to assail the flank of the French 47th, already under fire from the 4th Foot atop the ridge in the position Moore had assigned. At 4:30 P.M. the French abandoned their attempted enveloping move and retreated toward the Penasquedo Heights.

Unknown to Moore, the crisis of the day had now passed. He was, however, hard at work near Elvina, rallying the shattered 50th and 42nd—"Remember Egypt; think on Scotland!"—and organizing an attack by the Guards Brigade against Elvina and the main French battery on the ridge beyond. At 4:50 P.M. he was dashed to the ground by a cannon ball with a grave wound on his right side and shoulder, and command of the army passed to Hope. As he was carried from the field in a blanket amid his sorrowing staff, Moore frequently bade his bearers halt and turn him back toward the battle. In fact the day was practically won. After a further bitter struggle for Elvina, Hope finally regained the battered village and church using Manningham's brigade and part of Leith's. However, Hope did not feel the moment propitious for an all-out counterattack, even though Fraser's division was completely fresh. The final French attack came at 5:15 P.M. against the Piedralonga sector, but Delaborde was soon repulsed and the fighting petered out in the gathering dusk of a cold winter's day. For the loss of between eight and nine hundred men, the British had fought Soult to a standstill and inflicted about twice that many casualties. Soult decided to await the dawn, and, he hoped, the arrival of Marshal Ney, before attempting anything further against the red-clad ragged battalions.

Moore had been borne back to his headquarters overlooking the harbor. The surgeons declared his wound hopeless. When he learned of the French retreat he exclaimed: "I hope the people will be satisfied. I hope my country will do me justice." Shortly after 8:00 P.M. he died. Early on the morning of the 17th a hasty burial was performed by lantern-light in an unmarked grave on the landward ramparts, as all around the British regiments marched down to the waiting boats. His grieving staff then ". . . left him alone with his glory." He had not fought and died in vain. The embarkation was completed by 8:00 A.M. on the 18th, despite a battery moved forward by Soult to fire on the shipping, and by the last day of January, after surviving a severe gale at sea, 27,000 British troops had safely reached English ports.

Cotton, Admiral Sir Charles, Baronet (1753–1812). He first went to sea in 1772, and saw much active service between 1772–83 and 1793–1801. He was promoted to rear admiral in 1797 and to vice admiral five years later. He commanded naval units in the Tagus (1807–08), and commanded in the Mediterranean in 1810. His last appointment was the Channel fleet (1812).

Cotton, General (later Field Marshal) Sir Stapleton, Viscount Combermere (1773–1865). He entered the army in 1790, and four years later was a lieutenant colonel of cavalry. He served in Flanders (1793–94), at Capetown (1795), and in India (1799). He was promoted to major general in 1805, and became MP for Newark (1806–12). From 1808–12 he commanded cavalry in the Peninsula, fighting in many battles including Fuentes de ·Oñoro* (1811), but was sent home because of wounds. Cotton returned to fight in the campaign in the Pyrenees* (1813–14) and was created a baron in the latter year. In 1815 he commanded the Allied cavalry in France. He was Governor of

Barbados (1817–20), Commander in Chief in Ireland (1822–25), and in India (1825–30) was a full general. He captured Bhurtpore in 1826 and was made a viscount the next year. He became a field marshal in 1855.

Council of State. *See* **Conseil d'Etat**

Coups d'Etat (1794–1799). The latent instability of politics in a revolutionary era led to a series of *coups d'états* in Paris which, one way or another, affected the career of Napoleon and the fate of France.

On 27 July 1794, the coup of *9 Thermidor An II* took place. The extreme measures adopted by Maximilien Robespierre* and the Jacobin left wing of the Convention led to a strong reaction, and the "Dictator" and his main supporters were overthrown and eliminated by moderate elements led by Paul Barras* after an attack on the *Hôtel de Ville*. The "Thermidorian reaction" followed, and the "White Terror" saw the hunting down of Robespierre's confederates throughout France. Among the victims was Bonaparte, the protégé of Augustin Robespierre* since the siege of Toulon.* For part of August *général de brigade* Bonaparte was imprisoned in the Château d'Antibes on suspicion of treason.

The Jacobin cause was not yet wholly curbed, and on *12 Germinal An III* (1 April 1795) a mob invaded the Assembly but was dispersed by the National Guard. A further purge of left-wing leaders followed, and this inspired another insurrection by the Paris proletariat—that of *le Prairial* (20 May), which was again suppressed by the National Guard and the leaders guillotined.

It was next the turn of the royalists to lead a revolt. Following the publication of a new constitution placing power in the hands of a Directory* of Seven and further extending the life of the Convention by transferring two thirds of its members to the new Legislative Assembly *en bloc,* royalist sympathizers gathered at the church of Saint-Roche, and on *13 Vendémiaire* (5 October) prepared to march on the Tuileries. Barras was charged with the defense of the palace by his brother-Directors, and he sent for Bonaparte, whose guns soon scattered the crowd, causing possibly 600 casualties.

By 1797 the Directory was at the height of its unpopularity because of its venality and the breakdown of law and order, and once again crypto-royalists made a concerted attempt to sway the political scene, gaining important posts in the Assemblies. The Directors called in the army, and on *18 Fructidor An V* (4 September 1797) General Hoche* invested Paris, and a purge of the Royalists followed. In May 1798, another coup was mounted on 22 *Floréal,* this mite to thwart a new Jacobin conspiracy, and so the Directory continued on its way with apparently enhanced powers, but not for long.

Bonaparte's return from Egypt in October 1799 found the Directory in its last throes, and with the complicity of Roger-Ducos and Barras* (both of them Directors), Siéyès* and Talleyrand* resolved to achieve its overthrow. On *18 Brumaire** (9 November 1799), the *Conseil des Anciens** voted the transfer of the Legislature to Saint-Cloud and placed the troops in Paris under command of Bonaparte. The next day he presented himself before the Councils to announce the *coup d'état.* The *Anciens* were compliant enough, but the *Conseil des Cinq-Cents,** despite the efforts of its president, Lucien Bonaparte,* declared Napoleon a traitor and an outlaw. He was rescued from possible lynching by Murat's* troops, who turned the members out, and the same evening the Directory was dissolved and replaced by the Consulate of Three.* Napoleon was now well on the way to supreme power, and the turbulent period of French politics came to an unmourned conclusion.

Court, the Imperial. The creation of a court was linked to the setting up of a new nobility, a process carried through between 1804 and 1808. There was in fact a Consular Court, but only after the establishment of the Empire did Napoleon develop its organization, believing that it was a necessary, if often irksome, trapping of legitimate monarchy. An old courtier from *l'ancien régime* was brought out of retirement to teach a simplified etiquette, and the outcome was a phenomenally boring court that Napoleon often detested. Formal occasions were restricted to weekend receptions, evening entertainments, and occasional hunting parties. The authenticity of court life was much criticized by returned *émigrés,** who believed it to be a ridiculous sham. Napoleon, however, never permitted court politics to sway affairs of state. Duroc,* Grand Marshal of the Palace until his death in 1813, was the senior official of the court, assisted by hosts of chamberlains, equerries, and pages.

Couthard, Général Louis François, comte (1769–1852). After joining the army in 1791, he later served in Italy and at Rome (1798), and helped defend Genoa in 1800. After service in the *Armée du Nord* and the *Grande Armée,* he was made a baron in 1808. He was taken captive at Ratisbon,* 1809, and after release served in Spain. He became *général de brigade* in 1181. Next year he served in Russia and was wounded near Vilna* in December. He was retired as lieutenant general in November 1814, and was made a count in 1816. Recalled to service, he repressed a serious revolt in Brest (1821). He later had a political career (1827–30) but refused to serve under Louis-Philippe and resigned. He was formally retired in 1831. He was married to a cousin of Marshal Davout.*

Craonne, battle of, 7 March 1814. As Napoleon drove Schwarzenberg's* army away from Paris, Blücher* advanced with his 85,000-man Army of Silesia up the river Marne. Napoleon reacted vigorously and drove the Prussians and Russians over the river Aube. Blücher planned to form for battle on the plateau of Craonne and attempt an enveloping attack with Winzingerode's* corps and 11,000 cavalry, but before these plans could mature Napoleon pounced on Craonne on 7 March with 37,000 from the direction of Berry. Napoleon tried to pin the Allies' attention by a frontal attack while Ney* outflanked them from the north with strong cavalry forces, but the timing was wrong—Ney was badly mauled, and the Allies escaped. The Allies lost 5,000 casualties to the French 5,400. Blücher ordered Woronzow to disengage and fall back on Laon,* 15 miles to the northwest, where an important battle took place on 9 and 10 March.

Craufurd, Major General Robert (1764–1812). "Black Bob" first gained attention during the wars in India against Tippoo Sahib* (1790–92), at which time he was a captain. Promoted to lieutenant colonel in 1797, he served as Deputy QMG in Ireland during the revolt of 1798. He commanded the light brigade during the abortive campaign against Buenos Aires* (1807), and later served under Moore* with great distinction during the Corunna* Campaign, evacuating part of the army through Vigo. Back in the Peninsula under Wellington,* his mastery as a commander of light troops became legendary in such operations as the river Coa in 1810. Loved by his men despite his reputation as a strict disciplinarian, he rose to command the Light Division, and his death in the breach at the storming of Ciudad Rodrigo* was much mourned.

Cuesta, General Gregorio Garcia de la (1740–1812). Born in Old Castile, this Spanish commander first fought the French in 1793. Two years later he captured Cerdagne, and in 1798 became President of the Council of Castile. On the French invasion of Spain in 1808, he was appointed Captain General of Old Castile, but was defeated at Rio Seco and again at Medellin.* His attempts to cooperate with Wellesley* at Talavera* (1809) proved abortive, and on 12 August the old general retired after a stroke. He died in Marjorca.

Cuirassiers. *See* **Cavalry**

Czartoryski Family, the Polish. This princely Polish family, descended from 14th-century Grand Dukes of Lithuania, was a major power in their country's affairs. Adam Casimir (1734–1823), President of the Diet, accepted Russian intervention in Poland's affairs; his daughter, Maria, married Prince Louis Ferdinand of Württemburg in 1784, and his son, Adam George (1770–1861), was sent to Russia as a hostage after the Third Partition. Befriended by Alexander,* in 1801 he became the Tsar's minister for foreign affairs. He would never trust Napoleon's intentions toward Poland and bitterly opposed the creation of the Grand Duchy of Warsaw in 1807, after Tilsit.* In the next Tsar's reign he became involved in the Polish revolts of 1830 and 1831 against Grand Duke Constantine* and sought refuge in Paris.

Dalhousie, General Sir George Ramsay, Earl of (1770–1838). The ninth Earl Dalhousie commanded the 7th Division in the Peninsula and the south of France. Wellington* was sometimes critical of his performance, as during the retreat from Burgos* (1812), because of his tardy arrival on the battlefield of Vitoria* (1813), and for his misinformation about French intentions shortly before the battle of Roncesvalles.* Later in his career he became Governor of Canada and Commander in Chief in India.

Dallemagne, Général Claude, baron (1754–1813). He first joined the infantry in 1773, and after service in America (1778–83) rose to the rank of sergeant major in 1786. Commissioned in 1791, he commanded the grenadiers before Toulon,* and from 1794–95 served as a brigade commander in North Italy. Attached to Massena's* division in Italy (1796), he led the advance guard to success at Fombio and at Lodi,* and later did much to win the battle of Lonato.* Involved in the lengthy siege of Mantua,* he was promoted to *général de division* in August 1796. Later attached to the Army of England, and then the Army of Rome (1798), he was taken off the active list the next year at his own request and began a political career. After formal retirement in 1802, he was recalled in 1807 and served in Pomerania. In 1809 he helped in the repulse of the British Walcheren* expedition. He finally retired in 1813 and was made a Baron of the Empire shortly before his death.

Dalrymple, General Sir Hew Whitefoord, Baronet (1750–1830). Promoted to lieutenant in 1766, he became major in the 77th Foot in 1777. He was knighted two years later and promoted to colonel in 1790. From 1796 to 1801 he was Lieutenant Governor of Guernsey, and from 1806 to 1808 he served as Governor of Gibraltar. Sent to supersede Burrard* after Vimiero,* he signed the Convention of Cintra* and was recalled to face an enquiry. Nicknamed "Dowager," he became a full general in 1812 and was created a baronet in 1815.

Damascus, Ahmed, Pasha of. As ruler of one of the five *pashaliks* or regions of Syria, the Pasha spurned Bonaparte's offers of negotiations in 1798, and next year collected 35,000 troops with whom he attempted to interfere in the French siege of Acre.* He was, however, totally routed by Bonaparte and Kléber* at the battle of Mount Tabor.*

Danzig, siege of, 18 March–27 May 1807. Following the bitter battle of Eylau* in February, Napoleon ordered the army back into winter quarters, with the exception of the X Corps, which was sent under Marshal Lefebvre* to besiege the important port and fortress of Danzig on the Baltic coast of Prussia. The garrison comprised 14,400 infantry and 1,600 cavalry, supported by 349 guns of all types, and the Prussian Governor, General Kalkreuth,* was also fortunate to have full storehouses and stout defenses, both natural (marshes and streams) and man-made.

The French invested this redoubtable fortress on 18 March, and on 2 April the first parallel was opened against the western defenses. The second was established on the 14th, and the third on the 15th— by which time the French were close to the city's defenses. A number of sorties were beaten back and an assault seemed imminent, when on 10 May a Royal Naval and Russian squadron appeared off the mouth of the Vistula and landed 8,000 reinforcements under General Kamenskoi* at the small port of Neufahrwasser. The French were already in possession of the neighboring island of Holm, and this caused Kamenskoi to spend time establishing a fortified camp. This delay enabled Lefebvre to summon Lannes'* Reserve Corps (15,000) to the assistance of his own 20,000 men, and when Kamenskoi at last advanced toward Danzig on 15 May, the local French forces holding the outlying area of the .Frische Nehrung were able to defy the Russians until Lannes and Oudinot* arrived with reinforcements. Kamenskoi was then repulsed with 1,500 casualties, and thereafter his only thought was re-embarkation of his men, which was achieved on the 25th.

Kalkreuth had failed to make a major breakout attempt with his garrison to coincide with Kamenskoi's advance, but was still full of fight. On 20 May he led a determined sortie which did considerable damage to the French siegeworks. However, the next day Marshal Mortier* arrived at the head of his VIII Corps of 12,900 to further reinforce Lefebvre and Lannes. Aware that the Hagelsberg bastion was likely to be assaulted in the near future, and that this would surely doom the city, Kalkreuth opened negotiations with a French *parlementaire* on 22 May, and agreed to capitulate on the 27th. The Prussians were permitted to march out with the full honors of war, and marched off to rejoin their colleagues at Pillau. In

recognition of his success, Lefebvre was created *duc de Danzig* in 1808. So ended one of the relatively few major sieges (outside the Peninsula) of the Napoleonic wars.

Daru, Pierre Bruno, comte (1767–1829). After service in the Bourbon army from 1783, he became attached to the Ministry of War. He held a number of important posts in Paris, joined the Tribunate in 1802, and became a Councillor of State two years later. From 1805 he was *intendant-général* of the *Grande Armée,* charged with finding its supplies. A highly gifted administrator, Daru was reconciled with the Bourbons in 1819 and became a peer of France. Since 1806 he had been a member of the French Academy, and he wrote several works.

Davidovitch, General Paul von, baron (fl. 1796). This Austrian commander was assistant to Würmser* during both of his attempts to relieve besieged Mantua* in the second half of 1796, and to Alvintzi* in his November offensive. On 29 July, Davidovitch commanded 10,000 men in the central Austrian column that forced a crossing over the Adige at Dolce and impelled Bonaparte to abandon the line of the Adige, but the overall Austrian scheme was thwarted at Lonato* and Castiglione,* and Würmser retired to Trent. On 2 September, Bonaparte attacked Davidovitch near Trent, only to find that Würmser was advancing down the Brenta valley toward Bassano.* Massena* repulsed Davidovitch at Roveredo* on 4 September, as Bonaparte followed the main army. Lastly, in November, Alvintzi left Davidovitch to pin Joubert* near Rivoli during the Arcola* campaign.

Davout, Maréchal Louis Nicholas, duc d'Auerstadt and prince d'Eckmühl (1770–1823). Born the son of a cavalry officer of noble descent, Davout was commissioned into his father's regiment in 1788. He wel-

Davout

comed the coming of the Revolution, but his overenthusiasm, together with a mutiny, led to his arrest and resignation in 1791. A week later, however, he was elected lieutenant colonel of the 3rd Battalion of Volunteers of the Tonne, his home region, and he later fought at Neerwinden* (1793). When General Dumouriez* defected, Davout tried to arrest him and had his unit open fire. He was promoted to *général de brigade* on 25 July 1793, but again resigned the next month when the Assembly decreed that ex-aristocrats were not to serve in the field. He returned to the service in October 1794, and commanded cavalry on the Moselle and then the Rhine. After capturing Mannheim under Desaix's* overall command, he was taken prisoner when the town changed hands but was released on parole and subsequently exchanged. He next served in Ambert's division at Kehl and Haslach in 1796, and helped Desaix cross the Rhine at Diersheim in April 1797. He also captured Pichegru's* correspondence, which led to the disgrace of that general.

After being introduced to Bonaparte by Desaix, he was appointed to the staff of the Army of the Orient and fought at the Pyramids,* campaigned with Desaix in Upper Egypt against Murad Bey,* and took a leading part in the battle of Aboukir* (July 1799). On his way back to France in 1800 he was captured by the Royal Navy, but subsequently released from Livorno after one month. He was promoted to *général de division* on 3 July 1800. Later that year he commanded the cavalry of the Army of Italy.

Returning to France in July 1801, he was made Inspector General of cavalry and from November commanded the grenadiers of the Consular Guard. He was appointed a Marshal of the Empire on 19 May 1804, and became a colonel general of the Imperial Guard. After service near the Channel coast, in September he was appointed to command the III Corps of the *Grande Armée,* and he served with distinction in the War of the Third Coalition,* particularly at Zell* (or Maria Zell)* and at Austerlitz,* where he commanded Napoleon's right wing. The next year he earned great fame for defeating the Duke of Brunswick* at Auerstädt* on 14 October, despite being seriously outnumbered and deprived of the aid of Bernadotte's* corps. Napoleon allowed him to be the first to enter Berlin on 25 October in recognition of this feat, but was also somewhat resentful of his subordinate's achievement at Auerstädt, which to some extent detracted from the Emperor's own at Jena* the same day.

As the campaign of 1806 continued, Davout entered Custrin, Posen, and Warsaw, and won an engagement at Golymin* on 26 December. He commanded the French right wing at Eylau* in February 1807, where he was wounded, and later captured Königsberg. He was appointed Governor General of the Grand Duchy of Warsaw after Tilsit* and was created

Duke of Auerstädt in March 1808. After a brief period of command on the Rhine, he was given command of the III Corps of the Army of Germany on 30 March 1809, and in the war against Austria served at Eckmühl* (where his corps made the crucial attack), Ratisbon,* and Wagram,* where he commanded the French right wing with great drive and success. On 15 August he was rewarded with the title of Prince of Eckmühl; by this time he had also received grants and pensions worth more than a million francs a year. Some years before he had married General Leclerc's* sister.

In 1810 he commanded the French forces on the Rhine with headquarters at Hamburg, and became Governor of the Hanseatic Towns. In 1811 he was given command of the I Corps of Observation of the Elbe, which became the I Corps of the *Grande Armée de Russie* on 1 April 1812. With the invasion of Russia, he took over command of Jerome Bonaparte's* army when the King of Westphalia threw up his appointment, and in the course of the campaign occupied Minsk and Borisov and defeated Bagration* at Mohilev (23 July). After fighting at the battle of Smolensk* in August, he was wounded next month at Borodino.* Napoleon disregarded his plea on the eve of battle to employ an outflanking maneuver, and lived to regret his own decision to mount a frontal attack against Kutusov.*

With the retreat from Moscow, his fortunes declined slightly. Davout fought at Maloyaroslavetz* on 24 October, and was given command of the rear guard from 26 October to 3 November, fighting actions at Kolotsköi and Viasma, where Eugène Beauharnais* saved him from being cut off. However, the Emperor decided that Davout was marching too slowly, and thereafter awarded the post of honor to Ney.* Davout rejoined the main army after a stiff fight at Krasnoe* (17 Novem-

ber), but was unjustly criticized for Ney being cut off in his turn. By this time the I Corps, in June the best-equipped formation in the army, was down to one seventh of its original size (72,000), and after the hard-fought crossing of the Beresina* in late November it numbered only 3,000 survivors.

In the Campaign of Germany, Eugène appointed Davout to defend Dresden,* but he was then switched on Napoleon's order to occupy Hamburg,* which he did on 30 May. He held this great city for just under one year, winning the action of Lauenburg on 18 August 1813. He only evacuated Hamburg to the Allies on 27 May 1814 on receipt of a direct order from Louis XVIII,* a month after Napoleon's abdication.

Forbidden to enter Paris by the Bourbons, he lived on his estate at Savigny-sur-Orge until Napoleon returned from Elba.* He then became Minister of War from 20 March to 8 July 1815, and was made a peer of France. Napoleon also appointed him Governor of Paris—a key political appointment—but might have been better advised to give him command of the right wing of the *Armée du Nord* instead of Grouchy* during the Waterloo* Campaign, for no soldier was better qualified to face the Prussians. On 22 June Davout was given charge of the defense of Paris and checked Blücher's* advance on the capital, but on 3 July he agreed to evacuate the capital and marched the army to the Loire. Napoleon had re-abdicated on 22 June. On 14 July Davout submitted to Louis XVIII, and two weeks later was dismissed from all his posts, deprived of his peerage and exiled to Louviers under police supervision. In August 1817 he was reinstated, and readmitted to the peerage in March 1819. He died of consumption in Paris four years later on 1 June.

Davout was one of Napoleon's ablest and most loyal marshals. Dour and rough in manner, he was no courtier, and his severity was much criticized. His eyesight was weak, but his talents as a field commander were most pronounced. He never held a truly independent command, but as Napoleon himself wrote of this austere and commanding personality, "This Marshal displayed distinguished bravery and firmness of character, the first qualities in a warrior." Fittingly, his descendant was until recently director of the *Musée de l'Armée* in *Les Invalides*.

De Galles, Admiral. *See* **Morard de Galles**

Dego, battle of, 14–15 April 1796. After his success at Montenotte* in the Ligurian Alps, General Bonaparte had split his opponents and decided to follow the retiring Piedmontese forces of General Colli.* He left Massena* charged with holding off Beaulieu's* Austrian army by occupying a position around Dego. Massena found Dego occupied by a sizable force (possibly 5,000 Austro-Piedmontese) on the 13th, and next day assaulted the position, capturing 4,000 prisoners and taking 19 guns. On the 15th, however, Massena allowed his 8,500 troops to scatter in search of food, and in this unfortunate position was suddenly surprised by five Austrian battalions at daybreak, under command of General Wukassovitch. Massena was almost captured, and all his guns were taken. Bonaparte returned from pursuing Colli posthaste at the head of La Harpe's 8,000 men, and later on the 15th restormed the village for a loss of 1,000 French casualties. Then, his eastern flank again secure, Bonaparte set out once more toward Ceva* on the road to Mondovi,* intent upon defeating Piedmont.

Dejean, Général Pierre François, comte (1780–1845). The son of an engineer general, he served his father as ADC in 1795–96 and in 1800. In 1803 he became

Dejean

a dragoon and served in the campaigns of 1805–07, being promoted to colonel in 1807. Service in Portugal and Spain followed, and in 1811 he became *général de brigade*. After the Russian campaign, he was made ADC to Napoleon in 1813 and promoted to *général de division* in 1814. Briefly reconciled to the Bourbons, he rejoined Napoleon in 1815 and fought at Ligny.* After Waterloo* he was exiled until 1818. In later years, he frequently served as an Inspector General of cavalry.

Delaborde, Général Henri François, comte (1764–1833). Enlisting as a private in the *Régiment de Condé* in 1783, he rose rapidly during the Revolution. He was made *général de division* in 1793 and served with distinction at Toulon.* Service in the Pyrenees, on the Rhine, and in Germany followed (1794–1801), and in 1807 he commanded a division under Junot* in the invasion of Portugal. Defeated by Wellesley* at Roliça* in 1808, he later re-entered Spain under Soult,* and fought at Corunna* and Oporto.* After Russia he commanded a division of the Young Guard in 1813, but was badly wounded at Pirna.* Rallying to Napoleon in 1815, he became his Chamberlain and a peer of France.

Delancey, Colonel Sir William Howe (d. 1815). Of Huguenot origin, he was born in New York and by 1793 was a lieutenant in the 16th Light Dragoons. Service in the West Indies (1795) was followed by long years of duty in the Peninsula as Wellington's* assistant and later as Deputy Quartermaster General (1809–14). He was present at Ciudad Rodrigo* and Vitoria,* but was killed at Waterloo.* He had been made a Knight Commander of the Bath.

Delmas, Général Antoine Guillaume de la Coste (called Delmas) (1766–1813). First commissioned in 1784, Delmas was dismissed for insubordination in 1788. He re-emerged as a lieutenant colonel of volunteers in 1791 and served on the Rhine front, being promoted to *général de division* in September 1793. He later served under Desaix* (1796), fought at Rastadt and Neresheim, and was wounded in a cavalry charge at Neuburg. Transferred to North Italy, he replaced Rey* as divisional commander (11 March 1797), and later held various administrative posts there. In 1800 he fought at Moesskirch and Biberach on the Rhine, and later served once more in Italy. In December 1801 he became inspector general of infantry, but his irreligious attitudes caused his disgrace and unemployment from 1802–13. Recalled to service, he commanded a division under Ney* at Bautzen,* fought at Katzbach,* and was severely wounded at Leipzig.* He died of his wounds on 30 October 1813.

Delort, Général Jacques Antoine Adrien, baron (1773–1846). After joining as a volunteer in a Jura unit (1791) he was commissioned next year. After varied experience, he was attached to Sérurier's* staff in 1797 and served in Italy until 1801. He fought with distinction at Austerlitz,* receiving two wounds, served in Naples (1806), and from 1808–13 served in Spain, mostly under Suchet* in Catalonia. A dashing cavalry commander, he won many minor engagements. Made a Baron of the Empire in 1811, he helped cover Suchet's retreat from Spain in 1813. During the Campaign of France (1814), he was wounded at Montereau,* but was promoted to *général de division* on 26 February. In 1815 he charged at Ligny,* was twice wounded at Waterloo,* and lived in retirement until 1830. He then began a political career associated with military appointments, becoming an aide-de-camp to King Louis-Philippe (1832), and was made a peer of France in 1837. He headed several important commissions on military affairs.

Delzons, Général Alexis-Joseph, baron (1775–1812). After service as a volunteer, he became an officer of grenadiers (1792) and fought in Spain. In 1796 he fought under Bonaparte at Montenotte,* was wounded at Dego,* and served at Lodi* and Rivoli.* In Egypt he fought at Alexandria* and the Pyramids,* and aided Menou* in the defense of Alexandria (1801). The First Consul confirmed his promotion to *général de brigade* on his return to France (1801). In the following years he served in Austria, Dalmatia, and Illyria, and fought at the battles of Wagram* and Znaim* (wounded) in 1809. He was made a Baron of the Empire (1808) and promoted to *général de division* (1811). He invaded Russia with Eugène Beauharnais* and the IV Corps in 1812, fought at Ostronovo* and Borodino,* but was killed at Maloyaroslavetz* on 24 October.

Dennewitz, battle of, 6 September 1813. After his victory at Dresden,* Napoleon sent Ney* toward Berlin. He was marching with Oudinot's* corps some 40 miles southwest of his objective when he was ambushed by Bernadotte* (now fighting with the Allies) and General von Bulow* at Dennewitz. The Prussians attacked the French flank, and after a fierce fight Ney was driven back to Torgau on the Elbe with the loss of 10,000 troops. The Allies lost some 3,000 less. This setback persuaded Napoleon to concentrate his forces behind the Elbe in the general vicinity of Leipzig.*

Desaix, Général Louis Charles, Chevalier de Veygoux (so-called) (1768–1800). This distinguished French soldier was first commissioned in 1783. He quarreled with his noble family in 1791, and was soon serving the Republic on the Rhine. Promoted to *général de brigade* in September 1793, and to *général de division* next year, he served with great distinction on the Upper Rhine and in Germany, part of the time under Moreau,* fighting at Rastadt, Ettlingen, and Neresheim, and winning the battle of Biberach, all in 1796, and defending Kehl for several months. In early 1797 he joined Bonaparte in North Italy.

Desaix

Next year he sailed for Egypt, led the attack on Malta,* and won the battle of Ramanieh. After Bonaparte's departure for Syria, Desaix conquered Upper Egypt, fighting a very active campaign against Murad Bey.* He was nicknamed "the Just Sultan" by the local inhabitants. In 1800 he signed the Convention of El Arish,* but was captured en route to France by the Royal Navy and only gained his freedom in time to rejoin Bonaparte at Stradella in North Italy. As the crisis of the Campaign of 1800 approached, he was detached with two divisions to march on Novi,* but hearing the sound of the guns, returned in time to save the day at Marengo* on 14 June. He was killed leading the decisive attack. Much admired by Bonaparte, his death was widely mourned.

Desgenettes, Dr. Nicolas René Dufriche (1762–1837). Trained at Montpellier, this celebrated French surgeon served the Armies of Italy and of the Orient. At Jaffa* he courageously innoculated himself with the pus from plague victims, and boldly opposed Bonaparte's order for the mercy killing of the plague patients during the retreat from Acre.* In later years he was made Inspector General of the medical services, and served in both the Russian and the Waterloo* campaigns—being taken prisoner in the former but released on the Tsar's order. Until 1822 he was professor of the medical faculty at Paris, and was senior medical practitioner at *Les Invalides.** He was a distinguished member of the Academy of Sciences, and Napoleon greatly esteemed him, regarding him as second only to the great Larrey.*

Despinois (or Despinoy), Général Hyacinthe François Joseph, comte (1764–1848). A gentleman cadet of the *Régiment de Barrois* (or 91st) in 1791, he first rose to note at the siege of Toulon,* where he served as Dugommier's* Chief of Staff. He was badly wounded, and later promoted to *général de brigade*. In 1796 he fought at Mondovi,* and in June became *général de division*. He recaptured the citadel of Milan and was present at Lonato,* but was removed from his command by Bonaparte for refusing to engage the Austrians on 3 August. Thereafter, most of his posts were as garrison commander, for example, in Alexandria (North Italy) and Perpignan. He was formally retired in May 1815, but later emerged in 1830 when he vainly tried to check the new revolution at Nantes. He was arrested, released, and thereafter lived in retirement.

Dessolles, Général Jean Joseph Paul Augustin, marquis (1767–1828). Of noble birth, his early career from 1792 was stormy, but from 1796–99 he served in the Army of Italy, becoming a *général de brigade* in May 1797, and a *général de division* in 1799. In that year he fought at Novi,* and in 1800 at Biberach and Hohenlinden.* Service with Hanoverian forces led to a period in retirement (1804–08), as he would not serve under Lannes* out of loyalty to the disgraced Moreau,*

Dessolles

but in 1808 he was given a command under Ney* in Spain; he fought at Talavera* (1809) and Ocaña.* Recalled to France in 1811, he later served in Russia but was invalided home from Smolensk.* In 1814 he rallied to the Bourbons and did not rejoin Napoleon in 1815, but escorted Louis XVIII* to Béthune. In 1817 he was made a marquis, and in 1818 became president of the Council of Ministers and Foreign Minister. He was retired in 1819.

Dickson, Major General Sir Alexander (1777–1840). Commissioned into the Royal Artillery in 1794, he commanded the guns at the siege of Valetta in Malta* in 1800. He performed a similar role in Buenos Aires* (1807) and then served Wellesley* as a brigade-major at Oporto* the next year. He was attached to Portuguese forces under Beresford* and was promoted to lieutenant colonel, and from 1811 he was superintendent of Wellington's artillery in the Peninsula, earning his trust. In 1813 he commanded the guns at Vitoria* and two years later fought at Waterloo.* In 1822 he was appointed Inspector of Artillery and in 1833 he became Director General of the field-train department. He was made a major general four years later.

Diebitsch-Zabalkansky, General Karl Friedrich (1785–1831). Born a Prussian subject in Silesia, the son of an aide-decamp of Frederick the Great,* Diebitsch transferred to the Russian service after 1806. In late 1812 he commanded Russian troops that cut off General Yorck's* Prussian column near Tilsit—an event that led to the Convention of Tauroggen.* Promoted to lieutenant general in 1813, the next year he produced the plan for the Allied direct march on Paris. From 1820 he was the Tsar's Chief of Staff, and in 1825 quelled several plots against Tsar Nicolas. In 1828 he led a successful campaign against the Turks, capturing Adrianople. For this feat he was awarded the baton of field marshal. In 1831 he defeated the Polish rebels, but either committed suicide or died of cholera soon afterward.

Directory, the (1795–1799). Set up as the executive power by the Constitution of the Year III, the five Directors were elected by action of the Councils of Ancients (*les Anciens*)* and Five Hundred (*les Cinq-Cents*).* Replacing the National Convention from 27 October 1795, the Directory of Five tried to further the policies of the Thermidorian Convention, encountering both royalist and extremist Jacobin opposition. The Jacobin* Club was closed in 1796, and the Directory's foreign policy secured alliances with Spain, Sardinia, and Parma, and treaties of neutrality with Bavaria and Wurttemberg. The achievements of General Bonaparte in Italy led to the peace of Campo Formio* with Austria.

From 1797, however, the fortunes of the Directory rapidly declined. Unsatisfactory results in national elections led to several purges within its ranks, and a number of engineered *coups d'état* to set aside the electoral results—for instance those of 18th *Fructidor* and *Floréal* in 1797 and 1798 respectively. These irregular events indicated the insufficiency of the current constitution, and the Directory became increasingly discredited because of financial chaos at home and military defeat abroad in Germany, Switzerland, and above all in Italy at the hands of the Second Coalition.* Bonaparte returned from Egypt to serve as the "sword" of two Directors, Siéyès* and Barras,* who plotted the overthrow of their own government at *Brumaire*—just as the overseas military situation swung in France's favor with Massena's* victory at Zurich* and Brune's* at Bergen. These successes came too late to stop the tide of events at Paris, and the unmourned Directory gave place to the Consulate.*

Division. Military formation comprising two or more brigades of cavalry or infantry with appropriate artillery support. France had permanent divisions from the outset of the wars, largely on the advice of Dubois de Crancé,* but in the case of Great Britain these were only formally adopted from about 1809. Prior to that date, British divisions were *ad hoc* organizations with no permanent existence. Varying numbers of divisions went to make up army corps* in the French armies from 1799, and this pattern was widely copied by Continental powers from 1805–07, but not by Great Britain.

Djezzar Pasha, Ahmed (c. 1735–1804). Born a Christian in Bosnia, Ahmed fled to Cairo after a murder and became a Moslem. His patron, Ali Bey, used him to eliminate his foes, and his ruthless activities earned him the nickname of "the Butcher." After quarreling with the Mameluke* leader, he fled to Syria, where the Sultan appointed him Governor of Acre. Aided by Commodore Smith* and the *émigré* Phélypeaux* he successfully defied Bonaparte in the stalwart defense of Acre.*

Doctorov (or Dokhturov), General Dmitri Sergeivich (fl. 1812). This Russian commander led a division at Austerlitz,* and suffered heavy casualties near the Satschan lakes during the rout of Buxhowden's* vast column. In 1807 he fought in a similar capacity at Eylau,* and in 1812 he helped hold the outskirts of Smolensk.* In September he held a prominent post under Kutusov* at Borodino,* commanding the Tsar's VI Corps. When the French left Moscow in October, it was Doctorov who advanced from Tarutino to seize the important road junction at Maloyaroslavetz* to head off the *Grande Armée* from the direction of Kaluga.

Dolgoruki (or Dolgorouki), Count Peter Petrovich (1776–1806). A member of an established princely Russian family, Dolgoruki was the great favorite of Tsar Alexander I* and an opponent and rival of Adam Czartoryski,* the influential Polish noble and Russian Foreign Minister. In 1805, Dolgoruki served Alexander as aide-de-camp, and held an important interview with Napoleon shortly before the battle of Austerlitz,* which led the Allies to underestimate the French capacity.

Dombrowski, Général Jean Henri Dabrowski (so-called) (1755–1818). Born near Cracow in Poland, he first served in Saxon forces (1770–84) before entering the Polish army in 1791. He moved to France in 1795, raised a Polish legion that served in North Italy, the Cisalpine Republic,* and Naples, and after distinguishing himself at Novi* in 1799 he was promoted to *général de division* in 1800 (effective date). After further service in Italy, he organized a Polish division at Posen (late 1806), and with it served at Danzig* and Friedland* (1807). From 1809 Dombrowski commanded a division under Poniatowski* in the Grand Duchy of Warsaw. In 1812 he fought in Russia, losing Borisov to overwhelming Russian forces on 21 November, and being wounded at the Beresina* thereafter. In 1813 he fought at Mockern* and Leipzig,* succeeding to the command of the VIII Corps on Poniatowski's death. After Napoleon's fall in 1814 he returned to Poland, and was reinstated in his rank and made a senator by Tsar Alexander I.* He retired into private life in 1816.

Dommartin, Général Elzéar Auguste Cousin de (1766–1799). Commissioned into the French Royal Artillery in 1785, he later served at Toulon* (1793), and was promoted to *général de brigade* despite illness. He later served under Sérurier* and Massena,* fighting at First Loano (1795). The next year he fought at

Dommartin

Montenotte* and Mondovi,* suppressed the revolt of Pavia, and served at Castiglione* and Roveredo,* usually at the head of the horse artillery. In late 1797 he became artillery commander in the Army of the Rhine and, in 1798, of the Army of the Orient. As such he fought at Alexandria,* the Pyramids,* and at the sieges of El Arish* and Acre.* In 1799 he received wounds in an ambush on the Nile, and died of tetanus.

Domon, Général Jean Simon, baron (1774–1830). Joining the military as a volunteer in 1791, he soon earned a commission and a reputation in the cavalry. He fought at Jemappes* and in many other actions, usually with the hussars. In 1805 he was wounded at Elchingen,* fought at Jena* the next year, and later at Eylau,* Friedland,* and (in 1809) at Wagram* and Znaim.* He was made a Baron of the Empire in 1810. In 1812 he served at Ostronovo* and at Borodino,* and in October was promoted to lieutenant general in the Army of Naples. He returned there with Murat* in late 1813, and on the King's fall he moved to France, where his rank was confirmed. In 1815 he fought at Ligny* and was wounded at Waterloo.* After a period of eclipse, he re-emerged in 1820 as an inspector of cavalry, and in 1823 served in Spain, his last active service.

Donkin, General Sir Rufane Shaw (1773–1841). Commissioned into the 44th Foot in 1793, he served in the West Indies (1796), and in 1809 commanded a brigade at Talavera.* Two years later he was promoted to major general. He served in the Mahratta War (1817–18) before becoming acting governor of the Cape of Good Hope in 1820. He later entered Parliament and was promoted to full general in 1838. He was the author of a book on the river Niger.

Donzelot, Général François Xavier, comte (1764–1843). He became a soldier in 1783, and was first commissioned in the 21st Cavalry in 1792. He fought at Neerwinden* and from 1793–97 saw much service on the Rhine in various staff capacities. In 1798 he was transferred to the Army of the Orient and served on Desaix's* staff, fighting in many engagements in Egypt. He recaptured Cairo from rebels in April 1800, and was confirmed as *général de brigade* in March 1801. He unwillingly signed the surrender of Cairo to the British on 27 June 1801. After his eventual return to France, he held a number of staff posts, was promoted to *général de division* on 6 December 1807, and was made a Baron of the Empire in 1808. Service in Corfu and the Ionian Isles from 1807 came to an end in 1814 when he handed over the former to the British. In 1815 he joined d'Erlon's* I Corps and fought as a divisional commander at Waterloo.* Suspended in August 1815, he eventually was made Governor of Martinique in August 1817, a post he held until 1828. He finally retired in 1832.

Doppet (or Pervenche), Général François Amédée (1753–1799). After enrolling in the cavalry in 1770, he transferred to the *Gardes Françaises* the next year. He studied medicine at Turin, and in 1790 became an NCO of the Grenoble National Guard. Two years later he was elected lieutenant colonel, and in 1793, after various political appointments, he was promoted to *général de brigade*. Following service in the Alps he was made *général de division* in September 1793, succeeding Kellermann* in command. He was sent to recapture Lyons from the royalist rebels, and then to replace Carteaux* in the prosecution of the siege of Toulon,* a post he held only from 7 to 17 November, largely because of the machinations of Bonaparte. He was given a command in the Western Pyrenees, but illness interrupted his career. After various twists of fortune, he was put in charge of recruiting in the Moselle and Vosges regions (1795–96) before being retired in 1797. An attempt to enter the political arena in 1798 failed after his election to the Council of Five Hundred (*Cinq-Cents*)* was annulled.

Dornberg, General Wilhelm von (fl. 1815). Originally a colonel in Jerome Bonaparte's* Westphalian army, Dornberg deserted to the Allies in 1813 and was appointed to a command in the Hanoverian cavalry. On 15 June 1815, he intercepted near Mons a vital letter from Wellington's* chief intelligence officer, Sir Colquhoun Grant,* which revealed that Napoleon was advancing directly on Brussels from Charleroi, and not toward Mons. Instead of forwarding it to the Duke in Brussels, however, he returned it to its sender as being patently inaccurate. Vital news thus failed to reach Wellington until during the Duchess of Richmond's ball early on the 16th. Dornberg's later career is shrouded in (explicable) obscurity.

Douro, crossing of the (1808). *See* **Oporto**

Dragoons, the. *See* **Cavalry**

Dresden, battle of, 26–27 August 1813. After the breakdown of the Armistice of 1813,* the Army of Bohemia, comprised of some 230,000 Austrians and Russians, advanced on Dresden, capital of Napoleon's ally the King of Saxony. Napoleon was at the time trying to attack Blücher's* Army of Silesia, which was threatening Ney's* corps, and was moving east over the river Bobr—but the Prussians retired before him in accordance with their agreed strategy, the Trachenberg Plan.* The Emperor soon learned from Gouvion St. Cyr* (whose XIV Corps was the only French force near Dresden) of the Austro-Russian advance being led by Prince Schwarzenberg* (who was accompanied by the Tsar, the Austrian Emperor, and the King of Prussia), and at once set out for Dresden, followed by the troops of the Guard,* of Vandamme,* Marmont,* and Victor.*

On the 22nd, St. Cyr's advanced posts were driven in by the Allies, and next day Wittgenstein's* command was near the city, but a strong counterattack by St. Cyr on the 25th won the French a little more time, and the Allied attack on the city was postponed for one day.

Napoleon meanwhile was planning a strong attack on the Allied flank along the south bank of the river Elbe, but complications on distant sectors doomed this typical Napoleonic strategic maneuver— Oudinot's* defeat at Gross-Beeren* near Berlin being the most serious. Although he still hoped to launch his master stroke on the 26th, Napoleon was now worried about St. Cyr's ability to hold on at Dresden alone, and sent General Gourgaud* to report on the situation. He reported back late on the 25th that St. Cyr would go under unless reinforced at once. Napoleon therefore set out for the city with the Guard, the Reserve Cavalry, Marmont, and Victor, leaving Vandamme with only a single corps for the outflanking attack.

Napoleon entered Dresden early on the 26th, bringing the French strength up to 70,000 men. He found St. Cyr holding an extemporized defense line, and expecting to be attacked at any minute. The Allies' monarchs and generals, disconcerted by the cries of *"Vive l'Empereur!,"* were debating whether to abandon their attack, when the Allied troops decided the issue for their commanders by attacking before the orders could be canceled, and the battle opened.

The first day's fighting, mostly in the afternoon, saw St. Cyr taking the brunt of the action while Murat,* Ney, and Mortier* took command of special columns in his support. Somehow St. Cyr's line held, and at 5:30 P.M. Napoleon's counterstroke was launched, led by the Guard; almost every sector was recovered by nightfall. Overnight, the French forces grew to 120,-000 men as Victor and Marmont arrived with their corps. Schwarzenberg's strength rose only from 150,000 to 170,000, as the need to check Vandamme's attack away to the east (below strength though it was) had absorbed 38,500 men, and a further 21,000 were too far distant to reach the field in time.

On the 27th the Allies massed 120,000 men for a huge blow against the French center; Napoleon was planning the reverse—a holding action in the center, associated with two powerful attacks on the flanks, Ney and Mortier from the left, Victor and Latour-Maubourg's cavalry from the right. That left St. Cyr, Marmont, and the Guard (in reserve) to hold the center with about 50,000 men. A windy and wet night also had not improved Allied morale.

At 6:00 A.M. Napoleon seized the initiative, as Mortier and Nansouty* attacked Wittgenstein* and drove his men out of the Blasewitz woods; the Allied right wing

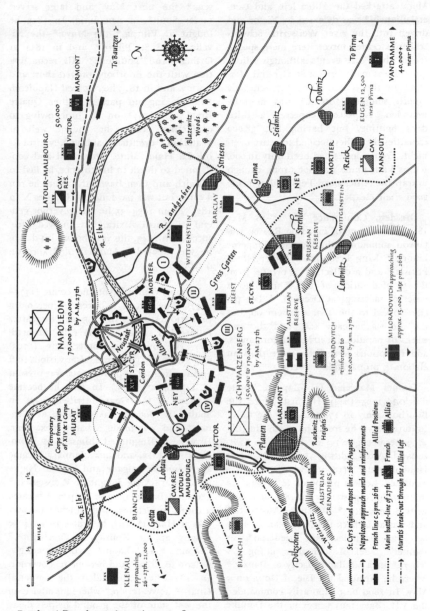

Battle of Dresden, 26–27 August 1813

soon began to give way. Simultaneously, Murat attacked the Allied left, and General Bianchi* was defeated by Victor and driven into the river Weisseritz. Schwarzenberg's center forces were mere spectators of these dire events, although a little ground was made against St. Cyr and Marmont in the center. Here the renegade French soldier, Moreau,* was mortally wounded. Napoleon expected a third day's fighting, but having lost 38,000 casualties the Allies decided to retire overnight. French losses had been only 10,000, but as Vandamme was not strong enough to trap the Allies near Teplitz they made good their escape.

Dresden, Conference of, 17–28 May 1812. On the eve of invading Russia, Napoleon summoned the Austrian Emperor Francis,* King Frederick William III of Prussia,* and a collection of princes from the Confederation of the Rhine* to a series of meetings at Dresden. A last pacific appeal to the Tsar was sent off, but the die was already cast, and the two weeks of parades, theatrical performances, and receptions were little more than an elaborate propaganda exercise.

Drouet, Maréchal Jean-Baptiste, comte d'Erlon (1765–1844). He first joined the Bourbon army in 1782. During the Revolutionary wars he rose rapidly, and in July 1799 became *général de brigade* in Switzerland. After fighting at Zurich* and at Hohenlinden* (1800), where he was wounded, he was promoted to *général de division* in August 1803. In 1805 he served with Bernadotte's* I Corps at Austerlitz,* and was at Lübeck the next year. In 1807 he was wounded at Friedland* as Lannes'* chief of staff after aiding Lefebvre* in a similar capacity at Danzig,* where he captured the Isle of Holm on 7 May. In 1809 he temporarily commanded the VII (Bavarian) Corps in the Danube theatre. In 1810 he was posted to Spain,

fought at Fuentes de Oñoro* under Massena* the next May, and later served under Soult* in Andalusia. In 1813 he fought at Vitoria,* the Maya,* the Nivelle,* and St. Pierre,* and in 1814 at Orthez* and Toulouse.* His reconciliation with the Bourbons proved short and stormy, and in 1815 he rejoined Napoleon. After taking no part at either Quatre Bras* or Ligny* on 16 June owing to conflicting orders, he fought well at Waterloo,* eventually aiding Ney* in taking La Haie Sainte. Proscribed and condemned to death in his absence, he fled to Munich and then Bayreuth (where he ran a café), but was pardoned by Charles X in 1825. From 1834–35 he was governor general in North Africa, but enjoyed little success. In 1843, the year before his death, he was created a Marshal of France on 9 April.

Drouot, Général Antoine, comte (1774–1847). The son of a baker, he became a probationer officer in 1793, and thereafter followed a successful career in the artillery. He fought at Hondschoote (1793) and Fleurus* (1794) and, after various staff and regimental appointments, was present at Trafalgar* (1805). In 1808 he became director of the Guard Artillery park in Spain. In 1809 he was wounded at Wagram* and was made a baron next year. Drouot distinguished himself at Borodino* in 1812, and next January became a *général de brigade* and aide to Napoleon. In 1813 he fought at Weissenfels,* Lutzen,* Bautzen,* and Leipzig,* became a count in October, and clinched the success at Hanau* with his guns. In 1814 he fought at La Rothière,* Vauchamps,* Craonne,* and Laon,* accompanied Napoleon to Elba,* and became its governor. In 1815 he commanded the Imperial Guard* at Waterloo,* where his advice on the wet state of the ground helped delay the opening of the battle. He was acquitted of high treason charges in 1816, and finally retired in 1825. Greatly respected, he died blind.

Dubois de Crancé, Général Edmond Louis Alexir (1747–1814). After service in the Royal Musketeers, he was elected to the States General in 1789. French *deputé-en-mission* and Jacobin politician as well as soldier, in 1793 he ordered the movement of troops to recapture Lyons and then to besiege British-occupied Toulon.* He persuaded the French Ministry of War to adopt a standardized all-arms divisional* system, the forerunner of the later *corps d'armée,** and he had also been behind *l'amalgame** of 1793, and advised the use of universal military service. In 1799 he was Minister of War, but disapproved of *Brumaire** and retired into private life.

Dubreton, Général Jean Louis, baron (1773–1855). Commissioned in 1790, he was stationed in La Vendée from 1794 to 1800. Posted to the West Indies in 1802, he was captured by the British in Santo Domingo in 1803. After his release Dubreton served in Poland and Spain, becoming *général de brigade* in 1811. Next year he greatly distinguished himself by successfully defending Burgos* castle against Wellington,* and was promoted to *général de division* in December. In 1813 he fought at Hanau* under Victor,* but then fell sick. He did not rejoin Napoleon in 1815, and was made a baron by Louis XVIII* in December 1815. He finally retired in 1831.

Duc, Le, Antoine (fl. 1806). As Muster-Master General, Le Duc served as a key member of Berthier's* "Cabinet," or private staff of a dozen experts, and did a great deal in ensuring the smooth running of the *Grande Armée* on campaign.

Ducos, Consul Pierre Roger, comte (1747–1816). A prominent lawyer in 1789,

he was elected to the Convention, where he voted for Louis XVI's* execution in 1793. He was President of the Council of Five Hundred (*Cinq-Cents**) during the *coup d'état** of 18 *Fructidor,* and thereafter took a high legal post in Landes. After the *Prairial coup,* he became a member of the Executive Directory* through the influence of his friend Barras.* He helped plan the *coup d'état* of *Brumaire** in 1799, and was briefly Third Consul in the Consulate* before being replaced by Lebrun.* Made vice-president of the Senate for a time, he later became a count and a senator. In 1814 he supported Napoleon's abdication. The Bourbons made him a peer of France in 1815, but as a regicide he was forced into exile next year. He died at Ulm as the result of a coach crash.

Dugommier, Général Jacques Coquille (so-called) (1738–1794). First commissioned in 1757, he spent much of the Seven Years' War in the West Indies (Martinique and Guadeloupe). In 1782 he left the army, and from 1789–91 pursued a mainly political career in the colonies. In late 1791

Dugommier

he returned to France and resumed a martial career, becoming a *général de division* in November 1793. He succeeded Doppet* as commander before Toulon* on 16 November, and aided by Bonaparte saw the siege through to a successful conclusion, being wounded twice. Service in the Army of the Western Pyrenees followed, but he was killed by a mortar bomb on 17 November 1794 on the Black Mountain.

Dugua, Général Charles François Joseph (1744–1802). Commissioned into the infantry in 1760, he left the forces in 1777. Holding a post in the *gendarmerie* in 1791, two years later he was nominated to be a *général de brigade* (August), and within three months was made *général de division* while serving as a senior staff officer before Toulon.* He next fought in the Pyrenees, but in late 1796 passed to the Army of Italy, where he commanded the cavalry reserve. He was wounded at Sacile,* and later occupied Trieste (March 1797). For two years he was a member of the *Cinq-Cents*,* but from 1798 he became Inspector of Cavalry and Infantry in the Army of the Orient. He helped take Rosetta, fought at the Pyramids,* and in February 1799 became commandant of Cairo. After eventual repatriation and a brief command at Toulouse, he was sent as Chief of Staff with the army of Leclerc* to Santo Domingo, and in early 1802 he was seriously wounded at Crête-à-Pierrot. Five months later he died of yellow fever.

Duhesme, Général Philibert Guillaume, comte (1766–1815). He emerged from a National Guard command in 1789 to serve in the Army of the North, 1792–94, and in the last year he became a *général de brigade* and distinguished himself at Fleurus.* After service on the Rhine and Moselle sectors, part of it under Desaix's* command, in 1798 he moved to the

Italian peninsula where he distinguished himself at the capture of Naples (January 1799). Until late 1807 he held various commands in Italy, but in early 1808 he was transferred to Spain. There he seized the citadel of Barcelona,* and as its Governor withstood a long if intermittent siege. In 1810 he was recalled to France in disgrace to face a multitude of charges of improper actions and malversation, and for a time lived in semiretirement. In 1813 he was made Governor of Kehl, and in 1814 was given a division under Victor.* Duhesme fought at Brienne* and La Rothière,* and was made a Count of the Empire in February. He rallied to Napoleon in 1815 and was given command of two divisions of the Young Guard. He fought at Ligny* and at Waterloo,* receiving a mortal wound near Plancenoit from which he died two days later as a prisoner-of-war at Jemappes.*

Dumas, Général Mathieu, comte (1753–1837). Of noble origin, he was commissioned in 1773, served in America as aide to General Rochambeau, and after diplomatic appointments in the eastern Mediterranean (1784–85), he eventually served both Broglie* and Lafayette* as ADC in 1789. He escorted the arrested Louis XVI* back from Varennes in 1791, and soon was combining military service along the Rhine with a hectic political life in Paris. He denounced Dumouriez* and others, and had to flee to Switzerland until after the *coup d'état*ature* of *Thermidor*. After a period in the War Ministry, he was proscribed in 1797 after *Fructidor*, and lived in Hamburg until *Brumaire*.* In 1800 he formed the Army of the Reserve at Dijon and fought under Macdonald* in Switzerland. Next year he was sent to Naples as ambassador and became a member of the Council of State.* Promoted to *général de division* in February 1805, he became the Emperor's quartermaster in September, and fought at Ulm,* Elchingen,* and Austerlitz.* In 1806 he served in Naples, and became Minister of War to Joseph Bonaparte,* both as King of Naples and later as King of Spain. In November 1808 he became assistant Quartermaster General to the French Army of Spain, and in December warned Napoleon of Moore's* advance on Valladolid. In 1809 he was assistant Chief of Staff in the Danube theatre, fighting at Essling and Wagram.* Next year he was made a Count of the Empire. As Intendant General of the Grand Army of Russia, he served throughout the Russian campaign, and in 1813 was taken prisoner at Leipzig.* During the Hundred Days he was charged with raising the National Guard, but was retired in September by the Bourbons. He soon resumed his political career and headed many important commissions. He was made a peer of France in 1831, and finally retired in 1832, almost blind and increasingly ill.

Du Merbion (or Dumerbion), Général Pierre Jadart (1737–1797). The son of an army officer, he first saw service in 1752. After fighting in Europe during the Seven Years' War, he spent the years 1765–73 in French colonial garrisons in America. In 1793, back in France, he became a *général de division* in May, and from January 1794 became Commander in Chief of the Army of Italy. Such success as he enjoyed was largely due to his senior artillery officer, Bonaparte, as he freely admitted. He handed over his command to General Schérer* in November 1794, and retired on pension the following May.

Dumouriez, Général Charles François du Perrier (so-called) (1739–1823). The son of a war commissary, he joined the cavalry as a volunteer in 1758. Severely wounded and taken prisoner in 1760, he was later employed in Corsica (1768) and

Dumouriez

on a number of secret missions to Madrid, Poland, and Sweden. He was promoted to major general in 1788. At the Revolution he commanded the Cherbourg National Guard and joined the Jacobin* party. In 1792 he was promoted to lieutenant general and commanded the Army of the North. He briefly held ministerial appointments, but his great achievements were in the field: he shared with Kellermann* (the Elder) the credit for Valmy.* Transferred to command the Army of Belgium he won the battle of Jemappes* and conquered the country. Restored to the Army of the North, in 1793 he invaded Holland, but was defeated at Neerwinden* in March. He began to plot with an Austrian colonel, Mack,* and on 2 April handed over to the Austrians the French *députés-en-mission* attached to his headquarters and also the visiting Minister of War. Deserted by his troops, three days later he evaded Davout* and crossed into the Allied lines. He was shunned by Tsar Paul* and other potential patrons, but in the end was given a refuge and a pension by Great Britain in 1800. He advised the Spanish leaders on the organization of the guerrilla* struggle (1808) and also was consulted by Wellesley.* He chose not to return to France with the Bourbons. A very able commander, his political ambitions caused him to betray his country.

Duncan, Admiral Adam, Viscount (1731–1804). After becoming a naval lieutenant in 1755, he saw much service in the Channel and West Indian fleets. He became an admiral in 1795, and from that year until 1801 was Commander in Chief in the North Sea. During the tricky naval mutinies of 1797 he prevented the contagion from spreading to his flagship, H.M.S. *Venerable*, and before the troubles were over led the fleet to a victory over the Dutch Admiral, de Winter, at Camperdown.* As a reward he was created first a baron, and then Viscount Duncan of Camperdown.

Dundas, General Sir David (1735–1820). Originally an artillery officer, he exchanged to the 56th Regiment in 1756. He served in several combined operations against French ports and in Cuba (1762). He was promoted to colonel in 1781 and to major general in 1790. From 1788 he wrote a series of drill books that became standard issue in the British Army, and his preference for Prussian concepts earned him the nickname of "Old Pivot." Promoted to lieutenant general in 1797, he took part in the Helder* Campaign two years later. Made a full general in 1802, he was Commander in Chief in England from 1809–11, and a Privy Councillor from 1809.

Dundas, Henry, First Viscount Melville (1742–1811). A Scottish lawyer and MP with much influence in Indian affairs, he was Home Secretary from 1791–94, and Secretary of War 1794–1801. He pushed through the British invasion of Egypt in

1801 against Pitt's* wishes, and it proved successful. He was created viscount in 1802, and was First Lord of the Admiralty (1804–05) but was impeached for malversation in 1806. He was found guilty of negligence but acquitted on the major charge. He was restored to the Privy Council (to which he had been first appointed in 1782) in 1807.

Dupont de l'Etang, Général Pierre, comte (1765–1840). A sublieutenant in the Dutch army (1784–90), he joined the French forces in 1791. After a turbulent career, he was confirmed as *général de brigade* in October 1795, and after running the Topographical Office became *général de division* in 1797. As Berthier's* Chief of Staff in 1800, he fought at Fort Bard* and Marengo* and signed the Convention of Alessandria* with Melas* after the battle. He later led a force to invade Tuscany. In 1805 he was attached to Ney's* corps and fought the actions of Haslach* and Albeck with great skill, rescuing Gazan's* division at Durrenstein.* In 1806 he served under Berna-

Dupont

dotte,* won the action of Halle, and next year that of Mohrungen. He was present at Friedland* in June 1807. Later that year he was transferred to the forces preparing to march on Portugal and made a reputation in several actions. He became a count on 4 July, but after being wounded was induced to surrender his corps to General Castaños* and the Spaniards at Bailen* on 22 July 1808. Repatriated to France he was at once disgraced, and served a considerable period in prison. In 1814 he emerged to become Minister of War after the fall of Napoleon, but had to flee next year. Returning to France after Waterloo,* he was made a Minister of State and pursued an active political career until his final retirement in 1832.

Dupuy de Saint-Florent, Général François Victor (1773–1838). Joining the army as a volunteer in 1791, he was commissioned in 1793 and served as Jourdan's* aide-de-camp. After service in Hanover and Batavia, he became a member of the *Grande Armée* (1805–08). Gravely wounded at Ulm,* he later served on Grouchy's* staff and was again hit at Jena* and Eylau.* Thereafter he held mainly staff appointments in Spain, Corsica, and through the Russian and Saxon campaigns of 1812–13. He was promoted to *général de brigade* in January 1814, and next year served in Vandamme's* III Corps during part of the Hundred Days, being made town-commandant of Philippeville. He was removed from the army in September 1815, but eventually was given full retired status in 1835.

D'Urban, Lieutenant General Sir Benjamin (1777–1849). As an officer of the Queen's Bays, he served in the Netherlands, Westphalia, and the West Indies. He transferred to the 25th Light Dragoons as major and by 1813 was a colonel

in the British Army and a major general in the Portuguese service. A distinguished cavalry commander, he fought in many Peninsula battles, including Salamanca.* In later years he was Lieutenant Governor of British Guiana and Barbados, and was promoted to lieutenant general in 1837. From 1842–47 he was Governor of the Cape of Good Hope, and in 1843 occupied Natal for the Crown. His last appointment was command of the troops in Canada, where he died.

Duroc (or du Roc), Général Geraud Christophe Michel, duc de Frioul (1772–1813). Trained as a gentleman cadet in early 1789, he was dismissed from the service in 1792 and became an *émigré.* He soon returned to France, however, and eventually became a lieutenant in the foot artillery* (1793). From 1793–98 he served with the Army of Italy, being present at Toulon,* later serving under Andréossy* with the bridging train (1796), distinguishing himself at Primolano (4 September 1796), and becoming an aide to General Bonaparte. In 1798–99 he

Duroc

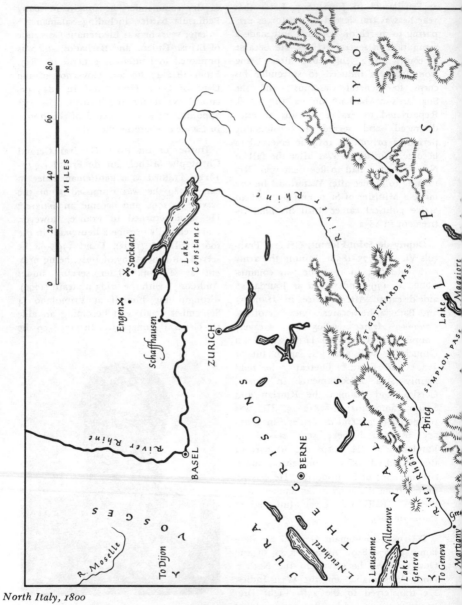

North Italy, 1800

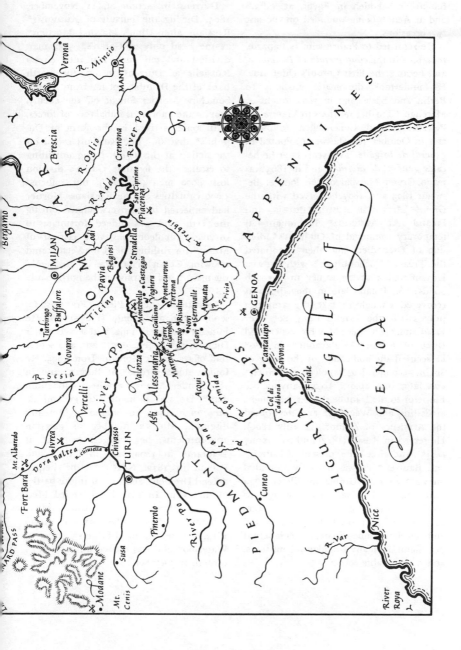

fought at Salahieh in Egypt, at Jaffa,* and at Acre,* being wounded on the last two occasions.

He returned to France with Bonaparte, took part in the *coup d'état* of *Brumaire*, and became the First Consul's chief aide. He undertook diplomatic missions to Berlin and Basle, and in 1800 fought at Marengo.* Further missions to Vienna, St. Petersburg, and Copenhagen followed, and in October 1801 he was promoted to *général de brigade*. Two years later he became *général de division*, and in 1805 was made Grand Marshal of the Palace. Between 1805 and 1807 he served with the *Grande Armée* in Austria, Prussia, and Poland. At Austerlitz* he fought in temporary command of Oudinot's* division of Grenadiers, and then negotiated the Treaty of Schonbrunn* with Prussia. He suffered a severe injury in a coach accident in Poland late in 1806, but was recovered enough to take the armistice proposals to the Tsar in June 1807 after Friedland.* The next May he was created Duke of Frioul. At Bayonne* in 1808 he secured the abdication of the King of Spain, accompanied Napoleon to Erfurt,* and later into Spain. Accompanying the Emperor to the Danube theater, he fought at Essling and Wagram,* and negotiated the Armistice of Znaim* (12 July 1809). He served in Russia (1812) and in Saxony (1813), and after being present at Lutzen* and Bautzen* he was mortally wounded on 22 May near Gorlitz in Silesia by a cannonball. He lived long enough to receive a visit from Napoleon. The Emperor missed him sorely: he was a trusted and efficient subordinate, a competent negotiator in many confidential missions, and a reasonable soldier.

Durrenstein, action of, 11 November, 1805. During the pursuit of Kutusov's* Russians after Ulm,* Marshal Mortier,* at the head only of Gazan's* 5,000-man division and ten guns, ran into 40,000 Russians at Durrenstein on the north bank of the Danube, not far from Krems. Somehow Mortier fought off the enemy, despite the enormous imbalance of forces, until relief arrived in the form of Dupont's* division. The Russians called off the action at this point, being unwilling to escalate the fighting. Gazan's division lost 3,000 men (or 60%), but inflicted 4,000 casualties on the Russians. Mortier had expected to be overwhelmed during the 11th, and was indeed fortunate to survive. Napoleon was very critical of Murat* for rushing ahead for Vienna and allowing Gazan to become isolated amid the main Russian army on the north bank.

Durutte, Général Pierre François Joseph, baron and comte (1767–1827). He joined the army in 1792, and served under Dumouriez* at Jemappes* and as a senior staff officer under Moreau* from 1795. He fought under Brune* at Bergen, and in 1800 under Moreau again at Hohenlinden.* He was promoted to *général de division* in 1803, but shared in Moreau's disgrace. After a number of garrison appointments, he emerged to fight at Wagram* in 1809, and in Russia and Poland in 1812. Next year he helped defend Dresden* and fought in the battles of that year. In 1814 he defended Metz with valor against 40,000 Russians. Made a baron in 1809, he became a count in 1813. He served in d'Erlon's* corps at Waterloo* and was retired on account of wounds in October 1815.

Ebelsberg (or Ebersberg), battle of, 3 May 1809. After the battles of Abensberg* and Eckmühl,* the Austrian army fell back toward Vienna, their retreat covered by General Hiller's* III Corps. At the river Traun he turned at bay, determined to win time for the organization of the capital's defense, massing 40,000 men and 70 guns. After a preliminary action at Wels on the 2nd, Massena* launched a strong frontal attack across the river Traun, apparently unaware that Lannes* and his extemporized corps were already moving to attack Hiller's rear.

After a costly storming of the bridge at 10:00 A.M., Claparède's division entered the town, but the Austrians remained in possession of the castle and its height, while beyond it was the ridge where Hiller had deployed his main forces. Claparède was soon fighting for survival, but at midday Massena was able to send part of the newly arrived Legrand's* division into the town, and after a bitter fight the 26th Regiment stormed the castle as the 18th and some Baden troops cleared the town. Hiller, surprisingly, did not counterattack, although the French never fielded more than 22,100 men. Their losses were 2,800 (Claparède alone losing 2,100 or 25% of his division), while Hiller lost an estimated 2,000 killed and perhaps 4,000 taken prisoner. Hiller retreated to Enns and then to Krems where he crossed to the north bank of the Danube, and on 13 May the French occupied Vienna. Napoleon criticized Massena for making such a risky attack, but the Emperor was soon to be guilty of an even rasher venture at Aspern-Essling.*

Eblé, Général Jean-Baptiste, comte (1758–1812). The son of an artillery sergeant, he became a gunner in 1773 and an officer 12 years later. After the battle of Hondschoote he became *général de brigade* in September and, after Wattignies,* a *général de division* in October 1793. After various appointments, he distinguished himself at the defense of Kehl in 1796. In 1799 he helped capture Naples and in 1804 commanded the artillery in Hanover. He next served under Bernadotte* in 1805, and next year fought at Halle and Lübeck. From 1808 he became associated with Westphalia, being made a Baron of the Empire that year, and was Jerome Bonaparte's* Minister of War until 1810. In that year he served under Massena* in Portugal, particularly at the sieges of Ciudad Rodrigo* and Almeida.* In 1812 he commanded the bridging train of the Grand Army in Russia, and after fighting at Smolensk,* saved the remnants of the army by bridging the Beresina* in November. He died of illness at Königsberg before his letters patent as *comte* could be issued, but his widow was made *comtesse* of the Empire in April 1813.

Ebro, the crossing of, June 1813. This great river in northern Spain was regarded as a major defense line by Joseph Bonaparte* and Marshal Jourdan* as they fell back before Wellington's* advance in strength from Portugal. The Allied army, after passing the river Esla, conducted a series of highly effective outflanking movements, many of them being executed by General Graham's* independent force, to compromise successive French defense lines. The climax came when the Ebro line was itself turned—an operation made feasible by Wellington's switch of his seaborne communications from Lisbon to Santander on the north coast of Spain. This success led directly to the climactic battle of Vitoria.*

Eckmühl (or Eggmühl), battle of, 22 April 1809. After regaining the initiative in the Danube campaign of 1809 at Abensberg* on 20 April, Napoleon sent the greater part of the Grand Army southward toward Landshut* in pursuit of what proved to be only the left wing of Archduke Charles'* army. The effect of this move was to leave Marshal Davout* at the head of only 20,000 men of his III Corps to face the main body of the Austrian forces—perhaps 75,000 strong in the Eckmühl sector—commanded by the Archduke in person. Charles ordered an attack on Davout's left wing (General Friant's* division) by the 40,000 men of Generals Rosenburg and Hohenzollern, while the corps of Kollowrath and Lichtenstein marched for Abbach with the intention of cutting the Grand Army off from the Danube.

Davout reinforced Friant with Pajol's* division and Montbrun's* cavalry, but by 1:00 P.M., after a slow start, the Austrian attack was gaining momentum and the French were losing ground. Help was on its way, however, for Napoleon had ordered Lannes* to hasten northward from Landshut with 30,000 troops to Davout's aid. At the approach of this force toward the Austrian left flank, Davout ordered an all-out attack by his tiring men to pin the Austrians. The important village of Leuchling and its neighboring wood were both captured at terrible cost, and two Bavarian divisions engaged the

Austrian right, while General Demont moved to cover the crossings over the river Gross Laber, where Lannes' leading troops were expected.

At about 4:30 P.M., while General Vandammer's* Württembergers took possession of Buckhausen, Lannes' two divisions fell with a will on the Austrian IV Corps, holding the eastern approaches to Eckmühl. Marshal Lefebvre's* VII Corps entered the fray on the farther flank, and by nightfall the French were masters of Eckmühl, and both Austrian flanks were thoroughly beaten and driven in. Having lost 7,000 killed and wounded and 5,000 prisoners, the Archduke Charles ordered a northward retreat after dark, crossing over the Danube and leaving only the garrison of Ratisbon* on the south bank. The success had cost the French 6,000 men in this, the third major battle in three days.

At Eckmühl, Napoleon's favorite grand tactical maneuver of a frontal attack linked with an outflanking column had worked with great efficiency. However, considering the weariness of his troops and after taking counsel with Massena* and Lannes at Egglofsheim, Napoleon decided against pressing ahead that night after the retreating Austrians, but sent 74 squadrons of cavalry to observe and harrass their movement. On the morrow, the infantry and guns would follow toward Ratisbon, still hoping that they would be in time to trap the Archduke south of the Danube. This, however, was not to be.

Edwards, Trumpeter John (fl. 1815). Aged 16, he was present at Waterloo* as field trumpeter to Lord Edward Somerset* (brother of Fitzroy-Somerset*). He blew the bugle call that launched the Union and Heavy Brigades of British cavalry into their devastating charge against the *cuirassiers* of Général Travers and the infantry of d'Erlon's* shattered I Corps.

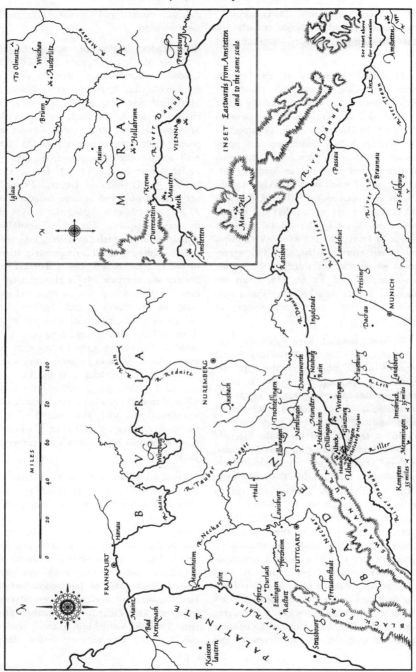

Danube Theater, 1805

He survived the charge, unlike most of his comrades, and his bugle is today in the Household Cavalry museum at Windsor.

El Arish, convention of, 28 January 1800. Following Bonaparte's return to France from Egypt, command of the Army of the Orient devolved upon General Kléber.* In December 1799, Commodore Sir William Sidney Smith* opened negotiations with the French on his own initiative, and arranged an armistice between the French and Turkish forces. Protracted discussions followed, but on 28 January it was agreed that the French would withdraw to the coastal ports of Egypt to be repatriated in Turkish ships, with their arms and baggage. This agreement was at once disowned by the British government, and on 20 March an infuriated Kléber attacked the Turks outside Cairo and won a great victory at Heliopolis.

El Arish, siege of, 8–19 February 1799. This fort, held by 600 Mamelukes* and 1,700 Albanian infantry, on the northeast coast of Egypt near the Syrian frontier, held up Bonaparte's Army of Egypt for 11 crucial days. General Reynier's* men stormed the village and outlying camp on the 9th, but the main defenses remained impregnable to direct assaults. Kléber* brought up his divisional 8-pounders on the 14th, but their fire made little impression. A Turkish attempt to relieve the garrison was foiled by his and Reynier's infantry on the next day. Bonaparte arrived in person on the 17th, deeply concerned for the havoc this unforeseen problem was wreaking on his timetable for the invasion of Syria, and at once ordered up a number of 12-pounders from the field park under General Dommartin.* That officer massed every available mortar against the fort, and after a devastating bombardment the 900 survivors of the garrison surrendered on the 19th; most were paroled.

El Bodon, action of, 25 September 1811. As Wellington* moved to besiege Ciudad Rodrigo* in late 1811, the French reinforced the garrison and Marshal Marmont* advanced with 58,000 men to challenge the Allies. Early on the 24th Marmont sent out strong cavalry forces to probe Wellington's intentions. On the 25th one of these patrols, 2,500 cavalry under General Montbrun,* found the British 3rd Division of General Picton* very strung out, and at once attacked at El Bodon without awaiting the arrival of infantry support. The five available squadrons of the 11th Light Dragoons and the 1st Hussars, K.G.L., desperately tried to hold their ground, but a Portuguese battery was overrun. Major Henry Ridge, however, brought up the 5th Foot and led them in an uphill attack against the French dragoons, which he scattered with three volleys before regaining the lost cannon. This check gave Picton time to withdraw his division in good order with the loss of 80 casualties. The blockade of Ciudad Rodrigo was eventually resumed when Marmont drew back, but Wellington was dissatisfied with this period of the Peninsular War. However, Ciudad Rodrigo would fall to him the following January.

Elba, island of. Off the west coast of Italy near Piombino, this island was the scene of Napoleon's first exile from 4 May 1814 to 26 February 1815. Carried to the island by H.M.S. *Undaunted,* Napoleon was in fact ruler of the 112,000 population, subject to the general supervision of Allied commissioners, and he was permitted a bodyguard of 400 troops (but in fact commanded 600 volunteers drawn from the Old Guard). His mother and sister Pauline* visited him in exile, and so did Marie Walewska* for a few days.

Former ministers and servants in Paris kept the fallen Emperor minutely informed of developments in France, and in late February 1815 he slipped away with about 1,000 men to begin the "Hundred Days."

Elchingen, action of, 14 October 1805. As the French ring closed around General Mack's* army in Ulm* the Austrian commander sent out 9,000 troops under Generals Werneck and Riesch with cavalry and 20 guns to try and break out of the ring by a drive along the north bank of the Danube in the hope of making contact with Kutusov's* approaching Russians. After a serious disagreement with Murat,* (the sector commander), Marshal Ney,* whose VI Corps had originally occupied Elchingen and its key bridge on the 10th, only to be ordered to abandon these gains by the Grand Duke of Berg on the 11th, prepared a new attack. Marshal Ney led the 6th Regiment of Loison's* division in a sudden advance against the bridge at

8:00 A.M. on the 14th and captured it despite heavy fire and serious casualties. A little to the north Dupont* drove Riesch's advance guard out of Langenau and Albeck. Ney then passed his light cavalry and more infantry over to assault the town of Elchingen with its large abbey on the steep ridge beyond. A serious fight raged for much of the morning around the villages and abbey, but the arrival of Mahler's division at 11:30 (which had crossed the Danube farther to the east) and the threat posed by Dupont, drove in the Austrian left flank and induced the Austrians to retreat through the *Grosser Forst* toward Ulm. Ney established his headquarters in the village of Oberelchingen and was congratulated by Napoleon on his achievement. The French lost 3,000 casualties, and inflicted 4,000 on the Austrians. It was at Elchingen, a few days later, that Napoleon received Mack to discuss surrender terms.

Ellesmere, Francis Egerton, First Earl

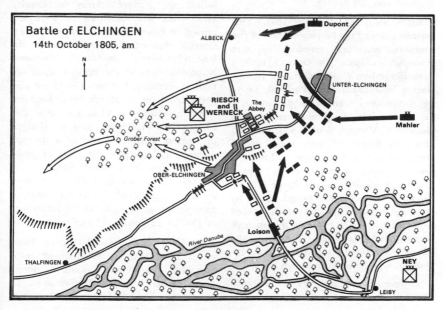

Battle of ELCHINGEN
14th October 1805, am

of (1800–1857). Ellesmere was a friend and confidant of the Duke of Wellington,* and wrote *Personal Reminiscences of the Duke of Wellington* (first published in 1903). A politician and scholar of some distinction, he translated German and Italian works and wrote poetry and works on archaeology. He became earl in 1846 and a Knight of the Garter in 1855.

Elliott, Sir Gilbert, First Earl of Minto (1751–1814). Educated in France and at Oxford, he followed a legal career and in 1776 entered Parliament. From 1794–96 he served as constitutional viceroy of Corsica, then in British hands, during which time he expelled the patriot Paoli.* Created Baron Minto in 1798, he led British diplomatic representation at Vienna the next year. In 1806 he became President of the East India Company's Board of Control, and was Governor General of India from 1807 to 1813, annexing Amboyna, the Moluccas, and Java (1811) in the Dutch East Indies. He became a viscount and earl in 1813.

Elvas, siege of, October 1808. This fortress guarded the Portuguese side of the southern corridor,* standing opposite Badajoz* in Spain. In October 1808 a French garrison (placed there by Junot* during his occupation of Portugal, 1807–08) surrendered to an Anglo-Spanish force. In 1810, after the French capture of Badajoz,* Marshal Soult* was held in check by Beresford* with 20,000 Allied troops operating from Elvas as his base, and attempts were made to regain Badajoz,* leading to the battle of Albuera.* Beresford was joined there by Wellington* and the bulk of the Allied army after his failure to take the Spanish fortress, and it was from Elvas that the ultimately successful attempt to recapture Badajoz was mounted in March 1812.

***Emigrés*, the.** French refugees, many of them of aristocratic families, left France during the violent phase of the French Revolution in order to escape persecution or death. Many settled in German states bordering the Rhine; others moved to England. A number of *émigré* military formations were organized (as at Mainz) to fight alongside France's enemies, particularly after the execution of Louis XVI,* and *émigrés* were involved in several of the plots against Napoleon's life—including the Cadoudal* affair. This led to the Enghien* incident of 1804. After this example of ruthless severity, Napoleon did all he could to attract back to France many of the *émigrés,* and a fair number complied (perhaps 40,000). The most diehard, however, returned to France only after the Bourbon restorations of 1814 and 1815.

Enghien, Louis Antoine Henri de Bourbon-Condé, duc d' (1772–1804). The son of a very ancient and prestigious French family with royal connections, he accompanied his parents into exile and joined the *émigré* Army of Condé. When this was disbanded in 1801, he retired to Ettenheim in Baden, and there secretly married Princess Charlotte de Rohan-Rochefort. Royalist plots induced Napoleon to order the Prince's arrest on neutral territory, and this illegal act was perpetrated on 15 March 1804. Enghien was hauled before a military court at the Château de Vincennes, tried on charges of treason without benefit of a defense counsel, and, despite the pleas of Josephine,* shot. As Fouché* allegedly remarked, ". . . it was more than a crime—it was a mistake." This act shocked Europe and was a factor in the formation of the Third Coalition* against France.

Enghien, cricket match of, 12 June 1815. The Duke of Wellington* took 16-year-old Lady Jane Lennox to watch a cricket match at this Belgian town. It is sometimes mis-stated that this event took place on the 15th, when Napoleon was attacking over the Sambre at Charleroi. The score of the respective British teams has not been recorded for posterity.

Engineers, the (or Sappers). French military engineers—*"la genie"*—were in short supply during the expansion of the army following the Revolution, and Bonaparte was 1,300 below establishment in the Army of Italy, 1796. Sapper functions included many tasks, from planning, supervising, and conducting sieges, to building roads, barracks, and bridges (aided in this last task by the *pontonniers*, many of whom were in fact members of the artillery service).

In the field, engineers were organized in separate battalions and commanded by such men as Carnot,* Chasseloup-Laubat,* Haxo,* and Caffarelli.* They performed many key services, of which only the sieges of Toulon,* Mantua,* Acre,* and Danzig* and the bridging activities associated with the battles of Aspern-Essling,* Wagram,* and the Beresina* can be mentioned here. Eventually there were seven battalions of regular engineers, some 10,000 men in all, but they were assisted in many of their tasks by the *pontonniers* and the battalions of pioneers, often made up of allied troops or even prisoners of war.

The topographical engineers were a small staff of picked engineers, charged with the surveying and making of maps and many other general staff duties. The *Bureau Topographique** of Carnot's War Ministry was staffed largely with engineer officers, although Bonaparte himself served with them for a spell in 1795.

In the British Army, the Royal Engineers had only come into existence as an independent corps in the 1760s, becoming separated from the artillery. Officers, NCOs of the Royal Engineers and the Royal Corps of Artificers, were often in desperately short supply in the Peninsular War. The whole scheme of the famous Lines of Torres Vedras* was undertaken by Lieutenant Colonel Richard Fletcher,* aided by Major Jones* and only 16 junior sapper officers and by a Portuguese labor force, in 1809–10. At the siege of Badajoz* in 1811 there were only three RE sergeants, as many corporals, and just 13 sappers in the whole besieging force. Colonel Fletcher and 18 RE officers, backed by 12 attached officers from the line regiments, were available for the siege of Ciudad Rodrigo* the following January, and all of 24 were present at the main siege of Badajoz in April 1812; the siege of Burgos* after Salamanca,* however, was severely understaffed. Nevertheless, Wellington's* engineers served him well in many a major operation, as for example at San Sebastian* in 1813. Endless duties came their way, many extremely dangerous—especially when mining was involved. Seven became casualties at Ciudad Rodrigo, 13 at Badajoz, 3 out of 5 at Burgos, and 11 out of the 18 present at San Sebastian, including Colonel Fletcher. Too often they had inadequate tools and equipment, and Wellington took public notice of the inadequate provision of his engineers in these respects. British engineer officers were trained mostly at the Royal Military Academy at Woolwich, founded in 1741.

Erfurt, Congress and Convention of, 27 September–14 October 1808. Within a year of the great conference at Tilsit* there was a marked deterioration in certain aspects of Franco-Russian relations. The effects of the Continental System* on the Russian economy were resented on one hand, while Napoleon distrusted Tsar Alexander's* ambitions vis-à-vis Constantinople on the other. However, faced by the event of Bailen* the Emperor was compelled to seek a new rapprochement with the Tsar in order to ensure, or so he hoped, the quiescence of central and eastern Europe during his forthcoming absence in Spain. Accordingly, a conference was arranged at Erfurt in the autumn of 1808. News of Vimiero* and the Convention of Cintra* increased the sense of urgency.

The French setbacks in Spain and Portugal strengthened the Tsar's bargaining position, and he certainly did not attend Erfurt in the status of a client ruler; it was Napoleon who was seeking the favors. Above all, he was seeking Russian guarantees of Austrian good behavior. In return for some very vague Russian stipulations on this point, Napoleon was forced to concede Russian possession of Moldavia and Wallachia and accept the Tsar's gains in Finland. The Tsar also induced Napoleon to strike off 20 million from the Prussian reparations imposed at Tilsit. For his part, Alexander agreed, in the event of Austria declaring war on Napoleon, "to make common cause with France."

Napoleon used every wile to impress Alexander: there were massive entertainments and parades and hosts of client princes were in attendance. But acute observers noted that there had been a subtle change of atmosphere—if anything, it was Russia who was calling the tune. After two and a half weeks of bargaining, the two emperors parted company after signing on 12 October a Convention embodying their agreements, together with another public appeal to George III* of Great Britain for reopened negotiations toward a general peace. The Franco-Russian special relationship had been shored up for a while, but within four months the cracks in the facade would become evident as Russia took virtually no steps to hinder provocative Austrian acts. Napoleon and the Tsar were destined never to meet in person again.

Erlon, Comte de. *See* **Drouet,** Maréchal Jean-Baptiste

Erskine, Major General Sir William, Baronet (1769–1813). Commissioned into the light dragoons, he distinguished himself with the future General Wilson* in 1793 in Flanders, when he helped save the Austrian Emperor Leopold from the French at Villers-en-Cauchies.* A Parliamentary career ran parallel to his military one, and in 1808 he was promoted to major general. In 1810 he commanded the Light Division at Torres Vedras* but earned a reputation for rashness. In 1812 he commanded Hill's* cavalry in the advance on Madrid but shortly afterward was declared insane and cashiered. He committed suicide the next year.

Esla, crossing of the river, 31 May–2 June 1813. As Wellington* advanced from Portugal into Spain, the swollen river Esla, a tributary of the Douro, lay across the path of Graham's* corps, which was marching well to the north of the main army carrying out the role of outflanking force. A ford was found at Almendra and the army was able to cross, but not without loss of life in the raging torrent. Eventually a pontoon bridge was established, and by 3 June the complete Allied army of 100,000 men was reunited at Toro, north of the Douro. The local French forces fell back, and Wellington's first strategic triumph of 1813 had been achieved. Ahead lay the road that would in due course lead to the Ebro crossing* and thence to Vitoria.*

Espagne, Général Jean Louis Brigitte, comte (1769–1809). After joining the Queen's Dragoons as a trooper in 1787, this able cavalry commander in due course served under Dumouriez* in the Alps, distinguishing himself at Mont Cenis (1794). Promoted to *général de brigade* in 1799, he fought under Jourdan* and then Moreau,* being present at Moesskirch and

Hohenlinden* (1800). After a period out of service, he was made *général de division* in 1805, and later that year served under Massena* in Italy, fighting at Caldiero* and in Naples (1806). After serving at the siege of Danzig* (1807) and being wounded at Heilsberg,* he was made a Count of the Empire in 1808. The next year, commanding the 3rd Division of Cuirassiers in Lannes'* II Corps, he was mortally wounded at Aspern-Essling* and died on the Isle of Lobau.

España, General Carlos José d'Espignac (so-called) (1775–1839). Born at Foix, he entered the Spanish service in 1792 and fought the French with varied success during the Peninsular Wars, earning Wellington's* bitter criticism for abandoning the bridge at Alba de Tormes* in July 1812—a mistake that enabled the French army to escape from the defeat of Salamanca.* A resolute absolutist, he was exiled in 1820, but the restored Ferdinand VII* made him Viceroy of Navarre. On Ferdinand's death he supported Don Carlos, but had to flee again. Allowed to retire in Catalonia, he was assassinated by an extremist of his own party.

Essen, General (later Field Marshal) Jean Henri, Count of (1755–1824). A Swedish soldier and statesman, he was aide-de-camp to King Gustavus III, and as such fought in Finland (1788). He vainly attempted to warn his master of the plotters surrounding him, and was present at his tragic death. In 1795 he became Governor of Stockholm, and of Pomerania five years later. His finest hour came in 1807, when he defended Stralsund* against the French for eleven weeks. Following the Swedish revolution of 1809 he was made a Councillor of State and led his country's embassy to Paris, signing peace with France in 1810. In 1814 he led the Swedish army against Norway, and after its occupation became its viceroy.

He was ultimately appointed a field marshal and, in 1817, Governor General of Scania.

Essen, General Pierre, Count (1780–1863). A Russian soldier and administrator of some talent, he fought at Eylau* and at Riga (1812). Made Military Governor of St. Petersburg in 1813, he was promoted to general of infantry in 1819 and made a Russian count in 1833. Nine years later he became a member of the Council of State, was made the Tsar's Chamberlain, and also Civil Governor of Livonia.

Eugen, Frederick Charles Paul Louis, Duke of Württemberg (1788–1857). The son of a general in the Prussian service, he accompanied his father (commanding the reserve of the Prussian army) during the disastrous Campaign of 1806, and then joined the Russian staff under Bennigsen.* Promoted to lieutenant general after Smolensk* (1812), he fought with great distinction at Borodino* and, during the French retreat, at Krasnoe.* The next year he was present at Lützen* and Bautzen,* and following the latter defeat he commanded the rear guard that enabled the Allies to retreat. He later fought General Vandamme* at Kulm,* distinguished himself at Leipzig,* after the invasion of France in 1814, at Arcis-sur-Aube,* and before Paris itself. Soon after Napoleon's first abdication he retired to his estates in Silesia, where he wrote a series of notable memoirs.

Eugène, Prince. *See* Beauharnais, Eugène

Evora, massacre of, 25 July 1808. General Loison's* division killed the entire population of the town of Evora, in Portugal, which had risen against French rule. This atrocity ensured an enthusiastic welcome for Wellesley's* shipborne army, and helped dissipate any Portuguese hesitation in accepting the proffered British aid.

Eylau, battle of, 7–8 February 1807. This followed the sharp but indecisive brush with General Bennigsen's* Russian army at Ionkovo.* The *Grande Armée* followed the retiring foe through bitter winter weather toward the township of Preussiches Eylau. On the afternoon of 6 February scouts brought word to Napoleon that Bennigsen had turned at bay at Eylau, and was offering battle with some 67,000 men and all of 460 cannon. Napoleon had 45,000 troops and only 200 guns immediately available, but two outlying corps—those of Ney* to the north and Davout* to the south, totaling a further 26,600 men—were within marching distance of the field. The only aid the

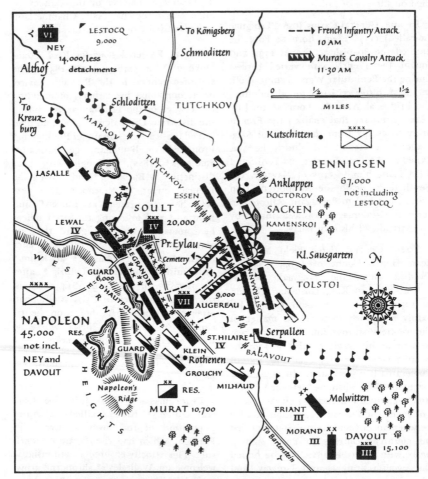

Battle of Eylau, 7–8 February 1807: Day One

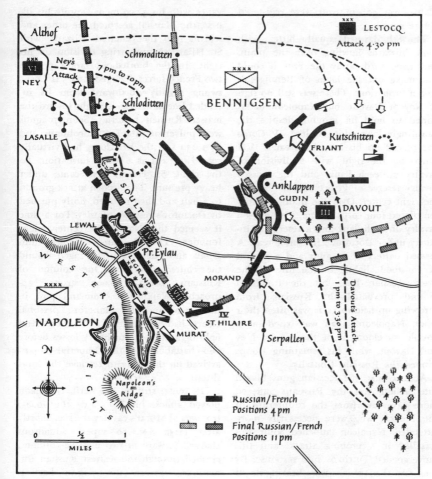

Battle of Eylau: Day Two

Russians might hope to receive was the force of 9,000 men under General Lestocq retreating ahead of Ney.

The main body of the French closed in upon Eylau on the afternoon of the 7th, and after a hard fight that raged on until well after dark they took possession of the town and its adjoining ridge. This action probably started by accident when part of the imperial trains—including the Emperor's own baggage—entered the town seeking quarters in total ignorance of the presence of the Russians. Each side lost about 4,000 casualties in this sharp encounter, the outcome of which provided many Frenchmen with at least a modicum of shelter for the night and doomed the Russians to a desperate night on the open plain—over 30° of frost were registered before morning.

The 8th dawned equally bitter, with snow blizzards howling over the plain, and 1,200 yards away the French could just make out the loom of Bennigsen's frozen formations. There was still no sign of Ney or Davout, but Napoleon determined to hold his ground, despite the dauntingly long odds. Soult's* IV Corps was placed on his left, Augereau's* VII Corps on the right, with a division of cavalry on each flank, and the massed cavalry reserve of Prince Murat* behind the right center. Over the plain, Bennigsen placed four corps in line, with massed cavalry on each flank and a reserve of infantry under Doctorov* in center rear. A massed battery of 70 guns and a second of 60 stood slightly to the fore of the main Russian line, but the iron-hard ground prevented the Russians from throwing up fieldworks as was often their wont. Napoleon's plan was based on a double envelopment of the foe by Ney and Davout, while his remaining troops pinned the Russians frontally.

At 8:00 A.M. the Russian guns blazed into action, but the Russians suffered more casualties from the counterfire of the French, who were necessarily more extended. Napoleon launched Soult and Lasalle* in a probing attack, and this move goaded Tutchkov into response. By 9:00 A.M. the Russians were bearing down in strength toward the French left wing, and Soult was hard pressed to keep Windmill Hill in his possession. At the same time a substantial force of Russian cavalry attacked the approaching troops of Friant's* division, which formed the advance guard of Davout's III Corps moving up from the south.

Soon both French flanks were in great peril. Napoleon decided to try to ease the situation by counterattacking in the center, and he ordered Augereau to ad-

vance with his 9,000 men. Despite his illness, the Marshal accepted the order and set off into the renewed blizzard, with St. Hilaire's* supporting division on his right. In the blotted-out landscape the two French forces diverged, and VII Corps swung slightly northward from its intended line of attack—straight toward the massed Russian batteries. Soon 70 guns were pulverizing the French columns, and by 10:30 A.M. the VII Corps had virtually ceased to exist as a viable formation. To the right, St. Hilaire also came under heavy pressure. The French attack ground to a halt and then recoiled, hotly pursued by Doctorov's reserve infantry. For a time it seemed that Napoleon's center might founder. The Russians swarmed into Eylau, and a desperate fight raged around the church cemetery. One column of Russians, perhaps 6,000 strong, approached Napoleon's command post in the town, and the Emperor's personal escort had to engage in hand-to-hand fighting and to accept heavy losses before two battalions of the Imperial Guard arrived on the scene to retrieve the local situation.

His center still in dire peril, Napoleon played almost his last card—the 10,500 troopers of Murat's cavalry reserve. Shortly after 11:30 A.M. 80 superb squadrons charged forward in two massive columns, crashed through the nearest Russian formations, overran the 70-gun battery, pierced the center of the Russian line, and then returned through the shattered center after reuniting into a single column of horsemen. It was one of the great charges of history, and for the loss of 1,500 cavalrymen Murat had earned Napoleon a desperately needed respite.

The battle raged on all afternoon. At 1:00 P.M., although there was still no sign of Ney from the north, Napoleon sent Davout into action from the south, and soon the Russian line was bent back into a hairpin configuration. Unfortunately for the French, Bennigsen received Lestocq's reinforcements before Ney could arrive, and the VI Corps, appearing shortly before dusk, came too late to enter the fray that day.

Overnight Bennigsen withdrew his troops, conceding Napoleon a technical rather than a true victory. In fact a draw would be the fairest assessment of the day's fortunes. Napoleon had lost at least 10,000 men; the Russians may have lost as many as 25,000. Certainly the French were in no position to pursue the foe next day, and soon both armies returned to winter quarters to await the advent of spring. Eylau was the nearest thing to a defeat Napoleon had experienced since his repulse before Acre* in 1799.

Fabvier, Colonel Etienne (fl. 1814). During the series of actions in the vicinity of Laon* in March 1814, Colonel Fabvier played a material part in averting the total rout of Marmont's* VI Corps as it fled toward the narrow Festieux Defile,* hotly pursued by Yorck* and Kleist* at the head of part of Blücher's* army. Hearing the din escalating to his rear as he marched westward to find the main French army, Fabvier gallantly countermarched his 1,000 infantry and two cannon, and managed to take Kleist in flank and drive him off the Rheims road. This feat of arms enabled the greater part of Marmont's men to rally and continue their retreat in some semblance of good order.

Fantassin, un. Common French term for an infantry soldier.

Ferdinand, Prince of the Asturias (later King Ferdinand VII of Spain) (1784–1833). The son of Charles IV* of Bourbon and his Queen, Marie-Louise of Parma, he was of a suspicious and resentful nature. Loathing the favorite Godoy,* he led an unsuccessful conspiracy against him in 1807, but then denounced his own accomplices. Constantly feuding with his father, both fearing that the other was attempting to dispose of him by poisoning or other means, in 1808 he became involved in a grave constitutional crisis in Spain which Napoleon exploited to the full, and at the Bayonne conference* both men were induced to abdicate their rights to the Spanish throne in favor (ultimately) of Joseph Bonaparte.* Ferdinand was then interned at Valençay, where he re-

mained until 1814. He at once revoked the liberal constitution of 1812, and after mounting the throne he eventually provoked the rising of 1820. The collapse of the Spanish overseas empire in South America and elsewhere led to more instability, and in 1823 the powers intervened to restore stability. Having no male heir, Ferdinand pressed the rights of his daughter Isabella at the expense of his brother Don Carlos, and this led to the gory Carlist Wars.

Ferdinand, Prince Louis of Prussia (1773–1806). Often referred to as Prince Louis-Ferdinand, he was probably the most gifted Prussian soldier of the post-Frederickan era. His promise was never fulfilled because of his tragically early death in action at the battle of Saalfeld* commanding 8,300 men against Lannes'* V Corps as the French left-hand column strove to break out from the Thuringerwald passes early in the Campaign of 1806. He was killed by Guindet,* quartermaster of the 10th French Hussars. As a prominent leader of the Prussian court war-party, his death was grievously felt.

Ferdinand, d'Este, Archduke (1781–1835?). An Italian prince closely related to the Habsburgs of Austria, he proved a quite able Austrian commander during the war of 1805 against France. He never approved of the plans of General Mack,* his superior, and refused to be bottled up in Ulm* with him, and on 15 October he evacuated the place at the head of 6,000 cavalry. Only some 1,900 reached Bohemia. At the time of the battle of Austerlitz* he was leading an Austrian corps toward Iglau. In 1809 he commanded a detached corps on the northern frontiers of Austria, defeated Poniatowski* at Raszyn (18 April), and advanced to the outskirts of Warsaw in the Grand Duchy. Pressing on toward Danzig in the hope of creating a major diversion, Ferdinand was ultimately forced to retreat after the belated entry of Russia into the war on the side of France, and by July he had been forced to evacuate most of Galicia.

Fesch, Joseph Cardinal (1762–1820?). An uncle of Napoleon (being half-brother to Letitzia*), he is credited with laying the foundations of the young boy's education in Corsica. His nephew arranged for his becoming a cardinal at the time of the Concordat* with the Papacy, and he later represented France at the Vatican. As Napoleon's mouthpiece, he bullied Pius VII without mercy. Before becoming Cardinal-Archbishop of Lyons in 1802 he earned a reputation for his supreme worldliness, but thereafter led an exemplary life and did much to improve the education of French priests. After the debacle of 1815, Fesch cared for *Madame Mère* in Rome until the end of her life, and in 1818 arranged for the sending of a priest to St. Helena* at Napoleon's express request.

Festieux Defile, action of, 10 March 1814. During the battle of Laon,* Marmont* made a very belated entry into the field and was seriously routed by Blücher's* army. As Marmont's men fled, a strong force of Prussian cavalry spurred ahead and tried to seize the Festieux Defile in the rear of Marmont. Had they succeeded, the VI Corps would have been doomed, but the heroic escort of a French convoy—just 125 men of the Old Guard*—managed to fight off the horsemen and kept the vital road toward Rheims open. This feat of arms, together with that of

Fabvier* a short distance to the north, indubitably saved Marmont.

Fiodoroivskoy, battle of, 3 November 1812. As the French *Grande Armée* retreated from Moscow, General Miloradovitch* abruptly attacked Davout's* I Corps, forming the rear guard near this town, about 50 miles west of Borodino. The Russians attacked in strength—perhaps 30,000 in all, including 20,000 cavalry and Cossacks—and Davout was soon cut off from the main French column and being assailed from all sides. The outlook for the 20,000 Frenchmen was bleak until Eugène Beauharnais,* next ahead of I Corps in the column, realized his colleague's peril and sent back two divisions of the IV Corps to his assistance. By breaking through the surrounding formations of Russians, these troops created a corridor that permitted Davout's survivors to move to the west toward the main army.

The Russians continued to press, however, and until yet another reinforcement, this time General Razout's division of Ney's* III Corps, was sent back from Viasma, it was still possible that a disaster would overwhelm the French. However, as the late-comers hove in sight Miloradovitch called off his formations, and the battered survivors of I Corps rejoined the main army. The cohesion of Davout's command was much shaken by this misadventure, and in fact its morale never recovered. Ney's III Corps assumed the role of rear guard in its place. It is estimated that Davout lost some 4,500 men.

Fiorella, Général Pascal Antoine (1752–1818). A native of Corsica, he was commissioned into the Royal Corsican Infantry Regiment in 1770. During the Revolution he served in the Alps and then, from 1794–99, in the Army of Italy. Confirmed as *général de brigade* in December 1795, he fought next year at

Mondovi* and Castiglione* (in temporary command of Sérurier's* division on the latter occasion), revealing his presence on Wurmser's* flank somewhat prematurely. Briefly a captive in November, he was exchanged and promoted to *général de division* in November 1797. In May 1799 he surrendered Turin to the Austrians, and after three years in captivity was restored only to the rank of *général de brigade* after release. He moved into the service of the Italian Republic in 1803 and became a lieutenant general in September 1804. He served under Eugène Beauharnais* with distinction at Venice (1805) and after further commands within Italy became a senator in 1809. A command in Corsica ended in August 1815, but two years later he was confirmed as a lieutenant general in the service of France.

First of June, naval battle of, 29 May–1 June 1794. Admiral Lord Howe,* "Black Dick" to his contemporaries, was all of 69 years old when he fought and tactically won this, the first major naval battle of the Revolutionary Wars, fought 400 miles west of Ushant. The French saw fit to claim a strategic success, since a crucial grain convoy of 130 sail from the U.S.A. safely reached Brest and that had been their purpose in putting to sea from Brest on 16 May, but tactically there is no doubt the honors lay with the Royal Navy.

Admiral Villaret de Joyeuse* sailed from Brest at a time when Howe was beating far out to sea watching for the arrival of the convoy. The French fleet totaled 26 sail-of-the-line, and Howe was soon in hot pursuit, capturing and burning two French corvettes on 25 May. He had been forced to detach a force of eight sail from his original force of 34 ships-of-the-line under Admiral Montagu to escort an outward-bound British convoy past Cape Finisterre, and this left him with 26 first-line vessels, but he was eager for action. On 28 May the *Queen*

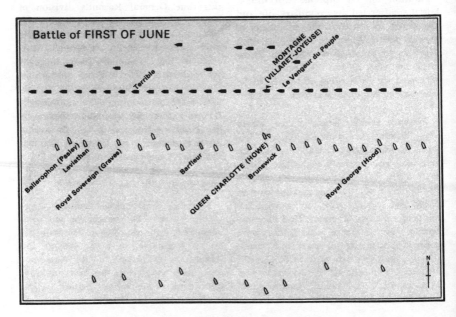

Charlotte (flagship) sighted the French ten miles to windward, but Villaret de Joyeuse did his best to avoid battle against so imposing a British force and tried to increase his lead. Howe detached Admiral Pasley with a group of ships to bring the French to battle, and soon four British vessels were in action and the French were forced to send the battered *Révolutionaire* back to France with an escort next day. By this time Howe was striving to get to windward of the French, and succeeded in catching up with the rear of their line and in cutting off the three last ships. To save them, Villaret de Joyeuse, under the glowering eye of a *deputé-en-mission*, Saint-André,* had to concede the windward advantage. To date the French had lost four ships from their line of battle to the British one, but could console themselves that the convoy was still safe.

On 30 May a reinforcement of four ships brought the French strength back to its original level, while Howe was still without Montagu's squadron. Mist concealed the position of the rival fleets, but this cleared on the 31st and Howe found his adversaries close by. He ordered battle for the next day. His plan called for the British fleet to bear down on the French bow to bow in order to smash their line in several places and defeat them in detail, confident that superior British seamanship would tell. He was to be proved correct.

Early on what would become known as "the Glorious First of June," the Royal Navy engaged the French. The six ships in Howe's van carried out his orders precisely—those to the rear with less effect—and soon the battle was joined. French confusion was great, and by evening six prizes were in British hands and another French ship had sunk. Villaret de Joyeuse was in full flight for Brest, but Howe failed to launch an all-out pursuit, earning some criticism thereby. His fastest ships were the most mauled, however,

and he was hoping that Montagu and a force from Plymouth might be in a position to cut off the French retreat; besides, he still hoped to find and destroy the French convoy.

Montagu did in fact sail for Brest and forestalled the French there, but unfortunately he drew aside and allowed Villaret de Joyeuse through into the *rade*, much to his relief. News then reached him that during the battle the convoy had slipped past the battle, and had safely reached harbor in France. Villaret de Joyeuse promptly claimed a victory. Back in Great Britain, however, King George III* was under no illusions as to where the success of the tactical battle indubitably lay, and the monarch instituted a special gold medal for the most deserving admirals and captains.

Fismes, battle of, 17 March 1814. As the Allies converged on Paris, Napoleon marched on St. Dizier,* hoping that this threat to their communications would distract their attention from the capital. In fact it was not to be, as the Allies captured a letter revealing the Emperor's plan. Meanwhile, Blücher* had defeated Marmont* in a sharp brush at Fismes, and both that Marshal and Mortier* at Rheims retired westward. News of this success persuaded the Allies to ignore Napoleon's maneuver and to press on for Paris.

Fleurus, battle of, 26 June 1794. This oft-fought-over ground (it had been the scene of major battles in 1622 and 1690) saw an important encounter between the French Revolutionary Army and the main forces of the First Coalition.* General Jourdan,* with 75,000 men, had captured Charleroi on the 25th, but as he moved deeper into the Austrian Netherlands he was next day attacked by 52,000 Austrian and German troops under command of Frederick Josias, Prince of Saxe-Coburg,* who advanced in five columns, the fourth being commanded by the young Archduke Charles.* Jourdan, with the aid of some balloons of the *corps aerostatier*, was eventually able to comprehend the Allied movements, which were poorly coordinated. The French volunteers fought well from rough entrenchments, and after six hours all Allied columns had been repulsed. Saxe-Coburg fell back over the Meuse to lick his wounds, although it later transpired that he had in fact suffered only half the casualties sustained by the French. The Prince lost 2,286 men, the French about 4,000. On the French side both Kléber* and Lefebvre* distinguished themselves. This considerable success proved the turning point of the War of the First Coalition, Austria abandoning the Netherlands.

Flotilla, for the invasion of England, May 1803—August 1805. Napoleon was planning to invade the British Isles at the head of 160,000 men, and the amount and type of shipping involved caused many problems. The main crossing would have to be by boats with oars as well as sails, owing to conditions of wind and tide. A thousand flat-bottomed boats, each capable of carrying 60–100 soldiers and two to four cannon, were ordered, and soon almost every port of France was hard at work producing its quota. As each batch of 30 to 60 were ready, they would be moved to the Pas de Calais area (where the Camp of Boulogne* was established) by canal or hugging the coast, special batteries being established to protect them from the Royal Navy, and field artillery moving along the cliffs in their support. These security measures proved effective. To receive the invasion barges, the port of Boulogne was deepened and extended, and the boats were moored along the quays nine deep. In addition, Vimereaux, Ambleteuse and Etaples took between

them 700 gun-vessels and transports, capable of lifting 62,000 troops and 6,000 horses, while a further 400 vessels massed at Calais, Dunkirk, and Ostend ready to move 27,000 more men and 2,500 horses, these forces forming the reserve. In fact this formidable armada would never put to sea, as a combination of British naval superiority and the machinations of the Third Coalition* never gave Napoleon the opportunity to launch it into action— if, indeed, he ever intended it to be more than a show of daunting force designed to cow British resistance.

Fletcher, Lieutenant Colonel Sir Richard (1768–1813). This very distinguished Royal Engineer saw early service in the West Indies and served with the Turks from 1799–1800, helping to build defenses at El Arish* and Jaffa.* He was later taken prisoner by the French but was released in 1802. In 1807 he took part in the Copenhagen* expedition, and from 1808 served Wellesley (later Wellington)* as chief engineer in Portugal. He fought well at Talavera,* but his greatest achievement was the construction of the Lines of Torres Vedras* (1809–10) near Lisbon. He fought at Bussaco* and ran the sieges of Ciudad Rodrigo* and Badajoz,* being wounded in the groin at the latter in April 1812. Next year he was made a baronet and awarded a pension. In 1813 he fought at Vitoria* and directed the sieges of Pamplona* and San Sebastian,* but was killed during the storming of the latter.

Flushing, capture of, 16 August 1809. The Walcheren* expedition mounted by the Earl of Chatham* as a diversion in northwestern Europe while Napoleon was far away fighting Austria on the Danube, proved a failure. Although 40,000 men were landed at the mouth of the river Scheldt, the effects of surprise were frittered away by the need to take the town of Flushing. The garrison put up a stalwart defense, and although they ultimately succumbed, enough time had been won for King Louis Bonaparte* and Marshal Bernadotte* to reinforce Antwerp in strength. Meanwhile, malaria (or "Walcheren fever") took its grim toll.

Fombio, combat of, 8 May 1796. This village just north of the river Po northeast of Piacenza was the scene of an indecisive skirmish on the evening of the 7th, and of a determined French assault. General Liptay's advance guard, at the head of Beaulieu's* army, was driven from its fortified village position by the French divisions of La Harpe* and Dallemagne*—perhaps 18,000 men in all —and were pursued for two hours toward Lodi.* Losses were proportionately heavy on both sides. The Austrians lost 280 killed and wounded and 700 prisoners; the French lost 150 killed and 300 wounded in the first volley alone. Colonel Jean Lannes* greatly distinguished himself in this action.

Fontainebleau, the farewell of, 20 April 1814. After accepting the Allied demands for his unconditional abdication and departure to the isle of Elba* (see next item), Napoleon reviewed the Old Guard for the last time in an emotional parade held in the Courtyard of the White Horse at the Palace of Fontainebleau. During its course he selected the 600 Guardsmen who were to be allowed to form his guard in exile. Many old soldiers were in tears, and at the parade's conclusion the Emperor embraced the eagle color of the Old Guard. He then entered his coach for the journey to St. Raphaël where H.M.S. *Inconstant* was waiting to carry him into exile.

Fontainebleau, treaties of, 16 April 1814. Forced to abdicate by the revolt of the marshals led by Ney,* Napoleon

awaited the pleasure of the victorious Allies. Caulaincourt,* Macdonald,* and Ney conducted the negotiations for the French, and several days of haggling took place. First the Allies extracted an unconditional abdication (6 April) whereby Napoleon renounced the thrones of France and Italy for himself and his heirs. On the 11th the final terms were agreed: Napoleon would receive Elba* and an annual allowance paid by the Allies. The principality of Parma was awarded to Marie-Louise and his son, and the other members of the family received pensions.

Fontainebleau had figured in several other important moments of the First Empire. On 13 October 1807 a decree signed there reinforced the Berlin Decrees* and the Continental System*; fourteen days later the first treaty of Fontainebleau was signed by Godoy* on behalf of the Spanish government, whereby France and Spain agreed to cooperate in the conquest of Portugal and the overthrow of the House of Braganza*—the country was to be partitioned into three sections, the northern area to go to the Queen of Etruria, the center (and Lisbon) to France, and the south to Godoy as a personal principality. In October 1810 further Fontainebleau decrees were issued tightening certain aspects of the Continental System's operation. But the treaty that bore the Palace's name in 1814 was the most significant, ending as it did the First French Empire.

Fouché, Joseph, duc d'Otranto (1759–1820). A religious youth who was given up by his materialistic parents as impossibly unworldly, the future Minister of Police was head of a school at Nantes run by the Oratorian Order in 1789. He embraced the Revolution when he realized it would succeed, and became deputy for the Lower-Seine Department in the Convention. For a time he was associated with Carnot* and Robespierre,* voted for the execution of Louis XVI,* and earned a reputation for hard work, thoroughness, and intrigue. He put down a revolt at Lyons aimed against Robespierre* with ruthless zeal, but on *9 Thermidor* (see *coups d'état*) he acted with equal vigor against his former Jacobin friends. He next served the Directory,* but in 1799 plotted its overthrow at *Brumaire** and promptly associated himself with Bonaparte's meteoric rise. Napoleon eventually confirmed him in his post as Minister of Police, and·in this capacity he eliminated much of the opposition to Napoleon within France—whether republican or crypto-royalist. He opposed the execution of the duc d'Enghien* in 1804 on grounds of expediency, but generally worked ruthlessly at his task. He remained Minister of Police until 1810, when he was replaced by Savary* following revelation of his intrigues with the House of Bourbon in exile. He was then employed on missions to Italy and Illyria, but his network of agents throughout France kept him minutely informed of all that was happening. On the restoration of the Bourbons he craftily followed a middle path and managed to maintain clandestine links with his former Emperor in Elba.* As a result, he was reinstated as Minister of Police during the Hundred Days.*

With his usual survivor's instinct, after news of the outcome of Waterloo* he abandoned Napoleon once and for all, and proposed the second abdication in the Chamber of Representatives. Louis XVIII,* once again restored to the throne of St. Louis, felt bound to reappoint Fouché to his old post—so comprehensive was his intelligence network throughout France—and on 9 July 1815 both he and that other expert in personal survival, Talleyrand,* were appointed to key posts. This provoked a strong reaction and bitter criticism among the King's ultra-rightwing supporters, and he was forced to re-

sign in September. As a sop, he was made head of the French legation at Dresden, but in 1816 he was removed from this post when a law was promulgated against all regicides. He moved to Prague and then to Trieste, where he lived out his days in great comfort, thanks to the vast fortune he had amassed, one way and another, during his years of power. So ended the career of a powerful and sinister man. His skill at discovering plots against Napoleon—both real and imagined—and the apparatus of police terror he built up, made him a feared and hated figure. In many ways he was a second-rate intellect, and Napoleon never gave him his fullest trust, with good reason.

Fourés, Mme. Pauline (1781–1869). Born Pauline Bellisle in Carcasonne, *"Bellitote"* later married Lieutenant Fourés of the 22nd *Régiment de Chasseurs* and managed to accompany the Army of the Orient to Egypt. The pretty blonde caught Bonaparte's eye, and an affair developed. Her husband soon found out and objected, whereupon his wife divorced him and continued from 1798 to 1799 as the general's chief mistress, called "Cleopatra" by the envious troops. She was not included in the party Bonaparte brought back from Egypt; aided by Kléber,* she secured a passage on an American vessel, but this was intercepted by the Royal Navy and she was returned to Egypt. In 1800 she managed to reach France and remarried. In 1811 she reputedly met Napoleon at a masked ball, and he awarded her a pension of 60,000 francs—but only for one year. She settled in the town of Craponne, where she scandalized the inhabitants by openly smoking a pipe. In 1816 she divorced her second husband and set off for Brazil with a former officer of the Imperial Guard. There she established a lucrative business in precious woods which kept her busy until 1837, when she settled in Paris in an apartment full of monkeys and parrots. She wrote two mediocre novels and lived until her late 80s, vivacious to the last. She ranks high among Napoleon's seven mistresses.

Fournier-Sarlovèse, Général François, baron, later comte (1773–1827). Originally a clerk, he was commissioned into the cavalry in 1792. Cashiered for fraudulent accounts and absence without leave in 1794, he was reinstated the next year. In 1797 he served as aide to Augereau,* commanded a unit of Guides in Germany (1797–98), and in 1800 saw some service with the Army of Reserve. In 1802 he was arrested for suspected complicity in a plot against Napoleon but was freed after three weeks. Posted to the West Indies in 1805, he sailed there but returned without landing aboard Villeneuve's* fleet. In 1806 he was attached to the Army of Naples, and in 1807 became Chief of Staff to General Lasalle.* He fought at Eylau* and Friedland,* was promoted to *général de brigade* in June 1807, and was made a baron next

Fournier

year. Posted to Spain, he fought in the Corunna campaign. After various appointments he fell seriously ill in 1811, but was sufficiently recovered to command Victor's* cavalry division in Russia (1812). He fought at Smolensk* and became *général de division* in November shortly before the Beresina,* where he was wounded. In 1813 he fought at Gross-Beeren* and Leipzig,* but was arrested after displeasing the Emperor. Reinstated in May 1814, he subsequently served the Bourbons in various capacities, including that of Inspector General of cavalry (1819).

Fox, Charles James (1749–1806). This British politician and statesman was the son of the first Baron Holland, was educated abroad and at Oxford, and entered Parliament in 1768. He became a Lord of Admiralty under Lord North in 1772, but was dismissed by King George III* two years later. Becoming a strong critic of British policy toward North America, in 1778 he joined the Rockingham Whigs and was particularly critical of naval affairs. He was wounded in a duel and was notorious as a gambler, running up huge debts.

In Parliament, however, Fox became a noted authority on economic and constitutional questions. He served Rockingham as Foreign Secretary in 1782, and helped found Grattan's Parliament in Ireland, but resigned when Rockingham fell the same year. A great favorite of the Prince of Wales, later George IV,* he was for that reason, *inter alia*, unpopular with the King. He got the Prince a financial grant despite royal opposition, and then busied himself with the affairs of the East India Company, helping to prosecute Warren Hastings in Parliament, 1786–89. During George III's first illness he secured the title of Regent for the Prince of Wales (1788). He became the inveterate opponent of the younger Pitt,* challenging his policies on the French Revolution, on the Eastern question, and on the matter of the treason and sedition bills. From 1792–97 Fox rarely attended Parliament, but was widely considered the most significant Whig politician. During this period he wrote his *History of the Revolution of 1688,* and in 1798 lost the status of Privy Councillor for toasting "Our Sovereign— the People" in public.

Napoleon had great hopes of a *rapprochement* with Great Britain should Fox become prime minister, and indeed met him in 1802 while Fox was traveling in France. In 1803 he made a three-hour speech in Parliament in favor of preserving the peace, but although proposed for a place in Pitt's cabinet after the fall of Addington,* this was vetoed by the king in 1804. After Pitt's death in 1806, Fox served as Foreign Secretary to Grenville, and sent information about a plot to assassinate Napoleon to Paris. A few days prior to his death, he moved the abolition of the slave trade in Parliament.

A man of uncouth habits and expensive pastimes, he was also a major intellect.

Foy, Général Maximilien Sebastien, comte (1775–1825). Commissioned into the gunners in 1792, he served with both foot and horse artillery. Sacked by the Revolutionary Tribunal for expressing bold views, he was restored to his rank and employment after the *coup d'état* of *Thermidor.* He fought in 1796 at the passage of the Rhine and at Offenburg,* and next year was wounded near Kehl. In 1799 he commanded Lorge's* guns at Zurich,* and in 1800 fought at Engen, Moesskirch, and Biberach. In 1803 he voted against the Life Consulate and the creation of the Empire, but was put in charge of coastal defense and of the mobile batteries associated with the Boulogne flotillas.* In August 1805 he was posted to Marmont's* II Corps, and two years later accompanied

Foy

Sebastiani* to Constantinople on a diplomatic mission. From late 1807 he served under Junot* in Portugal, being wounded at Vimiero.* In November 1808 he was promoted to *général de brigade,* and in 1809 fought under Soult* against Moore* at Corunna.* Defeated under Soult at Oporto,* he was later seized and imprisoned there by Portuguese militia but was eventually rescued. Made a baron in 1810, he was badly wounded at Bussaco.* Later that year he was sent by Massena* to explain to Napoleon the situation outside the Lines of Torres Vedras,* and he was promoted to *général de division* on the spot despite the unpalatable news he bore. He returned to Portugal in February 1811 to command a division of VI Corps. With this he served with great distinction at Salamanca* (July 1812), covering the retreat of the routed French army with skill, but being badly mauled at Garcia Hernandez.* In 1813 he defended Tolosa, won the action of Maya,* but was repulsed at the Nive,* and in February 1814 he was wounded at Orthez.*

He was accepted by the Bourbons and made an Inspector General, but in March

1815 he proclaimed Napoleon at Nantes, and thereafter served with Reille's* II Corps during the Hundred Days.* He fought at Quatre Bras* on 16 June 1815, but two days later was shot through the shoulder before Hougoumont during the battle of Waterloo.* He was retired from active service in August 1815, but subsequently served as an Inspector General and entered French politics as a liberal. He wrote a celebrated history of the Peninsular War, and died of a heart attack on 27 November 1825. A gallant soldier, Foy was one of Napoleon's ablest divisional commanders.

Francis I, Emperor of Austria (also Francis II of Germany) (1768–1835). He succeeded Leopold II in 1792 as Emperor Francis II of Germany, but dropped this title in 1806 when Napoleon dissolved the Holy Roman Empire, becoming Francis I of Austria. The first part of his long reign was dominated by unsuccessful wars, and during them Austria lost large areas of territory at the successive peaces of Campo Formio,* Luneville,* Pressburg,* and the Schonbrunn.* Despite these humiliations at the hands of France, in 1810 he married his daughter Marie-Louise* to Napoleon, and for three years remained an ally of the French Empire. However, in August 1813, advised by Metternich,* he joined the Sixth Coalition* at the end of the Armistice* of that year, and played a considerable part in the defeat of Napoleon, being present at Dresden* and Leipzig.* Following the wars, he adopted a conservative policy over home affairs, joined the Holy Alliance, and severely repressed burgeoning Italian nationalism in both 1821 and 1831. Not a particularly incisive ruler, he left most home affairs to Prince Metternich, and entrusted military aspects to his younger brother, the Archduke Charles.*

Frasnes, action of, 15 June 1815. As Napoleon crossed the Belgian frontier through Charleroi to begin the military phase of the Hundred Days,* Marshal Ney* in command of the two corps of the left wing advanced toward Quatre Bras.* In the early evening he was brought to a halt at Frasnes by the presence of a single battalion of Nassauers and eight guns, who boldly held their ground despite massive French superiority of force. Ney smelled a trap and halted for the night when Major Normann and Captain Bylefeld fell back to Quatre Bras, where further forces were collecting on the orders of Prince Bernhard of Saxe Weimar. The French closed up to the crossroads but took no further action that night, losing a great opportunity.

Fraser, General Alexander George, Baron Saltoun (1785–1853). An ensign in the 35th Foot in 1802, he served in Sicily (1806), at Corunna* (1809), in the Walcheren* expedition, and from 1812–14 in Spain and southern France. In 1815 he commanded the light companies of the Second Brigade of Guards at Quatre Bras,* and at Waterloo* held the garden and orchard of the chateau of Hougoumont against all French attacks, and late in the evening led the successful bayonet charge that finally routed the Middle Guard. In 1837 he was promoted to major general, and he played a leading role in the Chinese War of 1841–43. Promoted to lieutenant general in 1849, he was dubbed a Knight of the Thistle in 1852.

Fraser, General Alexander Mackenzie (so-called) (1756–1809). Commissioned into the 73rd Highlanders in 1778, he served as ADC to General Heathfeld during the siege of Gibraltar. As a lieutenant colonel he fought at Nimeguen (1794) and Geldermaisen (1795). In 1796 he went to the Cape of Good Hope with a battalion of the 78th which he had raised himself. He fought in the Mahratta Wars (1788–89) and was promoted to major general in 1802. The same year he entered Parliament, and next year assumed the name of Fraser. In 1807 he commanded an unsuccessful expedition to Egypt, but next year was transferred to the Peninsula. He served with Moore* through the Spanish campaign of 1808–09, and commanded a division at Corunna.* Later that year he took part in the Walcheren* expedition, where he caught fever and died.

Frazer, Colonel Sir Augustus Simon (1776–1835). The son of a military engineer, he entered the Royal Artillery in 1793. Under Dickson* he commanded the guns in the abysmal attack on Buenos Aires* in 1807, and thereafter was appointed to command the Horse Artillery as a member of Wellington's* staff during the years 1813 to 1815, including at Waterloo.* Knighted for his services in 1814, he was made a Fellow of the Royal Society in 1816. Only in 1825, however, did he receive his colonelcy, and he ended his career as Director of the Royal Laboratory, Woolwich (1828).

Frederick, William Charles, Prince of the Netherlands (1797–1881). The younger son of King William I, he was born in Berlin. He fought the Campaign of 1813 with the Allies, and was present at Waterloo.* In 1830 he failed to suppress serious rioting in Brussels, and retired from public life. He died at the Hague.

Frederick II, King of Prussia, the Great (1713–1786). One of the most notable commanders of modern history, Frederick the Great spent a miserable childhood that marked him for life. His artistic inclinations survived, but his brutal father was determined to make a soldier of him. Frederick emerged as a great general, and one whose military concepts were deeply admired by Napoleon throughout his life. Frederick led Prussia into the Silesian

War of pure aggression against Austria, and then "reaped the whirlwind" in the Seven Years' War (1756–1763) when he found all Europe, save Great Britain, ranged against him. Although he had his setbacks, he led his army to success, survived the hostile coalition until its cohesion snapped, and enabled Prussia to emerge exhausted but triumphant. At such battles as Rossbach and Leuthen he displayed great tactical skill and panache. He always tried to match his tactics to the terrain and relied on speed and shock to win his battles. The "oblique system" which he employed to bring superior strength against one part of the enemy line as a preliminary to piercing it or enveloping a flank helped form Napoleon's ideas of grand tactics.*

The King also produced a celebrated work on strategy—the *Secret Instruction* —which embodied much that Napoleon later practiced. The future Emperor always acknowledged his debt to Frederick, but observed that the contemporary Prussian army was not sufficiently flexible to do him justice. Frederick above all demonstrated that the will to survive is the most important national characteristic in a desperate war, and that good leadership can surmount the most daunting problems and perils. Once the wars were over he set about reconstructing Prussia. He achieved much, but his military descendants did not match the high and demanding qualities of "Old Fritz." After Jena-Auerstadt* Napoleon ordered Frederick the Great's personal insignia and weapons to be removed from Potsdam and transferred to Paris as trophies of war.

Frederick William III, King of Prussia (1770–1840). Born at Potsdam, he succeeded his father, Frederick William II, to the throne in 1797. He tried to remedy the repressive acts of his father's regime, reducing the censorship laws and encour-

Frederick William III of Prussia

aging religious toleration. The finances of Prussia were also put on a new footing. In 1805 he joined the Third Coalition* but backed out after Austerlitz.* Next year, driven by his masterful Francophobe wife, Queen Louise (a princess of Mecklenburg-Strelitz), whom he had married in 1793, he formed the Fourth Coalition,* and issued an ultimatum to Napoleon. Massively defeated at Jena* and Auerstädt,* Prussia was dismembered at Tilsit.* Forced into the status of a French client ruler, Frederick William was forced to send troops with the French into Russia in 1812, but after the disaster and the defection of General Yorck* at the head of the Prussian troops to the Russians, he threw over the French alliance and joined the ranks of the Sixth Coalition* in 1813. Thereafter, his troops fought in all campaigns against the French up to Waterloo,* the King being present at several battles, including Bautzen,* Dresden,* and Leipzig.* After the wars he refused to grant his people a liberal constitution or representative system, but helped create the Zollverein, or economic union of North German states. He also refused to share in Russia's repression of Polish nationalists.

Freire de Andrade, General Bernardino (1764–1809). A controversial Portuguese commander, who in 1793 took part in the campaign in Roussillon. In 1808 he organized an army to resist the French occupation forces of Junot,* but Wellesley* soon despaired of gaining real cooperation from him. However, he fought with Portuguese soldiers at Vimiero,* but next year he was killed by his own mutinous troops at the battle of Braga.

Freire de Andrade, General Gomez (1752–1817). Born in Vienna, the son of the Portuguese envoy, he eventually became a Portuguese commander of some note. He fought the French in the Roussillon Campaign, but unlike his namesake, in 1808 he entered the French service. He fought in Spain at the bitter siege of Saragossa (1808),* and in 1812 led a division into the Russian campaign. He was governor of Gloubokoie in Lithuania for much of the campaign, but rejoined the Grand Army at Smolensk* during the retreat. In August 1813 he was appointed Governor of Dresden, and was taken prisoner by the Allies when the city ultimately fell to them in November. He was freed the next May, went into retirement, and returned to Portugal. Hated as a collaborator, in 1817 he was accused of complicity in a conspiracy, tried, and shot.

Fréjus, landing at, 9 October 1799. This port on the south coast of France was Bonaparte's disembarkation point when he returned from Egypt on 9 October 1799, after a long and grueling sea voyage. This proved the first step toward the *coup d'état* de Brumaire.

Friant, Général Louis, comte (1758–1829). The son of a wax-polisher, he joined the French Guards in 1781, transferring to the National Guard of Paris in 1789. In 1792 he was elected lieutenant colonel and saw much service on the eastern frontiers and in Germany under Schérer* and Kléber.* In June 1795 he was promoted to *général de brigade,* and two years later passed to the Army of Italy, where he served in Bernadotte's* division at the Tagliamento and at Leibach. He sailed with Bonaparte to Egypt in 1798 and fought at many battles, including the Pyramids* and Heliopolis, and (in 1801) at the night battle of Alexandria against Abercromby's* army. After returning to France in late 1801 he served as Inspector General of infantry, and in

Friant

1805 commanded a division (he had become *général de division* in 1800 while still in Egypt) under Davout* at Austerlitz.* The next year he also distinguished himself, again under Davout, at Auerstädt.* In 1807 he was wounded at Eylau,* but was made a count the next year. In 1809 he fought at Eckmühl* and Ratisbon,* but was gravely wounded at Wagram.* Three years later he marched with Davout's I Corps to Moscow, being wounded at Smolensk* and twice at Borodino.* After the retreat, he became Chamberlain to Napoleon and commanded Guard formations during the campaigns of Germany and France, taking part in many of the battles. In 1815 he rallied to Napoleon, fought at Ligny* and was again wounded at Waterloo* at the head of the Grenadiers of the Old Guard. He retired from the service in September 1815.

Friedland, battle of, 14 June 1807. The town of Friedland, part of East Prussia in 1807, stands on the river Alle some 45 kilometers southeast of Königsberg (today Kaliningrad) and 26 kilometers east of Eylau.* It was the scene of a major Napoleonic battle that clinched the spring campaign of 1807 and induced Tsar Alexander* to suggest serious negotiations at Tilsit.* Its outcome spelled the end of the Fourth Coalition*—completing the work of Jena-Auerstadt* in October 1806 and reversing the impression given by the drawn battle of Eylau in February.

After leaving their winter quarters, the Russian troops of General Levin Bennigsen* had advanced on 5 June in an attempt to surprise the French stationed around Spanden and Lomitten. Napoleon had rapidly taken the necessary countermeasures and, regaining the initiative, pressed the Russians back through Heilsberg*—an indecisive battle fought on 10 June, the only result of which was to induce Bennigsen to continue his withdrawal to the Alle toward his forward base of Friedland. Believing that the Russians might be intending to retreat to the major fortress of Königsberg for sanctuary, Napoleon organized a web of fast-marching French army corps to cut the Russians off; a belief that Bennigsen was concentrating at Domnau proved erroneous, and it was only on the late evening of the 13th that a staff officer from Lannes'* V Corps arrived at Napoleon's headquarters with news that a large Russian force was massing near Friedland.

Lannes' reconnoitering parties were driven back in several hot actions by Prince Gallitzin's* squadrons during the evening of the 13th. Neither side was present in strength: Bennigsen had only 10,000 men west of the Alle bridges at this juncture, but the mass of his army was approaching. As for the French, even at 9:00 A.M. on the 14th Lannes had been joined only by Grouchy's* cavalry to bring their joint strength to 9,000 infan-

try and 8,000 cavalry, although Russian power had increased to 45,000 overnight. By 9:30 A.M., however, the arrival of Mortier's* troops brought the French up to 35,000.

Napoleon arrived at midday and at once decided to attack on the 14th, despite the advice of his staff who believed it would be wiser to await the arrival of Murat* and Davout* from their distant positions. The Emperor realized that Bennigsen was taking up a dangerous position in the bend of the river Alle with his troops facing the river. Furthermore, it was the anniversary of Marengo,* which he deemed a happy omen.

By four o'clock Napoleon was ready to attack. With the Imperial Guard and I Corps arrived on the scene, he was in command of some 80,000 men and perhaps 118 guns. His opponent Bennigsen, on the other hand, had only built up his force west of the Alle to 60,000 men and 120 guns, holding a four-mile line on

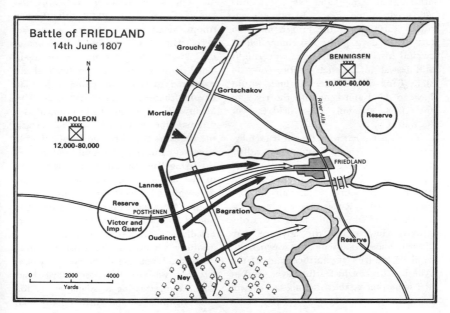

each side of the bisecting millstream which flowed into the Alle, his six infantry divisions being deployed in a double line, four to the north of the stream, two to the south. Cossacks and light troops held the northern and southern flanks around two woods. These dispositions largely determined Napoleon's dispositions and plan. To destroy the two Russian divisions of Generals Bagration* and Kologribov, Marshal Ney's* VI Corps, supported by Lannes holding the French center, was to advance northward and crush the Russians back against the river. Marshal Mortier was in command of the left wing, with d'Espagne's* and Grouchy's cavalry on his extreme flank. Victor's* I Corps and the Imperial Guard formed the centrally placed reserve. As Napoleon ordered, ". . . the advance must always be from the right, and the initiation of the movement must be left to Marshal Ney, who will await my order."

At 5:30 P.M. the French guns gave the prearranged signal, and Ney's divisions advanced to the attack. Bennigsen was totally surprised by the French move so late in the day, and he was compelled to rescind his latest order for an overnight withdrawal to a better position on the right bank of the Alle: his men would have to stand and fight with the river to their backs and only a few bridges over its waters.

The Russian left wing fought back magnificently. Marchand* and the leading French division cleared Sortlach Wood of Russian light infantry, and with the aid of Latour-Maubourg's accompanying cavalry repulsed a Russian cavalry counterattack launched on his flank by Kologribov. However, as the advance continued, massed Russian guns opened an enfilade fire from the further bank of the Alle which wrought fearful havoc, and at the same time enabled Bennigsen to send more horsemen over the millstream to

assault the hesitating French. Fortunately, the Emperor's keen eye had detected this possibility, and Marshal Victor and part of his corps were sent forward from reserve, led by General Dupont's* division. This welcome reinforcement arrived at the critical moment for Ney and fell on the flank of the Russian horsemen beyond Eylau wood. Once again the Russians pulled back.

The Russian army was fast becoming a mass of chaotic units, and now the French artillery exploited the situation. Victor ordered up 30 guns under General Sénarmont,* and, advancing by bold bounds, the gunners finally engaged the Russian masses at a range of only 150 yards, and ultimately at merely 60 paces. Whole companies of sweating Russian infantry were swept away while Latour-Maubourg disposed of the remaining Russian cavalry.

In a desperate attempt to distract the French from his crumbling left, Bennigsen launched Gortchakov* and his four divisions against Lannes and Mortier—but the attack was held by the French troops, aided by the cavalry of the Imperial Guard and Savary's* Fusiliers of the Guard. Ney was now once again marching northward at the head of his reordered divisions, sweeping a Russian bayonet charge into the waters of the Alle. Meanwhile, Dupont had resumed his original line of advance and was attacking the Russians to the north of the millstream to threaten the flank and rear of the tiring Russian center. Bennigsen now played his last remaining card—the Russian Imperial Guard—in a counterattack against Ney's flank as the French began to pour triumphantly into the outskirts of Friedland. A desperate struggle centered around a ravine, but the Russian Guardsmen could not check the rout. By 8:30 P.M. Ney was virtual master of Friedland, which the retreating Russians set fire to.

Meanwhile, on the further flank Bennigsen was trying to extricate his remaining troops over the Alle. Forty squadrons of massed French cavalry stood ready, but for some inexplicable reason Grouchy and d'Espagne let the opportunity slip, even though they faced only 25 Russian squadrons. Murat's absence from the field was now felt. However, Napoleon did not see fit to send in the unused Imperial Guard or the remaining two divisions of I Corps. Bennigsen's men had the good fortune to find a ford north of Friedland, and although three of their four bridges had been destroyed, a mass of defeated troops managed to cross the Alle covered by large batteries of guns along the riverbank. At 11:00 P.M. the battle at last drew to a close.

The French had lost between 8,000 and 10,000 casualties, and inflicted some 20,000 losses on the Russians and taken 80 guns. Napoleon had at last achieved his decisive victory. Ahead lay the conference table of Tilsit* and a victorious peace.

Frigates, naval. Fast vessels of between 28 and 36 guns, usually in a single gundeck, frigates were described by Nelson* as "the eyes of the fleet." Carrying crews of about 350 men, they were invaluable ships capable of independent action, of blockade* duties, or of cooperating with the ships-of-the-line in reconnaissance or pursuit roles, being handy and fast sailers. No navy ever had enough of them. British frigate design was superior to that of the French, but the Americans proved the best of all. By mounting larger naval guns in their frigates and developing a larger yet no less fast design, they brought off a number of spectacular successes in ship-to-ship duels during the War of 1812.*

Frimont, General Johann, Count of (1759–1831). An Austrian soldier who commanded the V Corps in 1813 and 1814, the next year he invaded Savoy, Sicily, and Provence and established himself at Dijon until 1818. The Holy Alliance sent him to repress the Neapolitan liberals (1821), and he restored Ferdinand I to the throne. As Governor of Lombardy, he similarly repressed revolts in Parma, Modena, and Ferrara. He was made President of the Austrian *Hofkriegsrath,* or War Council, (1831) but died that same year in Vienna.

Fructidor, *coup d'état de 18, An V* (4 September 1797). *See* **Coups d'état**

Fuengirola, action of, 15 October 1810. The Governor of Gibraltar, planning to distract Soult's* attention from the siege of Cadiz by threatening his lines of communication, and in the hope of causing a major popular uprising in Malaga, sent Major General Lord Blayney with a scratch force of 1,400 men (including four companies of the 89th, a Spanish regiment, and some 500 deserters of many nationalities from the French army) to make a sea landing at Fuengirola.

Conveyed in H.M.S. *Topaze,* the force landed two leagues west of Fuengirola on 14 October, but local response was minimal. The French-occupied fortress refused to capitulate and opened a damaging fire, and soon General Sebastiani* at the head of 5,000 French troops was heading for the scene from the interior. Instead of re-embarking his outclassed force, Blayney landed his guns—all four of them —and vainly tried to silence the fortress, encouraged by news that H.M.S. *Rodney* was about to arrive, carrying the 82nd Regiment. He chose a strong position with its back to the sea, stationing gunboats at each end of his line to guard the flanks; but as he was visiting the flotilla to make these arrangements the garrison made a strong sortie, and his foreign contingent promptly fled. The general rushed ashore, and at the head of the 340 men of the 89th made a brave charge which successfully regained his guns from the enemy. Seeing a new force loom nearby, and in the belief that they were Spaniards, Blayney ordered a cease-fire. His error was soon clear as Sebastiani's column appeared through the smoke, and Blayney at once charged again. This time he, and his entire force of the 89th, were compelled to surrender to *force majeur*. However, this event distracted the French, and the rest of Blayney's force was able to get off by boat, covered by two companies of the 82nd—the first of that regiment to reach the shore. This abortive but colorful and gallant action thus came to an end.

Fuentes de Oñoro, battle of, 3 and 5 May 1811. The battlefield lies between the rivers Des Casas, Turones, and Coa, around the village of Fuentes de Oñoro, which is today on the Spanish/Portuguese frontier, and the scene of the two actions lies partly in both countries. The battle was fought in May 1811 as Wellington* was determined to prevent Massena* from

resupplying the French garrison of Almeida,* some eight miles away, which was under close blockade by the Allies.

Massena advanced from Ciudad Rodrigo* on 2 May with four *corps d'armée* totalling 42,200 infantry, 4,600 cavalry, and 38 guns. Wellington at once took up an extended position along an eight-mile front, deploying his 34,500 infantry, 1,864 cavalry, and 48 guns to watch the possible routes the Prince of Essling might try to use for his breakthrough attempt. In fact, two of the Allies' six divisions saw little action, being placed to the north of Fuentes, but their presence there tied down three French divisions of Reynier's* II Corps for most of the battle.

On 3 May, Massena moved on the village of Fuentes de Oñoro with five divisions, while Wellington garrisoned the place with 2,260 men, mostly light infantry, and the 2nd battalion of the 84th Foot, all under Colonel Williams. Junot's* VIII Corps sent in ten battalions in an

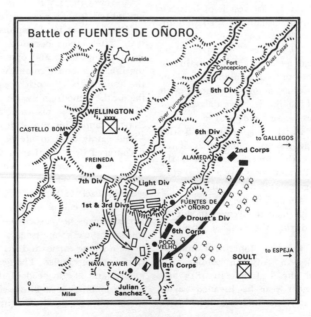

impetuous attack, and desperate fighting in and around the village lasted all day. The French drove Williams out in a second assault, but Wellington retook the village with three regiments, and after losing 259 British casualties to the French 652, the battle drew to a close at dusk with the Allies still masters of the church and narrow stone-walled lanes of Fuentes. The only other activity had been a minor diversion by Reynier against Wellington's left.

The 4th May passed with desultory outpost skirmishing. Early on the 3rd, Wellington had placed Picton's* 3rd Division above Fuentes on a ridge, with the 1st (General Spencer*), the Light Division* (Craufurd*), and Houstun's 7th Division in support and to the right, the southernment flank being entrusted to Cotton's cavalry and Sanchez's Spanish cavalry at Nave di Haver, five miles to the south of Fuentes itself. The left wing was formed by the 5th and 6th Divisions and some Portuguese troops holding Fort San Concepcion on the extreme northward end of the line, watching the main road to Almeida.

On the 5th, Massena launched a heavy blow at dawn against the Allied right near Nave di Haver. Sanchez was routed and Cotton repulsed near Poco Velho, and the 7th Division was also pushed back, as two divisions of VI Corps advanced over the river accompanied by Kellermann's* cavalry. The Light Division was brought up in the nick of time to check the French advance, and Wellington redeployed the 3rd and 1st Divisions, with a Portuguese brigade, to form a new line looking south in support of 7th Division. Craufurd fought a model withdrawal over two miles before superior forces, gaining time for the completion of these moves, but the British cavalry kept the French gunners at bay, and Ramsay's* troop of horse artillery made a celebrated escape from the midst of Junot's corps. The French outflanking force was eventually brought to a halt before the new Allied line, much of which was concealed behind reverse slopes.

Meanwhile a renewed and even more bitter battle had raged for most of the day around Fuentes, as Massena launched four major attacks, one after another, involving in all some 28 infantry battalions. Wellington was always able to reinforce the garrison of the village sufficiently to enable it to be held, but some grisly bayonet fighting took place in the narrow streets, and at one stage 100 French grenadiers were massacred in a cul-de-sac. At last, at 2:00 P.M., Massena ordered his troops to fall back to their positions. Wellington expected another attack, and uniquely dug his troops in, but Massena ordered a retreat on 10 May. The French had lost 2,192 casualties to the Allied 1,545 (both days).

Gallitzin, General Andréi, Prince (fl. 1806). This Russian cavalryman earned Napoleon's praise for the gallant fight he put up against formidable odds at the battle of Golymin* on 26 December 1806. The next year he commanded Bennigsen's* cavalry at Eylau* and was also present at Friedland,* where his horsemen were the first to engage Lannes'* corps, and he was commanding the Russian advance guard. The rest of his career is obscure.

Galuzzo, General Carlos (fl. 1807). A crusty political soldier of no great ability, Galuzzo was sent by Godoy* to occupy the part of Portugal apportioned to Spain by Napoleon in 1807. He earned notoriety for his local exactions, which continued long after the signing of the Convention of Cintra.* In 1808, when France attacked Spain, he was Captain General of Estremadura and commanded 13,000 troops around Burgos. He was recalled to answer charges of high treason before the Supreme Junta at Aranjuez in late October 1808, and was replaced by Count Belvedere, just before the launching of Napoleon's major offensive.

Ganteaume, Vice Amiral Honoré Joseph Antoine, comte (1755–1818). He first went to sea in a merchant ship in 1769, but was pressed into the Bourbon navy in 1778. He served under d'Estaing and Suffren in the West Indies during the American War of Independence, taking part in the siege of Savannah (1779). After a spell in command of a French East Indiaman he was briefly a captive of the British, but was freed and made *capitaine de vaisseau* in 1794. He fought at the Glorious First of June,* receiving three wounds, in 1794, and in 1796 was placed under Villeneuve's* command. As Admiral Bruey's* Chief of Staff, he sailed to Egypt in 1798, but escaped ashore when *l'Orient* blew up at the battle of the Nile.* Appointed rear admiral by Bonaparte in November, he served at Jaffa,* Acre,* and Aboukir,* and then sailed Bonaparte back to France aboard *La Muiron* in 1799. From 1800–02 he commanded the Brest fleet, sailing twice to Egypt in vain attempts to evacuate the French army. In 1802 he successfully led a naval force to resupply Haiti* and Santo Domingo* in the West Indies, and became vice admiral in May 1804. He was acting Admiral at Brest from 1804–05, and later shifted his flag to the Mediterranean, where he resupplied Corfu in 1808. Made a count in 1810, he was temporarily Minister of Marine. He became one of Napoleon's Chamberlains, and Colonel Commandant of the Sailors of the Guard (1811). He did not rally to Napoleon in 1815, and later voted for the death sentence for Ney.*

Garcia Hernandez, action of, 23 July 1812. After Wellington's* great victory at Salamanca,* the French were able to escape through Alba de Tormes,* but were hotly pursued by the Allied cavalry. On 23 July, four squadrons of heavy dragoons* of the King's German Legion* under General Bock* caught up with three battalions of General Foy's* infantry. In the ensuing action, the cavalry uniquely broke a formed square and also scattered a column in an uphill attack, inflicting 1,400 casualties and suffering 150 out of their 445 cavalrymen engaged. This setback forced Foy to place his division—the sole intact one after Salamanca—into a defensive position, but Wellington's infantry was not far enough forward to exploit the opportunity, and the rapid French retreat was resumed. Three days later, Wellington canceled the pursuit at Arevalo and headed for Madrid.

Gardanne, Général Gaspard Amédée (1758–1807). A coastal gunner in 1779, next year he joined the Bourbon *garde du corps,* from which he retired in 1784. In 1791 he was elected lieutenant colonel of Var Volunteers, and served in the Alps and Italy, and was present at the siege of Toulon* (1793). Much service in North Italy followed, and he was present at the Col de Tende in 1795 and at the battles of Borghetto* and Castiglione* in 1796, before being appointed Governor of Verona in October. In March 1797 he was confirmed in the rank of *général de brigade,* and served in Venice. Although nominated to a command in the Army of the Orient in Kléber's* division, he did not sail to Egypt but became governor of Alessandria in the Po valley instead, where he was in due course besieged and forced to capitulate in July 1799. He was soon exchanged for the Austrian General Mack,* took part in *Brumaire,** and was promoted to *général de division* in January 1800. He formed a division in the Army of Reserve and fought with great distinction at Marengo,* being awarded a saber of honor. In 1805 he commanded a division in Italy again under Massena,* and fought at Caldiero.* Transferred to the Army of Naples, he blockaded Gaeta (May to July 1806). For a time in 1807 he commanded a division in Ney's* corps in

East Prussia and Poland, but fell out with his commander and was switched to Lefebvre's* corps, with which he shared in the siege of Danzig* and the repulse of the Russian relief attempt. While on a mission to Silesia in 1807 to command Saxon troops, he caught a fever and died on 14 August.

Garnier, Général Pierre Dominique, baron (1756–1827). The son of a jobbing-architect, he served in the Bourbon infantry from 1773, and spent eight years in Guadeloupe in the West Indies. Back in France, he practiced as an architect briefly, and then joined the Marseilles National Guard in 1789. With them, he stormed the Tuileries Palace in October 1792. He later fought in the Alps, along the Rhine, and in Italy, becoming *général de brigade* in September 1793. He was present at Toulon,* returned to the Army of Italy in April 1794, and was promoted to *général de division* in August 1794. The next year he held an active command in the Alps, was transferred to the Army of Italy, and fought at Loano before being switched back again to the Army of the Alps. In 1799 he served in Naples and was made Military Governor of Rome. He defeated the Neapolitan army at Monte Redondo on 21 September 1799, but was forced to capitulate in Rome nine days later. He served under Suchet* in Italy in 1800, and retired in 1801. He was soon recalled to hold a number of reserve commands, and in 1811 became Governor of Barcelona,* before being retired again in July 1812. However, 1813 saw him back in the field, evacuating Fiume and Turin, but in December 1814 he retired for the last time, and was made a Baron of the Empire on the last day of that year.

Gassendi, Général Jean Jacques Basilien, comte de (1748–1828). Commissioned into the La Fère artillery regiment in 1768, as a captain, he had Lieutenant

Bonaparte under his command in May 1788. He served in the Pyrenees and North Italy, commanded the siege train at Toulon,* but fell foul of the authorities in Italy next year and only survived in employment thanks to Salicetti's* support. He commanded the artillery park of the Army of England in 1798, and was given the same post in the Army of the Reserve (1800). He was instrumental in getting the cannon over the Great St. Bernard Pass, and fought at Marengo.* In 1802 he became commandant of the Auxonne Artillery School, and was retired next year. However, he found employment in the Ministry of War in October 1804, became Inspector General of Artillery in 1805, and full *général de division* in September of that year. In 1806 he became a Councillor of State, in 1809 he was made a Count of the Empire, and in 1813 he became a senator. He voted for Napoleon's abdication in April 1814. Made a peer of France in June that year, he rallied to Napoleon in 1815 and was appointed a peer of France. Excluded from the House of Peers after Waterloo,* he was finally reinstated in November 1819.

Gaudin, Ministère Martin Michel Charles, duc de Gaeta (1756–1841). A former member of the Bourbon administration, he was a treasury commissioner during the Revolution. On the recommendation of Consul Lebrun,* Napoleon made him Minister of Finance, a portfolio he held from 1799 to 1814 without a break. He reformed direct taxation, introduced indirect taxation (*les Droits-Réunis*), founded the Bank of France and the *cour des comptes,* and established a system of rural rating. In recognition of his outstanding services, in 1809 he received a dukedom. In 1815 he was made a peer of France, and later that year was elected Deputy for the Aisne. As a politician he supported the constitutional party. He ended his career by becoming Governor of the Bank of France in 1820. He wrote a series of valuable memoirs.

Gazan, Général Honoré Theodore Maxime, comte de la Peyrière (1765–1845). Originally a coastal gunner, from 1786–91 he served in the *gardes du corps.* He also joined the National Guard of Grasse and later served on the Rhine, being wounded at Kehl in 1796; he later campaigned in Italy, along the Danube and the Rhine again. Promoted to *général de brigade* in April 1799, the next year he greatly distinguished himself under Massena* at Zurich* and was promoted to *général de division* on the field of battle (25 September 1800) (this was confirmed the next month). He next served in Switzerland and North Italy, was besieged in Genoa* with Soult* (1800), and later commanded a division in Italy under Suchet.* A period with the Army of the Ocean in 1805 was followed by an appointment in Lannes'* V Corps, with which he fought at Durrenstein,* Jena,* Pultusk,* and Ostrolenka between 1805 and 1807. The next year he moved to Spain under Mortier* and was made a count by letters patent. He served before Saragossa* and was wounded at Badajoz* and again at Albuera* (both in 1811). In January 1813 he took over command of the Army of Andalusia from Soult, and temporarily also that of the Army of the Center. In July 1813 he was appointed Soult's Chief of Staff in the Army of the Pyrenees, a post he held until April 1814. In January 1815 he was taken off the active list at his own request. In March he did not immediately rejoin Napoleon, but was eventually given the task of organizing defenses in the Somme area. He held various inspectorates between 1815 and 1831, became a peer of France in 1832, and finally retired in June 1832.

Gendarmerie Nationale, la. The French police force was reorganized in 1802, with detachments being placed in each commune under control of the Prefects. It later became a source of recruits for Napoleon's armies, especially after 1812, and much of its time was taken up in hunting down refractory conscripts.

Gendarmes d'Elite, les, of the Imperial Guard. Raised on 19 March 1802, this body was responsible for disciplinary and security aspects about Napoleon's person, including ceremonial occasions. Disbanded on 23 April 1814, the formation saw a last brief spell of existence from 8 April 1815 during the Hundred Days.*

Gendarmes d'Ordonnance, les, of the Imperial Guard. This unit proved the shortest-lived part of the Imperial Guard.* Raised on 23 September 1806, it was disbanded on 23 October 1807 after mounting pressure on the Emperor from within the Imperial Guard. Largely recruited from among the sons of influential returned *émigrés,** with the intention of binding their families more closely to the Empire, the young aristocrats were immediately highly unpopular with all other parts of the Guard, and for once Napoleon gave way to opinion.

Genoa, siege of, 20 April–4 June 1800. As the Austrians exploited their initial successes in North Italy, Generals Massena* and Soult* with 18,000 men were driven back by General Melas* into the port and city of Genoa, where they were soon closely besieged by General Ott's* corps, aided by a Royal Naval force blockading the port from the sea. News of this development forced Bonaparte to bring forward his own offensive with the forming Army of the Reserve. Despite his energetic crossing of the Alps, delays suffered before Fort Bard* made it impossible for the French to reach Genoa and relieve their beleaguered comrades in time. Despite his proud claim that "Genoa will be defended to the last extremity," Massena

knew that his powers of resistance were limited owing to shortage of rations, which were steadily reduced. Breakouts were attempted on 11 and 13 May (Soult being wounded and taken prisoner on the latter occasion). Although a smuggled message informed him that the Army of the Reserve was on its way, Massena, whose troops were reduced to eating even the hair powder, sought a parley on 1 June and opened negotiations. A convention was signed on the 4th granting the 8,110 French troops capable of marching out all the full honors of war and the right to free evacuation to join Suchet's* troops behind the river Var. Five privateers* were also allowed to sail from the port.

News of the fall of Genoa reached Bonaparte in a captured despatch near Piacenza on 8 June; and aware that the "pinning force" represented by Massena had collapsed, Bonaparte was forced to revise his plans and order movements that would lead to the battle of Marengo.*

George III, King of Great Britain (1738–1820). After succeeding his father on the throne in 1760, he determined to end the Seven Years' War, and sacked the elder Pitt, Earl of Chatham. He was soon deeply concerned with the revolt of the American Colonies, and fully backed Lord North's ministry. When the struggle spread to Europe, his conduct during the Gordon Riots of 1780 saved London from the mob, and, disillusioned by the Whigs and despairing of his son George,* Prince of Wales, he contemplated retirement to Hanover. North resigned in 1782. Later the King unwillingly backed the younger Pitt's* judgment as prime minister, but in 1793 threw all his influence behind Britain's entry into the War of the First Coalition* against Revolutionary France after the execution of Louis XVI.* Bouts of recurrent disabling illness (probably not amounting to mania, as has often been claimed) caused periodic crises, and from 1811 he withdrew from public affairs completely, his son becoming Regent. A popular monarch with the middle classes, who dubbed him "Farmer George," and much misrepresented by American propagandists, George III was a model family man although, as a ruler, inclined to be stubborn and obstinate. The tragic circumstances of his later years earned him his subjects' sympathy, and posterity is reassessing his reign and achievements.

George, Prince Regent, and later **King George IV** (1762–1830). A profligate gambler and roué from early youth, George quarreled with his father, George III,* and set up a separate household at Carlton House (1783). He secretly married Mrs. Fitzherbert in 1785, but denied the marriage to secure Parliament's aid with his crippling debts. He became closely associated with the Whigs under Rockingham and Fox.* His marriage to Caroline of Brunswick in 1795 proved disastrous, and he soon returned to Mrs. Fitzherbert. His ceaseless requests for leave to serve with the army were always refused. His father's recurrent illnesses involved periods of virtual regency, and in 1811 a restricted form of regency was officially proclaimed. He accepted the Tory ministry of Lord Liverpool* with bad grace, but generally backed the war effort against France. His later years were clouded by the divorce proceedings against Queen Caroline (1820) and by growing internal unrest; he opposed Catholic Emancipation but in the end gave way. He transformed Brighton into a fashionable watering place and showed considerable taste and discernment in artistic matters. Never a popular monarch, his reign saw a considerable diminution in both the powers and the repute of the Crown.

Gérard, Maréchal Maurice Etienne, comte (1773–1852). The son of a royal huntsman, he joined the army in 1791 and

Gérard

gained a commission the next year. He fought at Neerwinden* and Fleurus,* and in late 1796 began a long association with Bernadotte,* following him to Italy. He fought with distinction at Zurich* (1799), and later went to Hanover (1804). Wounded at Austerlitz,* the next year he was at the capture of Lubeck and was promoted to *général de brigade* in November 1806. In 1807 he fought at Mohrungen* and Eylau,* and from August became Bernadotte's Chief of Staff. He accompanied him to Copenhagen* (1808), and in 1809 became a baron and fought at Wagram.* Transferred to Spain, he fought at Fuentes de Oñoro* (1811), and after a period of sick leave, campaigned in Russia, fighting at Valuntina, Borodino,* and Maloyaroslavetz.* He had been made *général de division* in late September 1812, and took a prominent part in the retreat under command of Eugène Beauharnais.* In 1813 he commanded an infantry division under Macdonald,* fighting at Lutzen* and Bautzen* before being appointed to command the XI Corps. Wounded at Leipzig* in October, early the next year he fought at Brienne* and La Rothière,* and later took over II Corps from Victor.* He accepted Napoleon's abdication and was sent to replace Davout* at Hamburg* by the Bourbons, but he rallied to Napoleon in 1815. He captured the village of Ligny* on 16 June, and then under Grouchy* pursued the retiring Prussians. He failed to persuade his chief to march on Waterloo* on 18 June, and was wounded near Wavre.*

Forced to live in exile abroad until 1817, he returned to become a liberal deputy. In 1830 he became Minister of War and Marshal of France. In 1832, commanding the Army of the North, he invaded Belgium and besieged and took Antwerp. He was made a peer of France in 1833, and for several months in 1834 replaced Soult* as Minister of War and President of the Council. From 1842–48 he was Grand Chancellor of the *légion d'honneur*.* Napoleon III made him a senator in 1852.

Ghent, treaty of, 24 December 1814. This agreement brought to a formal end the War of 1812* between Great Britain and the United States. After protracted negotiations, the *status quo ante bellum* was restored on all fronts, but the question of the future of the islands in Passamaquoddy Bay was referred to a new commission. Commissioners were also to be appointed to survey and settle the U.S.-Canadian land frontier. Britain had earlier rescinded the Orders in Council* which had been a major cause of the war. News of the treaty arrived too late to prevent the fighting of the battle of New Orleans* in January 1815.

Girard, Général Jean-Baptiste, baron (1775–1815). Girard joined the army as a volunteer in 1793, and next year served as an unofficial staff officer under General

Monnier.* Commissioned in 1796, he was wounded at the Brenta in January 1797. Two years later he helped defend Ancona; in 1800 he became Monnier's Chief of Staff, and as such fought at Marengo.* After holding staff posts in France and Italy, in 1805 he joined Murat's* staff and fought at Austerlitz* and Jena.* In November 1806 he was promoted to *général de brigade* and passed to Suchet's* division of V Corps. He fought with this formation in Poland (1807) and next year became Baron of the Empire. Transferred to Spain, he commanded under Mortier* and distinguished himself at Arzobispo bridge* in August 1809, being confirmed as *général de division* in December. Girard was at the siege of Badajoz* (1811), fought at Albuera,* and captured Elvas,* but was taken by surprise at Arroyo dos Molinos.* In 1812 he marched into Russia under Victor's* command, fought at Smolensk* and at the Beresina,* where he was wounded commanding the rear guard. For a time in 1813 he commanded a Polish division, but was gravely wounded at Lützen.* He was besieged in Magdeburg (1813–14) before capitulating. In 1815 he commanded Napoleon's advance guard during the march on Paris, held a command in the Alps and then in the Army of the North, with whom he was serving when he was mortally wounded while storming the village of St. Amand at the battle of Ligny.* He died of his wounds in Paris 11 days later.

Gneisenau, General (later Field Marshal) Augustus Wilhelm, *Graf* Neithard von (1760–1831). The son of a Saxon officer, Gneisenau served in the Austrian and various minor German armies before joining the Prussian forces in 1786. He served in Poland, 1793–94, and in 1806 he distinguished himself defending Colberg against the French invading armies. This brought him to the notice of the reformer

Scharnhorst,* and between 1807 and 1813 he helped reform and modernize the Prussian army, organizing the *krumper* reservist system and transforming officer training, besides helping to establish a general staff. In 1813 he became Blücher's* Chief of Staff, and served him in this capacity until 1815. His sharp and acute mind ideally complemented the "hussar-complex" of his aging chief, and after Leipzig* he was admitted to the Prussian nobility. During the Hundred Days* he wished to retire on Namur after the defeat of Ligny,* but in fact retreated to Wavre* with important effects for the outcome of Waterloo.* After the wars he was made Governor of Berlin, and in 1831 he commanded the Prussian troops sent to suppress the Polish insurrection. Like Clausewitz,* he died of cholera at Posen. A gifted staff officer, he made up an ideal command team with Blücher.

Godoy, y Alvarez de Faria, Manoel, Prince of the Peace (1767–1851). A private sentinel in the Spanish Bourbon *gardes du corps,* Godoy became the favorite of Maria-Luisa of Parma, lascivious queen of Carlos IV.* Under her forceful patronage, he became a minister in 1791, and was created Duke of Alcudia and President of the Council the next year. He tried to dissuade the French Revolutionary government from executing Louis XVI* and then sought to avoid Spanish involvement in the war, but failed on both counts, and the struggle of 1793–95 against France bankrupted Spain. Godoy negotiated the Treaty of Basle by which Spain left the war of the First Coalition* in 1795, and was awarded the title "Prince of the Peace" in recognition. Later on, the French Directory* plotted his overthrow in 1798, but after two years he was back in the center of Spanish affairs. He inspired a short war against Portugal in 1801 and tried to maintain a posture of neutrality after the general pacification of Amiens.*

However, French bribes and blackmail drove him to lead Spain into an alliance with France against the Third Coalition— a decision that cost Spain her fleet at Trafalgar.*

In 1806 he intrigued with Prussia before Jena* and Napoleon extracted a Spanish corps under La Romana* for service in northern Europe as surety for Spain's continued good behavior. This treaty also led to Spanish involvement in Junot's* attack on Portugal in late 1807. Soon thereafter, however, the tensions within the Spanish Royal Family came to a head, with Godoy siding with the King against the heir apparent, Ferdinand, Prince of the Asturias.* Napoleon utilized this situation to effect the occupation of Madrid, and arranged the subsequent talks at Bayonne* which led to the abdication of both Carlos IV and Ferdinand. Godoy accompanied the old King into exile at Compiègne, and later lived in Marseilles and Rome. Although he was reinstated by Queen Isabella II, Godoy never again set foot in Spain, having too many foes. Venal and immoral, Godoy remained a sinister figure to the end of his days.

Goethe, Johann Wolfgang (1749–1832). Goethe trained to become a lawyer, but from 1771 devoted himself to literature. He is regarded as the greatest modern German poet. He soldiered in the Campaign of 1792–93, and later wrote about his experiences and the battle of Valmy.* After the Prussian catastrophe of 1806–07 he moved on the fringe of Napoleon's court circle, and in 1809 attended the Erfurt Congress* as Minister for the Duke of Weimar. There he was much lionized as well as patronized by the Emperor, to whom he presented several of his latest works.

Gohier, Ministre Louis Jerome, President of the Directory (1746–1830). A Breton lawyer by profession, he rose to influence after preparing the legal indictment against Louis XVI* on which he was tried for his life. In 1793 he was appointed Minister of Justice. Next year, following the fall of Robespierre,* he became president of the Criminal Tribunal of the Seine, and on 10 June 1799 became a member of the Directory.* He was soon appointed what was to be its last President, and as such interviewed Bonaparte on his unauthorized return from Egypt in late 1799. The *coup d'état** of *Brumaire* led to his being driven from power into obscurity, but he re-emerged in 1802 as French consul in Amsterdam. He wrote a set of notoriously inaccurate *Memoires*.

Golymin, action of, 26 December 1806. As Napoleon swept deep into Poland, the 26th December saw two notable battles. At Pultusk,* Marshal Lannes* fought General Bennigsen,* while 12 miles to the northwest Murat,* Augereau,* and eventually Davout* with all of 38,000 Frenchmen, took on the 18,000 Russian troops

of General Gallitzin.* Gallitzin was holding a good defensive position surrounded (except from the north) by woods and marshes, and he was aided by General Doctorov* (although not his full division) in a classic defensive action. Murat attacked Gallitzin's cavalry rear guard about 10:00 A.M., and as Augereau's VII Corps infantry marched up, the Prince sent in first Heudelet's* and then Desjardins' divisions against the extemporized Russian position, and deployed his two cavalry divisions against Gallitzin's meager horsemen. The Russians fought with the greatest gallantry and skill but were everywhere forced to give ground by weight of numbers after Davout's III Corps had appeared on the scene. The main Russian force then retired into a large wood, which Morand* cleared with difficulty. As they retired, Rapp* charged with dragoons in an attempt to cut their line of retreat up the Makov road, but the impetuous imperial aide-de-camp rode into a trap. He found himself opposed by Rus-

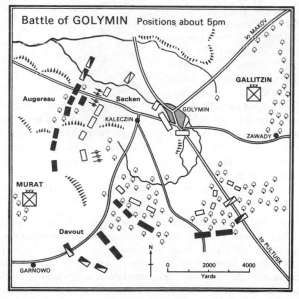

Battle of GOLYMIN   Positions about 5pm

sian infantry up to their waists in the marshes, and lost many troopers to their fire besides being wounded himself.

At nightfall the action ended, and overnight Gallitzin made good his retreat to Makov along a single road, almost completely surrounded by the French forces. He lost some 800 men—the French, it is thought, lost about the same. But against such long odds Gallitzin's achievement had been notable. Although he alone had been in a position to use artillery, the French had overestimated his strength at all of 50,000 men. The indecisive nature of this battle, together with that of Pultusk, persuaded Napoleon to send his men into winter quarters. They would not rest undisturbed: a month away was Eylau.*

Gomm, Field Marshal Sir William Maynard (1784–1875). First commissioned in 1794, he served with the 9th Foot in Holland (1799) under the Duke of York,* in the raid against Ferrol (1800), and in Hanover (1805). During the Copenhagen expedition* of 1807 he was assistant quartermaster general, and again in Portugal under Wellesley* and Moore* in 1808–09. He was at Corunna* and later that year at Walcheren.* From 1810–14 he served in the Peninsula, becoming a lieutenant colonel in 1812 after playing a fine role at Salamanca.* He served on Wellington's staff during the Hundred Days.* Promoted to major general in 1837, he held high posts in Jamaica, Mauritius, and India, where he became Commander in Chief. Promoted to full general in 1854, he received his baton 14 years later; his last appointment was as Constable of the Tower of London.

Gordon, Lieutenant Colonel Sir Alexander (1786–1815). After serving as aide-de-camp to his uncle, Sir David Baird,* at the Cape of Good Hope (1806), he fought at Copenhagen* the next year and thereafter shared in events in Portugal

and Spain until 1809. As a member of the abortive expedition to Buenos Aires,* he negotiated terms on behalf of General Beresford.* In 1813 he was promoted to lieutenant colonel. He was Wellington's* trusted aide both in Spain and during the Hundred Days* but was mortally wounded at Waterloo,* and died in Wellington's headquarters in the room next to where the Duke was penning his famous dispatch.

Gordon, General Sir James Willoughby, Baronet (1773–1851). Commissioned into the 66th Foot, by 1801 he had served in Ireland, the West Indies, Gibraltar, and North America. In 1801 he became lieutenant colonel of the 85th, and later of the 92nd. He was for a period Military Secretary to the Duke of York* and then quartermaster general in the Peninsula (1811–12) before being reappointed to a post at the Horseguards. A lieutenant general in 1825, he became a full general in 1841, and a Privy Councillor in 1830.

Gortchakov, General André Ivanovitch, Prince (1768–1855). Present at Friedland (1807), after distinguished service in the campaigns of 1812, 1813, and 1814 he was made General of Infantry in the Tsar's armies in 1819. He retired nine years later.

Gortchakov, General Pietre Dmitrievich (1789–1868). After taking a prominent part in the campaigns of Russia and Germany (1812–13) he commanded a division against Turkey in 1829. He was responsible for annexing much of the Amur region, and from 1839–51 was Governor of Eastern Siberia.

Gourgaud, Général Gaspard, baron (1783–1852). Educated at the Ecole Polytechnique, Gourgaud became an artillery officer and after several campaigns was appointed a personal staff officer to Napoleon in 1811. In 1813 he assessed the situa-

Gourgaud

tion at Dresden* before the battle, and in 1814 fought at Laon* and Craonne.* In 1815 he rallied to Napoleon, and after Waterloo* accompanied the fallen Emperor to St. Helena,* where he served as secretary while Napoleon dictated part of his memoirs. Severe disagreements with Baron Montholon,* however, caused Gourgaud to return to France in 1818, where he tried to gain for Napoleon better conditions of exile—but in vain. Louis-Philippe promoted him to general, and in 1849 he entered politics. He was the author of several books on the Imperial Army and on the exile of St. Helena.

Gouvion St. Cyr. *See* **Saint-Cyr,** Gouvion.

Goya, Francisco de (1746–1828). A brilliant Spanish artist who studied art at Saragossa and Rome, he became official court painter at Madrid from 1786. He painted Spanish life in all its forms, and among his best-known works are his paintings of the revolt of Madrid on 2 May 1808—and of its aftermath. His sketches, the "Horrors of War," reveal the full frightfulness and bitterness of an implacable guerrilla struggle. After the wars he returned to depicting country and bullfighting scenes, but eventually became the victim of deep depression bordering on lunacy. In 1824, disapproving of the absolute monarchy, he moved to Bordeaux.

Goya

Graham, General Sir Thomas, Baron Lynedoch (1748–1843). Educated at Oxford, he for many years lived the life of a Scottish landowner, playing cricket and breeding horses and cattle. The callous treatment accorded the corpse of his wife by the French revolutionary authorities after she had died of natural causes in France caused him to become a fanatical Francophobe. In 1793 he served as unpaid aide-de-camp to Lord Mulgrave at Toulon,* and next year raised at his own expense a unit of volunteers in Scotland and was appointed its unpaid lieutenant colonel. From 1794–1807 he was an MP of the Whig persuasion. In 1796 he served as a liaison officer with the Austrians in North Italy. He was prseent at the capture of Minorca (1798) and helped improve the defenses of Sicily. He served under Captain Ball RN* at the siege of the French troops in Malta* (1799–1800).

Through the influence of Sir John Moore* Graham at length secured a full military appointment and served as Moore's aide during the Corunna* campaign. Later in that year he commanded a brigade at Walcheren.* Promoted a lieutenant general in 1810, he won the battle of Barrosa* outside Cadiz, but resigned in pique when the Spanish generals claimed all the credit. Wellington* gave him a division, and he served at the siege of Ciudad Rodrigo* and Badajoz.* In the Vitoria* campaign of 1813 he commanded the left wing of the Allied army, marching independently to turn one French position after another. He fought at Vitoria and was wounded at Tolosa. His siege of San Sebastian* was at first unsuccessful, but he captured the city and fortress in the end. He was invalided home after the crossing of the Bidassoa* but was fit enough to command a British force sent to Holland in 1814. He was created a peer that year but refused a pension, and in 1821 he was promoted to full general. He was a chief founder of the United Services Club (the "Senior") in London—a task he achieved despite much official opposition.

Grand Strategy. This level of warfare relates to the formulation of policy and of realistic war aims, the creation and maintenance of alliances, and the overall organization of countries for waging successful war. The opening of the French Revolutionary Wars* in 1791 was almost fatal to the French government of the day, which deliberately challenged Europe but managed to survive through a combination of good fortune, mass enthusiasm, the blunders of the members of the First Coalition,* and the battle of Valmy.* Later, as confidence grew, France set herself the task of liberating the peoples of Europe from their old rulers and fought in Italy, Switzerland, Holland, and Germany for this purpose with mixed fortunes. Under Robespierre* and then the Directory* France was indeed organized on a war footing.

With the rise of Napoleon to power in 1799, a firmer policy became apparent. Aware of the exhaustion of France, he first fought for, and secured at Amiens,* a general peace which, however shortlived, did earn France a breathing space during which the First Consul reordered the economy and general administration and created the *Grande Armée*. Renewed war with Great Britain (from 1803) spread into general conflict in 1805, partly because of French diplomatic blunders (for instance the Enghien* affair) and unscrupulous territorial ambitions, and ten years of almost continuous wars followed. Napoleon—the supreme realist—proved most effective at destroying one hostile coalition after another, aiming always to destroy his enemies' main armies as rapidly as possible as the only sure means to a victorious peace. However, despite great diplomatic successes such as Tilsit* (and on a lesser scale the conferences of Erfurt* and Dresden*), and despite his paramount position on the Continent, Napoleon could never secure any lasting allies—except perhaps the Poles of the Grand Duchy of Warsaw. His demands in terms of men and money were always too exorbitant, and his thinly disguised scorn for the old rulers of Europe did not aid his cause. Thus the Austrian marriage alliance with Marie-Louise* did not bring more than two years of uneasy alliance with Francis I,* and even his relations with his own satellite kingdoms—Spain, Holland, Westphalia, and the Two Sicilies—were stormy and ultimately self-destructive.

At the level of Grand Strategy Napoleon made a number of mistakes that led to his downfall. His inveterate hostility toward Great Britain—which he saw with some reason as the implacable foe of France—and his frustration at his inability to come to grips with British forces because of the superiority of the Royal Navy led him to institute the Continental System* in 1806, which may be seen as the source of many of his future problems. It led him into the Portuguese and then the Spanish adventures, which ultimately merged to the insoluble problem of the "Spanish Ulcer" for the French—and which gave Britain a chance to strike back effectively at Napoleon on land. In large measure it also led to the Russian campaign of 1812, which doomed the First Empire. With simultaneous wars on two fronts, some 1,700 miles apart, France's resources could not for long stand the strain. Reliance on foreign contingents and unwilling allies to fill the ranks of the army led to a diminution of battle power, and once the list of disasters began to grow, his former confederates rapidly joined the victorious forces of the Sixth Coalition,* while Britain assumed the all-out offensive in Spain against the reduced French forces.

Although Napoleon "lost" the war at sea effectively from 1805, his naval strategy against Great Britain remained surprisingly effective. The severe defeats of the Nile (or Aboukir*) and Trafalgar* made it impossible for France to gain the real upper hand at sea in the conventional sense, but Napoleon played his remaining cards with skill. By keeping his surviving squadrons ready for sea (or capable of being rapidly made so) at Brest,

Rochfort, or Toulon, he kept the Royal Navy at full stretch on blockade* duties, and the task of hunting down a small French break-out force was incommensurately expensive in terms of vessels and effort. But such excursions—which were still taking place as late as 1809—could not be ignored by the British Admiralty while Ireland remained an inviting target for subversion and French military aid to the rebels. Again, Britain's dependence on seaborne commerce for her prosperity gave France the opportunity to mount a full-scale *guerre de course*, using numbers of privateers to pounce on merchant shipping in the Channel and its approaches. This placed a great strain on both the British economy and the Royal Navy, which was required to patrol the sea lanes and escort convoys in and out of British ports. Finally, by threatening to seize neutral navies, however small in themselves, Napoleon could compel Britain into desperate acts—such as the two Copenhagen* expeditions against neutral Denmark. By these means, Napoleon kept the Royal Navy at full stretch and almost broke its cohesion. From France's point of view as a continental power, this strategy had its culmination in the outbreak of the War of 1812* between Britain and the United States.

British Grand Strategy was based in the earlier parts of the war on an outdated version of the Elder Pitt's "maritime strategy," by which Britain used her wealth to create and subsidize coalitions of continental allies while she employed her navy and small army in securing control of the seas and then in mounting attacks on enemy colonies. This form of coalition warfare proved a repeated failure until as late as 1809, but from 1808 the British government added an element of "continental strategy" to its policy by exploiting the openings represented by Portugal and Spain to mount a growing military effort on the continent itself. This created an impossible problem for France, when taken in association with the military threats posed by the Sixth Coalition* from 1812. Britain's Peninsular War* was sustained by the Royal Navy at all stages, and the sea war was always of great significance. The naval and economic blockades of France and her satellites and the demand for the "Right of Search"* helped embroil Britain in the unnecessary and inconvenient minor War of 1812 with the United States (1812 to 1815), but this secondary struggle did not in the event have a determinant influence on the greater war. In sum, Great Britain was to a large extent seeking for the correct Grand Strategy for a number of years—and eventually came upon it through French mistakes. However, British persistence in challenging French power through thick and thin was consistent, and gave France's other enemies a rallying point and a source of financial and political assistance. Only in 1813 did the European powers achieve the necessary degree of cooperation and coordination of effort within the ranks of the Sixth Coalition to be able to achieve success. The degree of unity achieved was transient, as the history of the Congress of Vienna and post-1815 events would show, but the problem of defeating the power of France was solved after 23 years of almost incessant war.

Grand Tactics. The deployment of armed forces on the field of battle and the development of plans to make use of them to the full are in the realm of Grand Tactics. In the days of the early revolutionary wars, French grand tactics were often crude in the extreme, taking the form of the use of dense masses of ill-trained troops in all-out frontal attacks which, from Valmy* onward, nevertheless proved singularly effective against the hidebound 18th-century linear concepts of their opponents, who could not match the energy, drive, and enthusiasm of their French foes.

Under Napoleon, French grand tactics became highly sophisticated. Using the flexibility afforded by the *corps d'armée** system, he wedded grand tactics to strategic movement to a marked degree. Using the advance guard (however gravely outnumbered) to pin the enemy, he reinforced it with neighboring corps in a progressive fashion to attract enemy reserves into the frontal battle. Meanwhile, depending on intelligence information, he would often move a substantial force in great secrecy toward one or another flank of the enemy army, and mass his reserve (again concealed whenever possible) opposite the enemy troops holding the part of the battle line nearest to that flank (see diagram). When he was convinced that the moment was ripe—and almost all enemy reserves were committed to the fray—a signal would unleash the outflanking force from its concealment to threaten the enemy lines of communication. This disconcerting attack would coincide with renewed pressure along the front, and the enemy would be almost forced to weaken his army to produce troops to face the new threat from the flank—ideally from the closest sector of the battle line. When this occurred (Napoleon termed it "the event") the French reserve of heavy cavalry, massed artillery, and (on occasion) the Imperial Guard would be unleashed against the weakened sector, and the combination of psychological shock and the onslaught of these fresh troops would carve a gap through the enemy battle line, which the light cavalry would at once exploit.

Such was the essence of Napoleonic grand tactics. Of course, it was not an infallible formula for success, but in many adapted forms it did bring the French many battlefield victories from Castiglione* to Bautzen* and Champaubert.*

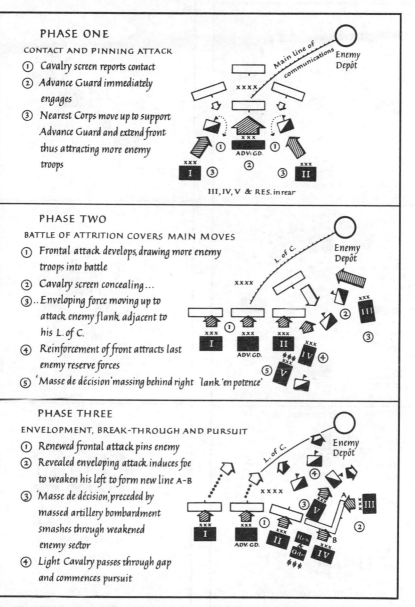

PHASE ONE

CONTACT AND PINNING ATTACK

① Cavalry screen reports contact
② Advance Guard immediately engages
③ Nearest Corps move up to support Advance Guard and extend front thus attracting more enemy troops

III, IV, V & RES. in rear

PHASE TWO

BATTLE OF ATTRITION COVERS MAIN MOVES

① Frontal attack develops, drawing more enemy troops into battle
② Cavalry screen concealing...
③ ..Enveloping force moving up to attack enemy flank adjacent to his L. of C.
④ Reinforcement of front attracts last enemy reserve forces
⑤ 'Masse de décision' massing behind right 'lank 'en potence'

PHASE THREE

ENVELOPMENT, BREAK-THROUGH AND PURSUIT

① Renewed frontal attack pins enemy
② Revealed enveloping attack induces foe to weaken his left to form new line A-B
③ 'Masse de décision', preceded by massed artillery bombardment smashes through weakened enemy sector
④ Light Cavalry passes through gap and commences pursuit

Grand Tactics: The Strategic Battle

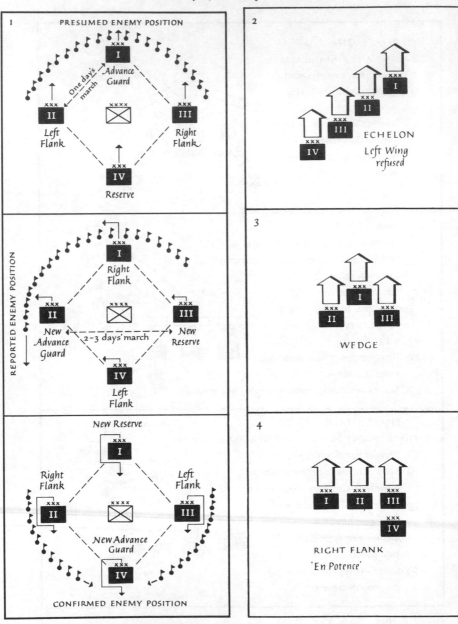

Grand Tactics: Le Bataillon Carré

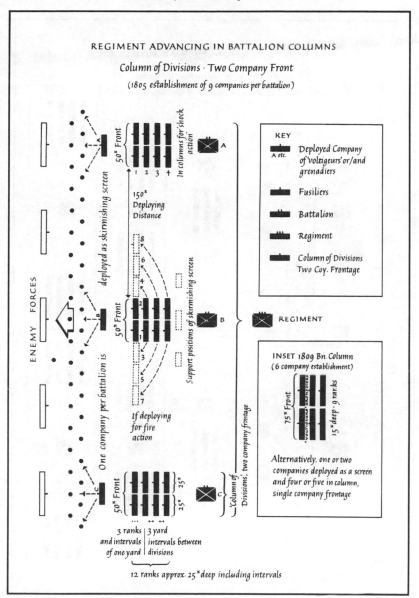

REGIMENT ADVANCING IN BATTALION COLUMNS

Column of Divisions · Two Company Front

(1805 establishment of 9 companies per battalion)

Grand Tactics

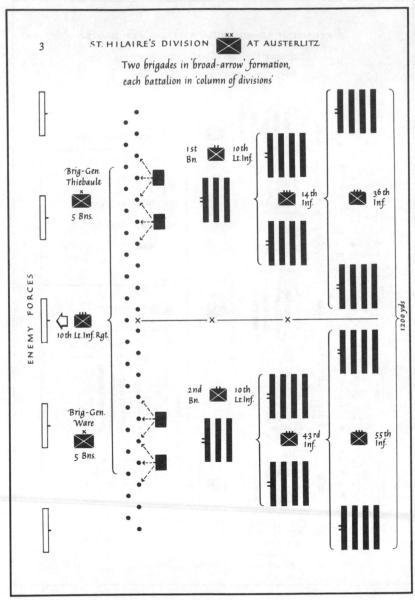

3   ST. HILAIRE'S DIVISION ⊠ AT AUSTERLITZ

*Two brigades in 'broad-arrow' formation,
each battalion in 'column of divisions'*

Brig-Gen.
Thiebault
×
5 Bns.

1st
Bn.   ⊠   10th
Lt. Inf.

14th
Inf.

36th
Inf.

ENEMY FORCES

10th Lt. Inf. Rgt.

Brig-Gen.
Ware
×
5 Bns.

2nd
Bn.   ⊠   10th
Lt. Inf.

43rd
Inf.

55th
Inf.

1200 yds

Grand Tactics

[182]

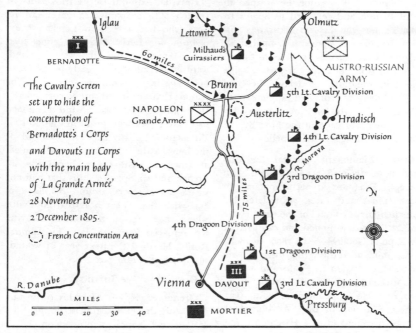

Grand Tactics: Cavalry Screen Concealing Davout's March to Austerlitz, 1805

As the years passed, however, France's foes learned what to expect, and the psychological impact of the method diminished. Similarly, they all (save Great Britain) remodeled their forces along French lines and could match French mobility and energy to a considerable degree. Also, in the hands of lesser commanders than Napoleon the French system could go wrong in many ways. This was convincingly demonstrated many times in the Peninsular War—for example at Vimiero,* Fuentes de Oñoro,* or Bussaco*—where a combination of Wellington's* skill at selecting good defensive positions with useful reverse slopes where his main forces could remain concealed until needed and French ineptitude at timing the various stages of their attack correctly, led to defeat after defeat. In 1815 it was the turn of the master grand tactician to meet his nemesis. At the battle of Waterloo* it was a case of the "biter bit": Napoleon's forces were sucked into the main battle against Mont St. Jean ridge, and then were taken in flank by the arrival of Blücher's* Prussians from the east in the midafternoon.

Grant, Lieutenant Colonel Colquhoun (1780–1829). Commissioned into the 11th Foot, he was captured at Ostend in 1798. Later, in the Peninsula, he served Wellington* as Deputy-Assistant Adjutant General and also as intelligence chief, proving very adept at breaking French codes. Captured again near the river Coa in 1812, he escaped from Bayonne to Paris, from where he managed to send a stream of intelligence information to Wellington. Disguised as a sailor, he escaped to Great Britain and returned to Spain. In 1815, he was the first to accurately discover Napoleon's plan of campaign in Belgium, and sent news of it from Condé to Wellington, but the arrival of this urgent information was delayed by General Dornberg.* Promoted to lieutenant colonel of the 54th Foot in 1821, he later commanded a brigade in the First Burma War. He died at Aix-la-Chapelle.

Grant, Lieutenant General Sir Colquhoun (c. 1764–1835). He fought with the 25th Dragoons at Seringapatam* in India (1799) and three years later became lieutenant colonel of the 72nd Highlanders. He was wounded and captured at the Cape of Good Hope in 1806. In 1808–09 he commanded the 15th Hussars during Moore's* campaign in Spain and retreat to Corunna,* serving with distinction at Sahagun.* He commanded the same regiment at Vitoria* in 1813. At Waterloo* he was in command of a Hussar brigade. He was promoted to lieutenant general in 1830 and served as an MP from 1831–32.

Grattan, Henry (1746–1820). Irish-born statesman and patriot, he entered the Irish Parliament in 1775. He championed Irish legislative independence from Westminster and the cause of Catholic emancipation. A bitter critic of parliamentary corruption, he refused office in Ireland several times, and after spending the period of the Irish revolt of 1798 in England did everything in his power to oppose the Act of Union in 1800. Later, as MP for Malton at Westminster (1805–06) and then for Dublin (1806–20) he consistently refused offers of ministerial appointments and continued to champion the cause of Catholic emancipation and support the continued prosecution of the war against France. He was considered a brilliant orator and speechwriter.

Gravina, Admiral Don Carlos, Duke of (1756–1806). A Spanish sailor of fair repute who had served in Lerclerc's* expedition to Haiti,* Gravina commanded the 12 Spanish ships that were to windward of Nelson's* fleet early on 21 October 1805, in two columns, but which for reasons that are still disputed surrendered the central position and wind advantage soon after daylight to form the van of Villeneuve's* main fleet. At the end of the long battle of Trafalgar* that ensued, at 5:05 P.M., Gravina gathered the six French and six Spanish ships that had not struck their colors around his flagship, and with them beat a retreat to Cadiz, where they arrived that night. Gravina was replaced four days later by Admiral Rosily. He died the next year of wounds sustained at Trafalgar.

Grenadiers. *See* **Infantry**

Grenoble, city of. After his confrontation with the 5th Regiment of the Line at Laffrey,* Napoleon pressed on the 15 miles to Grenoble, which he reached at 9:00 P.M. on 7 March 1815. Here, for the first time since his return from exile on Elba,* the Emperor was accorded a frenzied popular welcome. As he later remarked at St. Helena*: "Before Grenoble I was an adventurer; at Grenoble I was a prince." Two days later he set out for Lyons, with the road to Paris open before him.

Grenville, William Wyndham, Baron (1759–1834). This prominent British politician and statesman entered Parliament in 1782 and held various minor posts between that date and 1789, when he became Home Secretary. Two years later he became Foreign Secretary, a post he held for ten years. He led the war party in Pitt's* ministry but resigned with him over Catholic emancipation in 1801. Grenville refused to serve without Fox* in Pitt's second ministry, but headed the

Ministry of All the Talents (1806–07) after the Prime Minister's death. During his administration the slave trade was abolished. He subsequently refused offers of ministerial posts in various mixed ministries, but staunchly supported the continuance of the war against France up to 1815. He then supported Addington's* (Lord Sidmouth's) repressive legislation in 1816, and also the prosecution of Queen Caroline in 1820.

Gribeauval, Jean-Baptiste Vacquette de, comte (1715–1789). After entering the French artillery in 1732 he gained a commission three years later. After serving on attachment to the Austrian army during the Seven Years' War, he returned to France determined to reform the French artillery.* His main work began in 1765 (see **Artillery**) under the patronage of the duc de Choiseul, and by 1774 he had triumphed over many bitter opponents and his ideas were accepted and applied. His reforms touched every aspect—administrative and training as well as technological—of the artillery service, and he inspired a generation of notable artillerymen that included the du Teils* and of course Napoleon himself. He died on the very eve of the French Revolution.

Gronow, Ensign Rees Howell (1794–1865). After education at Eton, he gained a commission in the First Guards, with whom he fought in the Peninsula from 1813 and also at Quatre Bras* and Waterloo* in 1815. He wrote his *Reminiscences,* which form an important source of information on life in Wellington's* army. He died in Paris.

Gross-Beeren, battle of, 23 August 1813. As Bertrand's* corps, under Oudinot's* overall command advanced on Blankenfelde, the French found themselves facing General Tauenzien's* 13,000 men and 32 guns, including many raw *Landwehr.* While Bertrand sparred with the Prus-

sians, Reynier* advanced on Gross-Beeren at about 3:00 P.M. with 27,000 men to turn the Prussian flank. He captured the village and the Windmill Height beyond, but then allowed his men to make bivouacs. Suddenly he found himself attacked by Bülow's* newly arrived corps (38,000 men) amidst driving rain. Reynier, aware that Gross-Beeren on his right flank was his weakest point, placed a complete division in square to hold it, but the Prussians, despite heavy losses, captured the village and stormed the Windmill Height beyond. The French right wing collapsed as some Saxon troops fled after manfully trying to check the Prussian advance from the hill. Attempts to retake the ridge by the French troops of the center and left failed, and Reynier ordered a retreat. Both sides were again in bivouac when fighting suddenly was renewed when a French cavalry division fell upon the Prussian hussars to everybody's surprise. A confused running-fight developed that eventually ended in a stalemate. Over the day's events, the French and Saxons lost 3,000 casualties, 13 guns, and 60 wagons; the Prussian casualties were barely 1,000 men. The battle was of small strategic significance to either side but served to reinforce Oudinot's caution. Napoleon criticized Oudinot for allowing Reynier to become isolated, but soon Gross-Beeren would be eclipsed by news of Ney's* defeat at Dennewitz.*

Grouchy, Maréchal Emmanuel, marquis de (1766–1847). An aristocrat by birth, he was commissioned into the French artillery in 1781. Three years later he transferred to the cavalry, and in 1786 into the Scottish Company of the *gardes du corps du roi.* He soon espoused the cause of the Revolution and commanded cavalry in the Armies of the Center and Alps in 1792. Next year he helped repress the revolt in La Vendée* before being forced to resign his commission for a year on account of his

Grouchy

noble antecedents. Restored to service in 1794, he was promoted to *général de division* in June 1795, served under Hoche* in the west of France against the royalist rebels, and was present at Quiberon.* Next year he was second-in-command, again under Hoche, in the ill-fated expedition to Ireland. In 1799 he became Chief of Staff to Moreau,* received 14 wounds, and was taken prisoner at Pasturana. He protested from captivity against the establishment of the Consulate, but after being freed he commanded a division under Moreau at Hohenlinden* in 1800. Five years later he commanded a division under Marmont* in the *Grande Armée*, and fought at Ulm,* Lubeck, Thorn, Eylau,* and Friedland,* where it was felt he failed to exploit a favorable opportunity for the cavalry. Transferred to Spain, he put down the rising of Madrid depicted by Goya,* and after a period as governor of the city he was transferred to Italy and made a count (1809). He fought with distinction under Davout*

at Wagram* and was made colonel general of Chasseurs.

In 1812 he commanded the III Corps of Reserve Cavalry during the invasion of Russia, under command of Eugène Beauharnais.* He captured Orsha, fought at Borodino,* Maloyaroslavetz,* and Krasnöe,* and during the most desperate period of the retreat he commanded the "sacred battalion"* of officers in November. Ill health precluded much service in 1813, but he fought in most of the battles of 1814 in France. In 1815 he immediately rallied to Napoleon on his return from exile, and fought off the duc d'Angoulême's* royalist army in late March. Appointed a marshal on 15 April 1815 (in fact Napoleon's last such appointment), he was given command of the cavalry reserve of the Army of the North in early June, and then, possibly unwisely, he was transferred to command the right wing. With this he fought at Ligny* and Wavre* but refused to march on the sound of the cannon at Waterloo* (at the expense of his reputation), insisting on carrying out the letter of his latest orders. He then conducted an admirable retreat on the 19th, taking command of all the remnants of the army from 26 June, before handing it over to Davout.

Proscribed by the Second Bourbon Restoration, he lived for some years in Philadelphia, Pennsylvania, until allowed to return to France in 1820. Louis-Philippe restored his marshal's baton in 1831 and he became a peer of France the next year. Blamed by Napoleon on St. Helena* for the outcome of the battle of Waterloo, Grouchy's real *métier* was that of a skilled cavalry commander.

Guards. *See* **Infantry, Imperial Guard,** and **Cavalry**

Gudin, de la Sablonnière, Général Charles Etienne, comte (1768–1812). A noble by birth, he was educated at Brienne

Gudin

and entered the royal guards in 1782. From 1791–92 he served on the Santo Domingo* expedition, but after returning to France was posted to the Army of the North and then to that of the Rhine and Moselle. He served as Chief of Staff to Gouvion St. Cyr* and later under Lefebvre,* being appointed *général de brigade* in 1799. Transferred to the Army of Switzerland, he fought under Soult* but was defeated by Suvorov* in the St. Gothard Pass in September. With the Army of the Rhine he fought at Stockach,* Moesskirch, and Memmingen, and was confirmed as *général de division* in July 1800. In 1805 he commanded a division in Davout's* III Corps and fought through the Austrian and Prussian campaigns. He was wounded at Auerstädt* but captured Custrin and entered Warsaw. He fought at Pultusk* and Eylau.* He was made a count in 1808, and next year served in the Danube theatre at Abensberg-Eckmühl,* Ratisbon,* and Wagram* (where he was wounded four times).

Gudin invaded Russia under Davout in 1812 and fought at Smolensk,* but died of wounds sustained at Valutina.

Guerrillas. The feature of the Peninsular Wars that most baffled the French was the guerrilla struggle, which raged with great ferocity from mid-1808. It began in a spontaneous and localized fashion as bands of defeated Spanish regular soldiery linked up with bandits, peasantry, and priests to continue offering proud resistance to the conquerors of their country. It engulfed all parts of the country and soon no French courier or convoy was safe on the roads of Spain without an escort of 200 or more cavalry and dragoons. It is estimated that as many as 7,000 individuals were engaged in waging guerrilla "hit and run" warfare by 1812, operating from sanctuaries high up in the Cantabrian or other mountains of Spain; occasionally bands—the largest of which may have been about 150 strong—would join together for a wide-ranging raid on the plains, and even to attack middle-sized towns, but usually they fought in their independent groups, their leaders being quarrelsome, jealous, and divisive. Their effect on the French war effort in physical terms is hard to assess—guerrillas kept few records and their activities soon became absorbed into Spanish folklore—but it has been estimated that of the 200,000 casualties sustained by the French in Spain and Portugal between 1808 and 1814 at least 50,000 are attributable to guerrilla action. Even more important, and less disputed, is their effect on the morale of the French troops. Postings to Spain were as feared in the 1810s as transfers to the eastern front by German soldiers in 1943. As one Frenchman wrote: ". . . we fear to walk alone."

Many guerrilla attacks were aimed against Spanish collaborators—often the embryonic middle classes and parts of the senior clergy and aristocracy, who had originally welcomed the arrival of the French in 1808 with their relatively liberal ideas. This aspect of the struggle is often overlooked, but the bitterness of this internecine aspect was terrible.

Wellington,* however much he scorned Spanish regular forces following his early experiences of their so-called cooperation during the Talavera* campaign, was fully aware of the importance of the guerrillas to the war effort and did what he could to supply their leaders with money and arms. In return he gained much valuable intelligence, collected by such officers as Somers Cocks* or James Gordon* or handed in to his town-based "correspondents." He also realized the strategic dilemma the guerrillas presented to the French when associated with his small regular Anglo-Portuguese army. To control the guerrillas required the French to occupy the countryside, scattering their troops in garrisons, escorts, and punitive raiding parties. When Wellington advanced into Spain, however, the French had to concentrate to meet him, and thus lost control of the countryside. In the later campaigns the efforts of the guerrillas rose to even greater proportions. Thus, between January and April 1813 there were all of 53 encounters involving guerrillas in the area between Bayonne, Burgos, and Madrid alone—many of them amidst the Pyrenees but at least 20 along the intervening ridges and on the plains. The toll on French resources—and above all nerves—was great. The way in which atrocity bred counteratrocity as Napoleon ordered draconian punishments against whole communities is graphically demonstrated in Goya's* "Horrors of War."

The phenomenon of guerrilla or "little war" was not restricted to Spain, although there it found its widest expression. As early as 1805 the French had a foretaste of what was to come in Naples, where bandits rendered Calabria virtually ungovernable (and encouraged a British force to land and fight at Maida*) until Massena* took stern measures. Even then, 40,000 French troops were tied down in South Italy until 1808. Next, in 1809–10, patriots in the Tyrol rose against Napoleon's ally, Bavaria, under Andreas Hofer,* and even captured Innsbruck for a time. French and Allied troops were tied down there until 1814. In 1812 a widespread rash of partisan attacks led by Davydov harassed the lengthy French lines of communication leading back from (ultimately) Moscow to Poland, and the infuriated serfs wrought a terrible revenge on the French during their long retreat. Lastly, Germany was far from free of the contagion. In 1805 and again in 1809 spontaneous local risings threatened the French control of the Danube valley, and from 1806 on the *Tugenbund* of Prussian nationalists ran an intermittent guerrilla offensive against the French. This came to a head in 1813, but in Prussia popular resistance never reached the scale attained in Spain. Lastly, in 1814 parts of the Champagne rose against the Russian armies invading France when Napoleon issued the old battle cry of 1792—*"la patrie en danger"* —but the effort was spasmodic and achieved little. All in all, guerrilla war as a means to challenge an occupying power and keep alive a national spirit of resistance was used to a marked degree during the Napoleonic Wars, and the French never discovered a lasting answer to the contagion. Only in Catalonia did Marshal Suchet* and his wife make considerable progress with what today would be called a policy of "hearts and minds." Elsewhere the problem remained unresolvable.

Guibert, Général Jacques Antoine Hipployte, comte (1743–1790). The son of a governor of the *Invalides,* Guibert became a French military philosopher whose ideas greatly influenced the young Napoleon Bonaparte. His writings ranged from considerations of grand strategy* to minor tactics. At the former level he advocated short, sharp wars; at the latter, the use of *l'ordre mixte*, and he foretold the coming of a politico-military genius. The Comte de Guibert first rose to public notice by winning a prize for his *Essai de tactique générale* (1772), and later wrote his *Défense du système de guerre moderne* (1777), both of which became established textbooks. He saw active service during the Seven Years' War and was promoted to *maréchal-de-camp* (major general) in 1786. That year also saw his admission to the prestigious *Academie Française*.

Guides, les. Bodies of veteran cavalry forming the bodyguards and personal escorts of senior commanders, one such group was raised by Bonaparte in June 1796 after his near capture at Valeggio shortly after the battle of Borghetto.* Commanded by Captain (later Marshal) Bessières,* they formed the nucleus for what later became the *chasseurs-à-cheval* of the Imperial Guard.*

Guieu, Général Jean Joseph (1758–1817). After joining the artillery as a gunner in 1774, in 1791 he became a captain of volunteers and served in the Alps and Pyrenees. He served long campaigns under Augereau's* command and fought at the Black Mountain (1794). In June 1795 he was confirmed in the rank of *général de brigade*. He became a member of the Army of Italy in Sérurier's* division in 1796 and fought at Mondovi.* He greatly distinguished himself holding a building at Salo* for three days without rations, and later helped retake the town. Guieu fought with distinction at Arcola,* particularly at the Albaredo bridge, and in December 1796 was promoted to *général de division*. In 1797 he was defeated by Provera* at Anghiari, but won the action of Sacile* in March and later took

Palmanova. He left the army late in 1799 and retired in August 1803.

Guindet, *Maréchal-des-logis* (fl. 1806). As quartermaster of the 10th Hussars, Guindet engaged Louis Ferdinand,* Prince of Prussia and the most promising commander of the Russian army, in personal combat at the action of Saalfeld* (10 October 1806) during Napoleon's invasion of Saxony through the *Thuringerwald,* and killed him.

Guyot, Général Claude-Etienne, baron, later comte (1768–1837). After enlisting as a trooper in 1790, he gained a commission three years later and served on the Moselle, in La Vendée,* in Italy (1796), and Germany. In October 1802 he became a captain in the Consular Guard, and from 1805–07 served with the Guard cavalry, fighting at Austerlitz* and Eylau.* He was created a baron in 1808, and commanded the escort detachment of the *chasseurs-à-cheval* under Lefebvre-Desnouëttes* which accompanied Napoleon to Spain. In 1809 he was promoted to colonel after Essling, and he fought at Wagram.* He became *général de brigade* in August 1809, and an Imperial chamberlain the next March. Promoted to *général de division* in December 1811, he commanded the *chasseurs* of the Imperial Guard* in Russia. In 1813 he was wounded at Lützen,* fought at Bautzen,* and after being taken prisoner at Kulm* he was exchanged in time to fight at Leipzig.* Next year he commanded cavalry at Brienne,* La Rothière,* Champaubert,* and Craonne.* After Napoleon's abdication he became a Bourbon colonel of Royal Cuirassiers, but in 1815 rallied to his old master and received two wounds at Waterloo* in command of the heavy division of cavalry of the Guard. He was retired in 1816, but later held a few administrative posts before finally leaving the service in 1833.

Gyulai, Field Marshal Ignatius (1763–1831). Born at Hermanstadt, this Austrian soldier first rose to military prominence at the battle of Hohenlinden* (1800). Nine years later he commanded the rear guard of Archduke Charles'* army after the defeat of Wagram.* At Leipzig* (1813) he distinguished himself in the bitter fighting around the village of Lindenau. From 1823, the Emperor Francis II* appointed him governor of Bohemia. He died in 1831 at Vienna.

Haiti, troubles in, 1790–1807. Wracked by revolutionary fervor, the French colony of Haiti was in a state of political anarchy and social ferment for many years. A full-scale slave revolt gave Britain the excuse for occupying the island in 1794 and extirpating its nests of privateers* preying on British West Indian trade, but in 1797 the British troops were withdrawn by agreement with the native leader, Toussaint l'Ouverture.* For four years he imposed a measure of order and prosperity on Haiti. However, the French, who had received the eastern part of the island (Santo Domingo) from Spain by the Treaty of Basle* (1795) determined to regain it, and on 14 December 1801 (shortly after the Preliminaries of Amiens*) Bonaparte sent General Leclerc* and 20,000 troops, subsequently reinforced, to seize the island. L'Ouverture was overthrown (early 1802) and sent into exile in France, but Leclerc died of yellow fever in November 1802. Moreover, in 1803 a new major revolt broke out under Dessalins (established in 1802 as French puppet ruler of South Haiti), and General Rochambeau was forced to capitulate in November and withdraw his troops, 25,000 of whom had died. Dessalins became the Emperor James I in 1804, and from 1807 privateering again flourished.

Halkett, General Sir Colin (1774–1856). From 1792–95 he served in first the Dutch Foot Guards and later in their light infantry (albeit in British pay). In 1805 he took command of the 2nd battalion of the King's German Legion,* and at its head served in Hanover, Ireland, Spain, and at Walcheren.* Thereafter he returned to the Peninsula and fought at Albuera* (1811), survived the retreat from Burgos* the next year, and then served at Vitoria* and at many of the succeeding battles in the Pyrenees* and the south of France. During the Hundred Days* he commanded a British brigade at both Quatre Bras* and Waterloo.* After the Napoleonic wars he continued his career, being promoted to lieutenant general in 1830 and to full general 11 years later. Much time was spent in India, and from 1831–32 he was military commander of the Bombay presidency. In 1849 he became Governor of Chelsea Hospital.

Hamburg, siege of, 30 May 1813–27 May 1814. This city, the only truly strong fortress on the lower Elbe, was held with great skill and pertinacity by Marshal Davout* at the head of the XIII Corps, originally some 25,000 troops in all. During the later stages of the campaign of German Liberation in 1813 the duc d'Auerstadt fought an extremely active defense in the whole lower Elbe region, winning the action of Lauenburg (18 August) against General Walmoden and some 25,000 Prussian troops. As Napoleon retired from Germany, Davout found himself completely isolated, but offered as determined a resistance as ever. He continued to do so against growing odds, despite his own dwindling force and negligible munitions and supplies, until well after Napoleon's first abdication in

April 1814. In the end it required a personal message from Louis XVIII* conveyed by General Gerard* to bring him to accept a capitulation on 27 May 1814 after a defense that had lasted just under one year.

Hanau, battle of, 30 October 1813. After the mighty battle of Leipzig,* Napoleon extricated some 100,000 men and retired to Erfurt and then on toward the Rhine, harassed by the victorious Allies. His line of retreat was intercepted on the line of the river Inn by a Bavarian and Austrian force commanded by General Wrede,* Bavaria being the latest of the Emperor's former confederates to join the Sixth Coalition.* Wrede commanded some 43,000 troops and was determined to prevent the French from reaching their next sanctuary, Frankfort-on-Oder. Believing he was only tackling a flank column, he took up a hastily selected position on both banks of the river Kinzig, which had only a single bridge.

Napoleon soon appreciated this mistake by his opponent, and launched Macdonald* and Sebastiani* (perhaps 17,000 infantry and cavalry) through thick woods to attack the enemy's left. Marshal Victor* came up with more men, and by midday the battle was raging as Drouot* managed to pass some cannon through a dense forest. Soon 50 cannon silenced the 28 Bavarian guns, and Sebastiani's cavalry routed the horsemen holding Wrede's extreme left. Wrede had to fall back and lost many men around the single bridge over the Kinzig, but got away into Hanau town. For a loss of an estimated 6,000 casualties Napoleon inflicted 9,250 between 28 and 31 October (to include preceding and subsequent skirmishes). The road to Frankfort lay open before him, and beyond it the route to Mainz and safety. In addition to the battle losses, some 10,000 French stragglers fell into Allied hands during the last days of October, and this success at Hanau was

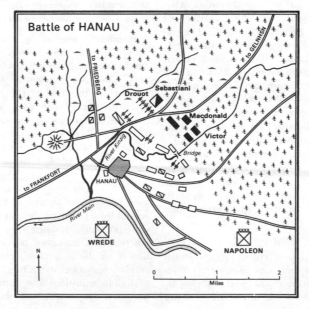

Battle of HANAU

only a slight encouragement to his tired survivors.

Hardenberg, Minister Karl Augustus, Prince (1750–1822). A Hanoverian by birth, in 1790 Hardenberg entered Prussian service. Employed as an administrator and diplomat, in 1795 he negotiated the Treaty of Basle with France and soon became, with Haugwitz,* the most trusted adviser of King Frederick William III* of Prussia. Working to build up a strong country, Hardenberg strove to moderate the warlike propensities of Queen Louise,* and after the disasters of Jena-Auerstadt* and the humiliation of Tilsit* he began to reconstruct the country, succeeding Stein* as Chancellor. By 1813 Prussia was capable of deserting the French alliance and joining the Sixth Coalition.* After Waterloo* Hardenberg represented Prussia at the Congress of Vienna* and achieved the return of Eastern Pomerania, part of Saxony, and also Westphalia and various areas along the Rhine to his adopted country. He was created a Prince for these considerable services, but his liberal sympathies clashed with the reactionary views of the Holy Alliance.

Hardinge, Field Marshal Sir Henry, Viscount (1785–1856). As deputy assistant quartermaster general to General Spencer* he fought under Wellesley* at Roliça* and Vimiero* (1808), and later served with Moore* in the Corunna* campaign, being at the general's side during his last moments. He fought at Albuera* (1811) and was wounded at Vitoria* two years later. He was sent to observe Napoleon's movements during the earlier part of the Hundred Days* and was British liaison officer, in the rank of colonel, attached to Blücher's* headquarters, and as such fought at Ligny.* He remained attached to the Prussian staff in France until 1818. In 1820 he

began a long political career, holding several minor posts and becoming a lieutenant general in 1841 and governor general of India (1844–47). He fought in the First Sikh War and was instrumental in 'having *suttee* abolished. He was promoted to full general in 1854 and appointed field marshal the next year.

Harris, General George, Baron (1746–1829). After serving with the 5th Fusiliers in the War of American Independence (he was wounded at Bunker Hill in 1775), he shared in the capture of St. Lucia in 1778. From 1790–92 he led troops against Tippoo Sahib* in India and again held a command in the Madras presidency from 1796–1800. His greatest achievements were the capture of Seringapatam* and the conquest of Mysore (1799). Promoted to lieutenant general in 1801 and to full general in 1812, he was made a peer in 1815.

Harris, Rifleman (fl. 1809). After enlisting in the 66th, he transferred to the 95th (later to become the Rifle Brigade) in 1805. With them he served at either Buenos Aires* or Copenhagen* (his regiment was involved in both expeditions during the same period of 1807), and then certainly fought in Portugal and Spain at Roliça,* Vimiero,* and Benavente* under Wellesley* and Moore.* He retreated with Craufurd* (his great hero) from Astorga to Vigo. Later in 1809 he fought at Walcheren,* but contracted the fever and never served again. He left famous *Recollections* which give a vivid account of life as a private soldier in 1808–09.

Haslach, combat of, 11 October 1805. Also known as the combat of Albeck, this engagement took place on the north bank of the Danube during the Campaign of 1805, as Napoleon closed in upon the forces of General Mack* and the Archduke Ferdinand* based upon Ulm.* The single division of General Dupont,* part of Ney's* VI Corps, found itself isolated on the north bank of the river near Albeck, faced by some 25,000 Austrian troops (including 10,000 cavalry), which Mack had sent out from Ulm to probe eastward along the riverbank. Dupont and his 4,000 men could only hope for assistance from Baraguey d'Hillier's* division of dragoons, and his exposed position was wholly due to a confusion in Prince Murat's* orders to Ney. With typical élan, Dupont ordered his men to attack the vastly superior Austrian forces, and by dint of gallant fighting managed to hold his own all day. As dusk fell, he found himself able to draw off his survivors toward Brenz. Meanwhile, Mack and Ferdinand, who had badly bungled the day's fighting, fell back into Ulm intending to renew their breakout attempt the next day. This was not, in fact, to take place. Despite a blazing altercation between Ney and Murat over Dupont's abandonment, on 13 October would be fought the important engagement of Elchingen,* which finally blunted the outclassed and bewildered Mack's resolve. A week later and he would surrender at Ulm.

Hatzfeld, General Franz Ludwig, Prince (1756–1827). By profession both a soldier and a diplomat, Prince Hatzfeld was born in Vienna but served the Prussian monarchy. After the devastating double battle of Jena-Auerstadt* he was appointed governor of Berlin. A few hours before the French reached the city he sent off a report on the French dispositions to King Frederick William III* which the French intercepted. When Hatzfeld reported to surrender the keys of Berlin to the Emperor, Napoleon accused him of spying and ordered his immediate court-martial. Only the intervention of Princess Hatzfeld, who pleaded for her husband on her

knees, saved Hatzfeld from instant execution. He served from 1822 as Prussian ambassador to the Court of Vienna, and it was in that city that he died.

Haugwitz, Minister Christian August Heinrich Curt, Count of (1752–1832). Born at Peuke in Silesia, he became Prussia's Minister of Foreign Affairs in 1792, and the next year negotiated the Second Partition of Poland. On the defeat of the First Coalition* he also helped draw up the Treaty of Basle* with the French. In 1804 he suffered temporary eclipse, being replaced by Prince Hardenberg,* but in 1805 he was reinstated. Haugwitz's last duty was to negotiate the Treaty of Schonbrunn* with France in 1805 after lengthy and personally humiliating negotiations with Napoleon, who kept the envoy dancing attendance at Vienna from 4 to 15 December awaiting the imperial pleasure, and then accorded him a blistering audience in which Prussia was forced to accept tough terms. Haugwitz was exhausted by this audience, and left public life in 1806 after signing the main treaty on 15 February 1806.

Hautpoul, Général Jean Joseph Ange, comte d' (1754–1807). After joining the royal dragoons as a volunteer in 1771 he was commissioned in 1777. Promoted to lieutenant colonel in 1792, he fought at Maubeuge. Two years later he was almost deprived of his rank for being of noble blood, but fought at Fleurus.* In 1795 he was confirmed as *général de brigade* and was wounded at Altenkirchen the next year. In 1797 he served at the passage of the Rhine, and two years later fought at Stockach.* Accused by Jourdan* of refusing an order at that battle, he was court-martialed but acquitted. In 1800 he served with Baraguey d'Hilliers* under Moreau,* distinguishing himself at the head of the cavalry reserve at Stockach and Hohenlinden.* After several ap-

D'Hautpoul

pointments in France he was given command of the 2nd Cuirassier Division in 1805, and at Austerlitz* drove in the Allied right center by a forceful charge. In 1806 he served at Jena* and was present at the fall of Lubeck.* He led several charges under Murat's* direction on 8 February at Eylau* but was mortally wounded. He died six days later after terrible suffering at the chateau of Vornen.

Haxo, Général François Nicolas, baron (1774–1838). Commissioned in 1792, he took part in the defense of Landau. After further training at the *Ecole Polytechnique* in 1796, he eventually was attached as an engineer to the Army of the Reserve in 1800, and served at Fort Bard* and Caldiero.* In 1805 he was on Massena's* staff, and two years later was sent to Constantinople to help the Turks fortify the Dardanelles. From 1808 he was in Spain, taking part in the sieges of Saragossa* and Lerida, and was promoted to *général de brigade* in June 1810. Next year he was made a baron and aide-de-camp to

Napoleon. After various tours of inspection Haxo was given command of the engineers attached to Davout's* I Corps in 1812, and fought at Smolensk* and Borodino* but was smitten by typhus after the long retreat. Recovered, he was made governor of Magdeburg in 1813, redesigned the defenses of Hamburg,* but was wounded and taken prisoner at Kulm.* Repatriated in 1814, he served the Bourbons for a while before rallying to Napoleon during the Hundred Days.* He was given command of the engineers of the Imperial Guard and fought at Waterloo.* In July he was chosen by Davout to negotiate with Louis XVIII* and in 1816 was appointed to the Council of War. Many posts as Inspector General of fortifications and schools of military engineering followed, but in 1831 he was appointed senior engineer of the Army of the North, and with it invaded Belgium. He besieged and took the citadel of Antwerp after a 24-day siege. He was made a peer of France in 1832 and retired from active service the following year.

Hay, Major General Andrew (1762–1814). In 1798 he raised the Banffshire Fencibles. He fought at Corunna* in command of the 3rd battalion of the 1st Royals, and later in 1809 commanded a brigade at Walcheren.* He later returned to the Peninsula under Wellington* and was promoted to major general in 1811. He died from wounds received during fighting outside Bayonne* in 1814.

Heilsberg, battle of, 10 June 1807. The French in Poland, now 220,000 strong, were preparing to resume the offensive when General Bennigsen* advanced on 5 June with 115,000 men. Within two days, however, the Russian attacks had been blunted and forced back, and Napoleon advanced in strength up the left bank of the river Alle. The Russians retired into a strong prepared position at Heilsberg

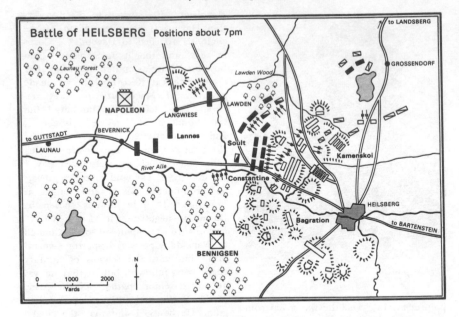

Battle of HEILSBERG Positions about 7pm

with 90,000 men. On 10 June Murat* attacked and took the outlying village of Launau, but was pinned by Russian artillery fire at Bevernick until Soult* could deploy his IV Corps and its guns. At 3:30 P.M. Bevernick was at last captured. Immediately afterward Bagration's* and Uvarov's cavalry counterattacked, and Murat and the Cavalry Reserve were routed. The arrival of General Savary* and two fusilier regiments with six guns saved the situation, and the Russian horsemen fell back, uncovering Bennigsen's right flank. Grand Duke Constantine* saw the danger and covered the gap with guns from the further bank of the Alle, and the fire from these cannon enfiladed Soult's divisions as they attempted to cross the Spuibach brook. The battle rapidly became one of sheer attrition. By late afternoon the French were falling back, despite Napoleon's presence, when the arrival of Lannes'* corps again reversed the situation. Lannes, in typically

hotheaded fashion, insisted on a night attack at 10:00 P.M. but lost 2,284 men for scant gains, and at 11:00 P.M. the firing died away. By then the day had cost the French 10,600 men, and the Russians some 8,000. Soult's corps alone had lost 8,268 killed and wounded. All expected a renewal of the battle the next morning, and Bennigsen brought down a heavy artillery bombardment. No close fighting developed, however, for Napoleon had decided to maneuver the Russians out of their strong position among the entrenched hills on both banks of the Alle. Mortier* and Davout* accordingly marched to turn Bennigsen's flank, and after nightfall on the 11th the Russians fell back toward Bartenstein, abandoning their wounded and stores. This battle showed little finesse—at least on the 10th —from Napoleon's point of view, and although a technical success, it was not decisive in any way. Heilsberg was occupied at 4:00 A.M. on 12 June. Two days away lay the great battle of Friedland,* which would at last clinch the Polish campaigns of 1806–07, and finally bring to an end the Fourth Coalition at Tilsit.*

Heudelet de Bierre, Général Etienne, comte (1770–1857). Commissioned a lieutenant of volunteers in 1792, he spent the next five years with the Army of the Rhine, becoming Gouvion St. Cyr's* Chief of Staff in 1795. In 1797 he fought at Kehl, and after further service was promoted to *général de brigade* in February 1799. In quick succession he was posted to the armies of the Danube and Switzerland, fought at Zurich* (1799) and Hohenlinden* (1800), and then returned to France. In 1805 he commanded the advance guard of Davout's* III Corps and served with distinction at Austerlitz,* being promoted to *général de division* on 24 December 1805. Commanding a division in Augereau's* VII Corps, he fought at Jena,* Golymin,* and Eylau,* where his command was virtually destroyed and he received a serious wound. After recovering in France and being made a Count of the Empire (1808), he served from November of that year in Spain, first under Junot* and then under Soult.* He captured Valencia, rejoined the Duke of Dalmatia at Oporto,* and for a time commanded the II Corps. In 1810, as a divisional general under Reynier,* he fought at Bussaco* and faced the lines of Torres Vedras.* In June 1811 he was allowed home on sick leave, and until 1812 was an Inspector General of infantry. In 1812 he rejoined Augereau on the Baltic coasts and helped cover the retreat of the remnants of the *Grande Armée* after the Beresina.* Besieged with Rapp* in Danzig,* he was taken prisoner. Repatriated to France in September 1814, he rallied to Napoleon the following March and served under Rapp in the so-called Army of the Rhine, but saw no action. After Napoleon's

abdication he withdrew to his estates. A few minor posts followed, and in 1848 he finally retired.

Hill, General Sir Rowland, Viscount (1772–1842). As a subaltern he studied at Strasburg, and in 1793 served as an aide-de-camp at Toulon.* In 1794 he became lieutenant colonel of the 90th Foot, fought in Egypt in 1801 (being wounded before Alexandria*), served in Ireland, and was promoted to major general in 1805. After service in Hanover, he was sent to the Peninsula, fought at Roliça* and Corunna,* and commanded a division at Talavera* (1809). His health broke down in 1810, but he returned to duty in 1811 and won an action at Merida. In 1812 he was promoted to lieutenant general and knighted, captured Almaraz,* commanded the right wing at Vitoria,* and blockaded Pamplona.* He fought with distinction at the Nivelle* and Nive* battles, as well as at Bayonne* and Toulouse.* He was created a baron in 1814. Next year he was sent on a mission to the Prince of Orange* and given command of the First Allied Corps. At Waterloo* he arrived in time to lead Adams' brigade toward the end of the battle. He was second-in-command of the Army of Occupation in France from 1815–18. In 1825 he became a full general and was Commander in Chief in England from 1825–29. His viscountcy dates from 1842.

Hiller, General Johann, baron (1754–1819). Born at Brody, he entered the Austrian artillery service in 1770. His first campaigns were against the Turks (1788–91), but over the following nine years he became deeply embroiled in the French wars. In 1809 he was in command of the force that was defeated at Abensberg,* but he won an action at Neumarkt during his subsequent retreat. Later in 1809 he fought with distinction at Aspern-Essling,* attacking the former village with skill. Never a popular commander with the Archduke Charles,* whom he bitterly disliked, Hiller surrendered command of the Austrian VI Corps to General Klenau on 26 May on grounds of ill health, but in early July he was briefly entrusted with command of the right wing—the part of the Austrian army that made the most progress against Napoleon on the second day of fighting at Wagram.* Four years later, Hiller contributed considerably to the Allied conquest of Illyria and parts of Italy.

Hilliers, Général Louis Barraguey d', comte (1764–1813). Commissioned in 1787, he rapidly rose to *général de brigade* by April 1793, but was arrested in July. Reinstated by the Revolutionary Tribunal the next year, his career remained checkered until May 1796 when he joined the Army of Italy. He fought at Rivoli* (1797) and led the pursuit. In March he was promoted to *général de division*, and the next year he accompanied the Army of the Orient to the East, taking part in the assault on Malta. He was captured by the Royal Navy but was released on parole, and after exchange became Chief of Staff to the Army of the Rhine. He fought at Engen and Biberach, and in 1800 occupied the key Valtelline Pass. In June 1804 he was appointed colonel general of dragoons and was given command of a dragoon division in August 1805. He served under Ney* at Elchingen* and later was made commandant of Ingolstadt. In 1806 he served in the Frioul, and remained in the eastern area of Italy until 1809, being made a count in 1808. Then he was posted to Catalonia until 1812, when he was given a staff appointment in Russia and became governor of Smolensk* during the invasion. Given command of a division in Victor's* IX Corps, he was badly mauled at Jelna in

D'Hilliers

November during the retreat. He was suspended pending a court of enquiry into his conduct, but died of a nervous fever at Berlin in January 1813 as he made his way back to France in disgrace.

Hoche, Général Louis Lazare (1768–1797). Originally a royal stable boy, he became a fusilier in the *Gardes Françaises* in 1784. At the Revolution he became a sergeant in the National Guard and took part in the march on Versailles. Commissioned in 1792, he served in the defenses of Thionville and Namur, but when his chief, Le Veneur, was indicted, he tried to defend him and was himself arrested—and acquitted (August 1793). Promoted to *général de brigade* that September, he served under Vandamme* in the Austrian Netherlands and captured Furnes and Ostend. On 23 October 1793 he was promoted to *général de division* and, on the same day, to Commander in Chief of the Army of the Moselle. Defeated at Kaiserslautern, he won the battle of Wörth in late December, but in March 1794 he again fell from grace and

Hoche

was jailed in the *Conciergerie*. Freed after four months, he was posted to Cherbourg and was soon in charge of internal security operations against the Vendean rebels. He defeated the *émigrés** at Quiberon* in July 1795, and later rounded up the Vendean leaders Stofflet and Charette. In July 1796 he was nominated commander of an army destined to invade Ireland and embarked in mid-December, but the expedition failed to get ashore at Bantry Bay* and was abandoned. In February 1797 he took command of the Army of the *Sambre et Meuse* and won the action of Neuwied before leading 15,000 men on a march toward Paris during the *coup d'état** of 18 *Fructidor*, when he besieged the capital. He was offered, but refused, the Ministry of War, and returned to his command. He died at Wetzlar from natural causes.

Höchstädt, battle of, 19 June 1800. After his success at Stockach,* Moreau* advanced from Baden into Bavaria, pushing back the Austrian army of General Kray von Krajowa* toward the fortified city of Ulm.* Moreau swung east and headed for the Danube 30 miles downstream near Höchstädt. On the 19th, Moreau attacked the 70,000 Austrians and caught them off balance. After 18 hours of confused fighting Moreau took the town and secured the left bank of the Danube, taking several thousand prisoners. Only about 1,000 men were killed or wounded, but Kray was forced to abandon Ulm and retreat to the river Inn. Following their dispirited opponents, the French in due course occupied Munich. Negotiations for a general pacification then created a pause in operations.

Hofer, Andreas (1767–1810). An innkeeper in the town of St. Leonard in the Tyrolean region, in 1809 he placed himself at the head of local patriots and led a revolt among the Alps against the inclusion of the area within the French puppet-kingdom of Bavaria. His efforts required large-scale French countermeasures, but in January 1810 Lefebvre's men captured him after a lengthy pursuit in the mountains following a tip-off. Hofer was tried for his life, condemned to death, and executed at Mantua. The Viennese government, which had originally encouraged his revolt and then abandoned him, ennobled his family nine years later.

Hohenlinden, battle of, 3 December 1800. The small Bavarian village of Hohenlinden stands about 50 kilometers to the east of Munich near the valley of the river Inn. It was the scene of a major French victory in late 1800, the effect of which was to crush Austrian resistance. As a result, Austria left the War of the Second Coalition* soon afterward.

The First Consul's victory at Marengo* in June 1800 led to intermittent negotiations between Paris and Vienna with a view to achieving a pacification. In the

meantime, however, General Moreau*
recommenced operations to exploit his
earlier advantages gained at Höchstädt*
(June) and the occupation of Munich the
following month. The pause was used to
build up the French Army of the Rhine
to a strength of 180,000 men, 100,000 of
whom were with Moreau. The Emperor
Francis II* meanwhile built up the Austrian forces behind the river Inn to
130,000, and brought in his brother the
Archduke John* to replace the less successful General Kray von Krajowa.* The
climax came in November 1800, when the
First Consul abruptly suspended the peace
talks and ordered Moreau to advance on
Vienna. Simultaneously, the Archduke
John crossed the Inn intending to attack
the French left flank, and for once the
Austrians had seized the initiative.

On 3 December the two armies met east
of Munich on very broken terrain. The
Archduke hoped to drive the French back
against the Bavarian Alps and sever their
links with France. Despite vile weather,
by 29 November the Austrians had reached
a position between Landshut and Neumarkt threatening Moreau's left, but their
own left wing was simultaneously forced
to concede some ground and French troops
were at places over the Inn. The Archduke
accordingly gave up his first idea of a
broad enveloping move and marched
straight on Munich down the only good
road in the area, which ran through the
forest of Hohenlinden. Advancing somewhat ponderously in four disconnected
columns, the Austrians ran headlong into
the French occupying a strong defensive
position—which the weather conditions
had made possible for Moreau to occupy
in strength along a six-mile front on each
side of Hohenlinden, with two divisions
poised to the south. The French general
continued to enjoy good fortune, thanks
in large measure to the determined and
skilled fighting of his key subordinates,
Ney,* who held the center against all

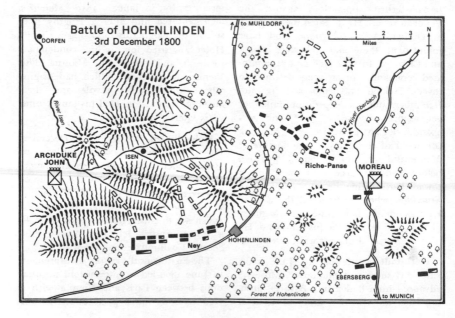

Battle of HOHENLINDEN
3rd December 1800

attacks, Grouchy,* and Richepanse—the true victors. The two left-hand enemy columns were shattered by a flank attack that was largely extemporized by Richepanse but was extremely effective, and the Austrian army reeled back, exhausted and dismayed. The Austrians lost an estimated 18,000 casualties; the French only 5,000 killed and wounded.

The Emperor Francis II hastily sent the Archduke Charles* to take over command from John, but nothing could hold up the French advance. Against minimal opposition Moreau advanced up the Danube valley through Salzburg and Linz to Steyr, barely one hundred miles from the Austrian capital, and there on 25 December an armistice was signed.

Meanwhile, in North Italy General Brune* had defeated Bellegarde on the river Mincio on 18 December, and by the new year the Austrians had lost the line of the river Adige. On 11 January the victorious French crossed the Brenta, while away to the north General Macdonald, after his famous winter crossing of the Splügen Pass, occupied Trent, and as in Bavaria, Austrian resistance collapsed. An armistice was signed at Treviso on the 16th. A third French force descended on the Neapolitans, regained Ancona, and an armistice was signed at Terni on the Neapolitan borders on 27 January.

This string of disasters meant the collapse of the Second Coalition,* and in February the Peace of Luneville* was duly signed. The First Consul, however, was somewhat displeased at the amount of popular acclaim accorded to Moreau after his victory.

Hohenlohe, General Friedrich Ludwig, Prince of (1746–1818). The scion of a noble Wurttemberg family, he entered the Prussian service in 1768 and rose to high military command during the wars against France. In November 1793 he won the battle of Kaiserlautern with the cooperation of the Duke of Brunswick,* but early the following year was forced to withdraw into the Palatinate by Hoche,* evacuating the whole area of the Rhine. In 1806 he was massively defeated by Napoleon at Jena,* but rallied the survivors of the Prussian army and withdrew with them into Pomerania, where he was eventually run to ground at Prenzlau on 28 October 1806 and forced to surrender. He remained a prisoner in French hands until 1808, when he was released and allowed back to Prussia. He played no further part in military affairs thereafter.

Hollabrünn, battle of, 16 November 1805. After the capture of Ulm,* the French marched eastward down the Danube valley attempting to trap the approaching Russian forces of Kutusov* south of that river. However, the Russians retreated through Mautern and Krems to the north bank by 8 November, and after a sharp fight around Durrenstein* on the 11th repelled the French attempt to establish a bridgehead. Murat* meantime rushed to occupy Vienna, where he seized the Tabor bridge from under the noses of an Austrian force and, hounded on by Napoleon, advanced on Hollabrünn with the intention of forcing battle on Kutusov before he could join Buxhowden's* approaching reinforcements. Aware that the French were now over the Danube in force, Kutusov was determined to retire northward toward a rendezvous with Buxhowden near Brünn, and ordered General Bagration,* commanding his rear guard, to delay the French. On the morning of the 15th Murat's advance guard confronted the Russians at the bridge of Schöngrabern, and the Prince proposed negotiations. Kutusov agreed, eager to gain time, and it was only when Napoleon sent Murat a furious order the next day to engage at once that the battle opened late on the 16th. It was fought largely at night, the infantry of Legrand* and Oudinot,* with Sebastiani's* cavalry, advancing against the crest held by 6,000 Russians. After a confused night action against heavy odds, Bagration withdrew his men toward the main army. The Russians lost 2,402 casualties (the French about 1,200), but Kutusov was able to reach Brünn in safety on 18 November, and next day made contact with Buxhowden.

Holy War, the, of 1798–1801. After the French victory at the Pyramids* and the subsequent occupation of Cairo, in October 1798 the Turkish Sultan issued a *firman* declaring a *jihad* or Holy War against the French infidels. On 21 October the Moslem population of Cairo rose in revolt against the French, and it took two days of stiff fighting for Bonaparte to restore order. The cost was 300 French lives. Over 2,000 Arabs were killed in the fighting, and many more were executed in French reprisals thereafter, including 6 sheiks and 80 pashas. The Holy War continued throughout the French period of occupation in Egypt, and considerably complicated Bonaparte's attempts to restore order in the country.

Hood, Admiral Sir Samuel, Viscount (1724–1816). Samuel Hood first entered the Royal Navy in 1741. He served under Rodney's command, and by 1757 had become famous for his skill at taking prizes. He was knighted in 1778 after making a further reputation in command of the North American station, 1767–70. In 1781 he fought under Admiral Graves against de Grasse at the Chesapeake, and repelled the same French sailor next year off Basseterre. He was second-in-command to Lord Rodney at Dominica, and was created a baron in 1782. From 1784 Hood became MP for Westminster; in 1787 he was promoted to vice admiral; and from

1788–93 he was a lord of the Admiralty. In 1793 he commanded the Allied force that occupied Toulon,* and when he was forced to evacuate the port owing to Bonaparte's artillery tactics he evacuated many refugees. In 1794 he captured Corsica, but owing to disagreements with the military commanders and to political factors he was recalled to Great Britain. In 1794 he became full admiral, and two years later he was created a viscount and appointed Governor of Greenwich.

Hope, General John, Earl of Hopetoun (1765–1823). From 1790 he was MP for a Scottish constituency, and in 1796 was Adjutant General under Abercromby* in the West Indies, and later in Holland (1799) and Egypt (1801), where he was wounded at Alexandria.* Promoted to lieutenant general in 1808, he was second-in-command to Moore* at Copenhagen* and during the Corunna* campaign. After Moore's death, he supervised the embarkation of the army. He commanded a division at Walcheren* later in 1809, and succeeded Graham* in the Peninsula, commanding the 1st Division at Nivelle* and the Nive* (both 1813), and conducting the blockade of Bayonne,* where he was wounded during the French sortie in 1814. He was created a baron, succeeded to his brother's earldom, and became a full general in 1819.

Hope, Lieutenant General Sir John (1765–1836). From 1778–82 he was in the Dutch service and was aide-de-camp to General Erskine in Flanders, 1792–93. From 1796–99 he commanded the 28th Foot (the Gloucestershire Regiment) and from 1799–1804 the 37th Foot. In 1805 he was Deputy Adjutant General under Lord Cathcart* in Hanover and again at Copenhagen* (1807). He commanded a brigade at Salamanca* (1812), was promoted to lieutenant general in 1819, and knighted two years later.

Hortense. *See* **Beauharnais,** Hortense

Hotham and Martin, naval battle of, 13–14 March 1794. As the French prepared an expedition of 18,000 men against Corsica, Admiral Martin* sailed from Toulon with 15 ships-of-the-line and 12 smaller vessels to ensure the transports' safe passage. Almost two thirds of his 12,000 men had never been to sea before. Admiral Hotham* had succeeded Lord Hood* in command of the British Mediterranean fleet at Leghorn, and on the 9th was incensed to learn that the French had captured the crippled H.M.S. *Berwick* two days earlier. The British fleet put to sea and closed with the French on the 11th, but bad winds made battle impossible. On the night of the 12th two French ships collided, and one had to leave the line, while the *Ça Ira* became a liability and was almost captured by Nelson* in the *Agamemnon*. She was eventually taken in tow by another French vessel. On the 14th the vans of the two fleets passed each other on opposite tacks within cannon range, and the British had the worse of the exchange of fire, two ships being badly mauled. However, the French lost contact with the *Ça Ira* and the *Censeur,* and both vessels were forced to strike their colors. So ended this tactically indecisive combat; nevertheless, the French decided to abandon the Corsican expedition and re-entered Toulon on the 24th. By then the British had lost H.M.S. *Illustrious* in a gale, so each fleet ended up having lost two ships.

Hotham, Vice Admiral Sir Henry (1777–1833). After succeeding Lord Hood in the Mediterranean, his first action was that called "Hotham and Martin"* (1794). He remained in the Mediterranean on mainly blockading duties until 1798, and then spent three years in the Bay of Biscay. In 1809 he managed to drive three French frigates ashore at Les Sables d'Olonne,

and destroyed a similar force off l'Orient in 1812. Knighted in 1815, his full knowledge of the Biscayan coastline of France thwarted Napoleon's hopes of escaping from Rochefort to the United States after Waterloo.* Hotham became a Lord of the Admiralty (1818–22 and again from 1828–30), being promoted to vice admiral in 1825. He died at Malta.

Howe, Admiral of the Fleet Richard, Earl (1726–1799). First going to sea with Anson in 1740, he took part in many naval actions during the wars of the Austrian Succession, the Seven Years' War, and the American Revolution. He succeeded to the viscountcy in 1758 and became a great expert at the skills of naval blockade* off the French coasts. In 1778 he resigned over discontent with the Ministry, but was promoted to admiral in 1782 and led the fleet that relieved the garrison of Gibraltar after its long siege. From 1783–88 he was First Lord of the Admiralty, and, despite attacks against his administration of the navy in Parliament he was created an earl in 1788. In 1794 he won the "Glorious First of June"* battle and became Admiral of the Fleet and General of Royal Marines in 1796. Next year he received the Garter. He retired in 1797, but intervened in the Nore* and Spithead* mutinies* at Portsmouth to ultimately good effect. He perfected the system of naval signaling.

Hume, Dr. John Robert, MD, LRCP (1781?–1857). Dr. Hume served throughout the greater part of the Peninsular War as Wellington's* personal doctor. In 1816 he gained his MD at the University of St. Andrews, and three years later became a Licentiate of the Royal College of Physicians. He continued as Wellington's medical adviser after the wars and was appointed a Commissioner in Lunacy in 1836.

Hundred Days, the, of 1815. This description of the Waterloo* campaign of 1815 was coined by the Comte de Chabrol-Volvic, Prefect of the Seine, who greeted Louis XVIII* on 8 July 1815 at the barrier of St. Denis on his return to Paris with the opening sentence: "A hundred days have passed since the fatal moment when Your Majesty left his capital . . ." In fact it was 110 days since the Bourbon court had fled from Paris on Napoleon's approach (20 March). However, the Emperor did ·actually leave Malmaison for Rochefort on the 101st day, but the actual attribution is as stated.

Hussars. *See* **Cavalry**

Hyder (or **Haider**) **Ali,** Nizam (1717–1782). Haider Ali Khan Bahadour, to give him his correct name, was the founder of the Moslem ruling dynasty in Mysore. Originally a soldier of fortune, he defeated the Mahrattas and Afghans and then became the client of the French, whose intrigues against British power in India he strongly supported. He beat a British and East India Company force at the battle of Perambaukum in September 1780, and among the prisoners he took was the (future) Sir David Baird.* Although he was ultimately defeated he proved capable of transferring his states to his son Tippoo (Tipou) Sahib.* He died at Arcot largely unlamented except by the French.

Hyderabad, the Nizam of (fl. 1798). The Nizam ruled the area around the Indian river Musi, a tributary of the Kistna. He was pro-British by inclination, but his army of 14,000 was officered by Frenchmen, and he was under the sway of Tippoo Sahib.* On the advice of Colonel Arthur Wellesley,* the Governor of the Madras presidency, Lord Clive, sent 6,000 troops to march on Hyderabad in October 1798. There was no fighting owing to a convenient mutiny against the French, who were forced to surrender. The Nizam soon signed a treaty with the East India Company whereby he accepted British officers for his forces and agreed to a garrison of 6,000 Company sepoys for his security (and paid for their upkeep) against Tippoo of Mysore and the Mahratta confederacy.

Ibrahim Bey, Emir of Egypt (1735–1817). Born in (modern) Czechoslovakia, he was sold as a slave to the head Mameluke* in Egypt, Abu-Dahab, who gave him his freedom and later made him governor of Cairo. On Abu-Dahab's death he became joint Emir-Mameluke and ruler of Egypt with Murad Bey.* His period of power came to an end with Bonaparte's expedition to Egypt in 1798, but he fought with great skill at the Pyramids* and Heliopolis. After the French evacuation he proved incapable of reasserting his rule in Cairo. In 1811 he successfully avoided Mehemet Ali's massacre of the Mameluke rulers, and died in obscurity six years later.

Ile Berthier, l'. A small island in the river Danube a few miles below Vienna, adjacent to Lobau Island, which Napoleon named "l'Ile Berthier" at the time of the battle of Wagram* in July 1809 as a tribute to his hard-working Chief of Staff, Marshal Alexandre Berthier,* who had largely planned the great battle.

Imaz, General José (fl. 1811). Following the death of the gallant General Menacho* leading a sortie against the French by the garrison of beleaguered Badajoz,* General Imaz succeeded to the command. Unfortunately the new commander was not of his predecessor's mettle, and on 9 March 1811 Imaz agreed to open negotiations with the besieging forces of Marshal Soult.* As a result, the Spanish garrison surrendered on the 11th, and Marshal Beresford*—sent posthaste by

Wellington* to sustain the fortress—arrived too late to affect the issue.

Imperial Guard, the. This, one of the most celebrated military formations in history, evolved from three sources. First, the *Guides** raised to protect General Bonaparte in 1796 became the nucleus of the cavalry* of the Imperial Guard. Second, selected members of the Guards of the Directory* and of the Legislative Assembly were added in 1799. Thirdly, these three cadres were combined to form the Consular Guard, which so distinguished itself at Marengo.* In 1804 the title was changed to the Imperial Guard, ready for Napoleon's coronation. In size it grew enormously over the years. In 1800 there were barely 3,000 grenadiers and mounted members. By 1804, it had grown to comprise 5,000 grenadiers, 2,000 *élite* cavalry, and 24 guns—about 8,000 in all. By Austerlitz* there were over 12,000, and by 1812 there were no less than 56,169 Imperial Guardsmen of one category or another. The peak was reached in 1814, when in the hour of France's crisis a vast expansion of the Young Guard made its total reach 112,482. At Waterloo,* however, the Imperial Guard's size had been reduced to 25,870 veteran soldiers.

The Imperial Guard evolved over the years from a small regiment to a complete army. Its organization was complex and always changing as subunits were added, disbanded, or brigaded with others. No less than 80 formations were involved, although not all simultaneously. The three main sections were as follows: the

Saxony, 1806

Imperial Guard Drummers, L'Ecole Militaire, Paris

Old Guard—the elite of the elite, comprising the Grenadiers and Chasseurs of the Guard, the mounted *grenadiers-à-cheval*, the *chasseurs-à-cheval* brigaded with the Mamelukes,* the *gendarmerie d'élite,** and the *marins de la garde*, besides artillery and engineer detachments. Next, in 1806, the Middle Guard was formed (a title it received later), eventually four regiments strong (two of fusiliers and two of flankers, or marksmen). Lastly, in 1809, the Young Guard came into existence, mainly comprising regiments of light infantry. Uniquely, its membership was made up from the cream of each annual conscript class. The older formations jealously guarded entry to their ranks: for the Old Guard, the minimum requirement was five years' service and two campaigns. Selection and transfer was a continuous process. Privileges of membership were considerable in terms of extra pay, rations, and other comforts, but

with ceremonial as well as military duties to perform, the Guard earned its keep. In later years it served as a training cadre for junior leaders: many an Imperial Guardsman found himself commissioned and sent off to command a unit in a line regiment in 1813 and 1814.

Napoleon, to the Guard's undisguised discontent, proved very chary about employing it in battle, but from 1812 it received its fill of action. In earlier years it was always held in reserve and often served as little more than spectators of great events. However, it was the *corps d'élite* of the French Army of the First Empire, and it earned a deserved reputation for valor, skill, and absolute loyalty to its creator and inspirer.

Infantry, the. The foot soldier was the basis of the Napoleonic army. In the days of the Revolution the old *Régiments* bearing provincial titles—*Navarre, Piedmont,*

[207]

the *Saar*, etc.—had been replaced by three-battalion *demi-brigades*. These, in the critical days of 1792 and 1793, comprised one experienced and two raw volunteer or *féderés* battalions by the rules of the *amalgame,** but in 1803 Napoleon reverted to the *régiments* based on a numbering system rather than the old names. The regiment thereafter remained the larger unit, made up of three battalions. Each battalion until 1805 comprised nine companies of about 140 men each (one company being a grenadier or *élite* group, and another one being a light infantry or skirmisher company). By 1808, however, an adjusted system was in the process of adoption, the new *régiment* being organized into four combat battalions of six companies apiece (two of which remained grenadiers and *voltigeurs* as before), supported by a depot battalion of four companies which trained the conscripts on their first arrival in the unit. Thus a regiment at full strength (very rarely attained) might contain 3,400 officers and men. Besides the line companies, there was a small headquarters, medical team, and a band. After 1801, the practice of attaching two 6-pounder cannons to each regiment lapsed, but from 1809, as the standard of

French 12-Pounder Cannon

conscript dropped, four 4-pounders were again introduced.

There were two main types of infantry formations in the French army—line and light. Both were armed with the Charleville 1777 musket, bayonets, and sabers, and every soldier carried a knapsack, water bottle, cooking pot, blanket or greatcoat, and entrenching tool, besides an ammunition pouch. Light infantry were mainly intended to fight in extended skirmisher order rather than in dense columns or shoulder-to-shoulder lines (see Tactics), and their later units contained a *carabinier* company instead of one of grenadiers, four *chasseurs-à-pied* (instead of fusilier) companies, and one of *voltigeurs*. In 1803 there were 90 line and 26 light (*léger*) regiments, but ten years later there were a total of 243 regiments (or theoretically 1,215 battalions to include depot formations), of which about 40 were light regiments.

Training remained rudimentary. The new conscript might receive two or three weeks of basic instruction at the depot, but he would fire on average only two musket shots a year in practice. Much stress was placed upon the attack with cold steel, the psychological threat posed by the 15-inch bayonet being more significant than its actual application. Most soldiers learned their profession at "the cannon's mouth" as of yore, but most officers passed through St. Cyr* or the *Ecole Militaire* until the mass commissioning of other experienced ranks was resorted to from 1813 onward. The drain this development imposed was serious on unit efficiency, and even more draining was the perpetual selection of the very best other ranks for transfer to the Imperial Guard.* It was amazing, however, what could be achieved with even the least experienced of troops. In 1813 and 1814, the fifteen-year-old "Marie-Louises"* or the incapacitated old men, with the

British 9-Pounder Cannon

odd *gendarme,* customs officer, and sailor thrown in, provided Napoleon with some of his staunchest infantry in battle, although these latter-day conscripts did not prove to have the marching stamina of their *grognard* (or "grumbler") predecessors of the great years of the Empire.

European infantry varied enormously in standard. Only the British clung uncompromisingly to linear concepts of tactics, although even in the British Army the work of Sir John Moore* and others saw the introduction of light infantry—including the famous 95th Rifles, armed with the Baker rifle rather than the standard Tower or "Brown-Bess" musket, the main firearm for almost every other infantry soldier. Although in the Revolutionary Wars the British infantry bore a mixed reputation, by the height of the Peninsular War it had been refined into the finest infantry in Europe, and Wellington's* redcoats were the terror of their opponents. The "red wall" with leveled muskets calmly awaiting the arrival of the French columns or cavalry squadrons became a byword.

Infantry employed by other continental powers than France underwent a transformation during the course of the Revolutionary and Napoleonic wars. In the 1790s the Habsburgs had over 200,000 infantrymen of many nationalities drawn from their wide-ranging empire. Some, like the Croats, fought as light infantry, but at first the concepts of linear drill ruled supreme, and their foes dubbed the Austrian infantry "walking muskets." However, they proved no real match for the French from 1795 on, the besetting problems of an antiquated and inefficient staff system, dominated by bureaucratic paperwork, hampering their effective employment. The regiment was the main formation. In June 1805 the Archduke Charles* reorganized these into four battalions apiece, one of grenadiers (600 men) and three of fusiliers (800 men each), or some 3,800 infantrymen in all. Only after Austerlitz,* however, did their rigid tactics begin to be modernized—again under the inspiration of Charles. By 1809 he had created an infantry arm of 279,000 men divided among 80 line regiments and nine

French Infantry

Jäger (or light infantry) battalions, backed by a *Landwehr* (or militia) of 240,000 men, at least on paper. A few improvements in the staff had also been achieved, and a proper divisional and army corps system (based on French lines) was introduced. This was the infantry that fought so well at Aspern-Essling* and Wagram,* later served under Prince Schwarzenberg* on the French side in Russia, and ultimately provided the bedrock of the armies of the Sixth Coalition.*

The infantry of Prussia in 1806 was "a museum piece," reflecting the great days of Frederick the Great,* imposing in appearance but decidedly disappointing in performance and outdated in training. This was evident as early as Valmy* in 1792, but few improvements had been wrought 14 years later. The cult of the past was unshakable, the tactics rigid, the

supply trains enormous, and a day's march of over 10 miles was considered excessive. Its leadership was also antiquated, except for Prince Louis-Ferdinand.* The disasters of Jena* and Auerstadt* and the succeeding weeks, and the humiliations of Tilsit* at length brought reform under the inspiration of Scharnhorst.* The French-imposed ceiling of 42,000 men was evaded by judicious use of the *krumpersystem*;* the best aspects of French organization and tactical forms were imitated, and a generation of good generals emerged, including Blücher,* Gneisenau,* and von Bülow.* By 1812 there were some 100,000 Prussian infantry (20,000 of whom took part in the Russian campaign as unwilling allies of Napoleon), and once General Yorck* had defected and Prussia joined the Sixth Coalition* in the spring of 1813, a rapid expansion took place, based on conscription. A Prussian *landwehr* of 110,000 came into existence, aided by *Freikorps* of foreigners, and the original 80,000 men offered to the Allied cause had swollen to all of 272,000 men under arms (including 228,000 infantry) by August 1813. Many weapons were antiquated, but a new spirit inspired the ranks; discipline had been modernized and was no longer based upon fear of condign punishment. Such were the troops that fought at Dresden,* Leipzig,* and Waterloo.*

The infantry of the Tsar was equally antiquated at first. Alexander* could boast of almost 500,000 men in 1805 (to include Cossacks and levies), and the infantry component, exclusive of the Russian Imperial Guard, was organized into 13 regiments of grenadiers, 77 line regiments, and 20 more of *Jäger* troops. An infantry regiment comprised 2,256 men divided between three battalions (one being a grenadier formation); the light infantry had an establishment of 1,385. Tactics were linear, based upon the platoon column. Once again, inspired leadership was generally lacking. However, the defeats sustained between 1805 and 1807 again produced a wave of reforming endeavor, much of it inspired by Barclay de Tolly.* A corps and divisional system based on the French model was introduced, and the green-clad *moujiks* of the Russian infantry began to take on a more modern appearance and developed into a tough opponent. In 1812 Tsar Alexander disposed of 14 regiments of grenadiers, 96 of the line, and 50 of light troops (all with two front-line battalions and one depot formation apiece), besides the Imperial Guard of six more regiments—perhaps 300,000 infantry in all, mostly "conscripts" serving for terms of 25 years. Good leaders and modern attitudes to the waging of war made the Tsar's infantry an effective force.

Such, then, were the infantry forces of the major powers. Those of smaller states such as Spain and Naples require no separate notice, while the mass of Germanic forces that became members of French satellite states such as Baden, Bavaria, and Westphalia after the destruction of the Holy Roman Empire closely modeled themselves, like all the great powers save England, on French practice.

Inkovo, battle of, 8 August 1812. As the French *Grande Armée* advanced on Smolensk,* General Sebastiani,* at the head of the 3,000 horsemen of the Second Cavalry Corps, engaged in a sharp action with Count Platov's* Cossacks, perhaps 7,000 strong. The French came off rather the worse in the fighting, losing several hundred casualties. Paradoxically, however, this success weakened rather than strengthened Barclay de Tolly's* nerve, and he placed the whole of his advance westward in abeyance for six days. As a result, Napoleon was able to launch his famous crossing of the Dnieper on a 15-mile front, an operation that led to the battle of Smolensk and which is rated among his masterpieces of strategic envelopment.

***Invalides,* les.** Founded by Louis XIV in 1670, and built by Bruant on the instigation of Louvois, this famous building was designed as a hospital for old French soldiers. In 1840, Napoleon's remains were placed in a special open crypt beneath the dome in a sarcophagus fashioned out of a single block of pink porphyry. It stands guarded by two huge statues, representing civil and martial power, and is flanked by 12 statues of Victories. The names of the great battles are inscribed around the walls. It was inaugurated on 2 December 1861 by Napoleon III.* In December 1940, the ashes of Napoleon II* were brought from Vienna by the Germans and placed beside the remains of his great father.

Ionian Isles, the. An archipelago in the Ionian Sea off the west coast of the Balkan Peninsula, they were removed from Venetian to French control in 1797, and were later occupied in turn by Russia, Turkey, and England. From 1815 until 1864 they formed an independent state under British protection, but in that year were assimilated into Greece.

Ireland. Traditionally the "Achilles' heel" of British home defense, Ireland lived up to its reputation during these wars. Its society was split among the small, influential group of officials of Dublin, the selfish ruling clique of the Anglo-Irish colony, and the mass of illiterate and half-starved Roman Catholic peasantry (the "bog-Irish"); trouble was endemic, and began to come to the fore again from the American War of Independence onward. The Irish Parliament was corrupt, inefficient, and wholly subordinate to Westminster, and the movement for an independent Irish Parliament was led by such able men as Grattan.* The strong Volunteer Force—raised to protect the country from the possibility (a recurrent fear and reality) of French invasion—also joined the clamor for legislative independence and the raising of the crippling economic constraints.

The outbreak of the French Revolution brought matters to a head. Wolfe Tone* raised the revolutionary United Irishmen movement in 1791, and once war with

France was a reality the Republican governments made a number of attempts to foment the Irish troubles. In December 1796 Hoche's* expedition failed to get ashore at Bantry Bay,* and in the following autumn a second expedition's sailing for Ireland was delayed by Duncan's* naval victory at Camperdown.* Without waiting for the promised French aid, in May 1798 Ireland exploded into a major violent rising against the British. A short but bloody campaign ended at the battle of Vinegar Hill, where the rebels were crushed. In July a French force under General Humbert at last landed but was easily defeated at Killala.

The revolt, although repressed, persuaded the British government that strong, definitive measures were imperative. The result was the Act of Union of 1801: the Irish Parliament was suppressed, and in return Ireland received 102 seats in the House of Commons and 45 in the Lords at Westminster. Certain steps were taken to adjust economic grievances as well, but Irish resentment remained smoldering, fanned by the long-fought issue of Catholic emancipation. More and more Anglo-Irish landlords and clergy moved to England, heightening the exploitation of the rural poor by ruthless agents. Nevertheless, Ireland remained a vital source of fighting men who swelled the ranks of the army: Wellesley* himself was of Anglo-Irish extraction and his family was deeply involved in Irish politics. Indeed, it would be none other than Wellington, as Prime Minister, who at last achieved Catholic emancipation in 1829.

Jacobin Club, the. In 1789, following the transfer of the Constituent Assembly to Paris from Versailles, a number of moderate representatives employed a one-time Dominican monastery in the Rue St. Honoré as their headquarters. Very soon the extreme republican left wing gained control of this group, and were nicknamed "Jacobins" after the former monks. Faction after faction of more moderate persuasion broke away—the *Feuillants* (constitutional monarchists), the *Girondins* (led by the Rolands and others), and the *Hébertists* (named after their leader Hébert)—and soon a bitter factional war was waging. The Jacobins formed the basis of the "Mountain," or left wing, and were soon notorious for their extreme opinions and ruthlessness. Their most prominent leaders were Danton and Robespierre,* the unleashers of the Terror. After the latter's fall and the Thermidorian reaction, the Convention finally ordered the Club's closure in November 1794.

Jaffa, storm and massacre of, 3–7 March 1799. Advancing into Syria on 23 February, the Army of the Orient captured Gaza and moved on to invest Jaffa. A direct assault was mounted after three days of preparation, and the garrison capitulated. When he learned that the garrison included 3,000 Turks who had only recently been released at El Arish* by the French on parole, Bonaparte ordered them all—together with a further 1,400 captives—to be executed. The massacre that followed was notorious, and Napoleon's reputation received a lasting stain which even the celebrated visit to the Pestiferies* four days later could not eradicate in the eyes of posterity.

Janissaries. These elite Turkish troops were originally recruited by the Sultans from among Christian slaves and formed their bodyguard. They grew into a small army over the centuries and were noted for their towering headgear, fierce bearing in battle, famous march, and for their capacity for intrigue in palace politics. By the late 18th century their power was but a shadow of its former strength.

Jay, John, American Plenipotentiary-Extraordinary (1745–1829). In late 1790 the British government had ordered the confiscation of all shipping—including that of neutrals—that touched French ports, whether in Europe or the colonies, and many American vessels had been taken. The United States' special envoy, John Jay, reached London in June 1794, and a Treaty of Commerce and Navigation was signed on 17 November that year which excluded American shipping in the West Indies area from the penalties and set up a joint commission to investigate grievances. France protested loudly to Washington over this negotiation, but at least a measure of Anglo-American harmony was restored which would largely survive until the War of 1812.*

Jellacic von Buzim, General Franz, Baron von (1746–1810). He first earned a reputation against the Turks in 1789. Seven years later he campaigned on the Rhine against Moreau,* and during the

War of the Second Coalition* he inflicted a check on Oudinot* at Feldkirch. Next year he was promoted to field marshal lieutenant in the Austrian army, but in 1805 he was surrounded by French forces and forced to surrender to Marshal Augereau* and the VII Corps.

Jemappes, battle of, 6 November 1792. After their unexpected success at Valmy,* the French National Convention ordered General Dumouriez* to take the offensive in Flanders during the autumn. At the head of a hastily gathered and ill-disciplined force of 40,000 men, Dumouriez encountered Duke Albert of Saxe-Teschen and 14,000 Austrian troops holding an entrenched position at Jemappes, west of Mons in the Austrian Netherlands. In an ill-coordinated but enthusiastic attack, the French infantry swarmed forward, employing *l'ordre mixte,* and stormed the position at bayonet point, in a direct attack, backed by artillery fire. This was the first real French victory on the field during the Revolutionary Wars and led to the French conquest of most of modern Belgium in the weeks that followed. Saxe-Teschen resigned his command after the loss of Brussels.

Jena-Auerstädt, battle of, 14 October 1806. Following his whirlwind passage of the Teutoburgerwald in early October 1806, Napoleon pressed north at the head of his *Grande Armée* of 180,000, seeking the main Prussian forces. His army moved in three main columns, Lannes* and Augereau* on the left along the river Saale; Soult,* Ney,* and the Bavarians on the right down the Elster; and Bernadotte,* Davout,* the Reserve Cavalry, and the Imperial Guard* with headquarters moved in the center toward Auma. For a time Napoleon expected to meet the Prussians in the general direction of Leipzig, but Murat's* questing cavalry found no sign of the foe in the northerly direction. However, the flexibility of the French *bataillon carré* formation and of

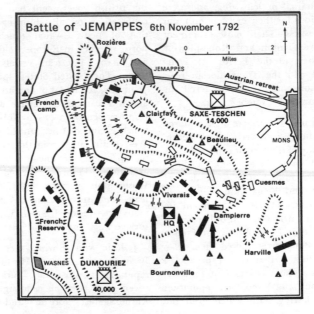

Battle of JEMAPPES 6th November 1792

its individual *corps d'armée** implied an ability to adapt rapidly to any situation, however unexpected.

And so it proved. On 13 October a message from Lannes leading the left-hand column revealed that he had encountered considerable enemy forces to the west of the Saale near the town of Jena. Napoleon at once set out to join the V Corps, and orders were sent to all major formations to veer west and head without delay for the Saale. At 4:00 P.M. the Emperor joined Lannes on the Landgrafenberg west of the river. What he could see convinced him that the main might of the Prussian army was before him and that it would probably retire west before offering battle at Weimar—perhaps in three days' time. In fact Napoleon miscalculated. Before him were only Hohenlohe's* 35,000 men (with 15,000 more under General Rüchel near Weimar); the main Prussian force (60,000) under Brunswick* and King Frederick William III* was in fact marching north toward Auerstädt and Naumburg.

All night and early the next morning hard-marching French formations made their appearance near the Saale while Napoleon supervised, by the light of flickering torches, the making of a road up the Landgrafenberg for his guns. Lannes was joined first by the Guard, but by 10:00 A.M. on the 14th this force had been doubled to 50,500 as Augereau appeared. By noon Soult's IV Corps provided a further boost, and with Ney's VI Corps and the Reserve Cavalry, the French strength at Jena itself would bring the total to over 90,000, with further forces joining. Napoleon meanwhile, deciding on his plan, had long before ordered Davout and Bernadotte to take their III and I Corps (47,000) toward Naumburg, ready to execute a classic envelopment attack while the Emperor pinned the main enemy force at Jena—or so he hoped. The next hours,

however, would hold substantial surprises.

The preliminary action at Jena opened at 6:00 A.M. as the French advanced to secure a larger area of ground to facilitate the deployment for battle of their arriving troops. This was entrusted to Augereau on the left, Lannes in the center, and Soult's leading division (St. Hilaire*) on the right. By 10:00 A.M., despite a slowly lifting fog and determined Prussian resistance, these aims had been achieved. By 9:00 A.M. Prince Hohenlohe had come to realize he faced more than the small French force of the previous night, and he sent urgent messages to Rüchel at Weimar for aid. The next stage of the battle centered around Ney and the VI Corps, held in central reserve. Resenting inactivity and chafing at delay, the Alsatian fire-eater eventually launched an unauthorized attack on his own account, and plunged forward into the fighting. The results were almost disastrous: charged by massed Prussian squadrons, Ney soon found himself almost cut off, and only a massive intervention by Lannes, Bertrand,* and the cavalry extricated VI Corps—at the cost of delaying Napoleon's overall development of the battle. Hohenlohe failed to make the most of this opportunity of French disequilibrium, and the chance passed by midday. By 1:00 P.M. every Prussian formation was in full-scale action, and Rüchel's arrival was desperately awaited as more and more French appeared on the field. At that hour Napoleon at last ordered the general advance. Hohenlohe's tired men could not withstand the strain for long, and by 3:00 P.M. they were streaming west from the field, and Rüchel's belated arrival shortly after 2:00 P.M. could not check the rout. Murat was soon leading a hell-for-leather pursuit toward Weimar, and by 4:00 P.M. the battle was over. Napoleon returned to his quarters convinced that he had just beaten the main Prussian army. For a loss of 5,000 Frenchmen he had inflicted possibly 25,000 casualties on the enemy.

At headquarters, however, surprising news awaited him. It now transpired that since early morning a desperate battle had been raging 15 miles north around Auerstädt, and that Davout, with only his 27,000 men of III Corps, had taken on and defeated a force of at least 50,000 Prussians. Napoleon now realized that he had fought only half of the Prussian army. Davout's achievement was immense by any standard. Carrying out Napoleon's order for an advance through Naumburg to cut off the anticipated Prussian line of retreat, Davout had faced bitter obstruction from the prickly Bernadotte whose I Corps was supposed to accompany Davout. Instead, Bernadotte had turned his men south and moved toward Dornberg down the east bank of the Saale—for the Gascon was˙not prepared to accept orders from his colleague, however tactfully couched. So it was that Davout, doggedly carrying out the letter of Napoleon's instructions, albeit on his own, suddenly found himself in the midst of Brunswick's forces as they moved north, and once the fog lifted a desperate battle ensued. In fact Davout husbanded his limited resources with care and fought with great tactical finesse, defeating each part of the foe's array in turn. The Prussians were late in attacking this exposed French force—the main action began at only 9:45 A.M. and was then extremely poorly coordinated. Much of the fighting centered around the village of Hassenhaussen, and in its vicinity Davout deployed his three outnumbered divisions. Attacks led by Schmettau, Wartensleben, and Orange were defeated in turn, Field Marshal Mollendorf* (aged 80) was mortally wounded, and when the French force boldly advanced shortly after 11:00 A.M., Prussian cohesion snapped and Frederick William III* ordered his generals to abandon the battle. By evening 13,000 Prussians and 115 guns had been accounted for; as for the exhausted but jubilant forces of III Corps, no less than 40% lay *hors de combat*. In sum, Jena and Auerstädt had shattered the main Prussian forces, and soon a contrite Bernadotte was leading a dramatic advance on Berlin.

Jervis, Admiral of the Fleet John, Earl of St. Vincent (1735–1823). Destined to emerge as possibly Britain's greatest sailor in this period after Nelson,* Jervis first served on a ship as an able-bodied seaman and midshipman. In 1755 he attained the rank of lieutenant, and in 1759 played a leading role in the capture of Quebec. During the American war he commanded vessels in the Baltic and off the northwest coast of France, helped in the relief of besieged Gibraltar, and was knighted in 1782. He gained flag-rank in 1787 and was promoted to vice admiral six years later. In 1794 he assisted in the capture of Martinique and Guadeloupe, and was made full admiral the next year and appointed Commander in Chief in the Mediterranean. He fought and won the battle of Cape St. Vincent* in February 1797 and was created an Earl. Blockading Cadiz, he sent Nelson* into the Mediterranean to watch the French expedition at Toulon* in 1798. After suppressing a mutiny, he earned censure by ordering Sir John Orde back to Britain, and this, together with ill health, caused his resignation in 1799. He soon re-emerged to command the Channel Fleet, and as First Lord of the Admiralty under Addington* planned the Copenhagen* attack against the Armed Neutrality* in 1801. He thereafter helped plan England's coastal defense and busied himself with naval administrative reform, inspiring the impeachment of Lord Melville. He quarreled with Pitt* over naval expansion but resumed command in the

Channel in 1806. He retired from the active list in 1807 and was promoted to Admiral of the Fleet in 1821.

John (or **Joao**) **VI, Prince Regent and later King of Portugal** (1767–1826). Son of Peter III of Portugal, he became regent in 1792 after a bitter row with his mother. He took the title of Prince of the Algarve and married the daughter of Charles IV* of Spain. His attitude toward both the Revolution and the Empire was one of hostility, and in 1807 Junot* invaded Portugal and the Regent and his government were forced to flee to Brazil. In 1816, on the death of his mother, he took the title of John VI but only returned to Europe in 1821. He faced much trouble from his sons Miguel and Pedro, and after exiling the former he ruled alone, introducing a form of constitutional monarchy.

John, Baptiste Joseph Fabian Sebastian, Archduke (1782–1859). The son of the Grand Duke of Tuscany (later the Emperor Leopold II*), in 1800 at age 18 he commanded an army in Bavaria but was defeated at Hohenlinden.* In 1809 he commanded in Italy and won the battle of the Raab. After 1815 he lived a modest and retiring life, and in 1827 he married the daughter of a postmaster.

Jomini, Antoine Henri, Baron (1779–1869). Born in the Swiss canton of Vaud, Jomini began his career in a bank but became a soldier during the Swiss Revolution. The Swiss army was organized along French lines, and in 1805 he received a post on Ney's* staff and served during the Austerlitz* campaign. In 1806 he so impressed Napoleon with his grasp of military strategy that he was attached to the Emperor's staff, and as a member of the Grand General Staff he was present at Jena* and Eylau.* Later in 1807 he became Ney's Chief of Staff and was made a baron in 1808. He was promoted to *gén-*

éral de brigade in 1810, and served on several missions to Russia, where the Tsar offered him employment. In 1803 Jomini had published his treatise on *Grand Military Operations*, and now in 1810 he began his classic *History of the Revolutionary Wars*, which he would eventually complete in 1824. His talents as a historian led him to several prestigious staff appointments. He fought with Ney in Spain but refused a major appointment in 1812 owing to his warm feelings for Russia, and ultimately served as governor of Vilna and then of Smolensk. In 1813 he resumed an active service role in Ney's III Corps and fought at Lützen* and Bautzen.* Ney wanted him promoted to *général de division*, but Berthier*—long jealous of his superior intellectual talents—had him arrested for failing to submit a fortnightly report of strength state. This led to Jomini joining the Allies on 15 August 1813, and the Tsar at once appointed him a lieutenant general and a personal aide-de-camp. He thereafter served as a senior staff adviser to the Allies until 1815. He was present at the Congress of Vienna,* and also at those at Aix-la-Chapelle (1818) and Verona (1822). From 1823 he spent six years as military tutor to the Tsar's heir. In 1828 he fought the Turks at Varna and later advised Tsar Nicolas II during the Crimean War. Much of the time he lived in Brussels, and there he wrote his great work, "Précis on the Art of War," which finally established his reputation as a military thinker as well as a historian of note. This was published in 1836, and although he was eventually overshadowed by his contemporary Clausewitz* as a military philosopher, his influence on several generations of officers—including the commanders in the American Civil War—was profound. Moving to Paris in his last years he wrote further works on Russia and its armed forces. In 1848 he retired from the Russian service and after several changes of living place he at last died at Paris in 1869 on 22 March.

Jones, Major General Sir John Thomas, Baronet (1783–1843). From 1798 to 1802 he served as adjutant of the Royal Engineers at Gibraltar but later returned to England where he became busy on anti-invasion preparations. In 1806 he was back in the Mediterranean, fighting under Stuart* at Maida* and capturing and refortifying Fort Scylla. From 1808 he served as aide to General Leith* with the Spanish army, but in 1809 he was transferred to take part in the Walcheren* expedition. Between late 1809 and late 1810 he designed and completed the famous Lines of Torres Vedras* outside Lisbon. In 1812 he was promoted to brevet lieutenant general and was wounded in the groin at the siege of Burgos fortress.* While convalescing he began his critical book on the "Sieges in the Peninsula." In 1815 he reported on the Netherlands fortresses as sole Inspector General and also held an appointment at Woolwich. Promoted to full colonel and appointed an aide-de-camp to George IV* in 1825, he became a baronet in 1831 and was promoted to major general six years later. During the war scare of 1840, he prepared plans for the defense of the United Kingdom and Gibraltar, and also drew up further reports on the fortifications in the Netherlands, besides writing several more works of military history. After his death, officers of the Royal Engineers erected a statue to him in St. Paul's cathedral.

Joseph, King of Spain. *See* **Bonaparte,** Joseph

Joseph II, Emperor of Austria (1741–1790). Joseph, who was born and died in Vienna, was an "enlightened despot," a ruler who patronized philosophers, economists, and artists and who worked for the amelioration of the lives of his subjects while insisting on the prerogatives of an absolute monarch. In 1764 he was crowned King of the Romans (in fact a subsidiary rank in the Holy Roman Empire), and next year succeeded his father as Emperor. For many years, however, he remained subject to the tutelage of his able and forceful mother, the Empress-Dowager Maria-Theresa. Austria shared in the partitions of Poland but failed to absorb Bavaria despite attempts to do so in 1779 and 1785—largely because of Prussian opposition. From 1780 Joseph was *de facto* ruler as well as *de jure,* and two years later he engaged in a massive contention over ecclesiastical privileges and appointments with the Papacy. During his reign he abolished serfdom and the use of torture and even declared the freedom of the press. In 1788, however, a war against the Turks failed to bring the desired territorial gains, and Joseph died a broken and disappointed man, to be succeeded by Leopold II.*

Josephine, Empress. *See* **Beauharnais,** Josephine

Joubert, Général Barthelemy Catherine (1769–1799). An artilleryman, he joined the *La Fère* regiment in 1784 after being expelled from school, but later resumed his studies. In late July 1789 he reemerged to matters military as a sergeant in the National Guard of Dijon and by 1791 was on the lower Rhine. Commissioned into the infantry in 1792, he soon attracted the favorable notice of the representatives of the people who forwarded his career. He fought in Italy from 1794 under Augereau,* was promoted to *général de brigade* in 1795, and took part in many of the battles and actions of 1796–97 including Montenotte,* Mondovi,* and Lodi* (after being transferred to Massena*). He fought well at La Corona and Castiglione* (now under Vaubois*) and

Joubert

led the pursuit to Trent. He fought with great skill at Rivoli,* and later in 1797 took part in the negotiations at Leoben* before being sent back to Paris with captured Austrian colors. In December 1796 he had been made *général de division,* and now in late 1797 he was put in command of the Army of Batavia* in place of Macdonald.* During 1798 he was also for a time commander of the Armies of Italy and of Rome, but these commands lapsed in early 1799. In August that year, however, he resumed command of the Army of Italy from Moreau* as the crisis of the War of the Second Coalition* approached, and in this position fought the Austrians under Bellegarde at Acqui (13 August) and the Russians under the great Suvorov* at Novi* (15 August). At the latter battle, Joubert was shot through the heart at the head of his grenadiers. He was greatly mourned, and a memorial was set up in his honor by his troops.

Jourdan, Maréchal Jean-Baptiste, later comte (1762–1833). The son of a surgeon, he became a private soldier in 1778 and

fought with the *Régiment d'Auxerrois* before Savannah (1779) during the War of American Independence. At the Revolution, he became a captain in the National Guard* of Limoges and was soon promoted to lieutenant colonel (October 1791). In this rank he fought at Jemappes* and Neerwinden,* and in 1793 was promoted both to *général de brigade* (May) and *général de division* (July), but was struck a glancing blow in the chest by a cannonball at Hondschoote in September. This did not prevent him from taking command of the Army of the North and winning the battle of Wattignies* in mid-October. Nevertheless, he was retired from the army and for a time became a grocer at Limoges. Soon recalled to harness, he took command on the Moselle in April 1794, replacing Hoche,* but later passed under the overall control of Pichegru.* On 26 June Jourdan won his greatest success at Fleurus,* and thereafter captured Brussels, Namur, Cologne, Coblenz, and Dusseldorf. Thus he was a well-established commander of distinction before Bonaparte appeared on the scene.

In 1796 he crossed the Rhine in association with events in Italy and took Frankfort, but ill health forced him to quit the field in July. Restored to health, he was defeated at Wurzburg in September and was recalled. He was then elected to the *Cinq-Cents,* soon becoming its president. In September 1798 he guided through the Conscription Law* that bears his name and then took up various commands in quick succession only to be defeated at Stockach* in March 1799. He returned to his political duties, joining the left wing, and as such opposed the *coup d'état* of Brumaire. He was arrested and almost deported, but the First Consul pardoned him and appointed him Inspector General of the infantry and cavalry in 1800. An ambassadorial post in the Cisalpine Republic* was followed by an ad-

Jourdan

ministrative position in Piedmont (1800–03), and in 1804 he received command of the Army of Italy and was created one of the original marshals.* He served Joseph Bonaparte* as Chief of Staff from 1806, and two years later transferred with him to Spain. For a while he commanded the IV Corps in place of Lefebvre* while remaining Chief of Staff, and was defeated by Wellesley,* with Victor,* at Talavera* in late July 1809. From 1811 he was Governor of Madrid, but he could not impress his strategic views on his fellow marshals. Commanding the Army of the Center, he shared in the massive defeat of Vitoria* in June 1813. He advised against fighting, but was later blamed by Napoleon for the outcome of the day, recalled to France, and retired from the service.

He never again held an active command, but rallied to the Bourbons in 1814. Next year, however, he rejoined Napoleon during the Hundred Days* and was made a peer of France, taking over command of the Army of the Rhine from Rapp* in late June. He again championed the Bourbon cause and presided over the

court that tried and condemned Ney.* In return he was made a count and (in 1819) a peer of France. His last post was as Governor of *Les Invalides** until his death on 23 November 1833.

Junot, Général Jean Andoche, duc d'Abrantes (1771–1813). He first took up a musket in 1790, and was wounded as a grenadier near Longwy in 1792 and by a musketball in 1793. As a sergeant, he served as Bonaparte's secretary at Toulon* and became his lieutenant aide-de-camp soon after. He served at his side in Italy (1794–95) and again as his senior assistant (1796–97). After taking captured colors to Paris, he escorted Josephine* back to Milan. He was grievously wounded in a combat in which he killed six men in August 1796, and was promoted to major. In 1798 he followed Bonaparte to Egypt and fought at Malta,* Rahmanieh, the Pyramids,* before Cairo,* and was made a provisional *général de brigade* in January 1799. Attached to Kléber* in Syria, he won a sharp skirmish at Nazareth in April and took part in the great success of

Junot

Mount Tabor* a week later. Returned to Egypt he fought at Aboukir* but was captured by the Royal Navy en route to France in October that year. He was freed, returned to France, and confirmed in his acting rank. In 1801 he was made *général de division*. After the Camp of Boulogne he was given high honors but not made a marshal, and in 1805 he became ambassador to Portugal. He left this post to rejoin the army in time for the battle of Austerlitz,* again serving as Napoleon's aide. In 1806 he became governor general of Parma and Piacenza and repressed a revolt in the Apennines. From October that year he became Governor of Paris for a spell, but was then appointed to head the force that entered Spain and invaded Portugal in late 1807. He narrowly missed capturing the Portuguese government in Lisbon, and was made Governor General of the country. Defeated by Wellesley* at Vimiero* the following August, he secured good terms at Cintra* and was repatriated to France with his army. He returned to Spain in command of the VIII Corps and later the III Corps, and conducted the siege of

Saragossa.* In June 1809 he was transferred to command the reserve army of Germany and fought on the Rhine. He returned to Spain in December at the head of the VIII Corps, took Astorga, and in 1810 served in Massena's* Army of Portugal, covering the siege of Ciudad Rodrigo* and commanding the center at Bussaco.* On 11 October he won the action of Sobral but was badly wounded early in 1811 at Rio Major. He took part in the retreat from Torres Vedras* to Pombal and fought at Fuentes de Oñoro.* In 1812 he served under Eugène Beauharnais* in Russia, commanding the II and IV Corps, and later the VIII Corps in place of Jerome Bonaparte.* He fought at Smolensk* but was much criticized for failing to reach Valutina in time to cut off the retreating Russians. Recalled to France in January 1813, he was briefly governor of Venice, but he became mad and was retired from all offices in July. He committed suicide on 29 July 1813. It is often claimed that Junot became a Marshal. Despite his close association with Napoleon for many years, this was not in fact the case.

Kalisch, Convention of, 28 February 1813. This involved the formal alliance of Prussia with Russia against Napoleon and set the seal on the work begun earlier in the year by General Yorck* at Tauroggen.* Frederick William III,* afraid of the repercussions on his country if news of his defection from the French alliance leaked out prematurely, tried to insist that the agreement be kept secret and inoperative until the Tsar's troops had reached Berlin. Kutusov,* however, refused to move without the guarantee of immediate Prussian aid, and in the end a compromise was reached whereby the King of Prussia directed Yorck, Bülow,* and Blücher* to follow the Russian forces to the river Oder, but to avoid open hostilities until war was formally declared. The French only got wind of the agreement on 15 March, and Prussia's definitive declaration of war against France only reached Paris on 27 March.

Kalkreuth, Field Marshal, Count von (fl. 1793–1807). A Russian soldier of obscure Germanic origins, Kalkreuth first earned fame for his conduct of the siege of Mainz in 1793 during the first major campaigns of the Revolutionary Wars. In 1807 he commanded the garrison of Danzig* and sustained a long and active defense of the important Baltic port and fortress against Marshal Lefebvre*; however, the inability of his compatriot, the junior commander Kamenskoi the Younger, to break through to his relief eventually compelled him to capitulate on 27 May, gaining generous terms by being

allowed to evacuate his men, arms, and baggage to Prussian-held Pillau.

Kamenskoi, Marshal Alexander, Count (1731–1807). As a junior general he had served with much distinction under the great Suvorov,* but by the time of the Campaign of 1806–07 in East Prussia and Poland he was far too old for the post of Commander in Chief of the Tsar's forces in the west. He proved incapable of holding up the French advance on Warsaw, leaving his subordinates to do most of the fighting at Pultusk* and Golymin,* but he did manage to extricate his army from the closing French trap in late December 1806, reaching safety near Ostrolenka. He owed this in large measure to Generals Bennigsen* and Buxhowden.* A man of violent temper, he was assassinated by a peasant on 9 January 1807.

Katzbach, battle of the river, 26 August 1813. While Napoleon was winning the great battle of Dresden* on the river Elbe, his subordinates were in trouble on other sectors of the front. Near Liegnitz, Marshal Macdonald* blundered into action at the head of the Army of the Bobr (about 101,000 strong) against Blücher's* 105,000 Prussians and Russians forming the Army of Silesia, which included the army corps of Generals Yorck,* Langeron, and Sacken.* Neither side expected a battle that day, believing the other to be on the defensive. The two forces clashed in a scrappy and confused battle near the river Katzbach. Macdonald tried to use 67,000 men to turn the enemy's right near Jauer, but his columns became too separated and were themselves trapped between the heights of Janowitz and the Neiss tributary. The main fight was sustained by 27,000 men of XI Corps under Lauriston.* The whole action was fought in pouring rain, so neither infantry could use fire-power. In the end Macdonald was driven off, after sustaining the loss of some 15,000 dead and prisoners and many cannon. Prussian losses are uncertain, but were probably about 4,000. This setback for the French, together with those sustained at Gross-Beeren* and Kulm* over the same period of time, vitiated all advantage that Napoleon could hope to derive from his great success at Dresden. Macdonald was not supposed to have been on the offensive at all; in the event he bungled it badly and was defeated in detail.

Keith, Admiral George Keith Elphinstone, Viscount (1746–1823). He is first known to have gone to sea on a voyage to China in 1767 and was a lieutenant three years later. During the American Revolution he served with distinction at Charleston (1780) and entered Parliament the same year. He served under Hood* at the defense and evacuation of Toulon* in 1793, became a rear admiral in 1794, and next year was sent in command of a force to take possession of the Cape of Good Hope from the Dutch. He won much prize money in this operation and became a wealthy man. In 1796 he helped in the capture of Ceylon, and the next year shared in the suppression of the serious mutinies, especially at Sheerness and Plymouth, which threatened to cripple the Royal Navy. In 1798 he was second-in-command in the Mediterranean and was blamed for the escape of Brueys* from Toulon. In 1800 he landed in Genoa,* and in 1801 he landed Abercromby's* army for the reconquest of Egypt. He quarreled seriously with Commodore

Smith* over the Convention of El Arish.* He was promoted to admiral in 1801 and commanded in the North Sea from 1803–07, and in the Channel from 1812–15. He was created a viscount in 1814, and next year was the British government's intermediary with Napoleon over his being exiled to St. Helena.* He was on board H.M.S. *Bellerophon* when Napoleon surrendered to the British.

Kellermann, Maréchal François Etienne Christophe, duc de Valmy (1735–1820). He entered the Bourbon army as a cadet in 1752 and next year was commissioned into the *régiment Royal-Bavarie*. He fought in Germany during the Seven Years' War and earned a reputation at Bergen* and Friedberg. In later years he carried out missions to the Poles and Tartars and helped organize the cavalry forces raised in the Palatinate of Cracow. Promotions came along steadily, and in 1792 he became a lieutenant general. Taking over the Army of the Center from General Luckner in August, he proceeded to play

Kellermann

the key role in the victory of Valmy,* thereafter recapturing Longwy and Verdun. After a period of political uncertainty during the Terror,* he eventually was given command of the Armies of the Alps and of Italy in 1793, but was arrested in October and was only restored to his rank in January 1795. Further service in the Alps and North Italy followed, but he retired from active command in September 1797. Thereafter he carried out many administrative duties. In 1799 he became a senator and later president of the Senate. He was created a Marshal of the Empire on 19 May 1804 although he never held a field command in that capacity. He carried out much work with reserve formations and the National Guard. In June 1814 the Bourbons made him a peer of France; Napoleon did the same in 1815, but the old veteran stayed away from the Emperor. He died in Paris on 13 September.

Kellermann, Général François Etienne, comte, later duc de Valmy (1770–1835). Commissioned into the Hussars in 1785, he was attached to the French Embassy in the U.S.A. in 1791. Slowly advancing his career, he returned to France in April 1793, only to be arrested with his father. He was released and returned to active service in July 1794. After serving his father as aide in 1795, he joined the Army of Italy in March 1796, took part in the repression of the revolt of Pavia, and fought before Mantua,* at Bassano,* Arcola,* Rivoli,* and the Tagliamento. In 1798 he served in the Army of Rome under Macdonald* and in that of Naples. He had been promoted to *général de brigade* in 1797 and led a celebrated charge at Marengo* in 1800, being promoted to *général de division* in recognition. Commands in Italy and Hanover gave way, in 1805, to service under Bernadotte* in the Ulm* and Austerlitz* campaigns, and he was wounded at the latter battle. In late

1807 he commanded Junot's* cavalry in the invasion of Portugal, and he was responsible for negotiating the Convention of Cintra* next year. Much service in Spain followed, including the pursuit of Moore* and action at Corunna.* He won several small actions and was several times in command of corps for short periods. In May 1811 he was recalled to France and appointed to a cavalry command in the Grand Army of Russia the next year. Unfortunately ill health intervened and he did not serve in Russia, but was retired at his own request in early 1813. However, not for long: in April he rejoined to command the cavalry under Ney,* fighting at Lützen* and Bautzen* (and being wounded at Klix in between) and also at Dresden.* After further fighting in France in 1814 he was reconciled to the Bourbons and served as a member of the Royal Council of War. In 1815, however, he rejoined Napoleon and fought with great distinction at Quatre Bras* (where he almost captured the crossroads) and at Waterloo,* where he was again wounded in the great charges. Retired from the service in August, he was recognized as Marquis de Valmy in 1817 and succeeded to the dukedom on the death of his father in 1820. Various high administrative posts came his way, but he finally left public life in February 1831.

Kempt, General Sir James (1764–1854). In 1799 he served as Abercromby's* aide-de-camp in Holland, and followed him to the Mediterranean and to Egypt in 1800–01. In 1806 he commanded the light brigade under Stuart* at Maida,* and later commanded a brigade under Picton* in the Peninsula. He was severely wounded in the storm of Badajoz* in 1812 but recovered to command a brigade in the Light Division through 1813 and 1814. At Waterloo* he assumed command of the 3rd Division on Picton's death. From 1820–28 he served as Governor of Nova

Scotia, and as Governor General of Canada for the next two years. Appointed a Privy Councillor in 1830, he became Master General of the Ordnance from 1834–38, and was promoted to full general in 1841.

Killala, action of. *See* **Bantry Bay** and **Ireland**

Kilmaine, Général Charles Edouard Saul Jennings de (1751–1799). Born in Ireland, he entered the French service in 1774, joining the *Royal-dragons* Regiment. Service in Senegal and America followed, and he was commissioned in 1780. After Jemappes* he was promoted to lieutenant colonel (1792) and next year he was made *général de brigade.* After service in the Ardennes he was arrested but was reinstated in 1795 and sent to command cavalry in North Italy under Stengel,* whom he replaced in April 1796. He fought well at Borghetto,* Castiglione,* and before Mantua,* but then illness interrupted his career. In 1797 he took command of the army of occupation left in North Italy and repressed several risings. In October 1798 he organized an abortive expedition against Ireland,* but ill health again struck him down and he died on 11 December 1799 of chronic dysentery.

Kincaid, Captain Sir John (1787–1862). After joining the 95th Rifles in 1799 as an ensign, he served in the Peninsula from 1811–14 with that corps. He took part in the storming of Badajoz* alongside his friend Harry Smith,* and fought at Waterloo* where he was gravely wounded. He was promoted to captain in 1826 and retired from the service in 1831. He became inspector of prisons and factories in Scotland in 1850, became a Yeoman of the Guard in 1852, and was knighted. He published two notable books, *Adventures in the Rifle Brigade* (1830) and *Random Shots of a Rifleman* (1835).

Kléber, Général Jean-Baptiste (1753–

Kléber

1800). The son of a mason from Strasbourg, Kléber abandoned ideas of becoming an architect for the profession of arms, and joined the Bavarian forces of the Holy Roman Empire in 1777. Despairing of promotion beyond lieutenant, in 1785 he returned to Alsace and became an inspector of public buildings at Belfort. In 1789 he joined the local National Guard, and in 1792 was lieutenant colonel of a volunteer battalion on the upper Rhine. In 1793 he distinguished himself at the defense of Mainz and was promoted to *général de brigade* (August) before being sent to serve against the rebels in La Vendée.* There he so shone at the actions of Cholet, Mans, and Chavenay (late 1793) that he was promoted to *général de division* in April 1794. After transfer to the Army of the Sambre-et-Meuse he fought well at Fleurus* and played a large part in the occupation of the Rhineland. However, disillusioned at not sharing the honors showered on Moreau,* Pichegru,* and Hoche,* Kléber thenceforward refused all offers of commands until Bonaparte, as First Consul, persuaded him to accept a division in the Army of Egypt (1798), where his compulsion for action could be satisfied. He was wounded leading the assault on Alexandria (2 July), but later directed his fierce energies against El Arish,* Jaffa,* and Acre,* and above all at the battle of Mount Tabor* (16 April 1799), where he withstood the attack of a vastly superior opponent until relief could reach him from the siege lines before Acre. After Bonaparte's return to France, Kléber became commander of the French forces in the Orient, but was soon chafing at the lack of opportunities for decisive action. Commodore Sidney Smith* induced him to sign the humiliating Convention of El Arish,* but this was repudiated by Sidney Smith's superiors, and the French found themselves confronting an increasingly critical situation, faced by a large British-supported Turkish army and a hostile population. Nevertheless, he brought off a major success at Heliopolis on 20 March 1800, which led to the recapture of Cairo and might have earned the French a breathing space, but Kléber was stabbed to death by a fanatic on 14 June that year. Despite political differences, Napoleon always evinced the greatest respect for this brilliant, but surprisingly self-doubting, commander of the Revolution.*

Kleist, Field Marshal Friedrich Heinrich Ferdinand Emil, Graf von Nollendorf (1762–1823). This notable Prussian commander was born in Berlin and earned a name for himself during the wars against the Revolution* and Napoleon. He emerged with particular distinction from the battles of Kulm* and Leipzig* in 1813. Next year he shared in the Allied invasion of France, and although defeated at Joinvilliers he is generally deemed to have won the battle of Laon* against Napoleon himself.

Korjietulski, *Chef d'escadron* Jan H.

(fl. 1808). This officer was commander of the 3rd Squadron of the Polish Light Horse, fulfilling the role of duty-squadron to the Emperor on 30 November 1808. He was ordered to charge the Spanish guns and regiments holding the crest of the Pass of Somosierra,* blocking the advance of the main French army upon Madrid. Accompanied by de Ségur,* Korjietulski set out to obey the nearly impossible order, and although the attack ultimately succeeded the cost was high for the Poles —7 officers (85%) and 74 troopers (36%) becoming casualties, including the *chef d'escadron,* whose horse fell at the outset of the charge up the narrow road. His formation, however, aided by *chasseurs-à-cheval,* captured all 16 Spanish guns and took 5 colors. This celebrated feat of arms earned some criticism for Napoleon, the direct instigator of the attack. Korjietulski survived with only severe bruising and concussion.

Korsakov, General Alexander Mikhailovitch Rimski (so-called) (1753–1840). This Russian soldier fought in Holland against the French in 1794 and two years later was sent to serve in Persia. Holding a high command under Suvorov* during the War of the Second Coalition,* he was decisively defeated by Massena* at the battle of Third Zurich* (1799). Appointed General of Cavalry in 1801, he later became Governor of Lithuania for almost 30 years. However, following the insurrection of 1830–31 he was recalled to St. Petersburg, and ultimately became a member of the Council of the Empire.

Krasnöe, battle of, 17 November 1812. This town, some 50 kilometers to the west of Smolensk, was the scene of an important action during the French retreat from Moscow. The Emperor was in the town from the 15th, waiting for his straggling column to close up, and his growing anxiety for the safety of the crucial highroad, which Russian forces were threatening, induced him to order first General Rapp,* then General Roguet,* to lead a surprise attack by the Imperial Guard* against Kutusov's* forces to the south of the town. The sudden onslaught caught the Russians completely by surprise, and the 16,000 French guardsmen soon had all of 35,000 Russians in full retreat. The results were that the road to the west remained open and that the rest of the army, except for the isolated Marshal Ney* and the rear guard, were able to join the Emperor by late that evening. This, one of the most celebrated actions by the Imperial Guard, demonstrated Napoleon's wisdom in not sending in his *élite* formations at Borodino* two months earlier.

Kray, General Paul, Baron Kray de Krajowa (1735–1804). Born at Kesmarch and thus a Hungarian, this commander earned a fine reputation during the Seven Years' War (1757–63). He successfully repressed the revolt of the Valaques in Transylvania (1788), and two years later was promoted to major general after sharing in a successful campaign against the Turks. He then fought a number of campaigns against the French. In 1799 he was temporarily in command of Melas'* army in North Italy during that general's illness, and during that period defeated Schérer* at Magnano (5 April) and recaptured Mantua.* Appointed Grand Master of the Artillery in the Austrian forces, he was sent to replace Archduke Charles* in command of the Army of Germany in 1800, but he was forced to give ground before the French and was removed from command.

Krumpersystem, the Prussian. Following the humiliations heaped upon Prussia at Tilsit* in 1807, her army was restricted to a ceiling of 42,000 men (increased with French permission to 75,000 in 1812). However, over the years from 1808 the Prussian military reformer, von Scharnhorst,* built up a secret reserve army by the simple expedient of retiring a fixed proportion of regular soldiers each year and replacing them with new recruits who received basic training and then were placed in reserve in their turn, making room for further replacements. By February 1813, when Prussia was on the verge of joining the Sixth Coalition* against France, this *krumpersystem* had produced a reserve of 33,600 trained soldiers over and above the stipulated limit. These provided a cadre around which the further expansion of Prussia's armed forces could proceed.

Kulm, battle of, 30 August 1813. The great defeat of Dresden* induced the Austro-Russian Army of Silesia to retreat through the mountains of the Erz Gebirge into Bohemia during the night of 27 August. Napoleon immediately detached a force of 32,000 troops under command of General Vandamme* with orders to intercept the left or eastern wing of Prince Schwarzenberg's* retiring army amid the difficult mountain terrain. After reaching Kulm, about 25 miles south of Dresden, Vandamme found his way blocked by 44,000 troops under command of Count Ostermann-Tolstoi,* drawn up in the vicinity of Priesten. A fierce frontal battle soon developed, in which Vandamme more than held his own, until 10,000 Prussians under General Kleist von Nollendorf* suddenly appeared after a concealed approach to attack the French rear at Kulm. This move was more accidental than deliberate, but it resulted in only half the French being able to escape from the trap. This victory cost the Allies 11,000 casualties but did much to restore morale in their councils and armies, coming as it did so opportunely after their massive debacle before Dresden.

Kutusov, Field Marshal Mikhail Hilarionovich Golenischev-Kutusov, Prince of Smolensk (1745–1813). The son of a military engineer, Kutusov received a com-

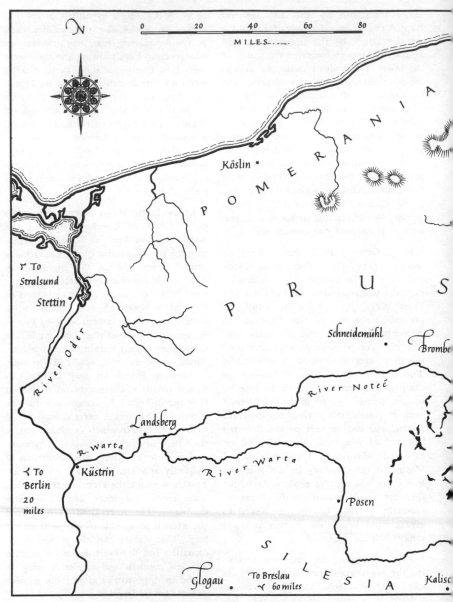

Poland, 1807

GULF OF
DANZIG

To Tilsit 20 miles

Königsberg

River Pregel

Pillau

R. Frisching

Wittenberg

FRISCHES HAFF

Brandenburg
Kreuzburg

Domnau
Lampasch

Allenburg
Friedland

Pr. Eylau
Landsberg

R. Alle

Danzig

R. Passarge

Bartenstein

Elbing

Hoff

Spanden
Lomitten

Wormditt
Launau

Heilsberg
Bevernick
Altkirch

Marienburg

Liebstadt

Güttstadt
Glottau

FOREST

Saalfeld

Deppen

Bergfriede

Wärtenburg

OF

Marienwerder

Möhrungen

Ionkovo
Mondtken
Allenstein

JOHANNIS-

Finkenstein

Osteröde

BURG

Passenheim

Lobau

Hohenstein

Ortelsburg

Niedenburg

Villenburg
Myszymec

R. Omulev

Lautenburg

Janova

R. Orzyc

Soldau

R. Narew

Mlava

Östrolenka

Bielshun

R. Ukra

Pryasnysz

Grodno
85 miles

Thorn

Makov
Rozan

Golymin

Brok

Moschin

Schensk

Pultusk

Schschotschin

Streshegozin
Novemteste

Plonsk

Nasielsk

Plock

Tscharnovo

Scherosk

River Vistula

Modlin

River Bug

Praga

WARSAW

AUSTRIAN
POLAND
[GALICIA]

mission in the Russian artillery under the Tsarina Catherine II. He later transferred into the newly raised *Jäger,* or light infantry, corps, which in due course he rose to command. From 1764–69 he fought with distinction in Poland and the Ukraine, and then from 1770–74 in the Crimea against the Turks, where he lost an eye in action. In further campaigns he fought against the Sultan's forces, was again shot in the head during the siege of Ochakov (1788), but was able to play an important part in the operations against the towns of Odessa, Benda, and Ismail and in the battles fought at Rimnik and Nashin over the following three years.

Sent as Russian ambassador to Constantinople, and later made Governor of Finland, he was appointed to command the main Russian army sent to aid Austria in the Danube valley during the War of the Third Coalition.* Arriving in the theater too late to prevent the Austrian disaster at Ulm,* he fought an effective rear-guard action against the victorious French, eluded one trap after another, and, thanks in no small measure to Murat's* errors of judgment, succeeded both in moving his army back to the north bank of the Danube and thereafter in linking up with Buxhowden's* reinforcements around Olmutz. Burdened by the presence of both Tsar Alexander I* and the Emperor Francis* at his headquarters, he allowed himself to be forced into what he considered to be a premature and ill-considered action at Austerlitz,* where the Russo-Austrian forces sustained a major defeat, Kutusov being wounded in the arm. He subsequently successfully extricated the survivors of the Russian army and beat a retreat into Poland. After a brief period of eclipse, he was sent by the Tsar to command the forces during the Russo-Turkish war along the lower Danube (1811–12), which he again did with great success.

In the late summer of 1812, Kutusov was summoned to take over command of the Russian armies in the west from Barclay de Tolly,* whose strategy—whether inspired or enforced—of continual retreat had forfeited the Tsar's confidence, and on 20 August he assumed command immediately after the defeat sustained by his predecessor at Smolensk.* The Tsar made this appointment more through court and aristocratic pressures than of his own initiative, for he was not a particular admirer of the 67-year-old Tartar, but Kutusov was destined to serve him well. Aware that he must stand and fight before Moscow, Kutusov selected a position at Borodino* and turned at bay. Although defeated at the end of the long battle that ensued on 7 September, Kutusov's army remained intact and was able to retire to the east and south of Moscow (which was abandoned to the French and subsequently largely burned to the ground by Russian incendiaries) to absorb reinforcements and await his chance. This came when Napoleon, despairing of bringing the Tsar to terms, decided to abandon Moscow. At the battle of Maloyaroslavetz* (24 October), he induced the Emperor to abandon his plan to retire through the fertile regions around Kaluga, and forced him back along his earlier line of advance, now much ravaged, through Borodino and Smolensk. Summoning more armies to his aid from the north, Kutusov decided to play a cautious waiting game, and instead of trying to force a major battle he contented himself with waging a harassing campaign against the retreating French, gradually driving them into a narrow central corridor from both flanks, waiting for the psychological effects of defeat and the destructive power of the approaching Russian winter to destroy the French cohesion. This caution earned Kutusov much criticism, but it proved the correct strategy. For although Napoleon was able to spring the surprise of Krasnöe* on his somewhat complacent opponent, the havoc wrought by the combination of the bitter weather and the depredations of the Russian Cossacks and partisans, who waged a dire guerrilla* war against the tiring and freezing French and their allies, gradually reduced the *Grande Armée* to a near wreck. However, Kutusov's intended master stroke and *coup de grâce*—the trapping of the French at the line of the river Beresina* following the capture of the French depots at Minsk and of the key bridge at Borisov—failed to come off, and after the long battle of 25–29 November Napoleon was able to continue his retreat into Poland, handing over its conduct to first Murat and then Eugène* from 5 December. Nevertheless, before the end of the year the last French troops had been expelled from Russian soil into Poland, and Kutusov was able to present his master the Tsar with over one hundred captured French colors at Vilna. In return he was made Prince of Smolensk —a reference to the fighting between that city and Krasnöe on 17 November which had, in fact, been more of a Russian defeat than a victory, although Russian propaganda chose to represent the outcome in a favorable light. However, the aging and ailing hero did not long continue to enjoy either the Tsar's favor or the highest command. In a decision that

combined a degree of realism, given Kutusov's state of health, with one of ingratitude, Tsar Alexander replaced him in the highest command by General Wittgenstein* in late April 1813, by which time the Russians, newly joined by the Prussians, had reached the river Elbe. The old warrior died of exhaustion and mortal illness in Silesia a few weeks later.

Although it has been fashionable for many historians to discount Kutusov's showing as a commander, there is little doubt that he was a general of great ability. He had the knack of playing upon the mystical side of the Russian character, resulting in his being able to inspire a high level of response among the peasant-soldiery of the Tsar. He was a cunning and able strategist, aware of the power that partisan forces could apply, and even his bitterest critics, who included the British General Wilson,* attached to his staff as a liaison officer, acknowledged his courtesy, shrewdness, general intelligence, and professional knowledge. If his energy was at times flagging, and his liking for the bottle and young women inordinate for one of his years, it was still because of Kutusov more than any other single person that Napoleon's invasion of Russia ended in cataclysmic failure—the first act in the collapse of the French Empire.

La Bedoyère. *See* **Bedoyère**

Lafayette, Général Marie Joseph Paul
de Motier, marquis de (1757–1834). Born
into the nobility, by the age of 13 he had
inherited a large fortune and in April
1771 he entered the Black Musketeers.
Two years later he transferred into the
Régiment de Noallies with a commission,
and in 1777, after negotiations with Benjamin Franklin, he formed a small volunteer force and sailed to North America,
where in July he was appointed a major
general in the Army of the United States.
After stalwart service he returned to a
hero's welcome in France in 1779, bought
the *Régiment des Dragons du Roi,* and
persuaded the king to send a larger force
to aid the American rebels against the
British. In April 1780 he returned to
rejoin George Washington and the next
year played an active role at Yorktown.
The same February he was promoted to
maréchal de camp by Louis XVI,* and
he returned to France in January 1782.
Following the pacification he made many
journeys, and in 1787 became deeply involved in the Assembly of Notables which
prepared the way for the States-General
meeting in 1789. Far from being a reactionary, Lafayette was regarded as a reformer.

When the States-General at last met, he
voted with the center-left as a member
for the First Estate, but threw in his lot
with the Third Estate at the first crisis
and was elected Vice-President of the National Assembly. On 16 July he formed
the National Guard* and attempted to
prevent the worst excesses in Paris. Next
day he persuaded Louis XVI to adopt the
tricouleur (the Bourbon white set between
the red and blue of the city of Paris) at the
Hôtel de Ville, and in October marched
to Versailles in time to save the royal
family from the mob. He escorted the king
back to Paris. Meanwhile he had been
co-founder of the Feuillant political club,
and for a time he backed Mirabeau's*
concepts. As events swept inexorably forward, he voted for the dropping of noble
titles and was made President of the
Assembly of *fédérés* and major general of
the Federation. When Louis XVI attempted to flee to Varennes, Lafayette
ordered his arrest and return to the
capital.

Promoted to lieutenant general on 30
June 1791, he slowly abandoned the
royalist cause. After refusing the post of
Administrator of the Upper-Loire, he was
sent to command the Army of the Center
in December; the next year he marched
on Namur but kept in close touch with
political developments in Paris. Transferred to the Army of the North in July
1792, he survived a vote of attainder in
the Assembly and then protested the suspension of the king in August. He arrested
the government's representatives at Sedan,
an act that earned him his dismissal and
a recall to Paris, and on the 19th he
crossed the frontier with his staff to join
the Allies. Far from being welcomed,
however, he was arrested and confined in
various fortresses including Olmütz. He
escaped but was retaken and was only
freed in September 1797 at the time of

the Preliminaries of Leoben.* He continued to live east of the Rhine, refusing the Consulate's offer of the post of ambassador to the U.S. In 1802 he formally retired and continued to refuse political offers. He opposed the Life-Consulate proposals and took no part in French affairs until 1814, when he was welcomed back to France by Louis XVIII.* During the Hundred Days* he was at last elected to the Chamber, but after Waterloo* was prominent in demanding Napoleon's re-abdication. He was appointed to negotiate with the Allies and thereafter lived for two years in retirement.

However, a long political career still lay ahead of him despite his advancing years. He was involved in the plot of Béfort in 1822, and from 1824–25 saw fit to make a long tour of the U.S. where he was feted. Returning to France in September 1825, he resumed an active role in politics; in 1830 he resumed command of the National Guard in the political crisis of that year and rallied behind the Duc d'Orléans. He thereafter was frequently in acrimonious dispute with the Orleanist monarchy. In 1834 he took cold at a funeral and died after a few days. A very important figure, Lafayette's role in the American Revolution was an important factor in preparing the way for the upheaval that overtook France in 1789.

Laffrey, the affair of, 7 March 1815. Just south of this small town in the French Department of Isère, some 25 kilometers south of Grenoble,* Napoleon and his escort, recently landed from Elba,* were confronted by a battalion of the Bourbonist *cinquième régiment d'infanterie de ligne,* sent out by the local commander to confront and arrest the newcomers. For some time it appeared that a fight was inevitable, but when Napoleon—sensing the mood of the rank and file of the 5ième—advanced alone toward them, opening

his coat and inviting them to fire, the men's enthusiasm for their old master broke through their discipline, and, heedless of their officers, they surged forward to greet and join the Emperor. This critical moment assured the success of Napoleon's bold return from exile, at least for a short time. He soon occupied Grenoble, to the plaudits of the hitherto cautious local population: "Before Grenoble I was an adventurer," he later declared, "at Grenoble, I was a prince." Many more rallied to his cause, including the 14ième *régiment* at Auxerre on the 16th, despite the avowed intention of Marshal Ney,* accompanying it, to return to Paris with Napoleon in an iron cage.

Lake Erie, naval battle of, 10 September 1813. In the second major phase of the War of 1812,* British control of Detroit hinged upon maintaining naval control of Lake Erie, as this continually threatened the Americans with a water-borne descent against their flank and rear behind the river Maumee in Ohio. Determined to free their hands of this implicit threat, the United States Navy sent Captain Perry* (aged 28), early in 1813, to take command of a flotilla of ten vessels under construction on the Sandusky River on the southern shores of the lake at Presque Isle. He completed the preparations with haste and put out to challenge the British shipping. On 10 September he was engaged in Put-in-Bay by a flotilla of six Royal Naval vessels commanded by Captain Barclay, mounting 65 guns between them and carrying 364 men, and a sharp engagement began at 11:45 A.M. Perry's squadron, manned by over 400 men but mounting only 55 guns, included heavier metal than the British, and the fight was both protracted and bloody. Early in the fray Perry lost his flagship, the U.S.S. *Lawrence,* but transferred his flag to the U.S.S. *Niagara,* and within three hours he had sunk or. captured the entire British flotilla. Barclay had 135 casualties, including 41 killed; Perry lost 123 men. The outcome of this victory was to force the British land forces to abandon Detroit a week later, and by the end of the month they were back in Ontario on Canadian soil, after also giving up Fort Malden.

La Maddalena, raid against, 23–25 February 1793. Lieutenant Bonaparte's first active service took place under command of Colonel Colonna-Cesari,* a relative of the Corsican patriot leader Paoli,* and it proved a fiasco. Sent with a scratch force from Corsica to attack this island at the northern end of Sardinia as a diversion for a larger attack on the town of Cagliari, Colonna-Cesari landed on 23 February, and after two highly confused days ashore, abandoned his project and re-embarked aboard his mutinous flotilla. Bonaparte, commanding the three guns attached to this expedition, bombarded the town of La Maddalena through the 24th, but then suddenly found himself deserted by his compatriots. He successfully withdrew his guns to the beach, but to his immense chagrin was forced to spike them there. Fortunately, some shipping was still at hand to take off the irate gunners, and they returned safely to Corsica—where Bonaparte's outspoken views on the misconduct of Colonna-Cesari did nothing to improve his relations with Paoli.

Lambert, General Sir John (1772–1847). After becoming an ensign in the 1st Guards in 1791 he was promoted to captain two years later, and became a lieutenant colonel in 1801. In 1808 he accompanied Wellesley* to Portugal, and then Moore* to Spain, and next year took part in the Walcheren* expedition. Appointed a brevet colonel in 1811, he spent the years 1811 to 1814 in the Peninsula,

being promoted to major general in 1813. Two years later he served at New Orleans* under the ill-fated General Pakenham but returned to England with dispatches in time to fight at Waterloo,* where he commanded one of the brigades of British Guards with distinction. From 1824 he was colonel of the 10th Foot, and he had been knighted in 1815. From Waterloo onward, General Lambert and his family became closely associated with Captain Harry Smith* of the 95th Rifles and his wife Juanita. In 1825 he became a lieutenant general, and a full general in 1841.

Landshut, battle of, 21 April 1809. Following the great French success at Abensberg,* the Austrian forces of Archduke Charles* split in two: Charles and the larger wing falling back on Eckmühl* to the east, General Hiller* and the left wing (perhaps 36,000 strong) retiring south over the river Isar to Landshut. In the mistaken belief that this second force comprised the bulk of the enemy army, the Emperor ordered Lannes to lead the greater part of the French Army of Germany in pursuit, and late on the 21st this force caught up with Hiller's rear guard as it prepared to evacuate Landshut. Marshal Massena's* force (comprising the IV and II Corps), some 57,000 men strong, after making a long march had successfully passed the Isar above the town at Mosseburg and was pressing down toward their objective along the eastern bank, but was somewhat behind schedule. Lannes,* with his own troops and the VII Corps, was advancing on the northern suburbs at 10:00 A.M. The Austrians fought with determination, but with Napoleon's personal arrival on the scene their fate was quickly settled. The suburbs were cleared, and then a picked force led by General Mouton* stormed over the burning timbers of the main Isar bridge and forced an entry into the town itself despite determined opposition. The impending arrival of Massena to cut their line of retreat at 5:00 P.M. finally forced Hiller to abandon his positions and retire toward Neumarkt, pursued by Marshal Bessières.* During this sharp action, the Austrians lost 10,000 casualties, 30 guns, 600 caissons, and 7,000 wagons and coaches, but Napoleon had failed to trap Hiller, whose survivors lived to fight another day—at Aspern-Essling.*

Lannes, Maréchal Jean, duc de Montebello (1769–1809). Of all the galaxy of martial talent that served Napoleon in the marshalate, none, save possibly Berthier,* was more highly regarded by Napoleon, both as soldier and friend, than Lannes. Certainly none surpassed his show of courage on the battlefield, and he received by far the most wounds of any of his colleagues. A native of Lectoure, he was apprenticed to a dyer but in 1792 enrolled as a volunteer, being appointed *sous-lieutenant* in a local regiment. For two years he served in the Pyrenees, receiving rapid promotion and the first of his many wounds, being shot through the arm in late 1793. Transferred to the Army of Italy, he fought at First Loano* (1795), and next year, under Bonaparte, at Ceva,* Millesimo,* and Dego.* He was given a force of grenadiers and at its head was first man over the river Po at Plasencia, subsequently fighting at Lodi.* He took a prominent part in the storming of the St. Georges suburb of Mantua* in early June, and later in the campaign fought with distinction at Bassano* and Arcola.* He had again been wounded in September, and received three wounds in three days at the last-named battle in November. Advancing with Bonaparte into the Frioul after the capture of Mantua, on 17 March his promotion to *général de brigade* was confirmed.

The year 1798 saw him en route to Egypt and Syria, where he served at the

Lannes

capture of Alexandria,* seized Rosetta, helped repress the Cairo* rising, and in early 1799 fought before El Arish,* Jaffa,* and Acre* (where he was shot in the neck). After the French retreat to Egypt he fought at Aboukir,* being wounded in the leg, and was one of the few officers selected to accompany his commander back to France. During the critical days of the *coup d'état* de Brumaire he played an important role, and in reward was appointed inspector general of the Consular Guard in April 1800 and a month later was confirmed as *général de division* (10 May)—a rank he had held provisionally since Acre. Commanding the advance guard of the Army of the Reserve, he led the advance over the Alps, bypassing Fort Bard* and taking Aosta and Chatillon, and in the second stage of the campaign winning the action at Montebello on 9 June—the preliminary to the great battle of Marengo* five days later, in which his dogged resistance to massively outnumbering Austrian forces gained enough time for Desaix* to reach the field to change the fortunes of the day, and for which Lannes earned a coveted saber of honor.

In 1802 he was sent on a diplomatic mission to Portugal but failed and returned to France, and as the Army of England prepared to cross the Channel he was given command of the large encampment at Ambleteuse in July 1803. Next year he became one of the original marshals, and a string of honors soon came his way, including his dukedom (bestowed in 1808). By that time he had given still further proof of his talents as a commander in the field. Commanding a corps, he marched on Austria in 1805, was present at Mack's* surrender at Ulm,* and at Austerlitz* on 2 December commanded the Santon hill and the French left wing, holding it against Bagration's* repeated attacks. In 1806 he won the action of Saalfeld* against Prince Louis-Ferdinand* of Prussia, was first on the scene at Jena,* and played an important role in command of the center in the ensuing battle. At Pultusk* in late December he received a minor wound, and then almost succumbed to a serious fever which forced him to leave his beloved V Corps for five months. Restored to health, he assisted Lefebvre* at the siege of Danzig* in May 1807, fought at Heilsberg,* and "opened the ball" at Friedland* on 14 June, commanding the center once again. Napoleon lavished rewards and pensions on his friend, and Lannes became a rich man.

He was given scant time to enjoy his privileges. In late 1808 he was commanding a corps in Spain, defeating General Castaños* at Tudela* before sustaining serious injuries in a fall from a horse which only Larrey's* skill was able to remedy. Again recovered, he took command of the siege of Saragossa* in late December and accepted its surrender in February 1809. As danger mounted on

the Danube Napoleon summoned Lannes to the German theater, and he was soon in action at Abensberg,* Landshut,* and Eckmühl,* and led the storm of Ratisbon* on 23 April. Appointed to command the II Corps of the Army of Germany, he was present at the occupation of Vienna, and then, in May, crossed the Danube to take possession of the village of Essling. As the battle of Aspern-Essling* rose toward its grim climax, he retained his hold on the town in the face of huge and repeated Austrian attacks, never losing control of the vital granary, but he needed the aid of the Young Guard to maintain his position on the afternoon of the second day, 22 May. As the French forces fell back on Napoleon's order toward the Isle of Lobau, a cannonball smashed both of Lannes' legs. His right leg had to be amputated, and nine days later, to the grief of Napoleon and the entire army, he died.

Lannes was the first of the marshalate to die of wounds sustained in action. Napoleon bitterly grieved for his friend— the only man he permitted to address him with the familiar "*tu.*" A fine fighting soldier of rather rough manners, Lannes was in no way a "political" soldier and had few equals as a battlefield commander, thus proving an ideal subordinate for the Emperor in the carrying through of his plans.

Laon, battle of, 9 and 10 March 1814. As the Allied armies marched deeper into France toward Paris, their northern thrust down the valley of the river Marne was deflected northward over the river Aisne. Napoleon, who was holding the central position between the two forks of the Allied advance, rushed northward with 47,600 troops, many of them raw conscripts, and after a stiff skirmish at Craonne* he pushed Blücher's* army of Russians and Prussians back to Laon.

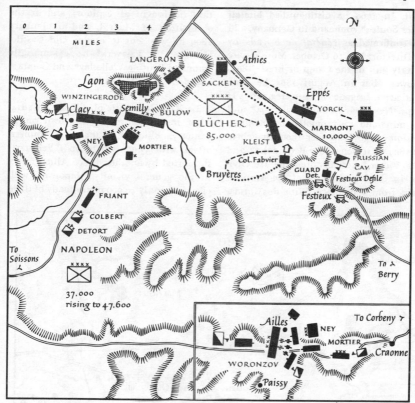

Battles of Laon and Craonne, 9–10 March 1814

Hoping to make the most of this situation, he ordered Marshal Marmont* to take the 9,500 men of his VI Corps to turn the eastern flank of the enemy army. However, Marmont dallied, and Blücher, now reinforced to all of 85,000 men, decided to force a major battle. On 9 March, General von Wartenburg* surprised Marmont and routed his force, which was saved from total collapse by a staunch fight put up by two small parties of the Imperial Guard* in the Festieux Defile.* Next day Napoleon held his position immediately below Laon on its steep hill, but decided to withdraw in the late afternoon. French losses are generally put at 6,000 men killed and wounded to the Allies' 4,000 casualties. Napoleon at once headed south to face Prince Schwarzenberg.*

Lapisse, Général Pierre Bellon, baron de Sainte-Hélène (1762–1809). The son of a tapestry weaver of Lyons, he joined the Bourbon army in 1778 and served from 1780–83 in America under Lafayette,* becoming a sergeant in 1784. At the Revolution, he was made a lieutenant in a Corsican light infantry unit in December 1789 and saw service in Italy and Piedmont. In 1799 he distinguished himself under Soult's* command in Germany, and was confirmed as *général de brigade* by the Directory* on 19 October. More service in Italy and in the Camp of Brest (1803) followed, but in August 1805 he commanded a brigade in Augereau's* VII Corps. Next year he fought at Jena* and Golymin* and was promoted to *général de division* on 30 December 1806. In February 1807 he served under Bernadotte* and later Victor,* commanding the 1st Division in the latter's corps of the Army of Spain from September. With this forma-

tion he fought at Espinosa and at the occupation of Madrid, and in January 1809 he was sent to occupy Old Castile. However, at Talavera* he was mortally wounded fighting Wellesley* and Cuesta,* and died at Santa Olalla.

La Rothière, battle of, 1 February 1814. After losing control of the town on 28 January, Blücher* launched a counter-attack with 53,000 troops on 1 February, supported by another 63,000 Allied forces in the general vicinity. Napoleon, with effectively only 40,000 men—many of them

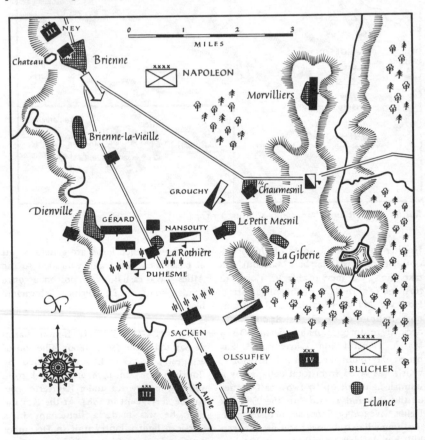

Battle of La Rothière, 1 February 1814

raw conscripts—planned to withdraw and avoid action, but the Prussian general forced battle. All day amid the snow a bitter engagement raged, but the French held their ground until nightfall, when they were skillfully disengaged. Each side lost an estimated 6,000 men.

Larpent, Mr. Francis Seymour (1776–1845). Educated at Cambridge, where he became a fellow of St. John's College in 1799, he was called to the bar and from 1812–14 served in the Peninsula as deputy judge advocate general. His later career was a distinguished one in the civil service; he became Commissioner for Customs in 1814, a civil and admiralty judge in Gibraltar, and also carried out secret service duties. From 1826–43 he was chairman of the Board of Audit of the Public Accounts.

Larrey, Dr. Dominique Jean, baron (1766–1842). The nephew of a doctor, Larrey qualified at Toulouse and in 1792 was appointed to the staff of the Army of the Rhine. In 1798 he accompanied Bonaparte to Egypt and Syria, and was appointed thereafter to the senior medical post in what became the *Grande Armée.* His ceaseless efforts for the sick and wounded earned him a vast renown, and after Aspern-Essling* and Wagram* in 1809 he was made a baron of the Empire. He marched with Napoleon to Moscow and achieved prodigies during the retreat. He remained loyal to Napoleon right through to Waterloo,* where he received a wound. He invented the first custom-built field ambulance for the easier evacuation of wounded. After the second Bourbon Restoration Larrey held many distinguished medical professorial posts and wrote extensively.

Lasalle, Général Antoine Charles Louis, comte (1775–1809). This distinguished cavalryman was born at Metz and entered the Bourbon infantry as a *sous-lieutenant*

Lasalle

in 1786. During the Revolutionary Wars* he enjoyed mixed fortunes, but came to General Bonaparte's notice at Vicenza in December 1796 and even more so at Rivoli,* where his squadron of hussars captured a full battalion of Austrians. In Egypt (1798) he performed prodigies of valor at the Pyramids,* earning further promotions and favor. He returned to France in mid-1800 and held posts in Italy and the Gironde before being promoted to *général de brigade* on 1 February 1805. He served in Klein's* division in Austria, fighting at Austerlitz,* and then against Prussia in 1806, fighting at Schleiz.* During the pursuit after Jena-Auerstadt* he forced Hohenlohe* to surrender at Prenzlau, and later bluffed Stettin into capitulating; he was present at the fall of Lübeck.* In December the same year he fought at Golymin* and was promoted to *général de division* on 30 December. Service under Murat* and Davout* followed. At Heilsberg* he first saved, and then was saved by, Murat. In 1808 he commanded Bessières'* division of light cavalry, winning a skirmish at Torquemada (6 June) and taking part in the battle of Medina del Rio Seco.* Later, at Medellin,* he saved the French army by breaking a Spanish square of 6,000 men at the head of the 26th Dragoons. He was made a Count of the Empire in March 1808. On 22 April 1809 he reported for duty in the Army of Germany, and under Bessières' command fought at Essling* and the siege of Raab (15–24 June). Finally, at Wagram* he was killed by a shot through the forehead while leading a charge. Thus France lost a talented and popular commander.

Las Cases, Emmanuel Augustin, comte (1766–1842). After fleeing abroad from France as an *émigré* and fighting at Quiberon,* Las Cases returned during the amnesty declared under the Consulate. After the publication of an acclaimed work on geography, he served as a volunteer during the defense of Holland against the British in 1809 (Walcheren*) and came to Napoleon's notice. High offices were awarded him. After Waterloo* he followed Napoleon to St. Helena,* but was expelled from the island in 1816 and for a time held a captive in the Cape of Good Hope. He later was permitted to live at Frankfort and then Belgium, but only after Napoleon's death was he allowed back into France. In 1823 he published his important *Mémorial de Sainte Hélène*. After 1830 he sat as a member of the Chamber of Deputies under the July Monarchy of Louis-Philippe.

Lauriston, Général (later Maréchal de France) Jacques Alexandre Bernard Law, comte (later marquis) (1768–1828). Born in India, he was commissioned into the artillery after training at the *Ecole Militaire* in September 1785. He served with the armies of the North, the Moselle, and the Sambre-et-Meuse (1792–95) but was dismissed in 1796. On rejoining in 1800 he became an aide-de-camp to the

Lauriston

First Consul and fought at Marengo.* After a mission to Cogenhagen and a period in command of an artillery regiment he was sent to London with the terms of the Preliminaries of Amiens.* In September 1802 he was promoted to *général de brigade* and served in the Army of the Ocean Coasts. In November 1804 he embarked in Villeneuve's* fleet at Toulon and was promoted to *général de division* (February 1805) before sailing to Martinique. On returning with the fleet, he fought on board against Hotham* off Cape Finisterre but returned to Paris before Trafalgar.* He held various governorships in Austria and occupied Ragusa in May 1806. Late in 1807 he became Governor of Venice and was made a count in May 1808 before being transferred to Spain in command of the artillery of the Imperial Guard.* In 1809, on Napoleon's staff, he fought before, and captured, Raab; at Wagram* he commanded the famous battery of 100 guns. In 1810 he escorted Marie-Louise* from Vienna to France. In February 1811, he replaced Caulaincourt* as ambassador to St. Petersburg, and in August 1812 rejoined the *Grande Armée* at Smolensk.* In October he was sent to negotiate with Tsar Alexander* but was not allowed through the Russian lines. He fought with the rear guard during the retreat. In 1813 he commanded a corps on the Elbe and fought at Mockern, Bautzen,* and Leipzig,* where he was taken captive. He was released in 1814, stayed loyal to Louis XVIII* in 1815, and became a marquis in 1817. In June 1823 he was appointed a marshal, and in September he took Pamplona. He was Minister of State from 1824.

La Vendée, risings in, 1793–96 and 1815. The troubles in a large area south of the river Loire arose out of local disagreement with two acts of the Revolutionary government in Paris, namely the civil constitution of the clergy and the demand for the raising of 300,000 men to fight in the revolutionary armies. In many instances the peasantry rebelled under the leadership of the nobility, but two exceptions were the peasant-commanders Cathelineau and Stofflet. The risings were local in nature but soon posed daunting problems for the authorities. The rebels met with great initial success, scoring six victories over Republican forces in March 1793 alone, the most significant being the wiping out of General Marcé's force at Pont-Charon by Sapinaud at the head of the Lower Poitou insurgents on 19 March. The capture of Noirmoutier and Pornic were further notable successes, and despite one setback at Les Sables D'Olonne (28 March) it seemed that the authorities would prove incapable of checking the revolt's spread. Troops were in short supply owing to the crises on the frontiers. However, after further rebel victories in Anjou during April, the Convention scraped together three armies based at La Rochelle, Brest, and Cherbourg, commanded by Generals Biron (soon replaced by Rossignol), Canclaux, and Wimpffen respectively. Little success awaited their arms until the rebel leadership began to quarrel, and although the republican authorities lost Saumur and Angers during mid-June, the rebels were checked before Nantes, where their leader Cathelineau was killed on 29 June. Then the arrival of Kléber* with the Army of Mainz to reinforce Canclaux tipped the balance against the insurgents, and the battle of Cholet on 17 October saw the death of a number of rebel leaders. A rebel army marched as far as Granville heading for the Channel and hoped-for British aid, but a counteroffensive forced it to retrace its steps to the Loire. Insurgents lost the battle of Mans on 11 December, and the subsequent massacre of survivors at Savenay implied the collapse of the main revolt. Generals Carrier and Turreau began a cruel policy of repression that caused the rebellion to continue by fits and starts, largely on a guerrilla basis, throughout 1794, but early in 1795 agreements of a sort were reached at La Jaunaire (17 February) and La Mabilais (2 May).

The flame was not completely extinguished, however, and news that a force of *émigré** troops had landed at Quiberon in Brittany, and of the arrival of the Comte d'Artois in the Ile de Yeu, caused a further flaring up of the rebellion. Lack of coordination led to a new collapse, and the leaders Stofflet and Charette were captured by the republican forces. Both were shot (February and March 1796), and once again the cause of La Vendée receded to near extinction. Not until Bonaparte's religious pacification did the region know real peace.

The return of Napoleon from Elba* at the beginning of the Hundred Days* caused a new rebellion to break out, but

General Lamarque soon had the situation under control. News of Waterloo,* however, led to the triumph of the rebels—at least ostensibly.

From first to last, the bitter struggle between the "Blues" (republicans) and the "Whites" (rebels) caused an estimated 600,000 deaths.

Leberton, Mme. Henriette Renique (fl. 1810). Also known as "Madame X," Henriette Leberton was Massena's* mistress, the pretty sister of one of his aides-de-camp. She accompanied him throughout the Campaign of 1810, including days of battle, fetchingly dressed as a cornet of dragoons decorated with the *légion d'honneur.** This little indulgence earned Massena bitter criticism from Ney* and Junot,* whose wife, the Duchess d'Abrantes, refused to sit at the same table with Henriette. She proved a not inconsiderable factor in the poor relationship between Massena and his corps commanders throughout the Bussaco* and Torres Vedras* campaigns in Portugal (1810–11), and Massena's tardy arrival at the former battle was blamed on his undue dalliance with his mistress.

Lebrun, Consul Charles François, duc de Plaisance (1739–1824). Under Louis XVI* he served as a royal lands inspector and as secretary to Chancellor Maupeou, but in 1789 Lebrun was elected a deputy to the States-General for Dourdan. During the Terror* he was imprisoned but was released under the Directory* and became a member of the *Conseil des Anciens.** During *Brumaire** he backed General Bonaparte, and together with Cambacérès became a consul. After Napoleon had assumed full authority, he was requested to reorder the Consulate's finances, with the appointment of Arch-Treasurer and a membership of the *cour des comptes.* He was later created duc de Plaisance, and following the abdication of Louis Bona-

Lebrun

parte* from the kingdom of Holland he took over the administration of Dutch affairs. In 1814 he joined the Bourbons, returned to Napoleon during the Hundred Days, and accordingly was exiled. However, he was pardoned in 1819. He was famous for his patience and ability, being highly experienced and yet advanced in his thinking.

Leclerc, Général Victor Emmanuel (1772–1802). A native of Pontoise, in 1791 he enlisted as a volunteer in a Seine-et-Oise battalion and the same year was elected lieutenant. The next year he served on the lower Rhine before transferring into the cavalry. He then became a staff assistant in the Army of Italy (1793), advancing to become Chief of Staff of a division under General Lapoype and serving before Toulon.* Further military service followed in the Ardennes, the Alps, and once more in Italy, where he fought at Castiglione* and Rivoli* in 1796–97. In 1797 he married Pauline

Bonaparte* and in April that year he was selected to carry the terms of the Preliminaries of Leoben* and captured Austrian colors back to Paris; he was promoted to *général de brigade* the same May. After a brief spell as provisional Chief of Staff to the Army of Italy, he served in the Army of Rome (early 1798). Appointed Chief of Staff to the so-called Army of Ireland that November, he was transferred to the same post in the Army of England. On 26 August 1799 he became *général de division* and helped further his brother-in-law's fortunes in the *coup d'état* de Brumaire. He served under Brune* in western France and under Lecourbe on the Rhine before being transferred to the Army of the Rhine under Moreau.* A severe fall from a horse temporarily interrupted his career, but he recovered in time to lead the 2nd Division of the Center Corps at Höchstädt* and at the capture of Landshut.* In March 1801 he commanded a corps sent to aid the Spaniards against Portugal but was recalled to Paris in October. There he was appointed Commander in Chief of the expedition to Santo Domingo,* sailing from Brest on 14 December. His army disembarked in Haiti* in February 1802, and after several months' fighting overcame Toussaint l'Ouverture.* Leclerc succumbed to an attack of yellow fever on 2 November.

Lefebvre, Maréchal François Joseph, duc de Danzig (1755–1820). The son of a miller, Lefebvre was born at Rouffach in Alsace. He enlisted in the *Gardes Françaises* in 1773 and by the Revolution had risen to sergeant. After involvement in several incidents about the royal family (being wounded during one), in 1792 he joined the 13th Light Infantry, was made a captain, and served in the Armies of the Center and of the Moselle. He was promoted to *général de brigade* in the

latter in December 1793, and greatly distinguished himself at Fleurus* in June 1794. Transferred to the Sambre-et-Meuse he won several engagements on the German front, 1794–97, serving under Hoche,* Kléber,* and Jourdan* in successive campaigns. Commands in the Army of England and the Army of Mainz followed—including temporary Commander in Chief of the latter—but following transfer to the Army of the Danube early in 1799 he was wounded in the arm leading the advance guard at Pfullendorf. During *Brumaire* he was in command of the Paris military area (following a failure to be elected to a vacancy among the Directors) and saved Bonaparte from the wrath of the Council of the Five Hundred (*Cinq Cents*)* by sending in his grenadiers to rescue the General. In 1800 he became a senator and later President of the Senate; in May 1804 he was also designated a member of the original marshalate. After holding an important post in the National Guard (1805–06), Lefebvre was given com-

Lefebvre

mand of the V Corps of the *Grande Armée*, succeeding Mortier* (4 September 1806), and from October also assumed command over the infantry of the Imperial Guard.* He fought at Jena,* and next spring was in charge of the long siege of Danzig,* which ultimately surrendered to him and earned him his dukedom (conferred in 1808). From late 1808 to January 1809 he led the IV Corps in the Army of Spain, defeating La Romana* at Durango, capturing Bilbao and Santander,* and defeating Blake* at Valmaceda,* all after launching a premature offensive ahead of the overall schedule, to Napoleon's considerable annoyance. Nevertheless, he assisted in winning the victory of Espinosa and in December occupied Segovia.

Transferred to command the Bavarian VII Corps in the reformed Grand Army of Germany in March 1809, he fought at Abensberg* and Eckmühl* but was repulsed at Rastadt in early May. After fighting a campaign against General Jellacic* in the Tyrol (May to October) he ultimately captured Innsbruck and got the better of the patriot, Andreas Hofer.* In April 1812 he was appointed to command the infantry of the Old Guard in the forming Army of Russia, and in September fought at Borodino.* He returned to France in January 1813, and later that year fought at the head of the Guard at Dresden* and Leipzig.* In 1814, during the Campaign of France, he performed wonders with the Guard in Champagne, and at Champaubert* and Montmirail.* Nevertheless, he voted in favor of Napoleon's abdication in April 1814 and was made a peer of France by the Bourbons. He rejoined Napoleon for the Hundred Days and was again made a peer, an honor that the Bourbons eventually restored to the veteran in 1819 after leaving him living in disgrace for four years.

Lefebvre was noted for his general fidelity to Napoleon and his cause. He was not grasping or avaricious and was celebrated both at court and in the army for his blunt plain speaking. In this last attribute he was outclassed by his wife, the former laundry maid Catherine Hubscher, who earned the nickname of "Madame Sans-Gene."

Lefebvre-Desnouëttes, Général Charles, comte (1773–1822). The son of a Parisian draper, he ran away three times from school to enlist. At the Revolution he became a *chasseur* in the Parisian National Guard, and after leaving the forces in 1791 re-enlisted in the Army of the Alps and was commissioned into the dragoons in February 1793. He served with various armies along the eastern frontiers (1793–97) and then transferred to Italy in 1797. In February 1800 he became an aide-de-camp to the First Consul and fought at Marengo.* From 1803 he served under Soult,* but in 1804 became an equerry to Napoleon and fought at Austerlitz* the

Lefebvre-Desnouëttes

next year with the 4th Dragoon Division. In September 1806 he was promoted to *général de brigade* and became first aide to Jerome Bonaparte* in the VIII Corps, taking part in several engagements and sieges. In November 1807 he passed into Westphalian service as full *général de division* and Grand Equerry to King Jerome, but returned to the French army in 1808, the year he was made a count. After serving as Bessières'* Chief of Staff, he fought in Spain at Tudela* and the siege of Saragossa,* where he was wounded during the assault. Newly promoted to *général de division,* he re-entered Spain under Lannes* with the *chasseurs-à-cheval* of the Imperial Guard* and fought under Bessières at Somosierra.* On 29 December, during the pursuit of Sir John Moore,* he was wounded by a pistol shot and taken prisoner under Napoleon's eyes at Benavente.* He escaped from England in 1812 and resumed command of the *chasseurs à cheval,* with whom he entered Russia, being wounded at Winkovo. He accompanied Napoleon back to France from Smorgoni. In 1813 Lefebvre-Desnouëttes fought under Mortier* at Bautzen* and later defeated Thielmann* at Merseburg, only to be overcome at Altenburg. He fought at Hanau* and was given command of the Young Guard cavalry from November 1813. At its head he fought in most of the battles of 1814 (receiving two bayonet wounds at Brienne*), and after the abdication escorted Napoleon into exile as far as Roanne. Next year, on Napoleon's return, he tried to bring over units to rejoin the Emperor with little success, but joined in person, and during the brief Belgian campaign he was given command of the Light Cavalry Division. Proscribed after Waterloo,* he moved to the United States and was condemned to death in France in his absence. After living in Alabama, he decided to move to the Low Countries,

but was drowned off Ireland when the *Albion* sank in a storm. A great favorite of the Emperor, Lefebvre-Desnouëttes was an inspiring leader of cavalry and much admired in the army.

Legendre, Général François Marie Guillaume d'Harvesse, baron (1766–1828). Born at Comeray, he first enlisted in 1787 but left the service as a sergeant in 1791 and may have taken Holy Orders. However, he re-enlisted in 1793 and was elected à captain. After service against royalists and *émigrés** in La Vendée* and Brittany, he fought under Augereau* in Italy from early 1797 and later joined the Army of England. Back in Italy in 1800, he fought at Marengo.* He did garrison service at Brest and St. Omer (1803–05) and then served under Suchet* at Austerlitz,* being promoted to *général de brigade* on 24 December 1805. He next served in Prussia and Poland, before being attached to Dupont's* staff on 9 November 1807. As his Chief of Staff, he signed the capitulation of Bailen* the following July and was repatriated to Toulon. The same September he was made a baron, but on 13 January 1809 he was publicly insulted by Napoleon at Valladolid, and he resigned his commission in February. Legendre was briefly arrested, then freed, and re-entered the service in Italy, but in 1812 he was summoned to Paris to face a further enquiry into Bailen, was imprisoned, and only emerged after the Bourbon restoration in April 1814. The Bourbons restored his rank, and he later served under Dupont at Tours. He finally retired in December 1824.

Légion d'Honneur, La. Feeling the need for a system of honors with which to reward loyalty to his person and achievement to the benefit of the nation, on 19 May 1804 Napoleon instituted the Legion of Honor. At first organized into 15 "cohorts" of 350 legionnaires apiece, with financial support, the first actual crosses were distributed to old soldiers and wounded veterans on 1 July 1804 in a splendid ceremony at the *Invalides;** the awards were open to civilians as well as to military men of distinction. The order with its five grades became the pattern for a multitude of other national orders, and as such was the prototype of the modern honors system. The five-pointed white enamel double-clefted star, surmounted by the imperial crown, on its red ribbon, became eagerly sought after. "It is with baubles that men are led," Napoleon once rather cynically remarked, but he was aware of the psychological impact of such signs of distinction. On 16 August 1804 Napoleon distributed many more crosses to the army at the Camp of Boulogne.* It has been estimated that over 50,000 crosses were distributed before 1815, but the value of the award never diminished.

Legrand

Legrand, Général Claude Juste Alexandre, comte (1762–1815). First enlisted in 1777, he rose to sergeant major by 1786. In 1790 he joined the National Guard as a private, but within two years he was a lieutenant colonel in the Army of the Moselle. After fighting at Fleurus* he was transferred to the Army of the Sambre-et-Meuse and fought on the Rhine front with distinction (having been a *général de brigade* since September 1793). After a spell with the Army of England he returned to the Rhine in 1799, now a *général de division,* and fought at Stockach, captured Offenburg, and served at Hohenlinden* the next year. After tours as an Inspector General of infantry and in the garrison of St. Omer, he fought in Austria (1805) at Wertingen, Hollabrunn,* and Austerlitz,* where he withstood the assaults of the Allied left wing in the Bosenitz valley. Next year he fought at Jena* and in 1807 at Eylau,* Heilsberg,*

and the siege of Königsberg. He was made a count in 1808, and in 1809 fought under Massena* at Ebersberg, Aspern* (where he was wounded), Wagram,* and Znaim.* In 1812 he served under Oudinot* in II Corps in Russia, fighting at Polotsk,* and was gravely wounded at the Beresina* during the retreat. Returning to France he became a senator, but in early 1814 returned to active service and organized the defense of Châlons-sur-Saone, holding it against one full-scale Allied assault before being forced to fall back before the second storming. In June 1814 he was made a peer of France. He ultimately died of the effects of his Beresina wounds in Paris on 9 January 1815.

Leipzig, battle of, 16–19 October 1813. This massive battle, the largest of the entire Napoleonic Wars, was nicknamed "the Battle of the Nations." During its course, the French forces involved grew from 177,000 to 195,000 men (with 700 guns), while those of the Allies escalated from an initial 257,000 to all of 365,000

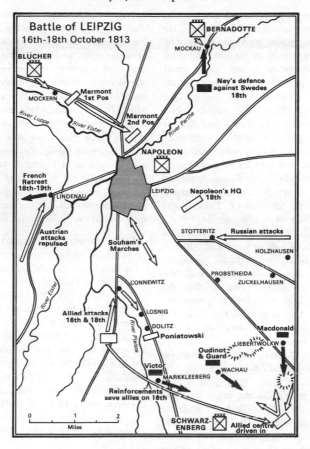

Battle of LEIPZIG
16th–18th October 1813

BERNADOTTE
MOCKAU

BLÜCHER

Ney's defence
against Swedes
18th

Marmont
1st Pos

MOCKERN

River Luppe

River Elster

River Parthe

Marmont
2nd Pos

NAPOLEON

French
Retreat
18th–19th

LINDENAU

LEIPZIG

Napoleon's HQ
18th

Austrian
attacks
repulsed

Souham's
Marches

STOTTERITZ   Russian attacks

HOLZHAUSEN

River Elster

CONNEWITZ

PROBSTHEIDA
ZUCKELHAUSEN

Allied attacks
16th & 18th

LOSNIG

River Pleisse

DOLITZ
Poniatowski

Macdonald

LIEBERTWOLKW

Oudinot
& Guard

Victor
MARKKLEEBERG

WACHAU

Reinforcements
save allies on 16th

0   1   2
Miles

SCHWARZ-
ENBERG   Allied centre
driven in

(with from 915 to 1,500 pieces of artillery). By its close, the French had lost 73,000 casualties to the Allies' 54,000, and its loss cost Napoleon all his positions east of the Rhine save Hamburg.*

The long Campaign of 1813 drew toward its inexorable climax as Napoleon, after failing for a second time to capture Berlin, began to regroup his forces west of the Elbe on 24 September. His new intention was to use Leipzig on the river Elster as his forward center of operations, or base, but this plan collapsed when Blücher*

forced a crossing over the Elbe at Wartenburg on 3 October while Bernadotte* of Sweden bridged the great river further downstream at a second point. Inspired by Blücher's dynamism, these forces began to close in on Leipzig from the north as Prince Schwarzenburg* at the head of another vast army marched up from the south, after masking the garrison of Dresden.* By 15 October Napoleon had concentrated 122,000 men around Leipzig and was facing the concentric advance of his opponents.

The battle opened early on the 16th, when Schwarzenberg sent Barclay de Tolly* with 78,000 men to attack the southern approaches to the city. By midday this poorly organized attack had petered out, and Napoleon at once counterattacked and regained all lost ground on the sector. Meanwhile Blücher had launched his 54,000 Prussians against Marmont's* positions in the North near Mockern, but VI Corps withstood odds of two to one and held its ground. Meanwhile, Bertrand's* IV Corps marched hither and thither, but ultimately helped in the fight for Lindenau.* Thus at the end of the first day's fighting the French were successfully holding their own, but the approach of further masses of Allies—and of only limited French reinforcements—was not encouraging. Had Napoleon beaten Barclay and Blücher decisively on this first day, the outcome might have been different, but as it was the forces of attrition were not in the Emperor's favor.

The 17th passed with little serious fighting. Napoleon spent the day reordering his 175,000 men within the Leipzig perimeter. On the other side, the arrival of Bernadotte and Bennigsen* from opposite points of the compass added a further 150,000 men to the Allied strength. On the 18th, the 355,000 Allies launched a multipart concentric offensive against all sectors of the French line. Such pressure was more than could be withstood, and after nine hours of grueling and often heroic fighting, Napoleon began a phased withdrawal through Leipzig and over the Elster. He was still very much in command of his men, and the Allies, despite their huge advantage, were slow in following up their success. The French evacuation might have ended in complete success, but the premature demolition of the single bridge over the Elster by a nervous engineer doomed 20,000 French troops of the rear guard who were still fighting in the city. Prince Poniatowski* drowned while trying to swim the river, and both Generals Lauriston* and Reynier* were taken prisoner. Napoleon retreated to the southwest toward Frankfort-on-Main, followed by the Allies. Bavaria changed sides and Wrede* tried to obstruct the French retreat at Hanau,* but Napoleon won the battle. Nevertheless, Leipzig effectively cost Napoleon control of Germany and brought his enemies to the frontiers of France. For a second year, fighting had cost the Emperor close to half a million men—such a strain could not be borne for much longer.

Leith, Lieutenant General Sir James (1763–1816). After being educated at Aberdeen and Lille, he became an ensign and served at Toulon* under Lord Hood* in 1793. Next year he was promoted to colonel, and ten years later to brigadier general. He fought at Corunna* under Sir John Moore* (1809), and from 1810–12 served as a divisional commander in the Peninsula under Wellington.* He was knighted in 1813 and promoted to lieutenant general. Next year he was made Commander in Chief of British forces in the West Indies and Governor of the Leeward Isles. He died at Barbados.

Lennox, Lady Georgiana (fl. 1815). The daughter of the Duke and Duchess of Richmond, she lived in Brussels from 1814. In 1815 she was a particular favorite of the Duke of Wellington.* She was present at the famous ball on the night of the 15th and left an excellent account of it. During the battle of Waterloo* she refused to heed Wellington's advice to quit Brussels, but spent the day making lint and bandages for the wounded. She later married Lord de Ros.

Leoben, Preliminaries of, 18 April 1797. Following up the capture of Mantua,* Bonaparte launched a campaign into the Frioul and pressed the Archduke Charles* back to the Semmering Pass, from which the spires of Vienna could be descried in the far distance. The French had occupied Leoben on 7 April. Nestled in the valley of the river Mur, this Styrian town stands 50 kilometers northwest of Graz. The French impetus was all but exhausted, but on 7 April the Austrians agreed to a five-day suspension of hostilities—subsequently twice extended. With customary bluster, Bonaparte, without the least authority, launched into full-scale negotiations, and on the 18th, when his bluff was on the point of being called, the Austrians suddenly agreed to sign the Preliminaries of Leoben. The terms were later, in somewhat modified form, embodied in the Peace of Campo Formio.*

L'Héritier, Général Samuel François, baron (1772–1829). In 1792 he became a grenadier and fought with, and later occupied minor staff posts in, the Army of the Rhine (1792–1800). In 1796 the Directory* gave him a commission back-dated to 1794. In 1800 he was wounded in the thigh at Marengo.* He soon became a famous cavalry commander in both the dragoons and the cuirassiers. Between 1805 and 1812 he served in Austria, Prussia, and Poland, being slightly wounded at Eylau.* He was created a baron in 1808 and shot in the shoulder at Essling* the next year. On 21 July 1809 he was promoted to *général de brigade,* and for two years he held posts in the cavalry inspectorate. In 1812 he served in Russia with Oudinot's* II Corps, fighting at Polotsk.* In March 1813 he became a *général de division* and was given command of the heavy cavalry forming part of the 3rd Cavalry Corps under Pajol.* He helped defend the Rhine crossings in late 1813 and the next year fought at Brienne,* La Rothière,* Troyes, and St. Dizier. He was placed on half-pay in June 1814 and held Bourbon posts subsequently, but rallied to Napoleon in 1815. Serving under Kellermann,* he was wounded at Waterloo.* Disgraced for some years, he became inspector of cavalry in 1819, and retired nine years later.

Liebertwolkwitz, action of, 14 October 1813. As the Allied forces converged upon Leipzig,* Murat,* commanding 32,400 infantry, 9,800 cavalry, and 156 guns (the II, V, and VIII Corps and two cavalry corps) engaged the advance guard of the Army of Bohemia to the south of the city. The morning passed in a fluctuating cavalry fight around Wachau and Markleeberg, but at 2:00 P.M. General Klenau attacked Liebertwolkwitz and captured the whole town save the church. That night the Allies evacuated the town. The action thus ended inconclusively, but it is regarded as the greatest cavalry contest of the campaign.

Ligny, battle of, 16 June 1815. As Napoleon advanced northward from Char-

L'Héritier

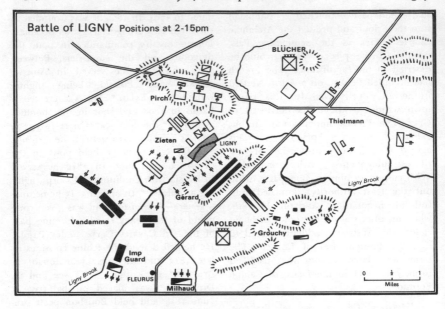

Battle of LIGNY Positions at 2-15pm

leroi and the river Sambre, he set himself the task of driving a deep wedge between the armies of Wellington* and Blücher,* hoping to defeat and destroy each in detail. While Ney* took two corps toward Quatre Bras,* Marshal Grouchy* led two more toward Fleurus and the neighboring village of Ligny. The Prussian army, on learning of Napoleon's sudden invasion of Belgium, had concentrated three of its four corps well forward in the vicinity of Ligny and St. Amand, and the Emperor realized that this offered him the chance of a telling success. Accordingly, he brought up his reserve corps, the Guard, and most of the cavalry in support of Grouchy's wing of the Army of the North, intending to pin Blücher with Gérard's* and Vandamme's* corps, bring in d'Erlon's* corps from Ney's wing to envelop the Prussian right wing, and then launch the Guard and reserves to smash the Prussian center and drive the rem-

nants away toward their base at Namur.

Blücher had drawn up his 84,000 men and 224 guns along a series of low ridges to the north of the Ligny brook, with strong detachments holding the various villages along its banks. About 2:30 P.M. Napoleon (with 80,000 men) launched his attack, and soon desperate fighting was raging among the villages. The Prussians gradually began to give way to the pressure, and Napoleon was about to launch the *coup de grâce* with the Guard when a dark mass of unidentified troops was noticed moving toward the French left rear. This was in fact d'Erlon, belatedly trying to fulfill his orders after some confusion, who had mistaken his objective and was moving along the wrong axis. Valuable time was lost by the French in identifying the newcomers, but at about 7:30 P.M. Napoleon launched the Guard forward. The Prussian resistance crumbled; Blücher in person led a cavalry charge to try and check the rout, but he was dismounted and ridden over several times. As night fell, Gneisenau,* with no knowledge of his chief's whereabouts, organized a general retreat toward Wavre,* due north, instead of toward Namur as Napoleon anticipated. In this fortuitous decision, which left the Prussians on the 17th and 18th within supporting distance of Wellington, lay the fate of the whole campaign. Thus, although the Prussians were decidedly worsted at Ligny, losing 25,000 casualties and inflicting only 11,000, the defeat was not decisive. The French follow-through after Ligny was tardy and ill-directed, and the Prussians were able to recover their cohesion as Blücher resumed command. The 18th would see the great double battle fought out at Waterloo* and Wavre.

Lindenau, battle of, 16 October 1813. This engagement formed part of the first day's fighting at Leipzig.* As a distraction from the main attacks being launched to the north and south of the city, General Gyulai* advanced with some 30,000 troops to attack the fortified village of Lindenau,* guarding the main bridge over the river Elster. The French garrison was commanded by General Arrighi, and by midday he was in serious trouble as the Austrians broke into the town. A desperate appeal for aid was sent to Bertrand,* whose IV Corps was en route to reinforce the southern battle area. Bertrand accepted the plea and turned his command to the west, and two divisions helped in the final repulse of the Austrians. Thus the vital French link with the west remained open, but at the price of diverting troops who had been vitally needed elsewhere.

Liverpool, Prime Minister Robert Banks Jenkinson, second Earl of (1770–1828). Educated at Oxford, he was in Paris during the storming of the Bastille, and next year was elected MP for Appleby (and from 1796 for Rye). Master of the Mint from 1799, in 1801 he began two years' service as Addington's* Foreign Secretary. He helped reconcile Pitt* and Addington, and served the former as Home Secretary from 1804–06. He led the opposition to Grenville's short ministry, and then resumed office as Home Secretary from 1807–09. Premier Perceval* appointed him Secretary for War and the Colonies (1809–12), and as a firm ally of Wellington* he greatly expanded the strength of the army. From 1812 he became Prime Minister; he disapproved of Catholic emancipation, but managed to prevent the issue from splitting his ministry; his greatest achievement was the pressing of the wars against Napoleon to a successful conclusion and the exiling of the Emperor to St. Helena.* The War of 1812–14 against the United States proved less successful. The latter years of his ministry were clouded by domestic problems of a social and economic nature.

Lloyd, Henry Humphrey Evans, marquis de (1720–1783). An adventurer of Welsh extraction, he received de Saxe's* patronage after the battle of Fontenoy for the design of a fine set of maps. In 1754 he reputedly betrayed plans of Marshal Belle-Isle's proposed invasion of the British Isles to London. He later fought in the Austrian army during the Seven Years' War and then transferred into the service of Prince Ferdinand of Brunswick.* He acted as a secret agent in Germany and later commanded a Russian division at the siege of Silistria. He traveled extensively in Italy and Spain before settling in Belgium, where he wrote a history of the Seven Years' War which attracted Napoleon's attention as a young man, and some ideas on the nature of battle were absorbed from this source and later applied.

Lobau, Maréchal Georges Mouton, comte de (1770–1838). Volunteered and appointed lieutenant in 1792, he served on the Moselle and the Rhine and in Italy (1795–1801), where he was twice wounded. He was at the siege of Mantua* and served as aide to Joubert.* After service at the camps of St. Omer and Compiègne he was promoted to *général de brigade* in February 1805, and next month was made an aide-de-camp to Napoleon, accompanying him at Austerlitz,* Jena,* and· Eylau* before being gravely wounded at Friedland.* In October 1807 he became *général de division,* commanded a division under Bessières* in Spain, particularly distinguishing himself at Medina del Rio Seco.* Later, under Soult,* he helped take Burgos,* but then reverted to his role as imperial aide and returned with his master to France early in 1809, and thence to the Danube theater. There he fought at Abensberg,* and at Landshut* led the party that captured the blazing bridge. After fighting at Eckmühl* he again distinguished himself at Aspern-Essling,* leading the Guard attack that regained the latter village at bayonet-point. While covering the retreat onto Lobau Isle he was wounded in the hand. In May he became a count and then fought at Wagram.* In 1812 he performed senior staff duty in Russia and was one of the few selected to accompany Napoleon back to France from Smorgoni. In 1813 Lobau fought at Lützen,* and at Dresden* took command of Vandamme's* corps. He was taken prisoner at the fall of Dresden, sent to Hungary, but returned to France in June 1814. Next year he rallied to the Emperor and commanded the VI Corps at Waterloo,* being taken prisoner at Plancenoit after again being wounded. After a period in England he lived in Belgium, but was allowed back into France in late 1818. Entering politics as a liberal he put down

Count of Lobau

Bonapartist rioters in 1831, and on 30 July was created a Marshal of France. He died in 1838 when an old wound re-opened. Count Lobau was well thought of by Napoleon, but was never appointed to the marshalate by his master.

Lodi, battle of, 10 May 1796. This Lombard town, 30 kilometers southwest of Mantua* on the river Adda, was the scene of a violent action in the second phase of the 1796 campaign when Bonaparte, after crossing the river Po near Piacenza, was making a determined effort to trap General Beaulieu* west of the Adda. In fact the French arrived too late to prevent the Austrian retreat, and at Lodi only fought Beaulieu's rear guard. Bonaparte in person sited and aimed 30 guns to sweep the eastern bank, and then Massena* led a gallant charge over the bridge which carried it at the price of 400 casualties. Further French columns under Beaumont and Ordener* forded the river upstream, and Beaulieu ordered Sebottendorf to abandon the town and head for Mantua. Each side lost some 2,000 casualties on the 10th, and from that date Napoleon's grip on his men was assured, however disappointing the outcome of the battle. Nicknamed *le petit caporal* (it was an artillery corporal's duty to align a cannon), Bonaparte moved on to occupy Milan, 20 miles to the northwest, on 15 May.

Loison, Général Louis Henri, comte (1771–1816). The son of a Deputy elected to the Constituent Assembly, Loison received a commission in 1791. After holding various line and staff appointments in the Army of the North, he emerged as a *général de brigade* in 1795 in the Army of the Rhine and Moselle. That October he cooperated with General Bonaparte at *Vendémiaire,* * headed the court-martial team that tried the ringleaders, and then followed his chief into the Army of the Interior. He did not, however, transfer to Italy, but after a period of nonemployment he joined the Army of Switzerland in January 1799 and achieved a fine reputation under Lecourbe and Massena,* who appointed him a provisional *général de division*—a promotion confirmed in October 1799. He recaptured the St. Gothard Pass and Reichenau before joining the Army of the Reserve in April 1800. As part of Victor's* corps he was entrusted with the reduction of Fort Bard* during the passage of the Alps, and consequently was not present at Marengo.* After service in Italy under Suchet* he joined the Camp of Compiègne, was given a division in Ney's* VI Corps, and fought with distinction at Elchingen* in 1805. After various governorships he besieged Colberg in 1807 and then was transferred to Junot's* army for the invasion of Portugal. He fought at Vimiero* next year, was repatriated to France after Cintra,* then returned to Spain under Soult,* and later Ney. In 1810 he took part in the sieges of Ciudad Rodrigo* and Almeida,* fought at Bus-

saco,* and in command of the VI Corps after Ney's departure defended Garda and fought at Fuentes de Oñoro.* In 1812 he was made Governor of Königsberg, but was then transferred to a divisional command in III Corps at Vilna, which he defended in late 1812. He was next Governor of Elbing and Tilsit, fought under Rapp* in 1813, and commanded the Wesel area. However, at this juncture he fell out of favor with Napoleon, who had him arrested for failing to accompany his division to the front. He received a severe reprimand, which effectively ended his active military career except for one brief appointment under Davout.* He went on the unemployed list in January 1815, and was finally retired in November of that year.

Lonato, first and second battles of, 2 and 5 August 1796. After occupying Milan in May 1796, Bonaparte set out to besiege the great fortress of Mantua,* to which General Beaulieu* had retreated after the battle of Lodi.* However, an Austrian relief army under General Würmser* marched south from the Alps and advanced in several columns to relieve Mantua. Würmser had over 50,000 men, and even after calling in all available detachments—including many from the Mantuan siege lines—Bonaparte had barely 43,000 in all, and Beaulieu had at least 12,000 men within its defenses. By early August the siege had been abandoned and many French siege guns spiked, and Würmser was able to pass in several convoys of food and munitions to the garrison. Meanwhile his westernmost column, 18,000 men under General Quasdanovitch,* was approaching the area down the banks of Lake Garda, and it seemed that Bonaparte might be caught between converging forces. Bonaparte at last decided to reinforce Despinois'* slender brigades with Massena's* division near Lonato, and in a stiff day's fighting

Quasdanovitch was repulsed while Augereau,* albeit massively outnumbered, held off Würmser's main force near Castiglione* some five miles away. Two days later, the French were able to mass against Würmser at Castiglione itself and inflict a defeat upon him. Quasdanovitch had by this time lost all of a division's worth of troops in renewed fighting near Lonato (the second battle), and soon the French were in a position to reimpose the siege of Mantua as Würmser retired up the river Adige toward Trent.

Loshnitsa, action of, **23** November 1812. As the Grand Army reeled back from Smolensk* in growing disarray, the Russian Admiral Tshitsagov* succeeded in capturing Borisov—the only bridge over the Beresina.* Marshal Oudinot* counterattacked with determination on the 23rd and won a stiff engagement against part of Tshitsagov's command on the plain of Loshnitsa, taking over 1,000 prisoners and a large store of supplies. Following up this success, Oudinot's II Corps reoccupied the town of Borisov, but the Russians retained control of the bridges. Nevertheless, Oudinot's success put a little heart into the demoralized main army and helped brace them for the forthcoming epic struggle of the Beresina crossing.

Louis XVI, King of France (1754–1793). The grandson of Louis XV, he succeeded his grandfather on the throne in 1774. Well-intentioned but lacking in willpower, he was dominated by his wife, Marie-Antoinette, and faced by the daunting legacy of half a century of near-national bankruptcy, he vacillated between courses of action, making the mistake of dispensing with the services of such able men as Turgot (1776) who might have discovered a solution to France's difficult economic problems, given proper backing. Then Louis led his country into involvement in the American

War of Independence in 1778, and his minister, Necker, had to add to the burden of national debts to finance this successful but expensive transatlantic venture. Another success was the solution of the Bavarian Succession crisis in 1779, but soon the economic situation at home was almost irremediable. Consequently, the King summoned the States-General, and in 1789 the meetings that began at Versailles soon turned into the French Revolution.* By 6 October that year Louis had been forced to take up residence inside Paris. He for a time put his trust in the Marquis de Mirabeau, but then dropped him. On 21 June 1791 the royal family attempted to flee to the Austrian Netherlands, but were arrested at Varennes. This action finally cost Louis the respect and trust of his people—and his willingness to take an oath to the new constitution on 9 September impressed nobody. In August 1792, as the Armies of the First Coalition* marched deeper into France, the Paris mob threatened to murder the royal family, and Louis was forced to seek sanctuary on the 10th within the building of the National Assembly. The monarchy was declared suspended. Brought to trial for alleged treason against France, Louis refused to plead and was eventually sentenced to death. On 21 January 1793 he was guillotined.

Louis XVII, King of France (1785–1795). The tragic son of Louis XVI, he never in fact reigned, but was imprisoned under the most harrowing conditions after his father's execution, and ultimately died of neglect and ill-treatment.

Louis XVIII, King of France (1755–1824). The grandson of Louis XV, brother of Louis XVI,* and uncle of the unfortunate Louis XVII,* he succeeded in escaping over the French frontier to Brussels in June 1791 and soon gravitated to the leadership of the army of *émigrés** collected at Coblenz, with the rank of lieutenant general. After the execution of his brother, he was for two years regarded as Regent-in-exile for the imprisoned Louis XVII, and on his death he was regarded by the supporters of the House of Bourbon as the rightful king of France. He established a small court at Verona but eventually, after the death of his wife, moved to England as French armies conquered North Italy. He long hoped that Napoleon would restore him to the French throne, but this never materialized. In April 1814 he returned to Paris, accepted the terms of the Treaty of Paris* (which limited France to her boundaries of 1792), and attempted to woo his people. However, surrounded by vengeful reactionary ex-*émigrés*, he soon found the situation slipping out of control, and in March 1815 was forced to flee back to Belgium as Napoleon arrived from Elba.* Restored after the Hundred Days* and Waterloo,* "in the baggage-wagons of the Allies," he was forced to accept the far harsher terms of the Second Treaty of Paris. The duc de Richelieu was his principal minister, and soon the "White Terror" was still further alienating sections of the French population. Louis acceded to the Holy Alliance, but the Ultras came to power after the death of the moderate duc de Berry in 1820. He died, old, sick, and dominated by Mme. du Caya.

Louise, Queen of Prussia (1776–1810). The daughter of the Duke of Mecklenburg-Strelitz and of Princess Fredericka Caroline of Hesse-Darmstadt, Louise married Frederick William,* Crown Prince of Prussia, in 1793. On his succession in 1797, she became Queen. From the first she gained the admiration of her subjects through her fine domestic qualities and downright patriotism. Prince Hardenburg* wielded a benign, moderating influence over Prussian policy for many years, but on his fall the Queen became strongly associated with the extreme patriots who

clamored for war against France, and the result was the disastrous struggle of 1806 and the virtual dismemberment of Prussia at Tilsit* in 1807. During the peace talks she employed every feminine wile to wring concessions out of Napoleon, but to little effect, although he dubbed her "the only real man in Prussia." For a time she lived in St. Petersburg and then at Königsberg and Memel, but in 1809 she returned to Berlin where she backed the clandestine work of reform and preparation being carried through by Stein* and Scharnhorst.* Before the struggle for Prussian liberation from French hegemony could truly begin, however, she died at the Castle of Hohenzieritz.

L'Ouverture, Toussaint de (1743–1803). The future Haitian statesman and general took an active part in defense of the Spanish royal authority during the Black Rising of 1791. He then passed into the Spanish service, but in 1794 reversed his allegiance and championed the French on account of their determination to stamp out slavery. In 1794 the French promoted him to *général de brigade*, and next year to full *général de division*. For years he was an Anglophobe, holding British ambitions in the area in check, but wishing to be the sole master in Haiti he sent the French Commissioners out of the country. In 1799 he similarly triumphed over the Spaniards in a new Black Rising, and occupied Santo Domingo (1801). Under his rule the united island began to enjoy a measure of prosperity, but that same year the First Consul sent his brother-in-law, General Leclerc,* at the head of an expedition to reconquer Haiti.* Defeated and taken captive, Toussaint was shipped back to France and imprisoned in the Chateau de Joux, where he died in a wheelbarrow of starvation and despair in 1803.

Lowe, Lieutenant General Sir Hudson (1769–1844). Gazetted an ensign in 1787, he was promoted to captain eight years later. He saw much service, being present at Toulon,* in Corsica, Elba, Portugal, Minorca, and Egypt. From 1805–12 he was in Italy in a liaison capacity, and he was later attached to Blücher's* staff in a similar capacity. Wellington* refused to have him on his staff in 1815, and he again served in Italy (having been promoted to major general in 1814). Late in 1815 he was appointed Governor of St. Helena,* responsible for Napoleon's custody and safety. He was knighted in 1817, but his unsympathetic and obstructive attitude toward his distinguished captive earned him much criticism. In 1821 he was recalled from St. Helena, and two years later was sent to Antigua as Governor. From 1825–30 he served in a staff capacity in Ceylon, being promoted to lieutenant general in 1830. His papers formed the basis for an early account of Napoleon's captivity, but as a very insensitive and even oafish man he had few friends.

Lumley, General Sir William (1769–1850). Educated at Eton, he entered the army in 1787 and rose to be a lieutenant colonel by 1795. Three years later he served in Ireland during the rebellion, and in 1801 saw service under Abercromby* in Egypt. In 1805 he was promoted to major general and next year served in the reconquest of the Cape of Good Hope and then in South America. From 1810–14 he served in the Peninsula, rising to the rank of lieutenant general. From 1819–25 he served as Governor and Commander in Chief in Bermuda, and in 1837 he was appointed full general.

Lundy's Lane, action of, 25 July 1814. As General Brown retreated with his 2,600 men to Chippawa, General Phineas Riall* sent Colonel Pearson in pursuit from Fort George. A mile from the Niagara Falls he halted at Lundy's Lane, aware that the Americans in the area were in superior strength. However, Riall and Lieutenant General Drummond both hurried reinforcements forward to bring Pearson up to a strength of 1,700 men. Meanwhile General Brown, fearful for his supply depot at Fort Schlosser, decided to advance north again as the best way to keep the British away from his stores. Late in the afternoon of the 25th General Scott's brigade of 1,000 Americans made contact with Riall and the latter decided to retreat, but this was countermanded by General Drummond, newly arrived upon the scene and knowing that another 1,200 men were close by. Scott never hesitated— at 6:00 P.M. he launched a frontal attack on the British position along a low ridge. The attack was successful and the British left gave way, Riall being wounded and captured. Elsewhere, however, Scott was less successful, and although he almost took the two British 24-pounder guns at one moment of the struggle, the battle was still continuing at 9:00 P.M. as darkness began to fall. Reinforcements reached both sides, the battle raged on into the night, and both American generals, Scott and Brown, were wounded. As a result, the third-in-command, General Ripley, ordered a withdrawal. The Americans had lost 172 killed, 572 wounded, and 110 missing; the British casualties amounted to 790 including 94 killed. Next day, the Americans fell back to Fort Erie.

Luneville, the Peace of, 8 February 1801. This treaty brought to a close Austrian participation in the War of the Second Coalition* against France. Talks had reopened after the Austrian defeat at Hohenlinden* by Moreau,* and the terms were surprisingly generous. The Habsburgs were required to do little more than reaffirm the terms of Campo Formio* in 1797, with its settlement of North Italian, Rhineland, and Swiss affairs. In return,

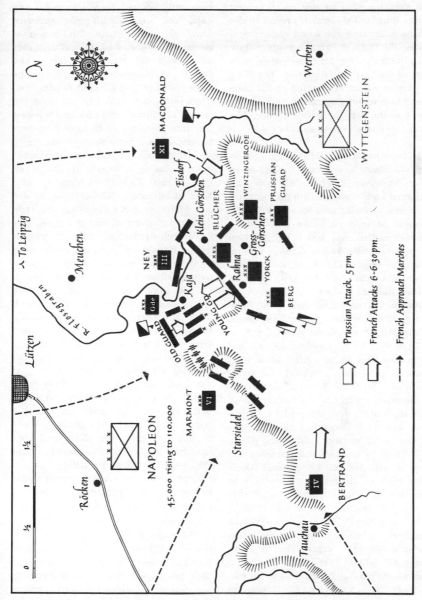

Battle of Lutzen, 2 May *1813*

the French agreed to pay compensation to the disinherited German princes in the Rhine valley from the seized ecclesiastical states; the Duke of Parma was given Tuscany in return for his principality, now part of the Cisalpine Republic. The King of Naples was to be restored to his kingdom. As a result, England stood virtually alone in the struggle against France. The road to Amiens* would soon be taken.

Lützen, battle of, 2 May 1813. Following the disasters sustained in Russia in 1812, Napoleon found himself facing an enlarged hostile Sixth Coalition* as Prussia threw in its lot with Russia in March, soon to be followed by Sweden. Soon a Russo-Prussian army was marching into Germany, and the War of German Liberation had begun. The Allied monarchs— Tsar Alexander* and Frederick William III*—established their headquarters in Dresden and entrusted their joint field-army, about 100,000 strong, to Count Wittgenstein* and General Blücher.*

In typical style, Napoleon determined to get his blow in first. After assembling some 120,000 troops behind the rivers Saale and Elbe, the Emperor crossed the former river on 30 April and advanced on Leipzig,* which was occupied by Lauriston* and the V Corps on 2 May. As news of the French advance reached the Allies, a force of 73,000 men and 500 guns was concentrated between Leipzig and Altenburg ready to advance on Lützen so as to threaten the French right flank if they continued to cross the Saale through Merseburg. Ney's* III Corps occupied Lützen itself on the 1st to protect the movement of the main army. That day saw some stiff fighting near Weissenfels,* during which Marshal Bessières* was killed.

Early on 2 May Ney, on Napoleon's order, set about occupying a number of villages south of Lützen. This induced Wittgenstein to order an attack upon the

apparently isolated French force holding Kaja, and after an all-night approach march the Allies swept into action at about 11:45 A.M. Led by cavalry, they suddenly found themselves facing two French divisions—Souham* occupying Gross-Gorschen and Girard* putting Starsiedel into a state of defense. Souham lost ground but Girard held firm, and this gave Ney time to ride over in haste from near Leipzig. Soon a fierce struggle was raging around the villages. Napoleon meanwhile was ordering up reserves to III Corps' aid, the Imperial Guard* coming up near Kaja, Macdonald's* XI Corps on the left, and Marmont's* VI Corps on the right during the course of the afternoon, raising French strength ultimately to 110,000 troops. Napoleon himself was on the scene at about 2:30 P.M., receiving a rapturous welcome from his men. Despite appeals for aid from both Ney and Marmont, Napoleon retained the Guard in reserve. Then Allied errors played into his hands; Blücher was wounded and his successor, General Yorck,* was no match for the French; Russian reserves were also late reaching the field. Accordingly, at 5:30 P.M., with the French outflanking forces almost in position, as Macdonald and Bertrand* came up on the left and right respectively, Napoleon ordered Drouot* to mass 70 guns near Kaja and then launched the Young, supported by the Old, Guard forward in a telling attack in the center. By 7:00 P.M. the enemy was in full retreat from the field, but Napoleon's crippling shortage of cavalry precluded all chance of an effective pursuit. The French had lost some 20,000 casualties in the day's fighting; Allied losses are computed at between 11,500 and 20,000—but their morale was shaken. Soon Napoleon was devising an advance toward Dresden* and, ultimately, Bautzen,* where another drubbing awaited the Allies. Napoleon had clearly seized the initiative.

Macdonald, Maréchal Jacques Etienne Joseph Alexandre, duc de Tarente (Tarentum) (1765–1840). Born at Sedan, he was the son of a Scottish Jacobite exile and joined the *Légion Irlandais* in 1784. The next year he served as a lieutenant in a French formation in the Dutch service, but in 1786 he transferred to the *Régiment de Dillon* as a volunteer, and by 1789 he had attained the rank of *sous-lieutenant*. In the early Revolutionary Wars he became ADC to General Dumouriez* and fought on his staff at Jemappes.* On. 27 August 1793 he was promoted to *général de brigade* on Pichegru's* recommendation, and next year fought at Turcoing and Hondeschoote. He was made *général de division* in November 1794.

Active service in Holland and with the Armies of the Sambre-et-Meuse and the North followed (1795–98), and in November 1798 he was transferred to Italy as Governor of Rome. A disagreement with General Championnet deprived him of this post, but in February 1799 he replaced that commander at the head of the Army of Naples. He was wounded while winning the combat of Modena but was compelled to retreat from Naples and was defeated at the river Trebbia. In late 1799 he was switched to the Rhine to serve as second-in-command to General Moreau,* with whom he struck up a close relationship. From 1801–02 he was sent as an envoy to Denmark, but fell from grace with Napoleon in 1804 when he defended Moreau's reputation in public against charges of treason.

The period of eclipse ended in 1807, when he was allowed to join the Neapolitan army. Commanding an Italian corps under Eugène* at the battle of the Piave in May 1809 he was wounded again, but recovered in time to lead his formation at Wagram* in the crucial attack on the second day, which smashed the Austrian center. This feat completed his reconciliation with Napoleon, who awarded him his baton on 12 July—the only marshal to be appointed on the battlefield. In December 1809 he was created Duke of Tarentum and awarded a valuable annuity. Service in Catalonia followed (1810–11), and in 1812 he received command of the X Corps for the invasion of Russia. Entrusted with the northern flank of this massive operation, he spent the months August to December in command of the unsuccessful siege of Riga, which led to General Yorck's* defection to the Allies at the head of the Prussian contingent. In the Campaign of Germany, Macdonald received command of the XI Corps, winning an action at Merseburg on 29 April. At Lützen* he commanded the French right wing, and he filled the same role at Bautzen.* Following the breakdown of the Armistice,* however, he was defeated by Blücher* at the river Katzbach where his corps was routed. At Leipzig* he narrowly avoided being captured while crossing the river Elster under enemy fire on the final day, but he survived to fight at Hanau.* Toward the end of the year he was made responsible for the defense of the lower Rhine area, but in the new year was forced to abandon Cologne and

Macdonald

retire to Châlons-sur-Marne, which again he had to quit under enemy pressure on 4 February. During the Campaign of France he fought in four minor engagements, but lost Troyes to the Allies in early March.

After the loss of Paris, Macdonald joined Ney* and two other marshals (Lefebvre* and Moncey*) in pressing for Napoleon's abdication, and took an active part in the subsequent negotiations with the Allies. The Bourbons made him a peer of France, and in March 1815 he escorted the fleeing Louis XVIII* to the Belgian frontier before returning to Paris. He refused all offers of a command under Napoleon, and lived in retirement until after Waterloo.* Upon the second restoration he was at once made Commander in Chief of the Army of the Loire, with orders to disband it. This tricky task he achieved with great tact. In later years he wrote his interesting memoirs, visited Scotland to see his ancestral home, and died at Courcelles-le-Roi on 7 September 1840. In later years he had served the

Bourbons as a Minister of State and as Grand Chancellor of the *Légion d'Honneur*.* His attitude toward Napoleon had always been correct, although he owed him little until 1809, as the Emperor freely admitted.

Macdonnell, General Sir James (17?–1857). He fought in a series of campaigns in Naples, Sicily, and Egypt (1804–1807) and was promoted to lieutenant colonel in 1809. From 1812–14 he served Wellington* in the Peninsular War,* and in 1815 he fought at Waterloo* and was made a Knight Commander of the Bath. From 1838–41 he was Commander in Chief in Canada, being promoted to lieutenant general in the latter year and to full general in 1854.

Mack, General Karl Freiherr von Leiberich (1752–1828). After distinguished service in the Austrian army in wars against the Turks he was promoted to general. As Chief of Staff to the Austrian Army of the First Coalition* his plans were thwarted by Jourdan* and Kléber* in the Campaign of 1794, but he helped negotiate Dumouriez' defection. In 1797 he was appointed commander of the Neapolitan Army of the Bourbons, but was defeated and taken prisoner by General Championnet. He escaped in 1800 and five years later was given the senior command on the Danube front. By this time he was quartermaster general of the Austrian army. He was totally outmaneuvered by Napoleon, however, and after the stiff fight of Elchingen* he was induced to surrender at Ulm* at the head of most of his army (20 October). This disaster cost him his command and almost his life, as he was condemned to death by the Habsburgs. This sentence, however, was commuted to imprisonment, and he was eventually pardoned in 1809.

Macquard (sometimes Macquart), Général François (1738–1801). After much experience dating from 1755, which included service as a grenadier and receiving four wounds at Minden (1759), he transferred to the dragoons and ultimately secured a commission in 1785. Promotion came faster under the Revolution, and during four years in North Italy (1792–96) he was promoted to *général de brigade* (1794) and *de division* (1795) after his success at Saorgio. He subsequently held several garrison commands before retiring from the service in 1797.

Magdeburg, siege of, 20 October–11 November 1806. This great Prussian fortress on the river Elbe was one of the few places to offer concerted resistance to the French after the battles of Jena* and Auerstadt.* After defying Murat's* summons to surrender, Prince Hohenlohe* escaped from the fortress on the 21st, leaving a garrison of 25,000 under the aged General Kleist* to withstand the troops of Ney* who, once Soult* had been summoned for further duties by the Emperor, commanded only 18,000 men. Little transpired except for outpost skirmishing, although on 4 November Kleist did attempt a half-hearted sortie that failed. Then, under threat of an intense bombardment, he opened negotiations; an armistice was concluded on the 7th, the capitulation was signed next day, and on the 11th the garrison marched out as prisoners of war.

Maida, battle of, 6 July 1806. Following Napoleon's deposition of Ferdinand IV, King of Naples, in favor of his brother, Joseph Bonaparte,* the British government ordered General Sir John Stuart* to land with an expeditionary force in Calabria, southern Italy. This body of troops, conveyed by Sir Sidney Smith's* squadron on Admiral Collingwood's* orders, left Messina in Sicily on 27 June, and three days later the force anchored off the Gulf of St. Euphemia. General Reynier,* French commander in

southern Italy, marched with 5,000 troops (including 1,000 cavalry) to challenge the invasion, although there was no sign of the popular uprising the British commanders were hoping for in their favor. Stuart's force was also about 5,000 strong but included no cavalry, and the two forces clashed near the village of Maida on 6 July. Reynier insisted on advancing to the attack over a river onto the open plain in column, and Stuart's infantry awaited them in silent linear formation, two deep, along a low ridge. The British held their fire and advanced in a menacing red line, then discharged a number of crippling volleys at point-blank range, following this up with a determined bayonet charge led by the light infantry. The French gave ground at once, and soon their left wing was totally routed. Retreat became flight, pursued by death-dealing British musketry, and Reynier lost 700 killed, 1,000 wounded, and an equal number of prisoners. British casualties amounted to 330. Stuart returned victorious to the landing beaches to rest his men. His subsequent action has been criticized —the British merely marched south ready to return to Sicily instead of trying to relieve besieged Gaeta with the navy's aid (the fortress fell to the French on the 18th), but the relations between the military and naval commanders were variable. However, Maida is important tactically as demonstrating the inherent superiority of British tactics over the French column of attack.

Maison, Maréchal Nicolas Joseph, marquis (1771–1840). After gaining rapid promotion in the National Guard of Epinay (1789–91), Maison served with a *fédéré* battalion at Jemappes,* earning distinction by retaking a color from the enemy. This notwithstanding, he was suspended for political reasons but re-emerged in the army in 1794 in a provisional capacity as captain aide-de-camp. Fully reinstated in

…

Maison

1796 he served first on the Rhine and then under Bernadotte* in Italy. Posted to Holland in 1799, he was wounded at Alkmaar —his seventh wound. After an assignment under Bernadotte in Hanover, he served as a senior officer on his staff in the 1805 campaign, fighting at Austerlitz,* and was promoted to *général de brigade* (February 1806). During the campaign of that year he fought at Schleiz* and Halle and at the surrender of Lubeck. In 1807 he served as Victor's* Chief of Staff in Poland, fighting at Friedland.* He was made a baron in 1808 and next served in Spain, fighting at Espinosa and being wounded outside Madrid. Next year he was transferred to the Army of Germany under Junot* and later to Holland. In 1812 he was assigned a command under Oudinot,* and after fighting at Polotsk* he was promoted to *général de division* in August and later greatly distinguished himself under Ney* during the retreat from Moscow. He continued to give good service in 1813, fighting at Bautzen* and in many minor actions, and was rewarded with the

title of count. After Leipzig* he was switched to the Army of the North, and in early 1814 defended Courtrai where he defeated General Thielmann* on 31 March—practically the last success of French arms before Napoleon's abdication.

Maison was rapidly reconciled with the Bourbons, who made him a peer of France, and he remained loyal to Louis XVIII* throughout the Hundred Days.* After the second restoration he sat in on Ney's* court-martial and held numerous important military posts, being made a marquis in 1817. In 1828 he led the French expedition to the Morea, and was appointed a Marshal of France in February 1829. During the troubles of 1830 he adhered to Louis-Philippe and for a period served as Minister of Foreign Affairs, and then (1831–1835) he served as French ambassador to first Vienna and then St. Petersburg. He ended his career as Minister of War (1835–36).

Maison, le. This flexible organization was the nerve center of Napoleon's staff system. It was divided into the Emperor's personal assistants—Berthier,* Duroc,* and Caulaincourt;* a dozen official general aides-de-camp led by Mouton,* Rapp,* and Savary;* the imperial servants (Constant the valet and Roustam* the Mameluke* bodyguard among others); and his *"cabinet,"* which held his key personal staff. Headed by General Clarke for many years, the *cabinet* held his personal secretaries (led at different times by Bourienne,* Meneval, and Fain), but its most significant part was the *Bureau Topographique,* or Map Room, which was presided over by General Bacler d'Albe.*

Malet, Général Claude François de (1754–1812). After a period in the Grey Musketeers of the Bourbon household troops (1771–75) he lived in Dôle until 1790, when he was made a captain in the

Malet

National Guard. After various staff and infantry appointments on the Rhine he was forced to resign from the service in 1793 as a former noble, but was recalled to a brigade staff appointment in 1796, serving in the Army of the Rhine and Moselle Elected to the Council of the Five Hundred (*Cinq Cents*)* for the Jura in 1798, his election was squashed. He then served in the Army of the Alps and was promoted to *général de brigade* in October 1799. Service in the Grisons and Switzerland followed, but he was soon out of favor with the authorities on account of voting against the Life Consulate and then the Empire. Service in Italy and then Naples was interrupted by his arrest for republican agitation in 1807. Over the following years he was in and out of prison several times but was eventually permitted to reside in a private mental institution in Paris. Escaping from this on 23 October 1812, he proclaimed that Napoleon had died in Russia and announced

the formation of a republican provisional government. A surprising number of officials believed him but, challenged by the Military Governor of Paris to authenticate his declarations, Malet shot him dead and was arrested, tried, and executed, together with 14 accomplices, on 29 October.

Maloyaroslavetz, battle of, 24 and 25 October 1812. After evacuating Moscow on 19 October, Napoleon and the *Grande Armée* headed southwest, intending to march toward the fertile region around Kaluga before heading westward toward Poland. The advance guard formed by the command of Eugène Beauharnais* had no trouble until the evening of the 23rd when, as it approached Maloyaroslavetz on the river Lusha, there were signs of Russian occupation. In fact Kutusov,* learning of the French approach, had rushed Doctorov's* corps from Tarutino. Eugène's 15,000 men faced 20,000 Russians but made a head-on assault against the bridge early on the 24th. In desperate fighting the bridge changed hands no less than seven times together with the township beyond. At one point Doctorov was almost defeated, but he received timely reinforcement from Raevski* at the head of the approaching main Russian army. Forced to send in his last reserves, Eugène made one last effort and regained control of bridge and town. Having sustained 6,000 losses (and inflicted perhaps 5,000 on the French), Doctorov drew off to the ridges overlooking Maloyaroslavetz, but although the French now had secured the bridge itself they could hardly claim to have secured a true bridgehead over the river. By midafternoon the main French army was in the vicinity, but Napoleon decided not to renew the action in strength. Next morning, as skirmishing continued, Napoleon conducted a personal reconnaissance of the south bank of the Lusha, and was narrowly saved from a surprise attack by a party of Cossacks. This event may have made up Napoleon's mind for him. After holding a discordant council of war, he ordered the army to abandon the march on Kaluga and to retrace its steps to Oshigovo and thence towards Mojaisk—the route used for the advance on Moscow early the previous month. This was to prove a crucial decision.

Malta, seizure and siege of, 1798–1800. En route to Egypt, Bonaparte and the Army of the Orient, conveyed by Admiral Brueys,* arrived off Malta on 9 June 1798. A pretext for occupying the island was fabricated from the supposed refusal of Baron Hompesch, Grand Master of the Order of St. John of Malta, to permit the entire French fleet to enter Grand Harbor at Valetta to replenish water supplies, and on the 10th General Reynier* landed a force to seize Gozo Island, while d'Hilliers* and Desaix* isolated Valetta. A little opposition was encountered, but this was rapidly overcome, and on the 12th Bonaparte in person supervised Vaubois'* assault which seized the acqueduct. Hompesch surrendered, and Bonaparte spent five days reordering the affairs of the island before sailing on toward Egypt on the 19th. General Vaubois was left with 4,000 men to garrison the island. Its capture had cost only three French lives.

Following the battle of the Nile* in August, a British naval blockade* was imposed by Admiral Nelson* and a British expeditionary force was eventually landed to support the revolt of the island's inhabitants against the French. On 24 October Nelson placed Captain Alexander Ball RN ashore as Governor and commander over all operations, with a squadron of five naval vessels under his command. Great problems were encountered over food supplies, and early in 1799 the blockade had to be virtually called off

during Bruix's* expedition down the Mediterranean. During the respite, Vaubois resupplied Valetta, and only in June 1800 was an effective series of operations against the French garrison recommenced, although the blockade had been restored a year previously. By June 1800, Colonel Graham* (later Lord Lynedoch) was at the head of 2,300 regular British and Neapolitan troops, besides some 4,000 Maltese militia. In May Vaubois drove part of the Maltese population out of Valetta as the pinch was again felt for food, and the siege continued in rather desultory fashion. Graham was superseded by General Pigot, who had arrived with 1,500 reinforcements, and in June General Stuart* visited the island. Growing famine at last forced Vaubois to treat for terms on 4 September, and a capitulation was signed next day. His garrison was permitted free evacuation to France. Subsequently, great diplomatic problems were encountered over the future of the island, British interests being challenged by the Order of St. John and the Russians.

Mamelukes, the. Since the 13th century, rule over Egypt had been in the hands of Mameluke Beys, warriors originating from the Caucasus. In the late 18th century rule was effectively in the hands of Ibrahim* and Murad* Bey, and Bonaparte encountered strong opposition from them during his conquest of the country in 1798. His victory at the Pyramids* broke their power, but they still proved very troublesome for a number of months. Admiration for their soldierly qualities induced Bonaparte to take one, Roustam,* for his personal bodyguard, and on 13 October 1801 he ordered Rapp* to organize a squadron of Mamelukes, up to 150 men. They retained their splendid Oriental dress but were commanded by French officers, and eventually became closely associated with the *chasseurs-à-*

cheval of the Imperial Guard,* forming part of Napoleon's escort. The formation was disbanded in 1814.

Mantua, sieges of, 1796–97. The focal point of the First Italian Campaign from May 1796 was the great city and fortress of Mantua on the river Mincio. Set among marshes, Mantua was notorious for its fever (probably malaria), but its garrison, initially comprised of some 13,000 Austrians with 500 cannon, was to hold out against Bonaparte for over eight months. The first French siege—or rather blockade —began on 4 June when Sérurier* sealed off the city with 9,000 troops. Early in July the French siege guns arrived before the defenses, but when General Würmser* advanced from Trent at the head of a new army to relieve the garrison, Bonaparte was forced to abandon the siege and spike most of his guns on 31 July in order to concentrate his outnumbered army.

After the French successes at Lonato* and Castiglione,* Würmser fell back up the Adige valley, but not before resupplying Count d'Irles (the governor of Mantua) and raising his strength to 15,000 men. The second French siege was imposed on 24 August and some headway was made against the suburbs of San Giorgio and La Favorita, but then a new crisis arose as Würmser set out a second time down the Brenta valley, determined to overthrow French ambitions in the Po valley. Bonaparte again took determined action, defeating the Austrians at Caliano and Bassano,* but after the last-named defeat Würmser led 12,000 men westward and forced his way into Mantua, assuming command of the defense. The presence of 23,000 Austrian troops within Mantua posed vast problems for the French, and when Würmser led a large sortie on 15 September, two days after his arrival, this was only repulsed with difficulty by Generals Kilmaine* and Mas-

sena*—although the Austrians lost 4,000 men and 27 guns in the breakout attempt.

As General Alvintzi* made his bids to regain North Italy in November 1796 and January 1797, Bonaparte managed to continue the prosecution of the siege despite the preoccupations with the Austrian field forces which led to the respective victories of Arcola* and Rivoli.* The last-named battle (14 January 1797) effectively dashed all hopes of Mantua being relieved, but an Austrian force under General Provera* fought its way as far as La Favorita before being crushed on the 16th. At last Würmser surrendered to Sérurier on 2 February 1797 and marched out at the head of 16,000 survivors. Over its length, the siege had cost at least 7,000 French and 18,000 Austrian lives, mostly from disease. This event freed Bonaparte's hands, and he at once assumed the offensive and advanced into the Frioul to challenge the Archduke Charles,* and ultimately to secure an armistice at Leoben.*

Marchand, Général Jean Gabriel, comte (1765–1851). A lawyer by profession, in 1791 he became a captain of volunteers. From 1792–99 he served in Italy, fighting at Loano (1795), Ceva,* and Caldiero* (1796), and was briefly a prisoner. As aide to Joubert* he was at his side when that general was killed at Novi* (1799), and in October that year he was promoted to *général de brigade*. After service on the Rhine, he served under Dupont* in 1805, fighting at Haslach,* Albeck, and Durrenstein* on the Danube before being posted to the Tyrol. Promoted to *général de division* in late December 1805, next year he fought at Jena* and Magdeburg,* and in 1807 at Freidland.* In 1808 he was made a count and posted to Spain under Ney.* He fought at Mayorga, took part in the pursuit of Moore,* and in 1810 served at the sieges of Cuidad Rodrigo* and Almeida* as well as at

Marchand

the battle of Bussaco.* In 1811 Marchand fought at Fuentes de Oñoro* and the following year, during the invasion of Russia, served as Jerome Bonaparte's* Chief of Staff and later as a divisional commander under Ney, fighting at Smolensk* and Borodino.* In 1813 he was present at Weissenfels,* Lützen,* Bautzen,* and Leipzig,* and in 1814 was entrusted with organizing the defense of Isère as the Allies invaded France. After the abdication he was retained in service by the Bourbons, and in 1815 tried to oppose Napoleon's return at Grenoble*—but in vain. After the second Bourbon restoration he was court-martialed on charges of having relinquished Grenoble to Napoleon, but was acquitted. He retired from the service in 1825.

Marchant, Major General John Gaspard Le (1766–1812). First commissioned in 1781, he became a friend of George III* and was well thought of by that monarch. After service in the ill-fated Flanders campaign of 1793–94 under the Duke of York,* he was promoted to major in 1795. He devised a new exercise with the sword for the cavalry, designed an improved pattern of weapon, and was promoted to lieutenant colonel in 1797. He next became a strong proponent of the need for formal military training for young officers of infantry and cavalry, and held responsible posts in the institutions that preceded the opening of the Royal Military College Sandhurst in 1812, of which he was the first Governor. However, that same year saw him called to the Peninsula to take up command, as a major general, of part of Wellington's* cavalry, and at the battle of Salamanca* he was killed in action after breaking a French square.

Marengo, battle of, 14 June 1800. The crossing of the Alps completed, the First Consul set about procuring a favorable battle situation. Advancing south of the river Po, an Austrian detachment was defeated at Montebello* on 9 June, but the previous day Napoleon had learned of the surrender of Genoa* on the 4th—a dire event that released the whole power of General Melas'* main army to challenge the numerically weaker Army of the Reserve. As the Austrians began to concentrate around Alessandria, the First Consul ordered a rapid advance over the river Scrivia toward the town and its neighboring village of Marengo. Unaware that all of 31,000 Austrians were nearby, on the 13th Napoleon detached two divisions, one to move northward to watch the river Po crossings, the other, commanded by Desaix* (some 5,300 men strong), to maneuver toward Novi in case Melas made an attempt to fall back toward Genoa. These detachments reduced the Reserve's battle strength to 23,700 men and merely 23 cannon. But its commander did not anticipate that his foe might take the initiative and attack.

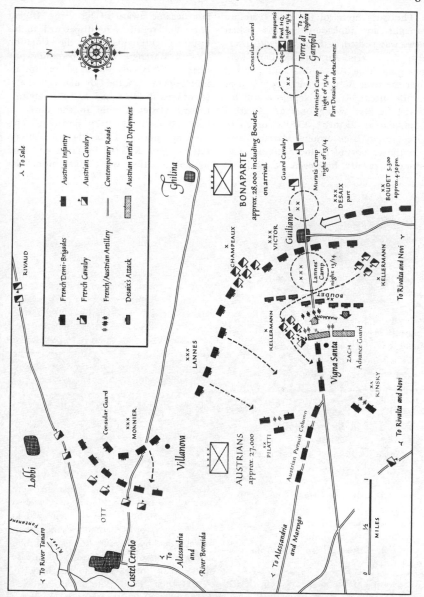

Battle of Marengo, 14 June 1800: The Afternoon Battle

The early hours of the 14th therefore brought an unpleasant surprise when news was rushed to French headquarters that three large Austrian columns were emerging from Alessandria and pouring over the river Bormida with every sign of hostile intent. At first Napoleon still believed he was facing only an Austrian bluff, but as Victor's* division began to give ground from around Marengo, despite the support of Lannes'* division and Murat's* cavalry, by eleven o'clock he at last became aware of his error. Urgent orders of recall were dispatched to his distant lieutenants, but the situation around Marengo was fast becoming precarious. Everybody was appealing for reinforcements, but the Consular Guard and Monnier's division had to be committed toward Castel Ceriolo in the north to head off General Ott's* threatened outflanking move. Thus there were no reserves whatever left by 11:30 A.M., and to make matters worse ammunition was

Battle of Marengo

running low. Fortunately a slight respite was earned between midday and 1:00 P.M. as the Austrians regrouped their triumphant forces for a new all-out effort against the tiring French.

When fighting resumed, the French line again began to give ground, particularly in the southern sector near Marengo. If its cohesion broke, a telling defeat would ensue. Confident that the day was as good as won, Melas handed over the battle to General Zach at 3:00 P.M. and retired to

rest in Alessandria. At almost the same moment, however, a mud-spattered General Desaix spurred up to the First Consul. "This battle is completely lost," declared the newcomer. "However, there is time to win another."

Fortunately Desaix had been held up during his morning march by floods, and consequently when the cannon opened fire at Marengo he was still not out of earshot. Without awaiting orders, Desaix at once ordered his column to retrace its

steps toward Marengo, and this intelligent act would prove the salvation both of the French army and of Napoleon's military reputation. By 5:00 P.M. the tired troops of Boudet's* hard-marching division were close at hand, coming up from the south. Zach proved dilatory in launching his *coup de grâce,* and this delay gave the newcomers just sufficient time to deploy behind Victor's shattered command on the French left wing.

Napoleon ordered Desaix to counter-attack without delay. Marmont* brought up a handful of guns, the younger Keller-mann* arrived at the head of his cuirassiers, and Boudet drew up his three *demi-brigades* in oblique order, the lead-ing and rearmost adopting *l'ordre mixte,* the central formation deploying in line. Desaix ordered the advance, but was almost immediately shot down near the hamlet of Vigna Sancta at the head of the attack. Boudet's men, staggered by this event, hesitated, but to the rescue came Marmont and his gunners. Rushing to the flank of the vast Austrian column that General Zach was belatedly getting under way, his cannon began to pour case-shot at point-blank range into the dense gray-coated masses. A lucky shot caused an Austrian ammunition wagon to explode. Stunned by the concussion, the Austrians hesitated, and sensing his mo-ment Kellermann charged home at the head of his handful of squadrons. The timing was perfect—and the psychological impact immense. Zach's 6,000 men began to shred away toward the rear, and the column degenerated into a mass of fugi-tives heading for the Bormida bridges, pursued by the bayonets of Boudet's jubilant infantry. The panic spread all along the Austrian line, and soon the whole force was racing for Alessandria, only Ott on the extreme left carrying out anything approaching a dignified retreat. The weary French battle-line surged for-ward and claimed the victory that had so nearly eluded their arms.

The Austrians lost almost 14,000 casual-ties (about half being taken prisoner). The French had lost at least 7,000 men—or a quarter of their total force (to include Boudet's men). The First Consul owed his success to Desaix's decision to return to the main army despite his orders, and to Marmont and Kellermann. He had been fortunate to avoid a telling defeat, which to some extent his early-morning rashness had invited. However, the abrupt reversal in the fortunes of war had taken all the resolve out of his opponents, and the next day Melas signed the Convention of Alessandria,* which restored much of North Italy to the French. The War of the Second Coalition* had still to be won by the French, but Marengo proved a telling blow.

Napoleon was determined that Marengo should hold a special place in the annals of his campaigns. It was his first major battle after becoming head of state, and therefore was important for political propaganda reasons. Over the years he insisted on a number of rewritings to the historians of the *Dépôt de la Guerre,* ad-justing the official record to cover up his mistakes and his great indebtedness to the dead hero, Desaix, and making it ap-pear that everything had gone according to his master-plan. This had not, in fact, been the case.

Marescot, Général Armand Samuel, comte, later marquis de (1758–1832). Com-missioned into the engineers in 1778, he was deeply involved in the defense of the northern fortresses in 1792, and in the capture of Antwerp. Next year he served with distinction before Toulon,* and in 1794 took an active part at the sieges of Charleroi, Landrecies, Valenciennes, and Condé, being promoted to *général de brigade* that September. After successfully conducting the siege of Maastricht the same November, he was made *général de division*. After service in the Pyrenees he helped defend Kehl in 1796, and successively held high engineer appointments in the Armies of the Rhine, Germany, England, and Switzerland. In 1800 he commanded the engineers in the Army of the Reserve, organized the passage of the Great St. Bernard Pass, besieged Fort Bard,* and was present at Marengo.* Supervision of the north coast of France's defenses was followed by service in Austria (1805). He was made a count in 1808 and conducted a survey of Pyrenean and Spanish fortresses. In July 1808 he helped negotiate the surrender of Dupont's* forces at Bailen,* and after repatriation was disgraced and imprisoned. Reinstated in 1814, he took no active part in the events of 1815 but was admitted to retirement in October of that year. Two years later he was made a marquis, and in 1819 a peer of France. He saw no further service.

Maret, Ministre Hughes Bernard, duc de Bassano (1763–1839). After conducting

Marie-Louise of Austria

many important diplomatic missions, Maret was created a duke in 1809, and from 1811–13 he was Minister of Foreign Affairs.

Marie-Louise of Austria, Empress (1791–1847). The daughter of the Emperor Francis I* and great-niece of Queen Marie-Antoinette, she was chosen, aged 19, by Napoleon to succeed the Empress Josephine* early in 1810. Marshal Berthier* carried out a marriage by proxy on 11 March that year at Vienna, and the young princess was transported to France. Despite her youth, her relationship with Napoleon became a very romantic one, and although she found it difficult to adjust to her new role as Empress at the Tuileries she earned her husband's gratitude by producing a son, the infant King of Rome, on 20 March 1811. Following Napoleon's abdication in 1814 she returned to Vienna with her son, and despite the Emperor's entreaties, never saw him again.

She was made ruler of the Italian principalities of Parma, Piacenza, and Guastalla by the Habsburgs, and took Count

Maret

Neipperg as her lover, subsequently marrying him in secret after Napoleon's death. She remained Duchess of Parma until the revolution of 1831, and after Neipperg's death married the Count de Bombelles, Master of Ceremonies at the Austrian court. Much criticized by her contemporaries for her neglect of Napoleon's son, the Duke of Reichstadt (or Napoleon II*), she was in fact an affectionate and sensible, but not overintelligent woman, who provided Napoleon with some genuine happiness during the four years of their effective marriage.

Marie Louises, les. Nickname given to the young conscripts, many of them in their middle teens, brought into the French service after the disasters of Russia and Germany. Despite their youth, they fought bravely and were devoted to the Emperor, but tended to be less capable of long marches than their predecessors.

Marmont, Maréchal Auguste Frederic Louis Viesse de, duc de Raguse (1774–1852). The son of a royalist officer, Marmont was commissioned out of the Châlons artillery school in 1792. After service in Italy, he came to Bonaparte's attention during the siege of Toulon.* Fighting under Desaix* at Mainz in October 1795, the next February he was appointed an aide-de-camp to Bonaparte and accompanied him throughout the Italian Campaign until October 1796, when he was sent back to Paris with captured Austrian colors. In 1798 he accompanied Bonaparte to the Orient and was provisionally promoted to *général de brigade* at Malta* in June after capturing the banner of the Knights of St. John. In Egypt he served in Bon's* division at the capture of Alexandria* and the battle of the Pyramids* and was a member of the select group chosen to return to France with his Commander in Chief. He played a part in the *coup d'état* de Brumaire, and was ap-

Marmont

pointed a Councillor of State by the First Consul.

In 1800, Marmont commanded the artillery at the battle of Marengo* with great skill and was promoted to *général de division* (still aged only 26) on 9 September. He fought in several more actions in Italy after the First Consul's departure for France, and signed the Armistice of Treviso in January 1801. Senior artillery posts followed, including command of the artillery in the camps around Boulogne* (1803–05), but he was not included among the original marshals, to his great chagrin, despite Napoleon's undoubted favor and his considerable talents.

In 1805 he was given command of the II Corps of the *Grande Armée* and fought at Ulm* and Weyer before being transferred to the Italian front. In July 1806 he was appointed Governor General of Dalmatia and drove the Russians away from Ragusa, a feat that was commemorated in the title of the dukedom awarded to him in 1808. Next year, again fighting in Italy and Croatia in command of the

XI Corps, he was wounded. Recalled to the Danube theater, he was in reserve at Wagram* in early July and went on to win the action of Znaim,* which earned him his long-coveted baton.

After two years in Illyria, in April 1811 he succeeded Ney* in command of the VI Corps under Massena,* and then became commander of the Army of Portugal in early May. In 1812 he fended off Wellington's* offensive into northern Spain with great skill, generally outmaneuvering him for a month, but overconfidence then led him to expose his army at Salamanca,* where he was severely wounded in the arm by a shell on 22 July. His wound took a long time to heal, and he saw no more active service until 1813. Commanding the VI Corps, he fought at Lützen,* Bautzen,* Dresden,* Leipzig,* and Hanau.* Early in 1814 he fought with skill at a number of engagements but was routed at Laon* in early March and earned Napoleon's severe censure. Falling back to the Heights of Montmartre,* he fought with skill alongside Moncey* and Mortier,* but then opened negotiations with the Allies and surrendered his corps on 5 April—the act of betrayal for which Napoleon never forgave him.

Louis XVIII* conferred on him a peerage of France, and understandably Marmont followed the King into exile in March 1815. After the second restoration, further honors were lavished upon him. He voted for the death sentence for Marshal Ney. In 1830 he played an equivocal part during the revolution of that year, and was effectively driven into exile, never more to return to France. He traveled to Russia, Turkey, Egypt, and throughout Italy, finally settling in Venice where he spent his last years writing his vindicatory *Mémoires.* He died there on 3 March 1852. A commander of considerable ability, his betrayal of Napoleon in 1814 left a permanent blot on his reputation,

and the verb *raguser* (to betray) entered the French language.

Marquisito, El, guerrilla leader. *See* **Porlier,** Colonel

Marseillaise, La. Revolutionary anthem, composed by Roger de Lisle, which the *fédérés* or volunteers chanted as they marched from Marseilles toward Paris in 1792 to offer their services for the defense of France. It soon became adopted as practically the national anthem of Revolutionary France, but Napoleon later banned its use as being excessively Jacobin in inspiration.

Marshalate, the. On 19 May 1804, Napoleon created 18 Marshals of the Empire. The rank of *maréchal* was technically an appointment rather than a rank, *général de division* remaining the senior promotion as such. Eventually, a total of 26 aspired to the honor, the last to be appointed being Grouchy* (3 June 1815). The original marshals, in alphabetical order, were Augereau,* Bernadotte,* Berthier,* Bessières,* Brune,* Davout,* Jourdan,* Kellermann,* Lannes,* Lefebvre,* Massena,* Moncey,* Mortier,* Ney,* Murat,* Perignon,* Sérurier,* and Soult.* On 13 July 1807, Victor* received his baton, and on 12 July 1809, Macdonald,* Marmont,* and Oudinot* were admitted to the hallowed band. On 1 July 1811, Suchet* became a marshal, as did Gouvion St. Cyr* on 27 August 1812. In 1813 Poniatowski* was created marshal on 16 October, three days before his death on the last day of Leipzig.* Most, although not all, members of the Marshalate received princely or ducal titles, and vast grants of money and other privileges.

Martin, Vice Amiral Pierre, comte (1752–1820). Born in Canada, he early adopted a maritime career and for many years served as a quartermaster on various vessels, becoming sailing-master of *Le Magnifique* for the naval campaign of d'Estaing in American and West Indian waters (1778–1781). He was commissioned in March 1788 and became a naval lieutenant in 1792 and captain the following February. The same November saw him promoted to rear admiral, and from February 1794 he commanded part of Villaret-Joyeuse's* Mediterranean fleet based in Toulon. He played a vigorous part in many forays against the Royal Navy, and in March 1795 captured H.M.S. *Berwick* (74 guns) but a week later lost two of his own vessels off Cape Noli and returned to Toulon. He briefly engaged Admiral Hotham* off the Iles d'Hyères on 13 July 1795, but broke off the action after the explosion of one of his ships. Promoted to vice admiral in March 1796, Martin commanded the naval forces at Toulon until October 1797, when he handed them over to Admiral Brueys.* He subsequently held various senior posts ashore at Rochefort from 1801–10, the year he was made a count. He was unjustly blamed for a naval disaster off the Ile d'Aix and was retired in late 1814. During the Hundred Days* he was restored as Maritime Prefect, but was finally retired by the Bourbons on 1 August 1815.

Massena, Maréchal André, duc de Rivoli, prince d'Essling (1758–1817). Destined to become one of the ablest generals of the Empire, Massena was born in Nice, the son of a trader, but was brought up by an uncle, a soap manufacturer. Aged 13 he went to sea as a cabin boy, but in 1775 he switched to a career in the army of *l'ancien régime,** being made a sergeant as early as 1777 (aged only 19), and seven years later he became a sergeant major. These appointments clearly indicated some military talents, but in 1789 he was discharged and re-entered civilian life. For a while he reputedly followed

Massena

the calling of smuggler as well as trading in fruit at Antibes. In 1791 he became a member of the National Guard and was rapidly elected lieutenant colonel of the Volunteers of Var (February 1792).

For the next six years he served with the Army of Italy, receiving rapid promotion. Made *général de brigade* in August 1793, his services at Toulon* earned him provisional promotion to *général de division* the same December—a rank confirmed nine months later. A period of illness interrupted his service in 1794–95, but served with distinction in the mixed Campaign of 1795, winning his first battle near Lonato* in June. Next March the Army of Italy passed under command of Napoleon Bonaparte, whom Massena had known a little in 1793, and he soon came to respect him as both general and man. During the brilliant campaign that followed, Massena played a central role in almost every phase and battle, fighting at, among others, Montenotte,* Lodi,* Castiglione,* Bassano,* Caldiero,* Arcola,*

Rivoli,* and in several operations near Mantua.* Somewhat worsted at First Dego* and Caldiero, he played a vital part at Rivoli (which would eventually be commemorated in his dukedom, March 1808), and at La Favorita, the last operation before the capture of Mantua, which earned him the nickname of *"l'enfant chéri de la Victoire"* from Bonaparte. He carried the terms of the Preliminaries of Leoben* to Paris.

After a period of relative quiescence, in April 1799 he took command from Jourdan* of the French forces in Switzerland, and soon found himself facing the great Russian General Suvorov* and his Russo-Austrian army. Massena's victory—the second battle of Zurich* in late September—proved his ability in independent command and did much to restore French fortunes in the War of the Second Coalition,* which up to that point had been going badly. Early in 1800 he became commander of the Army of Italy and was soon closely besieged in Genoa* by Melas* and the Austrians. He held out with the greatest intrepidity amid appalling conditions, but shortly before the First Consul could arrive to his relief from the Po Valley he was compelled to capitulate (4 June 1800) and was granted the honors of war. Marengo* followed, and when Napoleon returned to Paris he left Massena to command both the Armies of Italy and of the Reserve.

This appointment only lasted two months, for his barefaced plundering (an aspect of his character that persisted throughout his life) cost him his command. He retired for a while to Rueil and from 1803 became a member of the *Corps Législatif*, but it would be war rather than politics that would continue to claim his services.

Appointed a marshal in 1804 in the first such creation, the next year he was reappointed to command the Army of Italy, and while Napoleon was marching on Ulm* and Austerlitz,* Massena was fighting the Archduke Charles,* capturing Verona, and fighting an indecisive battle at Caldiero.* Recalled to the Grand Army, he briefly commanded the VIII Corps before being sent off to command against Naples in late December. Invading the Bourbon kingdom, he captured Capua and Gaeta and later attacked Calabria.

In January 1807 he was somewhat unwilling to be recalled to the Grand Army in Poland, where he took over the V Corps from Lannes.* One reason for his recall was the vast fortune he had accumulated in Naples—which Napoleon saw fit to confiscate. In July he obtained leave and returned to Rueil once more.

On 11 April 1809 Massena took over the IV Corps of the Army of Germany and proceeded to add further luster to his reputation in the weeks and months that followed. He fought with distinction at Landshut,* Eckmühl,* Ebersperg,* Aspern-Essling* (where he held the Aspern sector with skill and covered the retreat of the army onto the Isle of Lobau), and —despite a serious injury when his horse fell and rolled on him—at Wagram* (commanding the left wing), and at Znaim.* In November he was allowed back to France, and in January 1810 was made Prince of Essling. April brought an appointment to command the Army of Portugal, which eventually brought him face to face with Wellington.* The Campaign of 1810 in Portugal began propitiously enough with the capture of Ciudad Rodrigo* and Almeida,* but Ney* and Junot* proved awkward subordinates, while the presence on campaign of his mistress, Mme. Leberton,* disguised as a dragoon officer, was another complication. His bloody repulse by Wellington's Anglo-Portuguese Army at Bussaco* in late September proved the start of one of the least satisfactory periods of his military career. Surprised to find the British and their Allies impregnably positioned within the Lines of Torres Vedras,* an autumn and winter of increasing frustration followed. In March 1811 Massena was compelled to begin a retreat toward Spain, and by late April the only French post still held within Portugal was Almeida. Advancing to attempt its relief, Massena found Wellington again facing him at Fuentes de Oñoro,* and in the resultant battle the French were worsted. The result of this reverse was a recall to France and the end of truly active employment. In 1813 he was made governor of the 8th Military District at Toulon, and after unwillingly rallying to Napoleon in 1815, he commanded the Paris National Guard. After Waterloo,* he was military governor of Paris for a few days in July, but was then replaced by the Bourbon regime. He died in Paris on 4 April 1817, aged 59.

As a commander of men, Massena had shown great ability, not devoid of cunning and boldness. As a man, his greed and passion for women were legendary—and insatiable. As a general, Wellington once admitted at a meeting that "We were pretty even."

Massenbach, Colonel Rudolf (fl. 1806). An expert but unstable member of the Prussian staff, Massenbach produced a profusion of unlikely plans for the army and served as Chief of Staff to Prince Hohenlohe* during the disastrous Campaign of 1806. That commander's failure to attack the outnumbered Lannes* on the eve of Jena-Auerstädt* is laid at his door, and also the eventual surrender of the Prince—for no adequate reason—at Prenzlau at the height of the French pursuit. His nickname of "the evil genius of Prussia" is probably a trifle unjust, but he was certainly a liability to his superiors.

Maximilian-Josef, Elector, later King, of Bavaria (1756–1825). The son of a French general, he had become a *maréchal de camp* (1778) before the Revolution, but he retired to Mannerheim. In 1795 he became Elector of Bavaria and carried out many reforms. In 1801 he ceded certain territories west of the Rhine to France, and joined the League of the Rhine four years later. He allied himself to the Empire and his troops served in the Austerlitz* campaign. After the Peace of Pressburg* he assumed the title of King, and remained loyal to Napoleon until after Leipzig;* in late 1813 he signed the Treaty of Ried with the Allies. In 1817 he gave his country a constitution.

Maya, battle of, 25 July 1813. After Vitoria* the Allied army advanced to besiege San Sebastian* and Pamplona,* intent on removing the last French posts from Spanish soil. To guard against a French attempt to relieve their garrisons by a foray over the Pyrenees, Wellington* placed forces to watch the main passes—including Lieutenant General Sir William Stewart, under Lord Hill's* overall command, at Maya.

Marshal Soult* planned a double breakthrough, by way of the Roncesvalles* and the Maya Pass. The latter was entrusted to Drouet d'Erlon's* corps of three divisions aided by National Guardsmen, perhaps 20,000 in all. Advancing cautiously from Urdax, the French attacked at 10:30 A.M. on 25 July and soon drove in the British picquets. Stewart was some miles distant at the time, so command devolved upon Brigadier General Pringle, newly arrived from England, who fed his brigade into the fight from the valley unit by unit. He was aided by Cameron's brigade, and three battalions from Dalhousie's* 7th Division later made an appearance, but this only amounted to 6,000 men in all.

Pringle held up Darmagnac's division

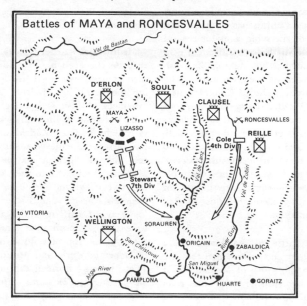

Battles of MAYA and RONCESVALLES

to the right of the road up the pass, but in the end was forced back. This left Cameron to withstand three French divisions; his men also lost ground, but at 2:00 P.M. Stewart arrived to take over command. A second position was taken up on a knoll overlooking a bend in the road, and a fierce fight raged over four Portuguese guns, which ultimately passed into French hands. By 3:00 P.M. the French were massing for the kill, when the opportune arrival of the three battalions from the 7th Division caused them to pause, wary of a British trap. The battle accordingly died away, and at 8:00 P.M. the British drew off southward toward Sorauren.* They had lost 1,347 casualties and inflicted some 2,000. But the French were free to continue their advance toward Pamplona.

McGrigor, Sir James, Baronet (1771–1858). After studying medicine at Aberdeen and Edinburgh universities (qualifying in 1788), he became surgeon to the Connaught Rangers in 1793 and saw service in Flanders, the West Indies, and India, and then in Egypt (1801) as superintending surgeon. In 1809 he was made Inspector General of hospitals, and in 1811 became Wellington's* head of medical services in the Peninsula. Despite fairly severe disagreements with his chief, he was knighted in 1814 and then served as Director General of the British Army Medical Services from 1815–51. He was made a baronet in 1830.

Medical Services. Provision of medical care for the sick or wounded was still rudimentary in most armies. A surgeon and a mate were attached to each battalion or equivalent formation but, with rare exceptions, were not luminaries of their profession. In the French army some progress was made on the insistence of Baron Larrey,* who introduced specially designed ambulance wagons, but the chances of surviving a major wound were only one in three—septicemia, gangrene, and blood poisoning, together with surgical shock, being the great killers. The British hierarchy included Commissioners for Sick and Wounded as well as surgeons and apothecaries general, and such officers as Dr. James McGrigor* (despite Wellington's* criticisms) gave selfless and efficient service in the Peninsula. Certain French senior officers—for example Marshal Davout*—earned reputations for misappropriating medical funds allotted to their commands.

Medellin, battle of, 29 March 1809. Marshal Victor* and 18,000 men took up a position to the south of Medellin near the Portuguese frontier with the river Guadiana to the rear, and there awaited the attack of General Cuesta* and the 24,000 Spaniards of the Army of Estremadura. Although outnumbered overall, the French had more cavalry and guns than their opponents. Cuesta advanced along a four-mile front, hoping to turn the French flanks, but the French fell coolly back to a compact position where Victor had determined to make his stand. Then the French hussars charged the Spanish lancers on Cuesta's left and they fled, taking more Spanish cavalry along with them. Cuesta was dismounted and almost captured, but was extricated with difficulty. His infantry, astounded by the collapse of their cavalry, was then charged by French dragoons at the right psychological moment, and the whole Spanish army dissolved into a mass of fugitives. Perhaps 10,000 Spaniards were killed or captured in the rout that followed. However, Cuesta somehow rallied his survivors, and Spanish resistance became more intractable on the popular front than ever. Later in the year Cuesta would fight

alongside Wellesley* at the battle of Talavera.*

Medina Del Rio Seco, battle of, 14 July 1808. As the French strove to re-establish their control over northern Spain following the revolt in Madrid* and in the provinces, Marshal Bessières,* charged with pacifying Galicia and keeping the vital highroad from Madrid to Burgos and France secure, achieved a substantial success against Spanish patriot forces at Medina del Rio Seco in the plain between the rivers Douro and Esla. Faced by Generals Cuesta* and Blake* commanding 24,000 Castilians and Galicians who were strongly positioned amid entrenchments at the top of a slope, the divisions of Generals Merle and Mouton*—barely 12,000 strong—stormed the position with the greatest *élan,* and after a fierce struggle, swept away Blake's Army of Galicia in full flight. Cuesta's refusal to commit his Castilian troops (about one quarter of the whole Spanish force) was partly to blame for this disaster. However, news of General Dupont's* disaster at Bailen* a bare week later would soon end French rejoicing.

Melas, General Michael Friedrich Benoit (1729–1806). Austrian soldier, born at Radeln in Transylvania, he entered the Habsburg forces in 1746. He saw considerable service in the Seven Years' War and gradually advanced his career, until in 1799 he was appointed to command the Austrian Army in Italy. Initially his campaign against the French was crowned with success, and in 1799 he won battles at Cassovo and Novi.* In early 1800 he besieged Massena* in Genoa* and forced him to capitulate. Melas was preparing to invade Provence when Bonaparte's arrival over the Alps into the Po valley at the head of the Army of the Reserve compelled a change of plan. Defeated at

Marengo,* Melas eventually evacuated the Austrian troops from North Italy. In 1803 he retired from Habsburg service.

Menou, Général Jacques-François de Boussay, baron de (1750–1810). The son of an officer, he joined the comte de Provence's *carabiniers* in 1766 and was commissioned two years later. After service in the Legion of Flanders and a number of staff quartermaster appointments, he became a lieutenant colonel in 1787. In 1789 he was a deputy for the nobility at the States-General and held various appointments. Two years later he commanded a regiment of *chasseurs-à-cheval* in the Army of the Rhine, and was promoted to *maréchal de camp* in 1792 and to *général de division* the following year. After being severely wounded at the taking of Saumur he was allowed to retire in 1793, only to be recalled to the colors in 1795. After holding several staff posts he commanded the Army of the Interior from July 1795, but he was arrested for negotiating with the Parisian insurgents on the eve of the *coup d'état* de *Vendémiaire*. A military court subsequently acquitted him, and after a period of inactivity he joined the Army of the Orient in 1798, commanding a division. He received seven wounds at the storming of Alexandria,* and later became Governor of Rosetta and then of Alexandria. After the battle of Aboukir* he commanded the siege of the castle. He succeeded Kléber* in command of the Army of Egypt in June 1800, but was defeated by the British expeditionary force at Canope and Alexandria and surrendered there in August 1801. Returned to France, he held a number of administrative and political posts as well as military appointments of an administrative nature. In 1808 he became a Count of the Empire and was Governor General of Tuscany and later of Venice.

Metternich

Metternich, Clemens Lothar Wensceslas, Count, later Prince of (1773–1859). Born at Coblenz, the son of a diplomat, his career at Vienna was forwarded by his marriage to a relation of the Chancellor Kaunitz. In 1801 he was appointed Habsburg Minister at Dresden, and then at Berlin (1803–06). After Jena* he was sent as ambassador to Paris for three years and sought a *rapprochement* with France in the belief that this was where Austria's best interests lay. Recalled to Vienna, in 1809 he was Minister of Foreign Affairs and Chancellor, and negotiated a new peace with France after Wagram.* Soon he was arranging the marriage of Napoleon to Marie-Louise* and again believed that he had created a special relationship with France. The disasters of 1812, however, convinced him of the fragility of Napoleon's position, so in 1813 Metternich negotiated with Russia and Prussia and in August brought Austria into the War of the Sixth Coalition* against France at the end of the Armistice.* After Napoleon's first abdication, he reached the summit of his political influence at the Congress of Vienna. After the Hundred Days* he became the virtual master of Austria for 34 years and the arbiter of Europe, reinforcing Habsburg absolutism internally, and externally striving to crush the forces of revolutionary nationalism through the Holy Alliance and the Congress system. Until 1848 he achieved a remarkable degree of success in these ambitions, but in the "year of revolutions" he miscalculated the strength of liberal feeling in Vienna and Milan, and resigned on 13 March at the demand of a determined opposition. For a while he lived in exile in Holland, but in 1851 he was allowed to retire to live on his estates.

Michelsberg Heights, surrender of. *See* Ulm

Midi, La, Revolt of, June–December 1793. Stung into rebellion by the repressive acts of the Revolutionary Government in Paris, first Marseilles, then Avignon and Toulon* revolted against Paris and espoused the cause of the House of Bourbon. The Revolutionary Government sent forces to suppress the rising under Carteaux,* and in due course Captain Bonaparte would make his name at the siege of Toulon.*

Milhaud, Général Edouard Jean Baptiste, comte (1766–1833). After a period in the National Guard following earlier service in the Bourbon Army, Milhaud became a deputy in the Convention and served on numerous special missions as an extreme republican. Tiring of political duties, he resumed a truly military career in 1796, fighting at Bassano.* He took part in *Brumaire** (1799), and next year was promoted to *général de brigade.* He commanded light cavalry formations in

Italy, at Austerlitz,* Golymin,* and later at Eylau,* having been promoted to *général de division* in December 1806. In March 1808 he was made a count, and was transferred to Spain, where next year he fought at Talavera* and Ocaña.* In 1812 he was attached to the staff of the *Grande Armée,* and next year fought in numerous actions in Germany including Hanau,* commanding a corps of cavalry. In 1814 he was much employed, but retired from the service in January 1815. Recalled after Napoleon's return, he commanded a division of cuirassiers in the Cavalry Reserve at Ligny* and Waterloo.* His later years held varied fortunes, including proscription as a regicide, but he was pardoned in 1817. He finally retired from the Reserve in 1832.

Millesimo, battle of, 14 April 1796. This small Italian village, some 30 kilometers northwest of Savona in Liguria, was the scene of General Augereau's* success over an Austrian-Piedmontese detachment during the initial phase of the Campaign of 1796. Thereafter, trying to advance on Ceva,* Augereau was first brought to a halt at Cosseria Castle.

Miloradovitch, General Mikhail Andreivitch, Count (1770–1835). After service with Suvorov* in Italy (1799), Miloradovitch served with distinction against the Turks and held a command at Borodino* in 1812. In 1813 he helped defeat Vandamme* at Kulm.* Appointed Governor of St. Petersburg in 1819, he was shot during an insurrection in the capital.

Minas, General Francisco Espozy (1784–1836). Born in Navarre, in later life Minas became a celebrated guerrilla leader against the French, and was promoted to general in 1813. He later turned against King Ferdinand VII, but was able to return to Spain in 1820 and was deeply involved in defending Barcelona* during the French invasion of 1823 and later in the Carlist wars. His nephew, Xavier (Minas the Younger, 1789–1817) also fought the French but was captured in 1810 and imprisoned at Vincennes until 1814.

Miranda, General Francisco (1752–1816). After service in the Spanish South Americas and under Rochambeau in the American War of Independence, Miranda moved to France in 1792, fought at Valmy,* and held a command in the Army of Belgium, occupying Antwerp (November 1792), having been promoted to lieutenant general the month before. However, defeats led to a series of charges and his career became a sorry tale of arrests, trials, and periods of exile. In 1806 he returned to the New World, and with Simon Bolivar he attempted the first risings in Venezuela (1806 and 1811). After being forced to capitulate in July 1812 he was imprisoned in Cadiz, where he died.

Mireur, Général François (1770–1798). A student of medicine who joined the Montpellier National Guard in 1789, he later served in the Army of the North and in Belgium. From 1795 he served on Bernadotte's* staff in the Army of the Sambre-et-Meuse, and next year after crossing the Rhine earned fame for his successful defense of the redoubt of Bendorf against heavy odds. Transferred with Bernadotte to the Army of Italy in 1797, he fought well at the passage of the Tagliamento in March and was promoted to *général de brigade* in April. Serving in command of a cavalry brigade in Egypt, he was killed near Damanhur on 9 July while riding from the camp to try out a new horse.

Missiessy, Amiral Edouard Thomas de Burgues, comte de (1756–1837). The son of a naval officer, he first sailed with his father in 1766. Twelve years later he served under d'Estaing during the War of

American Independence, fighting in several actions. A series of appointments and gradual promotion led up to the command of a frigate in the Mediterranean (1789–90) and the rank of full captain in 1792. Promoted to rear admiral in 1793, he was nevertheless arrested as a suspected nobleman in June, and was only fully cleared two years later. A series of important administrative appointments led to command of the Rochefort squadron (1804), and next year he was sent to the West Indies as part of the plan to lure the Royal Navy away from the Channel prior to the intended invasion. He relieved the French garrisons of Guadeloupe and Santo Domingo* and attacked Santa Lucia, but despairing of his intended link-up with Villeneuve* and Ganteaume* he returned to Rochefort in July 1805. In command of the Scheldt squadron from 1808, in both 1809 and 1814 he took a leading part in the defense of Antwerp. Appointed a count in 1811, he took no part in the Hundred Days.* After a number of high administrative commands under the Bourbons he retired in April 1832.

Mockern, battle of, 16 October 1813. *See* **Leipzig**

Mohrungen, action of, 25 January 1807. Marshal Buxhowden's* sudden attack in mid-winter compelled Napoleon to leave winter quarters in Poland and assemble his army. As Bennigsen* advanced, his advance guard under General Markov encountered Bernadotte's* retreating forces (or part of them) near Mohrungen at about noon on the 25th. With only parts of Dupont's* and Drouet's* divisions available (some 9 battalions and 11 squadrons in all), Bernadotte boldly decided to attack the position adopted by the Russians on some low heights north of Mohrungen. A cavalry engagement ended indecisively, but then Bernadotte attacked frontally, summoning Dupont to envelop and attack the Russian right wing. The main body made progress, but only as darkness fell did Dupont enter the action. The Russians were conceding the day when new fighting in a defile to his rear caused Bernadotte to retrace his steps, arriving just in time to drive off a mass of Russian cavalry that had surprised his baggage train in the streets of Mohrungen. Had Markov summoned aid earlier, Bernadotte might well have been doomed; as it was, each side lost about 2,000 casualties (including some 360 French prisoners captured in the Mohrungen surprise). Two weeks later would be fought the ghastly battle of Eylau.*

Molitor, Maréchal Gabriel Jean Joseph, comte (1770–1849). After serving as a volunteer in 1791, he was commissioned that August and after service on the Rhine, Moselle, and Danube fronts, he was made *général de brigade* in July 1799. He fought with distinction in Switzerland, repulsing Suvorov* at Naefels on 1

Molitor

October that year. In 1800, after fighting at Stockach,* he was again promoted. From August 1805 he served under Massena* in Italy, fighting at Caldiero* and occupying Dalmatia. He was made governor of Swedish Pomerania in April 1807 and took part in the siege of Stralsund.* Made a count in June 1808, next year he distinguished himself at Aspern-Essling,* occupying Lobau Island, and at Wagram.* From 1810–13 he held commands in the Hanseatic towns, Hamburg, and Holland, fought in the defense of Troyes under Macdonald* (1814), and commanded National Guards under Rapp* in 1815. He was made Inspector General of Infantry by the Bourbons and in 1823 fought in command of a corps in Spain, earning his marshal's baton. In 1847 he was appointed Governor of the *Invalides,* and he died in that office.

Mollendorf, Field Marshal Richard J. H. von (1724–1806). Born at Lindenberg, he made his reputation during the Seven Years' War, fighting with distinction at Leuthen and Torgau. He was made a general officer in 1762, and King Frederick William II made him a field marshal in 1793. The following year he commanded the main Prussian army in the field against the French, and defended Kaiserslautern from 23 May to 20 September in a notable siege. In 1806 he was senior commander in the field, but was mortally wounded at the battle of Auerstädt.*

Moncey, Maréchal Bon Adrien Jannot de, duc de Conegliano (1754–1842). The son of an advocate, he joined the Bourbon army in 1769, secured his discharge in 1773, but re-enlisted for two more years in 1774, serving in the *Gendarmes Anglais*. First commissioned in 1779, he was made captain in 1791, and from 1793–95 fought in the Pyrenees with great distinction. Provisionally promoted to *gén-*

Moncey

éral de brigade in February 1794, in under four months he was made *général de division,* and in August captured San Sebastian.* He was made commander of the Army of the West Pyrenees, a post he held until the autumn of 1795. After the *coup d'état* de *18 Fructidor* (1797) he was suspended as a suspected royalist, and remained on the unemployed list until 1799.

In 1800 he received a command in Switzerland but was transferred to the Army of the Reserve in North Italy and held various appointments there until August 1801. Made Inspector General of Gendarmerie by the First Consul, he accompanied Napoleon to the Low Countries. In May 1804 he was one of the original members of the Marshalate.*

Four years later he led III Corps into Spain, was created *duc* in early July, and served under Lannes* at Tudela* as well as during the siege of Saragossa.* He saw little action from 1809–14 but held high posts in Belgium and France. In 1814, however, he was appointed to command

the Parisian National Guard, and on 30 March fought at their head against the Allies at Clichy in the suburbs. Napoleon made him a peer of France during the Hundred Days,* but he seems to have taken no active part. However, after Waterloo* he refused to preside over Ney's* court-martial and was imprisoned for three months. He was restored to his rank and honors in 1816 and was soon in favor with the Bourbons once more. In 1823 he commanded the IV Corps and conquered Catalonia, winning several successes over General Minas.* Next year he was appointed Governor of the *Invalides.*

Mondego Bay, landing at, 1–8 August 1808. The area between Figueira da Foz and the sandy littoral to the south of the Rio Mondego, not far from Coimbra in Portugal, was the scene of the landing of the first British troops to enter the Peninsular War.* The force had sailed from Cork on 12 July under Lieutenant General Sir Arthur Wellesley;* Mondego Bay was selected for the landing because the neighboring fort was already in friendly Portuguese hands. On 1 August 8,500 troops and three artillery batteries were put ashore through the boiling surf, which claimed a number of lives. Stores took longer to land, but by 8 August some 13,500 men and 30 guns were ashore. Next day the expeditionary force set off for Leiria in conjunction with the patriots of Bernardino Freire,* ready to seek out the French forces of General Junot.* The road would lead to Roliça* and Vimiero.*

Mondovi, battle of, 21 April 1796. After the battles of Dego* and Ceva,* General Bonaparte pursued the retreating Piedmontese with vigor, leaving Massena's* division to hold off the Austrian forces of General Beaulieu.* With barely 13,000 men under command following their earlier setbacks, the forces of General

Colli* were faced by some 25,000 French troops, avid for booty. General Sérurier* launched three columns against the town's defenses and cleared the Piedmontese out of their positions. Two days later the French prepared to march on Turin, but the same day King Victor Amadeus II asked for terms, and on the 28th the Armistice of Cherasco* was agreed, ceding control of Piedmont to the French.

Monge

Monge, Ministre Gaspard, comte de Péluse (1746–1818). A Burgundian by birth, Monge studied at Beaune and then Lyons. After teaching mathematics at the military school of Mézières, he moved to Paris and was soon nominated to the Academy of Sciences. He welcomed the Revolution wholeheartedly, and in 1792 became Minister of Marine under the patronage of the Girondins. He survived the Terror* and busied himself founding the *Ecole Polytechnique*. In 1798 he was one of the *savants* selected to accompany the Army of the Orient to Egypt; the following August, he and Berthollet*

were selected to return with General Bonaparte to France. Elected a senator, Monge spent the rest of his days encouraging education and in writing learned works on mathematics, algebra, and geometry.

Montagu, Admiral Sir George (1750–1829). Himself the son of an admiral, George Montagu became a naval lieutenant in 1771 and was promoted to commander two years later. He saw much active service during the War of American Independence, earning a distinguished reputation. Promoted to rear admiral in 1794, he failed to intercept a French provision convoy but was nevertheless appointed vice admiral in 1795. Made a full admiral in 1801, he was Commander in Chief at Portsmouth for several years from 1803. He was awarded the Grand Cross of the Order of the Bath in 1815.

Montbrun, Général Louis-Pierre, comte (1770–1812). He first joined the cavalry in 1789, and was commissioned in 1794. Much service in Germany followed, with

Montbrun

steady promotion. From 1803–05 he was stationed at Bruges, but in 1805 accompanied Davout's* III Corps to the Danube and fought at Austerlitz.* In December he was promoted to *général de brigade.* Service in Naples and Silesia followed, and in 1808 he was made a baron. Next year he was promoted to *général de division,* served under Bessières* at Eckmühl,* and was made a count in August 1809. In 1810 he was placed in command of the cavalry in Massena's* Army of Portugal and served at Almeida,* Bussaco,* and Fuentes de Oñoro.* When Marmont* took over the army from the discredited Massena, Montbrun won the action of El Bodon.* He later served on the east coast of Spain. Recalled to France in 1812, he marched into Russia with the *Grande Armée* and was killed at Borodino.*

Montebello, battle of, 9 June 1800. Pressing ahead with the advance guard of the Army of the Reserve, Lannes* advanced from Pavia with 6,000 men and met the Austrian General Ott* at the head of 17,000 men and 35 guns. Lannes was at first repulsed, but Victor* arrived with 6,000 and enabled Lannes to resume the offensive and win the day, inflicting 4,000 casualties and suffering 500. Lannes later became duc de Montebello.

Montenotte, battle of, 12 April 1796. Advancing from the Ligurian coast to drive a wedge between the Austrian forces of General Beaulieu* and the Austro-Piedmontese forces commanded by General Argenteau, Bonaparte fell upon the latter's 6,000 troops with 9,000 French in the early hours of 12 April. La Harpe's men attacked frontally, while Massena* moved through the hills to turn the enemy right wing. Argenteau tried to evade the trap too late, and was scattered after losing 2,500 casualties. The French had thus secured the central position, and

marched on toward Dego.* This was General Bonaparte's first victory in the First Italian Campaign.

Montevideo, storming of, 1806. *See* **Buenos Aires**

Montereau, battle of, 18 February 1814. After his successes against the Army of Silesia along the river Marne at Champaubert,* Montmirail,* and Vauchamps,* Napoleon hastened back to the river Seine to confront the Army of Bohemia, which was threatening Paris from the southeast. Some French units marched 60 miles in under two days to check Prince Schwarzenberg's* advance at Mormant. The Austrians at once began to fall back, leaving the Prince of Württemberg* to cover the withdrawal at Montereau, at the confluence of the rivers Seine and Yonne. Marshal Victor* was dilatory in appearing before the town and was replaced by General Gérard.* The French massed guns to silence the Austrian batteries, and then launched a devastating attack on the town which captured both key bridges. The Allies lost 6,000 casualties and 15 guns, the French lost some 2,500 men. Napoleon was disappointed with the scale of the success, but the Army of Silesia had indubitably been repulsed and was heading back for Troyes in disarray.

Montholon, Général Charles Tristan, comte (1783–1853). This enigmatic and possibly sinister figure was educated at Brienne and later served as a brevet officer in Italy. It is known that he did serve as aide-de-camp to Joubert,* Championnet, Augereau,* Macdonald,* and Berthier* in turn between 1800 and 1809, and was appointed an Imperial chamberlain in late 1809. In 1812 he led a diplomatic mission to Würzburg, but was recalled in disgrace when his marriage to Albine de Vassal was revealed. Although he claimed to have been promoted to

Montholon

général de brigade in 1811 and to have been made a *général de division* on 15 June 1815 before serving as Napoleon's aide during the Waterloo* campaign, there is little evidence of these promotions and appointments, and it seems that he never became more than a colonel during the Napoleonic wars. He owed his employment to the influence and intrigues of his stepfather, and his claims to five wounds suffered in action are hard to substantiate. Nevertheless, fraud or no, in 1815 he was chosen, with his wife, to accompany Napoleon to St. Helena,* where he remained until the Emperor's death. He made many enemies among the rest of Napoleon's entourage, and one after another they were sent back to France. There is some circumstantial evidence that he may have been implicated in attempts to poison Napoleon on the orders of the

duc d'Artois. As an executor of Napoleon's will he eventually received a substantial sum, and his publication of the *Mémoires de Sainte Hélène*, contentious and plagiarized though most of them are, brought in more money. Nevertheless, he was frequently financially embarrassed; and despite the favor showed to him by the House of Bourbon and above all by Louis-Philippe, he joined Louis-Napoleon in his ill-fated *coup d'état* in 1840 and was imprisoned after its failure. He emerged in 1847 and was elected a deputy in the National Assembly.

Montmartre, action of, 30 March 1814. The Allied Armies of Silesia and Bohemia united at Meaux on 28 March and planned their culminating advance on Paris. With only the weak forces of Mortier* and Marmont* facing them—perhaps 23,000 men in all—and the defenses of the French capital in a very incomplete state, the 107,000 Allies made predictable progress toward their objective from the eastern and northern sides. Marshal Moncey* at the head of the National Guard made a brave stand at Clichy, but the two main corps were driven back by 4:00 P.M. to the heights of Belleville (held by Mortier) and the suburb of Montmartre (held by Marmont). Here what was to prove the final action of the Campaign of 1814 took place. At 2:00 A.M. on the 31st, Marmont opened negotiations with the Allies, and the train of events leading to Napoleon's first abdication were set in motion.

Montmirail, battle of, 11 February 1814. Following his repulse of Olssufiev on the 10th at Champaubert,* Napoleon marched west along the north bank of Le Petit Morin at the head of his small but determined army to confront corps of Sacken* and Yorck,* each some 18,000 men strong. Passing through Montmirail with 10,500 troops—basically the Old

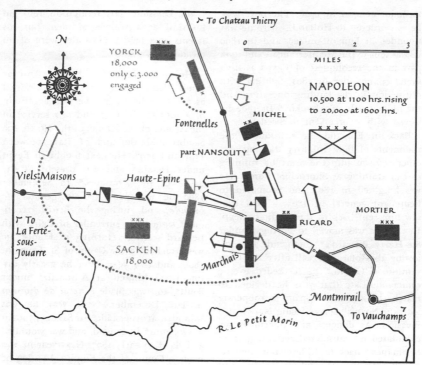

Battle of Montmirail, 11 February 1814

Guard and a few conscripts under General Ricard together with 36 guns—the Emperor sent in the latter against Sacken's corps which was trying to fight its way eastward to Montmirail, and posted further forces to watch for Yorck's expected arrival from the north. Fortunately Yorck was slow in appearing, and the arrival of Mortier's* Corps by 4:00 P.M. raised Napoleon's strength to 20,000. Now Napoleon could switch to the offensive, and soon Sacken's Russians had been badly beaten as Yorck's Prussians were repulsed by Mortier. The Allies lost 4,000 men and the French 2,000 casualties. Napoleon had badly shaken the Army of Silesia, and he continued the trend three days later at Vauchamps.*

Moore, Lieutenant General Sir John (1761–1809). The son of a Glasgow doctor, Moore was educated in part by accompanying the Duke of Hamilton on the Grand Tour. He was commissioned in 1776 and served in the American War of Independence. In 1784 he became an MP and in 1790 was promoted to lieutenant colonel. He was sent on a mission to Paoli* in Corsica in 1794 and aided in the conquest of the island. Serious dissensions with his naval and military superiors led to his recall to England in 1795, but he was shortly made a brevet colonel with local rank of brigade general. Service under Abercromby* in the West Indies ruined his health and almost caused his death, but he survived and was promoted to major general in 1798. The next year he was ordered to Holland, where he was wounded at Egmont-on-Zee, and in 1800 he was sent to the Mediterranean and took part in the reconquest of Egypt as divisional commander in 1801, fighting with distinction in the landing operation and the night battle of Aboukir.* In 1802 he served with a force sent to Sweden.

Back in England, he introduced the rudiments of light infantry training and other reforms into the army by running special training at Shorncliffe Camp. He was knighted in 1804 and promoted to lieutenant general in 1805, a year that saw him sent back to the Mediterranean. In 1808 he was moved to Portugal under Sir Harry Burrard's* command, and following that officer's recall after the Convention of Cintra,* he succeeded to the command. Late that year he decided to march the army into Spain to cooperate with the Spanish forces facing Napoleon's invasion. As dangers and difficulties accumulated he considered retreating from Salamanca* back to Lisbon, but then received news that Madrid was holding out against the French and that Marshal Soult's* command was widely deployed north of the capital and inviting defeat in detail. Consequently he moved deeper into Spain. In December he found that Napoleon had swung north from Madrid and had cut off his links with Portugal, and so Moore ordered the precipitate retreat to Corunna.* He held off the French pursuit despite bitter weather, and at length turned at bay at Corunna to face Soult and the French. In the battle that ensued the ragged British defeated the French, but Moore was mortally wounded and died. Although his strong Whig political leanings brought him some unpopularity with the home government, his training methods inspired a number of officers, and his Light Infantry Brigade ultimately became the

Light Division. His reputation rests on his skill as a trainer of men, but his talents as a field commander were of no mean order.

Morand, Général Charles Antoine Louis Alexis, comte (1771–1835). Trained as a lawyer he in fact became a captain of volunteers in 1792 and saw service in the Armies of the Rhine, of the North, the Sambre-et-Meuse, and of Italy between 1792 and 1797. He next fought in Egypt under Desaix* and was present at the battle of the Pyramids.* In September 1800 he was promoted to *général de brigade,* and during the British reconquest signed the surrender of Cairo with Belliard.* After returning to France, he was attached to the Camp of St. Omer in 1803, and two years later he greatly distinguished himself at Austerlitz* under Soult* and was made *général de division* in late December. Next year he was wounded at Auerstädt* in Saxony, fought at Golymin* in Poland, and was wounded at Eylau* in early 1807. Next year he was made a Count of the Empire. In 1809 he fought on the Danube at Abensberg,*

Morand

Eckmühl,* Ratisbon,* and Wagram,* where he was again wounded. In 1812 he commanded a division of Davout's* I Corps in the invasion of Russia, fought at Smolensk,* and was gravely wounded at Borodino.* In 1813 he served at Lützen,* Bautzen,* Dennewitz,* and at Hanau.* From December 1813 to April 1814 he commanded the defense of Mainz, before retiring to Fontainebleau. During the Hundred Days* he was made Napoleon's aide and commanded part of the Imperial Guard* at Waterloo,* recapturing Plancenoit from the Prussians. After retiring to the Loire he was exiled to Poland and condemned to death in his absence. On returning to France in 1819, however, he was acquitted and eventually retired in 1825, being made a peer of France in 1832.

Morard de Galles, Vice Amiral Justin Bonaventure, comte (1741–1809). After joining the Bourbon navy as a marine in 1757, a long career of service included one shipwreck and many expeditions before he was promoted to first lieutenant in 1777, and then to captain in 1781. With the coming of the Revolution* he was made rear admiral in January 1792 and vice admiral exactly one year later. He was cashiered and arrested as a suspected nobleman in November 1793, but was released and reinstated in March 1795. A short period in command of the Brest fleet was followed by appointment to the naval command in the projected expedition against Ireland, November 1796 to January 1797. Unfortunately his ship became separated from the rest in a fog, and by the time he reached Bantry Bay* the remainder of the fleet had abandoned the project and sailed for home. Thus General Hoche's* troops were never disembarked in Ireland. He later held a shore command at Brest, was made a senator in 1799, and a Count of the Empire in 1808.

Moreau, Général Jean Victor (1763–

Moreau

1813). The son of a lawyer, he was himself a legal student at Rennes, but in 1789 he formed an artillery company in the local National Guard and was appointed its captain. He transferred to a volunteer battalion as senior lieutenant colonel in 1791 and served under Dumouriez* in the Army of the North (1792–93). He distinguished himself at Neerwinden* and early in 1794 he was confirmed as a *général de brigade*. Within three months he was made *général de division* (April 1794). Patronized by Carnot,* his career continued to progress, and he succeeded Pichegru* as commander of the Army of the North upon that general's arrest in March 1795. Next year he was given command of the Army of the Rhine and Moselle, and advanced as far as the Danube before Jourdan's* defeat by the Archduke Charles* compelled him to retreat to the Rhine. However, his talents in the field were now widely recognized, and he further demonstrated them in Italy (1799), succeeding Joubert* in command of the Army of Italy after that officer's death at

Novi.* Transferred to the Army of the Rhine, in 1800 his conduct of the campaign and battle of Hohenlinden* won him fresh laurels. To some degree these successes—and the promptings of his over-ambitious wife—led him to overestimate his deserts, and although he supported Napoleon at the time of *Brumaire,** he soon began to constitute a rival to the First Consul, at least in the military sphere. He became involved in royalist intrigue, was imprisoned, and then exiled after the institution of the Empire. From late 1804 until 1813 he lived in the United States at Morrisville on the Delaware River, but was then induced to return to Europe by representatives of Tsar Alexander.* He accompanied the Tsar as military adviser during part of the Campaign of German Liberation, but was mortally wounded at his side at the battle of Dresden* and died five days later. A brilliant soldier, his political acumen was poor.

Mortier, Maréchal Adolphe Edouard Casimir Joseph, duc de Trévise (1768–1835). The son of a cloth merchant and half-English by birth, he studied at Douai before joining the National Guard of Dunkirk in 1789. In September 1791 he was elected a captain of volunteers and fought in the Army of the North at Jemappes* and Namur and in 1793 at Neerwinden* and then at Fleurus* (1794). He was then transferred to the Sambre-et-Meuse, distinguishing himself at Maastricht and the crossing of the Rhine. In 1797 he refused promotion to *général de brigade* but eventually received the rank in 1799. Service in Switzerland under Soult,* including the battle of Zurich,* earned him Massena's* recommendation, and in October he was confirmed as *général de division*. In early 1800 he was posted to a Paris appointment.

In 1803 he was sent by the First Consul to occupy Hanover, accepted the surrender

Mortier

of its army in July at Artlenburg, and in early 1804 was made colonel general of the Artillery and Sailors of the Consular Guard. He received his baton with the original creation of the marshalate* in May. In 1805 he was given command of the infantry of the Imperial Guard.*

During the Campaign of 1805 he commanded a provisional corps, earning great distinction at Durrenstein* against great odds, and after Austerlitz* he took over command of Lannes'* V Corps. A period in Paris followed, but in late 1806 he was appointed commander of the VIII Corps and with it conquered Hesse and Hanover. At Friedland* (1807) he commanded the left wing of Napoleon's army, and next year he was created Duke of Treviso.

From October 1808 he commanded the V Corps in Spain, fighting at Somosierra* and at the siege of Saragossa.* Later, under Soult's overall command, he fought at Arzobispo* and Ocaña,* where he was wounded. Service in Andalusia followed, including the siege of Badajoz,* and then in May 1811 he was recalled to France.

In 1812, appointed commander of the

Young Guard, he fought at Borodino* and was made governor of Moscow, but he refused to blow up the remains of the city when the retreat began. He fought at Krasnöe* and the Beresina* and assumed overall command of the remnants of the Imperial Guard in January 1813. During the campaign in Germany he again commanded the Young Guard at many battles, including Lützen,* Bautzen,* Dresden,* and Leipzig.* Next year he commanded the Old Guard at Montmirail,* Craonne,* and Laon* and then took part in the last stand before Paris. He was reconciled to the Bourbons.

The next year Mortier rallied to Napoleon after escorting Louis XVIII* from Lille to the frontier, but he fell ill at Beaumont and took no active part in the Waterloo* campaign. He unwillingly agreed to serve at Ney's* court-martial, but after this court declared itself invalid he was briefly in disgrace, then restored to a command in January 1816. In later years he served as ambassador to St. Petersburg (1830 and 1832), and in 1834 he was briefly Minister of War. On 28 July the next year he was killed by a bomb at a parade of the National Guard.

Moscow, French occupation and burning of, 1812. On 14 September, seven days after the battle of Borodino,* the French occupied an almost deserted Moscow. Kutusov* had ordered the abandonment of Russia's religious capital without a further struggle. Sebastiani's* cavalry, with Murat* to the fore, was the first into Moscow. Napoleon entered on the 15th and took up quarters in the Kremlin, but that very day fires broke out in several parts of Moscow—almost certainly the work of Russian incendiaries—and a two-day conflagration began in which three quarters of the city (but not the Kremlin quarter) was destroyed. Much looting surrounded these events. Plenty of quartering

remained for the French army, but a slowly growing awareness that Tsar Alexander* would not negotiate a peace and of his exposure far from Paris induced Napoleon to order the abandonment of the city on 19 October. The celebrated retreat had begun.

Mouton, Maréchal Georges, comte. See **Lobau**

Muffling, Major General Carl von, Baron (fl. 1815). A Prussian officer who, as a colonel, served as Blücher's* Subchief of Staff during the Waterloo* Campaign. He was Prussian liaison officer joined to Wellington's* staff over the critical days, and was instrumental in bringing in General Thielmann's* corps to reinforce the Allied left wing at the last crisis of the battle of Waterloo.

Muiron, La, French frigate. This vessel was used by General Bonaparte to bring him and a very select group of companions home from Egypt in 1799. In company with the frigate *La Carrère,* she sailed on 22 August under command of the flotilla leader, Admiral Ganteaume, and reached France after a voyage of 47 days.

Munro, Major General Sir Thomas, Baronet (1761–1827). A soldier who spent most of his career in India from 1780 and who contracted a lasting friendship with Colonel Arthur Wellesley,* later Duke of Wellington,* during his years in the subcontinent. He completed his career as Governor of Madras (from 1819), and was made a baronet for services in connection with the First Burma War.

Murad Bey (1750–1801). Together with his fellow-Bey, Ibrahim,* he was leader of the Mameluke* warriors caste effectively ruling Egypt in the late 18th century. He led the annual pilgrimage from Egypt to Mecca. Defeated with the Mameluke army at the battle of the Pyramids* by Bona-

Russian Campaign of 1812

St Petersburg

N

SKOFF

Velikye-Luki

otsk

Viesseldorp
Brilli
Sembin
Stachov
Borisov
Ucholodi
Sabashevitshi
Janikivi
Kostritsa
Studienka
Kamienska
Bobr
Tolotchino
Loshnitsa
Usha
R. Berezina

Inset to show
enlargement to twice linear
of River Berezina area.
See lower centre

Suraje
Vitebsk
Ostronovo
Biechenkowski
shashniki
Roudnya
Lyosno
Inkovo
Smolensk
Valutino
Lubino
Solovievo
Prudichevo
Yelna
Slavkovo
Viasma
Gzhatsk
Isarevo
Fiodoroivoskoy
Gridnevo
Mojaisk
Borisov
Vereja
Borovsk
Medyn
Afonassova
Kaluga
R. Oka
Maloyaroslavets
To Kolumna
Tarutino
Vinkovo
Voronovo
Oshigovo
Troitskoye
Desna
Pachra
Motsha
Borodino
MOSCOW

nen
Rudnia
Rosasna
Danikova
Vyrokorense
Krasnoe
Dubrovno
Kopiss
Orsha
Kochanov
nka
Kamienska
br
vitshi
ha
Mohilev
bobruisk
R. Dnieper

MILES

0   50   100   150

parte in 1798, he later quarreled with his Ottoman superiors and refused to take part with them in the fighting that culminated in the battle of Heliopolis. Pursued by Desaix* into Upper Egypt, he long eluded his pursuers, at the head of about 5,000 mounted warriors, from Cairo to Aswan and back. On 14 March 1800 he made an agreement with General Kléber,* ruler of Egypt after Bonaparte's departure. He died of plague in 1801 on his way to join General Belliard's* garrison of Cairo, but he may have been preparing to join General Hutchinson's British forces.

Murat

Murat, Maréchal Joachim, prince et roi de Naples (1767–1815). The twelfth child of an innkeeper, he was intended for the church but joined the cavalry as a trooper in 1787 as a way to escape his creditors after accumulating heavy debts. For one month in 1792 he was a member of Louis XVI's* Constitutional Guard, but then he reverted to the 12th Chasseurs and was commissioned *sous-lieutenant* in October that year. The energetic and self-confident young cavalryman then served with the Army of the North (1792–93). Known to be an extreme Jacobin at this time, he was almost purged after the *coup d'état* de 9 *Thermidor,* but he was reinstated by the Committee of Public Safety. On 4 October 1795 he was sent by Bonaparte to bring 40 guns from the park at Sablons, and thus played an important role in the suppression of the *coup d'état* de Vendémiaire. This earned him promotion and the appointment of senior aide to General Bonaparte for the First Italian Campaign. Promoted to *général de brigade* on 10 May 1796, he served with distinction, commanding a cavalry brigade under General Ney* and fought at the battle of Tagliamento* in March 1797. Next year he commanded a brigade of dragoons in Egypt, and in 1799 led a battle-winning charge at the second battle of Aboukir,* being seriously wounded in the jaw. He

was promoted to *général de division* on the battlefield. He returned with his master to France and helped Bonaparte in the crisis of *Brumaire,* thereby earning command of the Consular Guard. The next January he married Caroline Bonaparte.* His fortune was now made.

In 1800 he commanded the cavalry of the Army of the Reserve and fought at Marengo,* later receiving a saber of honor in recognition of his bravery. He was sent to occupy Tuscany, and after driving the Neapolitans out of the Papal States he signed an armistice with the King of Naples and commanded the army of observation in southern Italy. He held a number of appointments in various parts of Italy until June 1802. Two years later he was appointed governor of Paris, arranged the court-martial of the duc d'Enghien,* and was made a marshal on 19 May. He was made Grand Admiral and given the title of prince on 1 February 1805.

Murat played a prominent role in each of the great campaigns that now began. Commanding the cavalry reserve, he hounded the Austrian and Russian armies in the Danube valley, and if he earned

Napoleon's censure for his rash occupation of Vienna and for his acceptance of Bagration's* proffered armistice at Hollabrunn,* he also earned his praise for the bold capture of the Vienna bridge and for his conduct at Austerlitz.* On 15 March 1806 he became Grand Duke of Berg and Cleves. He fought at Jena,* headed the pursuit of the discomfited Prussians, occupied Erfurt and Prentzlau, and forced Blücher* to surrender at Lübeck. When the army turned east to seek out the Russians, he occupied Warsaw and fought at Golymin* in late 1806. The following February he saved the day at Eylau,* leading a vital charge to check the Russian advance, and later fought at Guttstadt and Heilsberg* before taking charge of the siege of Königsberg, which surrendered to him on 16 June 1806. He was present at Tilsit.*

In February 1808 he was appointed the Emperor's Lieutenant in Spain, and he repressed the Madrid rising of 2 May. Bad health forced him to give up this appointment, but upon his recovery he was appointed King of Naples on 15 July, replacing Joseph Bonaparte.* He was proclaimed King in Naples on 1 August and later captured Capri, but he failed in an expedition against British-occupied Sicily (1809). The next three years he spent in his kingdom, taking his royal role seriously.

In 1812 Murat left Naples to command the cavalry in the invasion of Russia, often commanding the advance guard, and fighting at Ostronovo,* Smolensk,* and Borodino.* He entered Moscow* late on 14 September. He had earned an almost mystical respect among the Russian Cossacks, but allowed himself to be fooled by Kutusov,* who launched a surprise attack against his positions at Vinkovo.* The long retreat followed, and when Napoleon left the army at Smorgoni* on 5 December to return to Paris he appointed Murat to command the survivors of the *Grande*

Armée. He brought the army back through Vilna, Kovno, Königsberg, and Elbing, but then handed over command to Eugène Beauharnais* on 18 January and returned to Naples.

Early in 1813 he opened secret negotiations with England and Austria, but in August he rejoined Napoleon and commanded the cavalry in Saxony, fighting at Dresden,* Wachau, and Leipzig.* He returned to Naples, ostensibly to raise new forces but in fact to reopen negotiations with the Allies, and in January 1814 he agreed to provide 30,000 to fight against France in return for a guarantee of his throne and possessions. Some fighting in North Italy followed, and he compelled Eugène to abandon the line of the Adige. After Napoleon's abdication he found that neither Metternich* nor the British were prepared to honor their obligations, and in 1815 he sought to regain Napoleon's good opinion by attempting to raise North Italy on his behalf. In fact this premature move still further annoyed his brother-in-law, who refused to employ his services. Defeated at Gaeta, he fled to France but was ordered not to travel to Paris. On news of Waterloo* reaching him at Lyons he eventually regained Italy by sea, but was arrested after a skirmish at Pizzo in Calabria and was tried, condemned, and shot half an hour after sentence, meeting his fate with customary courage and panache.

Murat was one of the most colorful figures of his time. His military talents on the battlefield, at the head of the cavalry, were considerable, but his rash initiatives robbed him of any chance of earning repute as a strategist. A vain and rather brainless man, given to devising splendid uniforms, he had many enemies among the marshalate but was greatly admired by the rank and file for his dash and undoubted charisma. He became the model for many another *beau sabreur* of the 19th century.

Nansouty, Général Etienne Marie Antoine Champion, comte de (1768–1815). Educated at Brienne and the *Ecole Militaire** in Paris, Nansouty was commissioned into the cavalry in 1785. In March 1792 he became lieutenant colonel of the 2nd *Chasseurs-à-cheval,* and from 1792–1801 served in the Army of the Rhine, being promoted to *général de brigade* in 1799 and fighting at Stockach* and Memmingen the next year. He became *général de division* in March 1803, served under Mortier* in Hanover, and after a spell at the Camp of Boulogne* was given the 1st Cuirassier Division under Murat* in August 1805, subsequently fighting at Wertingen,* Ulm,* and Austerlitz.* During the campaign in East Prussia and Poland he fought at Golymin* in late 1806 and at Eylau* and Friedland* (both 1807). Next year he became the Emperor's First Equerry and accompanied him to Spain and then back to Paris. In the Danube Campaign of 1809, again at the head of the 1st Cuirassier Division, he distinguished himself under Bessières* in all the great battles, including Aspern-Essling* and Wagram.* In 1812 he commanded the 1st Cavalry Corps in the Cavalry Reserve and fought at Ostronovo* and at Borodino,* where he was wounded in the knee. From July 1813 he commanded the Cavalry of the Imperial Guard,* fighting at Dresden,* Leipzig,* and Hanau,* where he was again wounded. In the same post he fought at La Rothière,* Montmirail,* and Craonne* during the Campaign of France

(1814). After the First Restoration he became an aide to the comte d'Artois, and captain lieutenant of the Grey Musketeers. He died in Paris on 12 February 1815.

Napier, Lieutenant General Sir Charles James (1782–1853). First commissioned in 1794, he was promoted to major in 1805 and served under Moore at Corunna,* where he was wounded and made prisoner. Exchanged the next year, he was posted to the Peninsula and fought at the Coa and Bussaco.* Promoted to lieutenant colonel in 1811, two years later he served against the United States. In 1822 he was in Greece during part of its independence struggle, but he declined the command of the rebels against the Turks. In 1837 he was made major general and in 1841 transferred to India, where he became famous as the conqueror of Sind in 1843, and thereafter as its gifted administrator. Promoted to lieutenant general in 1846, he retired from Sind the next year. Appointed to command in the Second Sikh War of 1849, he arrived back in India to find the war already over. Next year he resigned after a legal row arising from his suppressing a mutiny in the 66th Foot.

Napier, General Sir George Thomas (1784–1855). The brother of Sir Charles, he entered the army in 1800, becoming a captain four years later. He served under Moore* in Sicily, Sweden, and Spain. Made a major in 1811, he rose to become a major general 26 years later—the year he became Governor of the Cape of

Good Hope. Knighted in 1838, he was promoted to lieutenant general in 1846 and to full general eight years later.

Napier, General Sir William Francis Patrick (1785–1860). The younger brother of Charles and George, he joined the army in 1808, and in 1810 distinguished himself at the Coa. In 1819 he retired on half pay as a lieutenant colonel and began to work on his great history of the Peninsular War,* which was published between 1828 and 1840. Promoted to major general in 1841, be became lieutenant governor of Guernsey (1842–47). He conducted a long dispute with Beresford* over his portrayal of Albuera,* and also wrote several more books on his brother Charles' achievements in Sind.

Naples, King of. *See* **Murat**

Napoleon Bonaparte, Emperor (1769–1821). *NB: As practically every name mentioned in this key entry is treated elsewhere in this* Dictionary of the Napoleonic Wars, *it has been decided to suspend the practice of marking cross references with asterisks in this case.*

Napoleon Bonaparte

Of all the soldiers and rulers who have influenced the fates of nations and peoples through the millennia of recorded history, only two bear comparison with Napoleon—Alexander the Great and Genghis Khan. The range of Napoleon's abilities was immense, for besides his famous military achievements he was equally celebrated for his more constructive activities —codes of law and administrative measures—many of which have survived to the present day. Here was no common mortal, and this article can only indicate the main features in his dramatic career; for information on points of detail, the reader's attention is directed to the relevant entries that make up the greater part of this *Dictionary of the Napoleonic Wars*.

Napoleon's Early Years and Military Preparation. Napoleone Buonaparte (as he first spelled his name) was born at Ajaccio in Corsica on 15 August 1769, the second son of Carlo Buonaparte and Letizia (*née* Ramolino). His father was an impecunious lawyer of minor aristocratic connections but immense social and literary aspirations; he died in 1785 when Napoleon was 15. By that stage the family comprised *Madame Mère*, a strict and formidable figure, four other sons—Joseph (the eldest), Lucien, Louis, and Jerome and three daughters—Elisa, Pauline, and the baby of the family born in 1782, Caroline. No contemporary could have guessed that, of this numerous progeny, no less than four, excluding Napoleon himself, would one day wear crowns as rulers in their own right or as a Queen-Consort (Caroline), for in their earliest days the family circumstances verged upon genteel poverty.

In 1778 Joseph and Napoleon were sent to learn French at a preparatory school in Autun, and from there the latter proceeded to the school at Brienne for a state-supported education; he was soon noticed for his forceful temperament, ardent Corsican nationalism, and an aptitude for science and mathematics. In 1784 Napoleon transferred to the *Ecole Militaire* in Paris, and after a year's study he was commissioned into the *La Fère* artillery regiment. In the years that followed he served in a number of garrison stations, using his spare time for the intensive study of his profession and particularly military history and theory. The period he spent at Autun (1786) was probably the most formative of his life, under the benevolent tutelage and supervision of the commandant, Baron du Teil, who took a special interest in the young man. For the rest, long periods were spent on leave with his impoverished family in Corsica, and much of the support of his widowed mother and younger brothers and sisters fell upon the young officer's shoulders. He still remained an ardent Corsican nationalist.

The year 1789 saw the outbreak of the French Revolution. The young Napoleon welcomed the event and was present in Paris during the critical days of June and August 1792 which led to the fall of the House of Bourbon. He became deeply involved in the independence movement in Corsica, but after a bitter feud with his sometime hero, Paoli, he was compelled to leave the island with his family, whom he settled in the south of France.

So far his military experience had been limited to quelling a riot or two and serving in a fiasco of an operation against the island of La Maddalena off Sardinia. Now, in 1793, the siege of Toulon gave the captain of artillery the chance to rise from obscurity. For some months the famous city and naval arsenal was in British hands, but Napoleon—in his more-or-less self-appointed capacity of Director of Artillery to General Dugommier—executed a successful attack on the forts commanding the southwestern approaches to the town and harbor, and soon red-hot shot was compelling the British troops and fleet to evacuate their conquest (December 1793). Much of the credit for this success was justly paid to Napoleon, and he was promoted to brigadier general.

He spent much of the year 1794 campaigning in north Italy, gaining much local knowledge that would stand him in good stead two years later. But suddenly his whole future was placed in jeopardy. Following the *coup d'état* of 9th *Thermidor* in Paris, Napoleon, as a friend of the younger Robespierre, brother of "the Tyrant," was arrested and incarcerated in the Chateau d'Antibes. In typical fashion he spent his enforced leisure in study and the further formulation of his military ideas. Released in due course, he soon fell foul of the Revolutionary bureaucracy, which had a surplus of artillery brigadiers to employ, and long periods were spent kicking his heels in Paris, pressing for this or that decision. He became so disillusioned that he considered transferring his sword to the service of Turkey. Then he met the calculating politician, Paul Barras, a member of the Directory. On 5 October 1795, Barras employed Napoleon to defend the Convention against a march by royalist sympathizers. Sending a Captain Murat to bring guns from Sablons, the youthful brigadier soon sent the crowd about its business with the "whiff of grapeshot," and this broke, once and for all, the power of the Paris mob for a generation.

In reward for his services, the newly constituted Directory hastened to appoint their savior to command the Army of the Interior; but his eyes were already set on the Army of Italy, and in February 1796 he was transferred to its command in place of the incompetent General Schérer. Shortly before his departure for Nice, Napoleon married the widowed Josephine

Napoleon as General

de Beauharnais, Barras' cast-off mistress. He was now in his 27th year, and the opportunity for greatness lay just ahead, though few suspected it.

The Establishment of His Military Reputation and Rise to Power. The older generation of the Army of Italy received the "boy-wonder" and his staff of enthusiasts with considerable reserve and cynicism, but his promise of "honor, glory, and riches" kindled the imagination of the neglected rank and file. Between late March 1796 and October 1797, the long Italian Campaign unfolded through its many phases as a great success story, including victories at Montenotte, Millesimo, Mondovi, Castiglione, Arcola, Rivoli, and Mantua, which were among the most important. Little by little he perfected his strategic ideas and developed his battle techniques, but most of his victories were of a defensive

character, and a shortage of men deprived him of winning a really decisive battle at this stage. Nevertheless, he had so trounced a succession of Austrian generals by April 1797 that Vienna was induced to sign the preliminaries of peace at Leoben. The Directory, basking in their protégé's success and highly appreciative of the convoys of booty he frequently sent back to Paris, allowed him a surprisingly free hand, and he was entrusted with the negotiation of the Peace of Campo Formio in October the same year. Long before this his soldiers had come to practically worship *"le petit caporal,"* the hero of the bridges of Lodi and Arcola, and his officers were according him their fullest respect.

In December he returned to receive the plaudits of Parisian society (although some laughed at the lean and gangling young general, whom they nicknamed "Puss-in-Boots"), and he was elected a member of the Institute, France's most learned body. He was also appointed to command the "Army of England" massing on the Channel coast, ready to invade. Napoleon soon reported, however, that the Royal Navy's mastery of *La Manche* ruled out any chance of a successful invasion, and, loath to find himself condemned to inaction, he suggested instead the implementation of an attack upon Egypt, which would threaten Britain's commerce with the Levant and even the security of distant India. Once again he had his way, and in May 1798 Napoleon sailed from Toulon; in due course his expedition captured Malta and later, after narrowly missing Nelson's questing fleet, landed successfully in Egypt (1–3 July). The Battle of the Pyramids made short work of the feudal Mamelukes and won him Cairo, but Nelson's subsequent naval victory over the French fleet at Aboukir Bay (2 August) cut the expedition's links with France and greatly complicated Napoleon's task. Determined to forestall the impending Turkish counterattack, Napoleon invaded Syria in early 1799, but although he scattered the Army of Damascus at Mount Tabor, the defenders of Acre (aided by Commodore Sir William Sidney Smith RN) held out against all his efforts, and eventually forced the plague-ridden French to head back for Egypt over the Sinai desert. The army arrived in the nick of time to repress a rising in Cairo and to meet and destroy a second Turkish army sent from Rhodes at the land battle of Aboukir. The French position in Egypt was thus secured for the present.

Some time before this, however, Napoleon had secretly determined to leave his army and return to Europe, where the Directory was somewhat ineffectually trying to ward off the armies of the Second Coalition. He sailed, accompanied by a handful of friends, in great secrecy from Alexandria in August, and after a brief stormbound stay in Corsica (his last return to the land of his birth as it was to prove), he landed at Fréjus on 9 October after a near-brush with Lord Keith's battle fleet.

Napoleon's return to France coincided with the publication of his dispatches announcing the victory of Aboukir, and he found himself greeted with rapture by the populace. The Directory was distinctly icy in their attitude, however, especially as the overall war situation had taken an abrupt turn for the better with General Brune's victory at Bergen and that of Massena at Zurich. Nevertheless, all sections of the people were war-weary and disillusioned with the corrupt and inefficient Directory, and Napoleon, a born opportunist, found himself swept to power during the *coup d'état de Brumaire* (9 and 10 November 1799) as one of three Consuls. If his fellow conspirators, the Abbé Siéyès and Roger Ducos, had hoped to control their "sword" and retain him as a mere political nonentity they were soon disillusioned, for in a very few months their wily and ruthless colleague had maneuvered himself into the position of First Consul and induced his collaborators to retire into private life. Although he had not thought to climb so high so soon, Napoleon was now the *de facto* ruler of France.

To consolidate his hold on the country, it was vital to secure at least a temporary pacification, thus vindicating his reputation as the "Peacemaker of Campo Formio." The brilliant and rapid Second Italian Campaign of 1800 helped achieve this object. Placing himself (unofficially) at the head of the Army of the Reserve, he led his men over the Alps by the Great St. Bernard Pass to take the Austrian army in the rear, meeting them near Alessandria in the Po valley at the hard-fought battle of Marengo—a near-defeat for the French transformed into an important victory by the timely arrival of General Desaix's division at the crisis of the day (14 June). The same year saw General Moreau's success at Hohenlinden, which cleared the German front, and once again the crushed Habsburg court lost little time in negotiating the Peace of Leoben (1801). The Second Coalition having crashed in ruins, William Pitt resigned as Prime Minister of Great Britain, and his successors, despite the successful reconquest of Egypt, hastened to sign the preliminaries of peace, which were subsequently confirmed at Amiens in the spring of 1802.

For the first time in a decade France was at peace, and a grateful people showered honors on their deliverer. A plebiscite made Napoleon Consul for life, and he was sovereign in all but name. As great a statesman as he was a soldier, Napoleon proceeded to carry through a Concordat with the Pope (1801), thus returning (at least partially) republican France to the Catholic fold, and over a number of years he remodeled the national economy and administration of France. His greatest achievement was probably the Civil Code (1803–04). His popularity was fostered by his introduction of a system of civil and military awards, most notably the *légion d'honneur*, and was yet further increased by a number of royalist-inspired assassination attempts. These were used to foster a popular demand for a dynastic succession, and on 18 May 1804 Napoleon was duly proclaimed Emperor. The coronation was performed on 2 December, but although the Pope was brought to Paris for the ceremony, Napoleon symbolically insisted on placing the crowns on his own and Josephine's heads. He also had himself crowned King of Italy early in 1805. This was all a very far cry from the impecunious days of Ajaccio and Auxonne, but the new Emperor was barely 35 years old.

The Conqueror of Europe. Circumstances not wholly of Napoleon's making soon plunged Europe into a new series of bloody wars. Political, colonial, and commercial rivalries steadily mounted, but the legalized murder of the duc d'Enghien, a minor Bourbon prince, after his kidnapping from neutral territory, alienated much of influential European opinion once and for all and set the face of the old established dynasties against him. "It was more than a crime," opined Fouché, head of police, "it was a mistake." England, where William Pitt was once again at the helm, made the most of the opportunity to form the Third Coalition with Russia and Austria. War between England and France was declared as early as 1803, and Napoleon was soon massing 150,000 troops along the Channel coast for the "Project of England." This planned invasion was finally made impossible by Nelson's great naval victory at Trafalgar (21 October 1805), but months before that the newly rechristened *Grande Armée* was deep in central Germany, for Napoleon in typical fashion had weighed up the problems facing the invasion long before the naval battle and had determined to forestall his con-

Napoleon's Traveling Glass and Pocket Telescope

Napoleon as Emperor

tinental enemies before they could fully mass against him. By a brilliant strategic converging movement, Napoleon fell on the rear of General Mack's army with 210,000 men at and around Ulm, and forced him to capitulate in the field (20 October). Then the Emperor set out to catch the Russian Kutusov, but that wily general evaded his clutches and retired north of the Danube. Soon Vienna was in French hands, and Napoleon hounded his men northward after Kutusov, who was now heading for Olmütz to rendezvous with the Tsar and a second Russian army —a maneuver he successfully accomplished by late October. The French army was now at the limit of its advance and tiring rapidly, but with consummate mastery Napoleon tricked the Austro-Russian

army into attacking him to the west of Austerlitz (2 December), and the "battle of the Three Emperors" ended in cataclysm for the Allies when the French stormed the key Pratzen Heights in the center and thus sundered their opponents. The Peace of Pressburg resulted, by which Austria was obliged to cede her German and Italian possessions to France. From that moment, Napoleon's ambitions seem to have crystallized into a desire to re-create a vast West European Empire loosely patterned on that of Charlemagne. Thus Napoleon's aims became European at the very moment when his outstanding victory had finally set the seal on his hold over the French people.

These developing ambitions led to the hasty formation of a hostile Fourth Coalition, England once again serving as inspiration and paymaster, between Britain, Russia, and Prussia. The last named, however, for all its vaunted military reputation dating back to Frederick the Great, was eliminated after the *blitzkrieg* Campaign of 1806, which culminated in the double battle of Jena-Auerstädt (14 October), although peace did not follow. Instead, Napoleon had to fight a desperate winter campaign against the Russian armies, which survived the useless butchery of Eylau (2 February 1807) only to be decisively beaten at Friedland on 14 June. The Tsar was now eager to come to an arrangement with Napoleon, and following the famous meeting on a raft in the midst of the river Niemen near Tilsit, the two Emperors agreed to cooperate against England, and Prussia was forced to hand over territories to the west of the Elbe and in Poland. As a result of these treaties, the map of Europe was redrawn to include two new states, the Kingdom of Westphalia, awarded to Napoleon's brother Jerome, and the Grand Duchy of Warsaw, to fill the power vacuum left by Prussia's eclipse. Many historians regard

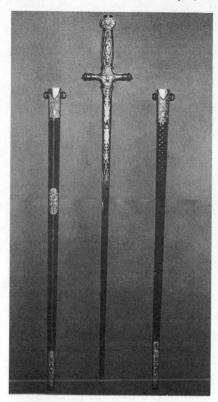

Napoleon's Court Sword

Tilsit as the high-water mark of Napoleon's career—his empire now stretched from the Atlantic to the Oder, from the North Sea to Sicily—but in fact various fatal decisions had already been taken which effectively dashed the hopes of a still-jubilant French people that a general European peace would ensue. These decisions were embodied in the Berlin and Milan Decrees, which enunciated an all-out policy of economic warfare against Great Britain. This, the so-called "Continental System," would prove the road to ruin for both France and its ruler.

Napoleon's aim was to ruin the British economy by closing all European ports to British trade. If the victorious Royal Navy could keep her shores inviolable, Britain's wealth appeared exposed to attack, and economic ruin would lead as inevitably as military conquest to the acceptance of a French-dictated peace, or so the Emperor hoped. In pursuit of this policy, Napoleon sent General Junot with an army to conquer Portugal (with a modicum of Spanish aid) in late 1807, with the intention of closing Lisbon to British trade and at the same time depriving her of England's "oldest ally." Next, unscrupulously seizing the opportunity proffered by the presence of his troops deep in Spanish territory, Napoleon abruptly turned on his erstwhile allies, the inefficient Spanish Bourbons, and induced the King to abdicate in favor of the Emperor's elder brother, Joseph. Within a few weeks the proud Spaniards rose in revolt, and a force under General Dupont was forced to surrender at Bailen. Meanwhile, an English army under Sir Arthur Wellesley was quickly sent out from the British Isles to exploit the new situation. After landing in Portugal, Wellesley swiftly forced Junot to surrender on terms and evacuate the country. These unanticipated events alarmed Napoleon, who held an emergency conference with Tsar Alexander at Erfurt (September 1808) in the hope of persuading Russia to watch an increasingly recalcitrant Austria while Napoleon turned his attentions to Spain. Napoleon rushed part of the *Grande Armée* to the Peninsula, and in a series of rapid strokes restored Joseph to the throne and defeated the Spanish armies. He then began to take steps to drive the British out of the Peninsula, but Lt. General Sir John Moore, Wellesley's successor, led the French a merry dance to Corunna, where the British were safely evacuated by sea. Several days before Moore died defeating Soult at Corunna

(16 January 1809), Napoleon had set out for France, summoned to Paris to face a new international crisis. He was never to return to the Peninsula, and he left his work undone, for thanks to Moore the southern part of the country, and Portugal, remained wholly unsubdued, and the British army would be able to return later in 1809 to reopen "the Spanish Ulcer," which would ultimately tie down between 200,000 and 300,000 French troops every year and cost them some 240,000 casualties by 1814. Thus one outcome of the Berlin Decrees was to provide Britain with a foothold on the Continent and impose a steady drain on French military resources. Here lay one root of eventual cataclysm.

Austria, meanwhile, had formed the Fifth Coalition with Great Britain and rashly undertook the invasion of Napoleon's ally, Bavaria. Napoleon's arrival on the scene transformed the situation, and soon the Archduke Charles found his armies defeated at Abensberg/Eckmühl and forced back over the Danube to the north bank, evacuating Vienna. Napoleon was almost defeated at the river-crossing battle of Aspern-Essling in May, but managed to cling to his narrow bridgehead in the Isle of Muhlau until large reinforcements could be summoned. He then proceeded to win the decisive battle of Wagram (July). Within a few weeks the Emperor Francis I was forced to sue for peace once more, which Napoleon quickly granted because of the questionable quality of his multinational army, the arrival of a British expedition in Walcheren, and signs of an incipient general German popular revolt. In October, by the Treaty of Vienna, Napoleon made peace with Austria, secretly agreeing to marry the Archduchess Marie-Louise of Austria after divorcing the childless Josephine, and exacting Austrian recognition of French rule over the Papal States,

Holland, Oldenburg, northern Hanover, and the Hanseatic towns. Territorial cessions also involved over three million Austrian subjects, and Austria agreed to exclude British trade. This campaign, however, had shown up a number of weaknesses in Napoleon's generalship, and it would seem that he was in the process of passing his prime as a commander.

Superficially, however, 1810 saw the First Empire at its peak in terms of size, grandeur, and apparent stability—but the cracks in the edifice were already becoming apparent to the discerning.

Decline and Fall. If the continuing struggle in Spain was one major reason for Napoleon's decline, his embroilment with Russia was indubitably a second. From Erfurt onward, Franco-Russian relations became increasingly strained over trade issues, the sudden marriage to the Austrian archduchess in 1810 following the divorce, the principality of Oldenburg (seized by the French in February 1811), intrigue over Poland, and the preferment of a French marshal, Bernadotte, to the position of Crown Prince of Sweden. Conciliatory overtures by both sides failed to make any progress, and from 1811 onward Napoleon was steadily building up a vast army east of the Oder. It seems he expected Alexander to come to terms at the mere threat of invasion, but in this the Tsar called Napoleon's bluff, and in June 1812 Napoleon had no option but to launch 600,000 men over the river Niemen into Russia. His armies were slower than formerly, and the Emperor could not adequately control all three plus two independent corps on the flanks, so the Russians were able to withdraw, trading space for time. "Scorched earth" and partisan activities began to affect French battle power as they advanced even deeper into Russia in search of the elusive major battle. The Russian armies managed to link up at Smolensk and then fell back to Borodino, where at last they turned to face the French. The resultant battle (7 September) cost many lives and was indecisive, but it delivered Moscow into Napoleon's hands.

Napoleon had hoped to find peace in Moscow, but he was to be disappointed. He had miscalculated Alexander's determination and the fervor of the Russian people. After several weeks of inaction around Moscow—which saw the burning of much of the city by incendiaries—he ordered the retreat. Repulsed unnecessarily from following a southerly route through Kaluga, Napoleon returned along his former line of advance, closely shadowed by Kutusov's armies. The weather turned from benign to deadly, and the retreat rapidly took on the overtones of an impending disaster. The army's cohesion began to crack, and deaths mounted rapidly. The crisis came late in November at the Beresina River line, but Napoleon proved capable of outwitting the Russian general and forced a crossing in a three-day action, but at further heavy cost. Almost 40,000 noncombatants perished at this point.

At this stage Napoleon learned of the Malet conspiracy in Paris and decided to leave his army. Quitting Smorgoni on 5 December, he was back in the capital 13 days later. His deserted army continued to wend its woebegone way back into Poland, but the Russian pursuit, which had never been very hard pressed by Kutusov and the main Russian army, slacked off. By early January, the last French survivor was out of Russia, but 570,000 of his comrades never recrossed the Niemen.

This disaster led to the War of German Liberation in 1813. As the Russians prepared to advance, Prussia threw off the French yoke and joined the Tsar, as did Bernadotte's Sweden. Napoleon somehow found another half million men by ruthless application of the conscription laws, but he never made good his losses of cavalry. In the campaign that followed in Germany, therefore, he was not able to exploit his successes won at Lützen (2 May 1813) or Bautzen (20 and 21 May); for their own purposes both sides proposed an armistice (2 June to 13 August), but it proved to France's detriment as Austria was persuaded to abandon her neutrality (since the spring) and join the Allies. The Allied commanders tried to avoid fighting Napoleon in person, concentrating on his detachments, but he forced a major battle at Dresden (26 and 27 August) where he administered a sound drubbing to Schwarzenberg's Austrians. This was counterbalanced by three smaller defeats elsewhere, however, and little by little the Allies converged on the main French army near the capital of Saxony. The resultant "Battle of the Nations" around Leipzig, 16 to 19 October, ended in a definite French defeat, and Napoleon was forced to withdraw his survivors to the west bank of the Rhine. Another 500,000 men had been swallowed up in central Europe, while away in Spain Wellington was now in full cry for the Pyrenees after decisively defeating Joseph and Jourdan at Vitoria. But still Napoleon would not admit defeat.

The Campaign of France lasted from January to April 1814. Faced by overwhelming numbers of Allied troops, and able to call upon the services of only scratch forces of conscripts and boy-soldiers, Napoleon performed wonders of defensive fighting, winning a series of minor battles on one sector after another. But the Allies were now aware of Napoleon's methods, and little by little they advanced on Paris. Then, in early April, the weary marshals mutinied against their old chief, and on 6 April 1814 Napoleon signed his first abdication.

Napoleon with the Old Guard Square at Waterloo

It seemed that Europe had found peace at last. While Napoleon set off for exile on the Island of Elba, Louis XVIII returned to Paris and the Allied statesmen met at Vienna to decide the readjustments necessary on the map of Europe. But as the months passed by, little was achieved, except that the Bourbons became increasingly unpopular in France itself.

Alerted to this development by his former friends, Napoleon decided to put everything at stake in one last gamble. Slipping away from Elba with 1,000 followers, he landed in France in early March. Successive forces sent to intercept him melted away as they came within range of the old magnetism, and on the 20th Napoleon was back in Paris, *de facto* ruler of France, while Louis XVIII was in flight for renewed exile. Slowly the aghast Allies remobilized their forces. For two months both sides prepared, but rather

than await his enemies around Paris as in 1814, Napoleon decided to use his slender resources in a desperate gamble against the only Allied armies currently assembled and in range—namely Wellington's Allied army and that of Field Marshal Blücher. On 15 June 1815, therefore, Napoleon launched *l'Armée du Nord* over the Sambre at Charleroi, and to a large degree surprised his adversaries. Unfortunately the initial momentum of his advance died away on the left, and although he won a considerable victory over the Prussians at Ligny on the 16th, Ney managed to bring off only a draw against Wellington's hastily assembled forces at Quatre Bras the same day. Wellington fell back toward Brussels, and, unknown to Napoleon, the Prussians retired parallel to their allies toward Wavre; on the 17th Napoleon himself failed to catch Wellington and force him to fight. At last on 18 June,

*Napoleon Bonaparte at the
Battle of Waterloo*

the great battle of Waterloo was fought near Mont St. Jean on a very restricted battlefield. Napoleon was slow to attack, and when the French did so, Ney threw away assault after assault through faulty dispositions, and Wellington hung grimly on, awaiting Prussian succor. It began to appear shortly after 1:00 P.M., thanks to Blücher's tireless efforts to help his friend, and by 4:00 P.M. a major Prussian attack on Napoleon's right flank and rear around Plancenoit was absorbing all of the Emperor's reserves and attention. About 6:00 P.M. Ney was at last about to crack Wellington's center near La Haie Sainte, but Napoleon could not send up the Imperial Guard to clinch the success until about 7:30 P.M. The famous attack that followed resulted in the repulse of the Middle Guard, whereupon the morale of the entire French army snapped, and it transformed itself into a horde of fugitives whose flight the Old Guard was hard pressed to cover.

Thus Napoleon's gamble ended in total failure, and within three weeks he was again compelled to abdicate as his ministers fell away once more. Condemned to

live out the remaining six years of his life on the remote and rocky island of St. Helena, Napoleon at last left the European stage forever. He died at Longwood on 5 May 1821. The flight of the eagle was over, but Europe would never again be the same, and the world would never see a greater soldier.

Napoleon II, François Charles Joseph Bonaparte, King of Rome (1811–1832). Napoleon's great desire for a son and heir was realized when the Empress Marie-Louise* gave birth to a boy on 20 March 1811. He was at once proclaimed as King of Rome. Aged only three, the young Napoleon left France forever in April 1814 at the abdication crisis of his father, and he was put under the guardianship of his grandfather, the Emperor Francis I.* He was given the title of Prince of Parma and, in 1818, created Duke of Reichstadt. He had briefly been recognized as Napoleon II by the Council of Five Hundred (*Cinq Cents*)* on 23 June 1815, and as such is

Napoleon II, King of Rome

regarded by all Bonapartists—including the Prince-President Louis-Napoleon when he assumed the title of Napoleon III in the mid-19th century. The young Prince was never allowed to communicate with his father on St. Helena, and his health rapidly deteriorated in Austria. Talk of making him King of the Greeks or of the Poles came to nothing, and *"l'Aiglon"* ("the Eaglet") died of tuberculosis on 22 July 1832 at the Schönbrunn.

Narbonne-Lara, Général Louis Marie Jacques Amalric, comte (1755–1813). Born in Italy, where his father was a court official to the Duke of Parma, he entered France in 1760 and later attended the Artillery School of Strasbourg, being commissioned in 1771. Promoted to colonel at age 25, at the Revolution he escorted members of the royal family to Rome. He was made *maréchal de camp* and held the post of Minister of War from December 1791 until March 1792, but his moderate views were denounced by the Jacobins and he was fortunate to escape, as an *émigré,** to England. After traveling in Switzerland and Germany he returned to France in 1800. A year later he was reinstated to the retired list in the rank of *général de division*. In May 1809 he was called for active service, made Governor of Raab, and later held a command at Trieste. Made a count in 1810, and an imperial aide-de-camp the next year, he was sent to Vienna as French ambassador in March 1813. His last appointment was as Governor of Torgau, where he died of typhus in November 1813.

Naval War, the. This complementary struggle to the campaigns waged on land was of the greatest significance to the course and outcome of the Revolutionary and Napoleonic Wars. At the outset, the French navy suffered from an exodus of officers, although the quality of their vessels was often superior to that of the Royal Navy. Britain entered the naval struggle aided by the Dutch and Spanish fleets—until 1795—and soon demonstrated its latent superiority. The loss of Toulon* to the British in August 1793 marked the nadir of French naval fortunes, and when Lord Hood* evacuated the port the same December all of 42 French naval vessels were burned. Then, under the inspiration of Jean Bon Saint-André,* a start was made on reconstruction. A purge of officers was instituted, and the first full trial of strength came with the battle of the First of June* (1794), in which Villaret de Joyeuse* lost the day but saved the convoy he was operating to protect. Thereafter the French navy abandoned democratic priorities in its choice of leaders and reverted to true professionalism.

By 1796 both Spain and Holland were allies of France, and French naval influence grew. An attempt to invade Ireland foundered at Bantry Bay* (December 1796), and a raid against Wales collapsed in February 1797. The same month saw Jervis'* great victory over the Spanish fleet off Cape St. Vincent,* but Britain's fortunes were low. Excluded from the Mediterranean, the unrest in the Royal Navy led to the critical Spithead* and Nore* mutinies. However, the morale of the fleet was not wholly on the ebb, as was demonstrated at the battle of Camperdown* during the same period, an engagement that destroyed a new attempt to launch an invasion of Ireland. The battles of St. Vincent and Camperdown restored the British naval ascendancy, and by the time of the collapse of the First Coalition* the French and their allies were largely blockaded in ports along the French, Dutch, and Spanish coastlines.

Meanwhile, the British policy of eliminating French colonies was both achieving results and causing problems. In 1794 British expeditions took possession of

Guadeloupe, St. Lucia, and the French part of Haiti,* thereby depriving France of many of the ports on which her West Indian trade depended, but the last-named success led to a native revolt led by Toussaint l'Ouverture.* Preoccupation with the need to defend India, together with the overrunning of Holland by the French and the subsequent treaty of alliance, led to further British expeditions to capture and occupy the Cape of Good Hope, Ceylon, Trincomalee, Pondicherry, and Malacca. Thus a stranglehold began to be applied to French and Dutch colonial trade, but the cost to Britain was far from negligible. By 1796, 40,000 troops had died—mainly of fever—in the West Indies alone, and the need to maintain garrisons in many far-flung outposts greatly reduced Great Britain's ability to mount serious operations on the continent of Europe.

The War of the Second Coalition* was dominated, from the naval point of view, by operations in the Mediterranean. Once the possibility of a French invasion of Britain or Ireland had receded in early 1798, all attention became focused on the voyage of the Army of the Orient from Toulon and other ports in May. Nelson* commanded a fleet sent out in pursuit, and although he twice missed the French at sea as they proceeded to capture Malta* and then head for Egypt, he at length caught up with Admiral Brueys* in Aboukir Bay* and destroyed his fleet at the battle of the Nile.* Thereafter General Bonaparte was largely isolated from France, and detachments of the Royal Navy under the overall command of Lord Keith* proceeded to harass the French invasion of Syria (as, for example, at Acre*) to prevent reinforcements from sailing down the Mediterranean, to support the force sent to regain Malta, and, ultimately, following Bonaparte's personal escape from Egypt

and return to France in late 1799, to prepare for and eventually mount the British invasion of Egypt under General Abercromby* which began in March 1801 and was completed by Hutchinson in September the same year.

Meanwhile, in the faraway Baltic, the Second Armed Neutrality,* which threatened to cut off Britain's vital sources of naval stores, resulted in Hyde Parker* and Nelson being sent to intervene, and the resultant battle of Copenhagen* (April 1801) led to its collapse that same year. The short-lived Peace of Amiens* proved no more than a brief respite in the Anglo-French struggle, and in 1803 hostilities were again resumed. Napoleon's apparent intention to mount a major invasion of the British Isles—as evidenced by the massing of troops in the Camp of Boulogne*—heightened the need for an effective Royal Naval blockade* of French and Spanish ports, but expeditions were nevertheless sent to capture Tobago and Guiana and to reoccupy St. Lucia and the Cape, while further forces were convoyed to India for the final elimination of French interests there. Other aspects of the naval war were also to the fore by 1805. Napoleon's attempts to interrupt British trade with the continent led to the British blockade of the Elbe and Weser, while the *guerre de course** reached a new intensity in the Channel.

However, the cross-Channel invasion possibility remained the dominant naval concern in 1805. Napoleon had collected 2,000 transports and 177,000 men facing England's shores, and British surveillance over the Texel, Brest, Ferrol, Cadiz, and Toulon reached a new intensity. In an attempt to divert the Royal Navy from the Channel, Villeneuve* broke out of Toulon in April, joined with a Spanish squadron, and sailed for the West Indies, pursued by Nelson. A general French naval concentration was planned to take place off Martinique, but when Ganteaume* (supposed to have broken out of Brest) failed to make the rendezvous and news of Nelson's approach arrived, Villeneuve sailed east hoping to unite with the squadron at Ferrol, bring Ganteaume out of Brest, and thereafter to clear the Channel. A chance encounter with a British brig in the Bay of Biscay alerted the Admiralty to Villeneuve's return, and a general fleet concentration was ordered off Ushant. A Royal Naval squadron under Calder* brushed indecisively with the French off Cape Finisterre on 22 July, and Villeneuve tried to head for Cadiz, but contrary weather blew him back into Ferrol. New orders from Paris drove Villeneuve to head for Brest once more, but he turned for Cadiz- instead. By this time (August) Napoleon had abandoned all thought of invading England, and Villeneuve was now instructed to sail to Naples. Nelson was waiting for him off Cape Trafalgar,* and on 21 October this decisive battle ended French aspirations to gain command of the seas.

Despite Trafalgar, the British government remained anxious about a possible future invasion threat, for French naval power remained considerable, though scattered. The danger of Napoleon assimilating neutral fleets led to the British seizure of the Danish fleet at Copenhagen in September 1807, and a similar operation in late November 1807 thwarted a French capture of the Portuguese navy in the Tagus. The strain of maintaining the blockade of European ports remained enormous, and the Continental System* and Orders in Council* stepped up the commercial and economic struggle.

Meanwhile the Royal Navy continued to eliminate hostile bases worldwide. In January 1806 General Baird* captured Capetown once and for all. The next month, naval operations off Santo

Domingo* crushed the remnants of the French West Indies squadron, and a similar success was scored in the Indian Ocean. British operations against Buenos Aires* and Montevideo* ended in failure (1806–07), as did an attempt to overawe the Sultan off Constantinople in March 1807, but these setbacks were offset by the capture of the Danish fleet in September and the occupation of Heligoland. The capture of Martinique and Santo Domingo in June 1809 were further successes, as were the seizure of Mauritius and Réunion in the Indian Ocean in late 1810.

The Royal Navy's most significant role after 1805, besides the maintenance of the blockade and the commerce war, was the support of anti-French operations on the continent of Europe. As early as June 1806, Sidney Smith* escorted a force to raid Calabria, culminating in the battle of Maida,* before evacuating the troops to Sicily. In July 1809 a larger force was convoyed on the ill-fated Walcheren* expedition. The major operation, however, was the movement of Sir Arthur Wellesley's* army to Portugal in 1808 and the subsequent maintenance and reinforcement of the British army in the Peninsula until 1814. Naval assistance in keeping Lisbon supplied was vital in 1810, and Sir Home Popham's* raiding force kept the north coast of French-occupied Spain in an uproar during 1812. Only in 1813, however, did the navy finally achieve total mastery over French coastal shipping and privateers,* and the transfer of Wellington's logistical base from Lisbon to Santander was made possible by control of the seas.

For the rest, the grinding upkeep of the blockades continued. The requirements of the British counter to the Continental System (most particularly the search of neutral shipping on the high seas) was one factor that led to the War of 1812* with the United States. Occasionally small

French squadrons escaped to sea and had to be hunted down, but the Royal Navy maintained the upper hand and all in all made a vital contribution to the ultimate defeat of Napoleon and the French Empire.

Neerwinden, battle of, 18 March 1793. After the execution of Louis XVI* the French government decided to forestall the inevitable international reaction and ordered General Dumouriez* to march into the Low Countries at the head of 45,000 men. He encountered the Austrian army of the Prince of Saxe-Coburg (effectively under command of the young Archduke Charles*), about 40,000 strong, at Neerwinden, 23 miles northwest of Liége. Dumouriez advanced in eight columns and attempted to turn the Austrian left but was repulsed in great disorder. Soon afterward Dumouriez defected to the Allies.

Nelson, Vice Admiral Lord Horatio, Viscount (1758–1805). The son of a Norfolk clergyman, Nelson entered the Royal Navy in 1770. Over the next 17 years he saw much service in the West Indies, and became a post captain in 1779. In 1787 he married a widow, Mrs. Nisbet, and then remained on half pay until 1793. In that year he was appointed to command H.M.S. *Agamemnon* in the Mediterranean, and the same August first met Sir William Hamilton, the British envoy at Naples, and his wife, Lady Emma. He served under the orders of Lord Hood* during the conquest of Corsica,* undertook the fortification of Bastia, and fought at the culminating action at Calvi, where some sand entered his right eye and eventually destroyed its sight (1794). From 1795–97 he commanded an independent squadron, harassing the French and Ligurian coasts and interrupting commerce, and was eventually promoted to commodore. He

Nelson

played an important role in the battle of Cape St. Vincent* in February 1797, carning his knighthood and promotion to rear admiral. The same July, having returned to his cruising and raiding mission, he attempted to capture a Spanish treasure ship at Santa Cruz, but the attack failed and he received wounds that resulted in the loss of his right arm.

Recovering from this serious wound, he rejoined the fleet in April 1798 and was put in command of the blockade of Toulon.* When Bonaparte and Brueys'* fleet slipped out from the port, he pursued the French down the Mediterranean and eventually brought Brueys to battle at the Nile.* This major victory earned him great acclaim and the title of Baron Nelson of the Nile. He operated with the Austrians from Leghorn and then returned to Naples, recovered the city from the Jacobins acting with the French (January 1799), and was created Duke of Bronté. About this time the famous liaison with Lady Hamilton began, and for some time Nelson lived at court at

Palermo, directing the blockade of Egypt and Malta.

On account of ill health Nelson accompanied the Hamiltons back to England overland in 1800, and separated from his wife. Promoted to vice admiral in 1801, he was sent under Admiral Hyde Parker* to the Baltic and effectively won the battle of Copenhagen* (April 1801), thus destroying the Armed Neutrality.* On returning to England he was made a viscount and lived with the Hamiltons in London and Merton. After Sir William's death (April 1803) he continued to live with Emma, who bore him a daughter. At the renewed outbreak of war with France he was sent to blockade Toulon once more.

When Villeneuve* broke out from Toulon in early 1805 and sailed for Martinique in the first stage of Napoleon's plan for a preinvasion naval concentration with the Spanish fleet, Nelson failed to intercept him. False intelligence and contrary winds delayed Nelson's pursuit, and by the time he had reached the West Indies Villeneuve had returned to Europe, brushing with Calder's* squadron off Finisterre. After a brief visit to England, Nelson resumed his command off Cadiz on board H.M.S. *Victory*, and on 21 October fought and won the celebrated battle of Trafalgar,* but was himself mortally wounded by a French sharpshooter and died at the moment of victory. His body was brought back to England and accorded a state burial in St. Paul's Cathedral.

Nelson holds a unique place among British sailors. His power to inspire his officers and men led to the formation of the so-called band of brothers, and this was matched by his grasp of naval strategy and tactics which amounted to genius. If his private life was deemed irregular in his day, his brilliant sea service earned him an undying place in the affections of his countrymen.

New Orleans, battle of, 8 January 1815. In mid-December 1814 a British fleet landed 7,500 troops under Sir Edward Pakenham in a bay to the east of New Orleans, as the southernmost prong of the British triple-offensive against the United States. The local commander, General Andrew Jackson, hurried 5,000 Americans from Baton Rouge to meet the threat. A night attack on 23/24 December checked Pakenham's advance some seven miles east of the city, and then Jackson fell back two miles to prepare a position around the hamlet of Chalmette. Felled trees and cotton bales were formed into a parapet between the raised banks of the Mississippi on the right and a cypress swamp on the left. On 8 January the British commander launched 5,300 men in a frontal attack against this position, but was brought up short by the American artillery and musketry. A renewed assault received the same treatment, and after losing 2,036 casualties within the space of half an hour, the British force retreated, Pakenham himself having been killed. The Americans lost only 8 killed and 13 wounded during the same engagement. In fact the Peace of Ghent between the U.S.A. and Great Britain had been signed on 24 December 1814, but news of this only reached New Orleans after the battle. The action made the reputation of Andrew Jackson, who would eventually become president.

Ney, Maréchal Michel, Prince de la Moskowa, duc d'Elchingen (1769–1815). Born at Sarrelouis, he joined a regiment of hussars in 1787. He rapidly rose through the noncommissioned ranks and served with the Army of the North (1792–94) with which he saw action at Neerwinden* and many other engagements. He was first commissioned in October 1792.

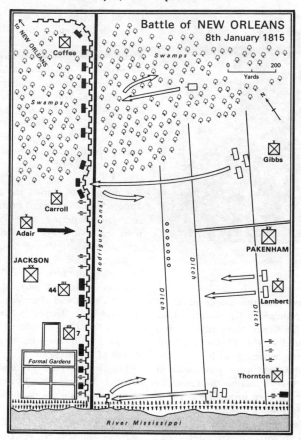

Transferred to the Sambre-et-Meuse in June 1794, he was wounded in the shoulder at the siege of Mainz. A veritable fire-eater, Ney was promoted to *général de brigade* in August 1796, and continued to command cavalry on the Rhine and German fronts. He was taken prisoner in April 1797 but was exchanged the following month. Spells in the Army of England and that of Mainz and the Lower Rhine (under Bernadotte*) followed, and after the capture of Mannheim he was promoted to *général de division* in March 1799. Later the same year he commanded the light cavalry in the armies of Switzerland and the Danube and was wounded in the thigh and wrist at Winterthur. After recovering, he was transferred to the Rhine and fought with distinction at Hohenlinden* under Moreau* in December 1800.

From September 1802 Ney commanded French troops in Switzerland and carried out diplomatic duties, before being re-

Ney

called to command the camps of Compiègne and Montreuil. On 19 May 1804 he received his baton. Next year he was given command of the VI Corps of the *Grande Armée,* marched with it to the Danube, and fought with great skill at Elchingen* after a major disagreement with Murat.* He then invaded the Tyrol, capturing Innsbruck from Archduke John* in November. In 1806 he fought at Jena*—somewhat precipitately—and then occupied Erfurt; later in that campaign he besieged and received the surrender of Magdeburg* on the Elbe. In early 1807, now in Poland, he arrived in the nick of time to save the day at Eylau,* and later that year fought at Güttstadt and, with distinction, at Friedland,* where he commanded the right wing. On 6 June 1808 he was created Duke of Elchingen.

Sent to Spain in August of 1808, Ney again commanded the VI Corps, won a number of small actions, and in 1810 accompanied Massena* in the invasion of Portugal. He took Ciudad Rodrigo,*

cleared the Coa, and fought at Bussaco.* His relationship with Massena was acrimonious, and during the retreat from Torres Vedras* he was removed from his command for insubordination. His red hair indicated his hot and impolitic temper. After kicking his heels in idleness commanding the Camp of Boulogne* in 1812 he was given command of the III Corps of the *Grande Armée* and took a leading part in the invasion of Russia. He was wounded in the neck at Smolensk,* fought doggedly in the center at Borodino,* and during the retreat from Moscow* took command of the rear guard at a critical period; after being cut off from the main army for a time he managed to rejoin it after a herculean effort, to Napoleon's delight. From this juncture he enjoyed the nickname, "the bravest of the brave." He took part in the battle of the Beresina* and after valiantly holding the bridge at Kovno, he was reputedly the last Frenchman to leave Russian soil. On 25 March 1813 he was proclaimed Prince of the Moskwa.

The Campaign of 1813 saw him back in action at Weissenfels,* Lützen* (where he was again wounded), at Bautzen* (where he commanded the left wing in the near-perfect envelopment battle), and—after suffering a setback at Dennewitz*—at Leipzig,* where he received another wound. Next year, commanding various formations, he fought at almost every battle, but at last, at Fontainebleau, he became the spokesman for the marshals and demanded Napoleon's abdication.

Early 1815 found Ney in high favor with the Bourbons, Commander in Chief of the cavalry and a peer of France, but on his old master's return—despite promises to return with him to Paris in an iron cage—the old magic proved too strong, and he rejoined Napoleon at Auxerre on 18 March. On 15 June he was given command of the left wing of the Army of the

North on the first day of the invasion of Belgium, fought Wellington* at Quatre Bras* (earning criticism for his slowness and relative passivity), and was then given the post of battle commander at Waterloo.* Some assert that his mishandling of the infantry and cavalry attacks during this battle led to the defeat. He returned to Paris and hoped to be allowed to retire, but the vengeful Bourbons had him arrested on 3 August. He was brought to Paris and tried before a Court of Peers on 4 December. Found guilty on the 6th, he was shot the next day, being allowed to give the signal for the firing squad to shoot.

Ney was much admired by the common soldier, and if he had certain shortcomings as a strategist he was extremely able as a commander in battle, displaying boundless courage and dash. His ideal level was that of a corps commander, and aided by Baron Jomini* he brought off many successes. The strains of the Russian campaign, and the eventual defection of Jomini to the Allies, affected his later performance.

Nielly, Contre-Amiral Joseph Marie, baron (1751–1833). The son of a merchant skipper, he first went to sea as a cabin boy at the age of seven in 1758. He graduated to the rank of powder monkey next year and was wounded in action off Belle-Isle. From 1771 until 1778 he served in the merchant marine, qualifying for a master's ticket in 1774 despite being under age. He was captured by the British in 1778 but escaped from Jersey after seizing a Dutch vessel. That September he was appointed lieutenant in a royal frigate and saw service in the West Indies and at Brest in various capacities. He was back in the West Indies as a First Lieutenant in 1792, was made commander of a frigate the next year, and promoted to captain. In November 1793 he was made rear

admiral and raised his flag the following January. He captured H.M.S. *Castor* (a frigate) and rejoined Admiral Villaret-Joyeuse* in time to command the rearguard squadron of the fleet in the First of June* battle (1794). For several years he commanded the French 3rd Squadron, and in November 1794 earned the Convention's thanks by capturing the British 64-gun ship-of-the-line, H.M.S. *Alexander.* In 1796 he took part in the abortive raid against Ireland, reached Bantry Bay,* but sailed back to Brest in March 1797. He later held important command positions at Brest and (from 1798) at l'Orient. He was made Maritime Prefect at Dunkirk in 1800 and retired from the service in September 1803. He was made a baron in 1814 and an honorary vice admiral in May 1821.

Nile, battle of the, 1 August 1798. After a long pursuit down the Mediterranean, Admiral Nelson* at the head of 13 British ships-of-the-line at last discovered the fleet of Admiral Brueys* (which had convoyed General Bonaparte and the Army of the Orient safely to Egypt) at anchor in Aboukir Bay, near the Rosetta mouth of the Nile Delta. The French fleet comprised 13 ships-of-the-line and 4 frigates.

Brueys had taken up what he considered to be an impregnable position, anchored in a two-mile line in a sandy bay protected by shoals, his left flank resting on a small island that held a battery, his right abutting the mainland, his four frigates being drawn up between his main battle line and the shore in shoaling water. He at once recalled his watering parties and cleared for action.

Although it was already late afternoon, Nelson ordered an immediate attack against the van and center of the French line, approaching from the northeast. This exposed the British to much French fire as they approached, but fortunately

Bequire Island mounted only six guns and two mortars—otherwise the advance to contact might have been very expensive. As it was the approach was unchecked, and Captain Foley on H.M.S. *Goliath* discovered that Brueys had left enough room for ships to sail around the head of the French line, so followed by H.M.S. *Zealous* he began to rake the inshore and largely unmanned sides of the French van. As dusk fell, Nelson came into action on board H.M.S. *Vanguard,* most of his fleet (save H.M.S. *Culloden* which ran aground) attacking the French ships from the seaward side. As the battle developed in the gathering night, several more British vessels discovered that the French had left large intervals between their vessels, which permitted British ships to penetrate the line, raking their opponents as they did so. Brueys' 120-gun flagship, *l'Orient,* pounded H.M.S. *Bellerophon* into a near-wreck in the center of the French line, but the British vessel managed to move clear, leaving the mighty *l'Orient* on fire and under attack by two more ships, one on each side.

Nelson was lightly wounded on the head

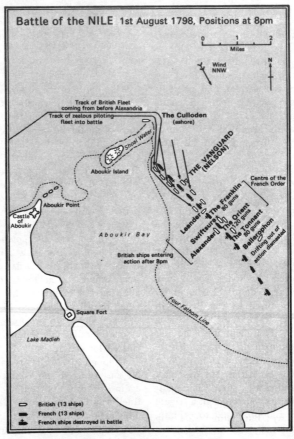

Battle of the NILE 1st August 1798, Positions at 8pm

and had to go below, but returned on deck in time to see the explosion, at 10:00 P.M., of *l'Orient*, which stunned the remaining vessels. After the battle had been resumed and brought to its conclusion, only two French ships-of-the-line and two frigates, under command of Villeneuve,* escaped from the Bay. Admiral Brueys perished in his flagship.

This great naval victory effectively isolated the Army of the Orient in Egypt, proved a turning point in the War of the Second Coalition,* and added greatly to Nelson's reputation.

Nive, battle of the, 9–12 December 1813. After the passage of the Pyrenees and the forcing of the Nivelle,* Wellington's* army found itself facing strong French positions defending the area between the Bay of Biscay and the rivers Adour and Nive leading northward toward Bayonne, held by Marshal Soult* with some 62,000 men. With only 64,000 troops available, Wellington realized there was a danger of being cooped up in a triangular salient unless he could force a crossing over the river Nive. Despite bad weather, General Lord Hill* led five divisions over the Nive near Ustaritz on 9 December, while the rest of the Allied army launched distracting attacks toward the Adour and Bayonne. Thereupon Soult led eight divisions from Bayonne to fall upon the forces west of the river Nive, achieving a measure of surprise on 10 December. The Light Division held its ground on a ridge behind Bassussary, but Reille's* attack farther west near Barroilhet almost broke through the Portuguese line, and a desperate battle centered around the *mairie*. However, the line held until reserves arrived from St. Jean de Luz at 2:00 P.M., whereupon Soult called off the attack. Both sides had lost some 1,600 men. Desultory fighting continued over the next two days, but neither side was seeking a major battle. However, a river

spate swept away a vital pontoon bridge newly constructed over the Nive near Villefranque on the night of the 12th, effectively isolating Hill's 14,000 men and 10 guns on the east bank just as the French were transferring their forces through Bayonne toward St. Pierre* with the intention of attacking on that sector the next day.

Nivelle, battle of the, 10 November 1813. Following his defeat at the Bidassoa,* Soult* fell back through the Pyrenees to hold a new line running from St. Jean de Luz on the Bay of Biscay, along the line of the river Nivelle, incorporating the large natural obstacles of La Grande and Le Petit Rhune to St. Jean Pied de Port in the interior. Expecting a renewed allied attack along the coast, Soult placed a full third of his 60,000 men to guard that sector. Wellington,* needing to get clear of the Pyrenees before the onset of winter, decided to mount a demonstration on the coast and make his main effort down the Nivelle valley, three divisions on each side of the river, while two more divisions were to assault the Petit Rhune. The preliminary moves were made after dusk on 9 November, and early next day the three forts on le Petit Rhune were captured by the Light Division as Beresford* with three divisions on the right occupied Amotz on the Nivelle. The French were driven back north of the Nivelle by mid-day, while Hill* and his three divisions made good progress on the far right. By dusk the Allies were masters of St. Pée, and Soult, after losing 4,450 men and 70 cannon during the day, ordered a retreat to the Nive* lines near Bayonne. The Allies lost 2,625 casualties to achieve this considerable success, which was somewhat marred by marauding on the part of the Spanish allies.

Nore, mutiny at the, 12 May–13 June 1797. The naval vessels anchored off the

Nore in the Thames Estuary mutinied against the conditions of service. Unlike the similar unrest at Spithead* a little earlier, the mutineers had political as well as economic and social aims, and they conducted their affairs with little moderation; the rioting and looting spread ashore. The elected representative of the mutineers, Richard Parker, was an educated ex-officer jailed for debt before being sent to sea. He declared himself "President of the Floating Republic," but following the collapse of the mutiny he was hanged at the yardarm on his ship on 20 June, while several of his associates were also executed or flogged round the fleet.

Normann-Ehrenfels, General Karl Friedrich Lebrecht, Count of (1784–1822). Born in Stuttgart, he entered the Austrian army in 1799. In 1803, he transferred to the Army of Württemberg with the rank of colonel, and nine years later he commanded the *régiment des chevaux-légers* in the Imperial Guard.* In 1813 he commanded a cavalry brigade at the battle of Kitzen, but deserted to the Allies on the third day of the battle of Leipzig* at the head of the Württemberg contingent. In 1816 he was made tutor to the son of the Landgrave of Hesse, and was killed at the battle of Missolonghi during the Greek War of Independence in 1822.

Novi, battle of, 15 August 1799. After losing most of northern Italy by the summer of 1799, the French Directory* sent General Joubert* to command the 35,000 remaining French troops in the hills north of Genoa, with orders to block the Russo-Austrian advance. On 15 August Marshal Suvorov* sent 45,000 troops to assault the French positions at Novi, midway between Genoa and Alessandria, and after 16 hours of the most ferocious fighting captured the fortified heights, inflicting 11,000 casualties on the French for the loss of 8,000. Joubert was himself among the slain. The whole of Bonaparte's gains in 1796–97 had been eliminated.

Obidos, action of, 16 August 1808. After landing in Mondego Bay* Wellesley's* army moved south to seek out the French Army of Portugal, moving through Leiria and Albocaca. On the 15th three companies of the 95th Rifles routed a French outpost at Brilos, but an overzealous pursuit brought them up against a French battalion of General Delaborde's* division on the outskirts of Obidos, and the riflemen had to be extricated. Next day, after a brief action, Delaborde evacuated Obidos and took up a position at Roliça.*

Ocaña, battle of, 19 November 1809. The Spanish Junta, as Wellesley* retired with his army into Portugal after Talavera,* collected 50,000 Spanish troops and entrusted them to General Juan Carlos Areizaga. In early November he advanced from the Sierra Morena at the head of this Army of the Center and reached La Guardia near Aranjuez. There he halted for 72 hours, affording Soult* sufficient time to concentrate Victor* and Sebastiani* with their divisions. As soon as his advance guard served notice of the French approach, Areizaga beat a hasty retreat, but his opponents, after crossing the Tagus, forced him to accept battle at Ocaña. A large cavalry engagement was the main feature of this battle, which utterly smashed the Army of the Center. The French left 4,000 killed and wounded and captured 15,000 Spaniards for a loss of some 2,000 men. This Spanish disaster laid southern Spain open to French conquest.

O'Donnell, General Joseph Henry, Count of La Bispal (1769–1834). A Spanish general of Irish descent, he played a leading part in the resistance offered to the French invaders during the Peninsular War.* In 1810 he won a minor victory at La Bispal in Catalonia, but was defeated by Marshal Suchet* outside Lerida on 13 April that year as he led 8,000 Spaniards to prevent the siege of that city. Three years later, after the battle of Vitoria,* O'Donnell was given the task of besieging Pamplona* with the 11,000 men of his Spanish division. Following his restoration, Ferdinand VII* appointed him Captain General of Andalusia and, from 1818, Governor of Cadiz. During the French invasion of 1822, O'Donnell was entrusted with the defense of Madrid against Bessières,* but after being accused of treachery by his own officers he fled to France, where he died.

Oldenburg, Peter Frederick Louis, Duke of (fl. 1810). After inheriting the secularized bishopric of Oldenburg in 1903, Peter Frederick joined the Confederation of the Rhine in 1808. This did not prevent the seizure of the territory by Napoleon in early 1811, who joined it to Hanover. As such, Oldenburg remained part of the French Empire until 1814. Tsar Alexander I,* the Duke of Oldenburg's brother-in-law, sought to gain him compensation—in vain—and this was one strand in the deterioration of Franco-Russian relations from 1811. The territories were liberated in 1813 and the

Duke restored, and from 1815 he assumed the title of Grand Duke.

Oporto, battle of, 12 May 1809. After resuming command of the Anglo-Portuguese forces at Lisbon on 22 April, Wellesley* determined to remove the current French threat to Portugal by attacking first Marshal Soult* on the river Douro and thereafter Marshal Victor* near Merida. Accordingly he marched north to a rendezvous at Coimbra, and the two marshals on 4 May advanced toward Oporto on the river Douro with 17,400 men. Soult felt secure behind the fast-flowing river, having removed all boats, and never envisaged a direct assault by the Allies against Oporto itself; he left only 11,000 men, including General Foy's* brigade and his trains, in its vicinity. However, after studying the northern bank from Serra Convent, Wellesley determined to use four barges that had been brought to the south bank by friendly townsfolk

to establish a bridgehead while General Murray crossed the Douro by a ferry at Barca d'Avintas four miles above Oporto to turn the French flank. At 10:00 A.M. the first troops slipped over the Douro unnoticed by the French and established themselves in a seminary on the northern bank. Several hundred men had crossed before the first French intervention under Foy at 10:30 A.M., but British guns drawn up near the convent brought down a heavy fire on the roads leading to the seminary, and French attacks were driven off by midday. More troops crossed the river, the bridgehead now being under command of General Hill,* and as the French sent battalions from the city to contain the threat the citizens flocked over with every boat to transport Wellesley's waiting formations. By 2:00 P.M. Soult realized that the situation was hopeless, and the French began a disorderly retreat to the north pursued by Hill. Unfortunately Murray's force was not prop-

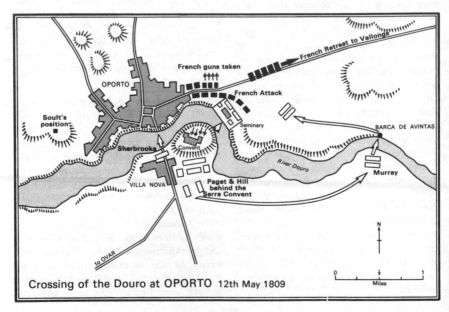

Crossing of the Douro at OPORTO 12th May 1809

erly positioned to intercept the French flight, and so Soult got away. Nevertheless, for a cost of 123 casualties, Wellesley had pulled off a masterly river crossing, inflicting a loss of possibly 600 men (including prisoners) and capturing 1,500 sick and wounded and 58 guns in Oporto.

Orange, William Frederick, Prince of, later King of the Low Countries (1772–1843). In 1806 he lost the principality of Nassau after refusing to join the Confederation of the Rhine,* but was awarded the Grand Duchy of Luxembourg and Limburg in compensation. In 1813 he became Sovereign Prince of the Low Countries, and two years later became king with the title of William I.

Orange, William, Prince of, later William II, King of Holland (1792–1849). The eldest son of William Frederick,* in 1815 he was given command of a corps in Wellington's* army and fought at Quatre Bras* and Waterloo,* where he was wounded. In 1816 he married Anna, a Russian princess, and succeeded his father as king of Holland in 1840.

Ordal and Villafranca, actions of, 12 and 13 September 1813. While Wellington* was fighting in the Pyrenees, Lord William Bentinck was operating against Marshal Suchet's* 30,000 Frenchmen in eastern Spain. After his check at Tarragonna* Bentinck fell back to a strong position behind the river Llobregat. Finding that Suchet would not attack, the Allied force advanced to Villafranca, sending 1,200 men under Colonel Adam ahead to secure the pass at Ordal. Suchet promptly attacked this detachment in moonlight, and despite a staunch defense by the 27th Foot, the French took the position and overwhelmed or scattered the survivors.

Suchet followed up his success by marching on Villafranca. Bentinck retired behind the town but soon found his force being enveloped by French cavalry on the 13th. Fortunately, one French division marching to turn the landward flank was held up by guerrillas, and when the French grew overbold against the retiring Allied center they suffered a sharp reverse when Bentinck turned at bay in a suitable gorge. However, Bentinck's main preoccupation was to get away without sustaining further damage, so at 3:00 P.M. he broke off the action, having lost 90 men on the 13th, and retreated to Tarragonna. He would soon re-embark for Sicily.

Ordener, Général Michel, comte (1755–1811). He joined the Bourbon army as a dragoon in 1773 and was commissioned into the *chasseurs-à-cheval* in 1792. He served on the Rhine and in Italy, fighting at Lodi* (1796). He was seriously wounded in Switzerland in August 1799, hit by eight saber blows, three bullets, and one cannonball. In July 1800 he received command of the *grenadiers-à-cheval* of the Consular Guard, and in August 1803 was promoted to *général de brigade*. In March 1804 he commanded the force sent to seize the duc d'Enghien* from neutral territory, and later served at the Camp of Boulogne.* From August 1805 he commanded the cavalry of the Guard in the *Grande Armée* and was seriously wounded at Austerlitz.* Promoted to *général de division* on 25 December 1805, he gave up active service the following May on account of his wounds. He was made a senator and formally left the service in October 1806. He was made Josephine's* First Equerry and (in 1808) a Count of the Empire. From 1809 until his death he was governor of the Palace of Compiègne.

Orders in Council, the British, November and December 1807. As a riposte to the Berlin Decrees of 1806, which instituted the Continental System,* Prime Minister Perceval* issued Orders in Council on 11, 15, and 25 November, and 18 December 1807. These decreed that any neutral vessel sailing to or from any hostile port would be required to unload its cargo in one of a list of designated British ports, to pay customs duties, and to purchase a special license if it proposed to trade with the enemy. These measures were designed to favor British colonial trade and shipping interests by preventing neutral traders from carrying foreign colonial produce to France or her allies without first paying British dues and license fees for the privilege of so doing. Napoleon soon riposted with the first and second Milan Decrees.*

Orthez, battle of, 27 February 1814. After the battles of the river Nive,* Soult* abandoned Bayonne* to its own devices and retired to the east over three river lines before taking up a position north of

the river Gave de Pau near Orthez. Wellington* advanced from the west along both banks of the river with 44,000 men and 42 guns. Soult had placed his 36,000 men and 48 guns to hold a long ridge running from St. Boes village in the west in a wide sweep to the east and then south down to Orthez on the river.

The Allied plan called for Lord Hill* to make a diversion against Orthez while the 4th and 7th Divisions under Beresford* attacked St. Boes and the Light, 3rd, and 6th Divisions assaulted the French center along three parallel spurs running up to the main ridge, under the overall command of Picton.* Wellington hoped that both French flanks would be turned by Beresford and Hill respectively and thus sever Soult's line of retreat as his center collapsed. Wellington supervised much of the battle from the ancient Roman Camp in the Light Division's sector.

By 9:00 A.M. on 27 February Beresford's

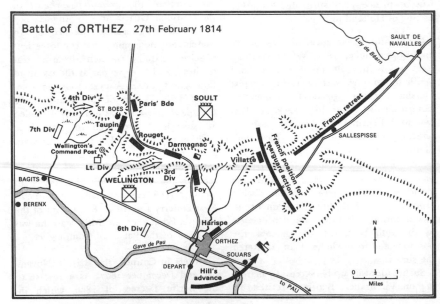

Battle of ORTHEZ 27th February 1814

attack was in full swing, and after a fierce fight St. Boes and its church were captured. Thereafter, however, the Allied left wing was checked by heavy and accurate artillery fire against the neck of ground leading onto the main ridge, and by midday Beresford was forced to pull back his troops before General Reille's* spirited counterattack. Meanwhile the Light Division was in firm control of the area around the Roman Camp, but both other divisions in the center were in trouble, and the French were in sight of victory as d'Erlon* advanced in the center. However, the observant Wellington noticed a gap developing between the two French corps and sent Colonel Colborne* and the 52nd Foot to assail Reille's flank and rear near a ravine, while he personally led up the 3rd and 6th Foot against Reille's inner flank as Beresford made one more attack with his nearly exhausted men against St. Boes. A salient was driven between Reille and d'Erlon, and the Allied center returned to the attack against Foy's* and d'Armagnac's divisions and cleared the central plateau. Beresford at last mastered the narrow neck of land beyond St. Boes, while away to the east Hill passed the river at Souars by means of a ford to threaten Soult's left and rear.

Soult now conceded defeat, but his escape depended on his reaching the bridge of Sault de Navailles eight miles up the St. Severs road before Hill could cut it. The French narrowly won the race, blew up the bridge after crossing, and marched away toward Toulouse.* The French had lost 4,000 men (including 1,350 prisoners), and many more took the opportunity to desert over the following days. The Allied casualties numbered 2,164, including Wellington himself, slightly wounded when a bullet drove his sheathed swordhilt into his thigh.

Ostermann-Tolstoi, General Ivan, Count

(1770–1837). The grandson of Tsar Paul I's Chancellor, Ivan Andreivitch Ostermann (whose daughter married a Count Tolstoi), he commanded with distinction part of the Russian army at Eylau* and Friedländ* (1807), at Ostronovo* and Borodino* (1812), and at Bautzen* (1813). He also defeated General Vandamme* at Kulm.* He died at Geneva.

Ostronovo, actions of, 25 and 26 July 1812. As Napoleon drove forward into the "River Gap" between the Dnieper and the Dvina, seeking a major action against Barclay de Tolly* near Vitebsk,* Murat* and the French cavalry encountered strong opposition near Ostronovo on the banks of the Dvina which persuaded Napoleon that the Russians had at last turned at bay. He paused for a day to await the arrival of the main army, but during the 27th Barclay retreated toward Smolensk,* seeking a junction with Bagration's* forces.

Ott, Field Marshal Peter Carl, Baron (1738–1809). This experienced Habsburg commander was born at Gran in 1738 and had a distinguished career in the Austrian service. He held high command against the Turks in 1789, fought the French in the Low Countries (1793–94), and served in North Italy in 1796. The following year he was appointed field-marshal-lieutenant. In 1799 he served with distinction under Suvorov,* fighting at Novi* and besieging Ancona. The next year, under Melas'* direction, he besieged Massena* in Genoa* and received his surrender. He was worsted by Lannes* at Montebello* and commanded the left wing under Melas at Marengo* on 14 June 1800, withdrawing his men in good order into Alessandria at the end of the battle. This proved to be his last active command.

Oudinot, Maréchal Nicolas Charles, duc de Reggio (1767–1847). The son of a

Oudinot

brewer, Oudinot joined the Bourbon infantry as a volunteer in 1784, serving for
three years. He became captain of a
cavalry troop in 1789, and next year
headed the National Guard of the Meuse.
From 1792–94 he served with the Armies
of the Rhine and the Moselle as lieutenant colonel, and received the first of
his 22 wounds at Haguenau in December
1793, being hit in the head. Valorous
service led to his provisional promotion
to *général de brigade* in June 1794 (confirmed one year later), but he had a leg
broken at Treves the same August. In
October 1795 he was taken prisoner near
Ulm* after sustaining six wounds in a
combat, but was exchanged the following
January. In September 1795 Oudinot was
again gravely wounded—at Ingolstädt—
receiving four saber cuts and a bullet
through the thigh. Appointments in the
so-called Army of England and in the
Army of Helvetia followed, and his battle
experience steadily grew. In April 1799

he was promoted to *général de division,*
only to be wounded in the chest near
Zurich* in June. Two more wounds were
sustained as Chief of Staff to the Army of
Helvetia and the Danube the same year,
but still his indomitable spirit burned. He
served Massena* as Chief of Staff during
the gallant but unsuccessful defense of
Genoa* in 1800, and later that year fought
under General Brune* at the passage of
the river Mincio. A few years of relatively
peaceful employment ensued.

In 1805 he commanded an *élite* division of grenadiers in Lannes'* V Corps
on the Danube, winning a combat at
Wertingen* but being badly wounded at
Hollabrünn.* After a year recovering and
carrying out mainly administrative duties,
he returned to the forefront of action at
Ostrolenka in February 1807, and then
served at the siege of Danzig.* Despite
having his leg broken by a horse fall in
May, he was fit to command his division
at Friedland.* In July 1808 he was made a
Count of the Empire. The next year he
fought on the Danube at Landshut,* was
wounded in the arm on the second day at
Aspern-Essling,* and was given command
of the II Corps *vice* the deceased Lannes
before fighting at Wagram,* where he
almost had an ear shot off. On 12 July
1809 the Emperor sent him the coveted
baton of a marshal, and in April 1810
he was made Duke of Reggio.

After service in Holland (during which
he supervised the incorporation of the
country into France on the enforced
abdication of Louis Bonaparte*) he
marched into Russia (1812) with his II
Corps, stormed the camp of Dunaburg,
and won the first day of the battle of
Polotsk* on 17 August, only to be badly
wounded in the shoulder that evening.
In October he was fit enough to resume
command of II Corps, and with it fought
at the Beresina* during the retreat but
was wounded in the side. Invalided home

to France, he almost fell into Russian hands when he was ambushed en route, but he organized a dozen men to defend a house successfully; the attack was duly beaten off, but a falling beam struck the redoubtable marshal.

In 1813 Oudinot commanded the XII Corps from April and was in charge of the extreme right wing at Bautzen.* Sent by Napoleon to march on Berlin after the breakdown of the Armistice* in August, he was defeated by Bernadotte* at Gross-Beeren* and later served in command of two divisions of the Young Guard at Wachau and Leipzig.* As the Allies invaded France in January 1814, Oudinot was again in the thick of the action, being wounded in both legs at Brienne.* He also fought at La Rothière* and Arcis* and there received his last wound—being struck full in the chest by a ball which was, however, deflected by the plaque of his Grand Eagle of the Legion of Honor. He joined in the mutiny of the marshals at Fontainebleau,* and after Napoleon's abdication served as a government commissioner in arranging a general armistice with the Allies.

The Bourbons made him commander of the Corps of Royal Grenadiers and governor of Metz. When Napoleon returned from Elba* he tried in vain to keep the local troops loyal to the Bourbons, but proudly refused to flee when his efforts failed. Summoned to Paris by Napoleon, he faced his master and was exiled to his estates. After Waterloo* the Bourbons made him commander of the Royal Guard and a member of the Privy Council. One more campaign awaited him, in 1823, when he led the I Corps into Spain and was for a time governor of Madrid. He ended his long and distinguished life as Governor of the *Invalides** from 1842. A fine and devoted fighting general, Napoleon once likened him to Bayard. He sustained more wounds than any other senior commander.

Paget, General Lord Henry. *See* Uxbridge

Pajol, Général Claude Pierre, comte (1772–1844). A native of Besançon, in 1791 he became sergeant major of a volunteer battalion and was commissioned into the line infantry the next year. Wounded several times at the head of grenadiers, he became aide-de-camp to General Kléber* (1794–97). He was then posted into the hussars, fought on the Danube, and was awarded a saber of honor in 1800. Garrison duty in Holland was followed by active service in Austria (1805), during which he fought before Ulm.* Transferred to Italy (1806–07), he was promoted to *général de brigade* in March 1807 and posted to Poland, where he fought at Güttstadt, Heilsberg,* and at the siege of Königsberg. He was made a baron in 1808, and serving under Montbrun* he distinguished himself next year at Eckmühl,* Ratisbon,* and Wagram.* In 1812 he was attached to Davout's* I Corps for the invasion of Russia, captured Kovno and Vilna* with his cavalry, defeated Bagration* at Ochmiana, and was promoted to *général de division* in August. He charged at the head of a light cavalry division at Borodino* but was seriously wounded two days later. He only recovered in time to fight under Gouvion de St. Cyr* at Dresden* but was again badly injured in a horse-fall at Wachau in October. Next month he was made a Count of the Empire, and after a period commanding National Guards on the river Yonne, he received a cavalry division with which he captured Montereau* in February 1814, where he was again wounded. He rallied to Napoleon during the Hundred Days* and fought under Grouchy* at Ligny* and Wavre.* Retired from the service in 1816, he helped organize a steamship company, but his violent anti-Bourbonist feelings caused him to become involved in the Revolution of 1830 as an insurgent leader. Thereafter he resumed his military career and was maintained on the active list, despite his age, until his death in Paris.

Palafox y Melzi, General José, Duke of Saragossa (1780–1847). As an officer of the

Palafox y Melzi

Spanish Royal Guard, he accompanied Crown Prince Ferdinand to Bayonne* in 1808 but escaped when his master was interned. He returned to Aragon, the region of his birth, and raised it against the French invaders. The rebels named him their general, and after being defeated at Tudela* with Castaños* he sustained and inspired the defense during two sieges of Saragossa* (1808–09). At the fall of the city to Lannes* he was taken prisoner and held in France until 1814. He returned to Spain that year and was made Captain General of Aragon and later Duke of Saragossa by Ferdinand VII. His brother, Francisco Palafox, also earned a fine reputation as a rebel leader but also proved something of an intriguer. In later years José Palafox proved to be a prominent anti-Carlist.

Palm, Jean-Philippe (1766–1806). The owner of a bookshop in Nuremberg, Palm marketed a pamphlet accusing Napoleon of being a tyrant. He was arrested, tried by court-martial, and executed immediately after sentence at Braunau-on-the-Inn.

Pamplona, blockade of, 30 June–31 October 1813. After Vitoria* the French forces headed into the Pyrenees, leaving strong garrisons in San Sebastian* and Pamplona, guarding the approaches to the Maya* and Roncesvalles* passes. Wellington* decided to concentrate against the former and sent the Spanish commander O'Donnell* with his 11,000 men to blockade Pamplona, which was defended by General Cassan and 3,000 men. When Soult* launched his offensive of the Pyrenees* in late July, his main effort was made toward Pamplona; after the actions of Maya and Roncesvalles the Allied troops fell back toward Pamplona under Picton.* On 27 July Cassan mounted a strong sortie, which caused O'Donnell to

spike his guns in panic, but the opportune arrival of d'España* and his division drove Cassan back within his position. Wellington also arrived, and the battle of Sorauren* was fought on the 28th almost within sight of Pamplona. A second engagement on 29/30 July led to the French falling back. The blockade of Pamplona was resumed under command of d'España, and on 31 October Cassan capitulated—and the last French post on Spanish soil was taken.

Pan Corbo, combat of, 31 October 1808. As Napoleon stood poised and ready to launch his major offensive into Spain, Marshal Lefebvre* and the 21,000 troops of IV Corps made a premature attack against General Blake's* 19,000 men as they straggled eastward from Reynosa* and Bilbao. The Spaniards suffered a sharp reverse, sustaining some 600 casualties to the French 200, and fell back westward—an eventuality Napoleon had been eager to prevent. Victor* and Lefebvre were ordered off in pursuit, but the former received a rough handling by Blake at Valmaceda* on 5 November, and only on the 11th, at Espinosa, was Blake defeated.

Paoli, General Pascal (1725–1807). Educated at the military school in Naples, Paoli was commissioned into the Regiment of Corsican Refugees commanded by his father. He was called to lead the Corsican patriots in their independence struggle against Geneva, and this led to two French interventions on the island, in 1756 and 1765. In 1768 Corsica passed under French rule, and next year Paoli, after being defeated at Ponte-Novo, went abroad into exile. He returned to Corsica in 1789 and for a time acknowledged French sovereignty, but then became disillusioned and commanded a new revolt—this time against Revolutionary France. This was based upon a miscalculation of the wishes of the bulk of the population and was denounced in Toulon by Lucien Bonaparte* and the Committee of Public Safety. Paoli opened negotiations with Great Britain which resulted in the British occupation of Corsica in 1794, but he soon fell out with his new allies, whom he believed to have betrayed him, and he went into exile in London where he died in complete obscurity. Paoli was the hero of the young Napoleon until the break in June 1793, when the Bonaparte family was compelled to move to Marseilles.

Paris, treaty of, 30 May 1814. After Napoleon's departure to Elba* after signing the treaty of Fontainebleau* the Allies set about agreeing to terms with the restored King Louis XVIII.* Although they exacted no indemnity, France was to be restricted to her frontiers of 1792; Talleyrand* managed to secure concessions over the retention within France of Montbéliard and Mulhouse, Chambéry and Annecy, and part of the Saar region. However, French colonial possessions were excluded from the agreement, and Britain took over Tobago, St. Lucia, the Ile de France, and the Seychelles Islands, and Spain recovered her half of Santo Domingo.* All other matters were postponed for the Congress of Vienna* to determine, but the French government was required to agree in advance to any territorial stipulations that might result.

Parker, Admiral Sir Hyde (1739–1807). The second son of Vice-Admiral Sir Hyde Parker, Bart., he served in North American waters during the War of Independence and was knighted in 1779. He commanded the Royal Naval forces stationed on Jamaica (1796–1800), and during the Second Armed Neutrality* he was sent with a fleet to overawe Denmark. His performance in the resultant battle of Copenhagen* was weak and undecided, and it was left to Nelson* to gain the

success in contravention of Parker's order for him to break off the action. Parker was recalled and received no further active commands.

Partouneaux, Général Louis, comte (1770–1835). A grenadier in the Paris Volunteers of 1791, he was commissioned into the infantry the next year. After some service he was wounded at Toulon.* In early 1796 he was sent to the Army of Italy and next year fought at Rivoli* and at Klagenfurt as General Rey's Chief of Staff. Promoted to *général de brigade* in April 1799, he was wounded and taken prisoner at Novi* but exchanged for General Zach. He was made *général de division* in August 1803, and in 1805 fought under Eugène* at Caldiero* and took part in the siege of Venice. Posted to serve under Massena* in Naples, he drove an English force away from Scylla in 1809. In 1812 he was attached to IX Corps for the Campaign of Russia under Victor.* On 26 November he was ordered to hold off Platov* and Wittgenstein* at the battle of the Beresina,* but to Napoleon's fury he bungled his role, was taken captive, and his men capitulated. On his return to France he received no appointments and took no part in the campaigns of 1813–15. The Bourbons made him a count in 1816, and he embarked on a long political and military career that only ended with his retirement in 1832. He died of apoplexy two years later at Menton near Nice.

Paul I, Tsar of Russia (1754–1801). The son of Catherine the Great and Peter III, he was twice married before succeeding to the throne in November 1796. He at once regulated the succession in the male line, but then proceeded to use his absolute power very unscrupulously. His loathing for the French Revolution reached a peak when Bonaparte occupied Malta* on his way to Egypt and declared himself Grand Master of the Order of St. John.

In 1798 he sent three armies to fight for the Second Coalition* in Holland, Switzerland, and North Italy, but despite the successes won by the great Suvorov* all failed in due course. With typical inconsistency, he regarded the British occupation of Malta as treachery and transferred his admiration to Napoleon as First Consul, forcing the Bourbon exiles to quit Mittau as an indication of his new feelings. However his increasingly unbalanced mind caused a court conspiracy to be organized, and on 12 March 1801 he was assassinated. "Mad Tsar Paul" was succeeded by his son, Alexander I,* who was privy to the conspiracy.

Pelet-Clozeau, Général Jean Jacques Germain, baron (1777–1858). Educated at Toulouse, he joined the army in 1799, and after a period as a sergeant he was transferred to engineering work in Italy in 1800, being commissioned into the Engineers the following year. In 1805 he was attached to Massena's* staff, was wounded at Caldiero,* and then saw service in Naples. In 1809 he was wounded at Ebersburg in the Danube campaign, and also fought at Essling* and Znaim.* From 1810–11 he served Massena in Portugal, writing an interesting account of the campaign. In 1812 he served on the staff of General Marchand* in Russia, fighting at Smolensk,* Borodino,* and at Krasnöe,* where he was severely wounded. Promoted to *général de brigade* in April 1813, he next served under Marmont* before being given a brigade of the Young Guard in August. He fought at Dresden* and Leipzig* and was then transferred to a high staff appointment in the Imperial Guard.* In 1814 he fought in almost every battle in command of Guard brigades. Kept in employment by the Bourbons, he rallied to Napoleon in 1815, fought at Ligny,* and at Waterloo* retook Plancenoit from the Prussians and held it

until the late evening. Three years of unemployment followed, but from 1818 a series of staff posts came his way including that of Director of the Staff College, with the rank of lieutenant general, in 1830. Pelet also pursued a political career, but was badly hurt by a bomb in 1835. In 1837 he was made a peer of France and continued in general staff appointments until his retirement in 1848.

Pellew, Admiral Sir Edward, Viscount Exmouth (1757–1833). Pellew joined the Royal Navy in 1770 and soon earned rapid promotion for his gallantry. In 1793 he was knighted after capturing the first French frigate in the war. Three years later he was made a baronet after he had rescued the crew of a transport driven ashore near Plymouth under the most perilous circumstances, and in 1797, with a fellow frigate captain, he destroyed the French 74-gun ship, *Les Droits de l'Homme*, in a famous action. He single-handedly quelled a potential mutiny in Bantry Bay* (1799). From 1802 he began a Parliamentary career, becoming a staunch Admiralty spokesman in the House of Commons. In 1804, with the rank of rear admiral, he commanded the East Indian Station, crushing the Dutch squadron in the Far East (1807). Promoted to vice admiral in 1808, he returned to England the next year to take up commands in the North Sea and the Mediterranean. Promoted to full admiral in 1814, he commanded the fleet that bombarded Algiers in 1816 and was subsequently made a viscount. From 1817–21 he was Commander in Chief at Plymouth. One of the most famous and colorful naval commanders of his day, Pellew was an inspiration to the Royal Navy.

Peninsular War, the (1807–1814). The eight years of incessant campaigns waged in Portugal, Spain, and parts of the

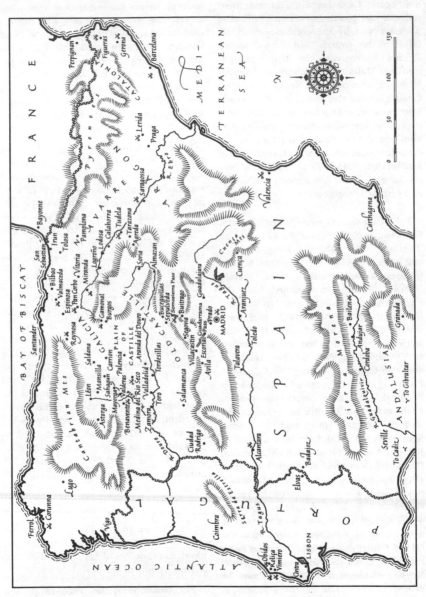

Spain, 1808–09

Pyrenees and of southern France that are collectively known as the Peninsular War were of central significance to the course and ultimate outcome of the Napoleonic Wars. What began in 1807 as an opportunistic invasion of a practically defenseless Portugal rapidly expanded into a major struggle involving whole populations as well as armies. Napoleon would come to rue the adventure, which cost France an estimated 100 lives a day on the average—or almost 240,000 casualties in all—besides enormous financial strains and general economic dislocation of the war effort. The "Spanish Ulcer" proved a major factor in the collapse of the Empire.

French involvement in the Peninsula developed for a number of reasons. Unlike Spain, Portugal under the rule of the Regent, John of Braganza* had consistently resisted France's alternate threats and blandishments, and remained loyal to the ancient relationship stretching back into the Middle Ages as "England's oldest ally." Portugal had either insisted on her neutral status or periodically allowed the Royal Navy to shelter, water, and resupply in the Tagus estuary. This in itself was enough to attract Napoleon's wrath and, when added to Portugal's absolute refusal to adhere to any part of the Continental System,* it is not wholly surprising that, after Tilsit* had cleared his hands of other continental commitments, the Emperor determined to settle old scores. From July 1807 Talleyrand* served a number of increasingly severe ultimatums on the Portuguese government, and although the Regent made a number of last-minute concessions to French demands, on 17 October General Junot* led 24,133 French troops into Spain, and on 19 November was passing through Alcantara into Portugal.

Three weeks earlier, the treaty of Fontainebleau* with Godoy* and the Spanish

government had assured Spanish connivance and participation in the aggression. Portuguese resistance was ill-coordinated, and although partisan-type operations caused a number of casualties, Junot was able to march into Lisbon on 30 November at the head of 2,000 men—only to find that Sir William Sydney Smith* of Toulon* and Acre* fame had once again intervened in Napoleon's affairs and persuaded the Regent, royal family, and other dignitaries to embark on a Royal Navy squadron and sail for South America, taking the Portuguese fleet and much of the state treasure with them—both items after which Napoleon hankered. This contretemps notwithstanding, Portugal was soon under French occupation and undergoing Franco-Spanish partition as agreed at Fontainebleau, and Napoleon could at least congratulate himself on closing the Tagus once and for all to the Royal Navy and on shutting Portuguese home markets (although not her considerable colonial ones) to British trade. Soon, however, signs of popular unrest began to become manifest.

All along, however, Napoleon had ulterior motives in his apparent cooperation with his Spanish neighbor, for he had long been dissatisfied with Spain's vacillating policy. She had fought against France from 1793–95 in the First Coalition,* then fought against Britain as France's ally from 1796 to 1802 (during which an invasion of Portugal known as the "War of the Oranges" had ended in minor Spanish advantages), and then again from 1803 she shared in the French engagements against Britain (including the great naval disaster of Trafalgar*). However, after the destruction of Admiral Gravina's* fleet, Franco-Spanish relations had noticeably cooled, and at the time of the outbreak of war between France and Prussia in 1806 even the French pensioner and lickspittle Godoy had prepared to change horses. Napoleon's spies soon learned of this, and the Emperor's countermeasures included the sending of a Spanish corps under La Romana* to serve as hostages in northern Europe with Bernadotte.* The Emperor was now determined to reform Spanish affairs (her government was corrupt and inefficient, to the detriment of the Continental System), and the alliance of late 1807 was little more than a blind to permit the introduction of French troops into key Spanish towns linking Bayonne to the Portuguese frontier—ostensibly as line-of-communication troops, but covertly as the first step toward a massive French intervention into Spanish internal affairs.

Franco-Spanish relations steadily deteriorated over the following winter as French agents played off King Carlos IV* and Godoy against the Crown Prince Ferdinand.* This was done with skill, and by the new year Napoleon was ready to act. His motives, besides an understandable repugnance for Godoy and the desire to bring Spain as well as Portugal into truly effective membership of the Continental System, consisted of the preparation of a grandiose strategic plan involving a three-pronged onslaught against British interests, including an attack on Gibraltar and the Barbary Coast through Spain as well as an onslaught against Sicily by Joseph Bonaparte* and another against Constantinople by Tsar Alexander I* in the Levant. Fringe benefits of a takeover in Spain would include the assimilation of the relics of the Spanish fleet, the nation's treasure, and possibly her overseas colonial markets. Napoleon had no idea of what his plans were in fact going to lead to.

The bubble burst on 16 February 1808. Announcing a policy of good-neighborly intervention to help set Spain's chaotic affairs in order, and his intention of mediating in the disputes dividing the royal family, Napoleon sent parties to seize key positions and fortresses in northern Spain to secure the pass exits from the Pyrenees. Then Prince Murat* marched on Lisbon at the head of 118,000 men commanded by Moncey,* Duhesme,* Dupont,* and Bessières.* The French were cheered by the town populations through which they passed, and soon Murat was in control of Madrid (24 March). When Carlos IV had tried to flee for Cadiz a few days earlier he was turned back by a mob. Napoleon announced his intention to summon all parties in the royal family dispute to a conference at Bayonne, and despite the first anti-French riots in Madrid on 1 April, the meeting duly opened in early May. Within a week Napoleon had maneuvered his unwilling brother Joseph onto the Spanish throne, and as the Spanish royal family set off for various places of exile it seemed that Napoleon's gamble might have come off.

However, he had badly miscalculated Spanish popular loyalty to the reigning house, the fervent distrust felt for France, and above all the ability of the British government to act. On 2 May serious riots broke out in Madrid which were savagely repressed, and before the end of the month major revolts had spread to Valencia, the Asturias, and Seville, and a wave of murders of pro-French Spanish liberals began. By 10 June every province was arming, and the Junta of Seville sent a formal appeal to Gibraltar for British assistance. Napoleon was thus faced with the need to conquer Spain—and to face a probable British intervention on the continent of Europe. With customary zeal he ordered Moncey, Dupont, and Bessières to lead strong columns to repress dissent, and above all to destroy Blake's* 30,000 men forming in Galicia and Castaños'* similar force gathering in Andalusia. The Spanish regular forces, some 100,000 in all, were scattered, poorly armed, and generally ill-led, but as Moncey marched on Valencia with 10,000 troops and Dupont with 13,000 on Seville, they met much obstruction and active hostility from the arming populace. By 18 June Murat had thrown up his overall command and set off for his new kingdom of Naples, leaving Savary* in temporary charge pending King Joseph's arrival in Madrid. This event took place on 20 July, and Joseph was greeted with the heartening news that Bessières had defeated Blake and Cuesta* at the battle of Rio Seco* a week earlier, and that the sieges of Saragossa* and Gerona were under way. Joseph, having sworn the Bayonne Constitution, felt optimistic.

Victory suddenly turned to disaster, however. The day after Lieutenant General Sir Arthur Wellesley* first set foot on Spanish soil at Corunna (1 July), General Dupont, caught amid the arid wastes of south-central Spain, was forced to capitulate with his full corps to Castaños at Bailen.* Hardly had this thunderclap been noted than news arrived that the British army had landed at Mondego Bay* in Portugal, defeated French detachments at Obidos* and Roliça,* and proceeded to defeat Junot* himself at Vimiero* on 21 August. Generals Burrard,* Dalrymple,* and Wellesley had then allowed themselves to be duped by the younger Kellermann* into agreeing to the Convention of Cintra* (30 August), but despite the free evacuation of his army there was no disguising that Junot had lost Portugal. In mounting panic the French abandoned first their sieges and then Madrid itself, falling back behind the river Ebro to regroup. Heartened by these twin successes, the Spanish Supreme Junta met at Aranjuez to plan future strategy.

News of these developments produced a violent reaction from Napoleon. Order-

ing Joseph and Marshal Jourdan* to hold Tudela, Burgos, and Navarre, the Emperor hastened to Erfurt* to confer with the Tsar, and then set out at the head of an army that would total 200,000 men once transfers from the Rhine and Danube were completed. Soon a massive armament was pouring over the Pyrenean passes, and on 6 November the Emperor took over command. He found to his annoyance that Lefebvre* had already fought an inconclusive battle on 31 October against Blake at Pan Corbo,* but next day launched his major offensive in the center, associated with outflanking attacks to west and east, designed to blast a way through Burgos toward Madrid.

All autumn the Supreme Junta had been arguing at Madrid. In the end seven armies under seven discordant captains general emerged, with no Supreme Commander. These forces numbered some 125,000 men in the front line supported by perhaps 75,000 more in reserve or garrisons, backed by possibly 30,000 guerrillas* in numerous independent bands and the 30,000-strong British army, now under command of General Sir John Moore,* in distant Lisbon. Eventually three armies under Blake (left), Castaños (center), and José Palafox* (right) were deployed, with some support from Generals Galuzzo,* Vives, and Redding elsewhere, but the Spanish plan was nebulous in the extreme, and the Junta's armies were soon to be shattered beyond redemption.

On 6 November the French swept forward from the river Ebro to execute a classical but far from straightforward strategy* of double envelopment. Despite Lefebvre's premature attack, the French were ultimately successful in their left hook against Blake. After sustaining a check on 5 November at Valmaceda,* Victor* and Lefebvre caught up with the Spaniards and crushed them at the two-day battle of Espinosa* (10–11 November), which scattered the Army of Galicia. In the center meantime, Napoleon was fulminating against Bessières' slowness in reaching Burgos, and he was replaced by the newly arrived Marshal Soult* on 9 November. Next day the battle of Gamonal outside the city of Burgos led to its occupation and sacking. His central position safely secured, Napoleon could now resume his master plan, and soon Soult was reinforcing the French right wing to smash Blake again at Reynosa* (14 November), while on the opposite flank Lannes* forced battle against Castaños at Tudela,* again securing a telling success but an incomplete one on account of Ney's* failure to close the Spanish line of retreat. Napoleon vented his mounting wrath on the heads of his sheepish marshals, but at least the road to Madrid lay virtually open before him with both flanks secure and with Junot's repatriated troops and Mortier's* reserves arriving in the rear. The new advance began on the 28th.

Meanwhile, Moore had been conducting a long march in three columns from Lisbon, intent upon giving aid to his Spanish allies who, however, were not wholly cooperative. Massing around Salamanca, Moore lingered for several weeks debating his best course of action, but although Napoleon knew of his presence in the area from the 21st of November, he determined to head for Madrid first. By the 29th the French were at the foot of the last mountain barrier before the capital. Next day, the controversial battle of Somosierra* took place, and with San Juan's* ultimate rout Madrid lay defenseless before the victorious French. On 3 December the Junta evacuated toward Badajoz, and next day the French assaulted the Retiro Heights and received the surrender of Madrid.

Napoleon's conquest was now almost complete. Rosas, on the east coast, fell in December, and the French garrison in Barcelona* was relieved. It only remained to deal with Moore and then to occupy the south of France and march again on Lisbon. A two-week lull ensued.

Suddenly dramatic news arrived at Madrid. Moore, whom Napoleon had thought to have been in full retreat for Portugal, was suddenly discovered to be in fact advancing from Salamanca to attack Soult's scattered divisions and thus to threaten the vital lifeline of the Madrid-Burgos-Bayonne highway. Napoleon at once galvanized his troops into action. Crossing the snow-clad Guadarrama Pass* in a blizzard, the Emperor set out to trap the impudent British soldier and his scorned army. Meanwhile Moore's cavalry, under Uxbridge,* had won a notable minor action at Sahagun* on 23 December, but immediately afterward news of Napoleon's advance had reached headquarters. Realizing that Madrid was not still offering resistance as he had been led to believe, Moore knew that he had no recourse but to order a precipitate retreat northward over the mountains toward Corunna and Vigo. His movement began on 1 January in the very nick of time. Aided by such minor rear-guard actions as Benavente* and Villafranca,* Moore kept his army just ahead of the pursuing French. Both armies suffered terrible privations amid the snowy and bitterly cold mountains, and the morale of Moore's army began to crack. Nevertheless, Napoleon judged that his prey had evaded him. Receiving alarming news of plots in Paris and of Austrian warlike preparations on the Danube, the Emperor decided to leave the army at Villafranca, and headed for France. He left Soult, supported by Ney's corps, to complete the destruction of the British army, and issued orders for the redeployment of the rest of the French army toward Portugal and southern Spain. He was never to return to Spain, refusing to accept either the hopelessness of the situation there or the fact that he had left the work of conquest incomplete. As events were to prove, he would have been better advised to have cut his losses and ordered the building of an impregnable military position north of the Ebro—but it was not Napoleon's way to acknowledge personal failure.

Meanwhile, having sent part of his army to Vigo under General Craufurd,* where they were evacuated by the Royal Navy, Moore reached Corunna with the main body ahead of his pursuers. However, no vessels awaited him. After several anxious days the expected sails at last hove in sight, and the embarkation of the cavalry and artillery began. Soult, realizing that his prey was about to escape, decided to attack without waiting for Ney to arrive, and in the ensuing battle of Corunna* (16 January 1809) he was defeated. Moore was killed, but his army escaped and returned to England to recover and prepare for future operations.

The French, under Joseph and Jourdan, now set about the further reduction of Spanish resistance. The second siege of Saragossa* had already been opened on 20 December, and it eventually fell after heroic resistance on 20 February. Three days before the battle of Corunna was fought, the Spaniards sustained a defeat at Uclés which permitted Joseph to re-occupy his capital. By the end of March, Soult had occupied Oporto in Portugal, and the hapless Cuesta had been defeated at Medellin. However, French affairs in the Peninsula were still bedeviled by popular resistance led by the guerrilla leaders, and very soon the British army would be returning to resume its role in thwarting French ambitions.

By early 1809 British policy concerning the Peninsula had largely evolved. The chance to hit back at France on land as well as by sea was welcomed; the state of the naval war* made it possible to convoy, supply, and reinforce the army wherever it was decided to place it ashore, but earlier campaigns in Flanders and Holland under the Duke of York* and at Copenhagen* under Lord Chatham* had proved disappointing. Only Egypt had been an unqualified success—and ahead lay the setback of Walcheren* (1809). But the transport of the army to the Peninsula was to prove the greatest British contribution to the winning of the wars against Napoleon. By tying down (at different dates) between 320,000 and 150,000 French soldiers in a hopeless and bitter struggle, the maintenance of a maximum of 50,000 British troops and perhaps as many more British-trained, armed, and equipped Portuguese regulars (as inspired by Marshal Beresford* and his team) was to prove highly cost-effective. It was also a demonstration both of Britain's resolve to defeat Napoleon and of the power of the Royal Navy. The message was clear for the rest of Europe to read. Furthermore, by breaking the stranglehold of the Continental Blockade in one area, Britain was gaining useful markets for her goods both in southwest Europe and the Americas.

On 22 April Wellesley again arrived at Lisbon, which had never been abandoned by its British defense force. He was in command of some 40,000 men in all, and at once set about training Portuguese formations. His view of his task was clear. By discreet use of his small army in support of the Portuguese and Spanish remnants of their regular armies and most especially in support of their partisan, *Ordonença,* and guerrilla forces, he hoped to make the French problem insupportable (see "Strategy"). Later, when and if conditions became favorable, he hoped to be able to switch from the defensive to the offensive, and undertake the liberation of the Peninsula and even the invasion of southern France. Everything had to be soundly based on effective preparation, training, and logistics. Soon realizing that little was to be hoped for in these respects from his Spanish allies, Wellesley began to build up the great administrative base of Lisbon, the linchpin of his triple supply system of later years—the movement by barge, ox-cart, and finally mule, of adequate supplies and munitions from Lisbon (and later Santander) to forward depots and thence to the front line.

The Defensive Phase of the Peninsular War. The immediate problem was to secure the safety of Portugal to permit the establishment of the Lisbon base. Advancing north in early May, Wellesley forced battle on Soult after a daring river crossing over the Duero (Douro) at Oporto.* This success effectively cleared the French from all but a few fortresses inside Portugal, and heartened by news of this success, Spanish forces compelled Ney to evacuate Galicia. Meanwhile French forces were undertaking the third siege of Gerona (which fell to them on 11 December), while Soult, redeployed to the south, began to move on Cadiz.* Elsewhere, however, more dramatic events were afoot. To aid the Spanish guerrillas and regulars, and to make the most of the Emperor's preoccupation with the campaign against Austria, Wellington (as we may call him from the Barony awarded after Oporto) marched into Spain and linked up with Cuesta's army. With this he fought and won the battle of Talavera* (27 and 28 July) against Joseph and Jourdan, but aware of French forces closing in upon him and totally disillusioned with Spanish promises of aid, he fell back into Portugal and ordered the secret construction of the celebrated Lines of Torres Vedras* just north of Lisbon. This proved a sensible precaution.

Napoleon, newly victorious from Wagram,* sent reinforcements to Spain and ordered that the great Marshal Massena,* soon to be Prince of Essling,* was to invade Portugal at the head of three strong *corps d'armée* to settle with the British once and for all. Meantime the Spanish General Del Parque pulled off a notable success at Tamames, leading to the temporary liberation of Salamanca from French control, but his colleague Areizaga was less fortunate, and after a rapid retreat from Aranjuez he was caught by the French at Ocaña* and soundly beaten in the largest cavalry battle of the Peninsular War. However, the major events of the next year (1810) were to be in Portugal and Andalusia.

During the first two months of 1810 Soult and the Army of the South undertook the formal conquest and occupation of Andalusia. The Junta abandoned Badajoz and fled to Cadiz, where they surrendered power to the Regency on behalf of the *Infante* Ferdinand. There the new government was promptly invested by Marshal Victor,* but British reinforcements arrived by sea from Gibraltar to assist General Albuquerque in the defense of the great naval port, and there he was later joined by Graham* and more British troops. The blockade of Cadiz would continue until 1812.

Meanwhile, Massena was ready to launch his offensive against Portugal. On 28 May he took over command at Salamanca, and after besieging and capturing Ciudad Rodrigo* and Almeida*—the two fortresses dominating the "northern corridor"* linking Spain with Portugal—he advanced over the river Coa and pressed Wellington back down the country. At Bussaco* the Anglo-Portuguese Army turned and inflicted a severe check on the pursuing French (27 September), before resuming their retreat unhindered into the Lines of Torres Vedras. The

The Peninsula

existence of this position came as a severe surprise to Massena, who arrived opposite the forward line on 11 October, and after a fruitless winter attempting to lure Wellington out of his prepared position, the starving French army began to retreat on 3 March 1811. This strategic defeat for the French was followed by the Allied blockade of Almeida, and by the defeat of Massena at Fuentes de Oñoro* on 5 May as Massena tried to succor his garrison. This further setback cost Massena his command, which Napoleon awarded to Marmont.*

In the south, the siege of Cadiz continued, but Graham's seaborne excursion from the defenses to raid the French rear areas led to his victory at Barrosa* (5 March) and successful withdrawal within the defenses. Meanwhile, however, Soult had captured the important fortress of Badajoz* from its Spanish garrison (February), and from it threatened to advance on Elvas* (the second fortress dominating the "Southern Corridor" from the Portuguese side of the frontier) and thence the Tagus opposite Lisbon. These events did not in fact take place, but it was thought politic to protect Lisbon from the Tagus side by undertaking the siege of Badajoz. Beresford was engaged on this when Soult advanced to relieve Philippon's* garrison. The result was the hard-won Allied victory of Albuera.* Badajoz was reblockaded from 19 May, but even Wellington's arrival from operations to the north along the river Coa did not bring a solution. Short of vital equipment, he abandoned the siege on 19 June as French forces converged upon him.

Elsewhere, the year 1811 saw Venezuela declare itself independent from Spain on 5 July (the previous 16 September had seen a major revolt in Mexico). In eastern Spain, Suchet* besieged Sagunto and defeated the resilient Blake between 23 September and 25 October. On 8 January 1812 the same commander surrendered Valencia to Suchet, who had received his marshal's baton from Napoleon in recognition of these considerable successes. Furthermore, Suchet and his wife proved most adept at "hearts and minds" treatment of the Spaniards in their area—the sole example of a French success in this type of psychological warfare.

With the advent of 1812 came an important switch of emphasis. As Napoleon began to turn all his attention toward the forthcoming Russian campaign, the French troop levels in Spain fell below 200,000 men. Wellington, his Anglo-Portuguese formations now fully trained and "blooded," was almost ready to take the offensive and undertake the liberation of Spain. First he needed to secure undisputed control of both corridors, and to this end he turned on Ciudad Rodrigo in the north and captured it after a brief winter siege on 19 January. Then, while Napoleon decreed that Joseph was to become Commander in Chief of all French forces in Spain, and the Cadiz *Cortes* passed a liberal constitution for the future governance of Spain, Wellington, now made an earl, prepared to take Badajoz. The fortress was finally stormed in a bloody onslaught on 6 April, and for three days the infuriated British soldiery ran amok against the unfortunate Spanish inhabitants. However, "the scum of the earth" had won for Wellington the last vital fortress he required. Now all was ready for the Allied army to assume a major offensive against the weakened French forces in Spain.

Wellington's Offensive Phase of the Peninsular War. With Marmont in the north and Soult in the south to choose between, Wellington selected the former, calculating that a threat toward Burgos and the vital highway back to France would be a sure way to force the major battle he was determined to obtain. Using the guerrilla chief Ballesteros and a force under General Hill* to harrass Soult in the south, a naval squadron under Sir Home Popham* to pin Caffarelli* to the north coast sector, a force from Sicily under Sir William Bentinck to divert Suchet's attention, and two more local leaders to harass Astorga and Toro lest Marmont get suspicious of the lack of activity on his central northern sector, Wellington was ready to march with 48,000 men (28,000 of them British troops) in late May from Ciudad Rodrigo. The advance began on 13 June, and four days later Salamanca had been occupied save for three forts. Then for a month a period of shadow-boxing with Marmont's main army began along the river Douro between Toro and Tordesillas, as both commanders strove to obtain a decisive positional advantage. The forts capitulated on 27 June, but Marmont was receiving reinforcements which brought his strength to 43,000 men, and there were signs that King Joseph and Suchet were both contemplating sending more aid—especially as Bentinck's expedition was very late appearing. However, the campaign of march and countermarch continued to the great dissatisfaction of many of Wellington's officers, but at last on 22 July the Earl found his battle opportunity, and the great battle of Salamanca* was fought and won. But for a Spanish failure to block the bridge at Alba de Tormes* the French defeat would have been total, but in the event their survivors escaped, although General Foy* was badly mauled at Garcia Hernandez on the 23rd.

North Spain was now at Wellington's mercy, but for political reasons he chose to march on Madrid (entered on 12 August) rather than on Burgos.* When at last he appeared before that fortress on 16 September he faced a determined garrison under an inspired commander,

Dubreton,* and the approach of two French relief armies forced him to abandon the siege. Meanwhile, Soult had left Cadiz (24 August) and was retreating toward Valencia, abandoning all of Andalusia, so the days of French rule appeared numbered. However, Wellington was constrained to spend the winter around Ciudad Rodrigo, absorbing reinforcements and planning the next campaign.

When this opened in June 1813 the overall situation was dramatically different. Napoleon's disastrous retreat from Moscow* the previous autumn and winter had given place to a no less desperate fight against the main forces of the Sixth Coalition* in Germany. King Joseph received orders to divert what was left of the Army of Portugal toward Biscay. However, not everything was going Wellington's way, as the abortive siege of Tarragonna* on Spain's east coast by General Murray* indicated. Nevertheless, Wellington's new offensive was masterly in both concept and execution. A combination of frontal pressure associated with an enveloping hook by Graham around the northern flank forced the French to fall back from river line to river line, until on 21 June the climactic battle of Vitoria* was fought, at which the remnants of three French armies under Jourdan were utterly routed. This success finally cost Napoleon Spain. Soon Soult was in full retreat from Valencia, and on 11 July he arrived at Bayonne with orders to take over all French troops in Spain. The Marshal was no ninny, and to attempt to relieve his last garrisons in Spain—besieged in San Sebastian* and Pamplona* respectively—he launched a sudden counteroffensive through the Pyrenean passes which took Wellington, newly made a field marshal, by surprise as the events at Maya* and Roncesvalles* demonstrated. However, Wellington rallied in time to meet and defeat Soult's columns at Sorauren* near Pamplona and Vera* near San Sebastian, and by early August Soult was back over the frontier. San Sebastian fell to a bloody assault in August, an event followed by another sacking, and some time later Pamplona also capitulated (31 October). Long before the last event, however, on 7 October Wellington had crossed the Bidassoa* onto French soil, and as Napoleon was fighting and losing the battle of Leipzig* in Germany, Wellington was probing toward Bayonne. On 10 November Soult was defeated on the Nivelle,* and a month later at the Nive* and St. Pierre,* but still he fought doggedly on. So bad was the behavior of the vengeful Spaniards on French soil that Wellington was forced to send them home.

Meantime, in a last attempt to influence the course of events on the southern front, Napoleon induced Ferdinand VII to sign the infamous—and unenforceable —Treaty of Valençay* on 11 December. The Campaign of 1814 began with the last French battle on Spanish soil— Molinos del Rey*—on the eastern sector, after which Suchet fell back into France. As Napoleon fought for his very existence around Paris against overwhelming odds, Ferdinand VII returned to Madrid after long years of exile. Wellington was still pressing after Soult deeper and deeper into France, winning battles at Orthez* and Tarbes.* Unbeknownst to either side, Napoleon abdicated on 11 April, but in the south the great battle of Toulouse* was fought six days later. The garrison of Bayonne* was the last to capitulate to the Allied army after a spirited final sortie. After eight years of perpetual conflict, the Peninsular War was at last over.

Those who hoped that the clock would be put back to mid-1807 were to be disappointed. Although the regime of Ferdinand VII soon rounded up the liberals in Madrid and elsewhere, in South America area after area refused to accept the imposition of metropolitan Spanish rule. A generation of revolution and disturbance and unrest lay ahead of both Spain and Portugal, but the menace represented by France had been dissipated in the "War of Liberation," 1807–14.

Perceval, Spencer, Prime Minister and Statesman (1762–1812). A lawyer by profession, he first entered Parliament as MP for Northampton in 1796. Under Addington* he was Solicitor General (1801) and Attorney General (1802) and was retained by Pitt* on his return to power. Under the Portland administration he served as Chancellor of the Exchequer with some success. In 1809 he succeeded Portland as Prime Minister but proved only moderately successful owing to problems with Castlereagh* and Canning.* His ministry survived the Walcheren* fiasco by forcing Lord Chatham* to resign. Despite the dislike of George,* Prince Regent, he was retained in office in 1811. He faced much criticism for keeping the British forces in the Peninsula short of financial support. In 1811 he introduced bank notes as legal tender. On 11 May 1812 he was assassinated by a bankrupt man, John Bellingham, in the lobby of the House of Commons.

Pérignon, Maréchal Catherine Dominique, marquis de (1754–1818). Probably the least known of the Marshalate,* Pérignon was first commissioned in 1780. Nine years later he became a lieutenant colonel of the National Guard, and in 1791 a deputy in the legislative Assembly. Released for military duty the next year, he served for three years in the Army of the East Pyrenees and rapidly made a reputation. On 18 September 1793 he was wounded by a bayonet and recommended for the rank of *général de brigade* the same day; within three months he was

Pérignon

promoted to *général de division*. From 1794–95 he commanded the army fighting in Spain, before being replaced by Schérer.* He was elected to the Council of Five Hundred* and appointed to hold coastal commands in the north and west of France. Instead he was sent to Spain as ambassador from 1795–97, and in 1798 he was transferred to the Army of Italy. After holding a command in Liguria, he led a corps at Novi,* where he was seriously wounded in the head and taken prisoner. He returned to France in 1800 and was made a senator the next year, becoming Vice President of the Senate in 1802. He was made a marshal in 1804 and served as Governor General of Parma and Piacenza from 1806–08. Made a count in 1808, he was transferred to the governorship of Naples and followed Jourdan* in command of the French troops stationed in that kingdom, where he remained until 1813. He rallied to the Bourbons and was at once employed by them, and Napoleon struck his name from the list of marshals in April 1815. However, Louis XVIII* restored his baton in 1816 and named him a marquis in 1817. One of the four honorary marshals created by Napoleon in 1804, he was not present at any of the great battles but proved an able administrator. His royalist sympathies were manifest from 1813.

Pero Negro. This small village in Portugal held Wellington's* headquarters in Portugal from October 1810 until March 1811. It was close to the first line of forts comprising the advanced position of the Lines of Torres Vedras,* from within which Wellington and the Anglo-Portuguese army defied Massena* and the Army of Portugal.

Perrée, Contre-Amiral Jean-Baptiste Emmanuel (1761–1800). After going to sea as a cabin boy in 1773, over the next 20 years he worked his way up to command a merchant vessel. He was transferred to the navy in 1793, and within a year had been appointed to the rank of captain. Two years later he conducted a successful cruise in the Mediterranean, capturing a British frigate, 2 corvettes, and 25 sail of merchant shipping. In June 1796 he was promoted to commodore. In May 1798 he sailed under Brueys,* commanding part of the fleet escorting Bonaparte and the Army of the Orient to Malta* and Egypt. He was put in command of the flotilla of boats that followed the army up the Nile, distinguished himself at Shubra Khit* in July by defeating the Moslem gunboats, and was awarded a saber of honor by Bonaparte. In November he was promoted to rear admiral. The next year he was charged with sailing the siege train to Jaffa* but was much hampered by Commodore Sir William Sydney Smith,* losing much of the materiel. In June 1799 he sailed for France with his flotilla but was intercepted by the British blockading forces and taken prisoner. Exchanged almost immediately, he commanded *Le Généreux* in a desperate attempt to pass supplies into Malta for the relief of the besieged French garrison, but was intercepted by Nelson* within sight of the island and accepted battle against hopeless odds to permit the other French vessels to escape. He was gravely wounded and forced to strike his flag when his ship foundered. He died on 18 February, ten days after the action.

Perry, Commodore Oliver Hazard (1785–1819). United States sailor, who built the flotilla on the Great Lakes and won the battle of Lake Erie* (1813) during the War ·of 1812.* He later helped build batteries and defenses along the Potomac River.

Pestiferies, the, of Jaffa, 1799. During the invasion of Syria, the French Army of the Orient was afflicted by an outbreak of bubonic plague. Some 300 cases were sick with the disease by the time the army reached Jaffa* on its march to Acre,* and were confined to hospital. On 11 March, ignoring the risk, General Bonaparte insisted upon visiting the wards in an attempt to rally the sinking morale of his army. Only 8% of the patients survived the dread disease. Bonaparte, returning defeated from Acre a few months later, gave orders for the remaining seriously sick—perhaps 50—to be poisoned. This elicited a warm protest from Dr. Desgenettes, and it appears that the order was not carried out, as the pursuing Turks found seven patients still alive, and many of the others had been evacuated with the retreating army.

Phélypeaux, Colonel Antoine le Picard de (1768–1799). Of aristocratic family, he was studying at the *Ecole Militaire* in Paris at the same time as the young Bonaparte, with whom he did not get on. He also entered the artillery. In 1789 he was promoted to captain, but in 1791 he became an *émigré* and served in Condé's army until 1795, when he returned to

France and attempted to raise a revolt for the royalist cause in the former province of Berry. He was arrested but escaped in 1797. He secretly returned to France and masterminded the rescue of Sir William Sidney Smith* from the Temple prison. Smith gained him a British commission as colonel, and in 1798 Phélypeaux accompanied him to the Levant, where he played a leading part in organizing the defense of Acre* against Bonaparte. After the successful thwarting of the Army of the Orient, he caught the plague and died.

Philippon, Général Armand, baron (1761–1836). Enlisting in the Bourbon army as a soldier (1778), by 1790 he had risen to the rank of sergeant major. In 1792 he was a captain of volunteers, served in Spain (1793–95) and later on the Danube (1799). Employed over succeeding years in Italy, Switzerland, and Hanover, he served with the *Grande Armée* from 1805–07, fighting at Austerlitz.* Transferred to Spain in 1808, he fought at Talavera* and at the siege of Cadiz.* In 1810 he was made a baron and also promoted to *général de brigade*. From March 1811 he was governor of Badajoz,* successfully defied Beresford's* and Wellington's* first siege attempts, was promoted to *général de division* in July, and in 1812 only surrendered after being wounded and after the costly storming of the city in April. He escaped from captivity in England and took part in the Russian and German campaigns, fighting under Vandamme* at Kulm* in August 1813. He retired from active service on 15 September of that year and was later reconciled with the Bourbons.

Pichegru, Général Jean Charles (1761–1804). The son of a peasant, he held a lowly teaching post at Brienne before joining the Bourbon army as a gunner in 1780. He fought in America, earned steady

Pichegru

advancement, and in 1792 was a senior lieutenant as well as an elected lieutenant colonel of revolutionary troops. Service on the Rhine followed, with rapid promotion to *général de brigade* and *général de division* in the same year (1793). For a period he commanded the Army of the Rhine, and then the Army of the North (1794) in place of Jourdan.* With this army he conquered Belgium, defeating the Duke of York* at Boxtel, overwhelmed Holland, and captured the Dutch Fleet on the Texel by launching a cavalry charge across the ice (1795). After a period commanding the Parisian National Guard, he was made commander of the Army of the Rhine and Moselle. He captured Mainz, but then allowed the Austrians to retake it, and resigned. He was then elected to the Council of Five Hundred* and became its president, but was proscribed at the *coup d'état** of *Fructidor* in 1797, and deported to Guiana. In 1798 he escaped and reached London. In 1803 he became deeply involved in the Cadoudal* conspiracy, but was arrested in Paris.

He was found strangled in his cell on 5 April 1804.

Picton, Lieutenant General Sir Thomas (1758–1815). Commissioned into the 12th Foot in 1771, he had risen to major via several regiments by 1795. Serving in the West Indies under Abercromby,* he took part in the captures of St. Lucia and Trinidad (1796–97). After some years as military governor of the latter, in 1801 he became civil governor as well, but resigned over charges concerning the use of torture. Promoted to brigadier general in 1801 and to major general in 1808, he took part in the siege of Flushing during the Walcheren* campaign (1809) and then was invalided home. Next year he joined the army in Portugal, and was given command of the 3rd Division by Wellington.* Picton fought at Bussaco* and Torres Vedras,* then headed the pursuit of Massena* and took a prominent part in the battle of Fuentes de Oñoro* (1811). He was in charge of the final siege of Badajoz* in 1812 and was severely wounded in the storming. He was knighted, and in 1813 promoted to lieutenant general. His division played a leading role at Vitoria* (1813). Seven times he received the thanks of the House of Commons for his military services, but in 1814 he was not raised to the peerage. In 1815 he commanded the veteran 5th Division during the Campaign of the Hundred Days,* fighting at Quatre Bras.* On 18 June he was killed leading his men to the charge at Waterloo.*

Pirch, Major General Georg Dubislaw Ludwig (1763–1830?). A native of Magdeburg, Pirch was given command of the Prussian II Corps in May 1815, replacing General Borstell, who had been disgraced for protesting about the treatment of some mutinous Saxon troops. His corps marched from Namur to Sombreffe to reinforce Ziethen,* and played a prominent part in the battle of Ligny.* On 18 June he followed Bülow's* corps through the Bois de Paris from Wavre* to fall on Napoleon's right flank at Waterloo,* arriving near Plancenoit at 6:00 P.M. His later career is obscure.

Pirna, battle of, 26 August 1813. After the breakdown of the armistice,* Napoleon planned a large-scale crossing over the Elbe to envelop the Allied right flank, but news of Oudinot's* defeat at Gross-Beeren* and anxiety for Dresden* caused him to switch all troops toward that city, leaving Vandamme* with the I Corps and an additional division to carry out the Elbe crossing and envelopment attack. By 5:00 P.M. on the 26th Vandamme had crossed the river by the Königstein bridges at the head of 34 battalions and Corbineau's* cavalry, but no guns. In a sharp evening engagement, Vandamme's 40,000 men defeated Eugen of Württemberg's* 12,500 Allied troops, guarding the main army's right flank, and drove them off the heights of Pirna and the neighboring plateau. Eugen's pleas for aid resulted in the diversion of Ostermann-Tolstoi* and his corps of 26,000 men to the scene from the Dresden front, and his supercession in command by that officer. As the victorious French army advanced from Dresden, Napoleon ordered Vandamme to sever the Allied line of retreat. The result was the defeat of Vandamme at Kulm,* and his capture, four days later.

Pitt, General Sir John, second Earl of Chatham (1756–1835). He began his army career in 1778, but as the eldest son of the great first Earl (Great Britain's victorious prime minister during the Seven Years' War) he soon became deeply involved in politics in his brother William's* governments. From 1788–94 he was First Lord of the Admiralty, being made a Privy Councillor in 1789 and a knight of the Garter the next year. From 1794–96 he was Lord

Privy Seal and Lord President of the Council from 1796–1801. In the last year, on the fall of his brother's government, he was made Master-General of the Ordnance, a position he held until 1806. He believed he should have been appointed to command in the Peninsula in place of Wellesley* in 1808, and in compensation was given charge of the Walcheren* expedition the next year. Proving wholly incapable, he tried to blame the naval commander for the fiasco that ensued, but was sacked by Prime Minister Perceval.* Promoted to full general in 1812, he was Governor of Gibraltar from 1820–35, but never lived down the Walcheren affair.

Pitt, William, Prime Minister and statesman (1759–1806). The second son of the great Earl of Chatham, he was educated at Cambridge and Lincoln's Inn, being called to the bar in 1780. Next year he entered Parliament, and in 1782 was appointed Chancellor of the Exchequer in the Shelburne ministry. In December 1783, on the fall of that cabinet, he was made Prime Minister at the age of 25 by George III,* who trusted him. In the face of repeated defeats in Parliament, he refused to dissolve despite his weak minority position until he judged the moment right, and then won an overwhelming majority in the general election of 1784. He spent much time reforming the national finances, instituting the Sinking Fund as a means of reducing the National Debt in 1786. When King George III became insane, the enmity of George,* Prince Regent, threatened his ministry, but the crisis passed with the King's temporary recovery. Pitt turned to colonial affairs and attempted to resolve the racial problem in Canada (1791).

At the outbreak of the French Revolution* he at first regarded it as no matter for British concern, but the execution of Louis XVI* and the French designs on the river Scheldt led to war in February 1793. The situation forced Pitt to suspend Habeus Corpus and many intended internal reforms, and the wars with France would take up the rest of his ministry and life. Between March and October 1793 he formed the First Coalition,* but although Britain gained successes at sea and made colonial gains, his continental allies met defeat. Pitt, under heavy pressure at home, tried to negotiate peace with France in March 1796, but in vain, and with the defeat of his allies and the grave economic strains of the struggle, Pitt's reputation was in a critical condition. All peace overtures failed, and with the crisis of the Irish Rebellion of 1798 he reached the nadir of his fortunes. However, the victory of Nelson* at the Nile* rallied national support and enabled him to create the Second Coalition in that year. To finance the war he introduced income tax and strengthened the property or land taxes.

In 1800 he united Ireland to England by the Act of Union, but his wish to secure Catholic emancipation was blocked by George III's complete opposition to the measure, and Pitt resigned in March 1801. He continued to support Addington's* ministry and approved the Peace of Amiens;* on the resumption of war he re-entered office as premier in May 1804, but without his former Whig allies' support. However, rallying the Addington supporters, he led a successful ministry and in 1805 created the Third Coalition against France. He raised the land tax by 25% to help finance the war, but attacks on his ministry's financial soundness began to undermine his health. News of Ulm* and then Austerlitz* led to a complete breakdown, and he died a broken man in January 1806.

An able party manager and financier, he was not as great a war leader as his father, his policy of supporting continental coalitions proving both costly and ineffective. Forced to abandon most of his concepts for internal reform, he nevertheless held the country together through a critical period, and at his death its naval reputation was at its peak and the colonial possessions of Great Britain had been considerably increased. Napoleon regarded him as one of his most inveterate foes.

Pius VII, Pope (1740–1823). Born Barnabas Luigi Gregorio Chiaramonti, in 1756 he became a member of the Benedictine Order. In 1782 he was consecrated Bishop of Tivoli and later translated to the bishopric of Imola (1785), the year he became a cardinal. On the death of Pope Pius VI he was elected Pope at Venice in March 1800. His pontificate opened auspiciously with the negotiation of the Concordat* with the Consulate (July 1801), and in late 1804 Pius was pleased to travel to Paris to crown Napoleon as Emperor. However, thereafter relations deteriorated: there was friction over the Organic Articles, and the Pope refused to adhere to the Continental System.* Pius had also refused (1805) to annul Joseph Bonaparte's* marriage. As a reprisal, Napoleon occupied Rome with a military force in 1808, and next year occupied the Papal States. Pius promptly excommunicated all concerned and was arrested. He was first confined in Genoa, then at Savona, and ultimately at Fontainebleau, where he was obliged to negotiate a new Concordat with Napoleon. The military disasters that befell France brought Pius VII his liberty, and in May 1814 he returned to Rome. The Congress of Vienna* restored the Papal States apart from Avignon. The Pope then proceeded to negotiate a whole series of concordats with European countries, and set in train a series of reforms within both the Holy See and the Papal States, raising a permanent army to defend his possessions.

Platov, General Matvei Ivanovich (1751–1818). Born at Azov, the future

Hetman of the Don Cossacks served with distinction under Suvorov.* He played a significant role with his Cossacks during the Campaign of 1812, especially during the French retreat. He fought at Leipzig* and in 1814 occupied Paris at the head of his unruly horsemen. He was something of a legendary figure among his tough Cossack warriors.

Plechenitski, action of, 29 December 1812. A force of Russian cavalry under General Lanskoi succeeded in outdistancing the French army as the survivors of the Beresina* marched slowly westward and they launched an attack against the town of Plechenitski to the west of Zembin. They surprised the small garrison, but the wounded Marshal Oudinot* organized 15 men into a defense force and successfully held a house until the Russians gave up and retired. Oudinot was, however, struck by a falling beam when part of the roof collapsed.

Polotsk, battles of, 17–18 August and 14 November 1812. This town near the river Dvina was twice the scene of important actions during the Campaign of 1812 in Russia. On 18 August Marshal Oudinot* and his II Corps, reinforced by Gouvion St. Cyr's* VI Corps to a total of 35,000 men, attacked General Wittgenstein's* Army of Finland after several weeks of indecisive maneuvering. Oudinot himself was *hors de combat* with a wound received on the evening of the 17th, but Gouvion St. Cyr commanded in his place the next day with some skill, and Wittgenstein was driven back over the Dvina. Napoleon awarded St. Cyr his marshal's baton for this achievement. Next, during the retreat from Moscow, Napoleon ordered Marshal Victor* to attack Wittgenstein with his IX and the wounded Oudinot's II Corps to avert the danger of the Army of Finland marching south to link up with other Russian forces at Minsk or on

the Beresina ahead of the retreating main French army. Victor had six divisions available, and Wittgenstein some 35,000, and the Russians came off decidedly the worse in the encounter, which centered around the village of Smoliani—by which name the battle is alternatively known. This imposed a delay on the Army of Finland, but Admiral Tshitsagov* won the race to the Beresina, and all forces were converging on that river line by the third week in November.

Poniatowski, Maréchal Josef Anton, Prince (1763–1813). Nicknamed "the Polish Bayard," Poniatowski was born in Vienna, the son of a senior Austrian commander. He was commissioned into the Austrian army in 1778, serving in the dragoons and carabiniers, and in 1788 he became an aide-de-camp to the Emperor Francis II* and was wounded fighting the Turks on the river Save. Leaving the Austrian service, he joined the army of his uncle, the King of Poland, and commanded the Polish forces fighting the Russians in the Ukraine in 1792, winning several engagements. Disillusioned by the peace terms, he left Poland and for a time lived in Vienna, refusing to serve under Russian orders. He later moved back to his estates near Warsaw, but saw little military or public service until 1806, when the King of Prussia made him Governor of Warsaw and Minister of War in the provisional Polish government. Following the French overthrow of Prussia, early in 1807 he was appointed to command the 1st Polish Legion in the French service and began his association with Napoleon. He became Minister of War of the Grand Duchy of Warsaw from 1808, and in 1809 he fought successfully against Archduke Ferdinand,* capturing Cracow in July. Returning to Warsaw, he founded military schools for the engineers and artillery and a military hospital.

In 1812 he commanded the Polish and

Poniatowski

Saxon troops forming the V Corps of the *Grande Armée* during the invasion of Russia, fought at Smolensk,* and commanded the right wing of the French at Borodino.* He was wounded at the Beresina* but recovered and set about reconstituting the Polish forces. Commanding the VIII Corps, he rejoined the Emperor in July 1813 and won a number of actions and lost several more in the fighting preceding Leipzig,* being wounded by a lance-thrust shortly before that battle. On 16 October he received his baton as a French marshal, and fought with élan during the great "Battle of the Nations." However, he was wounded four times trying to cover the retreat of the French to the river Elster, and after the bridge was blown he attempted to swim on his horse over the river to the French bank but was drowned.

Ponsonby, Major General Sir Frederick Cavendish (1783–1837). First commissioned in 1800, he was posted with his regiment to the Peninsula in 1809. After fighting with distinction at Talavera* and Barrosa,* he obtained command of the

11th Light Dragoons, whom he led for the rest of the Napoleonic wars. He fought at Waterloo,* where he was wounded. He went on half pay in 1820, but was promoted to major general in 1825, the year before he was appointed governor of Malta, a post he held until 1835.

Ponsonby, Major General Sir William (1772–1815). He obtained command of the 5th Dragoon Guards in 1803 and served in Spain (1811–14), commanding a brigade of cavalry at Vitoria.* He was knighted in 1815, shortly before the Hundred Days.* At Waterloo* he led the charge of the Union Brigade which shattered d'Erlon's* I Corps, but pressed too far, and after attacking the main French battery he was killed by Jacquinot's lancers as he tried to regain Wellington's* lines with his disordered horsemen.

Popham, Rear Admiral Sir Home Riggs (1762–1820). Entering the Royal Navy in 1778, nine years later he obtained a long leave of absence and busied himself in the East India and China trade. He was almost ruined when his vessel was seized for supposedly unlicensed trading. In 1794 he served under the Duke of York* in Flanders and was promoted to post captain. Service afloat in the Baltic followed, and later he commanded a squadron sent with Sir David Baird's* force to the Cape of Good Hope* (1806). Thereafter he was sent in a similar position with General Beresford* on an unsuccessful expedition to Buenos Aires* (1806), and for his supposed part in the disaster was replaced in command and censured by a court-martial (1807). He took part in the expedition against Copenhagen* in 1808. In 1812 he commanded a raiding squadron that kept the north coast of Spain in a ferment in conjunction with the guerrillas during the early stages of the Salamanca* campaign. Knighted in 1815, he was promoted to rear admiral and given command of the Jamaica station (1817–20), but his health broke down and he retired in 1820.

Porlier, General Juan Diaz, Marquis of Matoarosa (1783–1815). After serving at Trafalgar,* he fought against Napoleon in 1808 and became a famous leader of the Spanish guerrillas* operating in the Biscayan and Asturian regions. Porlier was the nephew of General La Romana* and from this he derived his nickname of *El Marquesito*. He fought at Gamonal, and in 1810 temporarily captured Santander in an amphibious operation with the aid of Commodore Popham* and his squadron, an exploit that was twice repeated over the next two years; the third attempt in 1812 was in fact repulsed. Later he became disillusioned with Ferdinard VII,* rebelled against his rule, and was eventually captured and hanged (1815) at Corunna.

Poserna, action of, 1 May 1813. As part of his master plan for the spring campaign in Germany, Napoleon ordered Ney* and Marmont* to advance through Weissenfels* toward Lützen.* On 1 May, after the French leading elements had passed through Weissenfels, there was heavy fighting between Poserna and Rippach, southwest of Lützen. Winzingerode's* cavalry attempted to block the passage of the stream near Rippach but was driven off by Ney's new conscript divisions. A heavy loss, however, was the death of Marshal Bessières,* killed by a round shot.

Potsdam, treaty of, 3 November 1805. This was an agreement signed between Tsar Alexander* and Frederick William* of Prussia, whereby the latter monarch agreed to make an offer of mediation to Napoleon, seeking a peace based on the Treaty of Luneville;* in the event of Napoleon rejecting this suggestion, Prussia would join Austria and Prussia in the Third Coalition* and contribute an army of 180,000 Prussian troops to the common

cause. In fact Prussia took no action whatsoever, and after Austerlitz* the French Emperor made unscrupulous use of his knowledge of the agreement to force Prussia into making humiliating concessions, embodied in the treaty of Schönbrunn.*

Pressburg, treaty of, 26 December 1805. Following the cataclysm of Austerlitz* the Emperor Francis* opened negotiations with Napoleon. The terms finally embodied in the treaty of Pressburg were harsh. Austria gave up all the Venetian territory acquired at the Peace of Campo Formio,* including Istria and Dalmatia. She also ceded all her possessions in south Germany, in the Tyrol, and in the Voralberg, receiving Salzburg in exchange (by arrangement with the Duke of Tuscany). France's allies in the late war, Bavaria and Württemberg, were recognized as independent kingdoms free of all feudal links with the Holy Roman Empire. The effect of these terms was to exclude Austria from Italy and from Germany proper, while Francis' title of Holy Roman Emperor became nothing more than a sham.

Privateers. Fast, well-armed raiding vessels, whose crews were permitted to prey on enemy merchant shipping for the profit of their owners by virtue of being issued a *lettre de marque*—virtually a license for piracy in time of war. They proved a source of serious losses to the British merchant trades. The *guerre de course* or commerce* war placed a considerable strain on the British economy, and the need for the Royal Navy to control the menace privateers represented proved no insignificant part of the naval war.*

Provera, General Johann, Marquis of (1740–1804). Born in Pavia, this Austrian commander fought with distinction against the Turks and was promoted to field-marshal-lieutenant in 1792. In 1796 he commanded a division in North Italy under General Beaulieu* but was defeated at Millesimo* and forced to surrender at Cosseria* in the first phase of General Bonaparte's offensive. Repatriated, he later took part in operations designed to relieve Mantua* in early 1797. He forced a crossing over the Adige with 9,000 men near Legnano and marched to within sight of Mantua. General Würmser* attempted to break out to join him on 16 January but was repulsed, and surrounded by converging French columns Provera was compelled to capitulate at La Favorita.*

Puebla, storming of the heights of, 21 June 1813. This feat of arms, forming the first stage in the battle of Vitoria,* was carried out by General Hill* in command of the British 2nd Division and General Morillo's Spanish troops, some 20,000 men in all. Forming the extreme right of Wellington's* line, Hill crossed the river Zadorra to secure the Puebla defile—and the neighboring heights that were its key —and thus gain entry to the plain of Vitoria from the southwest. Beginning at 8:00 A.M. on a drizzling morning, the fight against Maransin's Brigade was hard and bitter, but once Morillo had been reinforced by the 71st Regiment and the light companies the crest was carried and held against the counterattack by part of Conroux's division. Jourdan* was forced to redeploy two divisions from his center to create a new flank and reinforce Gazan,* and this had a great effect on the outcome of the main battle. Thus Hill's capture of the Heights and subsequent occupation of the village of Subijana de Alava were important developments that contributed to Wellington's notable victory.

Pultusk, battle of, 26 December 1806. The town of Pultusk stands on the west bank of the river Narew some 32 miles north of Warsaw in Poland. Following up

the wreck of the Prussian armies after Jena-Auerstädt,* Murat* occupied Warsaw on 26 November. The Prussians had been joined by a Russian army commanded by General Bennigsen,* and it was against this commander and his 35,000 men and 40 guns that Marshal Lannes* and his V Corps (perhaps 20,000 men initially) deployed at 10:00 A.M. The Russians were drawn up in three lines between Pultusk and Mostachin, their right commanded by Barclay de Tolly,* their left by Bagavut.* The weather was appalling—windy and wet—and thick mud covered the ground, but Lannes launched Claparède's* division against Pultusk itself, while Suchet* led his men against the Mostachin wooded heights. On both sectors the French made some progress despite the conditions and their numerical disadvantage, and captured the ridges forming the extremities of the Russian position. The Russian superiority in artillery soon told, and although the French at one moment got into the town they were unable to hold their ground there. At about 3:00 P.M. a division of Davout's* III Corps led by General d'Aultanne appeared up the Golymin road, bringing Lannes' strength up to 25,000 men, and Bennigsen wheeled back his right wing as Lannes and the newcomers pressed forward. The Russian cavalry poured 20 squadrons into a gap that appeared between Lannes and d'Aultanne, but they were met with infantry fire from squares of the 85th Regiment and gave ground. Dusk was falling and the French troops were in some confusion, so the battle petered out. The French fell back to their original battle line, having sustained some 8,000 casualties. Unbeknown to Lannes, Bennigsen (who had been ordered not to engage by his superior, Kamenskoi*) had decided to abandon his positions overnight, having lost possibly 5,000 men. The French were in no condition to pursue on the 27th,

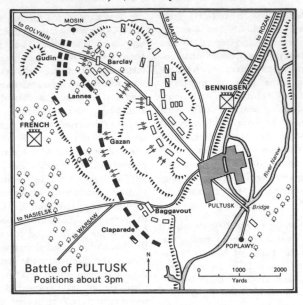

Battle of PULTUSK
Positions about 3pm

however, so the battle of Pultusk ended indecisively. The same day, moreover, had seen a second indecisive engagement between Sacken* and a Russian corps against Augereau* and Murat* at Golymin*—and Napoleon decided to halt his advance and place his troops in winter quarters. They were not to be long undisturbed there, however; in six weeks' time the terrible battle of Eylau* would be fought.

Pyramids, battle of the, 21 July 1798. Advancing up the west bank of the Nile toward Cairo, Bonaparte and the 25,000 men of the Army of the Orient found themselves facing the forces of the Mameluke* leaders, Murad* and Ibrahim Bey.* The Mamelukes had split their forces into two parts, divided by the Nile: near Cairo on the east bank stood Ibrahim with possibly 18,000 peasant infantry; on the west bank, Murad had placed most of his 15,000 infantry within en-

trenchments around the village of Embabeh near the river, together with most of his 40 guns; his elite Mameluke horsemen (perhaps 6,000 in all) were drawn up in the center, and further infantry stood on his left near the village of Biktil. Appreciating that the serried ranks of horsemen posed the real danger, Bonaparte was ready to draw up his five small divisions in large squares of his own devising, with his 30 guns deployed to cover the angles of each formation, and to place his meager cavalry and trains, together with headquarters and the savants,* inside the squares.

The French advanced from the direction of Omm-Dinar, having broken camp at 2:00 A.M., and came within sight of their foe 12 hours later. After an hour's rest, Bonaparte launched the divisions of Rampon* and Vial* against Embabeh and its defenses, and sent Desaix* on the desert flank to secure Biktil and pose a threat to the Mameluke left. The divisions of Dugua* and Reynier* were placed in support.

To avoid being penned in against the river bank about Embabeh, Murad Bey launched his Mamelukes forward in a series of fierce charges. The squares of Desaix and Reynier absorbed the brunt of these attacks, and closed their ranks just in time. The yelling horsemen could not penetrate the fire-fringed squares and wheeled away toward Biktil where a sharp fight ensued, the French garrison fighting from the rooftops. This distraction left the Egyptian infantry in Embabeh isolated —as Bonaparte had hoped—and the village defenses were stormed by Vial and Bon, supported by gunfire from Perée's* flotilla of boats on the Nile. The Egyptians broke and ran in panic, and large numbers were cut down, bayoneted, or drowned in the Nile. For some 300 casualties the French had inflicted an estimated 5,000 on Murad's army. The prize was Cairo, occupied the next day as Ibrahim abandoned the city without further ado while Murad withdrew with his 3,000 remaining cavalry toward Gizeh and Middle Egypt. The battle effectively won the French control of Lower Egypt. But Nelson's* great naval victory of the Nile* on 1 August would cut Bonaparte off from France.

Pyrenees, the (so-called) battle of, 25 July–2 August 1813. This "battle" in fact comprised Marshal Soult's* large-scale offensive, launched from the Pyrenees on Napoleon's order in the late summer of 1813 in the hope of relieving the French garrisons besieged by Wellington* in Pamplona* and San Sebastian.* Reforming the remnants of four armies into a united force of 88,000 men, Soult launched one corps under d'Erlon* to secure the Maya Pass* and two more under Reille* to take possession of the Roncesvalles Pass.* His initial target was Pamplona, and once that had been relieved he would swing westward toward San Sebastian on the coast. The French cleared both passes, driving back the meager British covering forces under Picton* and Cole* from Roncesvalles and its area and thus forcing Hill* to comply from Maya, and it seemed likely that Soult would reach Pamplona. However, the British and Portuguese rallied just north of the town on the hills above the village of Sorauren,* and there they were joined by Wellington. Soult was worsted in the resulting battle on 28 July, and again on the 30th when he attempted to defeat Hill further to the west. Despairing of success, Soult abandoned his offensive three days later and headed back toward France.

Quadrilateral, the. Four key fortresses in North Italy guarded the approaches to the most important passes over the Alps to southern Austria—those associated with the valleys of the rivers Chiese, Adige, and Brenta. The western pair were Mantua* and Peschiera, both situated on the river Mincio, linking the river Po and Lake Garda; the eastern pair, Legnano and Verona, were both on the river Adige. These fortresses and the strategic area contained within them figured importantly during the Campaign of 1796—most particularly Mantua, the military and administrative center of Austrian rule in north Italy.

Quasdanovitch, General Peter (fl. 1796). An Austrian commander of some note, he commanded the westward column of Würmser's* offensive in July 1796. Advancing toward Mantua* down the west bank of Lake Garda with 18,000 men, he was repulsed by Massena* at Lonato* on 3 August and retired to Trent. He similarly played a large role in d'Alvintzi's* campaign in early 1797. Advancing down the west bank of the Adige, he attempted to storm the Osteria Gorge at the climactic battle of Rivoli,* but in vain.

Quatre Bras, battle of, 16 June 1815. When the French crossed the Sambre on 15 June, heading for Brussels, Napoleon entrusted command of the left wing of *l'Armée du Nord* (the corps of Reille* and d'Erlon*) to Marshal Ney,* with orders to secure the crossroads, thus severing the main forward link between

Wellington's* army and that of Blücher.* Ney failed to reach Quatre Bras on the evening of the 15th thanks to the bluff played by Prince Bernard of Saxe-Weimar's slim force, which won time for Wellington to transfer troops overnight toward the threatened point.

Ney did not hurry even on the morning of the 16th, and it was only at 2:00 P.M. that Reille's divisions (20,000 men and 60 guns) advanced to the attack. They faced only Perponcher's 8,000 men and 16 guns at that moment, but proceeded with great caution. By 3:00 P.M. they had captured Piraumont and Gemioncourt farms on the Allied left and center, but the clearing of Bossu Wood to the west of the Brussels highroad was a tedious affair, involving half of Foy's* and all of Jerome Bonaparte's* divisions, and the defending Nassauers clung on tenaciously. Wellington arrived on the scene at this juncture, shortly followed by a cavalry brigade and Picton's* division of veterans, and these reinforcements raised the Allied strength to 17,000 men. The Prince of Orange's* attempt at a counterattack was repulsed with the loss of six guns, but the Duke of Brunswick* arrived by 4:00 P.M. with 4,000 more men, and Wellington could at last claim numerical parity with Reille's command.

However, in support of Reille should have been d'Erlon's 21,000 men of the I Corps. When Ney sent for d'Erlon to reinforce the front he discovered to his fury that this complete corps was marching away toward Ligny,* having been ordered

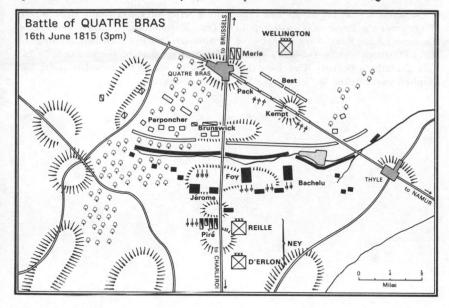

Battle of QUATRE BRAS
16th June 1815 (3pm)

in that direction by an imperial aide without prior consultation with Ney. Faced with an attack by General Alten's* division, Ney sent d'Erlon an order of recall, although he would only reach the Quatre Bras area after the end of the fighting. He then plunged back into the fighting. Ordering Kellermann* to charge the crossroads with his cavalry, around which Wellington could now deploy 26,000 men and 42 guns, Ney launched a furious attack. It almost succeeded. The British 69th Regiment was destroyed—caught in line owing to an order of the Prince of Orange—and the 33rd sadly disordered. Although Kellermann actually reached the crossroads, his advance was first checked and then routed by the guns of the King's German Legion and the musketry fire of the 30th and 73rd Foot. Kellermann only narrowly avoided being killed or taken prisoner.

Wellington, now reinforced to 36,000 men and 70 guns, launched a counter-attack at 6:30 P.M. that regained almost all the original Allied position by nine o'clock, when fighting ceased for the day. The Allies had lost 4,800 casualties, the French about 4,000, and the day had ended indecisively. Strategically, however, this was a serious check for Napoleon's plans. Even on the 17th, with d'Erlon present, Ney did not renew his attack until the afternoon, by which time Wellington had secretly withdrawn all his men, except for a rear guard of cavalry and horse artillery, toward his preselected position along the ridge of Mont St. Jean to the south of Waterloo.* Napoleon personally supervised the pursuit, but pouring rain and Wellington's considerable start enabled the Allies to reach their new position in safety. Meanwhile Blücher was retreating from Ligny toward Wavre.*

Quiberon, the landing at, 27 June 1795. To support the Bourbon sympathizers in La Vendée,* the Royal Navy landed 3,500 *émigré** troops on the Quiberon peninsula in southern Brittany. The rising they inspired was repressed by General Hoche* in a series of engagements in mid-July. The Revolutionary forces took 6,000 prisoners, and less than half the original force survived to be re-embarked. By the following March the complete rising had been crushed.

Raab, battle of, 14 June 1809. As Napoleon took steps to make good the chaotic opening of the Campaign of 1809 on the Danube front, Eugène Beauharnais* launched a complementary offensive against the Austrian Archduke John* in North Italy. After Napoleon's successes at Abensberg* and Eckmühl* the Archduke fell back into Hungary from the river Isonzo in May, but on news of the French check at Aspern-Essling* he determined to make a stand at Raab, 70 miles southeast of Vienna. The Austrians, probably 35,000 strong, took up a position on a height to the east of the river Raab, placing their local levies on the right, holding a village and two farms with the infantry, and placing their cavalry on the plain to the east. Eugène was advancing with 24,000 men, supported by Macdonald* with a further corps of 9,000 (which took no part in the fighting). Eugène placed Montbrun* and Grouchy* with their cavalry to face the Austrian left, and at 11:30 A.M. the French and Italian horsemen drove the Austrian outposts in upon their main body and then, supervised by Eugène, demonstrated against the Austrian cavalry so as to cover the main infantry attack led by Sarras, Durutte,* and Severoli against the height. This onslaught began at about 2:30 P.M. The Austrian center and right withstood the French onslaught against the farms and village of Kis-Megyer, but their cavalry on the left fled when the French horse artillery opened a withering fire. Eugène then led up Pacthod's division and the Italian Royal Guard from reserve,

and the French center was at last able to make some ground. At 5:00 P.M., aware that the French cavalry were threatening his line of retreat, the Archduke John called off the battle, sending his right wing into the fortress of Raab and the rest falling back northward in good order to Gönyö and Comoron. The Austrians had lost some 5,000 men to Eugène's 3,000. Eugène promptly invested Raab, which surrendered on the 25th, and then marched on to join Napoleon's main army at Vienna in time for Wagram.* Napoleon termed the Raab "a granddaughter of Marengo* and Friedland."*

Radetsky, Field Marshal Josef Wenceslas, Count (1766–1858). Born in Bohemia, Radetsky earned a reputation as a fighting soldier in campaigns against the Turks (1788–89) and against the French, whom he fought in the Low Countries, on the Rhine, and in Italy. After Aspern-Essling* in 1809 he was promoted to field-marshal-lieutenant and thereafter fought in all the campaigns against Napoleon from August 1813 to 1815. In 1831 he became Commander in Chief in Italy and was promoted to full field marshal. In 1848, the "year of Revolutions," he was driven out of Milan but regained the city and won a number of battles including Novara. Then, as Governor General of Lombardy-Venetia, he repressed Italian nationalist movements with some severity, finally retiring in 1857.

Raevski (or Great) Redoubt, the. This earthwork was the key to the Russian right center at the battle of Borodino,*

The Danube, 1809

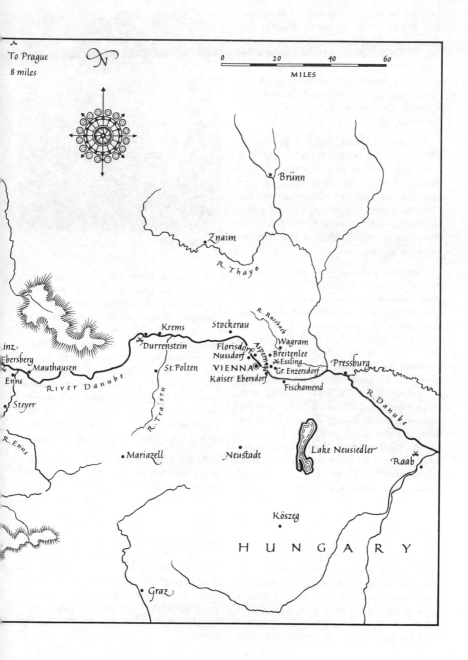

To Prague
8 miles

N

0   20   40   60
MILES

Brünn

Znaim

R. Thaya

R. Russbach

Krems
Durrenstein   Stockerau
                   Wagram
            Florisdorf   Breitenlee
            Nussdorf   Essling
inz   St.Polten   VIENNA   Gr. Enzersdorf   Pressburg
bersberg   Mauthausen   Kaiser Ebersdorf
Enns   River Danube   Fischamend
                                              R. Danube
Steyer

R. Enns   R. Traisen

Mariazell   Neustadt   Lake Neusiedler
                                              Raab

                    Köszeg

         H U N G A R Y

Graz

holding 18 guns. It was named after General Nikolai Raevski, whose Russian VII Corps had fought so well at Smolensk* and whose troops held the area of the redoubt to Semonovskaya to the south. Its defenders withstood several French assaults, but it was ultimately stormed by General Caulaincourt's* 5th Cuirassiers from the rear.

Rainier, Admiral Peter (1741?–1808). He entered the Royal Navy in 1756 and was promoted to post captain 23 years later. Between 1793 and 1804 he commanded the squadron serving in Far Eastern waters, capturing Trincomalee, Amboyna, and Banda Neira from the French and Dutch. He was promoted to admiral in 1805.

Rampon, Général Antoine Guillaume, comte (1759–1842). After joining the Bourbon infantry as a recruit in 1775, he had risen to the rank of sergeant major by the Revolution. Commissioned in 1792, he served with the Army of the West Pyrenees from 1793, being wounded and taken prisoner in December that year and only freed in October 1795. Commanding a *demi-brigade* in the Army of Italy from November 1795, he rapidly rose to notice next year under Bonaparte, who promoted him to provisional *général de brigade* in April. He fought at almost every major engagement over the next two years, from Montenotte* to Rivoli* and La Favorita,* doing particularly well at Arcola,* where his men repelled a counterattack by d'Alvintzi.* After fighting in Switzerland under Brune* in 1798, he accompanied the Army of the Orient to Egypt under Bon,* fighting at the Pyramids,* El Arish,* Mount Tabor,* and before Acre,* as well as at Heliopolis, returning to France (having been made *général de division* in 1800) after the French capitulation in late 1801. Awarded a saber of honor, he took his seat in the Senate from 1802

Rampon

and retired from the army. However, over the next years he held many important posts involving recruitment and National Guard commands and was made a count in 1808. In 1809 he served briefly under Bernadotte* in northeast France. After frontier-protection duties in the Pyrenees (1811), he defended Gorcum in Belgium in 1814 but was taken prisoner at its fall. In 1815 he rallied to Napoleon and was made a peer of France, and after a period of eclipse under the Bourbons he was restored to this dignity in 1819.

Ramsay, Major William Norman (1782–1815). He joined the army in 1798 and served in the horse artillery in Egypt under Abercromby* and Hutchinson (1801–02) and in the Peninsula under Wellington.* He particularly distinguished himself at the battle of Fuentes de Oñoro* (1811), evacuating his guns from the midst of the French with the greatest élan imaginable. Promoted to brevet major in 1813, he commanded a troop of guns at Waterloo* on the ridge above Hougoumont Chateau, where he was killed.

Rapp, Général Jean, comte (1771–1821). This much-wounded aide-de-camp of Napoleon was destined as a boy to become a Protestant pastor, but instead joined up in the cavalry in 1788. He was twice wounded in the Army of the Moselle under Hoche* in 1793 and was commissioned next year. He was wounded again several times in the Army of the Rhine and was appointed aide to General Desaix.* He accompanied him to Egypt, received more wounds, and then returned to France with his general and fought under him at Marengo* (1800) where Desaix perished in his arms. The next day he was appointed aide to the First Consul, and in 1801 was charged with raising the Mamelukes* of the Guard. In 1803 he was promoted to *général de brigade,* and in 1805 he captured Prince Repnine* at Austerlitz* after leading a charge to rout the Russian Imperial Guard, being wounded in the process. In December he was promoted to *général de division.* A number of governorships followed, but

Rapp

he was at Jena,* received a further wound at Golymin,* and then became governor of Danzig. Made a count in 1809, he led an attack with Mouton* to rescue Boudet's* division at Aspern-Essling.* After a period in disfavor for opposing Napoleon's divorce from Josephine,* he served in Russia at Smolensk,* Borodino* (four wounds), Krasnöe,* and the Beresina,* where he again was wounded. He defended Danzig* throughout 1813, surrendered on terms, but was imprisoned in the Ukraine until 1814. During the Hundred Days* he rallied to Napoleon and commanded the tiny Army of the Rhine, winning the combat of La Suffel near Strasbourg ten days after Waterloo* had been fought. He lay low until 1817, but thereafter held court posts under Louis XVIII* before dying of cancer.

Ratisbon, storming of, 23 April 1809. Ratisbon had seen much activity in the first days of the Campaign of 1809 when Davout* had avoided disaster by a hair's-breadth. However, after Napoleon's arrival on the scene the French situation had improved, and after his success of Eckmühl* the Emperor pressed after the retreating Archduke Charles,* who was making good his escape to the north bank of the Danube through Ratisbon. The defenses of the city were ancient, but the spirit evinced by the Austrian rear guard of 6,000 men was superb. A great cavalry engagement was fought outside the city and the first French attacks were repulsed, but Napoleon would not countenance the idea of a regular siege and ordered Lannes* to prepare an immediate all-out storming of the walls, supported by the troops of Lefebvre,* Davout, and Montbrun.* General Gudin* led the first assault at 1:00 P.M. but was repulsed. A four-hour pause ensued, during which Napoleon was wounded on the right ankle by a spent ball—to the consternation of the army until their master insisted on riding among them, his wound notwithstanding, to show that he was still alive. At 5:00 P.M. sufficient fascines had been made and ladders collected, and Morand* led his volunteers forward. After they had twice failed to make a lodgement, Lannes himself laid hold of a ladder and helped inspire a third assault, which succeeded. A postern gate was opened and the French swarmed into Ratisbon. By 7:00 P.M. the entire city and its nine battalions of defenders were in French hands, for the loss of 1,000 casualties. Archduke Charles had nevertheless made good his escape, although General Hiller's* corps was still south of the Danube. Sending Davout to the North bank, Napoleon prepared to march on Landshut*—and Vienna.

Reichenbach, Convention of, 19 July 1813. By the terms of this agreement, the Emperor Francis* of Austria agreed that his country would adhere to the Sixth Coalition* if Napoleon refused an offer of stipulated terms—namely the dissolution of the Grand Duchy of Warsaw and the Confederation of the Rhine, the return of the Illyrian provinces to Austria, and of her 1805 frontiers to Prussia. Napoleon rejected these terms with scorn, having recently won the battles of Lützen* and Bautzen,* and the Armistice* of 1813 came to a conclusion with a return to hostilities in mid-August. Austria honored its agreement and joined the Allies with 127,000 troops.

Reille, Général (later Marechal) Honoré Charles Michel Joseph, comte (1775–1860). A volunteer grenadier in 1791, he was commissioned while serving in the *Armée du Nord* (1792–93). After fighting at Toulon* he was a member of the Army of Italy until 1798. He was present at many battles in 1796, from Montenotte* to Arcola,* and fought at Rivoli* and La Favorita.* In 1800 he broke through the British naval blockade to join Massena*

Reille

besieged in Genoa.* In 1802 he was posted to Naples and promoted to *général de brigade* the next year. He accompanied Villeneuve* to sea in 1804 but was recalled to the *Grande Armée* in September 1805. Next year he fought at Saalfeld,* Jena,* and Pultusk,* and was promoted to *général de division* on 30 December. Appointed an imperial aide-de-camp, he fought at Friedland* and next year became a Count of the Empire (1808). Transferred to Spain, he was blockaded in Barcelona and later besieged and captured Rosas. In March 1809 he was recalled by Napoleon and fought at Essling* and Wagram* before being sent on a secret mission to Antwerp to observe the conduct of Bernadotte.* In 1811 he returned to Spain to serve under Suchet* before taking command of the Army of Portugal in October 1812, with which he fought at Vitoria* in 1813 under King Joseph Bonaparte* and Marshal Jourdan.* Later, under Soult,* he fought against Wellington* on the Bidassoa,* at Nivelle,* and at St. Pierre,* and in 1814 at Orthez,*

Tarbes,* and Toulouse.* In 1815 Napoleon gave him command of the II Corps, which formed part of Ney's* command, and he took a major part at both Quatre Bras* and Waterloo.* Restored to favor by the Bourbons in 1819, he held a number of administrative positions. In 1847 he was created a marshal, and in 1852 he became a senator.

Repnine-Volkonski, General Nicolas Grigorievitch, Prince (1778–1845). Russian soldier of noble lineage, he commanded the Russian Chevalier Guard at Austerlitz,* where he was taken prisoner by General Rapp.* He was present at the Congress of Vienna* (1815) and ended his career as Governor of Lesser Russia.

Revolution, the French (1789–1804). An understanding of the basic facts underlying the French Revolution is of importance for any study of the wars that grew out of that turmoil. The political background is a vital part of the grand strategy of any struggle or, as in this case, series of struggles, and the achievements of Napoleon—and the limitations he ultimately revealed—were in large measure bound up with the tradition and ethos of the French Revolution, one true starting point of the age of nationalism and European democracy.

The causes of the French Revolution were complex and need to be grouped under convenient headings. Some were of a long-term nature, others more immediate, but the dynamic train of events that was unleashed when Louis XVI* summoned the meeting of the States General in 1789 was one of the most important developments of modern history. At the time no one—least of all the king—foresaw where this seemingly minor concession, dictated by financial stringency, might lead. The situation was going to develop from crisis to crisis and ultimately result in the destruction of the monarchy and in the massive remodeling of French ways of life. Although under Napoleon and, after 1815, under the restored Bourbons, attempts would be made to reverse parts of the Revolution's work, France, Europe, and indeed the world would never be quite the same again.

The political causes of this immense upheaval are the first contributing factors that merit attention. France, for all the superb bureaucracy inherited from the days of Cardinal Richelieu and above all from the reign of Louis XIV, was politically an unachieved unity, ruled by a generally well-intentioned but distinctly reactionary monarch. The forces of conservatism centered around the court nobility and above all around the Queen, Marie Antoinette. The whole scene was dominated by the curse of privilege; many nobles were exempt from taxation to the detriment of the state; landowners still enjoyed medieval *droits de seigneur* on their estates to the detriment of their tenants; the Catholic Church was the most reactionary influence of all. But the all-pervasive malaise did not stop there. Within the government and civil service many offices either were hereditary or could be purchased. There was no standard fiscal system applicable throughout the country; the great provinces and cities, and even the subregions and minor towns, imposed their own standards of weights and measures and levied customs and excise charges. Particularism was rife, and jealously conserved. The municipalities, provincial assemblies, and regional Parliaments (legal institutions) clung to their local privileges, the most influential of all being the *Parlement de Paris*, which could exercise a very real stranglehold on tax grants. There were also very differing judicial systems in operation in different parts of France. In some areas Roman law (written) held sway, but there were

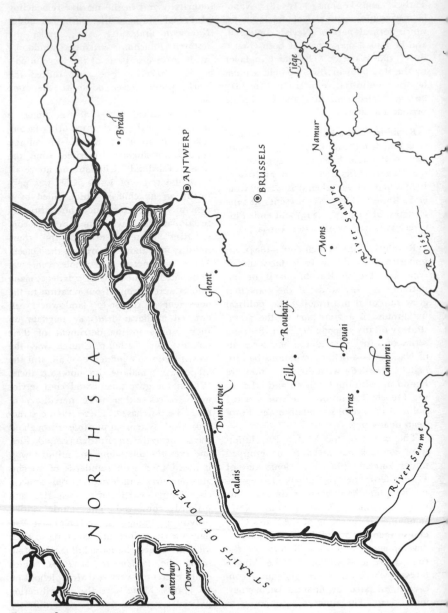

France, 1814

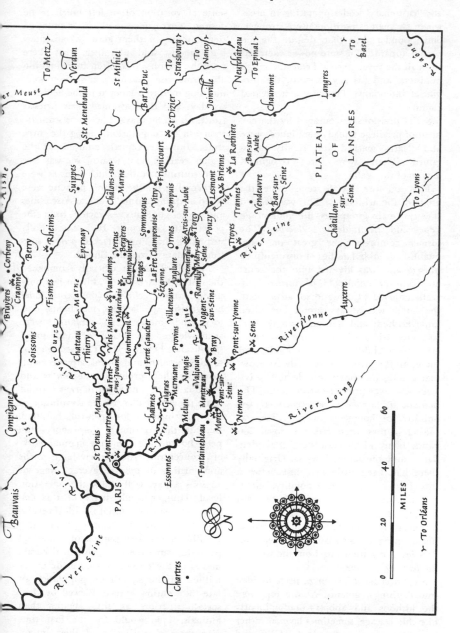

285 "customary" codes operating in areas where Germanic traditions were stronger. Small wonder then that, despite the imposing apparatus of state power exercised through the royal *conseil d'état,* the king's ministers, and his key servants, the provincial intendants, France was a divided country.

Social divisions, encouraged by the element of privilege already mentioned, were also clearly marked and rigidly maintained. There were three recognized Estates of the realm.

First on the social scene came the estate of the aristocracy. This was divided into two main groupings, the *noblesse de l'épée* and the *noblesse de la robe.* The former comprised the great or long-established noble families of distinguished lineage and was divided into the court and country nobility. The former generally enjoyed wealth and social prestige; the latter was always proud but often impoverished; and not surprisingly there was often friction between the two. However, every child was born a noble, and therefore the aristocracy was always growing; among the many considerable privileges was exemption from taxation. The *noblesse de la robe* were recently created nobility, of bourgeois origin. This was the class that produced the royal servants, many of the ministers, the intendants, and the senior lawyers. Originally there had been little love lost between this class and the ancient nobility, but in the difficult economic times of the 18th century there had in fact been much intermarriage—the ancient noble houses not scorning to marry ladies with generous dowries and settlements from the wealthy *noblesse de la robe.*

Second came the Church, itself divided into clashing segments. At the top were the bishops and abbots—predominently of noble lineage, sometimes laymen rather than clerics—whose standards of life and

sense of vocation often left much to be desired. Next came the *abbés,* or endowed clergy, many of them guilty of absenteeism, simony, and pluralism. Last there were the parish *curés,* often indistinguishable from the peasantry and often well-meaning men who labored in the fields for six days and then assumed their priestly functions on Sundays. There was scant interaction or cooperation among the three strata, but the Church enjoyed, at the higher reaches, vast wealth, yet was free from routine taxation. Such sums as were forthcoming for the aid of the state were voted at quinquennial General Assemblies and were generally extracted from the poverty-stricken *curés.* It is not wholly surprising that France lacked proper spiritual guidance from the Church.

The third Estate officially comprised the rest of French society, but in fact only its uppermost echelons (the professional bourgeoisie, the lawyers, merchants, doctors, and minor civil servants) were acknowledged as being of any social significance before 1789. This section was seeking wealth and social advancement, investing their profits in the *rentes* and National Debt, and from its ranks would come the first leaders of the Revolution— soon destined to lose control, however. Beneath the stratum of shopkeepers, the petty bourgeoisie, came the manual workers, concentrated in the few large towns and earning in 1789 an average wage of 10 sous a day, well below the starvation level. Hunger would make of this embryonic urban proletariat the ideal revolutionary instrument, particularly in Paris. Finally, at the very bottom of the social pyramid, came the huge, sullen, illiterate masses of the peasantry, who made up 21 million of the 25 million population of late-18th-century France. Viewed by their social superiors as little better than animals, 1789 would for the first time give them a realization of their importance and potential power, and from 1790 the French political scene would be dominated by this newly emerging class of society.

France still had a predominantly rural economy, and the peasantry comprised several types of workers. The highest stratum was that of the peasant-proprietor, owning his own land and saving every sou to acquire more from his financially embarrassed lords, who were in many cases selling off their patrimony for ready cash. This up-and-coming class of peasants bitterly resented the feudal privileges of the landowners—their monopolistic control over the local mill, wine-press, and bakery; their exclusive rights over game and hunting and the keeping of pigeons; and the still considerable legal powers of the seigneurial courts. Below them came the small class of *metayers*, small farmers without servile obligations but paying a fixed proportion of their profits to the lord. Lower still were the miserable copyholders, who formally rented their insignificant fields from the owner. They were only fractionally better off than the large numbers of serfs, found in the east and south of France, many of them owned by the Church, the more enterprising of them desperately trying to purchase their freedom but heavily burdened by dues and servile duties. The very last of all, the hapless landless peasant, was employed for a pittance by other, wealthier peasants.

Economic factors bulk large in any list of causes of the Revolution. France was undergoing a rapid growth in population, but agricultural methods were still feudal and not able to keep up with the expansion. Famine, therefore, was endemic, particularly hitting the urban poor, and a poor harvest was a major disaster leading to many deaths. If agriculture was hopelessly backward, still tied to crop rotation and farming of strips in the field, so were many aspects of trade, industry,

and commerce. The ancient trade guilds exerted a stranglehold on the expansion of established industries and the development of new ones, and when associated with endless state interference by a mass of petty officials and inspectors it is amazing to discover that France was second only to Great Britain in terms of industrial development, such as it was. Expansion was not aided by laws against usury, lending for profit being forbidden to most citizens. Variations in weights and measures and in local customs and excise regulations further discouraged the growth of trade and reinforced the deadening particularism.

At the root of many evils lay the chaotic taxation system, the burden of which was borne almost exclusively by the underprivileged. The levies fell very unevenly: *taille, capitation, vingtième*, and the hated *gabelle* were levied on property, households, profits, and salt (a state monopoly) respectively. The inefficiency of the official tax-collection machinery, allied to the chronic need for ready cash, had led to the pernicious system of tax-farming, whereby the government each year sold the product of a particular tax in a region for the best available price to entrepreneurs, who then collected as much as they could extort from the peasantry. It has been estimated that the state only received between half and a third of its due as a result. At the other end of the financial spectrum, the ceaseless depredations by tax-farmers and their ruthless agents forced the peasantry to assume the appearance of abject penury to avoid their ceaseless attentions. Nevertheless, if the total poverty was more apparent than real in many parts of France, it has been estimated that up to half the population was dependent in whole or in part on charity during most winters, and the generally low standard of living was not ameliorated by the practice of governmental speculation in grain, which caused spiraling inflation. So it was that begging and brigandage were frequently encountered aspects of the French social and economic scenes. Massive reform was long overdue in every sector, but the state was so burdened by inherited debts from the time of Louis XIV that the situation was almost hopeless, and the best endeavors of such able economists as John Law, Turgot, and Necker could only at best palliate the situation. Small wonder that shortly before his death Louis XV had uttered the famous phrase, *"Après moi le déluge."*

So much for the root causes that created the general situation out of which the Revolution developed. There were also a number of important specific and immediate causes. High upon any list of these must come the writings and influence of the *philosophes,* intellectuals often drawn from the upper classes of French society, inspired by the appeal to reason and the lure of perfectionism. Every aspect of French—and European—life was examined in the harsh light of "reason" by a number of outstanding men, who included Montesquieu, author of *L'Esprit des Lois,* a plea for a limited monarchical system; the bitter satirist Voltaire, the scourge of *l'ancien régime* in general and the Church in particular, the exponent of deism and the enemy of privilege; and the famous philosopher Rousseau, whose celebrated work, *Le Contrat Social,* was a mixture of poetic vision and near-lunacy, expounding the need for governments to accede to the "General Will" of the people. Two other groups also merit a mention: the Encylopaedists and the Physiocrats. The Encylopaedists, led by Diderot, editor-in-chief of the great *Encyclopédie* (a massive monument to learning and rationalism), pleaded for the abolition of feudalism's relics, of slavery, and of formal religion, and pressed for the development of constitu-

tional government and free trade. The Physiocrats, led by Quesnay, Mirabeau, and the economist Turgot, pressed for urgent agricultural reform, a greater degree of international commerce, and the abolition of internal trade barriers. The major effect of these writers, taken together, was to shake the confidence of the First Estate and thus psychologically prepare the way for its eclipse by encouraging the processes of decay from within.

The American Revolution also had a part to play. The attitudes of many influential men were affected by exposure to the phenomenon of American democracy and social equality. Many of the troops—and not a few of the officers—who served in America under Lafayette (himself a notable case in point) returned to France imbued with liberal ideas. The influence of the great Benjamin Franklin, U.S. ambassador to Versailles, helped propagate these ideas. Some were little better than sentimental concepts, but on a fiscal level there can be no doubt that participation in the War of American Independence greatly increased the national bankruptcy of France. Linked with this adulation for American liberty was, somewhat paradoxically, a genuine degree of admiration for the English model of constitutional monarchy. The writings of the English 17th-century philosophers, Hobbes and Locke, were much studied, and the position of the British middle-classes was particularly admired. Mirabeau's abortive concept of constitutional monarchy was largely founded on the British model.

In 1788 the French government, desperate for funds and aware that reforms would have to precede supply, called for the production of *cahiers* or lists of local and sectional grievances. The significance of these was that they made all parts of educated French society aware of the common nature and broad scope of their wrongs. Almost all *cahiers* included demands for the abolition of feudal relics; the need for Parliamentary control of taxation; the abolition of arbitrary arrest, censorship, and special courts; the total destruction of privilege and the abolition of serfdom; the preparation of a written constitution clearly defining the relative positions of King, Church, and People; and, as a first step, the immediate calling of a States General endowed with real legislative powers.

Faced by this evidence of seething discontent, Louis XVI decided to accede to this last demand and summoned the States General to meet at Versailles in May 1789. His motivation was a combination of a desire to thwart the power of the fractious *Parlement de Paris,* (an ancient thorn in the side of the Bourbon monarchy), a desire to share the intractable financial problems of the government with the three Estates, and a deeply felt wish to break the grip of the overly influential Second Estate as represented by the court nobility. Unfortunately, Louis XVI's attempt to place himself at the head of the reform movement contained one fatal flaw: he wished to tame the court nobility on the one hand, but he would listen only to reform proposals put forward by sections of the same First Estate.

The meeting of the States General took place in an atmosphere of great excitement. Following the opening meeting at which the representatives of all three Estates were present, the Third Estate immediately displayed its determination to take control of proceedings. The representatives insisted on further joint sessions, despite the king's expressed displeasure, and then took the famous "tennis-court oath," pledging themselves not to disband for any reason until their reforming work was done. Then, on the critical 14 July, the Paris mob rebelled and stormed the

Bastille prison-fortress, the symbol of oppression. This was a portent for the future, indicating that the common people, and especially the Paris mob, intended to use their muscle. In due course the lawyer-dominated "moderate" factions of the Third Estate would be swept aside by the ordinary people. The march of the women to Versailles followed, and Louis XVI publicly adopted the tricolor insignia and agreed to return to Paris, a semi-prisoner. The States General in a frenzy of excitement and fear abolished serfdom, feudalism, and noble and ecclesiastical privilege in a single sitting. The bourgeoisie was now alarmed by the developing extremism and formed the National Guard under Lafayette* in the hope of maintaining law and order—and of keeping overall control over events, a pious aspiration. In fact the radical trend was already firmly established, and the processes of the Revolution would soon pass out of the hands of the moderates, who would themselves be swallowed up in the catastrophe of their own making.

Here it is only feasible to mention the most important highlights and salient developments of the action-packed years of political ferment that followed. The abolition of feudalism was the signal for many acts of arson and indiscipline by the peasantry throughout the country, and a state of near-anarchy soon prevailed. The king hesitated to employ the army, part of which was in any case infected by revolutionary ideas. So first he tried to seek a face-saving compromise and lent at least a measure of tacit support to the noble reformer Mirabeau in his attempt to work out a form of constitutional government. When this attempt failed in late 1790, the voice of the moderates was increasingly drowned by the more extreme elements, which had allied themselves to the Paris *séctions* and operated out of the political clubs, the most important of which met at the former priory of the Jacobin* order. The threat of serious rioting was increasingly becoming the sanction behind the deliberations of the Legislative Assembly, which was effectively in the power of the Paris mob. Many aristocrats emigrated.

As the situation deteriorated, Louis took what proved the fatal step of trying to flee to the Austrian Netherlands, following the issue of the Declaration of Pillnitz by the European monarchs. The arrest of the royal party at Varennes and their humiliating return to Paris compelled the king to accept a dictated constitution, but he had now finally forfeited the trust of his people. As hysteria mounted, the Brissotin government declared war on the King of Bohemia in April 1791, and, following a series of defeats on the frontiers, the September massacres took place in Paris and the "Terror"* began. The monarchy was abolished on 21 September, and a republic proclaimed. Valmy* had temporarily saved the war situation, and a series of successes on several fronts later in the year made the extremists confident enough to stage the trial of the *çi-devant* king. He was duly condemned and eventually executed in January 1793, being followed to the guillotine by his wife, while the Dauphin died of neglect and ill treatment in the Conciergerie prison.

After a period of bitter factional infighting within the Convention, dog eating dog, Maximilien Robespierre* emerged as the predominant Jacobin leader of what became the Committee of Public Safety. The "Terror" reached new depths with the infamous Law of Suspects and the acceptance by the Revolutionary Tribunal of Fouquier-Tinville's demand for convictions on anomyous denunciations. Every day the tumbrils rolled their fresh loads of victims to the guillotine, and witch-hunts decimated both the administration and

the armed forces. However, the Committee did prove capable of imposing order on France and of directing a truly national war effort. Conscription* followed the *levée en masse,* and the conception of the nation-in-arms became a reality. The military situation slowly began to improve, the recapture of Toulon* in December 1793 being symbolic of a new national determination to support the government.

The following year saw the *coup d'état* de Thermidor* and the fall and execution of the feared Robespierre, "the Incorruptible," and his adherents. As the Thermidorian reaction set in a period of license and excess followed, the Directory* proving unstable, corrupt, and incapable of solving France's grave internal problems, foremost among which was a valueless currency made up of worthless paper *assignats* and *mandats.* The war, however, was going well, and the years 1795 and 1796 saw the gradual disintegration of the First Coalition,* and ultimately the conclusion of peace with Austria in October 1797. Internal upheavals continued, and the face of French politics was constantly shifting as one *coup* followed another, but at length the stroke of *Brumaire* in 1799 brought back a degree of true stability in the establishment of the Consulate and the rapid rise to pre-eminent authority of Napoleon Bonaparte.

First the Consulate brought a war-weary France the blessings of a period of peace following Marengo* and Hohenlinden* in 1800, and the conclusion of agreements with Austria at Leoben* (1801) and with Great Britain at Amiens* (1802). During the brief period of peace that ensued, Napoleon, First Consul and soon Consul for Life, carried through the first stages of his great reorganization of every facet of French life. At the same time, he proved the preserver, disseminator, and destroyer of the principles of the French Revolution. To give France stability he wooed the peasants, guaranteeing them the land settlement, and encouraged industry and commerce; his great legal Codes re-ordered the legal system. Despairing of the workings of the republican system, Napoleon gradually moved through the medium of popular plebiscites toward the assumption of the imperial purple in 1804. This process was bitterly resented and opposed by the staunch republicans, but Napoleon's control, through Nicolas Fouché,* of the press and of the secret police enabled him to crush all signs of incipient revolt, whether royalist or republican inspired, and France more or less willingly submitted to a new form of enlightened despotism as the price of economic stability, restored law and order, and general progress. However, there was another great price to pay—that of perpetual war. The struggle with Great Britain had resumed in May 1803, and by early 1805 a Third Coalition* of European powers was again challenging France and the new First Empire. From 1805 to 1814 France would be continually at war, great martial achievements being ultimately balanced by great failures. The restoration of the Bourbons after Waterloo* represented the final eclipse of the Revolution—but much in fact survived and still survives to the present day.

Revolutionary Wars, the French (1792–1801). The great but confused struggle that began when the French Legislative Assembly formally voted for a declaration of war on the "King of Bohemia" (a subordinate title of the Austrian emperor) on 20 April 1792 was to prove the first of the modern wars, a massive confrontation between rival political and social systems. As is the case with every war, its causation was complex rather than simple, and if at one level it was a matter of fundamental principles in collision—the rights of peoples against those of monarchs—at another it was a continuation of 18th-century contentions over the ancient issue of the balance of power within Europe.

What earned this struggle—which eventually grew to include every European power—its special revolutionary title was that it was concerned both with the rights of man and, at one remove, with the rights of nations. The claim of dynastic power as the fundamental basis of authority was being challenged by the concept of national existence based upon the rights of the common people. This revolutionary concept began as an internal French upheaval, but its implications were international almost from the outset, for once the Pandora's box of national liberalism, democracy, and the rights of the individual citizen had been opened, the dyke of European dynastic and aristocratic privilege had been well and truly breached, and all monarchs—even constitutional ones like (uniquely) George III*—felt themselves personally threatened. Thus, as politics within France progressed from the rational to the hysterical, from the liberal to the radical, and thence to the all-out revolutionary, the international implications of *"fraternité"* (the concept of the universal brotherhood of the common man and of Revolutionary France's sacred mission to aid in his liberation throughout Europe) eventually evoked a strong reactionary response. Both sides soon became involved in a bitter propaganda battle, leading to actual war.

This conservative reaction was embodied in the Declaration of Pillnitz, issued in April 1791 by the ancient monarchies of continental Europe, whose august heads had recently met to confer and deliberate. This was the moment of ideological parturition, when the battle lines were drawn and the main issues of rival principle declared, although formal war would not come for another year.

By the Declaration, the European powers served notice on France—still a nominal monarchy at that juncture—that unless they treated Louis XVI* with greater respect, unless they evinced less inflammatory policies (or in other words stopped "rocking the boat" of French and European affairs), then the powers would feel compelled to intervene to restore order and to re-establish the authority of the legal monarchy. It was hoped that this warning would be enough, that a war of words would suffice to reassert the former status quo. In fact it had the opposite, provocative effect, giving the French extremists the excuse they needed for leveling new charges against Louis XVI—now suspected of "treason" against his own country, in other words against himself, as royalists would regard this charge—and for claiming the existence of a great hostile international conspiracy (that perennial standby of extreme regimes who wish to disguise their own confusions and imperfections by whipping up feeling against an external threat, whether real or imagined) aimed against the rights of man and the other principles of the Revolution. Louis XVI's flight to Varennes and his arrest there played straight into the hands of the extremist factions and propagandists. The outbreak of hostilities could thereafter be only a matter of time.

There were other, more traditional, issues at stake that also were leading to open war. Pre-revolutionary France, for all its crippling economic, social, and mounting political problems, was still the most powerful nation in Europe at that time, hence the scale of the threat the revolutionaries posed to the rest of Europe once they secured effective power. France had great latent wealth, a large army and navy, and the most developed bureaucracy in the world, and taken in combination these advantages more than counterbalanced Prussia's theoretically greater

military efficiency or Tsarist Russia's vaster population. Traditionally, throughout the 18th century it had been Great Britain's task to keep France in order, but in the early 1790s British foreign policy was in total disarray following the loss of the American colonies and grave domestic and imperial problems associated with Ireland and India and the general working of the constitutional monarchy had effectively neutralized British power for the time being. The internal convulsions within France from 1789 equally neutralized her international influence for three critical years, and these internal preoccupations of the two greatest powers enabled Russia, Prussia, and Austria to assert themselves. The victim, inevitably, was hapless Poland, already partitioned by international conspiracy in 1775, and now again torn asunder by the rival central and east European powers in what their statesmen deemed to be an ideal opportunity now that the kingdom of Poland's traditional protector, France, was temporarily out of the arena. To this extent, therefore, the outbreak of the French Revolution was almost welcomed in Vienna, Berlin, and St. Petersburg. Thus, if the great monarchies were generally united in their apprehensions about events in Paris and their implications for the status of absolute kingship, they were equally divided among themselves over the future of Poland. The whole European scene was therefore extremely volatile and unstable in 1791, and international relations were abnormally unsettled. Under the pertaining conditions, it would not take much of a spark to start off a general European conflagration.

This was struck on 20 April 1792 when the Brissotin government in Paris, in a moment of ideological folly, declared war on the King of Bohemia, and by implication upon the whole of Europe. It was a rash action because France's army at that time was in a state of great confusion; many cavalry and infantry officers were fleeing abroad, many regiments were being suborned from all idea of discipline by extremist left-wing Jacobin* agitators, and only the bourgeois-created National Guard represented anything approaching stability—and yet its military experience was nil. On the other hand, the armies of the monarchies were not equipped to wage ideological warfare or to occupy and hold down a hostile population seething with revolutionary fervor. None of the French leaders knew the true state of their armed forces, or their capacity. They bravely called in the Legislative Assembly for 100,000 volunteers or *fédérés* and decreed the mobilization of the National Guard, but as early events were to prove, the defenses of France were in almost total disarray. A crusade to liberate the peoples of Europe was thus launched with the flimsiest of preparation.

The die, however, was cast. The Allied powers—Austria, the disjointed Holy Roman Empire, Prussia, and then Sardinia —began to move their armies toward the French frontiers. France was warned that Europe was arming to save civilization and refurbish the principle of monarchical power. In typical 18th-century fashion, however, the powers also settled, in secret articles, which choice bits of French territory each hoped to annex. At this stage Great Britain remained aloof. As a constitutional monarchy, although far from revolutionary in its sympathies and attitudes, Britain was not presently prepared to make common cause with absolutist monarchies in an attempt to crush what might be regarded as a French democratic and internal experiment in constitutional government. Charles James Fox* and the poet Wordsworth, among many more, had hailed the onset of the Revolution as a great and hopeful moment in the history

of mankind. Three years later Europe was at war.

France had flung down the gauntlet for several reasons. The solemn and overriding duty to spread the rights of man to the underprivileged populations of the rest of Europe was genuinely felt. Then again, amid the confusion and chaos of the domestic scene, there were those who saw a war as the best means to accomplish the final overthrow of the French house of Bourbon, which, since the Varennes episode, had been held in a state of suspended animation although it was still deemed necessary for Louis XVI to formally proclaim the war against the Emperor, his father-in-law. Others regarded a war as the only means truly to unite the people of France behind the government. In the most prosaic terms, the immediate reason was the need to do something about the burgeoning anti-revolutionary army of ` *émigré** officers that had been gathering in certain Rhineland principalities under the general protection of the Holy Roman Emperor. Hence the decision to declare war on Leopold* as king of Bohemia; even the Brissotin idealists did not want an all-out war at this juncture. However, having sown the wind they were about to reap the whirlwind with a vengeance.

The early events of the war shocked France to its very core. An attempt to send an army into the Austrian Netherlands ended in complete disaster. Whole units of the French army deserted to the Allies, and demoralized troops shot down their own officers when they sought to remonstrate with them. Then the forces of retribution began to mass. The Duke of Brunswick* assembled a combined Prusso-Austrian army around Coblenz and prepared to invade France up the Moselle Valley. In his Manifesto, published on 1 August 1792, the Duke threatened condign punishment for any Frenchman who harmed the royal family in any way. The immediate effect of this was to cause a further popular upheaval among the left-wing *séctions* of Paris nine days later, which compelled the moderate majority in the Legislative Assembly to formally vote the abolition of the monarchy and the imprisonment of the king and his immediate family.

Fortunately for France the Allies moved extremely slowly and cautiously. Brunswick's initial intention was to establish a military base area within France, in the hope that this would be enough to trigger a popular rising on behalf of Louis XVI. Both Prussia and Austria were at the time preoccupied with events far to the east, where a Tsarist army had moved into Poland, and consequently did not wish to become totally involved within France. However, wherever the Allies ponderously moved, success blessed their hesitant arms. The frontier fortresses of Longwy and Verdun fell at their approach, and it seemed indeed that Paris might be occupied. Hysteria gripped the capital as the September Massacres were perpetrated in the name of national security, and the extremist Jacobin faction ousted the Brissotin government.

Salvation, however unexpected, was at hand. Although only a jittery mob of *fédéré* troops stood at Châlons between Brunswick and Paris, General Dumouriez* managed to maneuver his Army of the Sambre-et-Meuse to threaten the Allied lines of communication. As Brunswick swung ponderously around to deal with this impertinence, Dumouriez was joined in the nick of time by General Kellermann* and part of the Army of the Center. The resulting Cannonade of Valmy,* following which Brunswick withdrew toward the Rhine, however inconclusive in military terms, was politically vital. From 20 September 1792 dates the recovery of French national morale and

also the salvation of the Revolution. It had been a near thing but now a positive success was within the French grasp. Dumouriez led his heartened men northward to fall upon the isolated Austrian army of General Clarfayt at Jemappes* on 6 November. The tide had turned with a vengeance, and by the new year of 1793 French forces were in Brussels, Frankfort, Nice, and Savoy; France was being organized for waging war as never before, as teams of all-powerful *députés-en-mission* (political commissars) toured the country to organize every aspect of life in support of the war effort. The evocative cry, *la patrie en danger,* produced an enthusiastic response as thousands of *sans-culottes* rushed to enlist. This enthusiasm would not last long—soon there would be a need for tough conscription laws—but it posed daunting administrative problems for the Ministry of War, which did not possess the resources or the machinery to equip, feed, and train the one and a half million men that flocked (by 1794) to swell the fifteen armies along the frontiers. The solution was at once desperate and brilliant. "War must be made to pay for war"; the troops must be encouraged to live off the countryside—and as it was preferable that these large armies, newly confident of success and aware of their power, should be kept as far away from Paris as possible to avert any danger of their commanders meddling in politics, the process of launching the struggle of liberation in central and southern Europe had to be brought forward and expedited. Thus, for once, principle and opportunism seemed to coincide, but in effect France was doomed to an incessant series of exhausting wars.

The main military crisis of the Revolution had still to be encountered, however. By the end of January, two very significant events had taken place. The first was the execution by guillotine of Louis XVI.

The new Republic henceforward bore the stigma of regicide to add to its already horrific reputation for excess. All chance of a compromise settlement was gone, or so it appeared. Secondly, Great Britain at last entered the war. The ostensible reason for this was the renewed French invasion of the Low Countries and the Jacobin government's absolute refusal to guarantee not to infringe on the rights of neighboring states. In the event, as in the previous September, it was the French government that actually declared war, but the effects were to be far-reaching. Britain was to prove France's most implacable and impregnable opponent. Her great wealth would enable her to raise a whole series of anti-French European coalitions;* her powerful navy would permit her to conquer virtually all of France's overseas possessions, to safeguard her own shores from the danger of invasion, and to convey the British army to the most advantageous points of the European coastline. Now, in early 1793, British diplomats lost no time in creating the First Coalition, welding together (albeit impermanently) by a series of bilateral treaties an alliance that included Austria, Great Britain, Prussia, Russia, Spain, and Holland. From the start, however, this was bedeviled by lack of common aims and riddled with internal disunity. Austria was already at loggerheads with Prussia and Russia after these powers had excluded her from participation in the Second Partition of Poland in 1792; moreover, none of the powers anticipated more than a short war designed to recover the Rhineland and the Low Countries from the French armies.

Eventually a reinforced Austrian army marched into Belgium, and a British expeditionary force under command of the Duke of York* landed in Flanders. Dumouriez failed to halt the Austrian advance at Neerwinden* on 18 March,

and then tried to march on Paris to overthrow the government upon whom he placed the blame for his defeat; thwarted in his purpose, he defected to the Allies, but as before their prevarication and disunity saved France. Prussia, with most of her army busy in Poland, attempted little west of the Rhine, while Britain and Austria failed to cooperate to any degree in Flanders. By this time the new French National Convention had decreed the drafting of 300,000 men—to be followed in August by the *levée en masse*—and the total subordination of French life to the needs of the war effort. Conscription was bitterly opposed in many parts of France, and serious risings amounting to civil war broke out in the pro-Bourbon region of La Vendée* and also in royalist Provence, where first Marseilles, and then the great naval arsenal and fortress of Toulon* defected and admitted Allied forces. By this time the government was appointing political commissars armed with full powers to serve alongside every commanding general to enforce discipline and loyalty to the Revolution and to reorganize the forces along more practical lines. Somehow the system worked: after the summary execution of a few dozen senior commanders, the armies began once again to achieve successes. Coerced and supervised at every stage by the teams of Citizen-Representatives, French armies forced the British to give up Dunkirk after the battle of Hondschoote (8 September), and a month later the Austrian advance was halted at Wattignies.* An army was found to repress the Vendean rebels, and another extemporized to quell Provence. Aided by a hitherto unknown artillery captain by the name of Bonaparte, this army ultimately forced Admiral Lord Hood* to evacuate Toulon* after a long siege in December.

With a million and a half men to feed, the French government was understandably eager to resume the offensive. This new energetic zeal coincided with a decline in Allied interest in the all-out prosecution of the war, and little by little the First Coalition began to fall apart at the seams. Continued trouble in Poland caused Russia to drop out in 1794 when faced by a large-scale Polish national rising. Dissension over the Polish question continued to bedevil Austro-Prussian relations, and as a result Prussian promises of military aid in the Low Countries proved valueless. This also incensed Great Britain, who decided to evacuate her forces from the Low Countries. A renewed French naval challenge was successfully met at the battle of the Glorious First of June* when Lord Howe* drove the French fleet back into Brest, but on all other sectors the initiative had plainly passed back into French hands. This was underlined on 26 June 1794 when a major Austrian offensive was repulsed by Jourdan* at Fleurus.*

Once again the French drove the unsupported Austrians out of the Netherlands, and by the end of 1794 their armies had invaded Holland, cleared the Allies out of the Rhineland, swept the Spaniards back over the Pyrenees into Rousillon, and occupied the western passes through the Alps as a precursor to a major offensive in North Italy. Everywhere success seemed to be blessing Carnot's* armies. Prussia, more worried about Russian ambitions than French ones, made peace with France in April 1795, and they were followed by the Dutch in May and the Spaniards in July. British expeditions were launched against Dutch colonies from late 1795 and against Spanish overseas possessions (early the next year) when these countries concluded actual alliances with France, and the Austrians successfully repelled a French attempt to launch an offensive over the Rhine in 1795; but the First Coalition, Great Britain and Austria

apart, was now a dead letter, and the most significant event of 1795 for the continental monarchies was the Third Partition of hapless Poland, which now completely disappeared from the map of Europe as an independent state.

France had survived the crisis, but the price had been heavy in terms of both casualties and economic dislocation of French life. The absolute authority and excessive use of power by the Committee of Public Safety under Robespierre* had bred the Thermidorian reaction, and Robespierre and his henchmen followed their countless earlier victims to the guillotine after yet another *coup d'état* in Paris in 1794. The first measures to be repealed were the draconian economic edicts that had been needed to support the huge armies. Now, however, the new government, the Directory of Seven,* found it impossible to pay and feed the soldiers, and inevitably discipline deteriorated, leading to more attempts and military-backed *coups* in riot-torn Paris. The Directory would have been glad to settle for France's "natural frontiers" (the Rhine, the Alps, and the Pyrenees) and to reach a general pacification on this basis, but the military machine was now so immense and all-demanding, and the emotional drive within the armies so strong, that although the struggle for national survival was now patently over, France was dragged willy-nilly into further military adventures. The expansionist period of the Revolutionary wars had begun.

The year 1795 had seen some inconclusive military efforts made in North Italy, and now in 1796 the Directory's war plan called for a major effort by Generals Moreau* and Jourdan* on the Rhine and Danube fronts, aided by a diversionary offensive by the newly appointed General Bonaparte in North Italy. The details of what transpired do not need to be reiterated here; suffice it to say that Napoleon's genius transformed the secondary into the main theater of war, and that it took a year-long campaign to bring Austria to the conference table seriously prepared to discuss peace terms. The costs of war had been at least partially reimbursed by the vast convoys of loot sent back from Italy by Bonaparte, but the price was the need to set up and police a whole string of small satellite republics in North Italy and Switzerland, and to mount expeditions against the Papal States and, eventually, Naples. However, the Peace of Campo Formio* in October 1799 at last brought the First Coalition to a close. Great Britain now stood alone. France had moved well and truly beyond the "natural frontiers" at the price of assuming major new responsibilities in the Rhennish areas of Germany and in north and central Italy. The resentment that the realities of "liberation" by the French inevitably incurred, together with the resentment felt at Vienna and Berlin over the French gains, were sure precursors of future trouble.

Great Britain, however, remained unbeaten and a prospective menace. The Royal Navy, despite the terrible troubles engendered by the Spithead* and Nore* Mutinies of 1797, retained its supremacy at sea. There were a few internal popular disorders to contend with as British republicanism was encountered, inspired by the brilliant writings of Thomas Paine, and Ireland remained in its endemic state of near-revolt, which would in fact flare into a major rising (with some French prompting) in 1798. On the other hand British sea power—reasserted at Camperdown* and in other actions—enabled her to conquer one overseas possession after another. All attempts at negotiation broke down.

In the hope of inducing a more compliant attitude at Westminster, the Directory created the Army of England and

threatened an invasion. When this proved beyond French naval resources to mount, the line of attack was switched partly toward Ireland but more significantly against British interests in the Levant and, by natural extension, in India. Bonaparte was sent off with the Army of the Orient to attack Malta,* Egypt, and eventually Syria. Once again the details need not detain us here. The loss of its fleet at Admiral Nelson's* victory at the Nile* in August 1798 effectively doomed the expedition to ultimate failure, but the French troops proved more than a match for the Turkish forces pitted against them until these were reinforced, long after Bonaparte's own return to France, by a strong British force under Generals Abercromby* and Hely Hutchinson. Long before this stage had been reached, a widespread European war had again broken out. Blatant French aggression and diplomatic tactlessness had enabled Great Britain, in December 1799, to bring into existence the Second Coalition, formed by Austria, Britain, and Russia. To begin with, the forces of the Directory suffered setback after setback, and of course their foremost commander was far away, isolated in Egypt and Syria. In early 1799 the Austrians forced the French out of most of Germany, while a strong Austro-Russian army led by the great Suvorov* pressed the French back in Switzerland, and another army regained most of Italy from the overextended French garrison. To make things still worse, an Anglo-Russian expedition landed in Holland. On all fronts the French were forced to give ground and retire, and antirevolutionary risings took place in Italy and were daily expected in Switzerland, Holland, and within France itself, where La Vendée was again restive.

It was news of these problems that persuaded Napoleon to desert his comrades-in-arms and return from the cul-de-sac of Egypt to France. However, by the time of his return France's situation had greatly improved. In June 1799 an internal *coup* had remodeled the Directory into a more effective pattern, and although it remained discredited by defeat, debt, and growing internal restlessness, it proved capable of crushing a revolt in southwestern France. Then Allied shortcomings again came to France's aid. The British made no progress against General Brune* in Holland; the Russians lent little practical aid, and the victory of Bergen restored the initiative to the French. Ultimately, receiving no encouragement from the Dutch, the British evacuated by sea. When Austria, without consultation or even notification, shifted large numbers of her troops out of Switzerland to reinforce her interests in Germany, General Massena* was able to defeat the isolated Russians at the battle of Second Zurich* and re-establish the French position. This, together with what he regarded as British bungling in Holland, so disgusted Tsar Paul I* that Russia recalled its armies and effectively left the coalition. Meanwhile in North Italy the French halted the Allied advance at the battle of Novi.* Thus the crisis had already passed for France when Bonaparte arrived back on the scene, ready to play a typically opportunist and effective role in the coup d'état, de Brumaire (9 and 10 November 1799), which replaced the decrepit and corrupt Directory with the Consulate of Three—one of whom was, of course, Napoleon Bonaparte.

The steps taken to destroy finally the cohesion of the Second Coalition need only be summarized here. The First Consul launched a double offensive, part over the Rhine under Moreau and Jourdan, and part over the Alps under his own *de facto* leadership. Although Massena's surrender of Genoa* almost led to a crisis, Napoleon's narrow victory over General Melas* at Marengo* on 14 June

1800 restored the French position in North Italy, while Moreau's subsequent victory at Hohenlinden* in the depths of Bavaria on 3 December finally broke the Austrian will to continue the struggle. The peace of Leoben* implied the isolation of Great Britain once again. For a further period Britain sustained the war effort alone, her strict policies of naval blockade* leading to a brief struggle with the Northern Powers of the Second Armed Neutrality,* until this was resolved by Nelson's victory of Cogenhagen* in April 1801. Bad harvests and an economic recession at last achieved what French arms had failed to do, and brought Britain to negotiate. Although the French Army of Egypt was forced to capitulate on terms, the subsequent Preliminaries and Peace of Amiens* (signed on 25 March 1802) proved favorable to French interests and brought the nine years of Revolutionary Wars to an unmourned conclusion. The general pacification, however, was destined to last only 14 short months.

Rey, Général Louis Emmanuel, baron (1768–1846). An infantry soldier from

Rey

1784, he was commissioned in 1792 and served in the Army of the Alps for four years, being promoted to *général de brigade* in 1796. He commanded the Camp of Boulogne,* or its remnant, from 1805–08 and was made a baron in the latter year. He served Gouvion St. Cyr* as Chief of Staff in Spain from August 1808, fighting at Barcelona* and Tarragonna.* From August 1811 he was governor of San Sebastian,* where he underwent a heroic siege from late June 1813, but he was ultimately forced to surrender on 9 September. In recognition of his gallantry Napoleon promoted him to *général de division* in November, although he was a prisoner of war at that time. He returned to France in May 1814 and was made Governor of Valenciennes during the Hundred Days.* After a period of enforced retirement he was recalled to head a Bourbon commission in 1830 for a period of three years.

Reynier, Général Jean Louis Ebénézer (1771–1814). Trained as a civil engineer, he became a volunteer gunner in 1792.

Reynier

He fought at Jemappes* under Dumouriez* and rapidly earned preferment, being promoted to *général de brigade* (after once declining the recommendation) in January 1795. After serving as Moreau's* Chief of Staff in the Army of the Rhine and Moselle in 1796, he was promoted to *général de division*. In 1798 he accompanied Bonaparte to Egypt, fought at the Pyramids* and at Heliopolis and Canope, but later quarreled with General Menou* and was shipped back to France. Continuing his feud, he published an attack on that general which the First Consul suppressed, and after killing General Destaing in a duel, he was exiled from Paris. Later service took him to Naples and Venice and then to Calabria, and in 1808 he was made Minister of War and the Marine in the Kingdom of Naples. In 1809 he served in the latter part of the Danube campaign, and in 1810 he was posted to Spain under Massena's* command. After covering the French sieges of Ciudad Rodrigo* and Almeida* (1810), he marched with the Army of Portugal to Bussaco* (where he commanded the French left wing) and thence to the Lines of Torres Vedras.* He won the action of Sabugal,* fought at Fuentes de Oñoro,* and was made a Count of the Empire in May 1811. In 1812 he took part in the Russian campaign and in 1813 fought at Bautzen,* Dresden,* Gross-Beeren,* and Dennewitz* at the head of the VII (Saxon) Corps, and also at Leipzig,* where his Saxon troops deserted to the Allies. He was taken prisoner, and after returning to France in February 1814 on exchange, he died in Paris two weeks later.

Reynosa, action of, 14 November 1808. As Napoleon launched his offensive over the Ebro, Marshal Soult* at the head of II Corps swept forward to take Burgos* and then headed to the southwest through Urbel intent upon trapping General

Blake* and the 12,000 survivors of the battle of Gamonal (fought outside Burgos on 10 November). However, Soult was only in time to catch the rear guard and convoys of the Army of Galicia as Blake abandoned his baggage and ordered his men to head into the mountains in the direction of Léon. At Reynosa, Soult joined up with Victor* and Lefebvre,* who had earlier fought Blake at Pan Corbo* and Valmaçeda.*

Rheims, battle of, 13 March 1814. Following the check received at Laon,* Napoleon fell back on Soissons and considered his next moves. Learning that St. Priest had occupied Rheims with 14,500 Allies on the 12th, and that Generals Yorck* and Gneisenau* were on the worst of terms, the Emperor decided on a rapid march to retake Rheims. Friant,* followed by Marmont,* Ney,* and some National Guard units, set out early on the 14th, and St. Priest—to his surprise—found himself facing Napoleon and a growing force to the west of Rheims at 4:00 P.M. Marmont's 8,000 men led the attack and St. Priest was killed. The French took the Soissons gate of the city, and the Allied corps fled with a loss of 3,000 men and 23 guns. Only some 10,000 of the 25,000 French had been engaged. Napoleon was now placed across the communications of Blücher* and Schwarzenberg.*

Rhine, Confederation of the, 12 July 1806. After Austerlitz* Napoleon began to reorder German affairs. Determined to do away with the anachronistic Holy Roman Empire, in January 1806 he proposed the formation of a federation of German states under his protection. Despite some hesitation by France's earlier allies, Württemberg and Bavaria, Napoleon had his way, and on 12 July 1806 some 16 princes announced their departure from the Holy Roman Empire

and formed themselves into the Confederation of the Rhine, promising France a contingent of 63,000 men. Prussia was highly suspicious of this new arrangement, and it formed one strand in the web of motivation leading to the outbreak of war with France later in 1806. After Jena-Auerstädt,* however, the Confederation was secure, and it formed an important part of Napoleon's Continental System,* closing central German markets from trade with Britain. As the years passed, Anhalt, Hesse-Darmstadt, and Nassau adopted many French-style reforms; Mecklenburg and Saxony rather fewer, but Napoleon did not force the pace. The Confederation fell apart during 1813 as one prince after another deserted Napoleon and joined the Allies.

Riall, General Sir Phineas (1775–1850). Commissioned into the British Army in 1794, Riall saw considerable service in the West Indies before being transferred to Canada as a major general in December 1813. He played a part in the battle of Lundy's Lane,* where he was wounded and captured. In 1816 he was appointed governor of Grenada. Knighted in 1833, he was promoted to full general in 1841.

Ricard, Général Etienne Pierre Sylvestre, baron (later comte) (1771–1843). Commissioned into the infantry in 1791, he served in Corsica and eventually became aide to Suchet* in the Army of Italy (1799). After command of various army bases, in 1806 he distinguished himself at Jena* and was promoted to *général de brigade* in December 1806. He was made a Baron of the Empire in 1808 and sent to Spain as Soult's* Chief of Staff in II Corps. Sent back to France from Portugal for intriguing, he underwent a period of semi-disgrace until Soult requested his services. Returning to Spain he served under Suchet at the siege of Tarragonna.* He took part in the invasion of Russia,

Ricard

occupying the Russian camp of Dunaburg. Promoted to *général de division* in September 1812, he was wounded at Krasnöe.* In 1813 he fought at Weissenfels,* Lützen,* and Leipzig* among other battles, commanding III Corps for a period. In 1814 he fought at Montmirail,* Vauchamps,* and Rheims,* and was wounded before Paris. He rallied to the Bourbons in 1815 and was made a count in 1817. Six years later he commanded a division under Lauriston* in Spain. From 1829 to his retirement in 1831 he commanded the infantry division of the Royal Guard.

Richery, Contre Amiral Joseph de (1757–1799). Of noble but impoverished family, he sailed as a cabin boy for nine years on merchantmen before transferring to the navy in 1774. He served under Admiral Suffren in the Americas and West Indies, earning a reputation for valor. After a shipwreck he returned to France in 1785. Sent to the Far East, he was promoted to *capitaine de vaisseau* in 1793, only to be suspended for a year

as a man of noble birth (1794–95). In September 1795 he was re-employed and given command of a squadron at Toulon, with which he attacked the British Levant convoy off Cape St. Vincent, capturing a warship and 30 merchantmen which he escorted into Cadiz where his crews, denied plunder, mutinied. However, in March 1796 he was promoted to rear admiral and sailed to Newfoundland later that year, where he wrought havoc with the British fishing fleets, capturing or sinking 80 vessels. In November 1796 he returned to Rochefort, where he was blockaded. He escaped to take part in the Bantry Bay* expedition (1796–97), his last active command.

Richmond, General Sir Charles Lennox, Duke of (1764–1819). Fourth Duke of Richmond and Lennox, he earned notoriety for fighting a duel with the Duke of York* in 1789. After service in the Leeward Isles, he became an MP (1790), and five years later was promoted to colonel. He had reached the rank of lieutenant general by 1805, and became duke in 1806. From 1807–13 he served as Lord-Lieutenant of Ireland, and was promoted to full general in 1814. On the night of 15 June 1815 he and his wife gave the celebrated ball in Brussels at which Wellington* learned the truth about Napoleon's advance. He was present at Waterloo* but not in a command capacity. In 1818 he was appointed Governor General of Canada, where he died.

Rivoli, battle of, 14 January 1797. In the new year of 1797 the Austrians made their fourth—and what was to prove their last—attempt to relieve their long-besieged garrison of Mantua.* General Alvintzi,* at the head of 28,000 men, marched south from Trent down the Adige Valley, while two diversionary attacks were made against Verona and

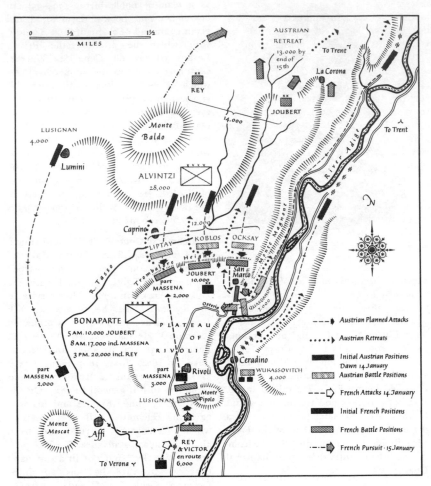

Battle of Rivoli, 14 January 1797

Legnano by Generals Bayalitsch and Provera* with 6,200 and 9,000 men respectively. General Bonaparte's fighting strength had grown to 34,500 men (exclusive of the 10,000 besieging Mantua), but it was only on 13 January that he became convinced that the main onslaught was that from the north. Both Massena* and Augereau* had reported enemy attacks on Verona and Legnano, but their commander, from his headquarters at Roverbella, refused to be drawn by these developments and awaited news from Joubert,* whose 10,000 men were stationed in the area between La Corona and Rivoli. In the afternoon of the 13th the tidings that Joubert had lost La Corona to heavy enemy attacks at length arrived, and Bonaparte at once began to concentrate troops to meet the revealed main threat. Massena with 7,000 men was summoned from Verona and Rey was called up from the shores of Lake Garda. By 2:00 A.M. Bonaparte had personally joined Joubert on the plateau of Rivoli, arriving in time to countermand that officer's intended withdrawal of his men. The enemy's campfires revealed that the Austrians were moving in five columns, two down the banks of the Adige along the only two roads in the area, two more to the east of Monte Baldo, and one to its west.

Much would depend on the timing of the Austrian attack the next morning, for both Massena and Rey were still distant. Alvintzi's plan was to employ Generals Liptay, Koblos, and Ocksay, with a joint 12,000 men, in a frontal attack over the river Tasso to seize the Trombalore Heights leading onto the plateau of Rivoli, while Quasdanovitch* brought 7,000 more to storm the Osteria Gorge from the Adige, supported by Wukassovitch and his 35 guns from the further bank of the river, to turn the French right flank. Finally, 4,000 more Austrians under Lusignan were to attempt to envelop the French left after a circuitous march.

Bonaparte took up the following dispositions. Joubert was ordered to send two brigades to hold the Trombalore Heights and to place his third to hold the village of San Marco and guard the Osteria Gorge on the right flank. By 6:00 A.M. on the 14th Massena's troops were appearing from the south, and orders were sent for one brigade to guard the French left from the Tasso near Monte Moscat, while the remaining two (5,000) were to wait around Rivoli to the rear of the plateau and serve as a reserve.

Shortly after daybreak Joubert was in action along the Trombalore Heights, sustained by 18 guns (one third provided by Massena), and the initial Austrian attacks were repulsed. However, the westernmost French brigade was outflanked by Liptay—a French unit panicked and fled—and Massena was brought up with 2,000 men from Rivoli to plug the gap and stabilize the situation. This was achieved by 8:00 A.M., the French strength having now risen to 17,000 men overall. Rey was still marching for the battlefield.

The crisis came in mid-morning, when both Austrian flank attacks began almost simultaneously. Massena was entrusted with the task of repulsing Lusignan on the left, and thus securing the French line of retreat toward Verona. Meantime, Quasdanovitch was making fair progress against Joubert's tiring men up the Osteria Gorge. Judging that the Austrian central attack was a spent force for the time being, Bonaparte realigned some of the men from the Trombalore Heights sector to meet the attack from the east and brought up some light guns. Shot and shell tore into the Austrian column and a lucky shot exploded a pair of power wagons; as the Austrians reeled under the concussion, Leclerc* and Lasalle* led forward 500 French troops in a determined charge, and soon the gorge was clear. There was just time for Bonaparte to send Joubert's men back to the Trombalore Heights to repulse a renewed onslaught by Koblos and Liptay. Meanwhile, Lusignan had found himself trapped between Massena and Rey's arriving troops, and 3,000 Austrians fell into French hands just south of Rivoli.

By 5:00 P.M. victory was assured, but Bonaparte was forced to march south with Massena's division to face Provera's column, which was forcing a crossing over the Adige at Anghiari. Rey and Joubert were left to follow up the victory, and a second day's fighting against Alvintzi's remaining 20,000 men resulted in the rout of three Austrian columns and the recapture of La Corona. The Austrians retreated toward Trent, leaving behind a further 5,000 prisoners of war. The two days had cost Alvintzi all of 14,000 men, or half his force; the French had lost some 5,000 casualties.

This notable success effectively doomed Mantua. A final success at La Favorita* on the 15th led to the surrender of Provera's column within sight of Mantua, and on 2 February Würmser* at last surrendered at the head of his garrison of 30,000 men (half of whom were sick). The conquest of the Po valley was at last complete.

Robespierre, Augustin Bon Joseph de (1763–1794). The younger brother of Maximilien (see below), Augustin practiced law at Arras up to the Revolution. With the coming of political turmoil, he administered the Pas de Calais area, and from 1793 became a *député* for Paris in the Convention. Entrusted with a number of key missions, in mid-1793 he was sent to investigate the unrest in the south and was one of the first to pick out Captain Bonaparte of the artillery near Toulon* as a promising officer whose practical skills and revolutionary fervor were just what the situation demanded. He continued to press Bonaparte's interests after returning to Paris to become Secretary of the National Assembly. He supported his brother through thick and thin, and on 9th *Thermidor* he tried to kill himself by leaping from a window of the Hôtel de Ville. The attempt failed and he was sent to the guillotine, carried to the scaffold already dying.

Robespierre, Maximilien François Isidore de (1758–1794). Also a lawyer in Arras, he was elected a *député* for the Third Estate in the States General, where he pressed strong democratic ideas. Nicknamed "the incorruptible," he became the political guide to the left-wing Jacobin* Club, but only slowly adopted republicanism personally. He came to full notice

in the National Assembly, leading the opposition to the Girondins. Made a *député* for Paris in the Convention and a member of the Commune, his power rapidly grew, and now a convinced republican, he voted for Louis XVI's* death. Appointed a member of the Committee of National Security, he used Dumouriez's* defection to the Allies to bring down the Girondins and led the insurrection that swept the Jacobins to power. From 27 July 1793 he was the most important member of the Committee of Public Safety, and he supported the Terror* as a means of achieving national unity at any price. In March 1794 Robespierre destroyed the Hébertist faction, and next month the supporters of Danton. Ruthlessly efficient, he directed the Committee's policies, supported by Couthin and St. Just. Hoping to restore morality, he supported the Festival of the Supreme Being. However, his cold and ruthless reputation earned him many foes, and when he proposed to pass laws to make the members of the Convention responsible to the law he triggered a revolt and a *coup d'état* against his rule on 9th *Thermidor*. Shot in the jaw by a policeman in the Hôtel de Ville, he was guillotined—placed face upward—the next day

Augustin Robespierre

(28 July 1794). Elegant, a good orator, self-denying, and totally dedicated to his ideals, he was executed along with his brother, Couthon, St. Just, and 17 key supporters. This event ended the Terror and caused the Thermidorian reaction.

Roguet, Général François, comte (1770–1846). The son of a locksmith of Toulouse, he joined an infantry regiment in 1789. After service in the Alps, from 1793–1800 he was a member of the Army of Italy. First commissioned as a regimental staff officer in 1793, he received several wounds serving under Joubert* and fought at Novi.* In 1803 he was promoted to *général de brigade,* and between 1805 and 1807 saw service at Elchingen* and Güttstadt, where he was wounded and taken prisoner. Released after Friedland,* he was made a baron in 1808 and sent to serve with IV Corps in Spain, where he fought at Durango. Recalled to France, he took command of the 2nd Grenadiers of the Imperial Guard,* and in 1809 fought at Essling* and Wagram.* He next led the Young Guard to Spain and fought there with success from 1809 to 1812, becoming *général de division* in 1811, serving under Dorscnne's* command. In 1812 he marched with the Guard into Russia, seeing action at Borodino* and Krasnöe.* In 1813 he was made a Chamberlain to the Emperor and fought at the major battles of that campaign, being wounded at Dresden.* Posted to the Low Countries, he fought with mixed fortunes in the defense of French interests, including at the siege of Antwerp. In February 1814 Napoleon made him a count. Despite a degree of Bourbon favor he rallied to Napoleon in 1815 and fought at Waterloo.* From 1815 to 1830 he saw no active employment, but thereafter held several important administrative posts on the French general staff. He was made a peer of France in 1831, and was only finally put on the staff reserve in 1839.

Roliça, battle of, 17 August 1808. Advancing from Mondego Bay,* Wellesley* set out for Lisbon to seek out Junot's* army. On 16 August a skirmish was fought with General Delaborde* at Obidos,* but that commander fell back to take up a strong position around the village of Roliça, where he deployed his 4,400 men and 5 cannon.

On 17 August Wellesley advanced to the attack from Obidos. Sending Colonel Trant* with 1,350 Portuguese along a spur to outflank the French from the west, and General Fergusson with 4,500 men and 6 guns to envelop them from the east, Wellesley advanced directly upon Roliça and its hill in the center at the head of his remaining 9,000 men. The British gunners opened fire prematurely, and Delaborde soon penetrated Wellesley's design; after a stiff fight around Roliça Hill he skillfully withdrew his men to a second position along a crest one mile to the rear. Four gullies led toward the summit, and once again, after a pause to reorganize, the Allies tried to repeat their plan of the morning—a double-envelopment associated with a frontal attack. The sequence became confused, and Colonel Lake and the 29th blundered up one of the gullies to suffer heavy casualties. Hill's* attempts to extricate Lake failed, and Wellesley had to order an all-out attack. In the end this succeeded, and Delaborde fell back again in growing disorder. The Allies had lost 485 casualties, the French some 700. The Allies were able to continue their march toward the Portuguese capital, and would soon fight an important battle at Vimiero.*

Romana, General Pedro Caro y Sureda, Marquis of La (1761–1811). A Spanish soldier of some note, he fought the French in Roussillon (1793) and in Catalonia two years later. In 1807 he was appointed to command a corps of Spanish troops incorporated into the *Grande Armée* on

Napoleon's insistence to serve as a guarantee of Spain's good intentions, and was sent to serve under Bernadotte* in northern Europe. However, after the revolt of Madrid* in 1808, La Romana and his men were spirited away from the Danish coast by the Royal Navy and returned to Spain. He played a leading role in the campaign that followed, but was defeated. He was appointed a member of the Supreme Junta that met at Seville after the loss of Madrid. From 1810 he became commander of a new Spanish army and operated in Portugal alongside Wellington* until his death in the following year.

Rome, Général François, chevalier (1773–1826). Commissioned into a Jura volunteer battalion in 1792, Rome served on the Rhine (1792–97), in Switzerland (1798–99), and in Germany (1800–01), taking part in many engagements including the battle of Hohenlinden.* As a captain of *voltigeurs*, he accompanied the *Grande Armée* to Austria, Prussia, and Poland from 1805, receiving wounds at both Auerstadt* and Pultusk.* He next served under Moncey* in Spain, fighting at Tudela* and at the siege of Saragossa,* but was then posted to the Low Countries (1809). In the Russian campaign he fought at Smolensk* and was wounded at Borodino.* Maloyaroslavetz* was his next action, and then in August 1813, after service in Germany, he was promoted to *général de brigade* and made a *chevalier* of the Empire. He helped Davout* defend Hamburg* (1813–14), holding the island of Wilhelmsburg against repeated Allied attacks. In 1815 he returned to the colors to command a division of Gérard's* IV Corps, fighting at Ligny* and, after Wavre,* covering Grouchy's* retreat to Namur. His active-list service ended in October 1815, but he later received an honorific post under the restored Bourbons, first at Calais, then (from 1821) at Strasbourg.

Rome, King of. *See* **Napoleon II**

Roncesvalles, battle of, 25 July 1813. As Soult* launched his counteroffensive through the Pyrenees,* he sent 40,000 men and 8 mountain guns under General Reille* from St. Jean-Pied-de-Port to drive the Allies from the Roncesvalles Pass. At 6:00 A.M. on 25 July, General Cole's* 4th Division, garrisoning the area as part of Wellington's* strategic deployment covering the siege of San Sebastian* and the blockade of Pamplona,* found itself under heavy attack by 20,000 French troops advancing along two parallel spurs on either side of the road running up the pass. Byng's* brigade to the east was driven in by Clausel's* division after a staunch three-hour fight that held up the entire French corps, but took up a new position on a height called the Altobiscar, while by 2:00 P.M. Cole was bringing up three more brigades to hold the pass and support the intrepid Byng. Fighting continued against long odds until 5:00 P.M., when a dense fog obliterated the battlefield just as a brigade of Portuguese infantry reached the scene. Despite his orders to hold at all costs, Cole decided to fall back toward Pamplona overnight. He had lost 450 men and inflicted some 200 casualties on the French, but his achievement was to delay Reille's advance for a complete day.

Rostopchin, General Fedor Vasiljevitch, Count (1763–1826). Appointed an aide-de-camp to Tsar Paul I,* his court career rapidly advanced him to the rank of general, Grand Marshal of the Palace, and Minister of Foreign Affairs (1798). In 1799 he was made a count. Under Tsar Alexander* he fell into temporary eclipse for opposing the French alliance in 1807, but as Franco-Russian relations cooled he reappeared at court in 1810. In 1812 he was made governor of Moscow, and after the evacuation of the city on Napoleon's approach is known to have ordered the burning of liquor stores, emptied the jails, and removed the fire engines, thus probably starting the great conflagration that eventually consumed two thirds of the city. He was reappointed governor in 1814 and was a member of the Russian delegation to the Conference of Vienna.* He was also a writer of some note.

Rothschild, the family. This famous Jewish banking family was founded by Mayer Anselm Rothschild (1743–1812) at Frankfort-on-Main, where he was entrusted with the financial affairs of William I, Prince of Hesse-Cassel. His sons and grandsons rapidly expanded the banking business into a European commercial empire. Anselm Mayer (1773–1855) followed his father at Frankfort, becoming Councillor of the Prussian commercial chamber and (from 1820) consul in Bavaria. Solomon (1774–1835) established the Vienna branch in 1826, while Nathan (1777–1836) operated from London and made a fortune in June 1815 by receiving early news of the outcome of Waterloo.* Charles (1788–1835) set up business in Naples (1820), and James (1792–1865) worked from Paris, where he performed great services for Louis XVIII,* Charles X, and Louis-Philippe. During the Napoleonic Wars the family was deeply involved in the financial dealings of all participants.

Roustam, Raza (1780–1845). This Mameluke* slave was the property of Salih Bey, but after his master was poisoned by Djezzar Pasha* at Acre* he made his way to Cairo, where he became part of Sheik El-Bekri's household. In June 1799 El-Bekri presented Roustam—together with a black stallion—to Bonaparte as a gift,

and from that time he served as Napoleon's personal bodyguard and valet, always dressed in Mameluke robes. He made a fortune selling favors but deserted his master shortly before the abdication in 1814. He later married a French girl, ran a state lottery office, and wrote some colorful and incredible memoirs, living a considerable time in London but returning to Paris in 1840 for the state funeral of Napoleon's body, brought from St. Helena.*

Roveredo, battle of, 4 September 1796. This small town 30 miles south of Trent in the Adige Valley was the scene of an engagement between the advance formations of the Army of Italy, commanded by Massena* and Rey,* and the larger part of Davidovitch's* Austrian force which General Würmser* had entrusted with the defense of the approaches to Trent while the main Austrian army headed east and south down the Brenta Valley in a second attempt to relieve besieged Mantua.* Massena's strength was about 10,200 men, and he faced 14,000 Austrians, deployed between the village of Marco and the important road junction of Roveredo. Sending one brigade to outflank Marco, Massena captured the main position, taking 6,000 prisoners and 20 guns for the loss of a couple of hundred men. As Davidovitch hastily retired toward the Tyrol, Massena occupied Trent on the 5th. Then, leaving Vaubois north of Trent with 10,000 men to guard against a renewed Austrian onslaught, Bonaparte ordered his army to follow Würmser down the Brenta Valley toward Bassano.*

Ruchel, General Ernest Philip von (1754–1823). Born in Pomerania, he entered the Prussian infantry in 1771 and served on Frederick the Great's staff. His admiration for his master lasted all his life. After campaigning in the Palatinate in 1793 he was promoted to general the next year and fought at Kaiserslautern. In 1796 he was made governor of Potsdam. In 1806, commanding one of the three main Prussian field forces, he arrived at Jena* too late for the main battle and was defeated between that town and Weimar, sustaining serious wounds. He survived, however, and later fought in Poland.

Ruffin, Général François Amable, comte (1771–1811). After volunteering for the army in 1792, he was within two days elected a captain and a month later promoted to lieutenant colonel. From 1792–94 he served 'in the Army of the North, fighting at Hondschoote. Staff appointments led to his becoming an aide to Jourdan* the next year, a position he sporadically held until 1798, when he served Ney* in a similar capacity. He fought on the Rhine and the Danube, becoming Ney's Chief of Staff in late 1799

and taking part at Hohenlinden.* Posted to the Camp of St. Omer in 1803, he was promoted to *général de brigade* in February 1805, and later that year he fought under Oudinot* at Austerlitz.* In October 1806 he briefly transferred to Oudinot's dismounted dragoons, but soon returned to staff duties. During the campaign in Poland he fought at Ostrolenka (February 1807) and then (under Lannes*) at Friedland.* In November that year Ruffin became *général de division*, taking over Dupont's* command in Victor's* corps. He was sent with Victor to Spain, where he learned that he had been made a count, and fought at Somosierra* and next year at Medellin and Talavera.* On 5 March 1811 he was mortally wounded at the battle of Barrosa* fighting against General Graham,* and taken prisoner. He died on board H.M.S. *Gorgon* off Plymouth on 15 May.

Saalfeld, battle of, 10 October 1806. As Napoleon led the *Grande Armée* through the Thuringerwald into Saxony at the outset of the war against Prussia, Prince Louis Ferdinand* advanced his 8,300 men and 44 guns over to the east bank of the river Saale to block the advance of the westernmost French column headed by Lannes* and supported by Augereau*—some 41,000 French troops in all. In fact Louis' superior, General Hohenlohe,* had countermanded this move on the orders of the Duke of Brunswick,* but the action had opened at 10:00 A.M. on the 10th before these new instructions reached the Prince.

As Suchet's* division emerged from the passes it came under artillery fire but, without waiting for Augereau, Lannes ordered an immediate attack. Suchet was sent through woodland to turn the Prussian flank, while covering troops attacked frontally. Louis saw the threat in time, reinforced his right wing, and advanced in the center to hold the village of Beulitz. After a fierce two-hour fight, French numbers began to tell. As his men were pushed back under the walls of Saalfeld, Prince Louis led five squadrons in a gallant charge against the French center—but he was cut down and killed by Quartermaster Guindet* of the 10th Hussars. This event ended Prussian resistance. The French killed 900 Prussians, captured 1,800 prisoners, and took 33 guns, all for a loss of 172 killed. Lannes and his V Corps were soon on the road for Jena.* Saalfeld, together with the action at Schleiz,* marked the satisfactory ending of the first phase of the campaign.

Sabugal, the action of, 3 April 1811. In pursuit of the retreating Massena,* Wellington* advanced from the strong Lines of Torres Vedras.* Learning that General Reynier's* corps was drawn up behind the Coa near Sabugal so as to cover the retreat of the rest of the Army of Portugal, Wellington ordered a frontal attack on the position by four divisions from the west while the Light Division and two cavalry brigades forded the Coa above the town to sever Reynier's line of retreat. This outflanking attack was to open the fight. Unfortunately, a dense fog threw the plans into confusion, surprise was lost, and the Light Division failed to pin Reynier's three divisions. Beckwith's brigade held a hill against all three French divisions, but in due course Reynier was able to draw off to the east amid torrential rain, having lost 760 casualties and one howitzer. The Light Division lost only 179 casualties. As Reille* retired, Massena fell back in conformity, and by 5 April only the garrison of Almeida* remained in French hands in Portugal. Wellington promptly blockaded it and awaited Massena's reaction around Fuentes de Oñoro.*

Sacile, battle of, 16 April 1809. The first battle of the War of 1809 took place in North Italy on the secondary front. Eugène de Beauharnais,* at the head of 37,000 French and Italian troops, somewhat rashly attacked the Austrian Arch-

Germany, 1813

duke John's* 40,000 men at Sacile near the head of the Adriatic. The fighting was confused, and when part of the Austrian army maneuvered so as to threaten his flank and rear, Eugène conceded defeat and fell back behind the river Piave and then retired over the Adige. Each side lost some 2,000 casualties. Little of note ensued, but later in the month events on the Danube front—as Napoleon advanced on Vienna from Eckmühl* and Ratisbon*—caused the Archduke John to be recalled into Hungary, and Eugène followed.

Sacken, General Dmitri Osten, Count (1790–1881). The son of a Russian general who fought with distinction at Eylau* (1807), in the Campaign of Russia (1812), and during the Campaign of France (1814), the young soldier shared in most of his father's military experiences. In later years he fought in the Caucasus, against Persia (1826–27), against Turkey (1828–29), and also served in Poland (1831), Hungary (1849), and in the Crimean War (1854–56).

Sackett's Harbor, action of, 28 and 29 May 1813. A considerable part of the War of 1812* between Great Britain and the United States centered around control of Lake Ontario. In the spring of 1813, the Governor General of Upper Canada, Sir George Prevost, led a determined attack on Sackett's Harbor, the American arsenal at the eastern end of the lake. The post was held by General Jacob Brown at the head of only 600 men, but he successfully repulsed two heavy assaults. Heartened by this success, the Americans sent off two columns to attack Montreal.

Sahagun, action of, 21 December 1808. As Sir John Moore,* still unaware that Napoleon was marching north from Madrid to intercept him, advanced toward Sahagun en route for Burgos in the hope of surprising the component parts

of Marshal Soult's* scattered corps, Lord Paget* and the cavalry advance guard set out to surprise General Debelle's force of dragoons and chasseurs billeted at Sahagun. Setting out from Mayorga, Paget advanced with the 15th and 10th Hussars. As soon as it was dark on the 20th, the cavalry began its final approach through the bitter cold to the town from Melgar de Abajo, on the way detaching Brigadier General Slade with the 10th Hussars and two guns away to the left over the river Coa—the plan being for him to attack the town from the west while the 15th under Paget awaited beyond the town to the south and east to cut off the French retreat.

After a difficult, icy journey, Paget arrived near the town to find no sign of the dallying Slade; the approach of the 15th was seen by a French picket, and the alarm was raised. Realizing that his original plan was impossible, Paget moved the hussars around the southeastern side of Sahagun, and in the early-morning gloom discovered Debelle evacuating the town with his 500 dragoons and chasseurs. In the belief that the newcomers were Spanish cavalry, Debelle faced about to challenge them and received a devastating charge by the 400 British Hussars. The first French line was shattered and the second soon gave ground, and the action developed into a mass of individual engagements. Debelle and his survivors fled east for the river Valderaduey to seek the road to Carrion, but many of his men were killed or taken along the riverbank. The French lost perhaps 120 men killed and a further 13 officers and 150 men taken prisoners; the 15th lost two hussars killed and 20 wounded. Slade arrived at the very end of the action but took no active part in this "brilliant little affair," which earned the British cavalry a high reputation. Moore and the main army reached Sahagun late on the 21st, but would very soon be in full retreat toward Corunna* as news of Napoleon's rapid approach at last reached them. The next notable cavalry action took place at Benavente* eight days later.

Saint-André, Commissioner Jean Bon (1749–1813). Also known as André Jeanbon and nicknamed "the Baron," he was born into a Protestant family of Montauban. After studying maritime subjects at Bordeaux he went to sea, but was shipwrecked. He then took holy orders, and in the Revolution was elected a *député* to the Convention. In due course he became a member of the Committee of Public Safety* and was sent to Brest as special naval commissioner. There he collaborated with Admiral Villaret-Joyeuse* in implementing important naval reforms. In later years he was French Consul-General in Algiers and then Smyrna. During the British reconquest of Egypt (1801) he was taken captive by the Turks, but later freed. Napoleon made him Prefect of Mainz, and he died there of typhus in 1813.

Saint-Cyr, *Ecole Spéciale Militaire de.* The Revolution closed the French military academies of the Bourbons, save for those at Châlons and Mezières for the artillery and the engineers respectively. Aware of the need to regularize the training of young officers, Robespierre* founded the short-lived *Ecole de Mars* in 1794, but this collapsed after four months. Bonaparte, as First Consul, signed a decree on 1 May 1802 creating an *Ecole Spéciale Militaire* at Versailles, and he took great personal care with the syllabus of instruction and training. Between 1805 and 1815 the school furnished the Emperor with about 4,000 young officers, of whom 700 were killed on active service, the first three to die falling at Austerlitz.* Seriously bombed in the Second World

War, Saint-Cyr was reopened at Coetiquidian in Brittany. The school's motto is "They study to conquer."

Saint-Cyr, Général Claude Carra, comte (1760–1834). Properly known as Carra Saint-Cyr, he was the son of an equerry. Commissioned into the infantry in 1774, he fought in America under Lafayette.* After holding various administrative posts in French garrisons he left the army for health reasons in 1792, but rejoined as a volunteer the same year. He was long associated with General Aubert-Dubayet, whose embassy to Turkey he accompanied in 1796 (having been promoted to *général de brigade* the previous year). He became Consul-General in Wallachia, returning to France in 1798 with the widow of his old chief, whom he married next year. Employed in the Army of Italy (1799), he was wounded in the thigh. Appointed to the Army of the Reserve, he fought in Monnier's division in 1800 at Marengo* after a period as commandant of Ivrea. In 1803 he was made a *général de division* and three years later he became Governor of Magdeburg. In 1808 he was made a Baron of the Empire. Next year he fought under Massena* with great distinction at Aspern-Essling* and was later made Governor of Dresden and, from 1810, Governor of Hamburg. In March 1813 he was disgraced by Napoleon for losing an engagement on the river Elbe near Hamburg, but was soon re-employed under Vandamme.* From 1814 until 1819 he was Governor of French Guiana, and finally retired from the service in 1832.

Saint Cyr, Maréchal Laurent Gouvion, comte and later marquis de (1764–1830). Properly known as Gouvion Saint-Cyr, he was an artist by profession, but volunteered in 1792 for the army. He rose rapidly, and in 1794 was promoted to both *général de brigade* and *général de division* after stalwart service in Germany. He played a leading role at the siege of Mainz (1795), and next year commanded the left wing corps of the Army of the Rhine and Moselle, taking over command of the army temporarily on the death of Hoche* in 1797. In 1798 he served in Rome, under Brune,* but was suspended for exceeding his powers. Transferred to the Army of the Danube in 1799, he fought at Stockach;* he then joined the Army of Italy under Joubert* and fought at Novi,* ending up as Governor of Genoa and with the award of a saber of honor. In 1800 he commanded under Moreau* on the Rhine, fighting at Engen and Biberach. The same year he was appointed a Councillor of State, and after a brief command in Naples was sent to Madrid as French ambassador (1801–03). After a further period in Naples (mid-1803) he was made Colonel General of Cuirassiers in 1804, but was not awarded his baton.

In 1805 he fought against the Archduke Charles* in North Italy, capturing an entire Austrian corps at Castelfranco. From 1806–08 he held high command in Naples and was made a Count of the Empire in the latter year. He was then sent to command in Catalonia, capturing Rosas, relieving Barcelona,* winning two small actions, and besieging Girona. However, he unwisely quitted Spain without awaiting the arrival of his appointed successor and was disgraced by Napoleon in November 1809. After two years he was appointed to the Council of State and given command of the Bavarian Corps of the *Grande Armée* before the invasion of Russia in 1812. That year he defeated General Wittgenstein* at the first battle of Polotsk,* being wounded in the process, and for this achievement Napoleon appointed him a marshal on 27 August 1812. However, he was then defeated at Second Polotsk* and threw up his command, having been seriously wounded in the foot, on 18 October. Next

Gouvion Saint-Cyr

year he served Eugène Beauharnais* as military adviser and was later made governor of Dresden. He fought at the battle of Dresden* in command of the center and later defended the town during the siege, but was forced to capitulate in November 1813. He returned to France in June 1814 and was reconciled with the Bourbons. In 1815 he did not rally to Napoleon. Later he served for various periods as Minister of War and of the Marine and was made a marquis in 1817. He retired in 1819 and busied himself with agricultural matters and in writing his memoirs.

St. Helena, exile upon, 1815–1821. After sailing aboard H.M.S. *Bellerophon* to Portland Bay in Dorset, Napoleon's appeals to the Prince Regent and Lord Liverpool's* government for sanctuary in Great Britain were ignored, and on 7 August the Emperor and his suite were transferred on board H.M.S *Northumberland,* which set sail next day for the south Atlantic island of St. Helena, designated by the British authorities as the place of exile. After a voyage of almost ten weeks' duration, the vessel arrived off the island on 15 October, and at 7:30 P.M. on 17 October (some authorities say the 16th), Napoleon went ashore.

As no suitable quarters were ready to receive the party, from 17 October until 10 December Napoleon occupied part of The Briars, the residence of William Balcombe and his family, where the former Emperor struck up a friendly relationship with the younger daughter, Betsi. Relations with the British authorities soon became strained, Napoleon refusing to recognize his being addressed as "General Bonaparte." However, on 10 December his household transferred to the newly adapted Longwood, destined to be Napoleon's final home. The arrival on the island of the new governor, Sir Hudson Lowe,* gravely exacerbated relationships, and after three stormy interviews Napoleon refused to receive him again. The long days, weeks, and months of exile passed somewhat dully, but the former Emperor was able to take some rides around the island (under escort by a British officer—another grievance) and spent much time dictating his memoirs to General Gourgaud* and others of his entourage. The household, run by Bertrand,* was not immune to jealousies and bitter quarrels, many of them centering upon or instigated by the sinister Montholon,* and first Las Cases* and then Gourgaud, followed by others, left the island to return to France. Dr. O'Meara was replaced eventually by Dr. Antomacchi as physician-in-ordinary (from September 1819 to May 1821), and new staff arrived from Europe to fill some of the vacancies caused by deaths or returns to Europe. Marchand the valet remained to the end, as did Bertrand (although his wife did not) and the Montholons. Napoleon's health began to deteriorate rapidly from 1819, and the case that he may have been subjected to forms of arsenical poisoning has recently been

deservedly reopened. From February 1821 Napoleon failed rapidly, despite the ministrations of his medical attendants. On 25 April he signed the final codicils to his will, and on 5 May, at five to six in the evening, he died. His final words were "Josephine" and "tête de l'armée."

His body was buried with fair ceremony in a simple grave, and there his remains rested until their transfer to Paris in 1840, where they were placed in Les Invalides.* So ended the life of Napoleon Bonaparte, who, as a small boy, had written in one of his geographical notebooks a cryptic sentence: "Sainte Hélène—petite île."

Saint-Hilaire, Général Louis Vincent Joseph le Blond, comte de (1766–1809). He joined the Bourbon army in 1777 and served in the West Indies, being commissioned in 1783. In 1792–93 he served in the Alps, and later in Italy, being provisionally promoted to *général de brigade* in September 1795. He was wounded at First Loano, losing two fingers, and successively served under La Harpe,* Massena,* Augereau,* and Vaubois,* fighting at Bassano* in 1796 and being wounded in both legs a few days later. A number of training and administrative posts followed, and in 1799 he was promoted to *général de division.* In 1803 he was attached to the Camp of St. Omer, and in 1805 fought in Soult's* IV Corps at Austerlitz,* where with Vandamme* he stormed the Pratzen Heights, again being wounded. In 1806 he fought at Jena* and in 1807 at Eylau* and Heilsberg.* In 1808 he became a Count of the Empire, and next year fought under Lannes* at Eckmühl,* Ratisbon,* and Aspern-Essling.* At the last-named battle his left foot was shot away, and he died of this wound in Vienna on 5 June 1809.

Saint Jean d'Acre. See **Acre**, siege of

Saint-Jean-de-Luz, action of, 9 November 1813. As part of his plan for the battle of Nivelle,* Wellington* ordered Lieu-tenant General Sir John Hope* (who had succeeded the wounded General Graham* as second-in-command of the Peninsular Army in October) to make a strong dem-onstration against Soult's* right wing—situated among the fortifications of this town on the north bank of the Nivelle—with 20,000 men as a feint to disguise the main allied attack inland. At first light, Hope attacked on the coastal sector preceded by an artillery bombardment, and captured the fortified villages of Urrugne and Socorri. This attack was the signal for the rest of Wellington's army to launch the main attack.

St. John, the Order of. This ancient and venerable organization of the Knights Hospitallers—the champions of Christen-dom against the Turks in the 16th-century struggles in the Mediterranean—had fallen on evil times by 1798 when their island of Malta* was attacked by the Army of the Orient on its way to Egypt. The last Grand Master, de Hompesch, was in-effective and weak, and his Order was un-dermined by traitors working from within. Bonaparte expelled the Order from Malta but paid the Grand Master some com-pensation for his dispossession.

St. Petersburg, Convention of, 5 and 9 April 1812. Soon after Bernadotte* had become Crown Prince of Sweden, he be-gan negotiations with Tsar Alexander I* with a view to making an alliance. In February 1812 Bernadotte's emissaries visited St. Petersburg and offered to dis-embark troops in Germany to attack Na-poleon's rear in the event of a Franco-Russian War, but stipulated Russian aid in the conquest of Norway. Alexander agreed, provided the King of Denmark (who also ruled Norway) was granted compensation in Oldenburg. The conven-tion was signed in Stockholm and St. Petersburg on 5 and 9 April.

St. Pierre, battle of, 13 December 1813. Defeated by Wellington's* army at the battle of the Nive* on 10 December, Mar-shal Soult* sought revenge by launching an attack against General Hill,* isolated at the head of 14,000 Anglo-Portuguese troops and 10 guns to the south of the river Nive after a sudden spate had washed away a vital pontoon bridge. Knowing that it would take at least 12 hours for aid to reach this force, Soult sent out four divisions from Bayonne,* supported by two more (some 42,000 men and 22 guns in all) to storm the ridge at St. Pierre d'Irube.

In fact Hill's position was strong, and the French attack was delayed by bridge congestion while crossing the Adour. Nevertheless, the battle was hard fought; one British unit left the field believing all was lost, but the gap was plugged by Hill and the engagement continued until Soult's men refused to launch a further attack. This near-mutiny coincided with Wellington's arrival at the head of the first reserves, so Soult fell sullenly back into Bayonne, having lost over 3,000 casualties and inflicted some 1,750 on Hill's command. Wellington credited his subordinate, Lord Hill, with the outcome of this gory postscript to the battle of the Nive.

Saint-Sulpice, Général Raymond Gas-pard de Bonardi, comte de (1761–1835). Born in Paris, he was commissioned into the Dragoons in 1777. His service during the Revolutionary Wars* was suspended in 1793 when he was sacked for two years on account of his noble birth, but he was reinstated in 1795 and served in Italy, Holland, and on the Rhine. He served at Wiesloch in December 1799 under d'Haut-poul, and four years later was promoted to *général de brigade*. In 1804 he became an Equerry to the Empress, and from 1805–07 served with the *Grande Armée* in Austria, Prussia, and Poland, being wounded at Eylau.* Promoted to *général de division* that same month, he took over command of d'Hautpoul's cavalry division. In 1808 he became a Count. In 1809 he fought under Bessières* and Davout,* taking part in Abensberg,* Ratisbon,* and Aspern-Essling.* After a year hunting down refractory conscripts in France, he went with the army to Russia in command of the Dragoons of the Guard. In 1813 he became Governor of the Palace of Fontainebleau, served in Saxony, and at Lyons next year. He retired in October 1815.

St. Vincent, battle of Cape, 14 February 1797. Admiral Sir John Jervis,* at the head of 15 sail-of-the-line, was on his blockading station outside Cadiz off Cape St. Vincent when a frigate signaled the approach of 27 Spanish naval vessels under command of Don José de Cordoba, heading for Cadiz from Cartagena. Despite their numerical superiority, the Spanish ships were very strung out over some 20 miles of sea, and Jervis formed his fleet into two columns and sailed to intercept the van. The battle began at 10:45 A.M., as Jervis re-formed a single line of battle so as to bring every gun to bear. By a skillful maneuver he interposed his fleet between the two widely separated parts of the Spanish armament and set about attacking the larger—18 vessels—as they passed on the opposite course, for the Spaniards had veered onto a northerly bearing. Captain Troubridge* aboard H.M.S. *Culloden* led the British column and tacked in pursuit of the enemy's main body, followed in turn by the succeeding ships. However, de Cordoba would have gained a significant start on his pursuers had not Commodore Nelson,* commanding H.M.S. *Captain,* at the head of the rearward three ships of Jervis' fleet, on his own initiative gone about so as to keep the enemy engaged and to head off the enemy's van. Shortly

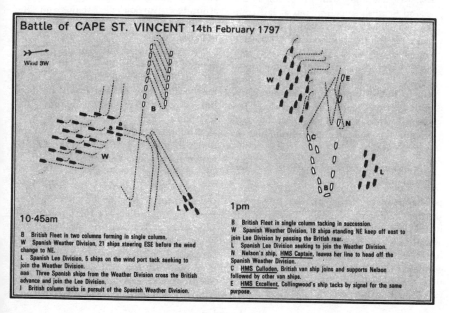

Battle of CAPE ST. VINCENT 14th February 1797

Wind SW

B

W

aaa

B

W

I

L

W

D E

N

C

L

B

10·45am

B   British Fleet in two columns forming in single column.
W   Spanish Weather Division, 21 ships steering ESE before the wind change to NE.
L   Spanish Lee Division, 5 ships on the wind port tack seeking to join the Weather Division.
aaa   Three Spanish ships from the Weather Division cross the British advance and join the Lee Division.
I   British column tacks in pursuit of the Spanish Weather Division.

1pm

B   British Fleet in single column tacking in succession.
W   Spanish Weather Division, 18 ships standing NE keep off east to join Lee Division by passing the British rear.
L   Spanish Lee Division seeking to join the Weather Division.
N   Nelson's ship, HMS Captain, leaves her line to head off the Spanish Weather Division.
C   HMS Culloden, British van ship joins and supports Nelson followed by other van ships.
E   HMS Excellent, Collingwood's ship tacks by signal for the same purpose.

after 1:00 P.M. Nelson boldly attacked the *Santissima Trinidad*, armed with 130 guns, the largest ship afloat at that date, and this action by a single British vessel caused the nonplussed Spaniards to change course again to the northeast. This evolution cost them a slight delay, which afforded time for Jervis' main line, headed by Troubridge, to catch up with the retiring foe. Then the melée of ship-to-ship duels began in earnest. The *Captain* was partially dismasted, but Collingwood* in the *Excellent* came to her rescue and blasted the *San Nicolas*, which promptly became entangled with the neighboring *San Josef*. As the *Excellent* sailed clear, Nelson used what little helmway was left to H.M.S. *Captain* to come alongside the *San Nicolas* and boarded first her, and then, after overcoming the ship's resistance, the *San Josef* beyond her—and thus captured two Spanish ships-of-the-line. Four Spanish vessels had now struck, and Jervis decided at 4:00 P.M. to draw away with his prizes, as the second Spanish squadron was at last coming up. The British had taken 3,000 prisoners for the loss of some 300 casualties—but no British vessel had been lost. Some have criticized Jervis for not pressing the battle further, but he had demonstrated British superiority, and the victory rallied British morale at a bad time. Jervis was created Earl St. Vincent, and Nelson was knighted and promoted to rear admiral.

St. Vincent, Admiral, Earl of. *See* **Jervis,** Sir John

Salamanca, battle of, **22 July 1812.** After capturing Ciudad Rodrigo* and Badajoz* earlier in the year, Wellington* was free to take the offensive as the French forces were reduced to provide troops for the Russian Campaign. He eventually selected Marmont's* Army of Portugal as his first target, and on 13 June advanced through the northern corridor* from the river Agueda. For a month the two armies maneuvered for the advantage, avoiding decisive action, but this enabled Wellington to reduce three forts in Salamanca (they fell to General Clinton* on 27 June); this still did not lure Marmont into attempting to relieve the garrisons as had been hoped. News of reinforcements about to reach Marmont forced Wellington, in mid-July, to seriously consider the need to abandon Salamanca and fall back toward Portugal, and on the 21st orders were indeed issued for the evacuation of the hospitals and rear stores. However, Marmont, now at the head of 50,000 men and 78 guns, believed that he had wind of Wellington's intention as well as his measure as a general, and the French army accordingly moved over the river Tormes to the east of the city and marched to Calvarrasa de Abajo. On the evening of the 21st there was fierce skirmishing between the French advance guard and the Light Division around Calvarrasa de Abajo and the neighboring chapel of Nuestra Señora de la Pena.

Next morning the Allied army, 48,569 men and 60 guns strong, was mainly drawn up in dead ground facing east on a north-south line; the last troops north of the river, Pakenham's division and d'Urban's cavalry, were summoned by Wellington to the south bank and ordered to make a march to Aldea Tejada, where they would be well placed, should the Allied army begin a full-scale retreat toward Ciudad Rodrigo, to serve as a covering force. During the morning Marmont took possession of the Greater Arapiles after at last securing the chapel and ridge near Calvarrasa, and was narrowly forestalled at the Lesser Arapiles. However, noticing the dust clouds caused by Wellington's evacuating convoys, the Marshal deduced that the Allies were in

Battle of SALAMANCA
22nd July 1812

general retreat, and in the late morning ordered his eight divisions to start a rapid march to the west, around what he took to be the right flank of Wellington's army drawn up near Los Arapiles,* in order to sever the line of retreat toward Portugal. Unbeknown to him (so well had Wellington concealed his formations on reverse slopes north of Las Torres), the bulk of the Allied army was now holding a line facing south and running east-west, leaving only the Light Division and one other in the original position. Wellington was lunching when news was brought to him of the French move, and he at once appreciated that Marmont was taking a great risk by moving parallel to the face of the Allied army, particularly as his column had become divided into three parts with considerable gaps developing between the first division (Thomières'* 7th) and the following two (Maucune and Clausel*), and then another gap between

them and the five remaining divisions. In other words, Marmont was inviting defeat in detail, one section at a time.

So it proved. After riding over to alert Pakenham of his 3rd Division's role, Wellington climbed the Lesser Arapiles to watch developments. At 4:45 P.M., Pakenham duly assaulted Thomières' isolated and unsuspecting division and scattered it. Just as its fugitives were encumbering Maucune's division one mile to the rear, Wellington unleashed the 5th Division and Le Marchant's* cavalry brigades at 5:00 P.M. Maucune in turn was smashed, but Le Marchant was killed while his cavalry broke up a number of imperfect infantry squares being formed by Brennier's* division, the next in line. Thus Wellington accounted for "40,000 French in 40 minutes," and Marmont was badly wounded by a shell, as was his second-in-command, General Bonet.*

However, General Clausel coolly assumed command, and when Coles'* 4th Division advanced against Bonet's command near Los Arapiles he was caught in a vicious cross fire and beaten back, while Pack's Portuguese likewise were defeated as they strove to storm the Greater Arapiles, the site of the 40-strong French main battery. Then, at about 5:45 P.M., Clausel unleashed a well-directed infantry and cavalry counterattack against the Allied 4th Division, which was routed. Boyer's cavalry pursued Coles' and Pack's survivors with élan, followed by the 12,000 infantry of Clausel's division. The crisis of the day had come, but Wellington was equal to it. As the French, scenting victory, drove a deep salient into the Allied center, Wellington brought up Clinton's 6th Division to seal off the northern shoulder of the intrusion, deployed Spry's Portuguese and some batteries to produce a telling cross fire, and backed these countermoves with the 7th and 1st Divisions placed in reserve. For five minutes a desperate battle raged deep in the Allied position. During it Clinton lost 33% of his effectives, but at its close Clausel's division was broken, and the Allied line of battle was soon restored. Now five out of eight French divisions had been shattered.

Wellington sent Clinton forward in the center. He was checked by Ferrey's division fighting in line, but only for a short time; Wellington rushed guns to the sector, which soon scattered Ferrey, and then Clinton successfully stormed the Greater Arapiles. Only Foy's* division now remained intact, and after fighting a staunch rear-guard action in the gathering gloom around Otero, its commander was able to break contact and head away toward the bridge over the distant river Tormes at Alba de Tormes*—a post that should have been occupied in advance by a Spanish force but which had not in fact been blocked, to Wellington's fury. However, for the loss of 5,214 men, the Allies had inflicted 14,000 casualties and taken 20 guns, and in the process shattered the French hold on north and central Spain.

Salicetti (or **Saliceti**), Commissioner Antoine Christophe (1757–1809). Born in Corsica, he was a lawyer by profession before being elected to the States General as a member of the Third Estate in 1789. He pressed for, and obtained, the full union of Corsica with France. A staunch Jacobin* in the Convention, he voted for Louis XVI's* death. On the revolt of Marseilles and Toulon* in 1793, he was sent by the Committee of Public Safety to supervise countermeasures, and in the process met Captain Bonaparte and became his supporter and patron, together with the younger Robespierre.* He survived the fall of Robespierre and was sent to the Army of Italy and later to Corsica; in 1797 he was elected to the Council of Five Hundred (*Cinq-Cents*.)* Two years later he was saved from the purge after the *coup d'état* *de Brumaire* by Bonaparte's personal intervention, and he was given diplomatic appointments at Lucca and Geneva (1801). From 1806 he served Joseph Bonaparte* as Minister of Police and Minister of War in Naples, putting down several insurrections. He found less favor under Murat,* who replaced him with Reynier,* but in 1809 he took a prominent part in the absorption of Rome into the Empire. Returning to Naples he suddenly died, probably from poison. Napoleon greatly esteemed his fellow-Corsican and once described him as "worth 100,000 men."

Sandhurst, the Royal Military College. Founded to train young officers for the infantry and cavalry, Sandhurst opened its doors in 1812. Its first Lieutenant Governor was Le Marchant.* The Duke of York* had inaugurated the plan for such an institution in 1799, and a small college had been opened at High Wycombe. In 1801 this had been divided into a senior and a junior department. The former, which stayed at High Wycombe, eventually became the Staff College at Camberley in the mid-19th century, but the latter moved to Marlow before finally being housed at Sandhurst. Some young officers were trained in time to take part in Wellington's* later campaigns, but not many. The Royal Military Academy at Woolwich,* an older institution, provided officers for the Artillery and Engineers.

San Juan, General Benito (1775?–1808). Entrusted by the Supreme Junta with the last-ditch defense of the road to Madrid against Napoleon's advancing army, San Juan took up a position at the Pass of Somosierra* and tried to hold the French in check. After being routed he tried to rally his men, but they only halted near Talavera,* where they turned on their commander and hung him from an elm tree.

San Marcial, combat of, 31 August 1813. In a last despairing effort to prevent the fall of San Sebastian,* Marshal Soult* planned a double onslaught against Wellington's* positions. While General Clausel* attacked at Vera,* General Reille* was sent with two divisions and two can non to ford the river Bidassoa to attack and take the ridge of San Marcial, defended by General Longa's Spanish division, and then press on (leaving a strong reserve to hold the ridge) to reopen the Royal Road, along which General Foy* would advance. At first Reille made progress, but when he tried to attack both flanks of the Spanish position on the mountainside his troops fell into disorder and were repulsed. Wellington rode over in person to encourage the Spaniards, and the 85th Regiment reached the field in time to give them support. Reille fell back to the river, called up Foy's division, and Soult also sent in Vilatte's division. Losses were sustained when the pontoon bridges had to be rebuilt, but the French

were about to renew their attack when news reached Soult that on another sector d'Erlon* was losing many casualties while San Sebastian itself was in the process of being stormed. Accordingly he called off the proposed new attack and withdrew his reserves. Reille continued to fight, but the Spaniards got the upper hand until a major storm blew up at 3:00 P.M., which ended the engagement. Under its cover, Reille recrossed to the north bank of the Bidassoa.

San Sebastian, siege and stormings of, 25 July–31 August 1813. After Vitoria,* Wellington* set off to besiege Pamplona* and San Sebastian, and by late June both places were blockaded. San Sebastian was a good port and near to one of the three roads leading into France on the western end of the Pyrenees. The siege was entrusted to General Oswald and the 5th Division, with Bradford's Portuguese Brigade, the overall operation, and the immediate covering force of British and Spanish troops being under command of General Graham.* Wellington's headquarters was not far away at Lesaca.

Wellington was much preoccupied with the siege, and on 25 July he was supervising the first attempted storming (which failed with heavy loss) when news reached him of Soult's* developing offensive over the Pyrenees.* The siege continued at a reduced level while the French relief attempt was beaten off at Sorauren* and elsewhere, but from 8 August the full siege was reimposed. By the 26th the heavy breaching batteries were in full action, and on the 31st a second all-out storm was ordered. The main attempt was made over the estuary at low tide, and great progress was made for the loss of 2,376 casualties, the town being cleared of the French. Five days of looting and excess followed, during which almost the whole town was razed to the ground, but the French garrison under General Rey*

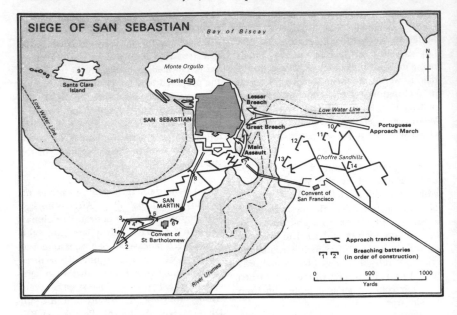

SIEGE OF SAN SEBASTIAN   *Bay of Biscay*

Santa Clara Island

Monte Orgullo

Castle

SAN SEBASTIAN

Lesser Breach

Great Breach

Low Water Line

Portuguese Approach March

Main Assault

Choffre Sandhills

SAN MARTIN

Convent of San Francisco

Convent of St Bartholomew

Approach trenches

Breaching batteries (in order of construction)

River Urumea

0   500   1000

Yards

held on grimly in the strong citadel atop Monte Orgullo. By 1 September Soult's last attempt at a relief had been defeated at San Marcial* and the bridge of Vera* and on the 5th the garrison commander agreed to negotiate. Three days later the garrison marched out with the full honors of war after having sustained a siege of 63 days of open trenches and having inflicted a total of 3,700 casualties on the Allies. Wellington was now free to plan his crossing of the river Bidassoa* into France.

Santander, city of. Situated on the north coast of Spain, the port and city of Santander figured several times in the early operations conducted by the French in the Peninsula. Between 1810 and 1812 the town was attacked three times by the guerrilla leader Porlier,* backed by Popham's* Royal Naval squadron, but the French only finally lost control of the place in late June 1812. Wellington* or-

dered the switch of his main lines of communication from Lisbon and Oporto to Santander as his liberation of Spain gathered momentum after Salamanca,* and the shorter distance by sea to Great Britain proved a considerable advantage to the logistical support of the army in the Peninsula in 1813 and 1814.

Santo Domingo, expedition to, 1804. This major island of the Antilles in the West Indies, second in size only to Cuba, had a history of connection with France dating back to 1697. Much prosperity came its way in the 18th century, but during the French Revolution a series of devastating sociopolitical wars disturbed its history. Originally called Haiti, it gradually received the name of Santo Domingo after the port of that name, and the Spanish part of the colony was ceded to France by the treaty of Basle in 1795. When the native population rebelled, a natural leader of great talents emerged in Toussaint L'Ouverture,* who created a kingdom and led the various races in a successful struggle against the French, who were expelled from the island in 1802. Haiti formally declared its independence from France on 1 January 1804, and Napoleon determined to regain the island, which was of some strategic importance in the West Indies. Accordingly, General Leclerc* was sent with an army from France, only to die with many of his men from the dreaded endemic yellow fever. Command devolved to General Dessalines, who successfully completed the reconquest of the island and captured L'Ouverture, who was sent back to France where he died a prisoner. Major troubles continued, and the island split into two countries until 1825, when France formally gave up all claims to the island. However, in 1844 the country was again split into halves.

Saragossa, sieges of, 1808–09. This city in northeast central Spain on the river Ebro had a population of 60,000, and when Marshal Bessières* detached General Lefebvre-Desnouëttes* with 6,000 men to occupy it, he anticipated little trouble, as José Palafox* had barely 1,500 men for its defense and 900 of those were volunteers. Although the Ebro protected it from the north, the southern approaches were wide open except for an old Moorish castle, the monastery of Santa Engracia, and the low hill, Monte Torrero. On 15 June 1808 the French attempted an immediate storming against the three southern gates, but the citizens swarmed out to the defenses, and although a Polish cavalry unit penetrated the Santa Engracia gate, overrunning the Spanish battery there, it was decimated amid the narrow streets of the city. Having lost 700 killed and several guns, Lefebvre-Desnouëttes pulled back and began a siege while awaiting reinforcements. Palafox's attempt to bring more volunteers into Saragossa was foiled by the French early on 24 June,

and he only returned to the city by a circuitous route on 2 July. General Verdier had meantime arrived with reinforcements to take over the siege, and soon captured Monte Torrero, from which his siege guns began to fire on the city and castle from 30 June. By this time the whole city was defended by a maze of barricades, and when on 4 July Verdier launched six columns against the defenses all were flung back after suffering a further 500 casualties. The attack on the Portillo Gate was foiled by Augustina Zaragoza, the "Maid of Saragossa," who manned and fired a deserted cannon at a critical moment and saved the day—being commissioned into the artillery forthwith. Verdier then had recourse to regular siege* warfare and by 4 August was again ready to attempt an assault, having at last captured the shattered monastery and established a bridgehead in the city's streets. His summons to surrender evoked Palafox's celebrated defiant reply: "War to the knife." A desperate struggle ensued, but by nightfall the French had lost another 2,000 men and were losing some of their initial gains. Both sides were utterly exhausted, but on 5 August Spanish reinforcements reached the city together with news of the great success of Bailen.* Disheartened by Dupont's* disaster, Verdier lingered around Saragossa until 17 August, when he broke off the siege and retreated to Tudela. The French had lost 3,500 since June; the defenders at least 5,000—but their heroic defense had become legendary.

Later that year, however, after Tudela,* Palafox gathered 35,000 men and 60,000 laborers to prepare Saragossa for a renewed onslaught that he knew must come. Provisions were collected, but too many defenders were crammed into the city. On 20 December Marshals Mortier* and Moncey* reimposed a siege at the head of 45,000 troops including 3,000 sappers and many guns. Within a month they had mined and blasted their way through the outer defenses, and then, on 16 January Marshal Lannes,* newly placed in overall command, began a systematic, street-by-street storming that lasted until 20 February, when the city at last fell. Disease had added to the horrors of the siege, and it was this factor that finally overcame the defense. This success cost the French 10,000 men, and the defenders all of 54,000.

Saumarez, Admiral James, Baron de (1757–1836). Born at St. Peter's Port, Jersey, he was promoted to lieutenant in 1776 and served in the Channel Fleet and in the West Indies. He was knighted in 1793 after capturing a French warship off Cherbourg, and from 1795–96 was on blockade duty off Brest. He fought at St. Vincent* (1797) and the Nile* (1798). In 1801 he was promoted to rear admiral and made a baronet. Much of 1801 was again spent on the Brest blockade, but on a foray to the Mediterranean approaches he was repulsed by a French force off Algeçiras; soon after that he defeated the Franco-Spanish squadron. After commanding the squadron off Guernsey (1803–07), he was promoted to vice admiral and second-in-command of the Brest blockade in 1807. From 1808–13 he commanded the British squadron in the Baltic and in 1814 was raised to full admiral. After Waterloo* further honors followed; from 1824–27 he commanded at Plymouth, and in 1831 he was raised to the peerage. In 1832 he was appointed general of marines.

Sauret, Général Pierre Franconin, baron de la Borie (known as) (1742–1818). After enlisting as a private soldier in 1756 he fought in much of the Seven Years' War, including the battle of Rossbach, and by 1763 had been made a sergeant. In 1780 he was commissioned as a junior officer of grenadiers, and by 1792 had become a captain. In the Revolutionary Wars* he

served in the Armies of the South and the Alps in 1792, but from 1793–95 was transferred to that of the West Pyrenees where he made his reputation. Promoted provisionally to *général de brigade* in October 1793, two months later he was made *général de division* after being wounded in the left leg at Villalonga. In April 1794 he won the action of Palau and was twice wounded at the siege of Roasa. In March 1796 he was posted to the Army of Italy and held a number of town commands, including that of Mondovi.* Between 29 July and 2 August he fought a series of actions around Salo in command of a division, but was ultimately worsted. Thereafter he held various town governorships, including Tortona, Alessandria, and (1800) Geneva, and from 1799 was elected to the *Corps Législatif*. His active service ended in May 1801, but from 1803 he was secretary of the *Corps Législatif* and in 1813 became a Baron of the Empire.

Savants, les (1798–1801). General Bonaparte organized a body of civilian professors and other experts to accompany the Army of the Orient to Egypt to carry out a number of scientific projects. In all, the Scientific and Artistic Commission numbered 167 members, most of them recruited by General Caffarelli* and the chemist Berthollet.* They included Monge,* Conté the balloonist, and the mineralogist Dolomieu. There were 19 civil engineers and 16 surveyors and cartographers, besides astronomers, botanists, surgeons (headed by Larrey*), pharmacists, archeologists, architects, and artists —even a minor composer. Most formed the membership of the Institute of Egypt which Bonaparte set up, and a great deal of archeological and surveying work was achieved during the expedition. Most were repatriated by the Royal Navy in September 1801.

Savary, Général Anne Jean Marie René,

duc de Rovigo (1774–1833). A native of the Ardennes region, Savary was educated at Metz on a royal bursary and in 1791 joined the cavalry as a volunteer, being commissioned in September that year. From 1792–97 he served with the Army of the Rhine, and from October 1797 he became Desaix's* aide-de-camp. He accompanied his general to Egypt and then, in 1800, to Marengo.* On Desaix's death, he was at once made aide to the First Consul and soon commanded his escort of *gendarmerie*. Promoted to *général de brigade* in August 1803, he was soon specializing in intelligence and undercover work, hunting down Cadoudal's* accomplices and organizing the execution of the duc d'Enghien* in 1804. The following February he was promoted to *général de division* and served on Napoleon's staff on campaign. In 1805 he was sent to visit Tsar Alexander I* before Austerlitz* and helped hoodwink that monarch. He was present at Jena* and led cavalry during the pursuit. He besieged and captured Hamelyn in November 1806, and for a time early the next year commanded Lannes'* V Corps, leading it to success in the action of Ostrolenka against General Essen.* At Heilsberg* he commanded the Fusiliers of the Guard, and he later fought at Friedland* and became governor of Königsberg. Missions to St. Petersburg and Spain followed, and Savary was deeply involved in the events at Bayonne* which led to the supercession of the Spanish Bourbon monarchy. He was made Duke of Rovigo in May 1808 and deputized for Murat* in command of French troops in Spain. The same year he accompanied Napoleon to Erfurt,* then campaigned with him in Spain and in 1809 followed him to the Danube again, fighting at Landshut* and Eckmühl.* From June 1810 to April 1814 he served as Minister of Police in succession to Fouché.* He was almost purged during the Malet* conspiracy in 1812. He

lived privately during the First Restoration, rallied to Napoleon for the Hundred Days,* and tried to accompany his master to St. Helena* but was arrested on board the *Bellerophon* and sent to Malta. With a sentence of death hanging over him he fled to Smyrna, but later lived at Graz in Austria and in London before returning to France in 1819. Pardoned, he retired in 1823 and settled in Rome. In 1831, Louis-Philippe recalled him to service, sending him to command troops in Algeria. Returning to Paris for health reasons in early 1832, he died there in March.

Saxe, Maréchal-général de France Hermann Maurice, comte de (1696–1750). Greatly admired by Napoleon, Saxe brought France great victories during the War of the Austrian Succession. His organizational experiments included the *légion,* an all-arm force in many ways the prototype of the later *corps d'armée.* His many successes over the British and Allied armies led to his appointment to the highest rank and to the governorship of Chambord. He also wrote *Mes Rêveries* (1732), for its day an advanced study of warfare.

Saxony, Frederick Augustus I, Elector and King of (1763–1827). This German prince early adopted a friendly relationship with Napoleon, and in 1806 was raised to the dignity of a crown. From 1807–13 he was also the personal ruler of the Grand Duchy of Warsaw. His alliance with France led to the Congress of Vienna* reallocating almost half of his inherited lands to other German princes.

Scharnhorst, General Gerhard Johann David, von (1755–1813). Born in Hanover, he entered its army in 1788 and taught at an artillery academy. In 1792 he fought under the Duke of York* at Hondschoote and Menin, but despairing of promotion in the Hanoverian service he transferred to Prussia in 1801. After a period instructing at the Berlin War Academy and as tutor to the Crown Prince, he fought at Jena-Auerstädt* as Chief of Staff to the Duke of Brunswick,* and also at Eylau* the next year. He was promoted to major general in 1807, after Tilsit,* and together with Stein,* Hardenberg,* and Gneisenau* began to rebuild the Prussian army as Director of the War Department. His strong sense of German patriotism inspired many he was associated with, but it also earned Napoleon's wrath, and King Frederick William IV* of Prussia was compelled to sack him in 1810. However, in 1812 he re-emerged as Blücher's* Chief of Staff, and in 1813 was mortally wounded at the battle of Lützen,* dying two months later at Prague. Long regarded as the epitome of German nationalism, he left many influential writings on military and political subjects.

Schérer, Général Barthelemy Louis Joseph (1747–1804). First commissioned in the Austrian army, he was wounded at Torgau in 1760. Twenty years later he transferred to the French army as an artillery captain and then saw service in the Dutch army from 1785 until 1790, when he left the service. In 1792 he rejoined the French forces and saw much service in the Army of the Rhine, being promoted to *général de brigade* (September 1793) and to *général de division* four months later. Under Jourdan* he undertook many sieges on the northeast frontiers, including those of Landrecies, Valenciennes, and Condé, and fought at the Ourthe—all in 1794. That November he was briefly commander of the Army of Italy in place of Dumerbion,* and next year held high command in the West Pyrenees before becoming Commander in Chief in Italy once more. He won the battle of First Loano, but piqued by what he considered to be governmental interference in his affairs he resigned command and left the Army of Italy on 27 March 1796, handing over to his designated successor, General Bonaparte. Administrative posts followed, including that of Minister of War (1797–99); in February 1799 he assumed command of the armies of Italy and Naples but only served with them for six weeks before again resigning. He was charged with profiteering, but these charges were dropped after the *coup d'état* de Brumaire. Reputedly fond of the bottle, he was not re-employed.

Schleiz, battle of, 9 October 1806. As the *Grande Armée* emerged from the defiles of the Thuringerwald as Napoleon launched his forces into Saxony, Marshal Bernadotte,* heading the central column, met the 9,000 Saxons of General Tauenzien near Schleiz. The Saxons intended to fall back on Auma, but Bernadotte forced action from about 8:00 A.M. and by 4:00 P.M. General Drouet* had defeated their rear guard and taken possession of the town. Bernadotte claimed a considerable success against a large force, but it seems the greater part of the action was against a rear guard only commanded by a Colonel Hobe; the Saxons lost some 570 men and a single cannon.

Schönbrunn, Peace of, 14 October 1809. Following the battles of Wagram* and Znaim,* the Austrians accepted an armistice on 12 July. Negotiations for peace were protracted, and it was not until Napoleon had served an ultimatum on the Emperor Francis I* that agreement was reached. By the terms of the treaty, Austria ceded the Inn region and Salzburg to Bavaria, handed over maritime Croatia, Fiume, Istria, and Trieste, with parts of Carinthia and Carniola, to France, and renounced rights over large areas around Lublin and Cracow in favor of the Grand Duchy of Warsaw, involving

1,500,000 inhabitants. The region of Tarnopol, with 400,000 inhabitants, went to Russia. In overall terms, Austria lost three and a half million inhabitants and all its points of direct access to the Adriatic. In addition, an indemnity of 75 million was to be paid to the victors. By refusing to support Tsar Alexander's* claims to large areas of Galicia, Napoleon demonstrated his displeasure with the poor Russian performance in keeping Austria in check as promised at the Conference of Erfurt* in 1809.

Schramm, Général Jean Adam, baron (1760–1826). From 1777 he enlisted in a Swiss regiment, becoming a sergeant major by 1786. From August 1792 he was a captain in a volunteer unit of the Army of the North, serving at the capture of Mons. In 1794 he was posted to the Sambre-et-Meuse for two years and was seriously wounded before Luxembourg. In early 1797 he fought under Bernadotte* in North Italy, distinguishing himself at Tarvis. Accompanying the Army of the Orient, he fought under Kléber* at the battle of Mount Tabor* in April 1799. After repatriation to France, he spent the years 1802–03 in garrison duty at Geneva, but in 1805 fought under Oudinot* at Austerlitz* and was promoted to *général de brigade* in December. He was commandant of Magdeburg* under d'Eblé in 1806 and next year, under Lefebvre's* command, he played a major role in the siege of Danzig.* In 1808 he was posted to Spain and served under Dupont* at the disaster of Bailen,* where he was again wounded. Repatriated to Toulon, he returned to Spain with the IV Corps and was made a Baron of the Empire in December 1808. Transferred to the Austrian front, he was gravely wounded at Ratisbon* in April 1809. He served in garrisons on the Rhine and then in Swedish Pomerania from 1809–12, and did not enter Russia. Returning to France in

April 1813, he commanded the National Guards in the Lower Rhine Department. The Bourbons retired him with the honorary rank of lieutenant general in March 1815, and he played only a minor role in the Hundred Days* around Strasbourg. He finally retired in August that year.

Schwarzenberg, Field Marshal Karl Philip, Prince (1771–1820). Born in Vienna, he entered the Austrian Imperial Army in 1788. The descendant of a Franconian family ennobled in the second half of the 17th century, the Prince first distinguished himself in campaigns against the Turks and then against the French in the Austrian Netherlands, fighting against Dumouriez* and Pichegru* in turn. He became a brigadier general in 1796 and commanded a division from 1800. In 1805 he escaped from Mack's* doomed army at Ulm* and rallied the survivors. From 1806–09 he served as Austrian ambassador to St. Petersburg, and after Wagram* and the Treaty of Schönbrunn* he was transferred to Paris and aided the negotiation of Napoleon's marriage to Marie-Louise.* In 1812 he commanded the Austrian corps placed on the extreme right flank of the *Grande Armée* during the invasion of Russia, and managed to bring many of his men out by forestalling the moment of crisis and retiring toward Poland. When Austria declared war on France in August 1813, he was made *generalissimo* of the Allied armies of the Sixth Coalition.* Defeated at Dresden,* he later commanded at the victory of Leipzig,* and during the invasion of France the next year led the Army of Bohemia with some success. In June 1815 he set out from Austria for the Rhine once more, but Waterloo* forestalled his arrival in force. Made a member of the Higher War Council, he was struck down by paralysis in 1817 and died three years later. As the commander of a great alliance he faced major problems, but managed to maintain the common cause through bad times as well as good.

Search, the Right of. One aspect of the British response to the development of the Continental System* through the Berlin and Milan Decrees* was to insist upon their right to stop and search neutral shipping on the high seas to examine papers and cargoes in search of contraband being conveyed to France or her allies and satellites. This policy did considerable damage to French commerce between 1807 and 1814, but the price paid by London was the growing irritation of the neutral powers over what many regarded as a high-handed and unjustifiable interference with their free use of international waters. It was one cause of the War of 1812* between Great Britain and the United States.

Sebastiani, Général (later Maréchal de France) Horace François Bastien de la Porta, comte (1772–1851). Intended for the priesthood, Sebastiani instead was commisisoned into an infantry regiment in 1789. He served in the armies of the Alps and of Italy, being wounded at Dego* (1796). He later fought at Arcola.* In 1799 he assisted Bonaparte in the *coup d'état* de *Brumaire,* and in 1800 fought at Marengo.* In 1801 he was sent on diplomatic missions to Turkey and Egypt, and on his return was promoted to *général de brigade* in 1803. Put in command of the cavalry of IV Corps, he occupied Vienna in 1805 and then fought at Austerlitz,* where was was wounded. In December of that year he became *général de division.* In late 1806 he was sent back to Turkey as ambassador and helped repel a British attack on Constantinople in February 1807. Recalled to France, he was sent to Spain in August 1808 under Lefebvre,* and from February 1809 assumed command of the IV Corps from that offi-

Sebastiani

cer, fighting at Talavera* and Ocaña* and then taking part in the conquest of Andalusia. In December 1809 he was made a Count of the Empire and continued in Spain until 1811. In 1812 he commanded cavalry in the invasion of Russia, at first under Montbrun;* after being repulsed by Wittgenstein* at Drissa he was taken by surprise by Platov* at Vinkovo,* by which time he had taken over Montbrun's command. He rallied the remnants of the cavalry during the retreat and in 1813 served under Eugène Beauharnais* in Germany, fighting at Wachau and Leipzig,* where he was wounded in the chest by a lance, and at Hanau.* In 1814 he commanded under Macdonald,* fighting at Rheims,* Châlons, and Arcis.*

His political career began during the Hundred Days,* but he held only a National Guard command in the Somme region. In August 1815 he visited England. From 1819 his political career began to burgeon. As a politician of the far left he first represented Corsica, but in 1830 he became Minister of Marine, and from

1830–32 he was Minister of Foreign Affairs. In later years he was ambassador to Naples and then (1835–40) to London. In October 1840 he was made a Marshal of France, while continuing his political career. He died at Paris and was buried in *Les Invalides.* *

Ségur, Général Philippe Paul, comte de (1780–1873). Enlisting as a hussar in 1800, he was commissioned the same year and became aide-de-camp to Macdonald* on the Rhine. He became attached to Duroc's* staff in December 1804, as part of Napoleon's household. In 1805 he negotiated Mack's* surrender at Ulm.* In 1806 he served in Naples at the siege of Gaeta. Returning to the *Grande Armée,* he was wounded in Poland and taken prisoner by the Russians, only being freed after Tilsit.* In Spain he was twice wounded at Somosierra* in November 1808. In 1809 he continued his service under Duroc in Germany and was made a count. Missions to Vienna and St. Petersburg followed, and in February 1812 he

Ségur

was promoted to *général de brigade* before serving in Russia. In 1813 he fought at Leipzig* and Hanau,* and next year at Montmirail* and Rheims (where he received bayonet and bullet wounds). He received several promotions and favors under the Bourbons, becoming a lieutenant general and a Peer of France in 1831. He retired in 1848.

Selim III, Sultan of Turkey (1761–1808). The son of Sultan Mustafa III and born in Constantinople, he succeeded his uncle Abdul-Hamid to the throne in April 1789. Despite the problems posed by the war with Russia, he attempted to implement internal reforms. The loss of provinces in the Danube region to Russia and Austria led to a troublesome internal revolt, and then the French invasion of Egypt in 1798 caused a further major distraction. Peace with France came in 1802. Four years later, under pressure from Sebastiani,* he declared war on Great Britain, and with the Frenchman's aid repelled a British attack on Constantinople the following year. In 1808, however, he was assassinated by disaffected Janissaries.

Semaphore, the. The visual semaphore —consisting of a series of intervisible signaling stations, each provided with three masts on which movable arms could be used to pass messages—was first developed by Chappe during the French Revolution to link the ministries in Paris with the frontiers. In good weather the passage of messages could be rapid, but fog or mist obviously interrupted the service, as during the critical days immediately before the opening of the Austrian Campaign of 1809.

The British developed a similar system, linking the Admiralty with Portsmouth. During the Peninsular War,* Wellington's* engineers employed semaphore stations to link the various sectors of the Lines of Torres Vedras.* Five stations were placed at intervals along the first line of forts, and four in the second line, and under good weather conditions a message could be passed from the Atlantic coast to the Tagus—about 22 miles—in a matter of seven minutes.

Senarmont, Général Alexandre Antoine Hureau de, baron (1769–1810). The son of an artillery officer, he was commissioned into that arm from the school at Metz in 1785. Service in the Armies of the Center and of the North followed (1792–93), and after a period at Douai he was sent to the German front, then to the Army of the Reserve to join Marmont* in 1800. He arranged a route around Fort Bard* for the guns during the passage of the Alps, and fought at Marengo.* In 1803 he commanded the artillery in the Camp of Brest and in 1805 became Assistant Chief of Staff (artillery). He was present at Austerlitz* and then, following promotion to *général de brigade* in 1806, became commander of the Artillery School at Metz before being recalled to the *Grande Armée* to serve in Poland under first Augereau* and then Bernadotte.* His handling of his guns at Friedland* earned him special commendation. From August 1808 he commanded the guns in Victor's* I Corps of the Army of Spain, having been created a Baron of the Empire the previous month, and in November served with distinction at Somosierra.* The same December he was promoted to *général de division,* and he fought at Ocaña in 1809. Next year he was killed by a howitzer shell at the siege of Cadiz.*

Seringapatam, siege of, 1792, and storming of, 4 May 1799. During the wars in India, French agents frequently inspired the native princes to rebel against the influence of the British East India Company and the forces it controlled. In 1790 Tippoo Sahib,* Sultan of Mysore, invaded

Travancore. Lord Cornwallis,* Governor General of India, declared Travancore to be under British protection, and in March 1792 laid siege to Tippoo's capital, Seringapatam. It fell on 19 March, and Mysore lost half its lands and paid a large monetary indemnity to the British.

Seven years later Tippoo again revolted against British influence. Lord Richard Wellesley* (brother of the future Wellington*), the Governor General at that time, ordered General Harris to assault the island fortress-city of Seringapatam. It was duly stormed on 4 May 1799, and Tippoo was killed. Thereafter the British hold on southern India was firmly established.

Sérurier, Maréchal Jean Mathieu Philibert, comte (1742–1819). He received a commission in the Laon Militia in 1755, and after transfer to a line regiment in 1759 fought in the Seven Years' War, being wounded at Warburg (1760) in Germany and later taking part in the expedition to Portugal. From 1770–74 he was a member of the French garrison of Corsica.

Sérurier

He was considering retiring from the service when the Revolution broke out. By 1791 he was lieutenant colonel of his infantry regiment, employed on garrison duty at Perpignan, and then, in 1792, on internal security operations against royalist sympathizers. Later the same year he was himself purged as a sometime-royalist, but was reappointed through the influence of Barras.* That wily politician also recommended him for promotion to *général de brigade* the next year while he was serving in Italy, and in December 1794 he was also provisionally promoted to *général de division* (confirmed the next June). In 1795 he fought with distinction at First Loano under Massena,* and next year captured Ceva* at the outset of the Campaign of 1796 before going on to win the battle of Mondovi,* which removed Piedmont from the war. He also fought at Borghetto,* and was then entrusted with the conduct of the siege of Mantua.* Sickness forced him to give up this command shortly before the battle of Castiglione* (General Fiorella* took over command of his division), but after a spell as governor of Livorno he recovered and resumed his duties from late December. He defeated General Provera* at La Favorita* just outside the besieged city on 16 January 1797 and then accepted Mantua's surrender early the following month. During Bonaparte's campaign in the Frioul he served at the Piave and at Tagliamento, but after his health again collapsed he was sent back to Paris with the captured Austrian colors.

By August he was back in Italy and was made Governor of Venice, a post he held until 1798. He continued to hold commands in Italy but was forced to surrender at Verderio to the Russian forces in April 1799. Suvorov* freed him on parole. He subsequently aided Bonaparte at the *coup d'état* de Brumaire that November, and was made a Senator.

His campaigning days were now over; he became vice president of the Senate (1802), in April 1804 he was made Governor of *Les Invalides*,* and in May he was appointed a marshal, one of the four honorific appointments. Four years later he was made a Count of the Empire. He carried out his duties at *Les Invalides* until the end of the First Empire, and on 31 March 1814 ordered the burning of the captured colors and other trophies of war as the Allies closed in on the French capital. An estimated 1,417 colors were publicly destroyed along with the insignia of Frederick the Great,* captured in 1806. The Bourbons made him a Peer of France —as did Napoleon* during the Hundred Days*—but after the Second Restoration he was replaced at *Les Invalides*. In January 1819 he was restored as an active Marshal of France, but died the same December, aged 77 years.

Seymour, Admiral Sir George Francis (1787–1870). The son of an admiral, he entered the Royal Navy in 1797 and was promoted to lieutenant in 1804. He served in the West Indies, where he was wounded at Santo Domingo* in 1806, the same year that saw him promoted to post captain. In 1809 he served under Lord Gambier at the action of the Basque Roads and was again on the West Indian station from 1813 to 1814. He was sergeant-at-arms in the House of Lords from 1819–41 and held appointments in King William IV's household (1830–37). Further distinctions and promotions came his way; made a rear admiral in 1841, he became Commander in Chief in the Pacific, a vice admiral in 1850, a full admiral seven years later, and lastly Admiral of the Fleet in 1866.

Sherbrooke, General Sir John Coape (1764–1830). After considerable years of service he emerged in command of the 33rd Foot in the campaign in the Netherlands under the Duke of York* (1794). Transferred to India, in 1799 he fought in the Mysore War and commanded the right-hand column at the storming of Seringapatam.* Between 1805 and 1808 he held various commands in Sicily, and in 1809 was appointed Wellesley's* second-in-command in the Peninsula, fighting at Talavera.* He was knighted following that victory but had to return to England because of ill health. During the War of 1812* he was Lieutenant Governor of Nova Scotia, and from 1816 to 1818 served as Governor General of Canada.

Shrapnel, Lieutenant General Henry (1761–1842). During service with the Royal Artillery in Flanders (1793) he was wounded at Dunkirk. An inventor of some note, he developed several improvements taken up by the artillery, most especially his shell—a hollow sphere packed with musketballs and explosive— which was first accepted in 1803. Used for the first time at Surinam in the East Indies (1804), Wellington* spoke highly of its value after Bussaco* (1810), and General Sir George Wood enthused over its properties after Waterloo.* From 1804 Shrapnel was senior Assistant Inspector of the Artillery and had attained the rank of major general by the time of his retirement in 1825. He was promoted to lieutenant general in 1837 and promised a baronetcy by William IV, but in fact never received this honor. His shell proved particularly effective against formed bodies of troops, whether infantry or cavalry.

Shubra Khit, action of, 13 July 1798. Advancing up the Nile River from El Rahmaniya, Bonaparte's five divisions of the Army of the Orient came in sight of Shubra Khit at first light on 13 July. Drawn up near the town were some 3,000 splendidly arrayed Mameluke* horsemen, supported by perhaps 10,000 servants and armed peasantry on foot. Bonaparte formed his 28,000 men into squares, and the Mamelukes made no impression; Murad Bey* soon called his men off and fell back toward Cairo, but on the river Nile itself Perée's flotilla of five craft had a desperate fight against the seven Moslem vessels supported by battery fire from the shore. Perée lost three vessels, and the *savants** on board his flotilla, including Monge* and Berthollet,* had to fight for their lives. Then a lucky shot destroyed the enemy flagship, and the Mamelukes broke off the action both ashore and afloat. Each side lost some 200 men. Bonaparte then continued his army's advance toward Cairo, and the battle of the Pyramids.*

Sidmouth, Lord. *See* **Addington,** Henry

Siege Warfare. Although regular sieges played a considerably less important part in the waging of warfare in the French Revolutionary and Napoleonic era than they had in the mid-18th century, they were nevertheless a significant feature of the military scene. Napoleon was directly concerned with four—Toulon,* the citadel of Milan, Mantua,* and Acre,* and indirectly with several more, including those of Danzig* and Königsberg. He disliked siege operations as time-consuming and wasteful. In the Peninsular War,* however, there were many sieges—at least 17—including those of Almeida,* Badajoz,* Ciudad Rodrigo,* Saragossa,* Burgos,* Pamplona,* and San Sebastian,* to mention only the most important.

Sieges came in three forms—not necessarily exclusive, as one frequently led to the next stage. First there were containments, or the posting of a force to observe the activities of forces within the town or fortress and to give early warning of any large-scale breakout so that it could be intercepted. Secondly there were blockades, a more elaborate affair involving more troops than a containment, the men being posted so as to deny the enemy free access into or egress from the place concerned—in other words the achievement of logistical isolation that could lead to the surrender of the town through starvation or sickness. Thirdly, and most complicated of all, there were regular sieges, in which the besieging force set about breaking a way into the objective by force in order to compel a capitulation. These were often lengthy and very expensive in terms of both lives and equipment within the siege area, and they also involved the services of a covering force capable of intercepting any attempt at relief by an enemy army. However, so elaborate had formal defenses become in the post-Vauban era that immediate all-out assaults could rarely be attempted without the prospect of horrific loss of life. Thus, unless a commander was prepared to ignore or merely contain a hostile garrison, there was no other alternative to a regular siege.

In terms of basic techniques, siege warfare had changed little since the days of Vauban. After collecting a sufficient force to provide both a besieging detachment and a covering army, the attacker moved the heavy siege guns and mountains of materiel toward the objective. After an investment had been established and the garrison expelled from any outworks and forced back within his main positions, the engineer officers would survey the defenses and choose two or more areas for attack: one to be the principal target, the others to distract the enemy's attention. Next, after the besiegers' camps had been established and the stores collected, a large trench would be dug running parallel to the chosen sector of the defenses at maximum cannon range, the parapet being strengthened with fascines and gabions. The sappers would then push forward zigzagging saps or approach trenches, and

establish a number of long-range batteries. Halfway to the objective a second parallel would be dug and more batteries established—and the process would be repeated a third, and occasionally a fourth, time until the trenches were very close to the enemy's outer line. To guard against sorties by the besieged, a considerable garrison had to be maintained under arms in the trenches, while underground mining galleries were driven toward his works. Sometimes enemy mines were encountered and these could cause much damage.

Once the edge of the main defenses had been reached, the large siege guns would be positioned as close as was both safe and effective and they would begin a heavy, ceaseless bombardment of the enemy bastions and walls, crumbling them away a little with every shot. Once a possible breach had been caused, the attacker would prepare to launch an assault. The old conventions of the 18th century whereby a defender could surrender with honor once a major breach had been driven through his defenses had largely disappeared, and unless disease or starvation was rampant within the position, a Napoleonic garrison commander was likely to insist on a fight to the finish. As was shown at Badajoz in 1812, even a prepared storming could be terribly expensive. Spanish garrisons, as at Saragossa, could also fight to the death. However, the besiegers could wreak a fearful penalty for a dogged defense if their storming was successful yet dearly bought —Badajoz and San Sebastian being the two prime examples, when Wellington's* rank and file went out of control.

Sieges, therefore, could be both time-consuming and expensive, affecting the progress and outcome of whole campaigns to a most marked degree. However, in countries like Spain and Portugal where roads were few and far between and fortified towns placed to guard vital passes or river crossings, they could not be avoided.

Sieyès, Abbé Emmanuel Joseph (1748–1836). Sent into the priesthood by his family on account of his poor health, Sieyès proved highly receptive to the new ideas that found expression in the French Revolution. As representative for Paris in the States-General* he played a determinant role on 20 June 1789 when the Third Estate, threatened with dissolution by Louis XVI,* voted itself indissoluble at a meeting in the tennis court at Versailles. He later became involved in founding the Jacobin Club,* the power base for the extreme left-wing republican

Sieyès

elements. He also was an influential drafter of the "Rights of Man" declaration. As representative for the Sarthe in the Convention, he survived the worst days of the Terror* and successfully undermined the position of Robespierre.* Then, under the Directory,* he was swept to positions of power and influence. He negotiated the treaty of the Hague (1795) with Holland, became President of the Council of Five Hundred (*Cinq-Cents*),* and ambassador to Berlin. Despairing of the Directory, he set about plotting its demise, planning the Consulate. He intended General Joubert* for the military role, but on his death at Novi,* Sieyès fell back in November 1799 on the available General Bonaparte, who became the "sword" behind the *coup d'état* de Brumaire. This brought Sieyès himself to power, briefly, as one of three consuls, but Bonaparte soon maneuvered himself to the leading position, and Sieyès was relegated to a gilded life without authority or power.

Smith, Major General Sir Harry George Wakelyn, Baronet (1788–1860). Commissioned into the 95th Rifles, he took part in the Buenos Aires* operations in 1807 and then accompanied Sir John Moore's* army to Corunna.* In 1811 he fought at Fuentes de Oñoro* and in 1812 served in the stormings of Ciudad Rodrigo* and Badajoz.* At the latter he rescued the Spanish girl, Juanita, from the drink-maddened British soldiery and later married her. She thereafter accompanied him on campaign as he fought on in Wellington's* army until 1814, including the battles of Salamanca* and Vitoria.* He took part in the War of 1812* in North America, fighting at Bladensburg, but returned to Europe just in time to fight at Waterloo.* Later he traveled to South Africa where he helped subdue the Kaffirs (1836); six years later he traveled to India to become General Gough's adjutant general, serving in the Gwalior and Sikh campaigns, leading the victorious charge that won the battle of Aliwal (1846), and commanding the 1st Indian Division at Sobraon (1846). He was made a baronet and promoted to major general, and in 1847 became Governor of the Cape. He fought and routed the Boers (1848) and subdued the Kaffirs (1859) besides successfully resisting the proposed establishment of penal colonies in South Africa. He left the country in 1852, but his name—and that of his wife—are commemorated in the names of the towns of Ladysmith and Harrismith.

Smith, Admiral Sir William Sidney (1764–1840). Known as "the Swedish Knight," he entered the Royal Navy in 1777 and three years later fought at the Battle of Cape St. Vincent.* In 1782 he took part in the capture of Dominica in the West Indies, and three years later he moved to Caen for two years to study French. In 1793 he served under Lord Hood* at Toulon* and destroyed much of the abandoned French shipping as the British withdrew, before being sent back to England with dispatches. He then served in the Swedish navy in the Baltic, receiving a knighthood. In 1796 he was taken prisoner during a daring cutting-out expedition off Le Havre and was imprisoned in Paris, narrowly escaping being convicted as a pirate. A daring escape from the Temple Prison brought him back to England, and he was given command of H.M.S. *Tigre* and sent as a commodore to serve under Nelson* in the Mediterranean. The two men did not get on well together, but Smith enjoyed a virtually autonomous command, and aided by Phélypeaux* he put fire into the defense of Acre* against Bonaparte from May 1799. Further service in the Mediterranean and from a base at Lisbon followed, and he was invariably energetic and dynamic. He was one of the few

British sailors present at Waterloo* in 1815, and he helped organize the evacuation of the wounded after the battle. In many ways the naval counterpart of the peppery General Wilson,* he was something of a braggart and given to theatrical gestures, and like Wilson he never received a British knighthood. However, in 1821 he was promoted to admiral, and he died in Paris 19 years later.

Smolensk, battle of, 17 August 1812. As Napoleon at the head of the *Grande Armée* drove into Russia in search of a decisive battle, the Russian army of Barclay de Tolly* abandoned one position after another as it fell back eastward, always seeking a junction with the forces of General Bagration.* Despite the brilliance of Napoleon's rapid crossing of the Dnieper beginning on 11 August, the two Russian commanders at last succeeded in linking their forces to make a joint 50,000 men, thanks in no small measure to General Neveroski's staunch fighting withdrawal along the south bank of the river, where his 9,500 men tempted Murat* into launching attack after attack to no purpose, and to General Raevski's skillful deployment of his 20,000 men and 72 guns beyond the city's suburbs.

The French moved up into contact with Raevski throughout the 16th, but Ney's* 18,000 infantry did not feel disposed to take on Raevski on their own, and only fierce skirmishing ensued that day. The 17th saw much confused fighting amid the suburbs as Napoleon launched three *corps d'armée* against the defenses, but although the city was in flames the Russians gave little ground. By dusk the French had sustained 10,000 casualties; the Russians had lost between 12 and 14,000 men over the two days of conflict. Thus the attack on Smolensk gained Napoleon very little.

Both armies lay in somber reflection during the 18th, and the relationship between Barclay and Bagration—never warm—became highly acrimonious. In the end Bagration began to retire to the east alone, and only in the late evening did Barclay accept the inevitable and begin to follow. Napoleon thus wasted an opportunity to catch his foes apart. When, on the 19th, he did at last bestir himself, it was already too late. The unpredictable General Junot,* ordered to march ahead and place a block across the roads at Lubino, failed to accomplish his mission, and the Russians got clean away. After a period of contemplation at Smolensk, Napoleon took what was to prove to be the fatal decision of the campaign. Instead of wintering around Smolensk he decided to press on after the foe, feeling sure they would turn and fight at the gates of Moscow. So the advance toward Borodino* began.

Somerset, General Lord Fitzroy James Henry, Baron Raglan (1788–1855). The youngest son of the Duke of Beaufort, he was appointed Wellesley's* aide-de-camp in 1808, and in this capacity fought at Roliça* and Vimiero.* He also served at Bussaco* (1810), Fuentes de Oñoro* (1811), and at the storming of Badajoz* (1812). At Waterloo* he was wounded at Wellington's side. After a long spell in military administration (1827–52), he succeeded Wellington as commander of the British home forces and was made Baron Raglan. In 1854 he commanded the British army sent to the Crimea, winning the battles of the Alma and Inkerman, but was soon in dispute with Lord Lucan over the misuse of the Light Brigade at Balaclava. He was then made the scapegoat for the terrible suffering experienced during the winter of 1854–55. The failure of an assault on the main defenses of Sebastopol on 18 June 1855 broke his spirit, and he died ten days later. A gentle, able man, he was an ideal subordinate

for Wellington but not really suited for independent high command.

Somerset, General Lord Robert Edward Henry (1776–1842). The elder brother of Fitzroy James Henry, and known as "Lord Edward Somerset," he served with cavalry during the campaign in Holland (1799) and later through all the Peninsular War.* At Waterloo* he commanded a cavalry brigade under the overall control of Lord Uxbridge.* He later commanded the British cavalry during the occupation of France and was ultimately promoted to full general in 1841.

Sommagices, conference of, 24 March 1814. After the battle of Arcis,* Napoleon had advanced to St. Dizier athwart the Allied communications, hoping that they would fall back from the approaches to Paris. This, indeed, was Prince Schwarzenberg's* first intention, but the capture of letters from Paris revealed the low state of the government's and the populace's morale, and so Tsar Alexander* at Sommagices induced Schwarzenberg to press on down the Marne without delay at the head of a joint army of 180,000 men to call Napoleon's bluff, while Winzingerode* made an appearance of complying with Napoleon's intention by moving at the head of 10,000 cavalry toward St. Dizier. This revised Allied strategy doomed Napoleon to ultimate defeat—and abdication.

Somosierra, battle of, 30 November 1808. Advancing toward Madrid, Napoleon encountered General San Juan's* 9,000 men and 16 guns holding the crest of the road passing over the Guadarramas —the last physical obstacle separating the French from the Spanish capital. A probing attack by General Savary* and a detachment of the Imperial Guard* on the evening of the 29th failed, and early the next morning Napoleon ordered General

Ruffin* to advance on the head of the pass with his infantry. Then, resentful of the inevitable delay, he abruptly ordered the Polish Light Horse squadrons of his escort to charge the guns up the road leading to the head of the pass. Despite the greatest gallantry, 60 of the 88 horsemen who attempted this task were killed or wounded by the Spanish cannons. Ultimately, a properly coordinated attack—Ruffin's infantry on the hillsides supported by more Poles and the *chasseurs-à-cheval* of the Guard, led by General Montbrun*—overcame Spanish resistance and San Juan's force was scattered. The French advance on Madrid recommenced, and on 4 December Napoleon occupied the capital.

Sorauren, battles of, 28 and 30 July 1813. Launching his campaign through the Pyrenees* with considerable skill, Marshal Soult* pushed back the small Allied forces at Maya* and Roncesvalles*

and marched southward at the head of 36,000 men toward blockaded Pamplona.* Wellington,* aware of the crisis, collected three divisions with all haste, perhaps 24,-000 troops, to meet the threat. He was almost captured on the 24th while writing orders in Sorauren village, but escaped up the hillside to the main Allied position above on the slopes of the Narval height.

Next morning Soult launched 25,000 men against the Allied line. The steep slope wearied his columns, but even so it took much desperate fighting for Wellington to hold the crest. Fortunately, the arrival of Pack's division from the west to reinforce the battered Allied line averted the crisis of the day as the newcomers took the French in the flank. Thereafter, by sheer "bludgeon-work, a second Bussaco" (as Wellington described it) the Portuguese regained Sorauren village, and after the arrival of Hill* and Dalhousie* the French sullenly pulled back. The

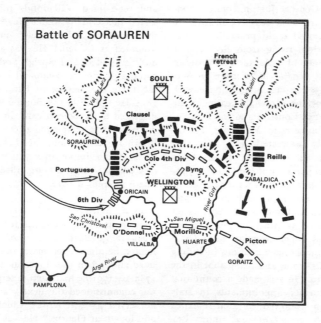

Battle of SORAUREN

Allies had lost 2,600 men to the French 4,000 casualties—and had prevented the relief of the French in Pamplona.

On the 29th Soult boldly decided to march west rather than retire north, hoping to sever the road from Pamplona to Tolosa and thus drive a wedge between Wellington and his forces under Graham* further west who were besieging San Sebastian* on the coast. He failed to break contact with Wellington, however, and on the 30th two further actions, known as the second battle of Sorauren, were fought. In the first, d'Erlon* made some headway against Hill at Tolosa but was ultimately held off, while Clausel's* attempt to leave the Sorauren area by night was spotted and a sharp action led by Pack caused 3,500 casualties. Soult thereupon called off his offensive and retired over the French frontier on 2 August. Pamplona fell to the Allies two months later.

Souham

Souham, Général Joseph, comte (1760–1837). Enlisted as a Royal Cuirassier in 1782, he enjoyed rapid promotion under the Revolution, rising from elected lieutenant colonel of volunteers in August 1792 to full *général de division* in September 1793. He saw much service with the Army of the North, defeating General Clarfayt at Courtrai and the Duke of York* at Turcoing in May 1794. He became closely associated with Moreau,* under whom he served in both the Army of the North and that of the Rhine (1799–1801), and when Moreau was disgraced he was arrested and imprisoned in 1804 and remained unemployed until 1807. After a brief period in Italy he next served in Catalonia under Gouvion Saint Cyr,* fighting in numerous operations including the siege of Girona and being shot in the head in 1810. He was made a count that year and further appointments in Italy and Germany followed; he then returned to Spain to serve (1811–12) under Bes-

sières* and Caffarelli.* He forced the raising of the siege of Burgos,* thus inflicting a rare defeat upon Wellington,* and reoccupied Valladolid. In 1813 he served in Germany under Ney,* winning the battle of Weissenfels* and being wounded at Lützen.* He was again seriously wounded at Leipzig* and only recovered in time to command under Marmont* in the defense of Paris in March 1814. He rallied to the Bourbons and was disgraced by Napoleon early in the Hundred Days.* Re-employed after the second Bourbon Restoration, he held various posts of fair importance (including that of Governor of Strasbourg, 1818–30), and finally retired in 1832.

Soult, Maréchal (and later Maréchal-Général de France) Nicolas Jean de Dieu (1769–1851). Born the son of a Gascon notary, he almost became a baker but instead enlisted in the Bourbon infantry in 1785. By 1791 he had risen to sergeant and was commissioned the next year. In 1794 he served as Lefebvre's* Chief of Staff and fought at Fleurus.* He was promoted to *général de brigade* in October the same year. He later served on the Rhine and in March 1799 fought at Stockach.* Next month he became *général de division* and fought well under Massena* at Zurich;* for a time he commanded against the great Suvorov.* Next year he aided Massena in the defense of Genoa* but broke a leg and was taken prisoner. Repatriated, he helped quell rebels in Piedmont.

Following a spell under Murat* in Naples, he was given command of the Camp of St. Omer (1803–05) and was created a marshal in May 1804. Next year he commanded the IV Corps in Austria, storming the Pratzen Heights at Austerlitz,* and earning the reputation of being "the best tactician in Europe" from Napoleon. He commanded the French right at Jena,* fought at Eylau* and Heilsberg,* and received the surrender of Königsberg (June 1807). He was now amassing titles and wealth, and became Duke of Dalmatia (June 1808).

For the next six years Soult saw much service in the Peninsular War.* In late 1808 he accompanied Napoleon to Spain and was given command over the troops that completed the pursuit of Sir John Moore* to Corunna,* where the French were defeated. Despite the escape of the British army back to England, Soult chivalrously put up a memorial to the fallen Moore. Next he invaded Portugal and, insatiable for further honors, began to aspire to the Portuguese crown. Any such hopes were rudely dashed, however, when he was sharply defeated by Wellesley* at Oporto* in May 1809, managing to save his men only by abandoning his guns and baggage. His later success over the Spaniards at Ocaña* re-established his reputation. After Talavera* (at which he was not present) he became King Joseph Bonaparte's* Chief of Staff in succession to Jourdan,* but did not find cooperation easy. In 1810 he invaded Andalusia, capturing Seville, Olivença,

and Badajoz* (early 1811), but failed to march up to Massena's aid during the episode of the Lines of Torres Vedras.* However, when Badajoz was besieged by Marshal Beresford* later that year he returned to try to raise the siege but was defeated at the gory battle of Albuera* in May. Soult fell back, and later invaded the kingdom of Granada before (early 1812) once again attempting to relieve Badajoz—but in vain, as it had already fallen to Wellington.

As the Allies exploited their success over Marmont* at Salamanca,* Soult was compelled to abandon the two-year blockade of Cadiz* and retreat northward to link up with Suchet.* He retook Madrid and pursued the retiring Wellington from Burgos* toward the Portuguese frontier.

He was recalled to France in early 1813 and succeeded to the command of the Imperial Guard* on the death of Bessières.* He fought at Bautzen* but was then hurriedly sent back to Spain when news reached Napoleon of the disaster of Vitoria.* From 12 July he took command of the remnants of all French forces and soon reorganized and reinspired them sufficiently to fight the tenacious campaign of the Pyrenees* against the Allies, winning the Maya* and Roncesvalles* actions but losing those at Sorauren* and Vera* in his attempts to prevent the fall of Pamplona* and San Sebastian.* He then set about delaying the Allied advance onto French soil but was fooled at the Bidassoa,* and after the hard-fought battles of Nivelle,* the Nive,* and St. Pierre,* Wellington compelled him to abandon Bayonne.* Pursuing him inland, Wellington inflicted another defeat at Orthez* (February 1814), and ultimately at Toulouse* on 10 April. Thus Soult had held off the Allies for ten months after the debacle of Vitoria.

Soult submitted to the Bourbons but was not employed by them in a senior position, and he at once rallied to Na-

Soult

poleon in March 1815. He was appointed Chief of Staff to the Army of the North but did not shine in this capacity during the short campaign in Belgium that followed. He was no substitute for Berthier.* After Waterloo* he gathered the army's survivors at Laon. The following January he was exiled and went to live at Düsseldorf, where he remained until 1819. Next year his rank was restored and he was made a peer of France in 1827.

A long, distinguished career still lay ahead of him. He was Minister of War from 1830–34, represented France at Queen Victoria's coronation in 1838 (where for the first time he met Wellington), became Minister of Foreign Affairs in 1839, and served two periods as president of the Council of Ministers (1832–34 and 1840–47), besides once again becoming Minister of War (1840–45). He was, at 71, the youngest of the surviving marshals to welcome the return of Napoleon's remains from St. Helena* in 1840. He retired from active life on 15 September

1847 and was proclaimed Marshal-General of France just eleven days later.

As a soldier it is perhaps arguable whether he fully merited this supreme distinction—one awarded previously only to Turenne,* Villars, and Saxe.* Even as a tactician he had been worsted by Moore and Wellington, and although his handling of the war in the Pyrenees had been able, it had ended in defeat. Nevertheless, he was greatly revered by the French nation and army, and even if his character was somewhat marred by excessive ambition and great avarice, he had been consistently loyal to Napoleon. He died at Soultberg on 26 November 1851. Soult indubitably merits a place alongside Davout,* Massena, and Suchet in the ranks of the Emperor's ablest commanders.

Soult, Général Pierre Benoit (1770–1843). The brother of the marshal, he joined the cavalry in 1788. He fought at Fleurus* and next year became his brother's unofficial aide-de-camp. In 1796 he was commissioned and served on his brother's staff until 1800, sharing all his fortunes. In September 1805 he served under Mermet in Italy, fought in Prussia (1806), and after being wounded at Heilsberg* (1807) he was promoted to *général de brigade* in July 1807. Much service in Spain followed; he was wounded at Bussaco* in 1810 and again at Alba de Tormes* in 1812. In March 1813 he became *général de division* and fought with distinction in the Pyrenees under his brother; he was at both Orthez* and Toulouse.* In 1815 he commanded a division of cavalry under Pajol.* He was not employed again but was retired in the rank of lieutenant general in 1825. Recalled to service, he acted in various capacities, both political and administrative, until his final retirement in 1836.

Spencer, General Sir Brent (1760–1828). This officer served with distinction in the

West Indies (1779–82 and 1790–94) and once again, as a brigadier general in 1797, in the campaign in Santo Domingo* against Toussaint l'Ouverture.* During the Helder Campaign (1799) he commanded the 40th Foot under the Duke of York.* Transferred under Abercromby* to the Mediterranean, he fought under Sir John Moore* at Aboukir* and Alexandria* in 1801. He was appointed an equerry to King George III* and served in the expeditions to Copenhagen* and Cadiz.* In 1808 he was second-in-command to Wellesley* at Roliça* and Vimiero.* In 1809 he received his knighthood and returned to the Peninsula the next year, fighting in command of a division at both Bussaco* and Fuentes de Oñoro* (1811). His command was taken over by General Graham* in 1811, largely on account of the pessimistic letters he sent back to England, which shook Wellington's faith in him. He became a full general in 1825.

Spithead, the mutinies at, 16 April–15 May 1797. Refusal by the British Admiralty to remedy the long-standing grievances of British sailors over pay (unchanged since the days of Cromwell), poor rations, and the generally abysmal conditions of service afloat led to a major crisis in 1797 when the Channel Fleet refused Admiral Lord Bridport's* order to sail from Spithead. The mutineers—led by a committee of delegates under Valentine Jones—handled matters with restraint, but after the breakdown of negotiations on 5 May some bloodshed occurred on board H.M.S. *London.* The Admiralty called in Lord Howe* to reopen negotiations, and Parliament passed the Seaman's Bill remedying many of the complaints—including the granting of pay parity with the army and militia at one shilling a day for the lowest ratings. Howe visited every ship in turn, and the Royal Pardon was read out. The ships' crews thereupon re-

turned to their duties. There were no reprisals. The later events involving naval shipping at the Nore,* politically motivated, were more serious and led to severe examples being made.

Stadion, Johann Philip Carl Josef, Count (1768–1824). This noted Austrian statesman entered the Habsburg diplomatic service in 1787. Retiring in 1794, he was recalled in 1801 to become Austrian ambassador in Berlin. From 1804 he filled the same post at St. Petersburg, where he helped negotiate the Third Coalition.* After the debacle of Austerlitz* he was made Foreign Minister. He soon became prominent in the court party seeking revenge for Austria's humiliations, and he helped plan the war of 1809. The defeat of Wagram* led to his second retirement, but in 1814 he reappeared in public life, being appointed Minister of Finance by the Emperor Joseph.*

Staël, Madame Anne Louise Germaine (*née* Necker), baronne de (1766–1817). The daughter of the Bourbon Minister of Finance, Necker, she early became a celebrated society hostess in the last years of the 18th century. She at first hailed the coming of the Revolution, but then became critical. After a period living near Lake Leman to care for her aging father, she moved back to Paris in 1797 and established a brilliant *salon* that became a major focal point of cultural and political life in the capital. The American Benjamin Constant was for a time her great favorite, but despite Mme de Staël's wiles, Bonaparte as First Consul would raise him no higher than to a seat in the Tribunate. She soon became disillusioned with Napoleon but gained great fame by publishing her novel *Delphine* in 1802, followed by a number of literary essays. She returned to Lake Leman as her father's death approached and established a cultured circle at the chateau of Coppet.

This soon became a hotbed of near-dissension against Napoleon, who formally outlawed her from Paris. She married twice more and traveled widely through Europe before returning to Paris, where she spent the rest of her days. A highly cultivated and gifted woman, Mme de Staël was perhaps the most important cultural influence of her day.

Stapps, Friedrich (1792–1809). The son of a Protestant pastor, this young Saxon was at first a great admirer of Napoleon but then became filled with hatred for him during the French invasion of Austria in 1809. He made a bold attempt to assassinate the Emperor with a knife, and was only intercepted in the nick of time by the watchful General Rapp.* Napoleon offered him his life if he would express regret for his attempted deed— but he declared that he would seize every future occasion to assassinate him. He was condemned to death and shot a few days later.

Stein, Heinrich Friedrich Carl, Baron, (1757–1831). Born a native of Nassau, Stein entered the Prussian civil service and in 1784 was appointed Director of Mining in Westphalia. He studied in England and later became President of the Westphalian Chambers of Commerce. From 1804–06 he was Minister of Trade. After the treaty of Tilsit,* Frederick William III called him to work on the reconstruction of Prussia's economy —work that he performed so well that Napoleon demanded his removal from office. Together with Scharnhorst* and Gneisenau* he helped refashion Prussian life, ending serfdom, reducing the power of the nobility, and making all men equal before the law. On Napoleon's insistence he was exiled and lived in Austria and Russia, where he worked on the creation of the Sixth Coalition.* Returning to Prussia in 1813, he traveled to Paris in 1814 and demanded stiff peace terms.

Mme. de Staël

After the Congress of Vienna* Stein rapidly became disillusioned with the absolutism of his royal master, and he retired from public life to live first at Frankfort and then in Westphalia. He was widely regarded as the model Prussian patriot.

Stengel, Général Henri Christian Michel, baron de (1744–1796). Commissioned into the Palatine Guards (1758), he became a French officer in the infantry in 1760. After fighting in Germany during the later years of the Seven Years' War (where he was wounded in the leg) he transferred to the hussars and then (1792) to the dragoons. That year saw him promoted to *maréchal de camp* under Dumouriez,* whose advance guard he commanded at Valmy.* Transferred to Belgium, he captured Aix-la-Chapelle in

1793 but then lost it. For this setback he was arrested and tried before the Revolutionary Tribunal, but was acquitted. He was retired in early 1795 but was called back to the service in March the same year. In June he was appointed *général de division* and sent to command the cavalry in the Army of Italy. Next year he was seriously wounded in the arm while leading the battle-winning charge at Mondovi* and died following an amputation operation.

Stockach, battles of, 25 March 1799 and 3 May 1800. As the armies of the Second Coalition* converged on French-held territory, General Jourdan* at the head of 40,000 men tried to withstand the advance of Archduke Charles* and 60,000 Austrians. The French were defeated and Jourdan was forced back over the Rhine with a loss of 5,000 men.

Next year, as part of the French grand strategic plan, General Moreau* led 50,000 French troops over the Rhine and invaded Baden in late April. He encountered General Kray* on 3 May and routed him. Each side lost some 2,000 men, and Kray fell back on Ulm.*

Stralsund, blockade and siege of, 30 January–29 April 1807. While the French main army was preparing to seek out the main Russian army of Bennigsen* (see Eylau), Marshal Mortier* was entrusted with the subjection of Pomerania, including the fortress of Stralsund. He advanced his men to open the blockade, which was effective from 30 January. Occasional minor actions and much sapping filled the next two months, but on 29 March Mortier was recalled with most of his corps from the siege, which was entrusted to General Grandjean's division of five regiments. The Swedish defenders, under General Essen,* promptly launched a major sortie in early April that drove the French back. This brought Mortier back to the scene from Stettin. Each side had

some 13,000 men deployed, but step by step the Swedes were driven back into their defenses by 17 September. Mortier then proposed an armistice which Essen accepted from 19 April. By this neither side was to renew hostilities without serving one month's notice. The Swedes also agreed not to move beyond the river Peene. Mortier was then reabsorbed into the army collecting along the Vistula.

Strategy. The art and science of planning campaigns so as to achieve the grand strategic purposes as economically and effectively as possible had few greater exponents than Napoleon. His methods were not truly original—except as regards their speed of execution and relentless application—but for more than a decade he had no equal. Basically, he employed two major strategic methods: the maneuver of the central position (or his "inferiority" strategy, employed when he was facing a numerically superior opponent or series of opponents), and the *manoeuvre sur les derrières* (or his strategy of "superiority," when the converse applied). In broad outline, the former involved the French in seizing the initiative and striking a blow designed to divide the opponents. Then, by reinforcing each wing in turn with his reserve (see Grand Tactics and *Bataillon carré*) Napoleon would build up a local superiority against each enemy force consecutively and defeat them in detail. This was the plan employed against Beaulieu* and Colli* on the Ligurian Coast in April 1796; it was also the strategy attempted in the Waterloo* campaign in 1815—with disastrous results for the French, as it turned out, although the concept that led to the preliminary battles of Ligny* and Quatre Bras* was as brilliant as ever.

The second strategy was based upon the possession of superior force and the principle of envelopment. Using a part of his army to distract the enemy's atten-

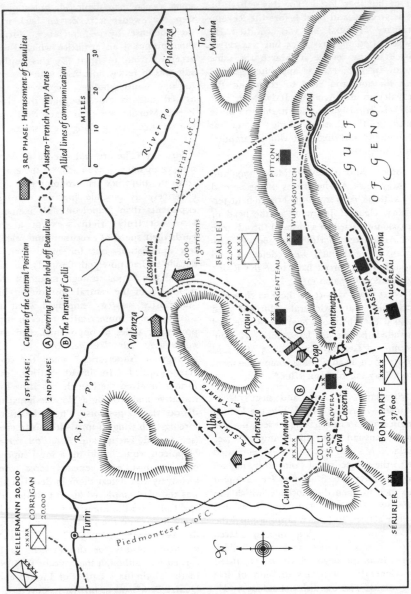

Strategy: Maneuver of the Central Position—The Attack at Piedmont, April 1796

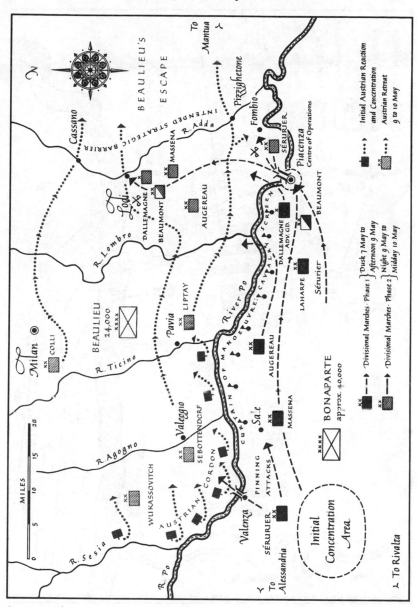

Strategy: The Maneuver Preceding Lodi

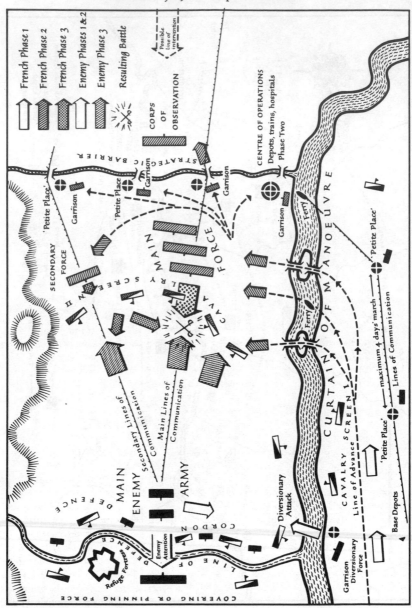

Strategy: The Maneuver of Envelopment (Schematic)

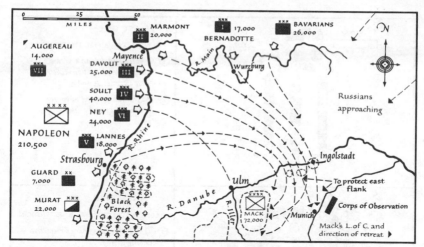

Strategy: Envelopment—French Advance to the Danube at Ulm, 1805

tion, Napoleon would rush the remainder by forced marches along a circuitous route to place a block on the enemy's lines of communications, severing his links with his bases. When the foe tried to force his way out of the trap he would find the French in a preselected battle position—and a "reversed-front battle" would theoretically be the result. In the event of a defeat, the enemy army had nowhere to retire upon—the pinning force now moving up against its rear—and the foe faced annihilation or surrender. First used during the Lodi* phase of the Campaign of 1796, variations on this theme were used almost 30 times, including at Marengo,* Ulm,* Jena-Auerstädt,* and Bautzen.*

Of course there were counters to these maneuvers. The Allies eventually learned that the way to defeat the strategy of the central position was to refuse to be driven asunder; if defeated, an army would move back toward or parallel to, its supporting army (as in the retreat by the Prussians on Wavre* after Ligny* during the Waterloo campaign of 1815). To defeat the maneuver of envelopment called for maintaining sufficient supplies and munitions close behind the army (thus reducing reliance on distant depots and bases), and then calling Napoleon's bluff, if such it was, by continuing a relentless pressure against the French frontal pinning force. This stratagem was well illustrated during the final advance by the Allies on Paris in 1814.

Wellington* was also an able strategist in his own right. In the earlier years of the Peninsular War* he appreciated that his Anglo-Portuguese army's role was to establish a secure base area (Lisbon) and then to take pressure off the Spanish and Portuguese guerrillas and partisans. By advancing into French-held territory, Wellington forced the French to concentrate their forces to meet him—and to fight a battle. During such a period, the guerrillas could operate unchecked against the French rear and isolated detachments. Thus, Wellington used the strategic offensive, seizing the initiative (as in the

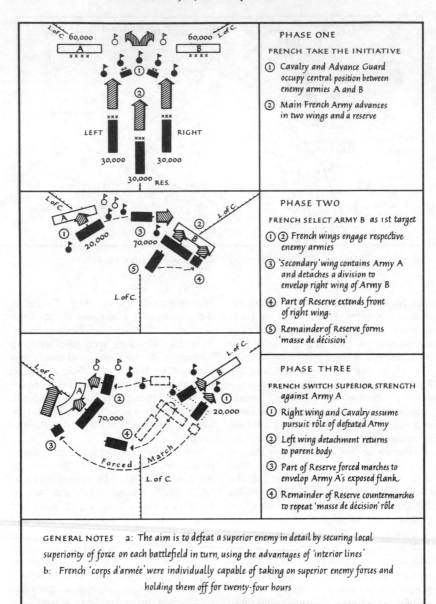

PHASE ONE

FRENCH TAKE THE INITIATIVE

① Cavalry and Advance Guard occupy central position between enemy armies A and B

② Main French Army advances in two wings and a reserve

LEFT   RIGHT

30,000   30,000

30,000 RES.

PHASE TWO

FRENCH SELECT ARMY B as 1st target

①② French wings engage respective enemy armies

③ 'Secondary' wing contains Army A and detaches a division to envelop right wing of Army B

④ Part of Reserve extends front of right wing.

⑤ Remainder of Reserve forms 'masse de décision'

20,000   70,000

PHASE THREE

FRENCH SWITCH SUPERIOR STRENGTH against Army A

① Right wing and Cavalry assume pursuit rôle of defeated Army

② Left wing detachment returns to parent body

③ Part of Reserve forced marches to envelop Army A's exposed flank

④ Remainder of Reserve countermarches to repeat 'masse de décision' rôle

70,000   20,000

Forced March

GENERAL NOTES   a: The aim is to defeat a superior enemy in detail by securing local superiority of force on each battlefield in turn, using the advantages of 'interior lines'

b: French 'corps d'armée' were individually capable of taking on superior enemy forces and holding them off for twenty-four hours

Strategy: Maneuver of the Central Position (Schematic)

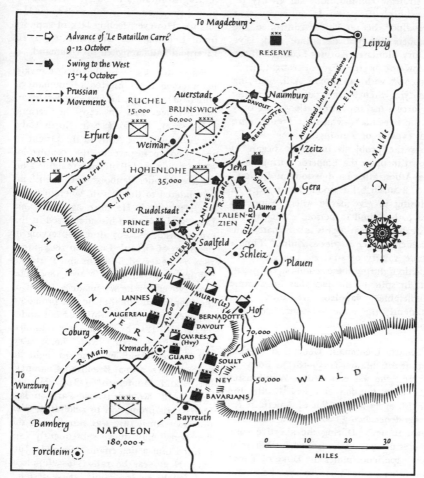

Strategy: The French Offensive, 1806

Oporto* and Talavera* campaigns) and then frequently (albeit not invariably) fighting defensively. In 1810 he reversed this strategic role and withdrew by way of Bussaco* to the Lines of Torres Vedras,* near his secure base of Lisbon, where he starved Massena's* Army of Portugal into accepting defeat by a combination of the strength of his position and the applica-

tion of "scorched earth" policy. The result was the ultimate destruction of the Army of Portugal and the discrediting of Massena.

Whether the Russians deliberately or through sheer necessity retreated before the mighty French invader in 1812 is still debated, but the effect was to deny Napoleon his decisive battle until the effects of strategic consumption had greatly reduced his battle-power. In consequence, at Borodino* he no longer controlled the numbers required to ensure a decisive victory. Similarly, Kutusov* controlled the follow-up of the French retreat from Moscow* with the utmost skill, worrying the dying French army rather than trying to force a major confrontation—save only at the Beresina*—which the French were still capable of winning.

As the problems of defeat began to crowd in upon the Emperor during 1813, the Allies, after hard lessons at Lützen* and Bautzen,* hit upon the strategy of refusing to give battle where Napoleon was to be found in person, concentrating instead on defeating his subordinate commanders at such battles as Kulm.* Thus a whole variety of strategic concepts were practiced during these action-packed years, but in spite of the fact that he became predictable, Napoleon remained preeminently the master-strategist until the final collapse in 1815.

Stuart, Lieutenant General Sir John, Count of Maida (1759–1815). Born in Georgia, he was educated at Westminster School in London and served with the British army in the War of American Independence, being taken prisoner at Yorktown in 1781. During the abortive campaigns of 1793–95 he gained further military experience under the Duke of York* and other commanders. In 1799 he fought at the capture of Minorca, and in 1801 he commanded a division at the battle of Alexandria;* it was his actions that in large measure won that engagement. In 1806 he commanded an expedition against Calabria and there defeated General Reynier* at the battle of Maida,* which demonstrated the full effect of linear over columnar tactics. This victory earned him a knighthood, a grant of £1,000 a year, and the title of count. He continued his successes in southern Italy in 1809 before

retiring to Messina in Sicily, where he repulsed the enemy invasion with great loss in 1810. However, feeling lack of support from England, he protested to Lord Liverpool* and resigned his command.

Subservie, Général Jacques Gervais, baron (1776–1856). Elected a lieutenant of volunteers in 1792, he first saw service in the Pyrenees and in 1797 he became aide-de-camp to Lannes* in North Italy. He sailed with the Army of the Orient in 1798 and took part in the capture of Malta,* but he fell ill and remained on the island under Vaubois* until the island surrendered to the British, whereupon he was repatriated. He once again became Lannes' aide, and at his side served in the campaigns of 1805–07 after first serving in the Army of Oceanic Coasts in 1804. From 1808–11 he served in Spain and Portugal, fighting at Medellin* in March 1809. The same November he was made a Baron of the Empire, and in 1811 he was promoted to *général de brigade* while serving under Suchet.* In 1812 he was severely wounded at Borodino* serving with the cavalry, but he recovered in time to fight in Saxony (1813) and at Brienne,* Champaubert,* and Montereau* (1814). He was again badly wounded near Paris in late March. His promotion to *général de division* on 3 April 1814 was annulled by the Bourbons, but they subsequently appointed him a lieutenant general in July 1814. Next year he rallied to Napoleon and fought under Pajol* at Waterloo.* He was removed from the active list in August and compulsorily retired in 1825.

Subservie had by that time become deeply embroiled in politics, and he took an active part in the Revolution of 1820. He combined an active political career with appointments as Inspector of Cavalry for the remainder of his long life.

Suchet, Maréchal Louis Gabriel, duc d'Albufera (1770–1826). Suchet was born the son of a silk manufacturer at Lyons.

Suchet

In 1791 he entered the National Guard cavalry and was commissioned. By September he had been elected to command a volunteer battalion, and he served at Toulon* (1793) with distinction, capturing Major General O'Hara.

Service in the Army of Italy under La Harpe followed, and he fought at Loano in 1795 and at Dego,* Lodi,* and Castiglione* the next year under Bonaparte, before being wounded. Despite his wound he fought outside Mantua* and later at Arcola* and Rivoli.* In 1797 he was again wounded near Neumarkt. His great talents were now receiving recognition, and for a period he served as Brune's* Chief of Staff in Switzerland. In March 1798 he was promoted to *général de brigade* and continued to serve as Chief of Staff in various armies. In 1799 he married the daughter of Joseph Bonaparte's* sister-in-law and the same year became *général de division* and Chief of Staff in the Army of Italy. He fought at Novi* under Joubert* and the following

January he held a command under Massena* in Italy, but was not besieged within Genoa*—a city he reoccupied for the French after Marengo.* More active service was followed by an appointment as Governor of Padua (1801). That year he also became Inspector of Infantry. In 1805 he served as a divisional commander in IV Corps (Soult*) before being transferred to V Corps (Lannes*). He fought at Ulm,* Höllabrunn,* and at Austerlitz,* where he helped command the French left wing near the Santon. Next year he was in action at Saalfeld* and Jena,* and in the succeeding Polish campaign he fought at Pultusk* and Ostrolenka before succeeding Massena in provisional command of V Corps. In March 1808 he was made a Count of the Empire.

For six years, from 1808, his military career took him to Spain where he earned an unmatched reputation among the marshals who served in that strife-torn country. Most of his service was in Catalonia, first as a divisional, then as a corps commander. He was involved in both sieges of Saragossa* and from April 1809 succeeded Junot* in command of III Corps, also known as the Army of Aragon. He proceeded to harry General Blake* in a series of battles; he failed to capture Valencia in March 1810, but captured Lerida, Tortosa, and Tarragonna*—the last achievement earning him his baton as Marshal of the Empire (awarded on 8 July 1811). He won a further series of engagements against Blake, being wounded at Sagunto and capturing Valencia early in 1812. The same January he was created Duke of Albufera.

In 1813 he was defeated at Castalla by General Murray, but he managed to break the Allied siege of Tarragona,* finally relieving the garrison in August 1813. From November he was appointed Governor of Catalonia as well as Colonel General of the Imperial Guard,* succeeding Bessières,* who was killed in Germany.

In this appointment he gained great repute as a fair administrator and, uniquely among the marshals sent to Spain, conducted an effective "hearts and minds" campaign with the able assistance of his wife, which had considerable effect on the local population. However, the disasters being suffered on other sectors compelled him to evacuate Catalonia in April 1814, after one last victory at Molinos del Rey (15 January). He carried out a model withdrawal into France and was appointed to command the Army of the South. Then came Napoleon's abdication.

He continued to serve under the Bourbons during the First Restoration but rallied to Napoleon in the Hundred Days.* He was given command of the minuscule Army of the Alps, and many commentators consider him to have been misemployed there, given his immense talents. Ultimately, after a brief offensive into Piedmont, he concluded an armistice with the Austrians in July, evacuating his hometown of Lyons. After a period in disgrace he was restored to favor by the Bourbons in 1819, but took little part in public life.

Suliman, El-Halebi (1777–1800). Born in Aleppo, he became a noted student of Islamic law and the Koran. He was incited by religious fanatics to assassinate General Kléber,* Governor of Egypt, on 14 June 1800. The French authorities condemned him to death by impaling.

Suvorov, Field Marshal Alexander Vasilievitch, Count Suvorov-Rimnisky, Prince of Italijsky (1729–1800). This famous Russian commander first rose to prominence during the Seven Years' War, being promoted to colonel in 1762 and to brigadier general within the next year. During the Russo-Polish wars (1768–72) he was made major general (1768), and in the campaigns against the Turks that were fought in the Balkans (1773–74) he won the battles of Orsova and Kosludscki.

Returning to Russia in 1775 he completed the repression of Pugachev's revolt. In high favor with Catherine the Great, he was appointed Governor of the Crimea in 1786 but was soon given a new field command against the Turks. He gained important successes for the Tsarina, capturing Ochakov at the mouth of the Danube after a siege (1787–88) as well as Chocim and Jassy (massacring the Turkish inhabitants of all three places), and winning battles at Focsani and Rimnik in 1789—for which he was created a count. Next year he stormed and sacked the city of Ismail in Bessarabia after a long siege. During the Third Partition of Poland (1794–95) he captured Praga and also meted out rough justice to the inhabitants of Warsaw, adding to his reputation for ferocity and effective leadership. Catherine II rewarded him with the baton of field marshal, but her death in 1796 led to Suvorov's eclipse.

With the advent of the War of the Second Coalition,* however, he was recalled to service (1799) and sent in command of Russian troops to North Italy. Three quick victories—at Cassano against Moreau,* at the Trebbia against Macdonald,* and at Novi* against Joubert* —undid almost all the work of Bonaparte's First Italian Campaign of 1796–97. For these successes Tsar Paul* created him Prince Italijsky (i.e., of Italy). However, the defeat of his subordinate, Gortchakov,* at Zurich* by Massena* compelled him to abandon North Italy, and he conducted a difficult retreat through the Alps into Austria. Returning to Russia in late 1799 he again fell from favor and died soon after.

Greatly beloved by the Russian rank and file, who probably approved of his coarse and brutal nature, he wrote a treatise called "The Art of Victory," in which he championed among other tactics the use of shock action with the bayonet in preference to firepower.

Tabor, battle of Mount, 16 April 1799. As the siege of Acre* continued, Bonaparte sent forces deeper into Palestine to investigate reports of Turkish movements. After Junot* had beaten off a strong force of Turkish cavalry near Nazareth, Kléber* was detached from the siege lines with 1,500 men to support Junot's detachment of 500 cavalry. On 11 April Kléber scattered 6,000 Turks near Canaan, but five days later he encountered the Pasha of Damascus at the head of possibly 35,000 troops (mainly mounted) near Mount Tabor. Realizing that retreat would be impossible, Kléber boldly attempted a surprise attack on the Turkish encampment at dawn the next day. His advance was, however, detected, and the French formed two small squares and fought desperately for their lives against

odds of 17 to 1. By 4:00 P.M., after eight hours of dogged fighting, French ammunition was running low when Bonaparte in person appeared at the head of his Guides* and General Bon's* division (2,500 strong), which he had marched up overnight from Acre, some 25 miles away. Arriving from the north, Bonaparte detached two cannon, which were positioned on a ridge overlooking the plain below, and then maneuvered around the Pasha's camp to position himself to the south of the battlefield. Then, judging the correct psychological moment, the cannon fired two shots as the newcomers advanced against the Turkish rear. Six volleys and the Army of Damascus dissolved into a horde of fugitives, seeking safety in the direction of the river Jordan.

The French claimed that Kléber had

Battle of Mount Tabor

lost only 2 men killed and 60 wounded in ten hours of action against 25,000 Turkish cavalry. Turkish losses are unknown. Bonaparte, satisfied that he had dealt with the only force capable of attempting the relief of Acre, forthwith returned to resume personal conduct of the siege.

Tactics. The evolution of French tactics and military organizations between 1792 and 1815 was in part haphazard and in part deliberate. In the early days of Valmy,* the problem of making effective use of unskilled *fédérés*—as often as not half-starved, underequipped, and semi-mutinous—had encouraged *l'amalgame,** the fusion of two raw and one experienced infantry battalions. The former mounted mass attacks in crude columns of attack; the latter provided the light infantry screen and musketry fire support drawn up in linear formation. This adaptation of Guibert's* *l'ordre mixte* involved the replacement of the old Bourbon regiments with three-battalion *demi-brigades,* combining the functions of shock and fire-action, and lay behind such notable successes as Jemappes,* thé first real victory of the Revolutionary armies. The cavalry of the Revolutionary forces was probably its weakest part, being worst hit by the emigration of officers and needing the longest period of time to recruit and train, but Hoche's* bold charge over the ice to capture the Dutch fleet in 1794 was a unique achievement. The artillery, on the other hand, was the most professional and effective arm of the service. Least affected by the departure of *émigrés,** and benefiting from the recent reforms of Gribeauval* and du Teil,* the guns silenced their opponents, then supported the French attacks, moving forward with them by bounds as the cavalry did its best to check the generally superior enemy cavalry and to exploit success when and if achieved.

Over the years the organization of French formations changed a great deal. The 1792-pattern battalion of three companies of 330 men apiece gave way by 1799 to the nine-company (including one of grenadiers and one of *voltigeurs*) establishment, holding 150–200 men each. By 1808 a simplification was ordered, the number of companies being reduced to six. From 1803 the old *régiment,* numbered rather than named, had been reintroduced. Numerous regiments of *tirailleurs* or light infantry were formed, there being 26 such regiments to 90 line in 1803 and over 40 (to 200 line regiments) by 1813.

The infantry company of attack was often organized on a two-company frontage, the front rank holding up to 75 men with some 11 ranks in close support. To fight in line, a unit deployed into three ranks. *L'ordre mixte*—personally preferred by Napoleon—was employed in various forms up to divisional level. Occasionally, columns of attack with only a company frontage (30 men or so) were resorted to in restricted areas. In theory, columns were supposed to deploy into line 150 yards from the enemy, but in practice they often charged home without pausing to re-form. The light infantrymen were usually deployed in a loose protective screen ahead of their columns, using sniping fire.

The cavalry rapidly improved under inspired leadership from Murat,* Kellermann,* Lasalle,* and others. The four-squadron (each of two troops of up to 116 troopers) cavalry *demi-brigades* gave place to cavalry regiments—heavy, dragoon, and light—on various establishments. There were eventually 17 regiments of *cuirassiers*, 30 of dragoons,* and as many more light cavalry formations. All cavalry were trained in various evolutions, including the slowly accelerating charge, and were taught to exploit success to the utmost but also to rally in good time.

The artillery* was divided into horse and foot, organized into *compagnies* (or batteries) of eight guns (six cannon and two howitzers) apiece. By 1800 there were eight regiments of foot artillery to six of horse; with both of these were brigaded companies of pontoon troops and battalions of train troops (eight by 1800). By 1805 France held over 20,000 cannons of all types and sizes, and by 1813 the artillery personnel numbered 103,000 men. Artillery tactics were based upon rapid fire (up to five rounds a minute from the smaller pieces) and progressive advances to close range in a succession of bounds— as carried out by Senarmont* to perfection at Friedland.* From 1806 the use of massed batteries of heavier 12-pounders was increasingly employed, and as the quality of the French infantry deteriorated so were more guns added at regimental and divisional levels. Numbers of horse artillery and *artillerie volante* (or galloper-guns), with some 12-pounders, were habitually kept in army reserve under the Emperor's personal control for use in special roles (see Grand Tactics). Firing round shot or canisters, or in the case of howitzers, fused shells, artillery played a vital part in the winning of many of Napoleon's battles. The massed batteries at Borodino* and Wagram* are two examples.

His opponents, clinging until after 1805 to 18th-century linear concepts for the infantry, were less imaginative, but for many years Austrian and Prussian cavalry had the edge over the French. Ultimately, all European powers remodeled their tactics along broadly French lines, and by 1813 were capable of defeating their former conquerors. British practice proved the exception. Although the cavalry remained a distinct liability—almost invariably charging too far without reforming (as at Vimiero* and Waterloo*), although Le Marchant's* handling of his horsemen at Salamanca* was a notable exception—the steadiness of the British infantry became legendary. Retaining the two-deep line as their standard fighting formation, the infantry of Moore* and Wellesley* proved more than a match for their opponents, particularly in Spain where the terrain and climate did not favor cavalry action. Wellington's skill at using reversed slope positions to hide his men from view and fire—supporting them with guns drawn up along the crest and with the riflemen of the Light Brigades deployed on the forward slopes to harass the approach of the French column—became fully established, and led to such notable victories as Talavera,* Salamanca,* and Vitoria,* and ultimately to Waterloo.

Napoleon evinced little direct interest in minor tactics, normally delegating such matters to his subordinates. However, in Egypt he did devise a form of divisional square as used at the Pyramids* and declared his preference for *l'ordre mixte* and ever-larger batteries of guns—the former for the use of the bayonet, the latter as dispensers of firepower. He always enjoined the need for bold, aggressive tactics proceeding from a sound defensive base.

Talavera, battle of, 27–28 July 1809. This battle was rated by Wellington* as one of the bitterest he ever fought. He commanded some 55,500 men and 60 guns, including 34,800 Spaniards under General Cuesta.* Opposed to them were 46,150 French troops and 80 guns commanded by King Joseph Bonaparte* and Marshal Jourdan,* organized into two corps. After liaison problems with his allies, Wellington had managed to withdraw the whole force west of the river Alberche, but on the morning of the 27th he had almost been taken captive at Casa das Salinas near the river. By afternoon, however, the Allies were holding a two-mile line running from the Medellin feature in the north (with cavalry on the

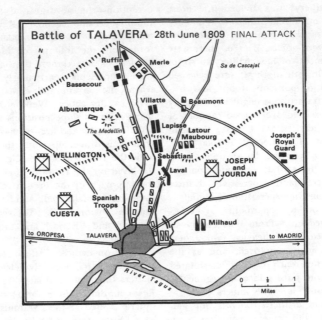

Battle of TALAVERA 28th June 1809 FINAL ATTACK

plain beyond keeping a wary eye for any sign of Soult's* anticipated intervention), along the line of the small Portina brook in the center (where an earthwork held a number of guns) to the walls of Talavera. The British held the left half of the line; the Spaniards the right, among entrenchments.

The evening of the 27th saw a panic among part of the Spanish forces when French cavalry were sighted, but it was only after dark that action suddenly blazed around the Medellin as General Ruffin's* division almost succeeded in a surprise attack against the key British position, which had been improperly garrisoned. General Hill's* counterattack with his 2nd Division drove the French back by 11:00 P.M. for a loss of 313 men, inflicting some 300 casualties upon the French. Both armies then passed an uneasy night.

Early on the 28th Joseph and Jourdan

decreed a major attack by 40,000 men against the British part of the line and the northern plain. Some 30 guns came into action at 5:00 A.M. from the Casjacal ridge. Three French columns advanced, but within two hours all had been beaten off. After a lull lasting until 11:00 A.M., the French advanced through the mounting heat of a scorching day to launch three more onslaughts against Wellesley's line, the main blows coming just south of the Medellin. The superior firepower of Sherbrooke's* 1st and neighboring divisions again repelled the French by 2:00 P.M., but when Sherbrooke advanced over the Portina brook he was badly mauled by the French second line formations. Wellesley extemporized a defense with Mackenzie's 3rd Division and eventually the threat to his center passed. Another French advance, this time into the northern plain in an attempt to turn the Allied flank, was met by fire from eight guns followed by a cavalry charge by Anson's brigade. Unfortunately the 23rd Light Dragoons charged into a ravine, but the survivors were extricated by the King's German Legion,* and the exhausted French recoiled. The discordant French commanders then decided (at about 4:30 P.M.) to retreat over the Alberche toward distant Toledo, and the battle was over. The British had lost 5,365 in all (or one quarter of their strength), the Spaniards 1,200, and the French 7,268 and 20 guns. Many wounded died tragically when a fire spread over the dry plain. Wellesley soon decided to retire to the west, aware that Soult was advancing to envelop his army from the north and thus cut him off from Portugal and his bases. In due course he was made a viscount for his conduct of the battle.

Talleyrand-Périgord, Charles Maurice de, L'Eveque d'Autun, Prince de Benavente (1754–1838). The ablest diplomat of the Napoleonic period, with a genius for personal survival which saw him through several changes of regime and *coups*

Talleyrand

d'état, he was educated for the priesthood at the Sorbonne. In 1775 he became an *abbé* in the diocese of Rheims and in 1788 he became Bishop of Autun, but the Revolution interposed and he represented the Second Estate at the meeting of the States-General. In 1790 he accepted the civil constitution for the clergy but resigned his bishopric in 1791 to take a full part in politics. Next year he was launched on his diplomatic career, traveling on missions to both London and the United States, thereby escaping the excesses of the Terror.* He returned to France in September 1795 after periods of residence in Holland and Germany.

Joining Barras,* he was appointed Minister of Foreign Affairs in July 1797, and then he transferred his opportunistic loyalties to Bonaparte, whose ambitious expansionist dreams he actively encouraged; thus he retained the portfolio for Foreign Affairs. In 1804 he was made Grand Chamberlain of the Empire and Duke of Benavente in 1806 as well as Arch-Chancellor and Grand Elector. In 1808 he accompanied Napoleon to meet the Tsar Alexander* at Erfurt* but was already sensing, from after Tilsit* in 1807, that Napoleon's fortunes were on the wane; he particularly disapproved of the involvement in Spain. He still retained Napoleon's confidence, but with the disasters of the Russian Campaign Talleyrand realized that cataclysm could not long be averted. To secure the best terms for France—and to ensure his own survival—he opened secret negotiations with the Allies and the *émigrés.** In 1814 he supported Napoleon's abdication and became temporary head of the provisional government before representing France at the Congress of Vienna,* where he skillfully played off the Allies against one another and secured notable concessions for Louis XVIII.* The Bourbons not unnaturally retained the services of so adept a minister-plenipotentiary, but restricted his political role. Louis-Philippe, however, sent him as ambassador to London where he worked to good effect improving Anglo-French relations and for the guaranteeing of Belgian independence. As he was then over 80, this proved his last success. In his active life he had served no less than eight regiments, and despite accusations that he was of obnoxious moral character, he was arguably, with Metternich,* the foremost diplomat of his day and the supreme realist of the European scene.

Tarbes, battle of, 20 March 1814. Following his victory at Orthez,* Wellington* —recovering gradually from the slight wound he had sustained—followed the French to St. Sever, separating Soult* once and for all from his garrison at Bayonne.* Pausing to detach two divisions under Beresford* to march on Bordeaux, where the authorities were made to capitulate, Wellington learned from his cavalry screen that Soult had marched away to the southeast and recrossed the river Adour at Maubourguet. The French were superior to the Allies at Aire, the latter having only five divisions on account of the Bordeaux detachment, but did not attack. However, it was evident that the French had been considerably reinforced, so Wellington called up half of Morillo's Spaniards from the siege of Navarren and Freire's force from before Bayonne to make good the numerical disadvantage. The 4th Division also returned to the main army six days after the occupation of that city on the 12th.

On the 18th Wellington could again advance. Wellington's aim was to trap Soult with his back to the Pyrenees, and the army marched south in three corps: Wellington commanded the center, Hill* the right, and Beresford the left (he had orders to outpace the other two in order to sever the three eastward-running roads that Soult might employ in an attempt to escape). On the 19th Beresford sev-

ered one of these roads and on the following morning severed a second. The trap was now fast closing around Soult's army, and the showy cavalry raid he mounted against St. Sever on the 17th and 18th (which produced 100 Allied prisoners) had clearly won him no time. However, on the afternoon of the 20th two French divisions managed to hold off the Light and 6th Divisions of Beresford's command for long enough to allow the bulk of Soult's army to slip away toward Toulouse* along the southernmost road. Fighting was very severe on a steep slope, crowned by a windmill, which constituted the main French position, their serried ranks placed one behind another down the hillside so that all could fire at once. French losses were put at 80 men in this action, those of the Allied at 120 (92 of them from the rifle battalions). Ultimately Soult made good his retreat to St. Gaudens and Monrejean, heading for Toulouse with the Allies hot on his heels.

Tarifa, sieges of, 19 December 1811– 5 January 1812. Marshal Soult,* deeply involved in the siege of Cadiz,* decided to occupy the nearby port and town of Tarifa. The Governor of Gibraltar, however, forestalled this move by sending an English force under Colonel Skerrett, assisted by an engineer officer, Colonel Smith, to organize the defense. The ancient defenses were strengthened by earthworks, and special positions were prepared on the peninsula jutting out to the south from the town. The Convent of San Francisco was fortified to the northwest of the town, the Catalina Hill on the neck of land to the south received a battery mounting a naval 18-pounder, and a line of naval shipping and gunboats was anchored so as to threaten the flank of any French force attacking from the northeast. The garrison comprised 2,500 men in all, including 600 Spanish infantry and 100 Spanish cavalry. Thirteen guns were sited on the peninsula and the "island" at its extremity, ten pieces were in the town itself, and five more placed among the outworks, but owing to the weakness of the ancient walls not all could in fact be brought into action.

On 19 December General Laval and 8,000 French drove in the outposts from the eastern approaches and next day the town was invested. On the 21st a French party was wiped out by a sortie from the Catalina fortification as it tried to reconnoiter the western side of the town, and after two more similar setbacks Laval determined to open his trenches against the northeast side of Tarifa; this was done on the night of the 22nd. Digging forward from 500 yards, the French trenches crept forward for four days. The French were aided by a gale on the 23rd that forced the naval vessels to put out to sea, and on the 29th their batteries opened fire against the town and their howitzers against the island. Soon a breach was battered in the center of the defenses near the Portcullis Tower. Colonel Skerrett wished to evacuate Tarifa without further ado despite Smith's opposition, but the shipping was no longer off the port so full attention was turned to preparing to repel any assault. The 87th Foot was to hold the breach, and preparations were made within the town to hold off the French attack. By the 30th the breach was 60 feet in extent, and practicable, but torrential rain precluded a storming attempt that day. At daybreak on the 31st, however, a column of French grenadiers attacked up the streambed against the Portcullis Tower but were defeated with heavy loss. The Allies lost only 36 casualties. Laval retreated on 5 January 1812, after losing 1,000 men to bullets and sickness against the total Allied loss of 150.

Tarragonna, siege of, 2–13 June 1812. Following his success at Castalla, General

Murray was ordered by Wellington* to attack the fortress of Tarragonna and thus keep Suchet* fully employed on the east coast while the main allied army struck in central Spain. Rear Admiral Hallowell's squadron duly landed Murray and his 16,000 men at Salou Bay (six miles to the south) on 2 June, together with some heavy guns. They were joined by the Spanish General Copons, and the total force soon numbered 24,000 men, half of them Spaniards.

To defend the extensive fortifications, General Bertoletti had only 1,600 men. He withdrew into the upper town at once, leaving two small bastions garrisoned by small forces. These positions engaged all of Murray's attention until 11 June, and as time passed he became increasingly anxious lest a French force should appear to relieve the garrison, although there were no clear indications of any such intent. On the 9th he went so far as to issue contingency plans for a possible re-embarkation of the force. Suchet, in fact, had marched north from Valencia with 8,000 men, intending to meet with General Decaen at Reus, but that commander was obsessed with the possibility of an Allied attack well to the north—being confirmed in this belief by a well-timed Royal Marine raid on the port of Rosas near the French frontier—and he only sent 6,000 men to the rendezvous inland from Tarragonna. Indeed, the French attempt did not materialize, for Suchet turned back when a Spanish threat to Valencia became manifest.

Rumors, however, swept through the Allied siege lines. General Copons was covering the northern approaches, while a British force held the Balaguer Pass to the south. Murray allowed himself to be taken in by appearances, and on 11 June cancelled the storm of Fort Royal and ordered the stores to be embarked on the squadron, to Hallowell's fury. As the re-embarkation of the cavalry and guns began amidst great confusion on the 12th, a serious dispute broke out between the Army and Navy, and Murray dithered about various priorities. However, at 1:30 P.M. he ordered the main transfer of troops from shore to shipping to begin, after receiving news that Decaen's 6,000 men were approaching. The troops of the Anglo-Sicilian force were taken on board in dire confusion, while Copons led his Spaniards toward the hills. The guns were spiked and abandoned. All this was unnecessary, for the French garrison was too exhausted to intervene, and Decaen's division, under General Mathieu, had actually given up the relief attempt when news from Tarragonna caused him to return. Lord Bentinck took over command from the unsatisfactory Murray and the force returned to Alicante.

Tascher, Josephine. *See* **Beauharnais,** Josephine de

Tauenzien, General Bolesas Friedrich Emanuel, Count von Wittenberg (1760–1824). After joining the Prussian army in 1775, he fought in the Campaign of 1793 and in 1801 was promoted to major general. In 1806 he fought Soult* at Schleiz* and later commanded Hohenlohe's* advance guard before sharing in the debacle of Jena.* In 1813 he conducted the siege of Stettin before being given command of IV Corps, with which he fought at Gross-Beeren* and Dennewitz.* After Leipzig* he besieged and took Torgau and then retook Wittenberg in a furious storming that earned him his title. In 1815 he was given command of VI Corps, but entered on operations after Waterloo* had been fought.

Tauroggen, Convention of, 30 December 1812. As Napoleon's main army staggered back from Moscow in growing disorder, on the distant northern flank Marshal Macdonald* had perforce to fall back from Riga on the Baltic coast.

Harassed by General Diebitsch,* the French retreat began on 18 December, heading for distant Tilsit, but on the 25th the Russians succeeded in cutting off General Yorck's* Prussian contingents (17,000 men and 60 guns) from the main French force. Negotiations were at once opened by Italian and German *émigrés* in the Russian army and continued for five days. On the 30th Yorck agreed to the terms of the Convention of Tauroggen, whereby he and his troops became neutrals in the struggle. Although Frederick William III* subsequently disowned this action, it marked the beginning of Prussian determination to quit Napoleon's cause and take sides with the forces of the Sixth Coalition.

Tarutino, position of, 1812. After abandoning Moscow* to the French following Borodino,* Prince Kutusov* fell back with the Russian army to this village and its area to the south of the capital on the road to Kaluga, occupying the position from 29 August. Earthworks were built there, and from these the Russian cavalry sortied forth to surprise Murat* at Vinkovo.* Thereafter the main Russian army occupied this position until after Maloyaroslavetz.*

Teil, Général Jean Pierre du (1722–1794). A royal artillery officer of some reputation, he fought in the Seven Years' War with distinction. Becoming a disciple of Gribeauval,* in 1776 he was promoted to colonel and in 1784 to *maréchal de camp*. As commandant of Auxonne he had a considerable influence over Napoleon as a young officer, furthering both his education and his professional knowledge by, for the day, enlightened methods. However, in 1793 he rallied to the Bourbon cause during the Revolt of the South against the Revolutionary regime in Paris, and was captured and executed at Lyons.

Teil, Général Jean de Beaumont, Chevalier du (1738–1820). The younger brother of Jean Pierre, he first served as an artillery supernumerary at Fontency under de Saxe* in 1745, and was commissioned in 1748. He advanced his career with appointments in the sappers and bombardiers, and in 1784 was promoted to lieutenant colonel in the Metz artillery regiment. Under the Gribeauval* system he moved with unit rotation to Auxonne (1788). He welcomed the Revolution, unlike his brother, and in March 1790 became commander of the Metz National Guard. In 1791 he was briefly sacked and retired, but was recalled in February 1792 to a senior staff appointment and in August was promoted to *maréchal de camp* and commander of artillery in the Army of the Rhine, before being transferred to the Alps and then to Italy. In August 1793 he was confirmed as *général de division*, and at Bonaparte's suggestion he was sent to command the artillery at the siege of Toulon* in late October. Despite the success there, he was suspended in January 1794 as a noble and was again retired from the service, obtaining a pension in November that year. In August 1799 he was recalled to fill the role of Inspector General responsible for raising auxiliary battalions. After a time as commandant of Lille, from March 1800 until his final retirement on 23 December 1813, he served as *commandant des armes* at Metz.

Tengen (sometimes **Teugen**), combat of, 19 April 1809. As Napoleon hastened to take command of the *Grande Armée* in the Danube valley, where it had been attacked by the Archduke Charles'* Austrian army, Marshal Davout* at the head of 47,850 marched southwest from Ratisbon* to evade the developing trap. While Montbrun fought off General Rosenberg's column near Dinzling, Davout came under heavy attack near Hausen-Tengen, Gudin's* and Morand's* divisions taking the brunt of the heavy attack by the Aus-

trian III Corps under Hohenzollern* at Post Saal, and St. Hilaire fighting doggedly at Tengen itself. Archduke Charles, although nearby, failed to reinforce Hohenzollern despite his urgent pleas, and as a result III Corps was badly mauled, losing 3,846 casualties. The French (all sectors) lost some 4,500 men but were able to proceed toward Abensberg,* and they were soon in touch with Lefebvre's* corps and the main army.

Terror, the. A term used to describe the period from early September 1792 to 27 July 1794 during which the Convention's extreme laws of suspects and denunciation were in full force. Faced by foreign invasion and internal treachery, France appeared in desperate straits, and on the proposal of Chaumette and the Paris delegates in the Convention the "Terror" was formally inaugurated on 5 September 1792. (NB: Some historians date the true "Terror" from 31 May 1793, following the defection of General Dumouriez,* others date it, as here, from the September Massacres of the previous year.) During its gory course the Terror led to the execution of an estimated 40,000 people throughout France, sentenced by the Committee of Public Safety or the Revolutionary tribunals.

Thielmann, General Johann Adolf, Freiherr von (1765–1824). A Saxon by birth, born in Dresden, Thielmann commanded a Saxon cavalry brigade under Latour-Maubourg in Russia (1812), fighting with distinction at Borodino.* In 1813 he had garrisoned Torgau for the Emperor, but when Napoleon summoned him and his Saxon division he defected to the Allies on 12 May. On 28 September he attacked and defeated Lefebvre-Desnouëttes* at Altenburg, operating against the French communications between Leipzig and Erfurt. In 1815 Thielmann commanded III Corps of the Prussian army.

Badly mauled at Ligny* holding Blücher's* left, he retired with the rest of the army to Wavre.* There, on 18–19 June, he fought a staunch rear-guard action with only 25,000 men against Grouchy's* two corps, enabling Blücher and the rest of the army to join Wellington* at Waterloo.*

Thomières, Général Jean Guillaume Barthelémy, baron (1771–1812). A volunteer in 1793, he was elected captain and served in the army of the East Pyrenees (1793–95). In March 1796 he joined the Army of Italy and fought at Dego,* Mondovi,* Lodi,* Bassano,* and Arcola* in staff appointments. He became Victor's* aide-de-camp in 1797 and again served in Italy (1799–1801), fighting at Montebello* and Marengo.* After a spell in Batavia he was posted to the Camp of St. Omer (1803–05), in which latter year he joined Andreossy's* staff. In January 1806 he became Lannes'* aide, serving in Austria, Prussia, and Poland. From May 1807 he joined Lannes' staff and was promoted to *général de brigade* that same July. In late September he joined Junot's* forces massing in southern France, and after taking part in the march on Lisbon he fought at Vimiero* in August 1808 against Wellesley*, being wounded there, and the next January fought under Merle at Corunna.* He was made a baron in June 1809 and continued to serve under Kellermann the Younger* in Spain. He invaded Portugal with Massena* in 1810, fighting in Solignac's division. In 1811 he was transferred to Maucune's division, and in July 1812 he was in provisional command of the 7th Division of the Army of Portugal when he was killed at Salamanca.*

Thouvenot, Général Pierre, baron (1757–1817). Trained as a royal geographical engineer, he was commissioned into the colonial artillery in 1780 and spent a long time in the West Indies (1780–88).

Recalled to France, he fought in Belgium, becoming a lieutenant colonel (1792), and later served as Dumouriez's* Chief of Staff in the Army of Holland. He defected with his chief in April 1793 and lived abroad in exile until 1800 when he was allowed back to France. Service in Santo Domingo* followed until 1803, and during this period he was promoted to *général de brigade* (October 1802). In 1804 he held a post in the Ministry of War and later served as commandant of Würzburg and of Erfurt (1806). Next year he was wounded at the siege of Colberg before becoming governor of Stralsund. Service in Spain followed under Moncey,* and for a period he was governor of San Sebastian. He was made a Baron of the Empire in 1811. As French rule in Spain crumbled, he commanded Reille's* 9th Division in the Army of the Pyrenees and eventually was made governor of Bayonne.* He fought at St. Pierre,* and after sustaining a siege (during which he was wounded), he signed a convention with the Allies on 5 May 1814—one of the last French generals to have continued resistance at so late a date. He remained at Bayonne until he was retired in September 1815.

Thurreau (or **Turreau**) **de Garambouville,** Général Louis Marie, baron de Linières (1756–1816). Originally a member of the comte d'Artois' *garde du corps,* and after a period in command of the Army of the West Pyrenees, in 1794 he ruthlessly repressed the rebels in La Vendée* with his "infernal columns." Several charges of misconduct led to his eventual arrest but in the end he was acquitted (December 1795). Service in Switzerland followed in 1799, and he temporarily commanded the French forces there between Massena's* departure and Moreau's* arrival. In 1800 he served with the Army of the Reserve on detached duty. In 1801 he was sent to Elba.* From 1803–1811 he was French Minister to the United States, and on his return he became Baron de Linières. He commanded Bourges under Augereau* in 1813 and then defended Würzburg against the Austrians, finally being forced to capitulate. He retired from the service in September 1815.

Tilsit, Peace and Treaties of, 7 and 9 July 1807. Following the battle of Friedland,* both Napoleon* and Tsar Alexander* wanted peace, and soon a great "reversal of alliances" was in the making. On 25 June the two rulers met for private discussions on a raft moored in the middle of the river Niemen. That peace would be made—and a Franco-Russian alliance emerge—was never in doubt. The only major issue of contention was the degree of severity of the terms that would be handed down for Prussia. Queen Louise* visited Napoleon on 6 July but all her considerable charm proved incapable of swaying Napoleon one iota. Similarly, it had early become clear that the Tsar was prepared to abandon his erstwhile ally of the Fourth Coalition* in the interests of an alliance with France, whose ruler he found fascinating.

On 7 July a series of instruments were signed at Tilsit, comprising a peace treaty, secret articles, and an agreement of alliance. Two days later a separate treaty with Prussia was added. In terms of territory Russia lost nothing, but Prussia lost all her territories west of the Elbe. Holland had absorbed East Frisia, and the Grand Duchy of Berg received certain Westphalian lands. Much of the rest was incorporated into a new Kingdom of Westphalia for Jerome Bonaparte.* All Prussia's Polish territories with a few minor exceptions were also wrested away. Reduced to merely four provinces, Prussia would eventually be evacuated by the occupying French troops—but only (by a

separate convention signed on 12 July) after a huge war indemnity had been fully paid. Prussia was thus humiliated.

The key to the Russian alliance centered upon the resolution of the Polish problem, but here the treaty was vague. Napoleon's original idea that all the former Prussian Polish provinces should go to Russia in exchange for Russian recognition of French acquisition of Silesia was not acceptable to the Tsar, and only Bialystok went to Russia. The remaining provinces were eventually, it was agreed, to be formed into the Grand Duchy of Warsaw ruled by the King of Saxony (and on 22 July Napoleon granted the Poles a constitution). A French force was to be stationed in the Grand Duchy, which, like Westphalia, was to be part of the Confederation of the Rhine. But Franco-Russian relations would eventually be placed under great strain by the existence of a French-controlled enclave so far to the east.

Alexander agreed to cede the Ionian Isles and other Mediterranean possessions to France, in return for France aiding Russia against the Sultan if Turkey refused to make peace within three months —in which case, all Turkey's European possessions would be forcibly taken over by Russia, except for Rumelia. The Tsar also agreed to mediate with Great Britain in the search for a general peace, particularly over the issues of the return of France's former colonies and of the freedom of the seas. If unsuccessful in this, the Tsar would use his influence to bring the Baltic countries and Portugal into the Continental System.* The Tsar would be allowed to take over Finland and parts of Turkey; France would extend the System to virtually continent-wide limits.

Such was the gist of the great treaties of Tilsit. Superficially, they brought Napoleon to the peak of his power, but beneath the surface grave flaws lurked. The issue of the Grand Duchy would be bound to recur, and Napoleon was also privately determined that Russia should never occupy Constantinople. Much depended on the continuation of Napoleon's personal hold over Alexander; the Emperor regarded Holy Russia as little more than a vassal state—not by any means a partner.

Tippoo Sahib, called Behadour, last Nabob of Mysore (1749–1799). The son of Hyder Ali, the creator of Mysore in India, he was educated by French officers and showed exceptional ability. Between 1777 and 1779 he emerged the victor in several campaigns against the Carnatic and the Mahrattas, and in 1782 he succeeded his father as Nabob. With French backing he expelled British influence from Mysore, but this support disappeared in 1783 with the Treaty of Versailles. The next year he accordingly made peace with Britain. In 1789 he failed to gain a treaty of alliance with France and set about increasing his domains at the expense of the Dutch and the Sultan of Travancore. The British intervened to support the latter. After two inconclusive campaigns, Tippoo found himself faced by the British, the Mahrattas, and the Nizam, and in 1792 he was compelled to sign a humiliating peace. Six years later, when Bonaparte was invading Egypt, he redeclared war but he was soon close-besieged by Lord Harris* in Seringapatam* and he was killed during the final British assault on the city.

Tolentino, treaty of, 19 February 1797. After the surrender of Mantua* Bonaparte found time, while his forces regrouped to pursue the Austrians into the Frioul, to lead an expedition into the Papal States. Invading the Romagna at the head of 9,000 men, Bonaparte soon bullied Pius VI into signing the Treaty of Tolentino, whereby the Papacy agreed to pay the Directory* 30 million francs to avoid "military execution" of its lands.

Tolly, General Barclay de. *See* **Barclay**

Tolstoi, General Ostermann. *See* **Ostermann**

Torgau, sieges of, 10 March–30 October 1813. Situated on the Elbe, the fortress of Torgau had been the scene of a major battle of Frederick the Great in 1760. In early 1813, following the disasters sustained in Russia and Poland the previous year, the French attempted to hold the line of the Elbe against the Russians. Torgau came within Davout's* sector, but the city itself was garrisoned by General Thielmann* at the head of some 6,000 Saxon levies. In the confused political situation prevailing at that time, he refused to admit either side within the city. In April the Allies began a blockade of Torgau, and after Lützen* Ney* was ordered to relieve the city. On 7 May Thielmann—respecting the King of Saxony's desire to retain neutral status—refused to admit Ney's relief column. Napoleon issued an ultimatum to Saxony, requiring, *inter alia*, that Thielmann be ordered to evacuate Torgau and place his men under Reynier's* corps. The King gave way and on 11 May Ney led 45,000 men over the Elbe through Torgau and the Saxon division was incorporated into the French forces, although its commander wasn't. The city's fortifications were modernized by the French, and on 4 October a Prussian force under General Wobeser reblockaded, and eventually occupied, the city.

Torrens, Major General Sir Henry (1779–1828). He was commissioned in 1793 and served under Abercromby* in the West Indies during the captures of St. Lucia and St. Vincent* (1796). Service in Portugal (1798) and the Netherlands

(1799) culminated in his being wounded at Egmont-op-Zee. From 1800–01 he commanded the Surrey Rangers in Nova Scotia. He fought in command of the 68th Foot in the Indian Mahratta wars, and in 1807 took part in the disastrous Buenos Aires* expedition. In 1808 he accompanied Wellesley* to Portugal in the capacity of Military Secretary, and fought at Roliça* and Vimiero.* In 1809 he was made Military Secretary to the Commander in Chief, the Duke of York,* and

in 1812 became an aide-de-camp of the Prince Regent. He was promoted to major general in 1814 and was knighted the next year. In 1820 he became Adjutant General and did much work revising the infantry regulations.

Torres Vedras, the Lines of, 10 October 1810–5 March 1811. The battle of Bussaco* checked the third French invasion of Portugal and won time for the Anglo-Portuguese forces to fall back into the

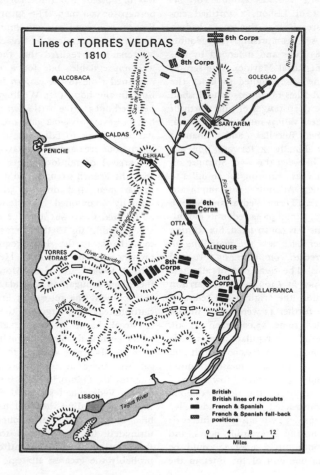

[443]

Lines of Torres Vedras to the north of Lisbon. Protected by the sea to the west and the Tagus estuary to the east, the triple line of forts had been constructed in great secrecy by Colonel Fletcher RE* and his 17 sapper officers, aided by 10,000 local laborers, who had begun their mammoth task in October 1809 on Wellington's* order. The last troops entered the defenses on 10 October 1810.

A total of 108 redoubts in three lines mounting 447 guns had been constructed. The rearward line was around Fort St. Julian, west of Lisbon, a fortified embarkation area in case the troops had to escape by sea, comprising 11 redoubts mounting 83 guns and defended by two battalions of Royal Marines. The second or main line was designed to block the four natural lines of approach to Lisbon through the steep ranges of hills north of the city. These valleys ran through Mafra, Montachique, Bucellas, and Alhandra respectively. Finally, a forward line was established between the river Sizandre on the Atlantic coast, running for 29 miles to the Tagus near Alhandra, with important focal points at Torres Vedras and Sobral. For this line, a total of 32 redoubts mounting 158 guns was constructed. Six to nine miles farther back was the main line already referred to, comprising 65 forts and 206 cannons. The total cost of all these works was put at £100,000. The garrison needed to hold the original 108 redoubts (to which a further 42 were added in late 1810) totaled some 25,000 men in all, mostly Portuguese regular and militia units. The main army (50,000 British and Portuguese troops) was massed around Mafra, ready to march toward any threatened sector of the defenses along specially constructed lateral roads. Five signal stations were established at intervals on dominant and intervisible peaks, and in good conditions a message could be passed from one end of the lines to the

other in seven minutes. Naval flotillas patrolled the Tagus. Ahead of the lines, Wellington had ordered a ruthless policy of "scorched earth" to be implemented to deny the French subsistence, but the length of time Massena* was able to stay near the lines indicates that this was not very thoroughly carried out. Partisan bands roamed the forward hills ready to harass stray French parties.

The French arrived before the lines on 11 October. Massena's Army of Portugal was organized into three corps, totaling perhaps 60,000 men. The surprise of the French was complete—no hint of these daunting preparations had reached them. Massena soon realized that the position was impregnable, but for a month he remained close to the eastern half of the lines in the hope that Wellington might be lured out to give battle. On 15 November, however, Massena gave orders for his starving troops to fall back to the more prosperous area around Santarem. Despite the arrival of reinforcements, by March 1811 the French strength had dwindled to 47,000 men, and on the 5th Massena formally abandoned his offensive when he realized there was no hope of Soult's* army coming up to the Tagus from the east, thanks to the slow progress of the French siege of Badajoz.* He began a retreat toward the river Mondego and thence via Sabugal* to Almeida.* Wellington followed the retreating French with caution, leaving it largely to the irregulars to wreak havoc on the stragglers. The Allies eventually blockaded Almeida and beat off Massena's attempt to relieve his garrison there at the bloody battle of Fuentes de Oñoro.* Thus the Lines of Torres Vedras had served their purpose well—safeguarding the vital base of Lisbon, blunting the French offensive, and ultimately forcing Massena to abandon the invasion of Portugal entirely. It was probably the greatest strategic victory of the whole Peninsular War,* and is often regarded as the turning point in the struggle.

Tott, François, baron de (1733–1793). The son of a Hungarian gentleman, de Tott rose to the rank of captain in the regiment of Bercheny. He emerged to prominence after appointment as secretary to the French minister, Vergennes, and eventually became French Consul in the Crimea, accredited to the Khan of the Tartars. Because of Russian hostility to his policy he was switched to Constantinople, where he reorganized the Sultan's forces to such good effect that they beat off Orlov's fleet from the Dardanelles, which he also fortified (1773–75). He was recalled to France in 1776 and made inspector of all French Mediterranean consulates. In 1779 he was promoted to *maréchal de camp* and appointed Governor of Douai, but in 1790 he became an *émigré** and eventually died in his native Hungary. His plans for a French attack on India were reinstated in 1798.

Toulon, siege of, 7 September–19 December 1793. French forces were everywhere on the defensive when a fresh blow was launched at the cause of the Revolution by the pro-Bourbon revolt in the south of France. First Avignon, then Toulon was infected, and on 28 August the citizens of France's greatest naval arsenal hoisted the Bourbon flag and admitted a force of British, Spanish, and French *émigré** troops under the overall command of Admiral Lord Hood.* The Committee of Public Safety could not ignore this challenge and strict orders were issued for the recapture of Toulon. The first attempts, commanded by unsuitable "political" generals such as Carteaux* and Doppet,* were patently unsuccessful, but the chance arrival on the scene of Captain Bonaparte at a moment when the senior

French gunner had just been wounded in a skirmish was to lead to a rapid improvement in the situation. Backed by the all-powerful *députés-en-mission,** Augustin Robespierre* and Salicetti,* who approved of Bonaparte's strongly pro-Jacobin* political sentiments, he was able to force through his ideas on the correct form for the siege. Promoted to *chef de bataillon* on 18 October, Bonaparte intrigued for the removal of Carteaux and his replacement by Dugommier,* who by mid-November had approved the young artillery officer's plan of operations. At his suggestion, Général du Teil* was also brought in as artillery adviser, and strong efforts made to build up the number of guns and men.

Bonaparte's military appreciation of the situation had convinced him that the key to the defenses of Toulon was the fort protecting Point l'Eguilette—a promontory commanding the outer harbor and the entry to the inner. Its possession would render Hood's fleet anchorage impossibly vulnerable to cannon fire, and he would have to evacuate. On 17 December, after weeks of careful preparation and a few setbacks the assault went in. Within a few hours Fort Mulgrave was in French hands, and before the day was out l'Eguilette was taken, Major Bonaparte receiving a bayonet wound in the thigh in the process. His intuition proved correct. Within a day Lord Hood had raised anchor and departed, conveying his troops and as many civilians as he could cram aboard his vessels with him, while Captain William Sidney Smith* burned and scuttled the captured French naval shipping within the harbor. On the 19th, republican forces reoccupied Toulon to claim the revenge of the Republic.

This was a politico-military success of great psychological importance for the struggling Republic. As a reward for his services the *députés* provisionally pro-

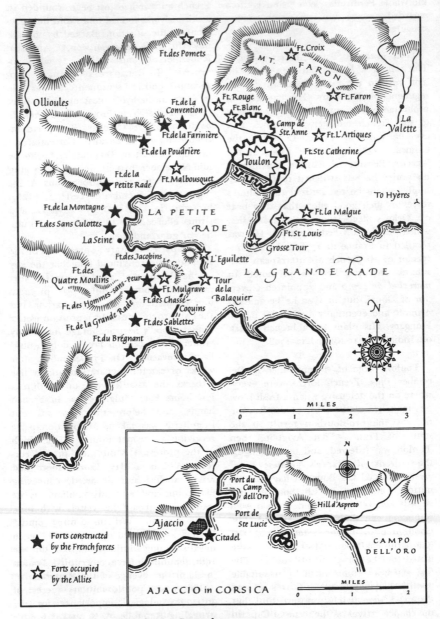

Siege of Toulon, 7 September–19 December 1793

moted Bonaparte to *général de brigade* on 22 December, and Paris in due course confirmed the grade. He was a little over 24 years old, and for the first time his name had been brought to public notice. Ahead of him stretched one of the most astounding careers recorded by history. Many future high commanders also served at Toulon, including Massena,* Marmont,* Suchet,* and Junot.*

Toulouse, battle of, 10 April 1814. Advancing from Tarbes,* Wellington* eventually reached the river Garonne, which was bridged on 4 April 11 miles downstream from the city, which Soult* was preparing to defend with his 42,000 remaining troops. Unknown to any contestant, the main Allied armies had entered Paris on 31 March, and Napoleon was on the point of unconditional abdication (6 April). Wellington had great trouble with his pontoon bridge, and from the 5th to the 8th he had 19,000 men isolated on the far bank, but Soult made no move. However, on the 8th a proper bridge was captured at Croix d'Orade, and soon thereafter Wellington had his 49,000 troops (including 10,000 Spaniards) closing in on the city.

The attack was timed for Easter Sunday, 10 April. Hill* with two divisions was to threaten the St. Cyprien suburb on the west bank of the Garonne, while the main army attacked southward toward the city between that river's east bank and the nearby river Ers. The target was the Height of Calvinet, which commanded the city from the east, but to reach this position involved a two-mile approach march under enemy fire. This unenviable duty was entrusted to Beresford* with the 4th and 6th Divisions, aided by cavalry on the flank. The two Spanish divisions were to attack the northern edge of the ridge, while the 3rd and Light Divisions advanced on the city itself. In all, 36,000

men were allocated to the main series of attacks between the Garonne and the Ers.

Soon after dawn Hill began his diversionary attack against the single division Marshal Soult had left in the St. Cyprien suburb. Hill contented himself with house-to-house fighting on the outskirts, and the street fighting, although intense at times, only cost him some 80 casualties. Picton,* on the northern outskirts, unwisely attempted to storm the fortified position at Pont Jumeaux and was repulsed with 400 men lost. By this time Soult had deployed Darmagnac's division to hold the area between the Languedoc Canal and the northern edge of the Heights of Calvinet, placed the divisions of Harispe and Villatte on the heights themselves, with Taupin's command in reserve, while his brother, Pierre Soult,* massed his cavalry to hold the eastern and southern approaches. A force of newly raised conscripts under General Travot was stationed along the ancient walls of Toulouse.

Beresford's march to turn Soult's right flank was badly delayed by muddy ground, and that general decided to leave his guns with orders to fire on the northeast corner of the ridge. The fire of these guns caused Freire's Spanish divisions, held in reserve, to move prematurely forward in the belief that Beresford's corps was now engaged, which was not the case. Accordingly, they received the full attentions of the French gunners and were driven back in confusion after heavy losses. Fortunately the Light Division was at hand to form a line behind which Freire's men rallied. At length Beresford was in position. The 6th and 4th Divisions ascended the slippery ridge with élan, but were driven back. Wellington rode over to encourage Beresford to make a second attempt, and this time the crest was attained. After a pause to drag up some guns with infinite difficulty, the force began to thrust its way northward, clearing the French from the position. The fighting was bitter. Two redoubts were won only to be lost again, and the 4th Division had to be brought through the ranks of the exhausted 6th to secure the center of the position. The Great Redoubt at the end of the ridge was thereupon evacuated by Soult as he pulled back into Toulouse itself, but the key heights were now in Allied hands and would provide a first-class artillery position once the guns had been brought up. Soult was aware of this, and after holding the town for one more day, at 9:00, P.M. on the 11th he retreated south toward Carcasonne. Next day the Allies entered the city and found it empty. That evening news arrived that Napoleon had abdicated some days earlier.

So ended the last major battle of the long Peninsular War.* It had been a costly one—4,500 Allies were killed or wounded, including 2,000 Spaniards (or 25% of Freire's strength). The hard-hit 6th Division accounted for 1,500 more (again about one quarter of its original strength). Soult had lost 3,236.

Trachenberg Plan, the, of 15 August 1813. This Allied plan emerged from a number of discussions among Russian, Prussian, and later Austrian senior commanders during the last days of the armistice* of 1813. Its main aspect was a decision to avoid direct field confrontations with Napoleon, drawing off when necessary (or feasible), and concentrating instead on inflicting minor defeats on subordinate French commanders.

Trafalgar, battle of, 21 October 1805. As part of his plan for launching an invasion of Great Britain, Napoleon conceived of his blockaded squadrons breaking out from Toulon and Brest, joining with their Spanish allies from Cartagena and Cadiz, and sailing for the West Indies in the hope of luring the Royal Navy's squadrons from the Channel in pursuit.

After uniting in the West Indies, the Franco-Spanish fleet would return to the Channel and win command of the Straits, which would be the signal for the invasion flotillas to put out from Boulogne* and the northeast coasts of France.

After a false start, thwarted by bad weather, Admiral Villeneuve* escaped from Toulon. Nelson* wrongly guessed his destination and waited for his fleet off Sardinia, but then learned on 18 April that his adversary had in fact passed the Straits of Gibraltar ten days before. Adverse winds and supply problems delayed the pursuit, and only on 16 May had Nelson reached Gibraltar. Even then a convoy had to be seen safely into the Mediterranean. At last, after learning that Admiral Cornwallis* was in full strength watching the Channel approaches, Nelson could head for the West Indies. Arriving there, faulty information sent him toward Trinidad; in fact Villeneuve, after contacting Gravina's* Spaniards from Cadiz, had sailed west only to double back toward Europe the moment he heard that Nelson was on his trail. Learning this, Nelson sent a fast brig back to England—which actually passed the Franco-Spanish fleet on passage—to alert the home defenses. Nelson, very disgruntled, returned to Gibraltar and thence to England.

Before he was home, a squadron under Calder* had fought an indecisive brush with the returning Villeneuve, who sought shelter in Ferrol. While Nelson spent three weeks in England, at Merton and in London, Napoleon was bullying his admiral to put to sea again. Several weeks before Nelson re-hoisted his flag aboard H.M.S. *Victory* on 14 September, Napoleon had abandoned his invasion plans and was planning the transfer of the newly named *Grande Armée* to the Rhine, preparing the campaign that would lead to Ulm* and Austerlitz.* Villeneuve was ultimately forced by Napoleon to put to sea and reached Cadiz, shadowed by Collingwood's* squadron. Learning of this, Nelson became more hopeful of finding a battle. He was soon discussing his tactical plan with his "band of brothers," launching his fleet in two columns (he would have preferred three, one to windward) to break through the enemy's line about one third from its van, thus forcing a pell-mell battle—"that is what I want"—that the superior British training and ship-handling would take full advantage of. Nelson rejoined the fleet off Cadiz on 28 September, confident that the Combined Fleet would soon put out to sea again.

Once again, Napoleon unwittingly played Nelson's game by driving the hapless Villeneuve to leave Cadiz for the Mediterranean, and on 19 October the Combined Fleet put out to sea. Unaware that the main British fleet was over the horizon, Villeneuve was only attempting to drive off Blackwood's blockading frigates—but then could not regain harbor. Soon all 33 French and Spanish ships-of-the-line (18 of them French) were at sea. Nelson, informed by his frigates, headed for the Mediterranean, determined to cut off the foe.

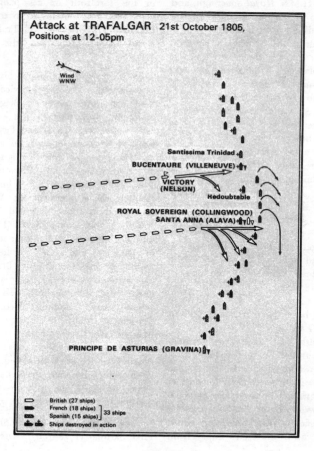

Attack at TRAFALGAR 21st October 1805, Positions at 12-05pm

Wind WNW

Santissima Trinidad
BUCENTAURE (VILLENEUVE)
VICTORY (NELSON)
Redoubtable
ROYAL SOVEREIGN (COLLINGWOOD)
SANTA ANNA (ALAVA)

PRINCIPE DE ASTURIAS (GRAVINA)

British (27 ships)
French (18 ships)
Spanish (15 ships) } 33 ships
Ships destroyed in action

Early on 21 October the two fleets were in sight of one another; Nelson's windward column closed up around him, the leeward section gathered under Collingwood's direction. Villeneuve reversed course, trying to regain Cadiz without a serious fight, but there was little chance of outsailing the cream of the Royal Navy. Nelson retired briefly to his cabin to compose the famous Trafalgar prayer, and then returned on deck to order a signal hoisted to the fleet: In its final form it read "England expects that every man will do his duty."

Shortly after midday Collingwood was in action in H.M.S. *Royal Sovereign,* and soon the rear of the Combined Fleet was fully engaged. An hour later and H.M.S. *Victory,* leading the windward column, was also in action, and the enemy line was pierced as planned. Villeneuve's van was separated from the remainder and could not return to the battle before the issue was decided. Ship after ship of the Franco-Spanish center and rear found itself being pounded by one or even two British ships at a time, and superior gunnery and training were soon wreaking havoc. At 1:15 P.M., however, while close by the *Redoubtable,* the *Victory's* quarterdeck came within the sights of a French sharpshooter—and the unmistakable figure of Nelson, his medals gleaming, was an obvious target. He fell, shot through the shoulder and spine. Carried below, he lived for three hours—long enough to learn that 18 French and Spanish ships had struck their colors and Villeneuve himself had been taken prisoner. Nelson died at 4:30 P.M.

The British had lost 1,500 seamen, killed or wounded, but not a single ship. The French and Spaniards lost 14,000 men and all of 18 vessels. Only four prizes reached Gibraltar, however, as a severe gale blew up off Cape Trafalgar, and it was with difficulty that the victors could save their own battered ships from foundering. But although Trafalgar was irrelevant in the immediate crisis, as the French had long since called off their invasion plans, in the long run it was of the greatest significance. French and Spanish naval pretensions lay shattered, and they would never again constitute a major challenge to British naval supremacy, although Napoleon would make clever use of the remnants of his naval power to keep Britain at full stretch at sea. Nelson's body was brought back to a sorrowing nation and accorded a state funeral and a resting place in St. Paul's Cathedral. His spirit, however, remained in the forefront of his people's consciousness, and remains so to the present day. Every anniversary of Trafalgar, all Royal Navy messes toast "the Immortal Memory."

Trant, Brigadier General Sir Nicholas (1769–1839). After early service with the 84th Foot and the Irish Brigade, with which he took part in the expeditions against Minorca (1798) and Egypt (1801), in 1808 he went to Portugal as military agent and fought with Portuguese troops at both Roliça* and Vimiero* under Wellesley's* control. He soon became commander of a considerable Portuguese force, and in 1809 he joined in the advance to the Douro which led to the battle of Oporto* and was made governor of that city. The same year he was promoted to captain in the British Staff Corps but continued to serve as a Portuguese brigadier general. His irregular forces scored notable successes over Massena's* Army of Portugal as it retreated from Torres Vedras* in late 1810, taking 5,000 prisoners. Next year the Portuguese Regency bestowed a knighthood upon him, but his British military career brought him only one more promotion, to brevet major in 1815.

Troubridge, Rear Admiral Sir Thomas, First Baronet (1758–1807). After entering the Royal Navy in 1773 he served in the East Indies, and in 1794 was for a period a prisoner of war. In 1797 he fought at Cape St. Vincent,* leading the line of battle with great skill. He was less lucky at Santa Cruz and at the Nile,* where his vessel struck a shoal. After posts at Naples and Malta* he was made a baronet in 1799 and a Lord of the Admiralty two years later. In 1804 he hoisted his flag as rear admiral, but in 1807 was lost at sea on H.M.S. *Blenheim* between Madras and the Cape of Good Hope.

His son, Sir Edward Thomas Troubridge (died 1852), entered the navy in 1797, fought at Copenhagen,* and served aboard H.M.S. *Victory* from 1803. He became a rear admiral in 1841.

Troyes, Treaty of, 22 February 1814. Following his series of successes against the army of Silesia in the northeast of France, Napoleon meted out similar treatment to Prince Schwarzenberg's* Army of Bohemia, winning a hard-fought battle at Montereau.* Schwarzenberg and Blücher,* despite the Emperor's intentions, were able to link their armies near Troyes. There a discordant council of war was held, at which the Austrian commander compelled the Tsar and King of Prussia to agree to a further withdrawal. A fulminating Blücher was sent back to command on the Marne, while the other Allies retired on Vandeuvre and the river Aube, thus depriving Napoleon of a near-certain battle on the 23rd. The Allies had clearly not yet learned the need for truly coordinated and united action. As for Napoleon, he believed he had the measure of his opponents, and all remaining chances of a negotiated settlement receded.

Tshitsagov, Admiral Pavel (1767–1849). An able Russian commander on land (his naval title was an honorific Tsarist appointment), he took over command of the forces in Moldavia from Kutusov* when

that general was recalled by Tsar Alexander I* in July 1812. At the end of the month he marched with 35,000 men from Bucharest to fight the French invader, and on 18 September he linked up with General Tormasov on the river Styr near Lourdsk where together they confronted Prince Schwarzenberg,* commanding Napoleon's detached corps on the extreme right wing. The Austrian commander was driven back into Poland to Brest-Litovsk, and thence (after a confrontation on 9 October) over the river Bug to Bialystok. Tshitsagov then maneuvered to capture Napoleon's supply base at Minsk; next he captured the town of Borisov on Napoleon's line of retreat and destroyed the bridges. This led to a great crisis for the *Grande Armée* (or its remnant) that only Napoleon's combination of good luck and military skill enabled it to surmount at the hard-fought battle of the Beresina,* where Tshitsagov was seriously defeated. Thereafter the Admiral followed the retreating French with more caution, but his forces were again mauled by the French IX Corps at Tchovitski on 30 November. The remainder of Tshitsagov's career is shrouded in relative obscurity, but it is known that he died in 1849.

Tudela, battle of, 23 November 1808. As Napoleon drove toward Burgos* and Madrid,* Lannes* was detached to the east to hunt down the armies commanded by Castaños* and Francisco Palafox.* The former had heard that he was being replaced in command on the 18th, and when Lannes attacked five days later at Tudela 70 kilometers west of Saragossa* he found the Spanish forces drawn up in disarray with wide gaps between their formations. A heavy defeat was rapidly inflicted which would have been total had Ney,* on a wide envelopment move with 9,000 men, arrived in time from Soria. As it was the Army of Aragon lost 4,000 casualties. General La Pena's 20,000-

strong Army of Andalusia had been little more than spectators, but at least his force "lived to fight another day" after retreating south into New Castile.

Tugenbund (The League of Virtue), 1808. Formed in Königsberg in the spring of 1808 by a group of Prussian patriots determined to work for the regeneration of national morale and the achievment of ultimate independence after the humiliations of the Tilsit* treaties, this society was run by a Committee of Six. With wide support from intellectuals, it carried out a propaganda campaign against Napoleon. The Emperor typically compelled Frederick William III* to order its suppression, in 1809, but it promptly moved underground. In the early months of 1813 the *Tugenbund* played an important role in Prussia's defection from the French alliance. However, in 1815 the organization was finally suppressed because of its increasingly liberal attitudes toward the future of Prussia.

Turenne, Maréchal-Général Henri de la Tour d'Auvergne, vicomte de (1611–1675). A commander much admired by Napoleon and placed by him among the great seven captains of all time, Turenne was the rival of the great Condé and a Protestant by birth, being a nephew of the great Maurice of Nassau. Wounded at Saverne in 1636, two years later he served with a Franco-Swedish force under Bernhard of Saxe-Weimar. For many years he brought off notable successes against France's Habsburg rivals. Involvement in the Second Fronde in 1650 proved a temporary setback to his career, and in 1653 he had to fight his old comrade and rival Condé, but aided Louis XIV to enter Paris and bring the civil disturbances to a close. At the battle of the Dunes, Turenne and the English Ironsides defeated Condé and the Spaniards. In 1672 he handed out heavy defeats to the Dutch, and three years later he won the battle of Turckheim after having conducted a brilliant winter campaign around Belfort the previous year. He was killed by a cannonball.

Ukase, The Tsar's, of 31 December 1811. This imperial decree of Tsar Alexander* placed heavy duties on all luxury imports into Russia, including those from France. It was in part an attempt to put Russia's chaotic finances in some form of order (an annual deficit of 100 million rubles was being experienced), and in part a deliberate flouting of the Continental System* and an act of defiance against Napoleon. It proved an important step in the long deterioration of Russo-French relations from the peak of Tilsit* to the actual outbreak of hostilities in June 1812.

Ulm, capitulation of, 20 October 1805. The great sweep of the constituent parts of the *Grande Armée* through central Germany from the Rhine to the Danube resulted in the Austrian forces of General Mack* and Archduke Ferdinand* (some 40,000 men) being cut off around Ulm with their links toward Vienna and the approaching armies of Tsar Alexander* severed. The French began to cross the Danube on 7 October, and over the next week Napoleon swung the bulk of his 210,000-strong army so as to converge on Ulm, while strong corps guarded his rear and watched for Kutusov's* arrival from the east. Mack made a number of strong attempts to break out, and tough actions were fought at Haslach* and Elchingen,* but all his efforts proved in vain. Penned into Ulm, and with no sign of the Russians arriving, the two Austrian commanders quarreled, and the Archduke rode out with his 6,000 cavalry to seek safety to the northeast. Mack and his remaining 27,000 men, despairing of relief, and with Napoleon at the gates of Ulm from 14 October, agreed to treat, and on 20 October they marched out of the city to lay down their arms at the foot of the Michelsberg Heights. The Archduke was eventually rounded up by Murat's* cavalry near Trochtelfingen, and a further 12,000 Austrians surrendered at Neustadt. In all, this campaign had cost Austria 50,000 men out of an original force of 72,000—and it forms one of the great examples of the Napoleonic strategy* of the maneuver of envelopment. The *Grande Armée* was soon on the road once more, heading east to seek out the formations of the Tsar.

Ulm, convention of, 17 October 1805. Trapped in Ulm,* General Mack* opened negotiations with de Ségur, the Emperor's representative. Mack demanded an eight-day armistice, but Napoleon only wished to grant one of five days. De Ségur, however, on his own authority agreed to Mack's terms, and an agreement was drawn up whereby Mack would surrender his forces on 25 October if no Russian military assistance had materialized by that date. De Ségur realized that Mack was in every way a beaten man, and in the end that general surrendered five days ahead of schedule on 20 October after learning of the capitulations of detachments at Heidenheim and Neresheim.

Undaunted, H.M.S. This British brig-of-war carried Napoleon and his suite from

St. Raphael to exile in the island of Elba* in April 1814. She sailed at 11:00 A.M. on the 28th and anchored off Porto-Ferrajo on Wednesday, 4 May. Napoleon disembarked at 2:00 P.M.

Usagre, battle of, 25 May 1811. As Marshal Soult* retired with his main army into central Spain leaving a garrison in Badajoz,* after the tough battle of Albuera* against General Beresford,* the French commander decided to send back a strong column under General Latour-Maubourg* to check the pursuing Allied cavalry. Advancing at the head of ten regiments (3,000 men in four brigades), Latour-Maubourg pushed back some Spaniards from Villa Garcia and then encountered General Lumley* at the head of 2,200 men comprising the 3rd Dragoon Guards, the 4th Dragoons, and the 13th Light Dragoons, four small Portuguese regiments, and a detail of Spanish cavalry on 25 May 1811.

The British commander concealed his cavalry with skill behind two rolling heights and watched as the French general sent his main column through the narrow main street of Usagre, which forced him to adopt a restricted front. Meanwhile, Latour-Maubourg also attempted to send a second column to outflank what he took to be Lumley's main position—and allowed his two columns to lose touch. This Lumley noted, and after skillfully positioning his outnumbered forces he proceeded to defeat the French in detail. Reaching the only exit from the town—a narrow bridge over a deep river gorge with steep banks—General Bron rashly advanced over this obstacle with two regiments. Timing his counterattack nicely, Lumley charged this isolated force with his cavalry and routed it utterly. By the time Latour-Maubourg had decided to call off the action, the French had lost 250 cavalry killed and wounded and 6 officers and 72 men taken prisoner. Lumley lost about 20 men. This cavalry action by the British regiments was their most notable achievement since Sahagun* and Benavente.*

Uxbridge, Field Marshal Lord Henry William Paget, first Marquis of Anglesey and second Earl of (1768–1854). Educated at Westminster School and Christchurch College, Oxford, Paget served in Parliament as MP for Carnarvon from 1790–96, and then for Milborne Port, 1796–1810. In 1793 he raised a regiment of infantry from his father's Staffordshire estates, given the number of the 80th Foot at the outbreak of war with Revolutionary France. He fought in Flanders (1794) and in Holland (1799), and commanded the cavalry of Sir John Moore's* army with great distinction in Portugal and Spain during the Corunna* campaign of 1808–09. He won two important cavalry engagements at Sahagun* and Benavente* and helped cover the disastrous retreat over the mountains to Corunna. In 1815 he was in command of the British cavalry and horse artillery under Wellington* and served in this capacity at Waterloo,* where he lost a leg (earning the nickname "One-Leg"). Later the same year he was created Marquis of Anglesey. In 1828 he was appointed Lord Lieutenant of Ireland, but only lasted a year because of his leniency toward the Catholics and his favoring of Catholic emancipation—matters that brought him into conflict with Wellington, now Prime Minister. However, he was reappointed by Lord Grey in December 1830. Back in Ireland, he faced stiff opposition from O'Connell and retired in 1833. In 1846 he was made a Field Marshal.

Valençay, treaty of, 11 December 1813. After the catclysm of Leipzig* Napoleon made a strong effort to clear his hands of the Spanish front. He sent La Forest, former ambassador to Madrid, to visit Ferdinand VII* (interned at Valençay since the Bayonne* negotiations of 1808). La Forest suggested that Napoleon recognize Ferdinand as King of Spain and the Indies, in return for his forcing the British to evacuate the Peninsula and subject to a trade treaty with France; collaborators with Joseph Bonaparte* were also to be pardoned. With some reluctance Ferdinand agreed, and a treaty was drawn up. This was sent to the Spanish Regency, which flatly refused to ratify the terms. Nevertheless, Napoleon decided to free Ferdinand in the hope that once back on his throne he might enforce the agreement, and on 24 March 1814 Ferdinand returned to Spain.

Valetta, battle of. See **Malta**

Valjouan, battle of, 17 February 1814. As Napoleon sought to stabilize the situation on the Seine front, after his virtuoso performance against the Army of Silesia at Montmirail,* Champaubert,* and Vauchamps,* he forced-marched the Imperial Guard* and Grouchy's* cavalry southward to join Victor,* Oudinot,* and Macdonald* near Guignes, where they were being worsted by Schwarzenberg's* Army of Bohemia. Early on the 17th, Gérard* and Grouchy decimated General Pahlen's command at Mormant and then fell upon General Wrede's* advance guard at Val-

jouan. Wrede was trounced in his turn and fell back in disarray from Valjouan to Nangis. Soon Schwarzenberg's offensive was in near-ruin, and despite Victor's poor cooperation Napoleon was soon heading toward Montereau.*

Valmaçeda, action of, 5 November 1808. After defeating General Blake* at Pan Corbo,* Victor* pursued the Spaniards overenthusiastically and in the process his forces became strung out. Blake, reinforced to 24,000 men by the arrival of General La Romana,* suddenly reversed his line of march and swept castward to succor a subordinate trapped in a defile by the French. Early on 5 November Blake attacked General Vilatte, drove him in total disarray from Valmaceda, and rescued his colleague. Vilatte was able to fight his way out in a large square, and was fortunate to lose only 300 men and one gun. Blake was soon in full retreat once more as Napoleon moved up Lefebvre* to envelop the Spaniards, but the Emperor issued Victor a stiff rebuke for his local setback. The Duke of Belluno, however, retrieved his reputation a few days later at Espinosa.

Valmy, battle of, 20 September 1792. At the intersection of the modern *Route Nationale 33* (Châlons-sur-Marne to Ste. Menehoud road) and *Route Nationale 31* not far northwest of Verdun, there stands a windmill and a monument to the elder General Kellermann.* On the bare hillsides around them was fought an action that better deserves the title "cannonade" than that of battle, for the opposing sides never came to grips on a large scale. Nevertheless, the political outcome was of crucial importance to the survival of the French Revolution, and Sir Edward Creasey was justified in including the action in his *Fifteen Decisive Battles of the World.*

In late 1792 it appeared that France was about to succumb to the armies of the First Coalition.* The Duke of Brunswick* captured Longwy and Verdun, severing the links joining the French Northern and Central armies, and it seemed that the politics-ridden French forces could offer no effective resistance. Panic gripped Paris, and the tide of executions of suspects rapidly mounted. Only a horde of ill-disciplined *fédérés* around Châlons stood between the Prussian army and the French capital.

Fortunately for France, General Dumouriez* rose to the occasion. He placed his inadequate troops across the Prussian army's communications near Ste. Menehoud, even though this meant abandoning his own links with Paris. Help was at hand, however, and on 19 September he was joined by General Kellermann (the Elder) at the head of part of the *Armée du Centre;* which brought the total French strength to 35 battalions, 60 squadrons, and some 40 cannon—or perhaps 52,000 men in all.

The Duke of Brunswick (accompanied by King Frederick William III*) moved south and east to eliminate this impudent force blocking the Châlons road, considering that 34,000 men and 36 guns would suffice for the task. The resultant clash would go down in history as the "cannonade of Valmy." The French eventually took up a semicircular position, with General Stengel commanding the right wing, Kellermann the center, and Chabot the left, with Dumouriez in reserve. The morning dawned misty, and the Prussians

loomed out of the fog early on the 20th to capture the village of La Lune from a small French outpost. They then drew up their forces in a line between that village and the hamlet of Somme Bionne, less than a mile from Kellermann's position atop a small hill surmounted by the windmill already mentioned.

Shortly after midday the rival batteries opened fire, the Prussians concentrating their shot and shell against Kellermann's sector, where he had brigaded single battalions of regular troops with two of *fédéré* volunteers in the hope of steadying these raw and inexperienced levies. Rather unexpectedly these troops withstood their ordeal well, chanting *"Vive la Nation! Vive la France! Vive notre général!"*

At about 1:00 P.M. the Prussian grenadiers deployed into line and began to advance but were met with such a hail of fire that they halted after covering only 200 yards. The French cohesion almost snapped when a lucky Prussian shot exploded three ammunition wagons behind the windmill, but Kellermann was at hand to rally the men, and Dumouriez sent forward two fresh batteries to reinforce the shaken sector. The Prussians failed to exploit their fleeting advantage —indeed, the aging Brunswick had already left the field. The action dragged on inconclusively until 4:00 P.M., when heavy rain put an end to hostilities.

Brunswick's seemingly inexorable advance on Paris had been halted, and within a month his forces would be in full retreat for the Rhine. At Valmy the French lost an estimated 300 casualties to the Prussian 180 killed and wounded, but the psychological importance of this limited success was immense, and French national morale quickly rallied. Thanks to Kellermann and his mixed *demi-brigades* and artillerymen, the Revolution had surmounted its first great external military challenge.

Vandamme

Vandamme, Général Dominique Joseph René, comte d'Unsebourg (1770–1830). After early service in a West Indian volunteer regiment, in 1791 he joined a regular French infantry formation. Next year he raised a company known as "Vandamme's chasseurs" and fought in Belgium and Holland. In September 1793 he was promoted to *général de brigade* and later fought under Moreau* at Turcoing and in several sieges. In June 1795 he was suspended for looting and bad language but was re-employed from September. Appointed to the Army of England, he was then switched to Mainz and became *général de division* in February 1799. Sent to the Danube theatre under Gouvion St. Cyr,* he fought at Stockach.* He returned to Holland to serve under Brune,* and he distinguished himself at Bergen and Alkmaar and later, with the Army of the Rhine, at Stockach again and Memmingen (1800). Recalled to France for financial irregularities, he later served for a time first under Macdonald* and then, at the

Camp of St. Omer, under Soult.* With IV Corps he played a vital part in storming the Pratzen Heights at Austerlitz* (1805), but after falling out with Soult was attached to the Staff in 1806. Then, under Ney,* he commanded Württemberg troops before Madgeburg* and Glogau, and before Breslau commanded two corps under Jerome Bonaparte.* Administrative posts at Lille and Boulogne followed, together with appointment as comte d'Unsebourg (1808). In 1809 he fought in Austria with VIII Corps at Abensberg,* Landshut,* and Eckmühl,* and commanded VII Corps, in place of Augereau,* at Wagram* where he was wounded. After a further spell at Boulogne, in 1812 he commanded the II and VIII Corps under Jerome in Russia, but was sacked for brigandage in July. Next year he fought under Davout* at Hamburg* and Magdeburg and took part in the action of Kulm* where he was taken prisoner. Interviewed by Alexander I* and charged with looting, he riposted that "At least I have never been accused of killing my father." He survived his imprisonment in Russia, however, and in 1814 returned to France, only to be exiled to Cassel by the Bourbons. He rallied to Napoleon during the Hundred Days,* being made a peer of France on 2 June, and then commanded III Corps under Grouchy* during the invasion of Belgium, fighting at Ligny* and Wavre.* During the retreat he commanded the rear guard back to the Loire. Again exiled by the Bourbons, he spent the years 1816–19 in the United States before returning to France, via Belgium, in December 1819. He was granted retired status in 1825. A blunt, venal, rough-spoken soldier, he was very loyal to Napoleon and was possibly unfortunate not to receive his baton. "So it is that I," he once stated, "who fear neither God nor Devil, tremble like a child when I approach him."

Vandeleur, General Sir John Ormsby (1763–1849). From 1781 to 1792 he served as an infantry officer but then exchanged into the dragoons. He fought in Flanders (1794–95) and the following year took part in the expedition to the Cape of Good Hope. In 1798 he was promoted to lieutenant colonel. Years of distinguished service in India followed (1803–05). Posted to the Peninsula under Wellington,* he commanded an infantry brigade in 1811 and a division in 1812–13, and then a brigade of cavalry. In 1815 at the battle of Waterloo* he commanded the 4th Cavalry Brigade on the Allied left flank and played an important part in steadying the center at the crisis of the battle. He was knighted in 1816, and in due course was promoted to full general (1838).

Vanstabel, Contre Amiral Pierre Jean (1744–1797). Born at Dunkirk, he served at sea during the American Revolution. In 1793 he was promoted to *capitaine-de-vaisseau,* and in command of the frigate *La Thetis* captured, burned, or sank 40 sail of British merchant shipping. On 12 November the Representatives provisionally promoted him to rear admiral, an appointment confirmed four days later. Commanding a squadron of the Brest fleet he successfully conveyed 170 grain ships from the U.S.A. into French ports in June 1794. He was appointed to command at Brest the next month, but was then sent to mount a naval descent on the Island of Walcheren,* during which he successfully forced the defenses of the river Scheldt.

Vaubois, Général Charles Henri, comte de Belgrand de (1748–1839). Commissioned into the French Royal Artillery in June 1770, he emerged in 1791 as a lieutenant colonel of volunteers. He served in the Army of the Alps and in September 1793 was promoted to *général de brigade.* He served at the siege of Lyons later that year, and in 1796 he was promoted to *général de division,* again in the Army of the Alps. Transferred to the Army of Italy, he took part in the siege of Mantua* and captured Livorno. Taking over command of Sauret's* division, he fought at Roveredo.* In January 1797 he was sent to Corsica and in May 1798 joined Bonaparte at sea en route to Malta,* where he took possession of the Old City of Valetta. Appointed commandant of Malta, he withstood a long British siege inspired by Captain Ball RN, but capitulated in September 1800. Returning to France, he was retired the next year. In 1808 he became a Count of the Empire, commanded a division of National Guards in 1809, and raised more units in 1812, but he did not rally to Napoleon in 1815.

Vauchamps, battle of, 14 February 1814. Following hard upon his successes at Champaubert* and Montmirail,* Napoleon learned that an enemy force had driven Marmont* out of Etoges. Calculating that the commander must be General Wittgenstein,* he realized that Blücher* must be short of troops under immediate command. Accordingly, leaving Mortier* to pursue the discomfited parts of the Army of Silesia away to the north, Napoleon marched overnight, leaving Chateau Thierry at 3:00 A.M. at the head of the Guard and Grouchy's* cavalry to join Marmont and bring the French strength in the area of Vauchamps to 25,000. Early on the 14th Blücher had advanced four miles toward Montmirail when he encountered strong French outposts near Vauchamps. With only 20,000 men under Generals Kleist,* Kapzevitch, and Ziethen,* the aged field marshal soon found his cavalry driven from the field and then discovered from a prisoner that Napoleon was approaching in person. His one hope of survival was precipitate retreat. The Prussians and Russians withdrew in good order, harassed by the French cavalry, which periodically got ahead of the Allied

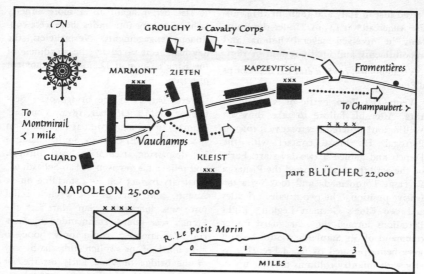

Battle of Vauchamps, 14 February 1814

columns. Fortunately for Blücher, the wet state of the ground hindered the deployment of the French guns and infantry, and he slipped away through Etoges. Napoleon halted the pursuit beyond that town and awarded his exhausted men a short rest. The events of the 14th had cost the French some 600 casualties; Blücher's losses were 7,000 men, 16 guns, and a mass of transport. The Emperor had now completed the discomfiture of the Army of Silesia and could turn his attentions against Schwarzenberg* and the Army of Bohemia to the south.

Vedel, Général Dominique Honoré Antoine Marie, comte de (1771–1848). Born at Monaco and the son of a royal officer, he enlisted as a private soldier in 1784 and was first commissioned in 1787. Under the Revolution he served in the Armies of the Center, the North, and of Italy (from 1793), and also in Corsica. In 1796, back in Italy, he fought at Lonato* and Salo, as well as at Bassano.* Attached to

Joubert's* division, he was wounded at Rivoli* in January 1797. He continued to serve in Italy until late 1799, when he was posted to the Army of the Grisons in Switzerland. From 1803–05 he was present at the Camp of St. Omer and then under Suchet* fought in the Danube Campaign. Vedel was briefly a captive at Ulm,* then fought at Austerlitz* and became *général de brigade* in December. In 1806 he fought at both Saalfeld* and Jena.* Wounded in the knee at Pultusk* in December 1806, the next year he fought under Lannes,* was twice wounded at Heilsberg,* and again at Friedland.* In November 1807 he was promoted to *général de division* and sent under Dupont* to Spain. There he obeyed his superior's order to rejoin him on 16 July 1808 and was forced to share in the capitulation of Bailen.* This brought him disgrace on his return to France. He was imprisoned from November 1808 and tried before a special court headed by Cambacérès.* He was reappointed to command in late 1813 and served first in Italy and then, in 1814, under Augereau* at Lyons. Under the Bourbons he received several honors and appointments, and finally retired in 1831.

Vendémiaire, *coup d'état de. See* Coups d'Etat

Venta Del Pozo, battle of, 23 October 1812. After his failure to take Burgos,* Wellington* ordered a retreat west toward Portugal. He broke contact with the French and gained a two-day start. Early on the 23rd the Army crossed the Pisuerga River at Torquemada and took up a defensive position. The two cavalry brigades and two King's German Legion* Light Battalions formed the rear guard under command of Sir Stapleton Cotton*—and were being pursued by 6,000 French cavalry with infantry columns moving up in support.

A near-disaster befell the rear guard at Venta del Pozo, as it was crossing a dry riverbed across a narrow bridge. Cotton ordered his troop of Royal Horse Artillery (commanded by Captain Norman Ramsay* of Fuentes de Oñoro* fame) to site their guns to sweep the bridge, and placed his rifle battalions for a similar role. Unfortunately Anson's cavalry brigade, after crossing safely, swung in front of the guns and the infantry, completely masking their fire. This gave the French their chance, and before Bock's* cavalry brigade could charge to prevent it, large numbers of French cavalry had swarmed over the bridge. A stationary sword and saber contest took place in restricted space. Then a force of French dragoons, who had crossed the riverbed higher up, charged down into the fighting mass on the British left flank. Both British cavalry brigades were forced to flee for their lives, but the two light battalions of the Legion saved the day by forming squares to receive cavalry, and inflicting 300 casualties upon the French horsemen. Behind the squares Cotton reformed his cavalry, and the retreat could

at last begin again in a more orderly fashion, but for four miles there were continuous engagements. Nevertheless, the day had been saved by the steadiness of the King's German Legion in a moment of crisis.

Vera, battles of the bridge of, 1 September and 7 October 1813. The preliminary to the main combat took place on 1 September 1813, when Soult* made a last despairing attempt to break through and relieve his garrison at San Sebastian.* That city in fact fell to a storming on 31 August, and part of the French relief force was defeated at San Marcial;* the French rear guard, commanded by General Vandamme,* could only hope to cross north of the swollen Bidassoa by way of the bridge of Vers. Early on the 1st September, 10,000 French troops approached the town from the south. The northern end of the bridge was defended by just 70 riflemen of the 95th under Captain Daniel Cadoux, and the nearest aid was Skerett's Brigade of the Light Division a full mile away. At 2:00 P.M. the French attempted to rush the bridge, killing the two sentries, but Cadoux's intrepid garrison repelled attack after attack, killing General Vandermaisen. The French were fairly trapped, but unfortunately Skerett declined to come to Cadoux's aid and ordered him to retire, which he refused to do; apart from the two sentries, he had amazingly suffered no casualties. He held his positions all night, but ran out of ammunition early on the 2nd. He then set out to obey Skerett's orders and retire, but in the open suffered 16 casualties—and was killed himself—while another 45 received wounds. The French accordingly were able to escape the trap, but were forced to leave all their guns south of the river.

On 7 October, during the crossing of the Bidassoa* operation, a diversion was planned from Maya by the 6th Division while four brigades of Allied troops launched a major attack northward over the river at Vera. The ridges north of the town were held by General Taupin. The main attack was launched by General Colborne's* brigade up the steep Bayonette Ridge to tackle Star Fort on the first crest. After a terrible struggle of varying fortunes the 52nd stormed the Fort and at once pursued the French to the next crest, which was also taken. Meanwhile Kempt's* Brigade attacked the neighboring Hog's Back; this was taken by the 3rd Battalion of the 95th Rifles, and with it the vital Puerto (or Pass) of Vera—the only direct route in the area leading to the Nivelle Valley—passed into Allied hands. General Longa's Spaniards attacked in the center between the two brigades, and after a series of flank attacks the French abandoned the whole area. Of their original strength of 4,700 the French lost 1,300 men; the Allies sustained 850 casualties out of 6,500 engaged and took 4 guns. On the 8th the Grande Rhune fell, and on the 30th Pamplona*—the last French garrison on Spanish soil—surrendered.

Vergennes, Charles Granvier, comte de (1717–1787). The last truly successful

Vial

minister and statesman of the pre-Revolutionary Bourbon period, Vergennes, a native of Dijon, had a distinguished diplomatic career. Although in eclipse during Choiseul's ministry, he re-emerged in 1771 as ambassador to Stockholm, and then from 1774 became Minister of Foreign Affairs. In this capacity he masterminded France's entry into the War of American Independence, secured the favorable Treaty of Versailles at its end (1783), and brought off such coups as the alliance with the Swiss cantons (1777), the preservation of European peace in 1779 during the crisis centering around Austria, and in 1786 the Franco-British trade agreement.

Vial, Général Honoré, baron (1766–1813). Originally a sailor (1788), he joined the infantry in 1792 and for two years served in Corsica. Transferred in turn to the Armies of the North (1794), of the Alps (1795), and then of Italy (1796–97), he soon attracted Bonaparte's attention and was provisionally promoted to *général de brigade* in August 1796 (confirmed in December). He fought at Arcola* under Massena* and at Rivoli* under Joubert,* and occupied Trent. In 1798 he was made Governor of Rome and then transferred to the Army of the Orient, fighting at Alexandria,* at the Pyramids,* before Acre,* and at the battle of Mount Tabor.* He returned to France in December 1800 and was sent as minister to Naples in 1802. Promoted to *général de division* in 1803, for five years he was French ambassador to Switzerland and then (1809) Governor of Venice. The year 1810 saw him made a Baron of the Empire. In 1813 he commanded a division under Victor* and fought at Dresden* and Wachau, but was killed at the battle of Leipzig.* He had a brother, Jacques Laurent (1774–1855), who was a distinguished cavalry general.

Victor, Maréchal Claude Victor-Perrin, (so-called) duc de Bellune (1764–1841). The son of a notary, in 1781 he enlisted in the artillery as a drummer-boy. In 1791 he served with the National Guard and then as a Volunteer, and soon began to emerge as a leader. From 1792–93 he served with the Army of Italy, distinguishing himself at the siege of Toulon* where he was badly wounded storming a British fort. On 20 December 1793 he was made a provisional *général de brigade* (but was not confirmed in the grade until June 1795).

By that time Victor had spent a year in the Army of the East Pyrenees, but was then posted to Italy to join Massena's* division. There he fought at Borghetto,* Lonato,* Dego,* Roveredo,* and was wounded at San Giorgio. In 1797 he fought at Rivoli* and La Favorita outside Mantua* and then occupied Ancona— being confirmed as *général de division* on 10 March 1797. After a spell under Kléber* he returned to Italy in mid-1798 and later fought at the Trebbia (again wounded), Montebello,* and Marengo,* where he was awarded a saber of honor. From 1800–04 he held high posts in Holland, and in 1805 was sent in a diplomatic capacity to Denmark. Next year he served under Lannes* at Saalfeld* and Jena,* captured Spandau, and later in the year fought at Pultusk.* In January 1807 he received command of X Corps but was taken prisoner near Stettin. Rapidly exchanged, he was given command of I Corps and fought at Friedland.* On 13 July 1807 he was awarded his marshal's baton. He was appointed Governor of Prussia and Berlin and received generous grants of money.

In September 1808 he was created Duke of Belluno. The title arose from a joke by one of Napoleon's sisters, who suggested that he should be called "Bellune" as his nickname was "Beau-Soleil" thanks

Victor

to his open and friendly nature. The name stuck. Meanwhile Victor had arrived to command I Corps in Spain, where he defeated Blake* at Espinosa, fought at Somosierra,* and emerged victorious at Medellin* (March 1809). However he was fairly trounced, alongside Jourdan,* by Wellesley* at Talavera* and again in 1811 by General Graham* at Barrosa* outside Cadiz.*

Victor returned to France in February 1812 but was soon given command of IX Corps for the invasion of Russia. He earned particular distinction for his conduct of the rear guard at the Beresina* during the retreat from Moscow.* In 1813 he fought at Dresden* and Leipzig.* In 1814 he served at Brienne* and La Rothière,* but earned bitter rebukes—and temporary suspension—for his dilatory behavior before the battle of Montereau.* However, he was soon given a Guard command and was badly wounded at Craonne. This ended his active service. In 1815 he stayed loyal to the Bourbons, who made him a peer of France, a Major General of the Royal Guard, and (1821–23) Minister of War. He continued to hold high appointments until his death in Paris, 1 March 1841.

Victor-Amadeus III of Savoy, King of Sardinia (1726–1796). He succeeded to the throne on the death of his father in 1773, and at once reformed the army along Prussian lines and founded the Academy of Turin. Bitterly opposed to the French Revolution,* he afforded asylum to French *émigrés*, including his brother-in-law the comte d'Artois. Not unnaturally he soon attracted French military attention, and in 1792 lost Nice and Savoy. The French invaded Piedmont, and in 1795 his forces suffered a further defeat at Massena's* hands at Loano. Next year, faced by Bonaparte, Victor-Amadeus' forces and their Austrian advisers were defeated at Montenotte,* Millesimo,* and at Mondovi.* This setback led to the signature of the Armistice of Cherasco,* which led to the Treaty of Paris* (18 May). By this instrument he agreed to the cession of Savoy and Nice to France. He died five months later.

Vienna, treaty of. *See* **Schönbrunn,** Negotiations of

Vienna, congress of, 1 November 1814–9 June 1815. After Napoleon's abdication in 1814, Russia, Great Britain, Austria, and Prussia summoned a top-level meeting of statesmen to convene at Vienna, there to settle the shape of post-Napoleonic Europe. Talleyrand,* representative of the Bourbons, played a brilliant diplomatic game to prevent the dismemberment of France, but he was faced by the equally able Metternich.* Despite the public impression of solidarity and gaiety, serious disagreements soon appeared dividing Prussia and Russia from Great Britain, and Talleyrand played upon these prob-

lems to extract the maximum advantage. Nevertheless, the terms of the Treaty of Paris* signed the previous 30 May were gradually worked out in practical terms, and a redrawn map of Europe began to emerge. However, in March news arrived that Napoleon had escaped from Elba,* and soon the powers dropped their diplomatic endeavors to form the Seventh Coalition* and to formally declare Napoleon an outlaw. The last formal session was held on 9 June 1815. The work of the Congress was resumed after Waterloo,* but it represented increasingly the triumph of the reactionary elements in Europe, taking little heed of national aspirations or demographic realities. As a result, many future problems were created and international disputes would soon proliferate.

Villafranca, action of, 3 January 1809. As Sir John Moore* led his ragged and crumbling army back from Astorga toward Corunna* its morale began to crack amid the bitter weather and the pressures exerted by the pursuing French, newly placed under the overall command of Marshal Soult* now that Napoleon had decided to return to France.

After staggering through the narrow streets of Bembibre, the army headed for Villafranca del Bierzo. The rear guard was at this time personally commanded by Sir John Moore. As the main columns of the 25,000-man main army reached Villafranca, where the wine cellars were looted with disastrous results, Moore and the rear guard were holding the bridge over the river Coa at Cacabellos some three kilometers outside the town. He was soon under attack by French dragoons under General Baron Colbert and a sharp engagement resulted borne in part by the 95th Rifles. Colbert was shot down and killed, whereupon the French pulled back, and at 10:00 P.M. the British blew up the bridge and recommenced their retreat. Rifleman Thomas Plunket fired the critical bullet at Colbert.

Moore was so horrified by the rampant indiscipline now prevalent in his army that he had paraded a division in the main square of Villafranca the previous day and made a strong speech about marauding, drunkenness, falling behind, and general indiscipline. Then, to make his point absolutely clear, a cavalryman was hung in front of the division for having broken into a rum store. This salutary lesson had little effect—the excesses continued—but the retreat toward Corunna went on.

Villaret de Joyeuse, Vice Amiral Louis Thomas, comte (1748–1812). Originally a member of the *gendarmes du roi*, the death of a rival in a duel forced him to flee to sea where from 1765 he began a new career. During the 1770s he accumulated great naval experience in the West and East Indies, particularly under command of Suffren. In 1783 he was for a short time a British captive at Madras. In February 1793 he was promoted to post captain, and between that year and 1796 he held high naval command at Brest, becoming rear admiral in late 1793 after successfully escorting into port a large convoy of American grain ships. Next year he confronted Lord Howe* and was badly defeated with the loss of eight vessels at the battle of the First of June.* Nevertheless, he was promoted to vice admiral the same September. In June 1795 he was again worsted by Admiral Bridport* and gave up his command in favor of a political career in the Council of Five Hundred (*Cinq-Cents*).* Proscribed as a crypto-royalist at the *coup d'état* de *Fructidor* in September 1797, he fled to the Isle of Oléron. Reemployed at Brest in 1800, in 1802 he commanded the fleet escorting General Leclerc's* expedition to Santo Domingo*

Villaret de Joyeuse

against Toussaint l'Ouverture.* From April that year he became captain general of Martinique and St. Lucia in the West Indies, a post he held until February 1809 when he was forced to capitulate to a British expedition. Napoleon ordered a commission of enquiry into this failure, and for a time Villaret de Joyeuse lived in semi-exile at Rouen. In 1811, however, he was restored to favor and sent to be Governor of Venice. He had become a Count of the Empire in 1808.

Villeneuve, Vice Amiral Pierre Charles Jean Baptiste Sylvestre de (1763–1806). He first entered the Bourbon naval service (*les gardes-marines*) in 1778 and served under de Grasse in the West Indies (1781–82), sharing in the capture of Tobago. In February 1793 he was promoted to *capitaine de vaisseau*, but was almost immediately suspended as a former aristocrat. Two years later he was restored to active service and became naval chief of staff at Toulon. In September 1796 he raised his flag as *contre amiral*, but sailed too late with his squadron to take part in the Bantry Bay* expedition against Ireland. In 1798 he sailed under Admiral Brueys* with the fleet escorting the Army of Egypt, and at the battle of the Nile* commanded the right wing, escaping to Malta* with two ships-of-the-line and two frigates. On Malta's surrender to the British in September 1800, he briefly became a prisoner of war. In May 1804 he was promoted to *vice amiral,* and in December was placed in command over all naval shipping at Toulon. On 30 March 1805 he set sail for the West Indies to execute Napoleon's plan for the distraction of the Royal Navy from the Channel, and in due course returned to brush with Admiral Calder* off Cape Finisterre before seeking shelter in Cadiz. Charged with cowardice by Napoleon, he sailed against his better judgment and was massively defeated by Nelson* at the battle of Trafalgar,* where he was taken prisoner. Freed on parole in April 1806 he returned to France, only to commit suicide (striking himself six times in the heart with a dagger) to escape the effects of his disgrace.

Villers-en-Cauchies, action of, 24 April 1794. This little-known engagement was in fact an astounding feat by the Allied cavalry forming part of the Prince of Coburg-Saalfeld's and the Duke of York's* army fighting in the Low Countries (1793–95). The Austrian General Ott,* learning that a French force was eight miles northeast of Cambrai trying to raise the Allied siege of Landrecies, collected four squadrons of light cavalry (two British and two Austrian) forming the Duke of York's advance guard, and marched to investigate. Not realizing that the four regiments of heavy cavalry sent in support were delayed, he suddenly found himself facing a large French mounted force with only 300 troopers. News then arrived that the Emperor Francis* and his suite were close by and all too likely to fall into French hands. Ott at once charged the enemy, who were holding a line between the village of Villers-en-Cauchies and a neighboring wood. After scattering a few *chasseurs-à-cheval,* the Allied cavalry were working up their charge when the enemy cavalry to their front wheeled aside to reveal a three-rank-deep line of infantry battalions supported by artillery. Despite the storm of grapeshot and musketballs, the gallant 300 charged home and miraculously overthrew the gunners and *fantassins.* They then fell upon the French cavalry as these tried to re-form in support of their fleeing infantry and soundly drubbed them too, before pursuing them for eight miles to near Bouchain. The French force—an estimated 12,000 men and 50 guns strong (according to the future General Wilson,* whose facts are sometimes a little suspect)—admitted a loss of 1,200 men and three guns. The Allies lost a total of 66 men, killed and wounded. The Austrian Emperor eventually issued a special gold medal to all officers present in this spirited action (and in 1801 Austrian knighthoods were also conferred upon them), including in their number the then newly commissioned Ensign of the 15th Light Dragoons, Robert Wilson.

Vilna, battle of, 28 June 1812. Six days after crossing the river Niemen, Napoleon made a strong attempt to force battle on Barclay de Tolly's* First Army of the West near Vilna. However, the French advance—particularly that of Eugène Beauharnais'* supporting army—had not been speedy enough, owing to the unaccustomed need to bring up supply convoys and to the appalling state of the roads in Russian Poland. Accordingly, the French hopes of securing the central position between the First and Second (Bagration's*) Armies and then forcing a determinant battle were thwarted. Early on the 26th, captured Russian dispatches seemed to indicate that both Tsar Alexander* and the First Army were still near Vilna, and as the French covering army was at last crossing the Niemen at Piloni, Napoleon felt free to act. Early on the 28th Murat* led his two cavalry corps and 60 horse artillery guns in a dash on the city, only to find the Russians in full retreat and the stores and bridges in flames, so only an artillery bombardment ensued. The Russians were out of the trap, and Napoleon had to advance further into western Russia.

Vimiero, battle of, 21 August 1808. As Sir Arthur Wellesley* led his 17,000-man Anglo-Portuguese army southward toward Lisbon following his defeat of General Delaborde's* division at Roliça,* the French Commander in Chief in Portugal, General Junot,* made a rapid advance from the capital at the head of 13,050 men and 24 guns to attempt to surprise the Allies before further reinforcements could reach them from England or Gibraltar.

Junot hoped to outflank the Allied position, but his columns were spotted early in the morning as they moved into position, and Wellesley redeployed his forces from their original sitings (his left being on Vimiero Hill above the village and his center and right on the West Ridge) so as to protect the beaches at the mouth of the river Maceira (today the Alcabrichel). As a result Vimiero Hill became his right center, while five brigades were moved from the West to the East Ridge to form his new center and left, leaving two brigades to form his right wing. In these adjusted positions he awaited the French attack, aware that his superior officer, General Sir Harry Burrard,* was on a vessel anchored off the Maceira.

Eventually Junot launched two sets of attacks against Vimiero Hill led by Generals Thomières* and Kellermann the Younger,* but the French columns were checked and then repulsed by the steady line volleys of the British formations, al-

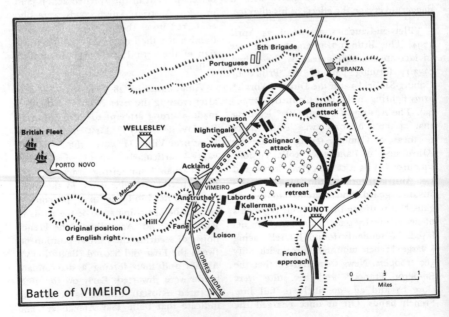

Battle of VIMEIRO

though at one stage a column did penetrate as far as Vimiero village. Wellesley launched the 20th Light Dragoons in a telling charge as the French retired in the center. Unfortunately, despite initial success, this formation charged too far and was decimated at about 11:00 A.M., losing 45 wounded and killed (including Colonel Taylor) and a further 11 taken prisoner out of a total 240 troopers.

Meanwhile the French outflanking force, led by Generals Brennier* and Solignac, was making its delayed approach march, but its attack was poorly co-ordinated with Junot's onslaught against Vimiero village. Two attacks against the hamlet of Ventosa on the Eastern Ridge were driven back with heavy losses. Having sustained over 2,000 casualties (including the loss of 13 guns), Junot fell back toward Torres Vedras. General Burrard, now arrived on the scene, forbade any immediate pursuit even though Wellesley had lost only 720 casualties. Soon an even more senior commander, General "Dowager" Dalrymple* appeared to take over command, and the French were able to negotiate the highly favorable Convention of Cintra,* which permitted them free and assisted evacuation of Portugal with all possessions. This led to a British enquiry that caused all three British senior generals to return to London, leaving Moore* in command.

Vinkovo, battle of, 18 October 1812. The very day that Napoleon made up his mind to retreat from Moscow,* Kutusov* pulled off a considerable surprise against Murat's* unwary cavalry screen near Vinkovo on the river Motsha 30 miles southwest of Moscow. Advancing from Tarutino, the Russian General Denisov and a strong cavalry force surprised General Sebastiani's* cavalry corps and defeated it, capturing six guns. Meanwhile Baggavout* advanced with infantry to attack Murat's center two miles from Vinkovo

and almost captured a defile in the King of Naples' rear. French *carabiniers* and *cuirassiers,* however, fought their way out of the near-encirclement, and Murat managed to bring his shaken force back to Voronovo. News of this setback reinforced Napoleon's determination to lose no time in falling back on Smolensk.*

Vitebsk, battle of, 28 July 1812. After the disappointment of Vilna* Napoleon redoubled his efforts to trap the elusive Russian First Army of the West and force a decisive battle. After actions at Mohilev and Ostronovo,* the Emperor believed the chance for his big battle had arrived but delayed by one day to allow reinforcements to arrive. During this short pause Barclay de Tolly,* realizing that Bagration* would not reach him with the Second Army of the West, decided to pull out again to the east. Thus, when the French advanced in strength on the 28th they found only a Russian rear guard holding Vitebsk—and once again the Russians had eluded the intended trap. Napoleon was now in possession of the important gap between the rivers Dvina and Dnieper, but he still needed a victory. Soon his men were on the road to Smolensk.*

Vitoria, battle of, 21 June 1813. Following his retreat from Burgos* via Venta del Pozo,* Wellington* wintered in Portugal, absorbing large reinforcements from England. In late May he led 30,000 men with Lord Hill* toward Salamanca once again, while the trusted General Graham* took some 40,000 troops on a long enveloping march through the Tras os Montes Mountains and region to the north, crossing the Douro and Esla river lines to continually make successive French defensive lines untenable. For the first two weeks in June, his main army now north of the Douro, Wellington followed the retreating French over the northern plains of Spain. He decided not to force battle south of the Ebro, but sent Graham with 20,000 men on a third great "hook" to the north, this time through the Cantabrian Mountains over rough tracks. King Joseph* and Marshal Jordan* ultimately gathered the remains of three French armies, some 50,000 men with 153 guns, behind the river Zadorra near Vitoria, intending to win time for their huge army trains to get clear toward the French frontier. Through an oversight, they neglected to destroy the river's bridges.

Stage by stage Wellington brought up 70,000 men and 90 guns, his army including all of 27,500 Portuguese and almost 7,000 Spanish regulars. The battlefield would extend for over eight miles; given the wet conditions of the day, it is amazing how any form of control was exercised over so vast an area, but Wellington was now at the peak of his martial form and had great faith in his key subordinates. Hill was to start an early attack from the south over the Zadorra to gain control of the steep Puebla Heights* dominating the main road to Burgos and Madrid; Wellington was to command the center of the army to the southwest; Graham was to bring his corps up over the mountains to form the left and try to cut French links with Irin, Bayonne, and Pamplona.

Hill's attack started at first light. A flanking column of Spanish troops worked their way around to the east as Cadogan's* brigade and some Portuguese painfully ascended the steep hillsides. At the crest they met General Gazan's* division that had just arrived there from the northern side. From 8:00 A.M. a fierce battle raged; Hill, for heavy losses, became master of the heights and held them against several tough counterattacks designed to regain the terrain and recapture the key village of Subijana de Alava—all in vain.

In the center the opening of the battle was delayed, as part of Graham's corps was late, but at about midday a peasant came to Wellington and revealed that there were no French guarding the bridge at Tres Puentes, which was well shielded by a convenient height. Kempt's* brigade was at once ordered to secure a bridgehead on the farther side. At about the same time Picton's* 3rd Division arrived on the scene from the north; growing impatient at the inaction, he took it upon himself to carry out orders intended for Dalhousie's* 7th Division, still delayed to the west, and crossed the river at Tres Puentes and Puente de Mendoza farther east. Here the troops found themselves attacking the flank of two French divisions with large batteries, but all French attention had been engaged in the fight proceeding against Hill, and soon Picton and Kempt between them had the French battle line in retreat. Gazan re-formed his line to try to keep control of the key Knoll of Ariñez,* but the arrival of the remainder of the Light Division and the 4th from over the Zadorra bridges again tipped the balance in the Allied favor and by 3:00 P.M., after a stiff combat around Ariñez, Picton, Kempt, and part of Dalhousie's newly arriving division, all under Wellington's personal command, stormed both the knoll and village. The French thereupon began to retreat on Vitoria, halting for a time along a low ridge near Armentia in the hope of giving some of the confused mass of refugees and baggage wagons time to get clear of the city.

Meanwhile Graham had advanced on the left from the direction of Bilbao through Murguia with two Anglo-Portuguese divisions and Colonel Longa's Spanish force under command. Longa fooled General Reille* into believing that he was simply a partisan leader, and this gained Graham time to launch a sudden

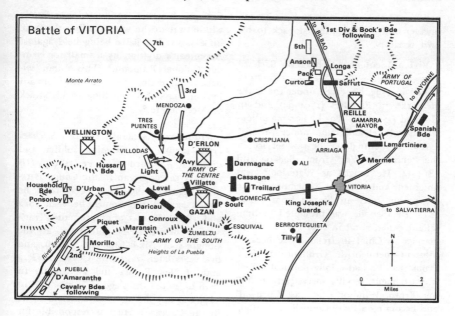

surprise attack on the hills overlooking the villages of Gamarra Mayor and Menor and Abachuco and the key Zadorra bridges beyond them. The Anglo-Portuguese stormed the ridge and soon took Gamarra Mayor, and another force occupied nearby Abachuco. In desperate fury the French tried to retake Gamarra Mayor, but in vain. Soon Graham was approaching the Zadorra bridges, but he was thwarted in securing a crossing by two well-sited French divisions that stood their ground with skill and courage for most of the afternoon. Only when Wellington's center broke through did these troops give ground, but Graham had in fact achieved his main purpose: Longa's guns, sited north of the Zadorra at Puente de Durana, effectively closed the old "Royal Road" toward Bayonne* to French traffic, forcing Joseph and Jourdan to order a pell-mell retreat toward Pamplona to the east. By late afternoon the battle was

gloriously won; it had cost Wellington some 5,000 casualties to inflict 7,500 on the French who now fled, abandoning fabulous masses of booty around Vitoria —the loot of six years of occupation. Jourdan's baton was found and sent off to England for the Prince Regent, who promptly returned the compliment in kind, thus promoting Wellington to the rank of field marshal.

The pursuit of the French was hampered by looting, slack discipline, and heavy rain; the marauding on this occasion gave rise to Wellington's famous remark about "the scum of the earth as common soldiers. . . ." However, this great, climactic battle once and for all cost the French Spain, although much fighting remained to be done around San Sebastian,* Pamplona,* the Pyrenees,* and in the south of France before the Peninsular War* was finally won. However, the great struggle of Spanish Independence was almost over, and the French invader and despoiler forced back to his own territory.

Vivian, Lieutenant General Sir Richard Hussey, Baron (1775–1842). First commissioned in 1793, he served under the Duke of York* in Flanders (1794–95) and in Holland (1799). In 1804 he became a lieutenant colonel and later, under Moore* and then Wellington,* he saw service in the Peninsular War* from 1808–09 and 1813–14. He fought at Waterloo,* was knighted, and served as a member of the occupation force in France from 1815–1818. In 1827 he was promoted to lieutenant general and in 1831 became Commander in Chief in Ireland. He became Master-General of the Ordnance in 1835. From 1820 he had a long political career in Parliament, serving successively as MP for Truro, Windsor, and East Cornwall and becoming a Privy Councillor in 1835. Already made a baronet in 1828, he was created Baron Vivian in 1841, the year before his death at Baden-Baden.

Voltri, combat of, 10 April 1796. As Bonaparte was preparing to launch his first campaign in North Italy, General Beaulieu* unexpectedly attacked the outlying brigade of General Cervoni* stationed at Voltri, ten miles west of Genoa. Two Austrian columns marched down the Bochetta Pass and Turchino Valley to envelop and destroy the French force.

Cervoni, however, conducted a masterly withdrawal to the west, eluding the trap, his exposed left flank being held against Argenteau's division by a small force under Colonel Rampon.* This minor setback induced Bonaparte to bring forward by four days the launching of his attack on Montenotte.*

Voronzov, General Prince Michael (1782–1856). This Russian soldier and diplomat was born at St. Petersburg. His military career began in the Caucasus region, fighting the Turk, and later he served against the French between 1812 and 1814. He was appointed the Tsar's special Minister-Plenipotentiary at the Congress of Aix-la-Chapelle (1818), and five years later was made Governor General of New Russia and Bessarabia. In 1828 he raised the siege of Varna, and in 1844 was appointed Commander in Chief in the Caucasus. He was responsible for building the greater part of the defenses of Sebastopol.

Voronzov, Count Semen (1754–1832). Russian diplomat of distinction, Voronzov was the Tsar's ambassador to London in 1789. Later he was instrumental in assisting Pitt* to create the Third Coalition* (Russian participation being assured through the Treaty of St. Petersburg of April 1805). He spent the last years of his life in England.

Wagram, battle of, 5–6 July 1809. After the *Grande Armée* had occupied Vienna (13 May) Napoleon had fought the unsuccessful two-day battle of Aspern-Essling* and been forced to retire to Lobau Island and the south bank of the Danube to reconsider his plans. The Archduke Charles* did nothing to follow up his success, and Napoleon was able to spend the next six weeks converting Lobau into an impregnable base for future operations, linking it to the southern bank by three well-protected and constantly patrolled bridges. During this period he also lost no time in summoning up outlying formations, including those led by Eugène Beauharnais* and Macdonald,* from the Italian front, and by early July no less than 188,000 French and Allied troops and 500 guns were in the vicinity.

Napoleon proved on this occasion that he could still learn from his mistakes, and the second crossing of the Danube was meticulously planned, with nothing left to chance. So it was that on the stormy night of 4/5 July a pontoon bridge was swung over the water separating Lobau Island from the north bank and troops were soon pouring over—to the great surprise of the Austrians, who had been lulled into a false sense of security by the previous weeks of apparent inactivity. At this juncture the Austrians had some 155,000 men and 450 cannon at their disposal in the Marchfeld area. The Archduke had anticipated a French attack, if at all, near Aspern, but Napoleon's crossing farther east near Gross-Enzersdorf completely fooled him. Although two

corps became entangled, Napoleon's master-plan continued to unroll and his army wheeled north and west, driving before them the ill-coordinated parts of the Austrian army which tried to intercept their line of march. By evening the French were in control of a vast salient some 15 miles long, extending from Aspern to Wagram in a great curve. Bitter fighting on the northern flank, where the Archduke Charles personally led up the reserve grenadiers to check the French advance near Gerasdorf, ended the day's battle, and both Commanders in Chief settled down to plan the morrow's events while the rank and file slept fitfully under arms, with frequent interruptions. Napoleon's main preoccupation was with how to win the victory on the 6th before the Archduke John could appear from the east, near Pressburg, with his 12,500 men.

Early the next morning it was the Archduke Charles who boldly seized the initiative. He started by a determined attack near Aderklaa, which defeated Bernadotte's* IX Saxon Corps, and Napoleon promptly sent Bernadotte off the field in disgrace. Meanwhile, Davout* was beginning the major French attack—an attempt to turn the Austrian left flank near Markgrafneusiedl—when Charles launched his main effort against the opposite French flank. This move caught Napoleon by surprise, and soon Boudet was reeling back in disarray. The links with Lobau Island seemed in peril, but Napoleon ordered Massena* to disengage from near Aderklaa and to march south to bolster the French left. This dangerous maneuver

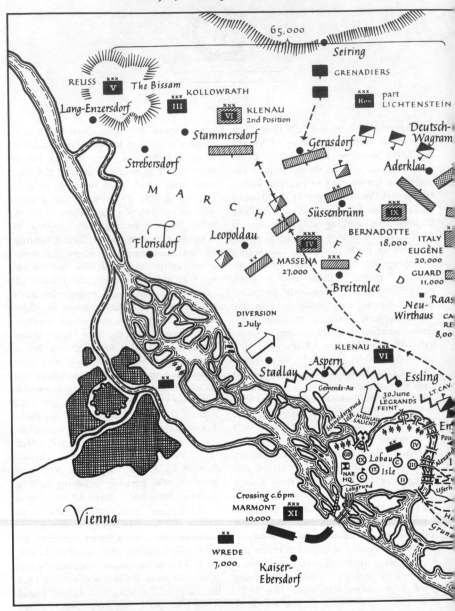

65,000

REUSS
V
The Bissam
KOLLOWRATH
III
Lang-Enzersdorf
VI
KLENAU
2nd Position
Stammersdorf
Streberdorf
Seiring
GRENADIERS
Res
part
LICHTENSTEIN
Deutsch-
Wagram
Gerasdorf
Aderklaa
IX
M A R C H
Süssenbrünn
Florisdorf
Leopoldau
BERNADOTTE
18,000
ITALY
EUGÈNE
20,000
IV
F E L D
MASSENA
27,000
GUARD
11,000
Breitenlee
Neu-
Wirthaus
Raas
DIVERSION
2 July
Stadlay
Aspern
Gemende-Au
KLENAU
VI
Essling
LT. CAV.
30 June
LEGRANDS
FEINT
En.
MÜHLAU
SALIENT
GD
IX Lobau
Isle
NAP
HQ
Lobgrund
IV
III
II
Crossing c.6pm
MARMONT
10,000
XI
WREDE
7,000
Kaiser-
Ebersdorf
Vienna

Battle of Wagram, 5–6 July 1809: Day One

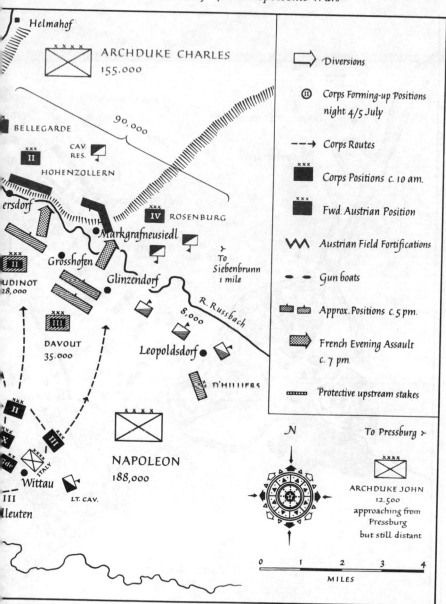

Helmahof

ARCHDUKE CHARLES
155,000

Diversions

Corps Forming-up Positions
night 4/5 July

BELLEGARDE

90,000

Corps Routes

CAV.
RES.

Corps Positions c. 10 am.

HOHENZOLLERN

Fwd. Austrian Position

ersdorf

Austrian Field Fortifications

IV   ROSENBURG

Markgrafneusiedl

Gun boats

Grosshofen

To
Siebenbrunn
1 mile

II

Glinzendorf

Approx. Positions c. 5 pm.

UDINOT
28,000

R. Russbach

French Evening Assault
c. 7 pm.

III

8,000

DAVOUT
35,000

Leopoldsdorf

Protective upstream stakes

II

D'HILLIERS

X

NAPOLEON
188,000

N

To Pressburg

Gde

ITALY

Wittau

ARCHDUKE JOHN
12,500
approaching from
Pressburg
but still distant

III

LT. CAV.

leuten

0   1   2   3   4
MILES

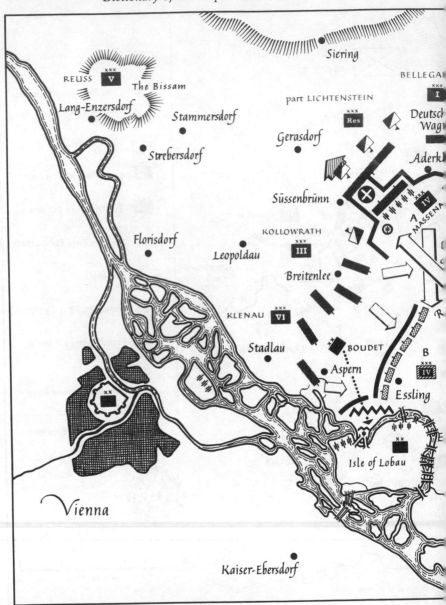

Battle of Wagram: Day Two

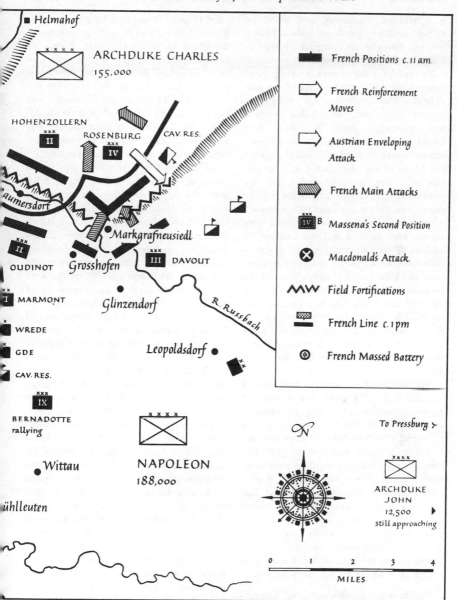

- Helmahof

ARCHDUKE CHARLES
155,000

HOHENZOLLERN
II

ROSENBURG
IV

CAV. RES.

aumersdorf

II

OUDINOT

Markgrafneusiedl

Grosshofen

III DAVOUT

MARMONT

WREDE

GDE

CAV. RES.

Glinzendorf

R. Russbach

IX

BERNADOTTE
rallying

Leopoldsdorf

Wittau

NAPOLEON
188,000

N

To Pressburg

ARCHDUKE
JOHN
12,500
still approaching

ühlleuten

	French Positions c. 11 am.
	French Reinforcement Moves
	Austrian Enveloping Attack
	French Main Attacks
IV B	Massena's Second Position
X	Macdonald's Attack
MW	Field Fortifications
	French Line c. 1 pm
	French Massed Battery

0 1 2 3 4
MILES

was brilliantly executed, and aided by massed artillery fire from Lobau Island, Massena brought the Austrian advance to a halt in the nick of time.

Meanwhile Davout was making good progress on the northern flank of the battlefield. The Austrian left wing was pressed back, and judging his moment with customary care, Napoleon then launched Macdonald's corps in a determined attack toward Gerasdorf against the hinge of the Austrian line. Fighting rose to a new intensity and a gap appeared in the French battle-line in the center, but this was plugged by a massed battery of 112 guns rushed forward from reserve and manned in large measure by soldiers of the Imperial Guard.* Macdonald's great attack slowly gathered momentum, and Charles could not withstand the pressure. His army was eventually split in two and the battle was lost for the Austrians. The Archduke John had not arrived in time to affect the issue, and when at 4:00 P.M. he at last made an appearance from the south it was to find the battle already lost.

Nevertheless, the Austrians had exacted a heavy price. Napoleon lost a total of 39,500 casualties (including 40 generals and some 7,000 prisoners), 4 eagles, and 21 guns. The Archduke Charles lost approximately 40,000 men and 20 guns, but the campaign had not many more days to run. Wagram, then, was a costly if ultimately decisive French victory, and Napoleon did Macdonald justice by awarding him his baton as a *maréchal* for his part in the battle, while the tireless Berthier,* mastermind of the crossing timetable on the 5th, added the title of Prince of Wagram to his many honors.

Walcheren, expedition to, 11 August–30 September 1809. In an attempt to create a major distraction in northern Europe, the British government sent a combined force of 40,000 troops under Lord Chatham* escorted by 35 sail-of-the-line and 23 frigates to make a landing on the island of Walcheren, part of Zealand in Holland at the extreme southwest of the archipelago in the Scheldt waterway, guarding that great river's entry into the North Sea. The town of Flushing* was captured on 13 August, but then the incompetent Chatham—a great courtier but no commander—made no attempt to exploit his indubitable initial success; instead of marching upon Antwerp, which would almost certainly have fallen to his arms, he kept his troops in deadening inactivity, preoccupied with supply problems, which gave the French and Dutch time to react. Fouché,* Minister of the Interior, appointed Bernadotte* (after his disgrace at Wagram*) to command the defense of Antwerp, and his troops were soon able to form a continuous front sealing off Walcheren—albeit with formations containing a high proportion of National Guard units. Soon the ravages of "Walcheren Fever" (a form of malaria) were decimating the British ranks amid the dykes and polders. Ultimately, on 30 September Chatham re-embarked his force, having lost 106 men killed in action and all of 4,000 dead through disease.

The original hope that this landing would result in a general German uprising against Napoleon proved wholly fallacious. Canning* resigned from the British government and fought his celebrated duel with Castlereagh,* while the Walcheren Enquiry soon began to implicate the royal family by producing details of the Duke of York's* mistress's involvement in the sale of commissions. Nevertheless, the Walcheren expedition also spread a fair measure of alarm throughout France's maritime provinces, and at least contributed to the war effort by causing large numbers of troops to be tied down in coast-watching duties.

Walewska, Marie, Countess (1789–

1817). This beautiful woman entered Polish history by becoming Napoleon's lover in early 1807, shortly after the French occupation of Warsaw. Offered up by her compatriots as a living sacrifice to the Emperor, she ended by becoming genuinely attached to him, and he to her, and the liaison continued on a sporadic basis for a number of years. The birth of their illegitimate son, Alexandre Florian Joseph, on 4 May 1810, is believed to have been one factor in deciding Napoleon to seek a divorce from Josephine* on the grounds of her infertility. Marie retained an affectionate loyalty to Napoleon to the end of her days, and in 1814 visited him on Elba.* She received the nickname of "the Emperor's Polish Wife."

Wallace, General John Alexander Dunlop Agnew (1775?–1857). First commissioned in 1787, he had become a captain by 1796 and received a lieutenant-colonelcy in 1804. Between 1789 and 1796 he served in India. In 1798 he took part in the attack on Minorca and then accompanied Abercromby* to Egypt, fighting at the night battle of Alexandria* and other actions (1801–02). From 1809 he fought with distinction in the Peninsular War,* earning special honor at the head of the 88th at Bussaco,* where he in large measure organized the repulse of Merle's* division of Reynier's* corps in the center of Wellington's* line. "Wallace," commented the Viscount, "I have never witnessed a more gallant charge." He also distinguished himself at Fuentes de Oñoro,* again at the head of the Connaught Rangers, recapturing the village with the bayonet. In 1819 he was promoted to major general; he was knighted in 1833, and finally attained the rank of full general in 1851.

Wallis, Admiral Sir Provo William Parry (1791–1892). Born at Halifax, Nova Scotia, he served at sea for all of 53 years,

Marie Walewska

having entered the Royal Navy as a midshipman in 1804. Promoted to lieutenant in 1808, he fought in the celebrated naval action between H.M.S. *Shannon* and the U.S.S. *Chesapeake* in 1813. The same year brought him promotion to commander, and in 1819 he became a post captain; in 1851 he hoisted his flag as rear admiral. After taking part in the Crimean War he was knighted in 1860, and ultimately became Admiral of the Fleet in 1877. Living to the ripe old age of 101 years, he holds the record for longevity among soldiers and sailors who fought in the Napoleonic wars and subsequently attained high rank.

Walter, Général Frederic Henri, comte (1761–1813). Enlisting as a hussar in 1781, he was first commissioned in 1789. Wounded at Neerwinden* in 1793, he transferred to the Army of the Alps where he was promoted to *général de brigade* in October 1793. In 1796 he commanded the cavalry attached to Augereau's* division of the Army of Italy. In 1700 he fought at Stockach* and next year, under Lecourbe, fought at Moesskirch on the Rhine and then with great distinction at Hohenlinden,* where he received his second wound of the campaign. In 1803 he was sent to Holland, and in August was promoted to *général de division,* taking over command of the cavalry attached to the Camp of Bruges. In 1805, commanding a dragoon division, he fought at Höllabrunn* and was wounded at Austerlitz.* On 8 February 1806 he was appointed a Chamberlain to the Emperor, and in May was given command of the Horse Grenadiers of the Imperial Guard.* At their head he served in Prussia and Poland, taking part in the great charge at Eylau.* In 1808 he became a count and the next year he commanded the Guard Cavalry at Wagram;* he fought throughout the Russian Campaign of 1812–13. His last campaign was fought in Saxony and his final battle was that of Hanau.* Three weeks later he died at Kusel on 24 November 1813.

War of 1812, the (1812–1815). This struggle was caused by a rise in tension between the United States and Great Britain over two main issues: the British claim to the right of search* on the high seas of neutral vessels suspected of carrying contraband or strategic materials to France and her allies; and American ambitions to assimilate those parts of Canada adjacent to the Great Lakes and the St. Lawrence River. Both were issues of considerable importance.

The war opened on 18 June 1812 with a small-scale American incursion over the Canadian frontier. This was driven back, and on 15 August in reprisal a British force captured Fort Dearborn (on the present site of Chicago) after a preliminary occupation of Fort Mackinac the previous month. At Detroit General Hull surrendered with 2,500 American militia-men to Major General Benjamin Brock's 700 Canadian and 800 Indian allies led by Chief Tecumseh on the 16th of the same month.

The next American invasion attempt in October met with little better success. General van Renselaer attempted to cross the Niagara River into Canada at Queenston on 15 October at the head of 900 regular troops and 2,270 militia. The shortcomings of the militia system, which was unpopular with the individual states, were again demonstrated when the militiamen, after watching the regulars cross over by boat, refused to follow them on the grounds that they were only contracted to serve on United States territory. In the ensuing battle of the Queenston Heights, Brock (at the head of 600 British regulars and 400 Canadian militia) inflicted 250 casualties and took 700 prisoners for minimal loss. Brock, however, was killed. The same story of U.S. militia intransigence was repeated in November the same year when an unsuccessful attempt was made to cross Lake Champlain.

In an attempt to interdict further American raids of this nature, General Proctor led an Anglo-Canadian and Indian force onto American soil early in 1813 to attack training camps commanded by General Harrison. This attack notwithstanding, by September Harrison had 7,000 reasonably trained troops available, but could not move to recover Detroit until naval control of Lake Erie was secure. By mid-1813 an American flotilla had been extemporized, manned by sailors from the seaward states, and on 10 September Commodore Perry,* employing Harrison's riflemen as marines, defeated the British flotilla on Lake Erie, and thus opened the way for a major American offensive. Harrison passed most of his men over Lake Erie on Perry's vessels and sent his Kentucky Mounted Riflemen around the shores of the lake and marched on Detroit, forcing Proctor to fall back into

Canada. Harrison caught up with him near the Thames River and on 5 October attacked Proctor's 800 regulars and 1,000 Indians. When Tecumseh was killed his braves fled the field, whereupon Proctor surrendered.

Meanwhile, on the eastern sector, General Pike had led an American force of some 1,600 men to burn York (modern Toronto), and in May Commodore Perry and Colonel Winfield Scott mounted a joint amphibious attack on Fort George guarding the mouth of the Niagara River and stormed the timber-built fort after inducing the defender, General Vincent, to retire his 700 men from the position by threatening to place 4,000 men across his lines of communication with the interior. The retreating British were pursued in a lackadaisical fashion by Generals Chandler and Winder, who allowed themselves to be surprised and defeated when Vincent suddenly rounded upon them. British fortunes were still none too bright at this juncture, for when Sir John Prevost, Governor General of Upper Canada, made an amphibious attack on Sackett's Harbor* he was repulsed by General Jacob's small garrison in ignominious fashion. To exploit their overall advantage, the Americans sent a force under General Wilkinson down the St. Lawrence and another under General Wade Hampton from Lake Champlain in a converging attack against Montreal, where a British army of 15,000 was gathering. Hampton was fooled into abandoning the enterprise by a small British force which sent out buglers into the woods to simulate the arrival of large bodies of troops, and accordingly retreated to Plattsburg for the winter. Wilkinson pressed on down the St. Lawrence with 8,000 men but was then routed in a model engagement at Frayser's Farm by a mere 800 British regular troops and Indian scouts. He, too, then retired into winter quarters. The British meanwhile captured Fort Niagara and un-

leashed their Indian braves to harass the American settlements, while General Drummond burned the township of Buffalo and destroyed the Black Rock navy yard.

Wilkinson's reputation was now shattered, and by order of the U.S. Congress he was replaced in April 1814 by General Jacob Brown. His program of training converted a rabble into a presentable force, and in early July 3,500 regular U.S. troops crossed Niagara River once again, captured Fort Erie, and defeated General Riall at the head of 1,700 British regulars at Chippewa, Winfield Scott's gray-coated regular brigade particularly distinguishing itself, and establishing the precedent for the full-dress uniform worn by the cadets at the U.S. Military Academy at West Point. British morale suffered as a result of this fresh setback. By this time, however, the British government was taking the situation seriously, and considerable numbers of Peninsular veterans, now available following Napoleon's first abdication, were arriving in, or on their way to, Canada. The first clash between the newcomers and General Jacob Brown came on 25 July 1814, when 3,000 British troops under General Sir Gordon Drummond came upon the Americans at the battle of Lundy's Lane*—perhaps the severest action of the war. It began in the early afternoon and raged on until long after nightfall, both sides claiming success. Both commanders were among the wounded, General Riall was taken prisoner, and each side lost about 900 casualties. However, it was the Americans who conceded the strategic advantage, falling back to Fort Erie where they were besieged by Drummond until 17 September, when a determined sortie broke through the surrounding troops. This proved the last major engagement on the Niagara front, and the Americans in due course abandoned Fort Erie.

By this time the British forces were

taking the initiative. As part of a complex strategy, in September General Prevost advanced from Montreal down Lake Champlain at the head of 14,000 Peninsular veteran troops to attack the American position around Plattsburg*—the last major obstacle blocking the route to the Hudson Valley. He was faced by only 1,500 regular American troops assisted by 3,000 militia under General Macomb, and he combined a frontal assault with a naval action against the gunboats and flotilla protecting Macomb's flank. The land assault was successful, but the naval engagement ended in complete success for the Americans, the British flotilla being compelled to strike its colors. This event ended the danger of a serious British invasion from the north, and Prevost withdrew his men in disorder, abandoning many of his stores.

The previous month had seen the landing of General Ross with 5,000 experienced troops in Chesapeake Bay. Against only minimal opposition, this force set out to march the 40 miles to Washington. The Americans—6,500 militia backed by 400 sailors and marines under command of General Winder—tried to hold up the British advance guard at Bladensburg on 24 August. The militia fled, and the naval gunners, after offering a spirited resistance, also had to abandon the position. On the 25th British troops burned down the White House and other public buildings. Flushed with success, Ross re-embarked his men and landed 14 miles from Baltimore on 12 September, intending to repeat the operation. He was faced, however, by a well-entrenched and determined body of Maryland militia, which beat off his attacks, during one of which Ross was mortally wounded. Fort MacHenry also underwent a British naval bombardment of considerable severity, but withstood the ordeal successfully. Thus a second part of the British offensive against the United States petered out.

There remained one last effort to be made. During the past two years contacts had been made by British agents with Creek Indians in Alabama, and a fierce struggle had been waged against these new British allies by Colonel Andrew Jackson. In late 1814 the newly promoted General Jackson was put in charge of the defense of New Orleans against a British expedition of 14,250 of Wellington's* best troops under command of the Duke's brother-in-law, General Sir Edward Pakenham. Convoyed from Jamaica by the Royal Navy, Pakenham landed on 13 December and pushed his advanced post to within seven miles of New Orleans, where he encountered an extemporized earthwork position extending from the Mississippi River to a swamp. Massively outnumbered though he was, Jackson harassed the British camp with night attacks over the period of a fortnight, these attacks raising the morale of his hybrid force, which comprised only 700 regulars, some Tennessee and Kentucky frontiersmen, a few New Orleans militia, and a party of Gulf pirates and privateers under their colorful leader Lafitte. When on 8 January Pakenham attempted a frontal assault with 5,300 men, the battle of New Orleans* led to the Americans inflicting no less than 2,000 casualties on the British, whose dead included Pakenham and two other generals. Jackson had lost only seven killed and six wounded. The British attack on the further bank of the Mississippi made some progress, but after the disaster on the east bank the British withdrew to their encampment and Jackson was content to see them go, attempting no pursuit.

In fact the war was already over when the battle of New Orleans was fought. On 4 December the Peace of Ghent* had been signed in Europe, but news of the pacification had not reached New Orleans before the climactic action had been fought. The battle of New Orleans holds a special and deserved place in American folklore, and in the person of Andrew Jackson the best commander of the war had emerged. Now this rather scrappy but drawn-out struggle, much of which had been fought out at sea (see the entry on "Naval War") in a series of celebrated frigate duels, had come to an unmourned conclusion. Neither side emerged from this struggle with much credit, only Brock and Jackson earning notable reputations. However, the national integrity of both the United States and Canada had been reasserted, and the raising of the British Orders in Council* with the ending of the Napoleonic Wars removed another source of longstanding grievances and opened the way for a rather happier period of British-American relations.

Waterloo, battle of, 18 June 1815. Three days after crossing the Sambre onto Belgian territory, and two days after the battles of Quatre Bras* against Wellington* and Ligny* against Blücher,* Napoleon fought and lost the most famous battle of modern history—Waterloo.

Late on the 17th Napoleon and his reserve had joined up with Ney's* left wing of *l'Armée du Nord,* leaving Grouchy* to take his two corps in pursuit of the defeated Prussians, who were ultimately located near Wavre.* Thus early on the 18th, Napoleon had 72,000 men (49,000 infantry, 15,750 cavalry, 7,250 gunners) and 246 guns at his disposal, while Grouchy had 33,000 men and some 80 guns about ten miles to the east. Facing them at first light were Wellington at the head of initially 68,000 Allies (only one third of them British) and 156 guns— 50,000 of his men being infantry and 12,500 being cavalry—and Blücher in command of 89,000 Prussians and 92 guns. Soon the latter was moving west to join up with Wellington at the head of three of his four corps (or 72,000 men and 44 guns), leaving General Thielmann* with just 17,000 and 48 guns to defy the French right wing over the Dyle at Wavre. Wellington relied upon Blücher to reinforce him on the ridge of Mont St. Jean by the late afternoon—and only on this assumption was he prepared to offer battle to Napoleon on the chosen ground.

The battlefield of Waterloo is small, stretching only four miles from east to west and perhaps two and a half miles from

Waterloo—Charge of the Scots Greys (North British Dragoons)

[481]

north to south. It is bisected by the Charleroi to Brussels highway, and Napoleon's aim was to be in the Belgian capital by nightfall. Wellington's position lay along the ridge of Mont St. Jean a mile south of his headquarters in the village of Waterloo, with three outposts stationed at the Château of Hougoumont (to the west), the farm and gravel pit of La Haie Sainte (on the highway), and the farms and hamlets of Papelotte and La Haie (to the east adjoining the Bois de Paris, linking the battle area to Wavre). These advance posts were held by the Guards' Light companies, part of the King's German Legion, and the 95th and Nassau troops respectively. His two main corps, commanded by Hill* and the Prince of Orange,* were interlaced along and behind the ridge, with the main force of cavalry under Uxbridge* in central reserve. A strong force had been stationed at Hal to the west to ward off the danger of a French envelopment, and the wedge-shaped configuration of the overall Allied battle line reveals the Duke's reliance on Blücher's arrival to reinforce his left wing. Many of his men were raw troops or former French Allies, and much would depend on the Prussians arriving in time.

Napoleon delayed opening the battle to allow the ground, made sodden by the previous night's heavy rain, to dry out, and this was in part Wellington's salvation. While the Allies dried out their muskets and equipment, the Emperor drew up his two main corps left (Reille*) and right (d'Erlon*) of the highroad along another low ridge running through La Belle Alliance. Massed cavalry was placed in the rear of each wing, and in central reserve stood Lobau's* VI corps and the Imperial Guard* with more cavalry; at about 11:30 A.M. the massed guns began to fire. Most of Wellington's men, on his order, were lying down behind the crest and so missed much of the fire, but By-

landt's Belgo-Dutch brigade left out in the open near the crossroads atop Mont St. Jean was decimated.

The French plan was simple—excessively so. After the initial bombardment and a diversionary attack by part of Reille's command against Hougoumont, d'Erlon's four divisions were to advance to pierce Wellington's (left center), after which the cavalry and reserves were to pour through the gap and head for Brussels amidst the shattered remnants of Wellington's army. There was scant subtlety in this scheme. Another error—as it proved—was to entrust the overall battle command to Marshal Ney.

The fighting comprised six main phases. First, the bombardment, which proved of little value; next, Jerome Bonaparte's* division of Reille's corps advanced against Hougoumont at about 11:30 A.M. This attack was supposed to distract Wellington's reserve to meet the threat, but in fact it achieved the opposite. A few extra companies of Guards were fed forward to reinforce the brave garrisons of the Château and its orchard, but by 1:00 P.M. all of two and a half French divisions had been drawn into the action. At one point the French broke into the central courtyard but were soon expelled, and even when the buildings were set on fire by French howitzer-fire in the midafternoon the British grip on the position never slackened. This, therefore, proved the first French fiasco of the day, and the last fighting of the day, like the first, was in the Château vicinity.

Meanwhile, at 1:30 P.M., the third phase of the battle had opened, as d'Erlon advanced to the attack. Shortly before this juncture, a captured Prussian courier had made Napoleon aware that Prussian forces were marching to Wellington's aid, and the Emperor ordered the VI Corps to march east and create a defensive flank from near Fichermont to the village of

Plancenoit, facing the Bois de Paris. Ney then launched d'Erlon forward. Through confused orders, three of his four divisions adopted a huge outdated formation that invited massive Allied artillery fire and duly received it. Then his men came up against Picton's* veteran division holding the hedgerow on the crest, and although that general was killed, the French attack petered out. A check became a bloody defeat as Uxbridge launched his cavalry into the hesitating masses, and soon d'Erlon's command, save one better-deployed division, was a mass of fugitives. The Scots Greys captured a French tricolor, and so did the Household Brigade charging on their right, but the former then attacked the French grand battery and were decimated as they tried to regain the Allied lines by Jacquinot's fresh lancers. Thus Wellington lost a full third of his cavalry—but the French grand attack had failed.

Major Baring* and the garrison of La Haie Sainte were all this time undergoing heavy attacks from General Alix's division, but held their position through thick and thin. About 3:30 P.M. Napoleon was watching the first indications of the arrival of Bülow's* IV Corps opposite Plancenoit when Ney launched a furious cavalry charge against Wellington's right center in the belief that he was evacuating his position. The cavalry attacks escalated until most of Napoleon's cavalry were involved, but the failure to send forward infantry and horse artillery supports, the sodden nature of the ground, the narrow funnel of ground between La Haie Sainte and neighboring Hougoumont, and above all the steadiness of Wellington's infantry squares and gunners resulted in another complete French failure, and Ney's cavalry was ultimately routed. The survivors were extricated on Napolcon's order by the remaining French horsemen with great difficulty, the rescue being led by Kellermann* at about 5:30 P.M. So Wellington, although some of his squares were battered, survived a second major crisis, and fighting was already escalating around Plancenoit, where Bülow had now been joined by Pirch's corps and Blücher in person. The fighting for the village swayed this way and that, but the French regained it and stabilized the situation only when Napoleon sent the Old Guard supported by most of the Young Guard to retake Plancenoit with cold steel. However, this meant that all the Emperor's reserves were committed.

The fifth phase began at about 6:00 P.M. The defenders of La Haie Sainte ran out of ammunition just as Ney at last led up a properly coordinated attack of infantry, cavalry, and guns, and the farm at last passed into French hands, together with the sand pit. Ney rushed a battery of guns up the highroad and soon was bombarding at point-blank range some Hanoverian battalions, already very shaken by the earlier cavalry attacks. The main crisis of the day had now come for Wellington. With his center visibly wavering before the storm of shot and shell, he could only extemporize some support by bringing over Vandeleur's* cavalry from the far left, which formed a single line of horsemen behind the shaken battalions. Ney was now bombarding the Emperor with requests for the Imperial Guard to be sent up to clinch the victory—but of course it was presently deployed facing Plancenoit and it took time to regroup even part of it ready to assail Wellington's center. In the hour that passed, the Duke received news that Ziethen's* I Corps was fast approaching his left wing (having mercifully been found by Baron Muffling* and redirected toward the crisis), and this made it possible to divert Allied infantry units to shore up the center.

At about 7:00 P.M. the sixth stage of the action opened with the dread approach of almost a dozen battalions of the feared Imperial Guard. Led up by first Napoleon and then Ney, for some undisclosed reason their two mighty columns veered west of La Haie Sainte and came up against Wellington's right center—where his steadiest infantry lay waiting in the corn. "Now, Maitland,* now's your time," called out the Duke. The scarlet lines of British Guardsmen rose out of the corn, and soon devastating volleys were pouring into the French Guard from three directions. Meanwhile, to wring a last effort from his other surviving troops, Napoleon had spread the deliberate falsehood that the newcomers appearing from the northeast were Grouchy's men, not Prussians. However, as the Guard began to reel downhill, so too did the newcomers open fire on the French, and the dreaded word "Treason" flashed through the French ranks, followed by the equally devastating phrase, "*Sauve qui peut!*" In an instant the whole French line began to disintegrate. Judging his moment with great nicety, Wellington charged his whole line with a spine-chilling cheer, and soon Allied bayonets were speeding the French flight as Blücher's Prussians also poured up from Plancenoit to threaten Napoleon's line of retreat. The Old Guard performed prodigies of cool valor, trying to cover the flight of their compatriots, but the day was irretrievably lost. Napoleon was persuaded to make good his escape toward Genappe, where he narrowly avoided capture by Prussian hussars.

Shortly before 9:00 P.M., as the light faded, Wellington met Blücher near the Emperor's former command post adjoining the inn of La Belle Alliance. The pursuit, led by the fresh Prussian cavalry, thundered off into the dusk and continued for most of the night. The Allies had lost 22,000 men to win this victory, but these losses they could absorb. Napoleon had lost 41,000 men, almost all of

them irreplaceable veterans. More, he had lost his reputation once and for all, and although he talked of new armies and more resistance, his political credit in Paris was exhausted. Ahead lay only renewed abdication and exile on St. Helena.*

Wattignies, battle of, 15–16 October 1793. The French armies of Carnot* headed for the Channel coast in the early autumn of 1793 intent upon relieving the garrison of Dunkirk. This done in September, the French turned toward Maubeuge, where the Prince of Saxe-Coburg at the head of 40,000 troops was besieging the last fortress barring the Allies from the road to Paris. Carnot ordered Jourdan* to take 50,000 men to avert this threatened cataclysm at all costs, and on the 15th they advanced against the Allied position, 26,000 men strongly drawn up on a plateau near Wattignies. The raw troops of the poorly organized French forces were driven back with considerable loss by the evening, but overnight Jourdan redeployed 8,000 men from his thwarted left flank to reinforce his right, facing Wattignies village. This enabled the French to outflank the Austrian left, and when the battle reopened early on the 16th it was not long before the Allied line was being rolled up. Saxe-Coburg and Clarfayt abandoned the siege of Maubeuge, recalling 14,000 men from the trenches, and fell back toward the Rhine intent upon entering winter quarters. So Paris was again saved, as it had been in September 1792 at Valmy.* The French lost an estimated 8,000 casualties and inflicted possibly 5,000.

Wavre, battle of, 18 June 1815. Napoleon prepared to attack Wellington* at Waterloo,* so Grouchy,* commanding the corps of Gérard* and Vandamme,* prepared to attack the Prussians facing him over the river Dyle between the towns of

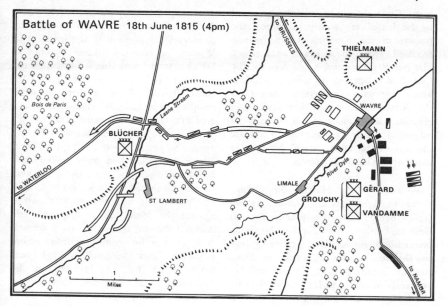

Battle of WAVRE 18th June 1815 (4pm)

Wavre and Limale. Although he was aware that from first light Blücher* was thinning out his forces and sending the greater part of them westward through the Bois de Paris toward distant Plancenoit, Grouchy insisted on obeying his last orders, which were to attack the Prussians where found. So, as the noise of battle opened up in the far distance, he refused his corps commanders' plea that he should "march on the sound of the guns" in the manner of Desaix* at Marengo* in 1800, and instead started a series of heavy attacks with his 33,000 men and 80 cannon against Thielmann's* rear guard of 17,000 men supported by 48 guns. The Prussians clung grimly to their positions despite the numerical odds, and bitter fighting raged around the bridge at Limale as Grouchy tried to storm over. However, the Prussians held out, covering Blücher's transfer of 72,000 men to Wellington's aid, and only at 5:00 P.M. did Grouchy receive an order from Napoleon recalling

him to the main army's aid. By that time it was far too late to intervene effectively, so Grouchy held his ground, and after a further burst of action on the morning of the 19th, began to fall back in good order when news of Waterloo's outcome arrived. He had lost 2,500 casualties and inflicted as many.

Weissenfels, action of, 1 May 1813. Fearing that the Allied army might take flight as the full might of the French army advanced toward Lützen,* Napoleon ordered his incomplete forces to press ahead to give Wittgenstein* no alternative but to accept battle. As part of this advance to contact, the Emperor ordered the III Corps and the Cavalry of the Imperial Guard* to march from Weissenfels on Lützen itself, supported by two divisions of VI Corps. So it was that Bessières* and the III Corps of Ney* entered onto a broad plain in some peril of being overwhelmed by the Allies, but when General Winzingerode* attempted to use his allies' cavalry to contest the passage of the Rippach stream he was repulsed. However, a round shot struck Marshal Bessières and killed him on the spot. The infantry of VI Corps, including many raw young conscripts, fought off the Russian cavalry in fine style, and Napoleon made much of this aspect of an otherwise minor engagement to inspire the rest of the army. Ahead lay the far more serious battle of Lützen.

Wellesley, Field Marshal Sir Arthur, Duke of Wellington, Viscount Douro (1769–1852). Born the fourth son of Garrett Wesley, First Earl of Mornington, who taught music at Trinity College in Dublin, he was educated at Eton, Brussels (1784), and a French military academy at Angers (1786). A delicate child, he shone at playing the violin and (like Frederick the Great*) showed few early signs of military proclivities; he was very much overshadowed by the brilliance of his elder brother Richard, later Marquess Wellesley.* He received a commission in the infantry in 1787 and became a Captain of Dragoons five years later. From 1787 to 1793 he served as aide-de-camp to the Lord Lieutenant of Ireland, and became MP for Trim (1790–95). Thanks to his ability to purchase them, his military promotions came very quickly: he became Lieutenant Colonel of the 33rd Foot in 1793 and next year commanded the regiment in the Duke of York's* Netherlands Campaign, fighting at Boxtel* and in general learning "what one ought not to do, and that is always something." Shocked by the general ineptitude of his brother-officers, from 1795 he began serious study of the military profession.

In 1797 he was sent with the 33rd to India, and in 1798 he was put in command of an expedition by his brother Richard, the new Governor General. In 1799 he commanded a division in the invasion of Mysore, committed some errors at Seringapatam,* and after being appointed governor of the town, quarreled with Sir David Baird.* These problems notwithstanding, his military competence and gifts as a civil administrator as well as his physical toughness (encouraged by an austere way of life) were developing apace. Illness prevented him from sailing with Baird for Egypt in 1801, but next year he was promoted to major general, aged 33. In 1803 he won two notable battles against the Mahrattas at Argaum* and Assaye,* showing those qualities of shrewdness, an eye for ground, careful reconnaissance, and personal courage that would reach full development in the Peninsular War.* He also came to appreciate the importance of logistics and began to pay much attention to everything connected with military supply. In civil affairs he set about purging local administration of tyranny, corruption, and double-dealing, and in the process made not a few enemies.

Resigning his Indian appointments, in 1805 he returned to England and married Catherine Pakenham, daughter of Lord Longford, which proved rather an unhappy match. A chance meeting with Nelson* in Downing Street impressed him with the sailor's ability beneath the bluster and vanity. In 1806 he became MP for Rye (and then successively for Mitchell and Newport), and he was (from 1805) in command of a brigade assigned to protect southeast England from the apparently impending French invasion. From 1807–09 he was appointed Chief Secretary for Ireland, but in 1807 he commanded a division in the expedition to Copenhagen* of that year, defeating a Danish force at Kiöge.

In 1808 he was promoted to lieutenant general and appointed to command the expedition sent to sustain the Portuguese. Thus began the series of campaigns that would finally establish his reputation as one of Britain's finest soldiers. After landing at Mondego Bay* he defeated General Delaborde* at Obidos* and Roliça* and then General Junot* and the main French army at Vimiero.* Superseded in command by Burrard* and Dalrymple,* he agreed to the terms of the Convention of Cintra* and was recalled with them to London to face an enquiry, from which he emerged without a slur or stain. Meanwhile Sir John Moore* conducted the Corunna* campaign in Spain, and in April 1809 Wellesley resumed command over the British forces in the Peninsula at Lisbon. Taking the offensive, he defeated Soult* at the daring river-crossing battle of Oporto* (on the Douro/Duero) and cleared the French out of Portugal. Later that year, lured by Spanish promises of cooperation, he advanced into Spain and fought with Cuesta* at Talavera,* a victory that earned him a viscountcy. Disillusioned with the Spaniards, however, he soon withdrew into Portugal. The ensuing Campaign of 1810 saw his triumph over Massena,* Ney,* and Junot. After checking their advance toward Lisbon at Bussaco,* Wellington (as he should now be called) retired into the carefully prepared Lines of Torres Vedras.* As a thwarted Massena retreated (1810), Wellington followed him up, blockaded Almeida,* and won the battle of Fuentes de Oñoro.* By now his officers' somewhat gloomy feelings for him had changed to full trust and admiration, and "Old Hookey," or "that Bugger that beats the French" was also greatly respected (but hardly loved) by his rank and file. Already, too, his fine appreciation of the realities of campaigning in the Peninsula

had led him to plan a deliberate strategy* based upon the Spanish guerrillas,* and a system of logistics was also being developed. Reorganizing the army into permanent divisions and incorporating Portuguese formations trained by Beresford,* he was fast creating a devastating, self-sufficient army. Meanwhile he had detached the trusted Graham* with a command to help sustain the Spanish government, besieged in Cadiz.*

Trying to secure the southern corridor into Spain, he reinforced Beresford (victor of Albuera*) at Badajoz, but was forced to abandon the siege on the advance of Marmont* and Soult in conjunction. He then moved north to besiege the northern-corridor fortress of Ciudad Rodrigo* but was once again thwarted by Marmont and Dorsenne. Much fighting took place along the river Coa, and Hill* led small forces to achieve successes such as Arroyo dos Molinos* and Maguilla, but in many ways most of 1811 proved frustrating. In January 1812, however, the capture of Ciudad Rodrigo* was followed with the bloody storming of Badajoz* in April, and at last the army was in a position to prepare a major offensive into Spain. As Napoleon withdrew troops in preparation for the invasion of Russia, so Wellington planned a devastating blow and ultimately launched the campaign that, after a month's maneuvering around the river Tormes, led to the great success of Salamanca* (July) over Marmont. However, the newly appointed Earl (for Ciudad Rodrigo) unwisely marched on Madrid, and consequently when he turned to besiege Burgos* he was repulsed and had to retreat rapidly as Soult and Souham* approached; he returned to winter in Portugal near Ciudad Rodrigo, establishing headquarters at Freinedas. Over the winter months he absorbed large numbers of reinforcements sent from Britain by

Lord Liverpool* and early in 1813 was ready to resume the offensive. Enjoying a considerable numerical superiority, he outmaneuvered the French from one river line to the next, and ultimately fought and won the great battle of Vitoria* where Joseph Bonaparte,* Jourdan,* and other commanders were badly defeated. This success compelled the French to evacuate the south and east of the country, and virtually cleared them from Spain. George IV sent Wellington his baton as field marshal and he was made a duke.

However, the battle for Spain was not yet over. San Sebastian* and Pamplona* still had to be taken, and Marshal Soult fought a tough campaign in the Pyrenees* which took all Wellington's skill to frustrate at such battles as Sorauren* and Vera.* By late July the French offensive had been thwarted, and soon Wellington was master of both towns (after a bitter storming of San Sebastian). Crossing the Bidassoa,* he at last passed onto French soil. A hard autumn and winter of maneuvering and fighting against the wily Soult followed, and major battles were fought at the Nive,* St. Pierre,* and Nivelle* outside Bayonne,* and farther to the east at Orthez,* Tarbes,* and, ultimately, at Toulouse*— an action that took place before news of Napoleon's first abdication reached the south of France. The occupation of France followed as the Bourbon monarchy was restored, but Wellington had already been forced to send his Spanish troops home for misconduct, while the greater part of the Peninsular Army's British units found themselves at sea heading for North America, there to take part in the War of 1812's* culminating stages.

Wellington returned to London to receive the plaudits of Regent, government, and people, and to hear five successive patents of nobility (baron to duke) read out in the House of Lords on a single day. Soon he was sent off to represent his country (with Lord Castlereagh*) at the Congress of Vienna,* but on Napoleon's return from Elba* he was sent to command the Anglo-Dutch and Allied forces in the Netherlands. There followed, in association with Blücher's* Prussian army, the dramatic events of the Hundred Days,* culminating in the four-day campaign in Belgium that held for Wellington the narrow success of Quatre Bras* and the final triumph of Waterloo,* achieved by dint of fine fighting techniques, staying-power, and selfless inter-allied cooperation. The invasion of France and the occupation of Paris ensued, and for Wellington his military career was at last over, although he remained Commander in Chief until 1852.

His political career, however, was about to open. After attending several international congresses, he became Master General of the Ordnance with a seat in the Cabinet from 1818–27. Honors were heaped on him and many important diplomatic missions followed, concerning Greek and Portuguese problems among others, while at home the Duke stood firm for the principles of aristocracy and was opposed to Catholic emancipation. He refused office under Canning* but in 1828 reluctantly agreed to become Prime Minister. Against his own convictions he accepted, and achieved, Catholic emancipation, but in 1830 resigned over constitutional reform proposals seeking a more democratic basis for the House of Commons. After the Great Reform Bill he returned in 1834 as Premier and Home Secretary, and in 1834 became Peel's Foreign Secretary. In 1848 he was called in to advise on the Chartist problems, but the use of force was avoided. He was a staunch supporter and friend of the young Queen Victoria and Prince

Albert and was a patron of the Great Exhibition and founder of Wellington College (opened in 1859 after his death). However, he was opposed to army reform, and his deadening hand on improvements would lead to the unprepared state of the forces at the outbreak of the Crimean War. Two years before this, however, he died at Walmer (1852), aged 83 years. So ended one of the most brilliant military and political careers enjoyed by any Englishman. If his true greatness lay in his military rather than his political attainments, he was nevertheless the outstanding Englishman of his generation, and his reputation as the commander who ultimately defeated Napoleon was indubitably his greatest claim to fame. An austere and rather humorless man, he never allowed his success to go to his head, and if at times he made unwise decisions, it is for his great store of common sense and ability for hard, sustained work that posterity has acclaimed him.

Wellesley, Sir Henry, Baron Cowley (1773–1847). The youngest son of Garrett Wellesley (Wesley), he was briefly in the army before becoming a diplomatic officer in Stockholm (1792). MP for Trim from 1795, he was also secretary to his brother Richard* in India until 1799, when he briefly returned to London. From 1801–02 he was Lieutenant Governor of British Oudh. From 1807 he was MP for Eyne and then First Secretary to the Treasury (1808–09). From 1809–22 he was British ambassador to Spain, then (1823–31) to Vienna, and ultimately to Paris (1841–46). Knighted in 1812, he was created Baron Cowley in 1828.

Wellesley, Richard Colley, Marquis (1760–1842). The eldest of Garrett Wellesley's (or Wesley's) large family, he was educated at Eton and Oxford and in 1781 he succeeded his father and became

second Earl of Mornington. In 1797, he was sent to India as Governor General, where he undertook the quelling of the Mahratta princes and the conquest of Mysore. In 1799 he was made a marquis. His long service in India saw the annexation of the Carnatic and part of Oudh, but he was often in dispute with the Directors of the East India Company and this led to his recall in 1805. In 1809 he was appointed ambassador to Spain, and from that year to 1813 was Foreign Secretary to Perceval.* He almost became Prime Minister of a coalition government in 1812, but gave place to Lord Liverpool.* He favored limited recognition of Napoleon as *de facto* constitutional ruler of France in both 1814 and 1815. From 1821–28 and again in 1833–34 he was Lord Lieutenant of Ireland. In 1835 he was appointed Lord Chamberlain and withdrew from public life.

Wellington, Duke of. *See* **Wellesley,** Sir Arthur

Wertingen, combat of, 8 October 1805. As Napoleon's net closed about General Mack* and the Archduke Ferdinand* in Ulm,* French dragoons forming the advance guard of the *Grande Armée* clashed with nine battalions and a single squadron of Austrian troops at Wertingen. Murat* and Lannes* took control of the spirited action that ensued, and by dusk the Austrian cohesion had been destroyed and the French were in possession of over 2,000 prisoners. News of this setback greatly depressed Mack, who forthwith withdrew all his forces north of the river. The result of this move would be the action of Haslach* (or Albeck).

Whinyates, General Sir Edward Charles (1782–1865). Commissioned from R.M.C. Woolwich, he became a gunner lieutenant in 1799 and a captain in 1805. He fought with horse artillery in the Peninsula, and in 1815, as a major, commanded the 2nd Rocket Troop RA at Waterloo.* He was knighted in 1823 and was promoted to lieutenant colonel in 1830. He was Commandant at R.M.C. Woolwich (1852–56) and was promoted to general in 1864.

Whitelocke, Lieutenant General John (1757–1833). Commissioned in 1778, he had risen to major ten years later and in 1791 was commanding the 13th Foot in Jamaica as lieutenant colonel. He fought against the French in Santo Domingo* (1793–94) and was promoted to colonel of the 6th West India Regiment and then to brigadier in 1795. Three years later he was a major general commanding in Guernsey (the Channel Isles), and in 1799 he began a period as Lieutenant Governor of Portsmouth. In 1805 he was made lieutenant general, and in 1807 he was placed in command of the force sent to attempt the recovery of Buenos Aires.* The disaster that followed his attempt to storm the city compelled him to treat for terms and to evacuate Montevideo.* This led to his court-martial on return to England, and in 1808 he was cashiered.

Wilson, General Sir Robert Thomas (1777–1849). Educated at Westminster and Winchester, this "slippery fellow" (as Wellington* later dubbed him) was commissioned into the cavalry in 1793. He played an important part in the "rescue" of the Austrian Emperor at Villers-en-Cauchies* in 1794 and later received an Austrian knighthood (1801) in recognition of this. In 1796 he purchased command of a troop of cavalry and served in the Helder Campaign and in Egypt,* writing a history of the latter campaign which was published in 1802. Two years later he was lieutenant colonel of the 19th Light Dragoons, transferring to the

20th the next year. He served at the Cape of Good Hope (1806) and at Memel (1807) and with the Russian army in the Friedland* Campaign. He claimed to have been present at Tilsit* and to have seen Napoleon. From 1808–09 he served in the Peninsula, creating the Lusitanian Legion, but did not see eye to eye with Wellington and went home. There George III* made him an ADC and a brevet-colonel (1810) before his departure as a member of a diplomatic delegation to Constantinople with the rank of acting brigadier general. There he found an excuse to travel to Russia and he served with Kutusov's army in a liaison capacity during the post-Borodino* events of the Campaign of 1812. He also became intimate with Tsar Alexander,* but his criticisms of Kutusov and other high commanders earned him much enmity. He was present at Krasnöe* and, in 1813 (now a major general), at Dresden,* and Kulm,* and ultimately at Leipzig.* In 1814 he served alongside Austrian troops in Italy. In 1818 he became MP for Southwark, a position he retained for three electoral periods, and earned some notoriety for championing Queen Caroline against George IV* during the divorce proceedings; he was later dismissed for dispersing rioters during the Queen's funeral (1821) but was reinstated by William IV and promoted to lieutenant general in 1830. Five years later he became colonel of the 15th Hussars, and in 1841 he was promoted to full general. From 1842 he took up the appointment of Governor of Gibraltar. He was a prolific historian and political writer but had a knack, like Sidney Smith,* for rubbing superiors the wrong way. A strong-minded individualist of great valor but comparatively little brain (his writings notwithstanding), he was vain and assertive—but at the same time a colorful and fascinating figure.

Wimpffen, General Georg Felix Baron (1744–1814). The son of King Stanislas of Poland's chamberlain, he was commissioned into the French army in 1757 and served through the Seven Years' War. Made a captain in 1766, he had two tours of duty in Corsica and became a colonel in 1774. Four years later he became *maître de camp* and took part in the capture of Minorca (1781) and the great siege of Gibraltar. In 1788 he was promoted to *maréchal de camp,* and he was a Deputy for Caen at the States General. He served under Lafayette* in 1792, and as a lieutenant general defended Thionville against the Allies. Commands on the Moselle and the Channel coasts followed, but he became commander of the forces of the denounced Girondin faction in June 1793 and was ultimately cashiered. He was accorded retired status by Napoleon in 1800 and made a baron in 1810 for the second time, as he already held that rank under the Bourbons.

Winzingerode, Field Marshal Ferdinand, Baron (1770–1818). As a member of the Austrian army he fought the French in several campaigns before transferring to the Tsar's service. As a diplomat he helped negotiate the Third Coalition* in Berlin and Vienna but was taken prisoner at Austerlitz.* Freed some time later, he openly opposed the Tilsit* accord between Russia and France and lived in obscurity until 1812 when he regained Tsar Alexander I's* favor. On 22 October 1812 he was again taken prisoner but was rescued on his way to France. He served throughout 1813 and 1814, taking part in the battle of Leipzig* but losing the battle of St. Dizier* to Napoleon in 1814.

Wittgenstein, Field Marshal Ludwig Adolf Peter, Prince of (1769–1843). The son of a Prussian general in the Russian service, he fought at Austerlitz,*

invaded Finland for the Tsar in 1809, and in 1812 was in command of the defenses of St. Petersburg. He commanded a large force at Leipzig* and fought through France. He was made a field marshal in 1825 and three years later was sent to fight the Turks. Evincing little enthusiasm for the task, he was retired.

Wrede, Field Marshal Carl Philipp, Prince of (1767–1838). Born a Bavarian, he entered the Elector's army and by 1795 had become a colonel. Fighting under the Archduke Charles,* he covered the retreat of the defeated Austrian army from Hohenlinden* (1800). In 1805 he was a Bavarian general and fought alongside French troops in 1805, 1809, 1812, and into 1813, in which year he commanded the Army of the River Inn. He concluded the Peace of Reid with the Allies, and after Leipzig* turned on the French. Attempting to intercept Napoleon's line of retreat to the Rhine, he was badly defeated at the battle of Hanau.* He later fought at La Rothière* and Bar-St.-Aube. In 1815 he attended the Congress of Vienna,* and seven years later was made President of the Bavarian High Council and generalissimo.

Würmser, General Dagobert Sigismond, Count (1724–1797). Born in Strasbourg, he was in the French army from 1745–47 before transferring to the Austrian service. In 1793 he undertook the siege of Mainz and in 1795 commanded the Army of the Upper Rhine, capturing Mannerheim. In 1797 he was sent to Italy and attempted to relieve Mantua.* This he achieved, briefly, but he was badly defeated at Castiglione* and then, during a second attempt to reach the city, at Bassano,* and ultimately he was forced to seek shelter within the besieged fortress. In February 1797 he was forced to capitulate.

Württemberg, Frederick I, Elector and King of (1759–1830). In 1780 he married a princess of the house of Brunswick-Wolfenbuttel. Becoming involved in the War of the First Coalition,* he lost Montbeliard to France in 1793. In 1797 he married his second wife, the Princess Charlotte, daughter of George II.* In 1803 he became Elector, and after Austerlitz* his country became a French satellite, being upgraded to a kingdom in 1806.

Xaintrailles, Général Charles Antoine Dominique, comte de Lauthier (1763–1833). After training as an artillery cadet, he was commissioned in 1779. When his regiment was disbanded (1783) he had to re-enlist as a simple gunner, and later as a light infantryman. By 1792 he had worked his way up to captain and was soon promoted to *général de brigade* on the Rhine front. He was twice suspended from duty and then reinstated. In 1796 he was commandant of the fortress-prison of Bitche and then became a commander under Desaix.* Promoted to *général de division* in 1796, he fought under Desaix in the Army of the Rhine and Moselle. Briefly retired in 1797, he was recalled the next year and fought on the Danube and in Switzerland, occupying the Valais region in 1799. He was acquitted on charges of peculation in 1801 and retired from the service. In 1813 he was hauled back into uniform and put in charge of the supply of the Bavarian corps of observation under Augereau,* but he was taken prisoner at Leipzig.* In June 1814 he returned to France. He died in abject poverty in Paris in 1833, the state being required to pay the funeral expenses.

Yorck, Field Marshal Johann David Ludwig, Count of Wartenburg (1759–1830). Born in Potsdam, he entered the Prussian army in 1772 but nine years later changed to the Dutch service. After six years he returned to the Prussian forces. In 1794 he took part in the campaign against Poland and 12 years later in that against France. He was taken prisoner by Bernadotte's* corps at Lubeck in the disaster following Jena-Auerstädt.* After Tilsit* he was promoted to major general and in 1812 was appointed to command the Prussian auxiliary corps in the *Grande Armée;* with it he invaded Russia, serving under Macdonald* on the northern flank. After the check before Riga, he negotiated the Convention of Tauroggen* with the Russians. Although King Frederick William* at first denounced this action, Yorck in fact had triggered the process of Prussia's defection from the French alliance, and he was soon promoted to general of infantry. He played an important part in the Campaign of 1813, fighting at Bautzen* and Leipzig* and in 1814 at Montmirail* and Laon.* He was made Count of Wartenburg in recognition of his services and was promoted to field marshal in 1821. His grandson Maximilian (1850–1900) wrote an important work on *Napoleon as a General* (1885).

York, Frederick Augustus, Duke of York and Albany (1763–1827). The second son of King George III,* he was elected the Lay-Bishop of Osnabruck through his Hanoverian lineage. In 1784 he was created Duke of York. He entered the British and Hanoverian armies and studied his profession in Germany. In 1789 he was involved in a scandal when he fought a duel with Colonel Lennox over a disparaging passage in the latter's speech in Parliament on the Regency Bill. In 1791 he married the eldest daughter of Frederick William II,* King of Prussia, and from 1793–95 commanded the British army in Flanders—with very mixed success, as the nursery jingle, "The Grand Old Duke of York," bears testimony. Nevertheless, in 1795 he was made a field marshal, and from 1789–1809 he was Commander in Chief of the British Army as a whole. His second attempt at command in the field, the Helder Campaign of 1799, also ended in failure, but his real métier was army administration. Although cautious and conservative in outlook, he did implement a number of reforms, backing some of Sir John Moore's* concepts, reducing disciplinary penalties to one hundred lashes (to the grave concern of many experts), and helping Le Marchant* found the Royal Military College, Sandhurst.* In 1803 he resigned his lay-bishopric, and in 1809 resigned the post of commander-in-chief because of commission scandals involving his mistress, Mary Anne Clarke. Reinstated in 1811, he received Parliament's thanks for his services in 1815 and was made guardian of his father, George III, during his last indisposition.

Zadorra, crossing of the river, 1813. *See* Vitoria, battle of

Zarragoza, sieges of. *See* **Saragossa,** sieges of

Zell (Maria Zell), battle of, 8 November 1805. As Napoleon and the *Grande Armée* advanced deep into Austria from Ulm,* attempting to trap Kutusov's* Russian army into accepting battle, Marshals Davout* and Marmont* launched a covering campaign toward the Alps to keep Austrian forces stationed in North Italy and the Alps from the main theater in the Danube Valley. Entering the northern foothills, Davout captured large quantities of Austrian stores and equipment among the Styrian gorges on 6 November, and two days later caught up with General Merveldt at Zell (or Maria Zell). A sharp battle was fought over the snow-covered ground, which resulted in the killing or capturing of 8,000 Austrians in the day's fighting; barely 2,000 escaped to Hungary.

Ziethen, Field Marshal Hans Ernst Karl, Graf von (1770–1848). Serving in the Prussian Queen's Dragoons from 1806, he fought against France during the Campaign of 1813 and 1814. In the first year he commanded a "brigade" (equivalent to a division) under General Kleist* and greatly distinguished himself at Leipzig.* In 1815 he was promoted to lieutenant general and in 1815, commanding the Prussian I Corps, he played an important role at Ligny* and Waterloo.* He was made commander of the Prussian army of occupation in France, and in later years was appointed Commandant General of Silesia. He was promoted to field marshal in 1835.

Zizandre, defense of the river, 1810. *See* Torres Vedras, the Lines of

Znaim, action and armistice of, 10–11 July 1809. Following up the defeated forces of the Archduke Charles* after the great victory of Wagram,* by late on the 9th July the French cavalry was threatening Znaim. There the Archduke determined to mount a strong rear-guard action in order to rally the remains of his army. Marmont* was the first on the scene, but Napoleon ordered Davout* to hasten up in his support. Marmont's Bavarian skirmishers were repulsed by the Austrian Reserve Corps, but Montbrun's* cavalry drove back the Austrian horseman. The divisions of Clausel* and Claparède* were soon hard engaged as the Austrian I Corps came up, and by 5:00 P.M. Marmont was in dire straits, opposed by 40,000 men. Overnight Massena* hastened up to Marmont's aid, and at 10:00 P.M. Napoleon in person reached the field, with Davout and Oudinot* close behind him. Fighting resumed, the French aim being to pin the Austrians until the major reinforcements could reach the field. This was achieved, but at about 7:00 P.M. fighting slackened and then stopped as officers cried out "Peace! Peace! Cease fire!"

On the 12th, Napoleon concluded an armistice with the Archduke Charles. It was to last initially for one month, the

Austrians agreeing to withdraw from Brünn, Graz, from the Tyrol and the Vorarlberg, and generally to territory behind the Bohemian and Moravian borders. The War of 1809 was virtually over, but negotiations for peace were only finally completed in the Treaty of Schönbrunn* (or Vienna) in mid-October.

Zurich, first and second battles, of 4–7 June and 26 September 1799. Massena,* at the head of initially 35,000 French troops, was hard-put to hold Switzerland against the offensive of the powers forming the Second Coalition,* fresh from successes in Germany and Italy. Archduke Louis* of Austria invaded Switzerland from Baden in the spring of 1799, and Massena moved 30,000 of his available men to Zurich to hold the 40,000 Allied troops. For four days the battle raged along a front stretching for some four miles. Both sides suffered heavy losses—3,400 Austrians to 1,730 French—but in the end Massena was forced to abandon the city, the key to north Switzerland. However, he clung to the hills behind Zurich near Limmat, where he was eventually reinforced. Soon he had Lecourbe

and Suchet* (Chief of Staff) and a plethora of talent among his divisional commanders, including d'Erlon,* Mortier,* Vandamme,* Ney,* and Soult.*

The renewed crisis came about three months later as the great Russian commander Suvorov,* fresh from successes in North Italy at Novi* and elsewhere, advanced through the St. Gothard Pass with 28,000 men into southern Switzerland. To protect his flank, he ordered General Korsakov* and his 30,000 Russians to block Massena until he could join him. Massena was not so green as to ignore the danger, and on 26 September, after detaching a division to harass the approaching Suvorov in the passes, he attacked Korsakov in strength and routed his force, capturing or killing 8,000 Russians and taking many guns and much baggage. Massena then fell upon Suvorov, who was soon in full retreat, losing almost half his command in the mountain ambushes before he extricated what was left of his army. This was Massena's greatest military achievement. Suvorov's defeat did much to induce Tsar Paul* to leave the Second Coalition* (22 October).

APPENDIX

Napoleon's Military Movements
1796–1815

THE TABULATED INFORMATION that follows attempts to trace Napoleon's personal movements from the date he left Paris to assume command of the *Armée d'Italie* in March 1796 until his arrival on St. Helena a little over nineteen and a half years later. It concentrates on moves associated with military purposes, although for general convenience the majority of campaigns are traced from his departure from Paris or St. Cloud until his eventual return there. Of course there are exceptions to this general rule—for instance the intervals between the campaigns of Jena-Auerstädt, Eylau, and Friedland were spent at Berlin and Finkenstein respectively, and not at the French capital. Moreover, when a long period was spent after the close of the military phase in negotiations or administrative reorganization (as were the months between April and November 1797) the information has been reduced to the barest minimum compatible with indicating continuity.

The main source of information for this section has been Albert Schuerman's incomparable *Itinéraire général de Napoléon Ier* (Paris, 1911), a work of great reliability. The compiler based his volume on many sources of information—the evidence supplied by the *Correspondance,* other official documentation, and the memoirs of the Emperor's intimates. Even his exhaustive researches were unable to fill in all the gaps during the earliest campaigns, when General Bonaparte's reputation was still in the making and his every move was not being observed and recorded the way it would be in later years.

In the interests of conciseness, certain conventions have been adopted. The Revolutionary Calendar has not been employed, and days of the week are only given for first and last days of each period considered and for days of battle or other major events. When Napoleon did not stop overnight but continued to travel in his sleeping coach, this is indicated by a note in the *"Events"* column and by placing the place name of the farthest point reached in parentheses. Actual times of departures and arrivals are only given when these are known with reasonable certainty. Journeys by sea are only described in the most general terms. Names of major engagements are given in capital letters; in those cases when Napoleon was not personally present (but the event described was of central significance to the campaign he was conducting), the happening is given in the *"Events"* column but placed in parentheses. When Napoleon is known to have bivouacked in the field, the fact is indicated by the abbreviation *"(biv.)."*

NAPOLEON'S MOVEMENTS: THE CAMPAIGN OF ITALY, 1796–97

Date	From	To	Via	Events
11 March 1796 (Fri.)	Paris	Italy		details of journey uncertain
12–13 March	en route	Chanceaux (6:00 P.M.)	Troyes	
14 March	en route			
15–16 March	en route	Villefranche		
17–20 March	en route	Marseilles		
21–23 March		at Marseilles		
24 March	Marseilles	Antibes	Toulon	
25 March		at Antibes		meeting with Berthier
26 March	Antibes	Nice (4:30 P.M.)		
27 March–1 April		at Nice		
2 April	Nice	en route		
3 April	en route	Menton		
4 April	Menton	Albenga	Oneille	
5–9 April		at Albenga		
10 April (Sun.)	Albenga	Savona		
11 April		at Savona		
12 April (Tues.)	Savona	Carcare		COMBAT OF VOLTRI
13 April		Carcare and area	Carcare	BATTLE OF MONTENOTTE
14 April		at Carcare and area	Cairo	BATTLE OF MILLESIMO
15–16 April		Carcare and area		

[498]

Date				
17 April	Carcare	Millesimo	Cairo	
18 April	Millesimo	Salicetto	Ceva	
19 April	Salicetto	Lesegno	Gandolfo	
20 April		Lesegno and area	Ceva, Gandolfo	
21 April (Thurs.)		Lesegno and area	Prata, Mondovi	BATTLE OF MONDOVI
22 April		at Lesegno		
23 April	Lesegno	Carrù		
24 April		at Carrù		
25 April	Carrù	Cherasco		
26–29 April		at Cherasco		ARMISTICE OF CHERASCO (28th)
30 April	Cherasco	Acqui	Cravanzana, Alba	
1 May		at Acqui		
2 May	Acqui	Bosco		
3 May	Bosco	Tortona	Sale	
4–5 May		at Tortona		
6 May	Tortona	Castel San Giovanni	Broni, Stradella	
7 May	Castel San Giovanni (4:00 A.M.)	Piacenza		crossing of Po River
8 May		Piacenza and area	Pizzighettone, Maleo	
9 May		at Piacenza		
10 May (Tues.)	Piacenza	Lodi	Zorlesco	armistice with Parma
11 May		at Lodi		BATTLE OF LODI

Date	From	To	Via	Events
12 May	Lodi (3:30 A.M.)	Pizzighettone		
13 May	Pizzighettone	Lodi		
14 May		at Lodi		many administrative measures
15 May	Lodi	Milan		
16–22 May		at Milan		
23 May	Milan	Lodi		
24 May	Lodi	Crema	Soncino	routs force of peasants
25 May	Crema	Binasco	Milan	
26 May	Binasco	Soncino	Pavia	
27 May	Soncino	Brescia		
28 May		at Brescia		
29 May	Brescia	(Calcineto)		no night stop
30 May (Mon.)	en route	(Valeggio)	Borghetto	BATTLE OF BORGHETTO almost captured
31 May	en route	Peschiera	Rivoli, Castelnuovo	
1–2 June		at Peschiera		
3 June	Peschiera	Roverbella	Verona, Castiglione	
4 June (Sat.)	Roverbella	Brescia	Mantua area, La Favorita	COMBAT OF ST. GEORGE suburb
5 June	Brescia	at Brescia, en route		no night stop
6 June	en route	Milan		signs treaty with Naples
7 June		at Milan		

Date				
8 June	Milan	Bologna		
9 June	Bologna	Milan		
10 June	Milan	Bologna		
11 June	Bologna	Milan		
12 June	Milan	Pavia		
13 June	Pavia	Tortona		
14–16 June		at Tortona		
17–18 June	Tortona	en route		
19 June	en route	Bologna	Modena, Fort Urbain	
20–24 June		at Bologna		signs armistice with Papacy (23rd)
25 June	Bologna	Pistoia		
26 June	Pistoia	en route		enters Tuscany; no night stop
27 June	en route	Livorno		
28 June		at Livorno		
29 June	Livorno	San Miniato		
30 June	San Miniato	Florence	Livorno	
1 July		at Florence		
2 July	Florence	Bologna		
3 July		at Bologna		
4 July	Bologna	Roverbella		
5–7 July		at Roverbella		
8 July	Roverbella	Verona		
9 July		at Verona		

Date	From	To	Via	Events
10 July	Verona	Porto Legnano	Marmirole, Roverbella	
11 July	Porto Legnano	Verona		
12 July		at Verona		
13 July	Verona	Milan		
14 July		at Milan		
15 July		at Milan		
16 July	Milan	Marmirole		
17–18 July		at Marmirole	Saint Georges	
19 July	Saint Giorgio	Castiglione		
20–22 July		at Castiglione		
23 July	Castiglione	Verona		
24 July		at Verona		
25 July	Verona	(Cassano)		Josephine joins him
26 July	en route	Brescia		
27 July		at Brescia		
28 July	Brescia	en route	Peschiera	no night stop
29 July	en route	(Montechiaro)	Desenzano, Castiglione Castelnuovo	no night stop
30 July	en route	Roverbella		
31 July	Roverbella	en route	Goito (for Brescia)	no night stop
1 August	Brescia	Montechiaro (4:00 P.M.)	Castelnedolo	
2 August		at Montechiaro		visits Brescia

3 August (Wed.)	Montechiaro	Castelnedolo	Castiglione	BATTLE OF FIRST LONATO
4 August	Castelnedolo	Castiglione	Lonato	
5 August (Fri.)		at Castiglione		BATTLE OF CASTIGLIONE
6 August		at Castiglione		visits Peschiera
7 August	Castiglione	Verona		
8–9 August	Verona	at Verona		
10 August	Brescia	Brescia		
11–15 August		at Brescia		
16 August	Storo	Storo		
17 August	Salo	Salo		
18 August	Brescia	Brescia		
19–24 (?) August		at Brescia, and area		some doubt on Bonaparte's exact moves from 21–24 August
25 August	Milan	Milan		
26 August	Verona	Verona		
27 August	Milan	Milan		
28 August		at Milan		
29 August	Brescia	Brescia		
30 August		at Brescia		
31 August	Desenzano	Desenzano		
1 September		Verona	Peschiera	
2 September		at Verona		visits Lazise
3 September	Verona	Ala	Seravalle	

Date	From	Via	To	Events
4 September (Sun.)			at Ala	BATTLE OF ROVEREDO
5 September	Ala		Trent	
6 September	Trent		Borgo di Val Sugana	ACTION OF PRIMOLANO
7 September (Wed.)	Borgo di Val Sugana		Cismona (biv.)	BATTLE OF BASSANO
8 September (Thurs.)	Cismona		Bassano	
9 September			at Bassano	
10 September	Bassano		Montebello	
11 September (Sun.)	Montebello		Cerea	SKIRMISH OF CEREA
				Bonaparte almost taken captive
12 September	Cerea		Ronco	
13 September	Ronco		Castellaro	
14 September (Wed.)	Castellaro		Due Castelli	ACTION OF ST. GEORGES (first day)
15–16 September			at Due Castelli	ACTION OF ST. GEORGES (second day)
17 September	Due Castelli		Verona	
18 September			at Verona	
19 September	Verona		Milan	
20–30 September			at Milan	
1–12 October			at Milan	creates *Cie. des Guides* (25th)
13 October	Milan		Modena	
14–18 October			at Modena	ill on 16th
19 October	Modena	Bologna	Ferrara	

Date				
20–21 October		at Ferrara		
22 October	Ferrara	Verona		
23–31 October		at Verona		
1–3 November		at Verona		
4 November	Verona	Montebello		
5 November	Montebello	Vicenza		
6 November (Sun.)		at Vicenza	Bassano	ACTION OF BASSANO rallies Vaubois' fugitives
7 November	Vicenza	Rivoli		
8 November	Rivoli	Verona		
9–10 November		at Verona		
11 November	Verona	Caldiero (biv.)		
12 November (Sat.)	Caldiero	Verona		ACTION OF CALDIERO
13 November	Verona	Villafranca		
14 November	Villafranca	Ronco		
15–18 November (Tues.–Thurs.)		at Ronco		BATTLE OF ARCOLA (3 days, 15–17 Nov.)
19 November	Ronco	Verona		
20–25 November		at Verona		
26 November	Verona	Villafranca		
27 November	Villafranca	Milan		
28 November–16 December		at Milan		
17 December	Milan	Verona		

Date	From	To	Via	Events
18–20 December		at Verona		
21 December	Verona	Milan		
22 December– 6 January 1797		at Milan		
7 January	Milan	en route		night stop uncerain
8 January	en route	(Mantua)	Bologna, Reggio	no night stop
9 January	en route	(Mantua)		no night stop
10 January	en route	Bologna	Verona	
11 January	Bologna	Roverbella	Borgo-Forte	
12 January (Thurs.)	Roberbella	Verona		
13 January	Verona (11:00 P.M.)	en route	San Marco	ACTION OF SAN MARCO
14 January (Sat.)	en route	Rivoli (2:00 A.M.)		BATTLE OF RIVOLI
15 January	Rivoli	Castelnuovo	Villafranca, Roverbella	
16 January (Mon.)	Castelnuovo	Mantua area	Roverbella	ACTION OF LA FAVORITA
17 January	Mantua area	Verona		
18–29 January		at Verona		
30 January	Verona	(Bologna)		
1 February		at Bologna		
2 February	Bologna	Imola	Sant'Antonio	(surrender of Mantua)
3 February	Imola	Forli	Faenza	
4 February		at Forli		
5 February	Forli	Pesaro	Rimini, Ancona	

Date			
6–7 February		at Pesaro	
8 February	Pesaro	Sinigaglia	
9 February	Sinigaglia	Ancona	
10–12 February		at Ancona	
13 February	Ancona	Loretto	
14 February	Loretto	Macerata	
15 February		at Macerata	
16 February	Macerata	Tolentino	talks with Papal representatives
17–19 February		at Tolentino	treaty with Papacy (19th)
20 February	Tolentino	Ancona	
21–23 February	Ancona	Bologna	Pesaro, Rimini, Ravenna, Imola
24 February–(?)		at Bologna	
1 March			
2 March	Bologna	Mantua	
3–8 March		at Mantua	
9 March	Mantua	Bassano	
10 March		at Bassano	
11 March	Bassano	Asolo	
12 March	Asolo	Ciano	
13 March	Ciano	Conegliano (biv.)	
14 March	Conegliano	Sacile	
15 March	Sacile	Pordenone	
16 March	Pordenone	Valvasone	crossing of the Tagliamento

Date	From	To	Via	Events
17 March		at Valvasone		
18 March	Valvasone	Palmanova		
19–20 March		at Palmanova		
21 March	Palmanova	Goritz	Gradisca	
22–26 March		at Goritz		
27 March	Goritz	Villach		
28 March		at Villach		
29 March	Villach	Klagenfurt		
30–31 March		at Klagenfurt		
1 April	Klagenfurt	Friesach		
2 April		at Friesach		visits Neumarkt
3 April	Friesach	Schiefling		
4–5 April		at Schiefling		
6 April	Schiefling	Judenburg		
7–9 April		at Judenburg		five-day armistice signed (7th)
10 April	Judenburg	Bruck (?)		
11 April	Bruck	Gratz		
12 April		at Gratz		
13 April	Gratz	Leoben		
14–21 April		at Leoben and Palace of Eggenwald		armistice extended preliminaries of Leoben signed (18th)
22 April	Leoben	Gratz		

Date				
23 April		at Gratz		visit to Palma
24–27 April		at Gratz and area		
28 April	Gratz	Laibach		
29 April	Laibach	(Trieste)		
30 April	Trieste	Palmanova		Austrians ratify terms
May–October	spent at Mombello, Milan, and Passariano (near Udine)			treaty of Campo Formio signed
26 October		at Treviso		appointed to command the "Army of England"
27 October	Treviso	Vicenza	Padua	
28–31 October	en route	en route for Milan		
1 November		Milan		
5–16 November		at Milan		
17 November	Milan	Mantua		
18 November	Mantua	en route for Turin		
19 November	Turin (2:00 A.M.)	en route for Chambéry (3:00 P.M.)		no night stop
		at Chambéry		no night stop
20 November	Chambéry	Geneva		
21 November	Geneva	Moudon		
22 November	Moudon	Berne		
23 November	Berne	Basle	Rolle	
24 November	Basle	Rastadt	Morat, Avenches	
25 November		at Rastadt	Soleure	
26–30 November			Offenburg	peace of Campo Formio ratified (30th)

Date	From	To	Via	Events
1 December		at Rastadt		
2 December	Rastadt	Nancy	Strasbourg	
3–4 December	Nancy	en route for Paris		
5 December (Tues.)	en route	Paris (5:00 P.M.)		

TOTAL DURATION OF NAPOLEON'S ABSENCE FROM PARIS: 643 DAYS

THE EXPEDITION TO EGYPT AND SYRIA, 1798–99

Date	From	To	Via	Events
4 May 1798 (Fri.)	Paris	Auxerre		
5 May	Auxerre	Châlon-sur-Saône		
6 May	Châlon-sur-Saône	Lyons		
7 May	Lyons	by boat	Valence	no night stop
8 May	Aix	Roquevaire		
9 May	Roquevaire	Toulon		
10–18 May		at Toulon		
19 May	Toulon (6:00 A.M.)	at sea		boards *L'Orient* (18th)
20 May–9 June		at sea	Hyères, Monaco, Calvi, Bastia, Corsica, Sardinia, Maritimo, Girgenti	
9 June	at sea	off Malta		fleet anchors

Date				
10 June	*L'Orient*	St. Paul on *L'Orient*		landing operation; sleeps on board
11 June				armistice talks
12 June	*L'Orient*	Valetta (1:00 P.M.) at Valetta		Order of St. John capitulates
13–18 June				reorders Maltese affairs
19 June	Valetta	*L'Orient*		sails for Egypt
20 June–1 July		at sea	Gozo, Crete	near-brush with Nelson, nights of 22/3 June and 26/7 June
2 July (Mon.)	Marabout (landing)	Alexandria at Alexandria		STORM OF ALEXANDRIA
3–6 July				
7 July	Alexandria	(El Karioun)		
8 July	en route	Damanhur (8:00 A.M.)	Beydah	no night stop
9 July		at Damanhur		
10 July (Tues.)	Damanhur	Rahmaniya at Rahmaniya		COMBAT OF DAMANHUR
11 July		Miniet-Salameh		
12 July	Rahmaniya	Shubra Khit (biv.)		
13 July (Fri.)	Miniet-Salameh			COMBAT OF SHUBRA KHIT
14 July	Shubra Khit	Chadour	Nekleh	
15 July	Chadour	Koum Chéryk		
16 July	Koum Chéryk	Algam		
17 July	Algam	Abou-Néchabéh		
18 July	Abou-Néchabéh	Wardan		
19 July	Wardan	at Wardan		
20 July	Wardan	Omm-Dinar		

Date	From	To	Via	Events
21 July (Sat.)	Omm-Dinar	Gizeh	Embabeh, Birtil	BATTLE OF THE PYRAMIDS
22 July		at Gizeh		surrender of Cairo
23 July		at Gizeh		
24 July	Gizeh	Cairo		reorders Egyptian affairs
25 July–7 August		at Cairo		BATTLE OF THE NILE (1 Aug.)
8 August	Cairo	El-Menair (biv.)		
9 August	El-Menair	Belbeis		
10 August	Belbeis	Koraïm (biv.)		
11 August (Sat.)	Koraïm	Salalieh		SKIRMISH OF SALALIEH
12 August	Salalieh	at Salalieh		
13 August		Belbeis (11:00 P.M.)	Koraim	
14 August	Belbeis	Cairo		learns of Battle of the Nile
15 August–17 September		at Cairo		
18 September	Cairo	Gizeh		
19 September	Gizeh	Cairo		visits the Pyramids
20 September–20 October		at Cairo		
21 October	Cairo	(Old Cairo)		learns of Cairo rising; returns
22 October	en route	Cairo		rising suppressed
23 October–23 December		at Cairo		
24 December	Cairo	Birket-el-Haggi (biv.)		

Date				
25 December	Birket-el-Haggi	Tree of Hamra (biv.)		
26 December	Tree of Hamra	Suez	Adjéroud	
27–29 December		at Suez		
30 December	Suez	Ajéroud		visits relics of old canal
31 December	Ajéroud	desert (biv.)		
1 January 1799	en route	Belbeis (biv.)		
2 January		at Belbeis		
3 January	Belbeis	Oasis of Saba-Biar	Abu-Néchabéh	revisits canal
4 January		at Saba-Biar		
5 January	Saba-Biar	Belbeis		
6 January	Belbeis	Cairo		
7 January–9 February		at Cairo		
10 February (Sun.)	Cairo	Belbeis		start of Syrian Campaign
11 February	Belbeis	Koraïm		
12 February	Koraïm	Pont du Trésor (biv.)		
13 February	Pont du Trésor	Katia		
14 February		at Katia		
15 February	Katia	Bir-el-Abd (biv.)		
16 February	Bir-el-Abd	Spring of Mesoudiah		
17 February	Mesoudiah	before El-Arish (biv.)		
18–20 February		before El Arish		
20 February (Wed.)	Camp	El Arish		FALL OF EL ARISH

[513]

Date	From	To	Via	Events
21 February	El Arish	at El Arish	Khan-Younès	near-brush with Mamelukes
22 February	Sheik-Zawi	Sheik-Zawi		
23 February	Khan-Younès	Khan-Younès		
24 February (Sun.)		before Gaza		SKIRMISH OF GAZA
25 February	Camp	Gaza		
26–27 February		at Gaza		
28 February	Gaza	Esdoud		
1 March	Esdoud	Ramleh		
2 March		at Ramleh		
3 March	Ramleh	before Jaffa		
4–6 March		before Jaffa		
7 March (Thurs.)	Camp	Jaffa		STORM OF JAFFA
8–13 March		at Jaffa		visits Pestiferies (11th)
14 March	Jaffa	Meski (biv.)		
15 March	Meski	Zeïtah		brush with enemy
16 March	Zeïtah	near Mt. Carmel (biv.)		
17 March	Camp	near Haifa (biv.)		
18 March	Haifa area	banks of Bélus River		
19 March (Tues.)	Bélus River	height before Acre		Siege of Acre begins
20–31 March		before Acre		assault fails (28th)
1–6 April		before Acre		assault fails (1st)

Date				
7–14 April		before Acre		sortie repulsed (7th)
15 April	Acre	Heights of Safoureh (biv.)		
16 April (Tues.)	Safoureh	Nazareth	Gebat, Mt. Tabor	BATTLE OF MOUNT TABOR
17 April	Nazareth	Mount Tabor		
18 April	Mount Tabor	before Acre		
19–30 April		before Acre		new assault fails (24th)
1–19 May		before Acre		many attacks fail
20 May (Mon.)	Acre	desert (biv.)		siege abandoned; retreat begins
21 May	en route	Tantourah		
22 May	Tantourah	Caesarea		
23 May	Caesarea	El Haddar River (biv.)	Haifa	some skirmishing
24 May	El Haddar River	Jaffa		
25–27 May		at Jaffa		
28 May	Jaffa (3:00 P.M.)	Ebneh (midnight)		
29 May	Ebneh (5:30 A.M.)	El-Mechdin (1:30 P.M.)	Esdoud	
30 May	El-Mechdin	Gaza		
31 May	Gaza	Khan-Younès		
1 June	Khan-Younès	El Arish	Refah, Sheik-Zawi	
2 June	El Arish	at El Arish		
3 June	El Arish	desert (biv.)	Mesudieh	
4 June	en route	Ka'ia	Bir-el-Abd	

Date	From	To	Via	Events
5 June	Katia	Om-Farez	Pelusa	
6 June	Om-Farez	Katia		
7 June	Katia	Dattiers		
8 June	Dattiers	Salheyed		
9 June	Salheyed	Kasatir		
10 June	Kasatir	Belbeis		
11–12 June		at Belbeis		
13 June	Belbeis	El-Merg		
14 June	El-Merg	Cairo		triumphal entry into Cairo
15 June–13 July		at Cairo		
14 July	Cairo	Pyramids (biv.)		news of Turkish landing at Aboukir
15 July	Pyramids	Gizeh		
16 July	Gizeh	Wardan		
17 July	Wardan	Terraneh		
18 July	Terraneh	Chabour		
19 July	Chabour	Rahmaniya		
20–21 July		at Rahmaniya		
22 July	Rahmaniya	Berket-Gitas		
23 July	Berket-Gitas	Alexandria (10:00 P.M.)		
24 July	Alexandria (3:00 P.M.)	desert (biv.)		
25 July (Thurs.)	desert (biv.)	Aboukir		BATTLE OF ABOUKIR

Date				
26 July	Aboukir	at Aboukir (biv.)		
27 July		Alexandria		
28 July–4 August		at Alexandria		
5 August	Alexandria	Berket-Gitas		
6 August	Berket-Gitas	Rahmaniya		
7–8 August		at Rahmaniya		
9 August	Rahmaniya	Nile		takes boat
10 August		on the Nile		
11 August		Cairo		
12–17 August	en route	at Cairo		
18 August	Cairo	Menouf	Boulak	decides to leave Egypt
19 August	Menouf	on the Nile		takes boat
20 August	en route	Rahmaniya		
21 August	Rahmaniya	Berket-Gitas		
22 August	Berket-Gitas	Alexandria		
23 August (Fri.)	Alexandria	La Muiron	Beydah	
24 August–8 October	at sea	at sea	Malta, Lampedusa, Cape Bon, Ajaccio	leaves Egyptian soil
9 October	Saint-Raphäel	Saint-Raphäel		lands; no night stop
10 October	en route	en route	Aix	no night stop
11 October	Avignon	Avignon		
12 October	Valence	Valence	Montélimar	
13–15 October	Nevers	Nevers	Lyons, Châlons	
16 October (Wed.)		Paris (6:00 A.M.)		

TOTAL DURATION OF NAPOLEON'S ABSENCE FROM PARIS: 531 DAYS

CAMPAIGN OF MARENGO, 1800

Date	From	To	Via	Events
6 May 1800 (Tues.)	Paris (4:00 A.M.)	Avallon (7:30 P.M.)	Sons	
7 May	Avallon	Dijon (6:00 A.M.)		
8 May	Dijon	Geneva	Auxonne and Dôle	
9–11 May		at Geneva		
12 May	Geneva	Lausanne	Vidy	
13–15 May		at Lausanne		(15th Army starts Alpine crossing)
16 May	Lausanne (5:00 P.M.)	Saint-Maurice	Vevey	
17 May	Saint-Maurice	Martigny		
18–20 May		at Martigny		(19th: advance guard at Bard)
20 May	Martigny	Etroubles	Liddes, St. Pierre, Great St. Bernard Pass, La Vacherie, and St. Rémy	passage of the Great St. Bernard Pass
21 May	Etroubles	Aosta		SIEGE AT FORT BARD BEGINS
22–25 May		at Aosta		
25 May	Aosta	Verrès	Fort Bard	
26 May	Verrès	Ivrea	Fort Bard	assault fails
27 May	at Ivrea			
28 May	Ivrea	Chivasso		
29 May	Chivasso	Ivrea		
30 May (departs early A.M.)	Ivrea	Vercelli		

Date				
31 May	Vercelli	Novara		
1 June		at Novara		
2 June	Novara	Milan	Buffalora (Tessin River)	(4th: Genoa falls) (5th: Fort Bard falls)
3–8 June		at Milan		meeting with clerics (5th)
9 June (departs 8:00 A.M.) (Tues.)	Milan	Stradella	Binasco, Pavia	BATTLE OF MONTEBELLO
10 June	Voghera	at Stradella		Desaix's arrival
12 (?) June (departs 5:00 A.M.)	Voghera	Torre-di-Garofoli		
13 June	at Torre-di-Garofoli	at Torre-di-Garofoli		reconnoiters Marengo area
14 June (Sat.)	Torre-di-Garofoli	at Torre-di-Garofoli		BATTLE OF MARENGO
15 June				armistice
16 June		Milan		visits Marengo
17 June		at Milan		
18–25 June				18th: Te Deum at the Duomo 24th: Order of Day issued
25 June	Milan (midday)	Vercelli		
26 June	Vercelli	Turin		
27 June	Turin	Bussolengo		
28 June	en route	Lyons (5:00 P.M.)		no night stop
29 June	Lyons	at Lyons		
30 June	Dijon	Dijon		
1 July	Nemours	Nemours		
2 July (Wed.)		Paris (2:00 A.M.)		

TOTAL DURATION OF NAPOLEON'S ABSENCE FROM PARIS: 57 DAYS

CAMPAIGN OF ULM AND AUSTERLITZ, 1805

Date	From	To	Via	Events
24 September 1805 (Tues.)	Saint-Cloud	La Ferté-sous-Jouarre		
25 September	La Ferté	Nancy	Bar-le-Duc	(first troops cross Rhine)
26 September	Nancy	Strasbourg		
27–30 September	Strasbourg	at Strasbourg		
1 October	Strasbourg	Ettingen		
2 October	Ettingen	Louisburg	Durlach, Wilferdingen, and Pforzheim	
3–4 October	Louisburg	at Louisburg		
5 October	Louisburg	Gmund	Asberg and Schorndorf	
6 October	Gmund	Nordlingen	Aalen, Unterkochen, Wildhausen, and Bopfingen	(Danube crossings seized)
7 October	Nordlingen	Donauwörth		(combat of Wertingen)
8 October		at Donauwörth	visits to Burgau and Pfaffenhoffen	
9 October	Donauwörth	Zusmarshausen	Mettingen, Wertingen	
10 October	Zusmarshausen	Augsburg		
11 October		at Augsburg		(combat of Albeck/Haslach)
12 October	Augsburg	Burgau	Lech River crossing	
13 October	Burgau	Pfaffenhoffen	Gunsburg	
14 October (Mon.)	Pfaffenhoffen	Oberfahlheim	Hildenhausen and Elchingen	COMBAT OF ELCHINGEN

[520]

15 October	Oberfahlheim	Elchingen Abbey	Michelsburg Heights and Haslach	SECOND COMBAT OF HASLACH
16–19 October		at Elchingen Abbey		surrender of Mack, 2:00 P.M., 19th
20 October (Sun.)		at Elchingen Abbey		surrender of Austrian Army
21 October (Mon.)		at Elchingen Abbey		BATTLE OF TRAFALGAR
22 October	Elchingen	Augsburg		
23 October		at Augsburg		
24 October	Augsburg	Munich		
25–27 October		at Munich		(French cross Isar River, 25th)
28 October	Munich	Haag (near Wels)	Hohenlinden	
29 October	Haag	Braunau	Muhldorf, Inn River crossing and Burghausen	
30–31 October	Braunau	at Braunau		
1 November	Ried	Ried		
2 November	Haag	Haag (near Wels)		
3 November	Lambach	Lambach		
4 November	Linz	Linz	Wels	
5–8 November		at Linz		(action of Amstetten)
9 November	Enns	Enns	Ipps River crossing	(action of Maria Zell, 8th)
10 November	Meelk	Meelk Abbey		news of Trafalgar arrives
11 November	Saint-Polten	Saint-Polten		(combat of Dürrenstein)
12 November		at Saint-Polten		
13 November		Schönbrunn Palace	Pukersdorf	(capture of Vienna)
14–15 November		at Schönbrunn Palace		(armistice of Hollabrünn, 15th)

Date	From	To	Via	Events
16 November (Sat.)	Schönbrunn	Hollabrünn		BATTLE OF HOLLABRÜNN
17 November	Hollabrünn	Znaim	Tesswirtz visit	pursuit of Russian rear
18 November		at Znaim		
19 November	Znaim	Poehrlitz		
20 November	Poehrlitz	Brünn	Latein visit	(combat of Wischau)
21 November		at Brünn	Wischau visit	selection of battle site
22–27 November		at Brünn		
28 November	Brünn	Posorzitzer-Post	(Olmutz/Austerlitz road junction)	night spent on terrain
29 November	Austerlitz	Kristchen (biv.)		interview with Dolgorouki
30 November		at Kristen (biv.)	Visits to Aujest Markt, Pratzen, and Jirschikowitz	full inspection of battle site
1 December	Kristen (biv.)	Zurlan (biv.)		torchlight procession
2 December (Mon.)		at Zurlan (biv.)	Chapel of St. Antony and Posorzitzer-Post	BATTLE OF AUSTERLITZ
3 December	Zurlan area	Austerlitz Castle		bulletin issued
4–6 December		at Austerlitz Castle		meeting with Emperor Francis, 4th; armistice, 6th
7 December	Austerlitz	Brünn		
8–11 December		at Brünn		
12 December	Brünn	Schönbrunn Palace		
13–27 December		at Schönbrunn		(Peace of Pressburg signed, 26th)

Date				
28 December	Schönbrunn	Mölk Abbey		
29 December	Mölk	Passau		
30 December	Passau	Braunau	Scharding	
31 December	Braunau	Munich		
1–16 January 1806		at Munich		marriage of Eugène Beauharnais (14th)
17 January	Munich	uncertain		
18 January	uncertain	Stuttgart		
19 January		at Stuttgart		
20 January	Stuttgart	Karlsruhe	Entzburg	
21 January	Karlsruhe	Ettingen		
22 January	Ettingen	Strasbourg		
23–24 January		at Strasbourg		
25 January	Strasbourg	Châlons-sur-Marne	Bar-le-Duc	
26 January (Sun.)	Châlons-sur-Marne	Paris (10:00 P.M.)	Epernay, Dormans, Château-Thierry, and Meaux	

TOTAL DURATION OF NAPOLEON'S ABSENCE FROM PARIS: 124 DAYS

CAMPAIGN OF JENA-AUERSTÄDT, 1806

Date	From	To	Via	Events
25 September (Thurs.)	Saint-Cloud (4:30 A.M.)	non-stop	Châlons-sur-Marne	
26 September	(Verdun)	non-stop	Metz, Saint-Avold, and Saarbrucken	
27 September	(Saarbrucken)	non-stop	Kaiserslautern	
28 September	(Kaiserslautern)	Mainz	Oppenheim	
29–30 September		at Mainz		
1 October	Mainz (10:00 P.M.)	non-stop	Frankfort	
2 October	(Frankfort)	Würzburg	Hessentheim and Triefstein	
3–5 October		at Würzburg		
6 October	Würzburg (3:00 A.M.)	Bamberg (1:00 P.M.)	Burgenwenheim	
7 October		at Bamberg		
8 October	Bamberg (3:00 A.M.)	Kronach (9:00 A.M.)		reconnoiters Saalburg Defile
9 October (Thurs.)	Kronach (3:00 A.M.)	Ebersdorf	Nordhalben, Hailigen-Ebersdorf, and Schleiz	COMBAT OF SCHLEIZ
10 October	Ebersdorf	Schleiz		(COMBAT OF SAALFELD)
11 October	Schleiz (3:00 A.M.)	Auma	Gera	
12 October	Auma	Gera		
13 October	Gera	Landgrafenburg	Roda, Lobeda, Koestritz, Ziegenshein, and Jena	supervises road building
14 October (Tues.)		at Jena and area		BATTLE OF JENA-AUERSTÄDT

[524]

15 October	Jena (1:00 P.M.)	Weimar		
16 October		at Weimar		
17 October	Weimar	Naumburg	Auerstädt	visits battlefield
18 October	Naumburg	Merseburg	Rossbach	visits battlefield of 1757; destroys Prussian monument
19 October	Merseburg	Halle		reviews Imperial Guard
20 October	Halle	at Halle		
21 October	Dessau	Dessau	Zorbig	
22 October	Wittemberg	Wittemburg		Prussia asks for peace
23 October	Kropstadt (5:00 A.M.)	Kropstadt		
24 October	Potsdam	Potsdam	Marzahn and Beliz	
25–26 October	Charlottesburg	Charlottesburg	Spandau	visits tomb of Frederick (26th)
27 October		Berlin		triumphant entry
28 October to 24 November (Mon.)		at Berlin		(pursuit and capitulation of Prussian units; last on 6 Dec.)

TOTAL DURATION OF NAPOLEON'S ABSENCE FROM PARIS (to date): 61 DAYS

WINTER CAMPAIGN OF EYLAU, 1806–07

Date	From	To	Via	Events
25 November (Tues.)	Berlin (3:00 A.M.)	Kustrin (10:00 A.M.)	Muncheberg	
26 November	Kustrin	Meseritz	Landsberg, Erzebiszewo, and Schwerin	
27 November	Meseritz	Posen	Beksche, Lewice, Pinne, and Bytyn	
28 November–		at Posen		
15 December				
16 December	Posen (3:00 A.M.)	Klodawa	Wreschen	
17 December	Klodawa (2:00 A.M.)	Sompolno	Kutno	
18 December	Sompolno	Blonie	Lowicz and Sochaczew	
19 December	Blonie	Warsaw (1:00 A.M.)		
20–22 December		at Warsaw		
23 December	Warsaw (1:00 A.M.)	Czarnovo	Praga, Jablona, Okumin (bridge over Bug River), and Ukra River to Bug River confluence	full reconnaissance
24 December	Czarnovo	Nasielsk		pursuit of Russians
25 December	Nasielsk	Lopaczyn	Slostovo, Novemiasto, and Lopaczyn	
26 December (Fri.)	Lopaczyn	Paluki	Golymin (after getting lost)	(BATTLE OF PULTUSK) (COMBAT OF GOLYMIN)
27 December	Paluki	Golymin		
28 December		at Golymin		

[526]

Date				
29 December	Golymin	Pultusk		
30–31 December	Pultusk	at Pultusk		
1 January 1807		Warsaw	Bronie	first meeting with Marie Walewska
2–29 January		at Warsaw	Pultusk	army ordered into the field (27th)
30 January (Fri.)	Warsaw (6:00 A.M.)	Pratnitz		SIEGE OF STRALSUND BEGINS
1 February	Pratnitz	Villemburg		
2 February	Villemburg	Passenheim		
3 February (Tues.)	Passenheim	Getkendorff	Passenheim	COMBAT OF BERGFRIEDE
4 February (Wed.)	Getkendorff	Schlitt	Passenheim and Allenstein	BATTLE OF ALLENSTEIN or INKOVO
5 February	Schlitt	Arensdorf	Walersdorf and Deppen	
6 February	Arensdorf	Gross Glandau	Freymarkt, Stabuken, and Landsberg	(combat of Hof)
7 February	Gross Glandau	Ziegelhof		fight for Eylau
8 February (Sun.)	Ziegelhof	bivouac near Eylau		BATTLE OF EYLAU
9–16 February		at Eylau		visits the field (9th)
17 February	Eylau	Landsberg		
18 February	Landsberg	Freymarkt		
19 February	Freymarkt	Liebstädt		
20 February	Liebstadt	at Liebstädt		
21 February		Osterode		
22–28 February		at Osterode		army resumes winter quarters

Date	From	To	Via	Events
1–31 March		at Osterode		(siege of Danzig opens, 18th)
1 April	Osterode	Finkenstein		
2–7 April		at Finkenstein		
8 April	Finkenstein	Marienwerder		
9 April	Marienwerder	Finkenstein		
10–24 April		at Finkenstein		interviews Blücher (21st)
25 April	Finkenstein	Marienburg		
26 April	Marienburg	Finkenstein		
27–30 April		at Finkenstein		interviews Persian Ambassador (27th); Stralsund falls (29th)
1–7 May		at Finkenstein		signs treaty with Persia (7th)
8 May	Finkenstein	Elbing		
9 May	Elbing	Finkenstein		
10–30 May		at Finkenstein		(capture of Danzig, 27th)
31 May	Finkenstein	Oliva, near Danzig		
1 June	Oliva	Danzig		
2 June	Danzig	Marienburg		
3 June	Marienburg	Finkenstein		

TOTAL DURATION OF NAPOLEON'S ABSENCE FROM PARIS (to date) : 191 DAYS

THE CAMPAIGN OF FRIEDLAND, 1807

Date	From	To	Via	Events
4–5 June (Thurs./Fri.)		at Finkenstein		
6 June	Finkenstein (8:00 P.M.)	Saalfeld		
7 June	Saalfeld	Deppen (biv.)		
8 June	Deppen	Alt-Reichau		
9 June	Alt-Reichau (3:00 A.M.)	Guttstadt (8:00 P.M.)		COMBAT OF GUTTSTADT
10 June (Wed.)	Guttstadt (6:00 A.M.)	bivouac on the field		BATTLE OF HEILSBERG
11 June		at Heilsberg		
12 June	Heilsberg (2:30 A.M.)	Preussiche-Eylau		
13 June		at Preussiche-Eylau		
14 June (Sun.)	Preussiche-Eylau	Postenen (biv.)		BATTLE OF FRIEDLAND
15 June	Postenen	Paterswalde, near Wehlau		
16 June	Paterswalde	Wehlau		builds bridges over Pregel River
17 June	Wehlau	Drusken (near Klein-Schirrau)		
18 June	Drusken	Gross Skaisgirren	Schwartzlaucken	
19 June	Gross Skaisgirren	Tilsit		
20–21 June		at Tilsit		
22 June–8 July		at Tilsit		armistice agreed (21st); effective 23rd; Niemen interview (25th); sees King of Prussia (26th); TREATIES OF TILSIT SIGNED (8th)

Date	From	To	Via	Events
9 July	Tilsit (6:00 P.M.)	on the road		
10 July		Königsberg (4:00 A.M.)		
11–12 July		at Königsberg		
13 July	Königsberg	on the road	Marienwerder	
14 July		on the road	Moligno and Posen	
15 July		on the road	Glogau	
16 July		on the road		
17–22 July		at Dresden		
27 July (Mon.)		Saint-Cloud	Leipzig, Weimar, Frankfort, Mainz, Bar-le-Duc, and Epernay	

TOTAL DURATION OF NAPOLEON'S ABSENCE FROM PARIS: 306 DAYS

THE CAMPAIGN OF SPAIN, 1808–09

Date	From	To	Via	Events
29 October (Sat.)	Paris (11:00 A.M.)	Rambouillet	Chateaurenault	no night stop
30 October	Rambouillet (4:00 A.M.)	(Tours)		no night stop
31 October	(Tours)	(Angoulême [11:00 P.M.])		no night stop
1 November	(Angoulême)	(St.-André-de-Cubzac) (10:00 A.M.) and Bordeaux (11:00 P.M.)		
2 November	Bordeaux	Mont-de-Marsan		
3 November	Mont-de-Marsan	Marrac (3:00 P.M.)	Bayonne (2:00 A.M.)	enters Spain
4 November	Marrac (midday)	Tolosa (6:00 P.M.)		
5 November (Fri.)	Tolosa	Vitoria	Salinas	takes over command
6–9 November		at Vitoria		
10 November	Vitoria	Cubo	Arminon	
11 November	Cubo (1:00 A.M.)	Burgos (5:00 A.M.)		reviews troops
12–22 November		at Burgos		(BATTLE OF TUDELA)
23 November	Burgos (1:00 P.M.)	Aranda de Duero (6:00 P.M.)		
24–28 November		at Aranda de Duero		
29 November	Aranda de Duero	Boceguillas		
30 November (Wed.)	Boceguillas	Cerezo de Arriba (6:00 A.M.) and Buitrago	Boceguillas	ACTION OF SOMOSIERRA

Date	From	To	Via	Events
1 December	Buitrago	San Agostino	La Cabrera	bivouacs at Chamartin
2 December	San Agostino	Madrid		in bivouac
3 December		before Madrid		Madrid capitulates
4 December		before Madrid		
5–8 December		at Chamartin Chateau		
9 December	Chamartin	Madrid		(ACTION OF SAHAGUN, 21st)
10–21 December		at Chamartin		
22 December	Chamartin (2:00 P.M.)	Guadaranina	Guadarrama Pass	passages of the Pass
23 December	Guadaranina	Villacastin		
24 December	Villacastin (1:00 A.M.)	Arevalo (3:00 P.M.)		
25 December	Arevalo	Tordesillas		
26 December		at Tordesillas		
27 December	Tordesillas	Medina del Rio Seco (9:00 A.M.)		
28 December	Medina del Rio Seco	Valderas	Aguilar del Campo	ACTION OF BENAVENTE
29 December		at Valderas		
30 December	Valderas	Benavente	Castro Gonzalo	
31 December		at Benavente		
1 January 1809	Benavente	Astorga		news of Austrian plots
2 January		at Astorga		decides to return to Paris
3 January	Astorga	Benavente		

Date				
4–5 January	Benavente	at Benavente		
6 January	Benavente	Valladolid	Medina del Rio Seco	reviews army
7–16 January		at Valladolid		
17 January	Valladolid (7:00 A.M.)	(Vitoria)	Burgos	no night stop
18 January	(Vitoria)	(Tolosa)		no night stop
19 January	(Tolosa)	(Bayonne [4:00 A.M.])		no night stop
20 January	(Bayonne)	Bordeaux	Mont-de-Marsan	
21 January	Bordeaux (4:00 A.M.)	Cubzac	the Dordogne	
22 January	Cubzac	Vendôme (5:00 P.M.)	Poitiers	
23 January (Mon.)	Vendôme	Paris (8:00 A.M.)		

TOTAL DURATION OF NAPOLEON'S ABSENCE FROM PARIS: 87 DAYS

THE CAMPAIGN OF WAGRAM, 1809

Date	From	To	Via	Events
13 April (Thurs.)	Paris (4:30 A.M.)	en route	Bar-le-Duc (3:30 A.M.)	no night stop
14 April		en route	Strasbourg (4:00 A.M.), Kehl, Rastadt, Durlach, Stuttgart	no night stop
15 April		(Ludwigsberg)		7-hour pause at Strasbourg
16 April	(Ludwigsburg)	(Dillingen)		no night stop
17 April	(Dillingen)	Donauwörth (2:00 A.M.)		
18 April	Donauwörth	Ingolstadt (4:00 P.M.)	Rain	
19 April	Ingolstadt	Vohburg	Wellenburg, Neustadt	
20 April	Vohburg	Rohr	Abensberg, Bachel	BATTLE OF ABENSBERG
21 April (Fri.)	Rohr (4:00 A.M.)	Landshut	Rottenburg, Pfaffenhausen, Holzhausen, Altdorf	ACTION OF LANDSHUT
22 April (Sat.)	Landshut (6:00 A.M.)	Alt-Egglofsheim	Schierling, Eckmühl	BATTLE OF ECKMÜHL
23 April (Sun.)	Alt-Egglofsheim	Ratisbon		STORMING OF RATISBON (Napoleon wounded in right foot)
24–25 April		at Ratisbon		
26 April	Ratisbon (8:00 A.M.)	Landshut (1:00 P.M.)		
27 April	Landshut (midday)	Muhldorf (6:00 P.M.)		
28 April	Muhldorf	Burghausen		
29 April		at Burghausen		reviews light cavalry

Date				
30 April	Burghausen		Salza River	
1 May	Braunau	Rannshofen (near Braunau)		
2 May	Ried	Ried (8:00 P.M.)	Traun River	
3 May (Wed.)	Lambach	Lambach	Wels	(COMBAT OF EBELSBERG)
4 May	Ebelsberg	Ebelsberg		
5 May		at Ebelsberg		visits Amstetten
6 May	Enns	Enns		
7 May		at Enns		
8 May	Mölk Abbey	Mölk Abbey		
9 May		St. Polten Abbey		
10 May	St. Polten Abbey (4:00 A.M.)	at St. Polten Abbey		
		Schönbrunn Palace	Sieghardskirchen	
11–17 May		at the Schönbrunn		surrender of Vienna (13th)
18 May	Schönbrunn	Kaiser-Ebersdorf		
19 May		at Kaiser-Ebersdorf		supervises bridges
20 May	Kaiser-Ebersdorf	Isle of Lobau		
21 May (Sun.)		at Isle of Lobau		BATTLE OF ASPERN-ESSLING (first day)
22 May	Isle of Lobau	Kaiser-Ebersdorf		BATTLE OF ASPERN-ESSLING (second day); defeat
23 May–4 June		at Kaiser-Ebersdorf		visits wounded and defenses, death of Lannes (31 May)
5 June	Kaiser-Ebersdorf	Schönbrunn Palace		
6–30 June		at the Schönbrunn		many visits to Lobau Island and area

Date	From	To	Via	Events
1 July	Schönbrunn (4:00 A.M.)	Isle of Lobau		supervises crossing preparations
2–4 July	Isle of Lobau	at Isle of Lobau		
5 July (Wed.)		near Aderklaa		BATTLE OF WAGRAM (first day)
6 July (Thurs.)		near Aderklaa		BATTLE OF WAGRAM (second day)
7 July	Aderklaa	Kaiser-Ebersdorf		
8 July	Kaiser-Ebersdorf	Wolkersdorf		
9 July		at Wolkersdorf		
10 July	Wolkersdorf (4:00 A.M.)	Laa	Wilfersdorf	(ACTION OF ZNAIM)
11 July	Laa (2:00 A.M.)	near Tesswitz (near Znaim)		
12 July (Wed.)	Znaim	near Tesswitz		AUSTRIANS SIGN ARMISTICE
13 July		Schönbrunn Palace at the Schönbrunn		
14 July–30 August	Schönbrunn	at the Schönbrunn		many reviews and decrees
31 August		Raab	Pressburg, Kistee, and Altenburg	
1 September	Raab	Schönbrunn Palace at the Schönbrunn		
2–7 September		at the Schönbrunn		
8 September	Schönbrunn	Krems	Gottweiz and Mautern	
9 September	Krems	Schönbrunn		
10–14 September		at the Schönbrunn		
15 September	Schönbrunn	for Moravian tour		no night stop

Date				
16 September	en route	Brünn		
17 September		at Brünn		reviews Davout's corps
18 September	Brünn	Angen		
19 September	Angen	Schönbrunn		
20–30 September		at the Schönbrunn		
1 October	Schönbrunn	Baden Spa		
2–15 October		at the Schönbrunn		
16 October	Schönbrunn	Mölk Abbey		
17 October	Mölk Abbey			no night stop
18 October	en route	Passau		
19 October (Thurs.)	Passau	(Freysing)	Scharding, Pfarkirchen, Landshut	RATIFICATION OF PEACE TREATY
20 October	en route	Nymphenburg (8:30 A.M.)		visits King of Bavaria
21 October		at Nymphenburg		visits Munich
22 October	Nymphenburg (5:00 A.M.)	en route	Augsburg	no night stop
23 October	en route	(Stuttgart [7:00 A.M.])		no night stop
24 October	en route	(Strasbourg)	Karlsruhe, Rastadt	no night stop
25 October	en route	Bar-le-Duc [10:00 A.M.])	Epernay	no night stop
26 October (Thurs.)	en route	Fontainebleau (9:00 A.M.)		no night stop

TOTAL DURATION OF NAPOLEON'S ABSENCE FROM PARIS: 197 DAYS

CAMPAIGN OF RUSSIA, 1812

Date	From	To	Via	Events
9 May 1812 (Sat.)	Saint-Cloud (6:00 A.M.)	Châlons-sur-Marne (8:00 P.M.)		accompanied by Empress Marie-Louise
10 May	Châlons-sur-Marne	Metz (3:00 P.M.)		
11 May	Metz (2:00 A.M.)	Mainz (1:00 P.M.)		
12 May		at Mainz		
13 May	Mainz (dawn)	Würzburg (5:00 P.M.)	Frankfort, Aschaffenburg	
14 May	Würzburg (8:00 A.M.)	Bayreuth (9:45 P.M.)	Bamberg, Hollfeld	
15 May	Bayreuth (8:00 A.M.)	Plaven (5:30 P.M.)		
16 May	Plaven (4:30 P.M.)	Dresden (11:00 P.M.)	Freiberg	
17–28 May		at Dresden		major international conference; Empress leaves (25th)
29 May	Dresden (3:30 A.M.)	(Buntzlau 5:00 P.M.)	Reichenbach, Görlitz	no night stop
30 May	(Buntzlau)	Posen (8:00 P.M.)	Glogau	
31 May–1 June		at Posen		
2 June	Posen (3:00 A.M.)	Thorn (6:00 P.M.)		
3–5 June		at Thorn		
6 June	Thorn (3:00 A.M.)	(Marienburg)	Gradenz, Marienwerder	no night stop
7 June	(Marienburg)	Danzig (8:00 P.M.)	Dirschau	
8–10 June		at Danzig		
11 June	Danzig	Marienburg		
12 June	Marienburg	Königsburg	Elbing	reviews I Corps

Date				
13–16 June		at Königsburg		
17 June	Königsburg (2:00 A.M.)	Insterburg (4:00 P.M.)	Wehlau	
18 June	Insterburg (2:00 P.M.)	Gumbinnen		
19–20 June		at Gumbinnen		
21 June	Gumbinnen	Vilkowischi	Stalluponen	
22 June	Vilkowischi	Naugaraidski	Pilwischi	
23 June	Naugaraidski	Kamen (biv.)	Shawtdy, Pissa	
24 June	Kamen (3:00 A.M.)	Kovno (9:00 P.M.)		personal reconnaissance of east bank of Niemen River
25–26 June		at Kovno		
27 June	Kovno	Owzianiskia	Jewje	army crosses the Niemen
28 June	Owzianiskia	Vilna (midday)		
30 June–15 July		at Vilna		ACTION OF VILNA / military reviews
16 July	Vilna (1:00 P.M.)	en route for Gloubokoie	Sventsiani	no night stop
17 July	Sventsiani (late P.M.)	en route for Gloubokoie		no night stop
18 July	en route	Gloubokoie (1:00 P.M.)		
19–21 July		at Gloubokoie		
22 July	Gloubokoie (9:00 P.M.)	en route for Ouschatsch		no night stop
23 July	en route	Kamen (11:00 P.M.)	Ouschatsch (1:00 P.M.; 4-hour stop)	

Date	From	To	Via	Events
24 July	Kamen	Biechenkovski (2:00 P.M.)		
25 July (Sat.)	Biechenkovski	Ostronovo area (biv.)		(FIRST COMBAT OF OSTRONOVO)
26 July (Sun.)	Ostronovo area	Koukovitchi (biv.)	Komarchi	SECOND COMBAT OF OSTRONOVO
27 July	Koukovitchi	Vitebsk area (biv.)		
28 July (Tues.)	Vitebsk (1:30 A.M.)	Agaponowszezyna (biv.) Souraje	Souraje	pursuit of Russians
29 July	Agaponowszezyna	Vitebsk (8:00 A.M.) at Vitebsk		(BATTLE OF VITEBSK) (action of Inkovo, 8th)
30 July–12 August				
13 August	Vitebsk	Rosasna (biv.)		
14 August (Fri.)	Rosasna	Boyarinkova (biv.)	Siniaki	COMBAT OF KRASNÖE
15 August	Boyarinkova	Koroutnia		Napoleon's 43rd birthday
16 August	Koroutnia (8:00 A.M.)	Smolensk area (biv.)		BATTLE OF SMOLENSK
17 August (Mon.)		in Smolensk area (biv.)		
18–23 August		at Smolensk		COMBAT OF VALUTINO (19th)
24 August	en route	en route		no night stop
25 August	en route	Dorogobouje (P.M.)	Lubino, Pniewno	
26 August	Dorogobouje (11:00 P.M.)	en route		no night stop
27 August	en route	en route	Slavkovo (stop from 5:00 A.M.—11:00 P.M.)	no night stop

Date				
28 August	en route	near Viasma		
29–30 August		at Viasma		
31 August	Viasma	Weliczewo	Rubki	
1 September	Weliczewo	Gzhatsk	Tsarevo-Zaimizeze	
2–3 September	Gzhatsk (1:00 A.M.)	at Gzhatsk		
4 September	Gridnevo (6:00 A.M.)	Gridnevo (biv.)		
5 September (Sat.)	Schivardino	Walonewa area (biv.)		COMBAT OF SCHIVARDINO
6 September		Walonewa area (biv.)		reconnoiters Russian positions
7 September (Mon.)	Borodino area	Borodino area (biv.)		BATTLE OF BORODINO
8 September		in Borodino area		tours the battlefield
9–11 September	Mojaisk	Mojaisk		ill for three days
12 September	Petelina	Petelina		
13 September	Berowska	Berowska	Nikolskoye	
14 September	Moscow (1:00 P.M.)	Moscow (3:00 P.M.)	enters Moscow	fire of Moscow begins
15 September		at Moscow		moves to Kremlin (7:00 A.M.)
16 September	Petrowskoie	Petrowskoie		
17 September		at Petrowskoie		
18 September	Moscow	Moscow		returns to Kremlin
19 September–18 October		at Moscow		
19 October		Troitskoye (near Desna)		start of the retreat

Date	From	To	Via	Events
20 October		at Troitskoye		
21 October	Troitskoye	Ignatievo	Krasnöe	
22 October	Ignatievo	Fominskoie		
23 October	Fominskoie (9:00 A.M.)	Borovsk (7:30 P.M.)		
24 October (Sat.)	Borovsk (10:00 A.M.)	Ghorodnia (biv.)		COMBAT OF MALOYARO-SLAVETZ
25 October		at Ghorodnia (biv.)		Emperor almost captured by cossacks
26 October	Ghorodnia	Borovsk	Maloyaroslavetz	changes line of retreat
27 October	Borovsk	Vereya		
28 October	Vereya (6:00 A.M.)	Oupenskoje (biv.)	Mojaisk	
29 October	Oupenskoje	Gzhatsk	Gorki, Kolotskoie, Gridnevo	crosses battlefield of Borodino
30 October	Gzhatsk (midday)	Weliczewo (5:00 P.M.)		
31 October	Weliczewo	Viasma (4:00 P.M.)		
1 November		at Viasma		
2 November	Viasma (midday)	Semlevo (7:00 P.M.)		
3 November (Tues.)	Semlevo	Jaskovo	Slavkovo (3:00 P.M.)	(ACTION OF FIODOROIVSKOY)
4 November		at Jaskovo		
5 November	Jaskovo	Dorogobouje (5:00 P.M.)		
6 November	Dorogobouje (8:00 A.M.)	Mikhailovska (midday)		learns of Malet conspiracy

Date				
7 November	Mikhailowska (6:00 A.M.)	Pnievo (near Slobpneva)		
8 November	Pnievo (7:00 A.M.)	Beredikino		
9 November	Beredikino (7:00 A.M.)	Smolensk		first serious frost
10–13 November		at Smolensk		
14 November	Smolensk (8:30 A.M.)	Koroutnia		(SECOND BATTLE OF POLOTSK)
15 November	Koroutnia (9:00 A.M.)	Krasnöe		
16 November		at Krasnöe		
17 November (Tues.)	Krasnöe	Liadouï		ACTION OF KRASNÖE
18 November	Liadouï (5:00 A.M.)	Doubrovna (5:00 P.M.)		
19 November	Doubrovna	Orsha		
20 November	Orsha (midday)	Baranouï		
21 November	Baranouï	Kamienska	Kokhanovo	Ney's survivors reach Orsha
22 November	Kamienska	Tolotchino		
23 November	Tolotchino	Bobr		
24 November	Bobr (8:00 A.M.)	Loshnitsa	Kroupki	creates "Sacred Squadron"
25 November	Loshnitsa (9:00 A.M.)	Staroi-Borisov	Borisov	
26 November	Staroi-Borisov	Studienka		orders two bridges over the Beresina
27 November (Fri.)	Studienka	Zaniwski (near Brilli)		BATTLE OF THE BERESINA (first day)
28 November (Sat.)		at Zaniwski		BATTLE OF THE BERESINA (second day)
29 November	Zaniwski (7:00 A.M.)	Kamen (5:00 A.M.)		bridges destroyed
30 November	Kamen	Plechenitzi		

Date	From	To	Via	Events
1 December	Plechenitzi (7:00 A.M.)	Staïky (2:00 P.M.)		
2 December	Staïky	Sedlicz	Ilija	
3 December	Sedlicz	Molodetchna		
4 December	Molodetchna (9:00 A.M.)	Bienica (3:30 P.M.)		
5 December	Bienica (9:00 A.M.)	(Smorgoni)		takes leave of the army
6 December	en route	(Vilna)	Sedaniski, Ochmiana, Rownopol, and Miedniki	no night stop
7 December	en route	(Maryampol)	Kovno, Wilkowichi	takes to a sledge
8 December	en route	(Loniza)	Goldapp, Grajevo	no night stop
9 December	en route	(Pultusk)	Przasznio, Mokov	no night stop
10 December	en route	(Warsaw)		no night stop
11 December	en route	(Nassau)	Lovicz, Kutno, Lusace	no night stop
12 December	en route	(Posen)		no night stop
13 December	en route	(Bautzen)	Posen	no night stop
14 December	en route	(Meissen)	Dresden (2:00 A.M.)	no night stop
15 December	en route	(Erfurt)	Leipzig	no night stop
16 December	en route	Mainz	Vach	crosses Rhine
17 December	Mainz	(Verdun)	Saint-Avold	no night stop
18 December (Fri.)	en route	Paris (11:00 P.M.)	Château-Thierry, Meaux	

TOTAL DURATION OF NAPOLEON'S ABSENCE FROM PARIS: 224 DAYS

CAMPAIGN OF GERMANY, 1813

Date	From	To	Via	Events
15 April 1813 (Thurs.)	Saint-Cloud (4:00 A.M.)			no night stop
16 April	en route	Mainz (midnight)	Mars-la-Tour, Metz	
17–24 April	Mainz (8:00 P.M.)	(Hanau)	Frankfort	no night stop
25 April	en route	Erfurt (9:00 P.M.)	Fulda, Eisenach, Gotha	
26–27 April		at Erfurt		
28 April	Erfurt	Eckartsberg	Weimar	
29 April	Eckartsberg	Naumburg		
30 April	Naumburg	Weissenfels		
1 May	Weissenfels	Lützen		(ACTION OF POSERNA)
2 May (Sun.)		at Lützen		BATTLE OF LÜTZEN
3 May	Lützen	Pegau		visits battlefield
4 May	Pegau	Borna (5:00 P.M.)		
5 May (Wed.)	Borna	Colditz	Lauwigk, Ballendorf	(ACTION OF COLDITZ)
6 May	Colditz	Waldheim		
7 May	Waldheim	Nossen		
8 May	Nossen	Dresden		
9–17 May		at Dresden		
18 May	Dresden (2:00 A.M.)	Hartau (near Bischofswerda)	Schmiedefeld	
19 May	Hartau	Kleinförstchen	Bischofswerda	

Date	From	To	Via	Events
20 May (Thurs.)	Kleinförstchen	Bautzen	Bautzen area	BATTLE OF BAUTZEN (first day)
21 May (Fri.)	Bautzen	Klein Purschwitz		BATTLE OF BAUTZEN (second day)
22 May		at Nieder-Markersdorf (near Görlitz)		organizes pursuit
23 May	Nieder-Markersdorf (9:00 A.M.)	Görlitz (1:00 P.M.)		
24 May	Görlitz	at Görlitz		
25 May		Bunzlau		
26 May		at Bunzlau		
27 May	Bunzlau	Liegnitz	Michelsdorf	
28 May		at Liegnitz		
29 May	Liegnitz	Rosenig		
30 May	Rosenig	Neumarkt		
31 May–4 June		at Neumarkt		ARMISTICE SIGNED (2 June) for 2 months
5 June	Neumarkt	Liegnitz	Rothkretsham	
6 June	Liegnitz	Hanau		
7 June	Hanau	Bunzlau		
8 June	Bunzlau	Görlitz		
9 June	Görlitz	Bautzen		
10 June	Bautzen	Dresden (5:00 A.M.)		
11 June–9 July		at Dresden		interview with Metternich (26 June)

10 July	Dresden (3:00 A.M.)	Wittemberg	Torgau	
11 July	Wittemberg (3:00 P.M.)	Dessau		
12 July	Dessau	Magdeburg		
13 July	Magdeburg	Leipzig		
14 July •	Leipzig (6:00 P.M.)	(Dresden)		no night stop
15–19 July		at Dresden		
20 July	Dresden (midday)	Luckau		
21 July	Luckau	(Dresden)	Luben, Guben	no night stop
22–24 July		at Dresden		
25 July	Dresden (2:30 A.M.)	(Frankfort)		no night stop
26 July	en route	Mainz (10:30 P.M.)		
27–31 July		at Mainz		
1 August	Mainz (6:00 P.M.)	en route		no night stop
2 August	en route	(Bamberg)	Zelle, Wurzburg	no night stop
3 August	en route	(Hof)	Bayreuth	no night stop
4 August	en route	Dresden (9:00 A.M.)		
5–14 August		at Dresden		armistice broken (11 Aug.); Austria joins Allies (12 Aug.)
15 August	Dresden (5:00 P.M.)	Bautzen		
16 August		at Bautzen		
17 August	Bautzen	Reichenbach		renewed hostilities
18 August	Reichenbach	Görlitz		
19 August	Görlitz	Zittau	Gabel	

Date	From	To	Via	Events
20 August	Zittau	Lauban	Görlitz	ACTION OF BUNTZLAU
21 August (Sat.)	Lauban	Löwenberg	Gruben	follows Allied retreat
22 August		at Löwenberg		(ACTION OF GROSS-BEEREN)
23 August	Löwenberg	Görlitz		
24 August	Görlitz	Bautzen (3:00 P.M.)		
25 August	Bautzen	Stolpen (7:00 P.M.)		
26 August (Thurs.)	Stolpen	Dresden		BATTLE OF DRESDEN (first day)
27 August (Fri.)		at Dresden		BATTLE OF DRESDEN (second day)
28 August—		at Dresden		(BATTLE OF KULM, 30th)
2 September	Dresden (6:00 P.M.)	Hartau		
3 September	Hartau	Hochkirch	Spillwitz	
4 September	Spillwitz	Bautzen		
5 September	Bautzen	Dresden (7:00 P.M.)		
6 September		at Dresden		(BATTLE OF DENNEWITZ)
7 September				
8 September (Wed.)	Dresden	Dohna	Sedlitz	ACTION OF GROSS-SEYDLITZ
9 September	Dohna	Liebstadt	Toplitz, Ebersdorf	
10 September	Liebstadt	Breitenau	Peterswalde, Gieshubel	
11 September	Breitenau (11:30 A.M.)	Pirna		
12 September	Pirna	Dresden		
13–14 September		at Dresden		
15 September (Wed.)	Dresden	Pirna	Gieshubel	ACTION OF GIESHUBEL

Date				
16 September	Pirna	Peterswalde		
17 September	Peterswalde	at Peterswalde		
18 September		Arbesau		
19 September	Arbesau	Pirna		
20 September	Pirna	at Pirna		
21 September	Dresden	Dresden		
22 September	Dresden	Hartau	Weissig	
23 September		at Hartau		
24 September	Hartau	Dresden		
25 September–6 October		at Dresden		(ACTION OF WARTENBURG, 3rd October)
7 October	Dresden (6:00 A.M.)	Seehausen	Meissen	
8 October	Seerhausen	Wurzen		
9 October	Wurzen	Eilenburg		
10 October	Eilenburg (10:00 A.M.)	Düben		
11–13 October		at Düben		(SECOND ACTION OF COLDITZ, 12th)
14 October	Düben (7:00 A.M.)	Reudnitz	Hohenossig, Leipzig	
15 October	Reudnitz	at Reudnitz		(ACTION OF LIEBERT-WOLKWITZ) reconnoiters Allied positions
16 October (Sat.)		Wachau (biv.)		BATTLE OF LEIPZIG (first day)
17 October (Sun.)		at Wachau (biv.)		BATTLE OF LEIPZIG (second day)
18 October (Mon.)	Wachau	Leipzig		BATTLE OF LEIPZIG (third day)
19 October	Leipzig	Markranstadt		army retreats
20 October	Markranstadt (3:00 A.M.)	Weissenfels	Lützen, Röcken, Rippach	

Date	From	To	Via	Events
21 October	Weissenfels (3:00 A.M.)	Eckartsberg (9:00 A.M.)		
22 October	Eckartsberg	Ollendorf	Buttelstadt	
23 October	Ollendorf (midnight)	Erfurt (3:00 A.M.)		
24 October		at Erfurt		
25 October	Erfurt	Gotha		
26 October	Gotha	Vacha	Eisenach	
27 October	Vacha	Hünfeld	Dornsdorf, Buttlar, Rastord	
28 October	Hünfeld	Schlutern	Fulda, Neuhof	
29 October	Schlutern (4:00 A.M.)	Isenburg (7:00 P.M.)	Wurtheim, Gelnhausen	
30 October (Sat.)	Isenburg	Hanau (biv.)		ACTION OF HANAU
31 October	Hanau	Frankfort		
1 November	Frankfort	Hochst		
2 November	Hochst	Mainz (5:00 A.M.)		
3–6 November		at Mainz		
7 November	Mainz (10:00 P.M.)	en route		no night stop
8 November	en route	(Verdun)	Metz	no night stop
9 November (Tues.)	Verdun	Saint-Cloud (5:00 P.M.)	La Ferté	

TOTAL DURATION OF NAPOLEON'S ABSENCE FROM PARIS: 209 DAYS

THE CAMPAIGN OF FRANCE, 1814

Date	From	To	Via	Events
25 January 1814 (Tues.)	Paris (6:00 A.M.)	Châlons	Château-Thierry	
26 January	Châlons	Vitry-le-François		
27 January (Thurs.)	Vitry-le-François	Saint-Dizier		SKIRMISH OF ST. DIZIER
28 January	Saint-Dizier (11:00 A.M.)	Montier-en-Der	Eclaron	
29 January (Sat.)	Montier-en-Der	Maizières	Brienne	BATTLE OF BRIENNE
30 January		at Brienne		
31 January		at Brienne		
1 February		at Brienne		BATTLE OF LA ROTHIÈRE
2 February	Brienne (4:00 A.M.)	Piney	Lesmont	French in retreat
3 February	Piney (9:00 A.M.)	Troyes (3:00 P.M.)		
4–5 February		at Troyes		
6 February	Troyes	Ferreux		
7 February	Ferreux	Nogent-sur-Seine		
8 February	Nogent-sur-Seine (10:00 A.M.)	Sézanne	Barbonne	
10 February (Thurs.)	Sézanne (9:00 A.M.)	Champaubert		BATTLE OF CHAMPAUBERT
11 February (Fri.)	Champaubert (5:00 A.M.)	Montmirail		BATTLE OF MONTMIRAIL
12 February	Montmirail (8:00 A.M.)	Nesle	Vieux-Maisons	
13 February	Nesle	Château-Thierry		

Date	From	To	Via	Events
14 February (Mon.)	Château-Thierry (3:00 A.M.)	Montmirail		BATTLE OF VAUCHAMPS
15 February	Montmirail (10:00 A.M.)	Meaux	La Ferté-sous-Jouarre	
16 February	Meaux (8:00 A.M.)	Guignes	Ozouer-le-Vougis	
17 February	Guignes (7:00 A.M.)	La Baraque		
18 February	La Baraque	Montereau at Montereau		
19 February				
20 February	Montereau	Nogent-sur-Seine at Nogent-sur-Seine	Bray	
21 February				
22 February	Nogent-sur-Seine	Châtres	Méry-sur-Seine	
23 February	Châtres	Pouilly		
24 February	Pouilly	Troyes (10:00 A.M.) at Troyes		Allies offer peace
25–26 February				
27 February	Troyes (midday)	Herbisse	Arcis-sur-Aube	
28 February	Herbisse (6:30 A.M.)	Sézanne	Semoine, La Ferté Champenoise	
1 March	Sézanne	Jouarre	La Ferté-Gaucher	
2 March	Jouarre	La Ferté-sous-Jouarre		
3 March	La Ferté-sous-Jouarre (2:00 A.M.)	Bézu-Saint-Germain	Château-Thierry	
4 March	Bézu-Saint-Germain	Fismes	Raucourt	

Date				
5 March	Fismes	Béry-au-Bac	Gernicourt	
6 March	Béry-au-Bac	Corbény		
7 March (Mon.)	Corbény	Braye		
8 March	Braye (10:00 A.M.)	Chavignon		ACTION OF CRAONNE
9 March (Wed.)	Chavignon	at Chavignon		BATTLE OF LAON (first day)
10 March		at Chavignon	Clacy	BATTLE OF LAON (second day)
11 March	Chavignon	Soissons	Saint-Brice	
12 March		at Soissons		
13 March	Soissons	near Rheims (biv.)		BATTLE OF RHEIMS
14–16 March		at Rheims		
17 March	Rheims	Epernay		
18 March	Epernay	La Fère-Champenoise		BATTLE OF FISMES
19 March	La Fère-Champenoise	Plancy	Méry-sur-Seine	
20 March (Sun.)	Plancy	Arcis-sur-Aube		BATTLE OF ARCIS-SUR-AUBE (first day)
21 March (Mon.)	Arcis-sur-Aube	Sommepuis		BATTLE OF ARCIS-SUR-AUBE (second day)
22 March	Sommepuis	Orcomte	Vitry-le-François, Frignicourt	
23 March	Orcomte	Saint-Dizier		
24 March	Saint-Dizier	Doulevant		
25 March		at Doulevant		
26 March (Sat.)	Doulevant (2:30 A.M.)	Saint-Dizier		ACTION OF VALCOUR

Date	From	To	Via	Events
27 March	Saint-Dizier	at Saint-Dizier	Vitry-le-François	
28 March	Saint-Dizier	Doulevant (5:30 P.M.)	Vandoeuvres, Dolancourt, Troyes	
29 March	Doulevant	Pouilly		
30 March	Troyes	Fromenteau-Juvisy	Sens, Moret, Fontainebleau	(ACTION OF MONTMARTRE)
31 March	Fromenteau-Juvisy	Fontainebleau (6:00 A.M.)		(Allies enter Paris)
1–19 April		at Fontainebleau		mutiny of the Marshals (3 April); first abdication (6 April); takes poison (13 April)
20 April (Wed.)	Fontainebleau	Briare		last Guard inspection; departs for Elba
21 April	Briare (midday)	Nevers (8:00 P.M.)	Cosne, La Charité	
22 April	Nevers (6:00 A.M.)	Rouanne	Moulins	
23 April	Rouanne (midday)	(Lyons, 10:30 P.M.)		no night stop
24 April	en route	(Donzère)	Vienne, Valence, Montélimar	no night stop
25 April	en route	Calade (near Aix)	Orange, Avignon, Orgon	
26 April	Calade (4:00 A.M.)	Luc	Tourves	in disguise
27 April	Luc	Fréjus		
28 April	Fréjus (8:00 P.M.)	Saint-Raphaël		boards H.M.S. *Undaunted*

29 April	Saint-Raphaël (11:00 A.M.)	at sea		
1–3 May	at sea	Porto-Ferrajo		anchors off the port
4 May (Wed.)	H.M.S. *Inconstant*	Porto-Ferrajo (2:00 P.M.)		lands on Isle of Elba

THE CAMPAIGN OF THE HUNDRED DAYS, 1815

Date	From	To	Via	Events
26 February (Sun.)	Porto-Ferrajo (5:00 P.M.)	France		aboard *Inconstant*
27–28 February		at sea		
1 March	Golfe Juan (5:00 P.M.)	Cannes area (11:00 P.M.)		bivouacs at Mouans
2 March	Mouans	Seranon		
3 March	Seranon	Barrême	Castellane	
4 March	Barrême (7:00 A.M.)	Malijal	Bédéjun	
5 March	Malijal	Gap (9:00 P.M.)	Sisteron	
6 March	Gap (2:00 P.M.)	Corps		
7 March	Corps	Grenoble (9:00 P.M.)	La Mure, Laffray, Vizille	meeting with 5th Line Regiment
8 March		at Grenoble		
9 March	Grenoble (2:00 P.M.)	Bourgoin	Rives	
10 March	Bourgoin	Lyons (9:00 P.M.)		
11–12 March		at Lyons		

Date	From	To	Via	Events
13 March	Lyons (1:00 A.M.)	Mâcon (7:00 P.M.)	Villefranche	
14 March	Mâcon	Châlon-sur-Saône (10:00 P.M.)	Tournus	
15 March	Châlon-sur-Saône (10:00 A.M.)	Autun		
16 March	Autun (10:00 A.M.)	Avallon	Vermenton	
17 March	Avallon	Auxerre		interview with Ney
18 March		at Auxerre		
19 March	Auxerre	Pont-sur-Yonne		
20 March	Pont-sur-Yonne (1:00 A.M.)	Paris (9:00 P.M.)	Fontainebleau	
21 March–11 June		at Paris and area		
12 June	Paris (4:00 A.M.)	Laon (midday)		
13 June	Laon	Avesnes		
14 June	Avesnes	Beaumont		
15 June (Thurs.)	Beaumont	Charleroi	Gilly	ACTION OF CHARLEROI
16 June (Fri.)	Charleroi	Fleurus		BATTLES OF QUATRE BRAS and LIGNY
17 June	Fleurus	Farm of Le Caillou (Quatre Bras area)	Marbois, Genappes	
18 June (Sun.)	Le Caillou			BATTLES OF WATERLOO AND WAVRE
19 June	en route	(Mézières)	Charleroi, Philippeville, Roeroi	no night stop
20 June	en route	(Laon)	Berry-au-Bac	no night stop

Date			
21 June	en route	Paris (8:00 A.M.)	second abdication (22nd)
22–24 June	Paris	at Paris	
25 June		Malmaison	
26–28 June		at Malmaison	travels incognito
29 June	Malmaison (5:00 P.M.)	Rambouillet	no night stop
30 June	Rambouillet	(Tours)	no night stop
1 July	en route	Niort (10:00 P.M.)	Vendôme
2 July	Niort	(Saint-Louis)	St-Maixent, Poitiers
3 July	en route	Rochefort (8:00 A.M.)	Mauzé, Surgères, Muron
4–7 July		at Rochefort	
8 July		Frigate La Saale	
9–11 July	Rochefort (4:00 P.M.)	on board La Saale	
12 July	La Saale	Ile d'Aix	
13–14 July		on the Ile d'Aix	Visits Ile d'Aix
15 July	Ile d'Aix (6:00 A.M.)	H.M.S. Bellerophon	meeting with Joseph
16 July–6 August		on board H.M.S. Bellerophon	Torbay, Plymouth
7 August (Mon.)	H.M.S. Bellerophon	H.M.S. Northumberland	
8 August–16 October		on board H.M.S. Northumberland	sets sails for St. Helena
17 October (Tues.)	H.M.S. Northumberland	Jamestown (7:30 P.M.)	reaches Jamestown (15th)
			NAPOLEON DISEMBARKS

Bibliography

NOTE: The books listed below relate to the naval, peninsular, and North American campaigns as well as to the specific activities of the French Revolutionary and Napoleonic armies. No attempt has been made to distinguish among these subjects. Similarly, only rarely has information on specific editions been included. The list is selective and is in no way a comprehensive guide to the past literature on the period.

Abbott, J. S. C., *The Life of Napoleon Bonaparte* (London: 1899).

Adams, H., *A History of the United States Army during the Administrations of Jefferson and Madison* (9 vols.; New York: 1889–91).

Adlow, E., *Napoleon in Italy* (Boston: 1948).

Adye, Sir J., *Napoleon of the Snows* (London: 1931).

Albemarle, G. Thomas, Earl of, *Fifty Years of My Life;* revised edn. (London: 1877).

Aldington, R., *Wellington* (London: 1946).

Allen, J., *Journal of an Officer of the Royals in Spain* (London: 1811).

Almack, E., *The History of the Second Dragoons, 'Royal Scots Greys'* (London: 1908).

Ambert, J., *Esquisses de l'Armée Française* (Brussels: 1840).

Anderson, J., *Recollections of a Peninsular Veteran* (London: 1911).

Anon., Les Fastes de la Gloire ou Les Braves (Paris: 1825).

Antommarchi, C. F., *Mémoires, ou les derniers moments de Napoléon, 1819–21* (Paris: 1898).

Anton, J., *Retrospect of a Military Life . . . of the Last War* (Edinburgh: 1841).

Arnott, A., *An Account of the Last Illness . . . of Napoleon Bonaparte* (London: 1822).

Askenazy, S., *Le Prince Joseph Poniatowski* (Paris: 1921).

Atkinson, C. T., *History of the Royal Dragoons, 1661–1934* (Glasgow: 1934).

Aubrey, J., *Sainte Hélène* (Paris: 1935).

Aubry, O., *Napoléon* (Paris: 1964).

"Avrillon, Mlle." (Villemarest, M. C. de), *Mémoires* (2 vols.; Paris: 1833).

Badcock, L., "A Light Dragoon in the Peninsula . . . 1809–14." *S.A.H.R. Journal* (London: 1956).

Bailleul, J. C., *Examen critique* (Paris: 1822).

Bainville, J., *Napoleon* (London: 1932).

Bannantyne, N., *History of the 30th Regiment 1689–1881* (Liverpool: 1923).

Barnett, G., *Bonaparte* (London: 1976).

Barralier, Capt., "Adventure at the Battle of Salamanca." *United Services' Journal* (London: 1851 and 1852).

Barras, P., *Mémoires de Barras;* ed. by G. Duruy (4 vols.; Paris: 1895).

Barrett, C. R. B., *The 85th King's Light Infantry* (London: 1913).

Batty, R., *Campaigns in the Western Pyrenees and the South of France* (London: 1823).

Beamish, N. L., *History of the King's German Legion* (2 vols.; London: 1832).

Becke, A. F., *An Introduction to the History of Tactics* (London: 1909).

———— *Napoleon and Waterloo* (single volume edn.; London: 1939).

Bell, Sir G., *Soldier's Glory . . .* (London: 1956).

Belloc, H., *Napoleon* (London: 1932).

Berthezène, E. F., *Souvenirs militaires* (Paris: 1855).

Bertrand, H., *Les Cahiers de Sainte Hélène* (3 vols.; Paris: 1949 and 1959).

Bigarré, A., *Mémoires du . . . aide-de-camp du Roi Joseph* (Paris: n.d.).

Bingham, D. A., *Selection from the Letters and Despatches of Napoleon* (3 vols.; London: 1844).

Blakeney, S. J., *A Boy in the Peninsular War.* . . . (London: 1899).

Blakiston, J., *Twelve Years Military Adventure* (2 vols.; London: 1840).

Bonnal, H., *La manoeuvre de Jéna* (Paris: 1904).

────── *La manoeuvre de Landshut* (Paris: 1905).

Bonaparte, J., *Mémoires.* . . . (10 vols.; Paris: 1853–54).

Bonaparte, L., *Mémoires . . . secrets;* ed. by T. Jung (2 vols.; Paris: 1836).

Boothby, C., *Under England's Flag from 1804 to 1809* (London: 1900).

────── *A Prisoner of France.* . . . (London: 1898).

Botta, C., *Storia d'Italia del 1789–1814* (8 vols.; Rome: 1826–40).

Bourcet, P., *Mémoires historiques sur la guerre, 1757–1762* (Paris: 1792).

Bourgogne, A. J. B. F., *The Memoirs of Sgt. Bourgogne;* new edn. (London: 1979).

Bourienne, M. de, *Memoirs of Napoleon Bonaparte,* English edn. (3 vols.; London: 1844).

Boutflower, C., *The Journal of an Army Surgeon during the Peninsular War* (London: 1912).

Bragge, W., *Peninsular Portrait;* ed. by S. A. C. Cassells (London: 1963).

Brannan, J., *Official Letters . . . in the Years 1812, 1813, 1814 and 1815* (Washington: 1822).

Brett-James, A., *General Graham, Lord Lynedoch* (London: 1959).

────── *Wellington at War, 1794–1815* (London: 1961).

────── *The Hundred Days* (London: 1965).

────── *1812* (London: 1966).

────── *Europe against Napoleon* (London: 1970).

────── *Life in Wellington's Army* (London: 1972).

Broglie, Duc de, "Instruction." *Archives de la Guerre* (Paris: 1761).

Brookes, D. M., *The St. Helena Story* (London: 1960).

Brossier, Adjt. Cdt., *Journal* (Paris: 1901).

Broughton, S. D., *Letters from Portugal, Spain and France.* . . . (London: 1815).

Brown, R., *The Republic in Peril* (New York, 1964).

Browne, D. G., *The Floating Republic* (London: 1963).

Brunon, J., *Les Maréchaux de France à travers neuf siècles d'histoire* (Paris: n.d.).

Bryant, A., *The Age of Elegance* (London: 1950).

────── *The Years of Endurance* (London: 1942).

────── *The Years of Victory* (London: 1944).

────── *Jackets of Green* (London: 1976).

Buckham, P. W., *Personal Narrative of Adventures in the Peninsula.* . . . (London: 1827).

Bucquoy, E. L., *Les Gardes d'Honneur du premier Empire* (Nancy: 1908).

Bugeaud, T. R., *Aperçus sur quelques détails de la guerre* (Paris: 1846).

Bunbury, T., *Reminiscences of a Veteran* (3 vols.; London: 1861).

Burgoyne, J., *Life and Correspondence of Field Marshal Sir J. Burgoyne* (2 vols.; London: 1873).

Burroughs, G. F., *A Narrative of . . . the Retreat from Burgos.* . . . (Bristol: 1814).

Burton, R. G., *Napoleon's Invasion of Russia, 1812* (London: 1914).

Butterfield, H., *The Peace Tactics of Napoleon* (Cambridge: 1929).

Cadell, C., *Narrative of the Campaigns of the 28th Regiment . . . since . . . 1802* (London: 1835).

Callender, G. and Hinsley, F. L., *The Naval Side of British History, 1486–1945* (London: 1945).

Camon, H., *Génie et métier chez Napoléon* (Paris: 1929).

—— *La guerre Napoléonienne—les systèmes d'opérations* (Paris: 1907).

—— *La guerre Napoléonienne—précis des campagnes* (2 vols.; Paris: 1925).

—— *Quand et comment Napoléon a conçu son système de bataille* (Paris: 1935).

Campbell, Sir N., *Napoleon at Fontainebleau and Elba*. . . . (Edinburgh: 1869).

Carlyle, T., *Critical and Miscellaneous Essays* (4 vols.; London: 1843).

Carr, R., *Spain—1808 to 1939* (Oxford: 1966).

Carss, J., "The 2nd/53rd in the Peninsular War." Ed. by S. H. F. Johnstone, *S.A.H.R. Journal* (London: 1948).

Cary, A. and McCance, S., *Regimental Records of the Royal Welch Fusiliers* (3 vols.; London: 1921).

Casse, A. du, *Mémoires du Roi Joseph* (2 vols.; Paris: 1854–55).

Castelanne-Novejean, E. V. E. B. de, *Journal*. . . . (5 vols.; Paris: 1895–97).

Castlereagh, Lord, *Correspondence of Viscount Castlereagh;* ed. by Marquess of Londonderry (London: 1851).

—— *Despatches* (12 vols.; London: 1848–53).

Caulaincourt, A. de, *Memoirs* (3 vols.; London: 1950).

Cerf, L., *Lettres de Napoléon à Josephine* (Paris: 1929).

Chandler, D. G., *The Campaigns of Napoleon* (New York: 1966).

—— *Napoleon* (London: 1974).

—— *The Art of Warfare on Land* (London: 1974).

Chaptal, J. A., *Mes souvenirs de Napoléon* (Paris: 1893).

Charles-Roux, F., *Napoleon* (London: 1937).

Charras, Lt. Col., *Histoire de la campagne de 1815* (London: 1857).

Chastenet, J., *Godoy, Minister of Spain* (London: 1953).

Chesney, C. C., *Waterloo Lectures*. . . . (London: 1868).

Chuquet, A., *La jeunesse de Napoléon* (3 vols.; Paris: 1897–98).

Clausewitz, K. von, *La campagne de 1796 en Italie* (Paris: 1899).

—— *The Campaign of 1812* (London: 1843).

—— *On War;* ed. by M. E. Howard (London: 1974).

Cléry, R. de, *Lasalle* (Paris: 1899).

Clowes, W., *History of the Royal Navy* (7 vols.; London: 1897–1908).

Cobban, A., *A History of Modern France* (3 vols.; London: 1961).

Codrington, E., *Memoir of the Life of Admiral Sir Edward Codrington*. . . . (2 vols.; London: 1873).

Cockburn, G., *Napoleon's Last Voyage* (London: 1888).

Coignet, J. R., *The Notebooks of Captain Coignet;* ed. by J. Fortescue (London: 1929).

Cole, G. L., *Memoirs of Sir Galbraith Lowry Cole* (London: 1934).

Coles, H. L., *The War of 1812* (Chicago: 1965).

Colin, J., *La campagne de 1796–97* (Paris: 1912).

—— *L'éducation militaire de Napoléon* (Paris: 1906).

—— *Les grandes batailles de l'histoire* (Paris: 1915).

—— *The Transformations of War* (London: 1908).

Collingwood, G. L. N., *A Selection from the* . . . *Correspondence of Vice-Admiral Lord Collingwood* (London: 1829).

Comeau, S. J. de, *Souvenirs des guerres d'Allemagne* (Paris: 1900).

Connely, J., *Napoleon's Satellite Kingdoms* (New York: 1965).

Cooke, J., *Memoirs of the Late War* (2 vols.; London: 1831).

Cooper, J. S., *Rough Notes of Seven Campaigns in Portugal, Spain, France and America* . . . *1809–1815* (London: 1896).

Corbett, J. S., *The Campaign of Trafalgar* (London: 1910).

—— *The Spencer Papers*, Vols. 1 and 2, *The Navy Records Society* (London: 1913–14).

—— *Fighting Instructions, 1530–1816, The Navy Records Society* (London: 1905).

——— *Some Principles of Maritime Strategy* (London: 1911).

Corwallis-West, G., *The Life and Letters of Admiral Cornwallis* (London: 1927).

Costello, E., *Adventures of a Soldier;* ed. by A. Brett-James (London: 1967).

Cowper, L. I., *The King's Own—the Story of a Royal Regiment,* Vol. One (Oxford: 1939).

Craig, G., *Problems of Coalition Warfare: The Military Alliance Against Napoleon, 1813–14* (Colorado Springs: 1965).

Craufurd, A. H., *General Craufurd and his Light Division* (London: 1891).

Croker, C., *The Croker Papers* (3 vols.; London: 1885).

Cronin, V., *Napoleon* (London: 1971).

Crouzet, E., "Blockade and Economic Change in Europe, 1792–1815." *Journal of Economic History* (London: 1964).

——— *L'économie Britannique et le blocus continental* (2 vols.; Paris: 1958).

Cugnac, G. J. M. R., *La campagne de l'armée de réserve en 1800* (2 vols.; Paris: 1900–01).

Dallas, A. R. C., *Incidents in the Life of the Rev. Alex R. C. Dallas* (London: 1873).

Dalton, C., *The Waterloo Roll-Call* (London: 1904).

Daniell, J. E., *Journal of an Officer in the Commissariat Department. . . .* (London: 1820).

Davies, G., *Wellington and His Army* (Oxford: 1954).

Debidour, M., *Recueil des actes du directoire exécutif* (2 vols.; Paris: n.d.).

Debrière, E., "Projets et tentatives de débarquement aux Iles Britanniques." *Archives de Vincennes* (1793–1805).

Delavoye, A. M., *Life of Thomas Graham, Lord Lynedoch* (London: 1880).

Delderfield, E. F., *The March of the Twenty-Six* (London: 1962).

——— *Imperial Sunset* (London: 1968).

Dernelles, C., *Constant, mémoires intimes de Napoléon Ier* (Mainz: 1957).

Desaix de Veugoux, L. C. A., *Journal de voyage de Général Desaix en Suisse et en Italie* (Paris: 1797).

Deutsch, H. C., *The Genesis of Napoleon I* (Cambridge, Mass.: 1958).

Desorière, E., *The Campaign of Trafalgar* (London: 1907).

Dickson, A., *The Dickson Manuscripts . . . from 1809–1815;* ed. by J. H. Leslie (Woolwich: 1907).

Dodge, T. A., *Napoleon* (4 vols.; New York: 1904).

Doguereau, J. P., *Journal de l'expédition de l'Egypte* (4 vols.; Paris: 1904).

Donaldson, J., *Recollections of the Eventful Life of a Soldier* (Edinburgh: 1845).

Douglas, N. D., "The Diary of Captain Neil Douglas, 79th Foot, 1809–10"; ed. by A. Brett-James, *Journal of S.A.H.R.* (London: 1963).

Downman, T., "The Diary of Major Thomas Downman, RHA in the Peninsula." *Journal of S.A.H.R.* (London: 1927).

Drouet, Comte d'Erlon, *Mémoires* (Paris: 1884).

Ducasse, J. N., *Mémoires et Correspondence . . . du Roi Joseph* (10 vols.; Paris: 1854 et seq.).

Duffy, C. J., *Borodino* (London: 1972).

——— *Austerlitz* (London: 1977).

Dufrische-Desgenettes, R. N., *Histoire médicale de l'armée d'Orient* (2 vols.; Paris: 1802).

Dumas, M., *Précis des événements militaires* (Paris: 1826).

Dundonald, Lord, *Autobiography of a Seaman* (2 vols.; London: 1860).

Dunn-Pattison, R. P., *The History of the 91st* (Edinburgh: 1910).

Dupont, M., *Napoléon et ses grognards* (Paris: 1945).

——— *Murat* (Paris: 1934).

Dupuy, R. E. and T. N., *The Encyclopaedia of Military History from 3500 BC to the Present* (London: 1970).

D'Urban, R. I. J., *Peninsular Journal of Maj. Gen. Sir Benjamin D'Urban* (London: 1830).

Dwelley, W., *A Muster-Role of the British NCOs and Men present at . . . Waterloo* (Fleet: 1934).

Dyneley, T., "Letters written by Lt. Gen. Thomas Dyneley, CB, RA . . . 1806–1815." *Proceedings of the R.A. Institution* (London: 1896).

Earle, E. M., *The Makers of Modern Strategy* (Princeton: 1943).

Egglestone, W. M., *Letters of . . . Lt. John Brumwell (43rd Regt.)* (Durham: 1912).

Elchingen, le Duc d', *Documents inédits sur la campagne de 1815* (Paris: 1840).

Ellesmere, F., *Personal Reminiscences of the Duke of Wellington* (London: 1904).

Ellison, Sir G., "Army Administration." *Army Quarterly* (London: 1921).

Esposito, V. J. and Elting, J. R., *A Military History and Atlas of the Napoleonic Wars* (New York: 1964).

Faber du Four, C. W. von, *La campagne de Russie, 1812* (Paris: 1895).

Fain, A. J. F., *Manuscrit de 1812* (2 vols.; Paris: 1908).

—— *Mémoires* (Paris: 1884).

Falls, C., *The Art of War from Napoleon to the Present Day* (London: 1961).

—— (ed.) *Great Military Battles* (London: 1964).

Fernández Duro, C., *Armada Española* (6 vols.; Madrd: 1896–1900).

Fée, A. L. A., *Souvenir de la guerre d'Espagne* (Paris: 1856).

Fernyhough, M., *Military Memoirs of Four Brothers. . . .* (London: 1829).

Ferrero, G., *The Gamble: Bonaparte in Italy, 1796–97* (London: 1961).

Fezensac, R. A. P. J. de, *Souvenirs militaires* (Paris: 1863).

Fisher, H. A. L., *Napoleon* (London: 1950).

Fitchett, W. H., *Wellington's Men: Some Soldier Autobiographies* (London: 1912).

Forester, C. S., *The Naval War of 1812* (London: 1952).

—— *Nelson* (London: n.d.).

Forshuvfvud, S., *Who Killed Napoleon?* (London: 1961).

—— and Weider, B., *Assassination at St. Helena* (Vancouver: 1978).

Fortescue, Sir J., *A History of the British Army;* vols. 6–10 (Oxford: 1910–20).

Foucart, P., *Campagne de Prusse: Jéna* (2 vols.; Paris: 1887).

Fouché, J., *Mémoires* (Paris: 1945).

Foy, M. S., *Histoire de la guerre de la Péninsule* (4 vols.; Paris: 1827).

—— (ed.), *Vie militaire du Général Foy* (Paris: 1900).

François, C. F., *Journal* (3 vols.; Paris: 1903–04).

Fraser, E., *The Sailors Whom Nelson Led* (London: 1913).

—— *The War Drama of the Eagles. . . .* (London: 1912).

—— *The Soldiers Whom Wellington Led* (London: 1913).

Fraser, Sir W., *Words on Wellington: The Duke—Waterloo—the Ball* (London: 1902).

Frazer, A. F., *Letters;* ed. by Maj. Gen. E. Sabine (London: 1859).

Frederick II, King of Prussia, *The Instructions of Frederick the Great for his Generals, 1758;* tr. by T. R. Philips (Harrisburg: 1960).

Fremantle, A., *The Wynne Diaries* (3 vols.; London: 1935–40).

Fuller, J. F. C., *The Conduct of War, 1780–1961* (London: 1961).

—— *The Decisive Battles of the Western World* (3 vols.; London: 1954–56).

Gardyne, C. G., *The Life of a Regiment . . . the Gordon Highlanders . . . 1794–1816* (Edinburgh: 1901).

Garrett, R., "A Subaltern in the Peninsular War." Ed. by A. S. White, *S.A.F.R. Journal* (London: 1934).

Gavin, W., "The Diary of William Gavin . . . 71st Highland Regt. . . . 1806–1813." *The Highland Light Infantry Chronicle* (Edinburgh: 1920).

Geyl, P., *Napoleon* (London: 1946).

Gibney, Dr. T., *Eighty Years Ago, or the Recollections of an Old Army Doctor* (London: 1896).
Gleig, G. R., *The Subaltern* (London: 1825).
────── *The Light Dragoon* (London: 1850).
────── *Personal Recollections of the First Duke of Wellington* (Edinburgh and London: 1904).
Glover, M., *Wellington's Peninsular Victories* (London: 1965).
────── *The Peninsular War, 1807–1814* (London: 1974).
────── *Wellington's Army* (London: 1977).
────── *A Very Slippery Fellow . . . Sir Robert Wilson* (London: 1977).
Glover, R., *Peninsular Preparation* (London: 1963).
Godoy, M., *Memoirs of Don Manuel Godoy* (2 vols.; London: 1836).
Gohier, L. J., *Mémoires* (Paris: 1824).
Gomm, Sir W., *Letters and Journals. . . .* (London: 1881).
Gonneville, M. de, *Souvenirs militaires* (Paris: 1895).
Gordon, A., *A Cavalry Officer in the Corunna Campaign, 1808–09* (London: 1913).
Gough, R., *Life and Campaigns of Hugh, First Viscount Gough* (2 vols.; London: 1903).
Gourgaud, G., *La campagne de 1815* (Paris: n.d.).
────── *Journal* (2 vols.; Paris: 1899).
Graham, D. A. M., *Life of Thomas Graham, Lord Lynedoch* (London: 1880).
Grandmaison, G. de, *L'Europe et Napoléon* (3 vols.; Paris: 1908–31).
Grattan, W., *Adventures with the Connaught Rangers, 1809–1914* (London: 1902).
Green, J., *The Vicissitudes of a Soldier's Life . . . 1806–1815* (Louth: 1827).
Griess, T. E. and Luvaas, J., *Strategy, its Theory and Application* (Westport: 1971).
Gronow, R. H., *Reminiscences and Recollections* (London: 1900).
Grunwald, M., *Alexander I* (Paris: 1955).
Guedalla, P., *The Duke* (London: 1935).
────── *The Hundred Days* (London: 1934).
Guibert, J. A. H. de, *Essai général de tactique* (Liège: 1775).
Gurwood, J., *The General Orders of Field-Marshal the Duke of Wellington. . . .* (London: 1837).
Hales, E. E. Y., *Napoleon and the Pope* (London: 1962).
Hamilton, Sir F. W., *The Origin and History of the First, or Grenadier, Guards* (3 vols.; London, 1874).
Hampson, F., *La marine de l'an II, 1793* (Paris: 1960).
Hardinge, R., "Letters from the Peninsula, 1812–14." *Journal of the Royal Artillery* (London: 1958 and 1959).
Harris, *The Recollections of Rifleman Harris;* ed. by C. Hibbert (London: 1970).
Hautpoul, A., *Mémoires* (Paris: 1906).
Hay, W., *Reminiscences 1808–1815 under Wellington* (London: 1901).
Hayward, P., *Surgeon Henry's Trifles: Events of a Military Life* (London: 1975).
Hecksher, E. F., *The Continental System: An Economic Interpretation* (Oxford: 1922).
Heilmann, J., *Feldmarschall Fürst Wrede* (Leipzig: 1881).
Henderson, H. N. B., *A Dictionary of Napoleon and His Times* (London: 1920).
Herbert, J. B., *Life and Services of Admiral Sir T. Foley* (Privately printed: 1884).
Herold, C. J., *The Age of Napoleon* (New York: 1963).
────── *Bonaparte in Egypt* (London: 1963).
────── *The Mind of Napoleon* (New York: 1955).
Herring, H., *A History of Latin America* (London: 1968).
Hitsman, J. M., *The Incredible War of 1812* (Toronto: 1965).
Holzing, K. F. von, *Unter Napoleon in Spanien* (Berlin: 1937).

[563]

Horsman, R., *The War of 1812* (New York: 1969).
—— *The Causes of the War of 1812* (New York: 1962).
Hourtoulle, I. G., *Soldats et uniformes du premier Empire* (Paris: n.d.).
Houssaye, H., *1814* (Paris: 1888).
—— *Waterloo* (Paris: 1893).
Howard, J. E., *Letters and Documents of Napoleon* (London: 1961).
Howard, M. E., *War in European History* (Oxford: 1976).
Howarth, D., *A Near-Run Thing* (London: 1968).
Hudson, W. H., *The Man Napoleon* (London: 1915).
Humble, R., *Napoleon's Peninsular Marshals* (London: 1973).
Humphreys, R. A., *Liberation in South America* (London: 1952).
Jackson, T. S., *Logs of the Great Sea Fights* (London: 1900).
Jackson, W. G. F., *Attack in the West* (London: 1953).
—— *Seven Roads to Moscow* (London: 1958).
James, C., *A Universal Military Dictionary in English and French* (London: 1816).
James, W., *The Naval History of Great Britain*, first 4 vols. (London: 1886).
Johnson, D., *Napoleon's Cavalry* (London: 1978).
Jomini, A. H., *The Art of War* (Philadelphia: 1875).
—— *Histoire des guerres de la Révolution* (Paris: 1838).
—— *Life of Napoleon* (Kansas City: 1897).
Jones, Sir J. T., *Journals of sieges . . . in Spain . . . 1811 to 1814* (3 vols.; London: 1846).
Jones, R. B., *Napoleon, Man and Myth* (London: 1977).
Jonquière, C. E. de la, *L'expédition d'Egypte* (5 vols.; Paris: 1889–1902).
Jourdan, J. R., *Mémoires militaires* (Paris: 1899).
Keegan, J. D. P., *The Face of Battle* (London: 1976).
Kelly, C., *Memoirs and Wonderful Achievements of Wellington the Great* (London: 1852).
Kemble, J., *Napoleon Immortal* (London: 1959).
—— *Gorrequer's Journal* (London: 1969).
Kennedy, Sir J., *Notes on the Battle of Waterloo* (London: 1865).
Kennedy, L., *Nelson's Band of Brothers* (London: 1951).
Kennedy, P. M., *The Rise and Fall of British Naval Mastery* (London: 1976).
Kincaid, J., *Adventures in the Rifle Brigade* (London: 1852).
Kircheisen, F. M., Memoirs of Napoleon I (London: 1929).
—— *Napoleon* (London: 1931).
Kohn, H., *The Mind of Germany* (London: 1961).
Kotzebue, A. F. F. von, *Mes souvenirs de Paris en 1804* (The Hague: 1805).
Kurtz, H., *The Trial of Marshal Ney* (London: 1957).
—— *Talleyrand* (London: 1958).
Lachouque, H., *Jéna* (Paris: 1961).
—— *Napoléon à Austerlitz* (Paris: 1960).
—— *Napoléon—vingt ans de campagnes* (Paris: 1964).
—— *Waterloo* (London: 1975).
—— and Brown, A. S. K., *The Anatomy of Glory* (London: 1965 and 1977).
Laird-Clowes, W., *The Royal Navy* (3 vols.; London: 1898).
Landmann, Col., *Recollections of My Military Life* (London: 1854).
Lanrezac, C. L. M., *Mémoires—Lützen* (Paris: 1904).
Larchey, L., *The Narrative of Captain Coignet, Soldier of the Empire* (London: 1897).
La Roncière, C. de, *Histoire de la marine française* (6 vols.; Paris: 1930–32).
Larpent, F. S., *The Private Journal of . . . Judge-Advocate-General* (2 vols.; London: 1853).
Larrey, Baron, *Madame Mère* (2 vols.; Paris: 1892).

Las Cases, E., *Memoirs of the Emperor Napoleon* (London: 1836).

—— *Le mémorial de Sainte-Hélène* (2 vols.; Paris: 1951).

Lauerma, M., *L'art de campagne Français pendant la guerre de la Révolution* (Helsinki: 1956).

Laughton, J. K., *The Naval Miscellany*, vols. 1 and 2 (London: 1900 and 1910).

Laugier, D. J. C., *Mémoires* (Paris: 1853).

Lawford, J. C., *Napoleon's Last Campaigns* (London: 1977).

—— and Young, P., *Wellington's Masterpiece—Salamanca* (London: 1974).

Lawrence, W., *The Autobiography of Sergeant William Lawrence. . . .* (London: 1886).

Leach, J., *Rough Sketches of the Life of an Old Soldier* (London: 1831).

Le Barrois, d'O., *Le maréchalat de France des origines à nos jours* (2 vols.; Paris: 1932).

Lecestre, L., *Lettres inédites de Napoléon Ier* (Paris: 1897).

Lefebvre, G., *Napoléon* (2 vols.; Paris: 1953 and London: 1969).

—— *The French Revolution* (2 vols.; London: 1965).

Leith, H., *A Narrative of the Peninsular War* (2 vols.; London: 1934).

—— *Memoirs of the late Lt. General Sir James Leith* (London: 1919).

Lejeune, L. F., *Souvenirs d'un officier sous l'Empire* (3 vols.; Paris: n.d.).

Le Normand, M. A., *The Historical and Secret Memoirs of the Empress Josephine* (2 vols.; London: 1895).

Lettow-Vorbeck, O. von, *Der Krieg von 1806 und 1807* (Berlin: 1892).

Levavasseur, O., *Souvenirs militaires* (Paris: 1914).

Lévy, A., *The Private Life of Napoleon* (London: 1894).

Lewis, M., *History of the British Navy* (London: 1959).

—— *England's Sea-Officers* (London: 1939).

—— *The Navy of Britain* (London: 1948).

—— *A Social History of the Navy from 1793–1815* (London: 1960).

Leyland, J., *The Blockade of Brest, 1803–05* (2 vols.; London: 1898 and 1901).

Liddell Hart, B. H., *The Ghost of Napoleon* (London: 1933).

—— *The Strategy of the Indirect Approach* (London: 1954).

Livermore, H. V., *A History of Portugal* (Cambridge: 1947).

Lloyd, G., *L'introduction à l'histoire de la guerre en 1756* (Brussels: 1784).

Lloyd, G., *Nelson and Sea-Power* (London: 1973).

Londonderry, C. W. V., *Narrative of the Peninsular War, from 1808 to 1813* (2 vols.; London: 1829).

Long, R. B., *Peninsular Cavalry General (1811–13);* ed. by T. H. McGuffie (London: 1951).

Longford, E., *Wellington, the Years of the Sword* (London: 1969).

Lovell, W. S., *Personal Narrative of Events, 1799–1815* (London: 1879).

Ludwig, E., *Napoleon* (London: 1926).

Lunt, J., *Scarlet Lancer* (London: 1964).

MacDonald, J. E. J. A., *Souvenirs* (Paris: 1892).

Macdonnell, A. G., *Napoleon and His Marshals* (London: 1950).

Mackay, E. S., *History of American Privateering* (New York: 1899).

Mackesy, P., *The War in the Mediterranean, 1803–10* (London: 1957).

—— *The Strategy of Overthrow* (Oxford: 1974).

Mackinnon, H., *A Journal of the Campaign in Portugal and Spain . . . 1809–1812* (London: 1812).

Madelin, L., *Le Consulat et l'Empire* (2 vols.; Paris: 1932).

—— *The French Revolution* (London: 1946).

Mahan, A. T., *The Influence of Sea-Power on the French Revolution and Empire* (2 vols.; London: 1892).

—— *Sea-Power in its Relation to the War of 1812* (Boston: 1895).

—— *Naval Strategy* (London and New York: 1911).

Mainwaring, G. and Dobree, B., *The Floating Republic* (London: 1935).

Malmesbury, Earl of, *A Series of Letters* (3 vols.; London: 1870).

Manceron, C., *Austerlitz* (Paris: 1962).

Marbot, M. de, *Mémoires;* ed. by Gen. Koch (3 vols.; Paris: 1891).

Marchand, L., *Mémoires de Marchand (2* vols.; Paris: 1952 and 1955).

Marcus, G. J., *A Naval History of England*, vol. 2 (London: 1971).

Markham, F., *Napoleon and the Awakening of Europe* (London: 1938).

—— *Napoleon* (London: 1963).

Marmont, A. F. L. V., *Mémoires* (9 vols.: Paris: 1857 *et seq.*).

Marshall-Cornwall, Sir J., *Marshal Massena* (London: 1965).

—— *Napoleon as Military Commander* (London: 1967).

Martineau, G., *Napoleon's Last Journey* (London: 1976).

—— *Napoleon's Saint Helena* (London: 1968).

—— *Madame Mère* (London: 1977).

Martinien, A., *Tableaux par corps et par batailles . . . 1805–15* (Paris: 1899).

Masefield, J., *Naval Life in Nelson's Time* (London: 1905).

Massena, A., *Mémoires* (7 vols.; Paris: 1847–50).

Masson, F. and Biagli, G., *Napoléon inconnu* (Paris: 1895).

—— *Napoléon chez-lui* (Paris: 1884).

—— *Napoléon et les femmes* (Paris: 1894).

Maude, F. N., *The Jena Campaign, 1806* (London: 1909).

—— *The Ulm Campaign* (London: 1912).

Maudit, H. de, *Les derniers jours de la Grande Armée* (Paris: 1847).

Maxwell, Sir H., *The Life of Wellington* (2 vols.; London: 1899).

Maxwell, W. H., *Life of Field Marshal His Grace the Duke of Wellington* (3 vols.; London: 1839–41).

McGrigor, Sir J., *Autobiography and Services . . .* (London: 1861).

Méneval, C. F., *Mémoires* (Paris: 1894).

—— *Napoléon et Marie Louise: souvenirs historiques. . . .* (3 vols.; Paris: 1844).

Mercer, C., *Journal of the Waterloo Campaign* (London: 1870).

Metternich-Winneburg, C. W. L., *Mémoires* (2 vols.; Paris: 1880).

Military Panorama or an Officer's Companion (London: 1813).

Milne, A., *Metternich* (London: 1975).

Mockler-Ferryman, A. F., *Regimental War Tales, 1741–1918* (Edinburgh: 1913).

Mollien, M., *Mémoires d'un ministre du trésor publique* (Paris: 1845).

Montholon, C. J. F. T. de, *Mémoires de Napoléon* (Paris: 1823).

—— *Histoire de la captivité de Sainte Hélène* (Longwy: 1846).

—— *Récits de la captivité de Sainte Hélène* (Paris: 1847).

Moore, Sir J., *Diaries;* ed. by Maj. Gen. Sir J. F. Maurice (2 vols.; London: 1904).

Moore, J., *Narrative of the Campaigns of the British Army in Spain. . . .* (London: 1809).

Morris, T., *Military Memoirs: the Napoleonic Wars;* ed. by J. M. Selby (London: 1967).

Morrison, A., *The Hamilton and Nelson Papers* (2 vols.; London: 1899).

Morvan, J., *Le soldat impérial* (2 vols.; Paris: 1904).

Müffling, F. C. E. von, *Passages from My Life* (London: 1853).

—— *History of the Campaign of 1815;* new edn. (Leeds: 1970).

Munster, Earl of, *An Account of the British Campaign of 1809 in Portugal and Spain* (London: 1831).

Nadaillac, La Marquise de, *Mémoires* (Paris: 1912).

Napier, Sir W. F. P., *History of the War in the Peninsula . . . 1807–1814* (6 vols.; London: 1851).

Napoleon I, *Commentaires de Napoléon Ier* (6 vols.; Paris: 1867).

—— La correspondance de Napoléon Ier (32 vols.; Paris: 1858–70).

—— Les maximes et pensées de Napoléon; ed. by B. Weider (Montreal: 1976).

Naval Chronicle, vols. 1–15 (London: various dates).

Naylor, J., Waterloo (London: 1960).

Neale, A., Letters from Portugal and Spain (London: 1809).

Nelson, Sir H., Despatches and Letters of Vice-Admiral Lord Viscount Nelson; ed. by Sir H. Nicolas (7 vols.; London: 1846).

Ney, M., Documents inédits du duc d'Elchingen (Paris: 1833).

—— Mémoires (2 vols.; Paris: 1833).

Nicolson, H., The Congress of Vienna (London: 1946).

Norvins, J. de, Souvenirs d'une histoire de Napoléon (Paris: 1897).

Odeleben, E., Relation de la campagne de 1813 (Paris: 1817).

Olivier, D., The Burning of Moscow, 1812 (London: 1967).

Oman, Sir C., Wellington's Army, 1809–14 (Oxford: 1912).

—— A History of the Peninsular War (7 vols.; Oxford: 1902–30).

Oman, C., Nelson (London: 1947).

—— Moore (London: 1950).

O'Meara, B. E., Napoleon in Exile (3 vols.; London: 1823).

Ompteda, C., A Hanoverian-English Officer a Hundred Years Ago. . . . (London: 1892).

Pakenham, E., The Pakenham Letters, 1800 to 1815 (London: 1914).

Palmer, A., Napoleon in Russia (London: 1967).

—— Russia in War and Peace (London: 1972).

Palmer, R. R., Twelve who Ruled: the Committee of Public Safety during the Terror (Princeton: 1941).

Paret, P., Yorck and the Era of Prussian Reform (Princeton: 1966).

—— and Howard, M. E., Clausewitz (Princeton: 1976).

Parker, W. T., Three Napoleonic Battles (Durham, N.C.: 1944).

Parkinson, C. N., Life of Lord Exmouth (London: 1951).

Parkinson, R., Moore of Corunna (London: 1975).

—— The Hussar General (London: 1976).

—— Clausewitz—a Biography (London: 1972).

—— The Peninsular War (London: 1974).

Parquin, D. C., Souvenirs de gloire et d'amour (Paris: n.d.).

—— Napoleon's Army; tr. and ed. by B. T. Jones (London: 1969).

Pasquier, E. D., Histoire de mon temps (Paris: 1893).

Patterson, J., Camp and Quarters: Scenes and Impressions of Military Life (2 vols.; London: 1840).

Pelet, J. J., The French Campaign in Portugal, 1810–11; ed. by D. Horward (Minnesota: 1973).

Perkins, B., Prologue to War, England and the United States 1805–12 (New York: 1961).

—— Castlereagh and Adams; England and the USA 1812–23 (Berkeley: 1964).

Petit, J. M., Histoire des campagnes de l'Empereur (3 vols.; Paris: 1843).

Petre, F. L., Napoleon's Conquest of Prussia; new edn. (London: 1977).

—— Napoleon's Campaigns in Poland, 1806–07; new edn. (London: 1976).

—— Napoleon and the Archduke Charles; new edn. (London: 1976).

—— Napoleon's Last Campaign in Germany; new edn. (London: 1974).

—— Napoleon at Bay, 1814; new edn. (London: 1977).

Pettigrew, T., Memoirs of the Life of Vice-Admiral Lord Viscount Nelson (2 vols.; London: 1849).

Phillimore, A., Life of Admiral of the Fleet Sir William Parker (London: 1876).

Phipps, R. W., The Armies of the First French Republic (5 vols.; Oxford: 1926–39).

Picton, Sir T., *Memoirs;* ed. by H. Robinson (2 vols.; London: 1835).
Plotho, C. von, *Der Krieg in Deutschland und Frankreich* (Berlin: 1818).
Pocock, T., *Journal of a Soldier of the 71st . . . from 1806 to 1815* (Edinburgh: 1828).
Polnay, P. de, *Napoleon's Police* (London: 1970).
Porter, Sir R. K., *Letters from Portugal and Spain* (London: 1809).
Porter, W., *History of the Corps of Royal Engineers* (3 vols.; London: 1889).
Quimby, R. W. S., *The Background of Napoleonic Warfare* (Columbia: 1957).
Rapp, J., *Mémoires* (Paris: 1821).
—— *Mémoires écrites par lui-même* (Paris: 1823).
Read, J., *War in the Peninsula* (London: 1977).
Reiche, L. von, *Memoiren* (Leipzig: 1857).
Reichel, D., *Davout et l'Art de la Guerre* (Neûchatel and Paris: 1975).
Reinhard, M., *Avec Bonaparte en Italie* (Paris: 1946).
—— *Le Grand Carnot* (2 vols.; Paris: 1950).
Rémusat, C. de, *Mémoires* (Paris: 1893).
Richardson, F., *Napoleon, Bisexual Emperor* (London: 1972).
Richardson, R. G., *Larrey: Surgeon to Napoleon's Imperial Guard* (London: 1974).
Richmond, Sir H., *Statesmen and Sea-power* (Oxford: 1946).
—— *The Spencer Papers;* ed. Navy Records Society, vols. 3 and 4 (London: 1923 and 1924).
Rigondaud, A., *Le Plumet* (illustrations of uniforms) (Paris: n.d.).
Roberts, D., *The Military Adventures of Johnny Newcome* (London: 1904).
Robertson, F. L., *The Evolution of Naval Armament* (London: 1921).
Robespierre, M., *Correspondance;* ed. by G. Michon (Paris: 1941).
Rocca, M. de, *History of the War . . . in Spain* (London: 1815).
Rodger, A. B., *The War of the Second Coalition* (Oxford: 1964).
Roeder, H., *The Ordeal of Captain Roeder* (London: 1960).
Roederer, P. L., *Oeuvres* (Paris: 1854–59).
—— *Autour de Bonaparte* (Paris: 1909).
Roos, H., *Mémoires d'un médecin de la Grande Armée* (Paris: 1913).
Roosevelt, T., *The Naval War of 1812* (2 vols.; Boston: 1904).
Rose, J. H., *Life of Napoleon* (2 vols.; London: 1902).
—— *Lord Hood and the Defence of Toulon* (Cambridge: 1922).
—— *The Personality of Napoleon* (London: 1912).
—— *William Pitt and National Revival* (London: 1911).
—— *Pitt and the Great War* (London: 1911).
Roskill, S. W., *The Strategy of Sea-power* (London: 1962).
Ross, C., *The Correspondence of Charles, 1st Marquess of Cornwallis,* ed. (3 vols.; London: 1859).
Ross, Sir J., *Memoirs and Correspondence of Admiral Lord de Saumarez* (2 vols.; London: 1838).
Rothenburg, G., *The Art of Warfare in the Age of Napoleon* (London: 1977).
Rousset, C., *Recollections of Marshal Macdonald, Duke of Tarentum* (London: 1893).
Rovigo, Duc de, *History of the Emperor Napoleon* (2 vols.; London: 1828).
—— *Mémoires sur l'Empire* (8 vols.; Paris: 1828 et seq.).
Rudorff, R., *War to the Death—the Siege of Sarragossa, 1809–09* (London: 1974).
Russell, Lord, *Knight of the Sword* (London: 1964).
Sainte-Denis, E., *Souvenirs du . . . Ali* (Paris: 1926).
Sargent, H., *Napoleon Bonaparte's First Campaign* (London: 1895).
Saski, C. G. L., *La campagne de 1809* (3 vols.; Paris: 1899–1900).
Savant, J., *Napoléon raconté par les témoins de sa vie* (Paris: 1954).
—— *Tel fut Napoléon* (Paris: 1953).
—— *Les amours de Napoléon* (Paris: 1954).

—— *The Prefects of Napoleon* (Paris: 1958).
Saxe, M. de, *Mes Rêveries* (2 vols.; Paris: 1757).
Schaumann, A. L. F., *On the Road with Wellington: the Diary of a War Commissary.* . . . (London: 1924).
Schlieffen, Graf von, *Cannae* (Berlin: 1919).
Schwartz, B., *The Code Napoleon and the Common Law World* (New York: 1956).
Seeley, Sir J., *A Short History of Napoleon I* (London: 1899).
Ségur, P. de, *Histoire et mémoires* (Paris: 1857).
—— *History of the Expedition to Russia* (2 vols.; London: 1825).
Seton-Watson, R. W., *Britain in Europe, 1789–1914* (Cambridge: 1955).
Shanahan, W., *Prussian Military Reforms, 1788–1813* (New York: 1945).
Sherer, M., *Recollections of the Peninsula* (London: 1824).
Siborne, H. T., *Waterloo Letters* (London: 1891).
—— *The Waterloo Campaign, 1815* (London: 1900).
Sidney, E., *The Life of Lord Hill, GCB* (London: 1845).
Simmons, G., *A British Rifleman . . . during the Peninsular War and the Campaign of Waterloo* (London: 1899).
Six, G., *Dictionnaire biographique des généraux et amiraux français de la Révolution et de l'Empire* (2 vols.; Paris: 1934).
Sloane, W. M., *Life of Napoleon Bonaparte* (4 vols.; London and New York: 1896).
Smith, D. B., *The St. Vincent Papers* (2 vols.; London: 1921 and 1926).
Smith, Sir F., *History of the Royal Army Veterinary Corps, 1796–1919* (London: 1919).
Smith, Sir H., *The Autobiography of Sir Harry Smith, 1787–1819* (2 vols.; London: 1901).
Smith, J. G., *The English Army in France.* . . . (London: 1831).
Southey, R., *Life of Nelson* (London: 1813).
—— *A History of the Peninsular War* (London: 1823).
Sperling, J., *Letters of an Officer of the Corps of Royal Engineers . . . 1813 to 1816* (London: 1872).
St. Chamans, O. de, *Mémoires* (Paris: 1896).
St. Cyr, G., *Mémoires* (Paris: 1829).
Stanhope, P. H., *Conversations with the Duke of Wellington* (London: 1899).
Steevens, C., *Reminiscences of my Military Life from 1795 to 1818* (Winchester: 1878).
Stepney, Sir J. C., *Leaves from the Diary of an Officer of the Guards* (London: 1854).
Stirling, A. M. W., *Pages and Portraits from the Past: the private papers of Admiral Sir William Hotham* (2 vols.; London: 1919).
Stocqueler, J. J., *The Life of Field Marshal the Duke of Wellington* (2 vols.; London: 1852).
Stothert, W., *A Narrative of the Principal Events . . . of 1809, 1810 and 1811* (London: 1812).
Suchet, L. G., *Mémoires* (Paris: 1834).
Surtees, W., *Twenty-five Years in the Rifle Brigade* (Edinburgh and London: 1833).
Swabey, W., *Diary of Campaigns in the Peninsula . . . 1811, 1812 and 1813* (Woolwich: 1895).
Tale, W., *Jottings from my Sabretasch by a Chelsea Pensioner* (London: 1847).
Talleyrand-Périgord, C. M., *Memoirs* (London: 1891).
Tarlé, M., *Napoleon's Invasion of Russia, 1812* (London: 1942).
Terraine, J., *Trafalgar* (London: 1976).
Thibaudeau, A. C., *Mémoires* (Paris: 1913).
Thibaudeau, A. C. (fils), *Napoleon and the Consulate* (London: 1908).
Thiébault, A. C., *Memoirs;* tr. by A. J. Butler (3 vols.; London: 1896).
Thiers, L. A., *A History of the Consulate and Empire* (20 vols.; London: 1845 et seq.).
Thompson, J. M., *The Life of Napoleon* (Oxford: 1952).

Thoumine, R. H., *Scientific Soldier: a Life of General Le Marchant, 1796–1812* (London: 1968).

Tomkinson, W., *The Diary of a Cavalry Officer . . . 1809–1815* (London: 1894).

Tour du Pin, Marquise de la, *Journal d'une femme de cinquante ans* (Paris: 1913).

Tramond, J., *Manuel d'histoire maritime de la France des origines à 1815* (Paris: 1957).

Tucker, J. S., *Memoirs of Earl St. Vincent* (2 vols.; London: 1844).

Tulard, J., *Napoléon* (Paris: 1977).

Turner, A. E., *The Retreat from Moscow and Passage of the Beresina* (Woolwich: 1898).

Vachée, A., *Napoleon at Work* (London: 1914).

Verner, W., *History and Campaigns of the Rifle Brigade*, Pt. 2 (London: 1919).

Vertray, M., *Journal d'un officier de l'armée d'Egypte* (Paris: 1883).

Very, E. W., *Navies of the World* (New York: 1880).

Vidal de la Blache, M., *L'évacuation de l'Espagne* (2 vols.; Paris: 1914).

Vivian, C., *Richard Hussey Vivian, First Baron Vivian—A Memoir* (London: 1897).

Wairy, Constant, *Mémoires* (5 vols.; Paris: 1898).

Wall, A., *Diary of the Operations in Spain under Sir John Moore* (Woolwich: 1896).

Walsh, H., *The Concordat of 1801* (Columbia: 1933).

Ward, S. G. P., *Wellington's Headquarters* (Oxford: 1957).

Warden, W., *Letters from St. Helena* (London: 1816).

Warner, O., *Great Sea Battles* (London: 1963).

—— *Portrait of Lord Nelson* (London: 1953).

—— *Lord Nelson—a Guide to Reading* (London: 1955).

Warner, P., *Napoleon's Enemies* (London: 1976).

Warre, Sir W., *Letters from the Peninsula, 1808–12* (London: 1909).

Wartenburg, Y. von, *Napoleon as a General* (2 vols.; London: 1902).

Watteville, H. de, *The British Soldier* (London: 1954).

Weller, J., *Wellington in the Peninsula, 1808–14* (London: 1962).

—— *Wellington in India* (London: 1972).

—— *Wellington at Waterloo* (London: 1967).

Wellesley, H., *Diary and Correspondence of Henry Wellesley, 1790–1846* (London: 1930).

Wellington, Lord, *The Dispatches of Field Marshal the Duke of Wellington. . . .* (12 vols.; London: 1834–38).

—— *The General Orders of . . . Wellington* (London: 1837).

—— Supplementary Dispatches and Memoranda of . . . Wellington (15 vols.; London: 1858–64).

Weygand, M., *Histoire de l'armée Française* (Paris: 1938).

Wheatley, E., *The Wheatley Diaries. A Journal and Sketchbook. . . .* (London: 1964).

Wheeler, W., *The Letters of Private Wheeler, 1809–1828* (London: 1951).

Whinyates, J. T., *The Whinyates Family Record* (2 vols.; London: 1894 and 1896).

Wilkinson, S., *The French Army before Napoleon* (Oxford: 1915).

—— *The Rise of General Bonaparte* (Oxford: 1930).

Williams, G. T., *The Historical Records of the 11th Hussars. . . .* (London: 1908).

Wilson, Sir R., *Narrative of Events during the Invasion of Russia* (London: 1960).

—— *British Observations on the Character and Campaigns of the Russian Army* (London: 1870).

Wood, G., *The Subaltern Officer: a Narrative* (London: 1825).

Yaple, R. L., *The Regiments and Uniforms of the British (and other) Armies, 1802–15* (Dayton, Ohio: 1975).

Young, N., *Napoleon in Exile* (Philadelphia: 1915).

Young, P., *Napoleon's Marshals* (London: 1974).

—— and Lawford, J. (eds.), *A History of the British Army* (London: 1974).

Zhilin, P. A., *Gibel' Napoleonovskoi Army S Rossy; new edn.* (Moscow: 1974).

Ziegler, P., *A Life of Henry Addington, 1st Viscount Sidmouth* (London: 1965).